The
RIVERSIDE
READER

The
RIVERSIDE
READER

EIGHTH EDITION

Joseph F. Trimmer
Ball State University

Maxine Hairston
University of Texas at Austin

Houghton Mifflin Company   Boston New York

Vice President and Publisher: Patricia A. Coryell
Executive Editor: Suzanne Phelps Weir
Senior Development Editor: Sarah Helyar Smith
Associate Project Editor: Lindsay Frost
Editorial Assistant: Teresa Huang
Composition Buyer: Sarah Ambrose
Senior Photo Editor: Jennifer Meyer Dare
Senior Manufacturing Coordinator: Marie Barnes
Marketing Manager: Cindy Graff Cohen

Cover image: Daryl Benson, Gum Tree Forest and River, Western Australia
© Masterfile.
Chapter opening art: Luke Eidenschink

Acknowledgments appear on pages 699–703.

Printed in the U.S.A.

Library of Congress Catalog Card Number: 2003110163

ISBN: 0-618-43385-6

12345678-QUF-08 07 06 05 04

CONTENTS

   A noted essayist who became a paraplegic tells the story of a grueling summer as a seventeen-year-old in Louisiana when he developed muscle, stamina, and courage as he worked alongside seasoned ditch diggers and earned their friendship and respect.

PROCESS ANALYSIS   95

DIVISION AND CLASSIFICATION 245

In this short story, we see a wise and compassionate mother choose sides in a conflict between her two dramatically different daughters, and in so doing she defines and endorses the way she has chosen to live her own life.

CAUSE AND EFFECT   399

Reflecting on experiences such as coming upon an accumulation of discarded light bulbs in a remote corner of the Red Sea and finding pollution from mercury waste in a remote native village in British Columbia, a journalist concludes that often the causes of environmental problems are so complex that we feel hopeless.

This science writer reports on research showing that the record-breaking performers in any field, whether sports, music, or chess, are those who start early and practice intensively over long periods of time.

Columnist and novelist Anna Quindlen explains how her early passion for reading has endured into her adult life, enriching it immeasurably and shaping her values.

In this profile of Stanley Kaplan, the energetic entrepreneur who created the Kaplan program to coach students for their College Boards, Gladwell shows how Kaplan's success has undermined the standing of the Educational Testing Service and raised serious questions about college admissions practices.

PERSUASION AND ARGUMENT   475

RESOURCES FOR WRITING   571
Discoveries—A Casebook

The Senses of Place: A Visual Essay

THEMATIC TABLE OF CONTENTS

The Other

Women

Heroes

Work

Science and Technology

Ethical Issues

PREFACE

For two decades, *The Riverside Reader* has set the standard for rhetorical readers. Its explanations of purpose, audience, and strategies have enabled a generation of students to read prose models effectively and to write their own essays successfully. Indeed, its thorough coverage and thoughtful advice about the many issues and problems embedded in the reading and writing processes have established this book as one of the core texts in the college composition curriculum.

The eighth edition of *The Riverside Reader,* like its predecessors, presents essays by acknowledged masters of prose style, including George Orwell, Flannery O'Connor, and Lewis Thomas, along with many new voices such as Garry Wills, Jill McCorkle, Malcolm Gladwell, and Francine Prose. Almost one-half of the selections are new to this edition. As always, introductions, readings, study questions, and writing assignments are clear, creative, and cogent.

THE *RIVERSIDE* TRADITION

The first seven sections in this reader are arranged in a sequence familiar to most writing teachers. Beginning with narration and description, moving through the five expository patterns, and ending with persuasion and argument, these sections group readings according to traditional writing strategies that are central to the Advanced Placement English Language and Composition course.

The readings within each section have been chosen to illustrate what the section introductions say they illustrate: there are no strange hybrids or confusing models. Within each section, the selections are arranged in an ascending order of length and complexity. The ultimate purpose of *The Riverside Reader* is to produce good writing. For that reason, the writing assignments in this book are presented as the culminating activity of each section. Six assignments at the end of each section ask students to write essays that cover a range of writing tasks from personal response to analysis and argument.

FEATURES NEW TO THE EIGHTH EDITION

- **Seven Visual Texts.** To demonstrate the increasing importance of visual literacy in our culture, each rhetorical section features a visual text—such as a cartoon, an icon, an advertisement. Each of these texts is followed by an assignment that encourages students to look more closely at the image, discuss its significance to the chapter's rhetorical strategy, and write about what they have discovered.
- **Photographic Essay.** *The Senses of Place*: This eight-page color insert also emphasizes the power of images to evoke insights and ideas. The images present the places where we live, work, play, struggle, and reflect, and are followed by assignments that encourage students to connect what they see with a possible writing topic.
- **A Case Study.** *Discoveries*: This mini anthology presents variations on the theme of discoveries—personal, geographic, medical, archeological, and scientific. The seven essays and one short story, which are arranged to repeat the pattern presented in the seven rhetorical chapters, illustrate how such strategies enable writers to investigate a theme

from a variety of perspectives. The writing assignments following each reading encourage students to use what they already know or can discover to *respond, analyze,* and *argue* about the texts.

REVISIONS TO THE ENDURING FEATURES

At the core of *The Riverside Reader* is our desire to assist students in their reading and writing by helping them see the interaction between the two processes:

- The **connection between the reading and writing process** is highlighted in the general introduction. The familiar terminology of *response, purpose, audience,* and *strategies* provides a framework for the introduction and for subsequent study questions and writing assignments.
- **Guidelines for Reading an Essay** is paired with **Guidelines for Writing an Essay** to enhance and advance the students' understanding of the reading/writing connection.
- A **new annotated essay** on the subject of reading appears in the general introduction: "Beginnings" by Gloria Naylor. The annotations illustrate how a reader responds to reading by writing.
- A **new student essay** on the subject of writing—Kristie Ferguson's "The Scenic Route"—discusses the beginning experiences of one student writer. The essay is followed by commentary on what the student discovered about her writing and by writing assignments that encourage similar discoveries.
- In each section introduction, an **annotated paragraph by a professional writer**, such as an excerpt from Maxine Hong Kingston's "A Song for a Barbarian Reed Pipe," concisely demonstrates reading and writing at work.
- In each section introduction, a **paragraph by a student writer**, such as Lauren Briner's "Deloris," is followed by questions about writing strategy.

- A **Points to Remember** list concludes each section introduction and provides a convenient summary of the essential tasks and techniques of each strategy.
- This eighth edition of *The Riverside Reader* contains thirty-one new selections, among them Sister Helen Prejean's "Memories of a Dead Man Walking," Barbara Ehrenreich's "Scrubbing in Maine," and Andrew Sullivan's "Virtually Normal." The complete collection, which includes popular essays from previous editions, provides a variety of readings to engage the interest of all students on subjects as wide ranging as the taste of fast food, the impact of ethnic stereotypes, and the devastation at Ground Zero.
- A **Thematic Table of Contents** is provided for teachers who wish to organize their course by themes or issues.
- Selections in the **Persuasion and Argument** section are paired to present different perspectives on the issues such as race, family, and the popular Harry Potter books. This feature reflects our continuing emphasis on analytical and interpretive reading and writing.
- A **short story** concludes each section to provide an interesting perspective on a particular writing strategy and to give students opportunities to broaden their reading skills. New to this edition are Ann Beattie's "Janus" and Arthur C. Clarke's "The Star."
- **Study questions and writing assignments** throughout the text have been extensively revised.
- The chapter on **using and documenting sources** provides expanded instruction on using and documenting sources in the format of the latest Modern Language Association (MLA) style. Special attention is given to the problem of plagiarism and the citation of electronic sources. The chapter concludes with an annotated student paper, Blythe Rogers's "Assessing Coffee's Health Problems," that uses both print and electronic sources.
- The **Glossary** provides extended definitions of key rhetorical terms. Each definition refers students to a particularly effective example in the text.

SUPPLEMENTS FOR
THE RIVERSIDE READER

Web Site

A dynamic web site encourages further exploration by students into the themes and topics of the book and supplies considerable support to students' writing. Features include suggested assignments or exercises, sample student essays, links to extensive and reliable resources for research, links to always-useful resources for writing, a writing guidelines checklist, and an online handbook of grammar and usage.

The web site for instructors supplies the on-line version of the comprehensive Instructor's Resource Manual.

For both sites, go to **http://college.hmco.com/english.**

Instructor's Resource Manual

The *Instructor's Resource Manual* by Rai Peterson of Ball State University includes extensive rhetorical analysis of each essay and story, reading quizzes and vocabulary lists, and additional student essays and writing assignments. The manual also includes advice on teaching reading and writing strategies.

A correlation from the reader to the Advanced Placement course description ("acorn book") for English Language and Composition is available from your McDougal Littell representative.

ACKNOWLEDGMENTS

We are grateful to the following writing instructors who have provided extensive commentary of *The Riverside Reader* for this edition:

Lynnette Beers, Santiago Canyon College
Martha J. Craig, Bradley University

Heather Eaton, Daytona Beach Community College
Louis Gallo, Radford University
LeiLani Hinds, Honolulu Community College
Fred Kille, Western Nevada Community College
Kris Kurrus, Spokane Falls Community College
Derek Parker-Royal, Texas A&M University–
    Commerce
Patrick S. J. Ruffin, Community College of
    Philadelphia
Max Smith, Normandale Community College
Jeffrey L. Snodgrass, Prince George's Community
    College
Sandra Stephenson, South Plains College

We are also grateful to our students for allowing us to reprint their work in this edition: Kristie Ferguson, Lauren Briner, Sara Temple, Nathan Harms, Gareth Tucker, Jason Utesch, Emily Linderman, Jim Saloman, and Blythe Rogers.

A special thanks goes to our long-time friend and development editor, Lynn Walterick, and to our new friend and art editor, Susan Holtz, for helping us to create and prepare the illustration program. And, of course, our debt to all of our students is ongoing.

J.F.T.
M.H.

The
RIVERSIDE
READER

INTRODUCTION

People who do well in college are nearly always good readers and good writers. They have to read well to absorb and evaluate the wealth of information they encounter on line and in books and articles, and they have to write well to show that they're learning and thinking. In this book we try to help you connect your reading and writing and become skillful at both crafts. For they are complementary skills, and you can master both of them through practice.

what about math?

BECOMING A GOOD READER

- Step One. When you're reading a piece of writing you need to master, go over it quickly at first to get the main ideas and the flavor of the piece. Just enjoy it for what you're learning. Unless you get lost or confused, don't go back to reread or stop to analyze the writer's argument.

I definitely don't do that.

- Step Two. Now slow down. If you're reading from a book or magazine you don't own, photocopy the essay. If you're reading off the Internet, print out the piece. Now go back over it, this time underlining or highlighting key points and jotting notes in the margins—summaries of the main points in the left margin, questions or objections in the right one.

What about long pieces?

- Step Three. On a separate piece of paper or in a separate file, jot down your response to the reading. What about the writer's ideas appeals to you? What puzzles you? What elements in the piece remind you of some of your own experiences? Remember that there's not necessarily one "right" reaction to what you're reading. Each reader brings different experiences to reading a piece of writing—sees it through his or her unique lens, so to speak. So every response will be individual, and each reader will have a slightly different perspective. The notes you take will help you if you go on to write about the piece or discuss it in class.

Then how do you receive a grade?

The annotated sample essay, "Beginnings," which you will find further along in this introduction, shows how one reader responded to an essay by African-American writer Gloria Naylor. In that essay the writer shows how her mother overcame poverty and discrimination to move to a place where her children would have the opportunity to become readers and writers. Naylor also emphasizes her early exposure to books.

READING TO BECOME A BETTER WRITER

Many people have learned to improve their performance in a sport or activity by watching a professional at work and then patterning their activity on that of the professional. We believe that in the same way student writers can sharpen their skills by paying attention to how professional writers practice their craft. We've organized this book around that assumption. Thus you will find tips about what to look for as you read these authors and questions that give you insight into their writing process. Here are three things to look for:

- What is the writer's **purpose**? What does he or she want to accomplish? How does the writer communicate that purpose? For instance, in "The Scenic Route," the sample student essay that comes right after Guidelines for Writing an Essay, the writer's purpose is to explain how she developed her own writing process.
- Who is the writer's **audience**? Why has he or she chosen that audience? In "The Scenic Route" the author, Kristie Ferguson, is writing for other novice writers who might empathize with her struggles to develop as a writer.
- What are the writer's **strategies**? What can you tell from the way the writer starts out? Does he or she tell stories, argue, give examples, cite personal experience, or empathize with a person or group? In "The Scenic Route" Kristie Ferguson draws on personal experience and narratives to make her point.

But every writer is different

When you get in the habit of asking these questions when you read, you'll begin to understand how writers work and, we hope, also begin to master some elements of the craft for your own writing.

READING TO LEARN ABOUT WRITING STRATEGIES

In *The Riverside Reader* you will find essays and short stories that comment on events and circumstances that affect all our lives. Here are just a few of the topics you may read about.

- The environment
- Racial discrimination and problems
- Capital punishment
- Ethnic conflicts
- Family patterns and values

Any descriptive, fiction stories?

- Academic testing
- Popular entertainment
- Classical archeology

[handwritten: I'd like to see creative writing]

The essays connect to other strands in your college education and are as pertinent to courses in women's studies, architecture or archeology, history, or education as they are in a college writing course. In the short stories you can see how fiction writers explore human problems through narratives.

Common Writing Strategies

The essays in *The Riverside Reader* are arranged according to common patterns of development that we encounter every day.

- Narration and description
- Process analysis
- Comparison and contrast
- Division and classification
- Definition
- Cause and effect
- Persuasion and argument

[handwritten: I don't really agree w/ that]

As you read and get a sense of how professional writers develop their ideas by using one or more of these patterns, you'll probably see how you can adapt these strategies to your writing. For instance, when you see how William Langewiesche uses dialogue, anecdotes, and sketches of behavior to define David Griffin's character in "American Ingenuity," you might see how you could define someone through the same strategies.

We've chosen essays for this reader that provide strong examples of each strategy in action, but you don't have to limit yourself to a single pattern for an entire piece of writing. Certainly professional writers don't. But frequently they do structure an essay around one dominant strategy, using other strategies to supplement it. For example, Paco Underhill focuses on comparison and contrast in "Shop like a Man," but he also depends on description to make his point. Malcolm Gladwell concentrates on cause and effect in "Examined Life," but he also uses narration to tell the story of Stanley Kaplan.

Is it possible to have only one?

Strategies for Your Writing

You can also use these traditional strategies as tools of discovery to generate material for your first draft. Suppose you want to write about wind farms as an alternate energy source. Here are some strategies for getting started.

> **Narration and description:** Describe a wind farm.
>
> **Comparison and contrast:** Contrast wind power with hydroelectric power.
>
> **Process analysis:** Analyze how wind farms work.
>
> **Cause and effect:** Show wind power as a clean energy source. Show why it is needed.
>
> **Persuasion and argument:** Argue for the special benefits of wind power compared to nuclear or coal-generated power.

What about making a paper interesting?

You can see that when you begin to think of writing with these patterns in mind, you'll have an easier time getting started.

USING *THE RIVERSIDE READER*

Before you begin to read essays from a section of *The Riverside Reader*, look over the introduction to that section to get a feel for what to expect. The introduction will suggest how you might incorporate the pattern into your own writing and will also illustrate how a professional writer used the pattern and how a student writer incorporated it into a paragraph. Each introduction concludes with a highlighted list of Points to Remember.

Where do they choose the student pieces?

Before each essay or story you'll find a headnote about the author's background and work. Following each essay is a set of questions to help you analyze key elements of the piece; after each story, a "comment" discusses some of its high points. After each section, you'll find writing assignments that connect with the section's essay pattern.

On pages 7 to 8 we give Guidelines for Reading an Essay, and after those Guidelines you will find a sample analysis of Gloria Naylor's short essay "Beginnings." This introduction to *The Riverside Reader* closes with Guidelines for Writing an Essay, followed by the student Kristie Ferguson's essay.

Guidelines for Reading an Essay

I. READ THE ESSAY THROUGH CAREFULLY

Didn't it say earlier to shim

a. Consider the title and what expectations it raises.
b. Note when the essay was written and where it was first published.
c. Look at the author information in the headnote and consider what important leads that information gives you about what to expect from the essay.
d. Now go back over the essay, underlining or highlighting key ideas and jotting down any questions you have.

II. THINK ABOUT YOUR RESPONSE TO THE ESSAY

a. Note what you liked and/or disliked about it and analyze why you had that reaction.
b. Decide what questions you have after reading the essay.
c. Think about the issues the essay raises for you.

III. WRITE A BRIEF STATEMENT OF WHAT SEEMS TO BE THE AUTHOR'S PURPOSE

a. Consider how the information about the author's life and experience may account for that purpose.
b. Decide to what extent you think the author achieved his or her purpose.

IV. AS FAR AS YOU CAN, IDENTIFY THE AUTHOR'S ORIGINAL AUDIENCE

a. Make a guess about what those readers' interests are.
b. Compare your interests and experiences to those of the readers the author had in mind when writing the essay, and decide how similar or different they are.

what if you don't have time to do all of this?

V. LOOK AT THE STRATEGIES THE WRITER USES TO ENGAGE AND HOLD THE READER'S INTEREST

a. Look at the lead the author uses to engage the reader.
b. Identify the main pattern the writer uses in the essay, and consider how that pattern helps to develop his or her main idea.
c. Pick out the descriptions, events, or anecdotes that make a particular impression, and consider why they're effective.
d. Identify passages or images that you find especially powerful.

VI. REFLECT ON THE ESSAY, AND TRY TO STATE ITS CONTENT AND MAIN ARGUMENT IN TWO OR THREE SENTENCES

What if you found the piece dull? extremely

Sample Analysis of an Essay

GLORIA NAYLOR

Distinguished African-American writer Gloria Naylor was born in New York City and continues to live there. The winner of several fellowships, in 1983 she received the American Book Award for her novel *The Women of Brewster Place*. The seven stories that make up that novel were later adapted for a television mini-series by ABC. Two later novels are *Mama Day*, published in 1989, and *Bailey's Cafe*, published in 1992. Naylor's other novels are *Linden Hills* (1985) and *The Men of Brewster Place* (1998). Most recently she has edited and published *Children of the Night: The Best Short Stories by Black Writers, 1967 to the Present.*

Naylor's short essay reprinted here was originally given as a talk at the Folger Shakespeare Library in Washington at a gala sponsored by the PEN/Faulkner Foundation, an organization dedicated to supporting and promoting literary writers. For this inaugural gala in 1989, twenty-one fiction writers were asked to speak for no more than three minutes on the topic "Beginnings." The talks from that year and from similar galas in following years were published in 2000 under the title *Three Minutes or Less: Life Lessons from America's Greatest Writers.*

Beginnings

While I am by birth a native New Yorker, I've often mentioned publicly that I was conceived in Robinsville, Mississippi, because, for me, that

Her topic conception was the beginning of my writing career. It was through my mother's genes that I

Powerful image to show her mother's strength

inherited my passionate love of books. But since she was from a sharecropping family that could not afford the luxury of buying books, and the public libraries in the South were closed to black Americans, she would take her spare Saturday afternoons and hire herself out in someone else's fields to earn the money to send away to book clubs. And she made a vow to herself that all of her children would be born in a place where you could be poor and still read.

Does one inherit a love of books?

Was race or poverty the bar here? Really both

Library is access to learning. Reading and writing the key

Library becomes a haven where she can find herself

She kept that promise, and my earliest preschool memories are of being taken to a low brick building in the Bronx with dark walnut shelves that stretched high over my head, shelves that seemed to a four-year-old to almost stretch into eternity. And she told me that once I could write my name, all those books would be mine. She would repeat this ritual with her second daughter and then the third. My sisters were average readers; I became an avid one. I was the shyest of the three, painfully shy, and fortunately I was taught early to revere a place that would be the repository of all my unspoken fears and my unspoken needs.

Why does she stress that she is shy?

Mother's example gave her courage and determination

And today with my own writing, that's basically what I'm giving back. Words that attempt to make some order out of the inarticulate chaos I have within. But writing for me is also about dreaming, and I grew up encouraged to dream by a woman who, in spite of her very limited personal circumstances, somehow managed to find a way to hold on to a fierce belief in the limitless possibilities of the human spirit.

This paragraph is confusing. What is she giving back? How do her dreams fit in here?

Comment The reader begins her analysis of the essay by underlining what seem to be key sentences, then summarizing the main points Naylor is making in notes in the left margin. In the right margin, she notes questions that occur to her, questions that she might like to ask the author. Such under-lining and notes come from the reader's digging into the es-say and giving it serious thought; they will provide good ma-terial for writing a response, either on line or in a paper.

First the reader circles the topic: "the beginning of my writing career." It's an assigned topic, "Beginnings," but one that could go in many directions. Naylor narrows it immedi-ately, going back to the time before she was born and intro-ducing us to her mother, whom she sees as the single most important influence on her life and subsequent career. In the rest of the essay she uses her narrative skills as a novelist to show us the drama of her mother's life. We see the sharecrop-per who worked extra hours to buy books that were denied to her because she was black; who schemed to move her chil-dren out of the South so they would have the freedom to read; who found the public library in New York and intro-duced her daughters to the great treasures that lay before them when they learned to read; and who gave her daughters the example of a black woman who, against great odds, cre-ated a new life for herself and her children through hope and grit and determination.

In this way Naylor shows us that her career as a writer be-gan with her mother; she says nothing of her own efforts. The last paragraph is a little fuzzy. Phrases like "inarticulate chaos" don't tell us much about herself as a writer, but she seems to suggest that she sees her work as a kind of tribute to her mother, her books as evidence that another black woman has overcome odds to succeed. The essay is powerful, a mov-ing drama sketched in just a few words.

I don't agree w/ all of the points highlighted in the sample + they missed some

Guidelines for Writing an Essay

Before you begin a college writing assignment, you need a plan. Here are some suggestions that will get you started and help you work through to a piece of finished writing.

I. ANALYZE YOUR WRITING SITUATION

Any writing task has three components: (1) a topic, (2) a purpose, and (3) an audience. Before you start, analyze these basics and write out the results.

- Decide on your topic and the basic points you want to make. Put your ideas in writing.
- Decide on your purpose, what you want to achieve.
- Identify your audience and their interest in your topic.
- Plan how you will appeal to that audience.

II. SELECT AND NARROW YOUR TOPIC

- If you can choose your own topic, look for one that interests you and on which you already have some knowledge.
- Brainstorm with your classmates about the topic and talk to friends to get ideas for developing it.
- Check the on-line catalog in your library for leads, and look on the Web for other resources.
- Write a tentative thesis sentence to get you started; it can always be modified later.

III. FINE-TUNE YOUR PURPOSE

- Decide what outcome you want to have.
- Consider what conclusion you want your readers to come to.

IV. ANALYZE YOUR AUDIENCE

- If your readers are going to be your instructor and classmates, consider what will help you appeal to them.

- Also identify a publication where your essay might be published, and analyze the readers of that publication.
- Write out the questions your readers are likely to have.

V. DECIDE ON A PLAN OF ORGANIZATION

- Make a rough outline to put your ideas in order.
- Choose a tentative writing pattern to get you started. Depending on your purpose, you might try narration, comparison and contrast, or cause and effect.
- Consider what kinds of supporting evidence you need.

VI. WRITE A DRAFT, GET FEEDBACK ON IT, REVISE, EDIT, AND PROOFREAD

Where are the tips for proofreading?

Student Essay

KRISTIE FERGUSON
The Scenic Route

What is the scenic route?

As a writer, I always seem to take the scenic route. I don't plan it that way. My teachers provide me with detailed maps pointing me down the most direct road, but somehow I miss a turn or make a wrong turn, and there I am—standing at some unmarked crossroads, head pounding, stomach churning, hopelessly lost. On such occasions, I used to curse my teachers, my maps, and myself. But recently, I have come to expect, even to enjoy, in a perverse way, the confusion and panic of being lost. Left to my own devices, I have learned to discover my own way to my destination. And afterwards, I have a tale to tell.

Is she lost in the topics?

Sure, we were all lost in 2nd grade.

I did not learn this all at once. In the beginning, I was confused about where I was going. One day in the second grade, Mrs. Scott told us that if we wrote a brief theme, we could go to a movie. I grabbed my #2 pencil and listened for directions. "You may not use erasers or dictionaries. I may ask for do-overs." Lost! I was the worst speller in the class. My first draft was "Too sloppy. Misspelled words." My second, "Misspelled word. Do it over." Now I was really lost. One misspelled word. They all looked right—and then they all looked wrong. Blind luck led me to one of those "ie" words. I rubbed out the letters, reprinted them, and put the dot between them. "Kristie, you erased," she hissed. "No ma'am." She eyed my paper and then me again, and with a sigh waved me to the auditorium. Collapsing next to my best friend, Karla, I arrived in time to watch

What is this assignment

a film about dental hygiene. Teeth? All that for teeth!

My next problem was trying to figure out where I was going. Mrs. Pageant, my fifth-grade teacher, was the source of my confusion. Seemingly unaware of my errors, she wrote enthusiastic notes on all my papers, suggesting on one, "Kristie, you're so creative. Why don't you write a book?" Why indeed should the second-grade dummy begin on such a perilous journey? "You should, Kristie. You really should. You could even write a fantasy book like the one we read today." Luckily, fantasy was my forté. I used to make up stories about the family of squirrels in my backyard. And so I wrote *Squirrel Family Starts a Grocery Store* in which, after the hoopla on page one, the squirrels run out of food on page three and close their store on page five.

Her use of dialogue is confusing?

I love fantasy!

As she read my book to the class, Mrs. Pageant could hardly contain herself. "What a delightful story, Kristie. You must write another one immediately." My head pounded. My stomach churned. I had stumbled into one story, but why keep going? Because Mrs. Pageant "just loved" those dumb squirrels. So there was the *Squirrel Family Starts a Bank,* in which the dumb squirrels run out of money, and *Squirrel Family Starts a Newspaper* in which they ran out of stories. I couldn't think of another squirrel story, and Karla told me that if she had to listen to one more, she would throw up.

I think Karla is jealous

What a nice comment

When I got to the eleventh grade, I knew for the first time where I was going and why. The poster on Mr. Logan's bulletin board announced a writing contest: "Threats to the Free Enterprise System." Sponsored by the Blair County Board of Realtors. First prize $200. Now my problem was

how to get there. Mr. Logan took us to the
school library where he mapped out the first half
of his strategy. Look up sources in the data base.
Take notes. Organize notes into an outline for the
first draft. It seemed like a sensible plan, but, as
usual, I got lost at the first turn. I logged on to
Google, but it was pointless. The screen displayed
hundreds of sources on free enterprise, but I
couldn't find out who was threatening it.

I know
that
feeling

As the deadline for the first draft approached, I
was so desperate I asked my parents for directions. "Ask some local business people what they
think." Not bad for parents. I borrowed my father's tape recorder and made the rounds—the
grocery store, the pizza parlor, the newspaper.
Most of the people seemed a lot like me—lost.
They talked a lot, but they didn't focus on the
question.

That's a lot
of work for
a paper.

Maybe I was asking the wrong question. I listened to the tape a couple of times and picked out
some common themes. Then I rewrote my question: "How do taxes, government regulation, or
foreign competition threaten your business?" The
next time around, people seemed to know what
they were talking about. I organized their answers
under my three categories, wrote out my draft,
and made the deadline.

In class, Mr. Logan announced the second half
of his strategy. Read draft. Listen to student and
teacher responses. Write another draft. Mail essay.
Karla went first. She quoted every book in the
school library. Looking down at my paper, I saw
myself stranded again. After a few more papers, I
felt better. All of them sounded alike. I knew my
quotes would be different—the guy at the pizza
parlor, the newspaper editor. "You didn't do any
research," Karla complained. "I bet you didn't
read one article." A chorus of "yeses" came from

Who is
Karla?

she's a snob.
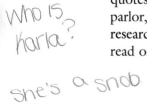

the guys in the back row. Mr. Logan didn't say anything for a while. Then, smiling, he looked at Karla. "What is research?" Now Karla looked lost. The guys looked at their notebooks. Silence. Finally, the bell. What's the answer? What am I supposed to do? Mr. Logan never said. I thought about what I had done, considered my options, and, with a sigh, mailed my essay.

A few weeks later I was standing not at some unmarked crossroads, but in the center of town— behind a lectern in front of a room full of people. A man from Blair County Board of Realtors handed me a trophy and an envelope and asked me to tell how I wrote the paper. I started to panic, and then I smiled. "Well . . ." I caught Mr. Logan's eye. "I asked a lot of people what they thought. At first they didn't know what I was talking about. Neither did I. Then I fixed up my question and they helped me figure out what to say." I looked at Mr. Logan one more time. "I guess I did research."

Comment   This engaging essay by Kristie Ferguson also tells of one writer's beginnings. It takes readers on a tour of her development as a writer and highlights three memorable experiences along the way. Although the narrative focuses on her personal experiences, they conjure up memories for many fledgling writers. First, the Nazi teacher from the second grade who demands perfection and loves to punish mistakes. Then the sweetie-pie teacher from the fifth grade who gushes and lavishes praise on stuff the writer knows is junk. Finally, the practical and organized eleventh-grade teacher who outlines a writing process and guides the students through it.

But Kristie finds out that one size doesn't fit all. She has to try various approaches and adapt the process to her own style. When she does and trusts her intuition to take her in a direction that feels right to her, she succeeds and writes a winning essay that comes from listening to people talk about their own concerns. She enlivens her account with anecdotes and personal stories, creating a persona that amuses her readers and engages their sympathy. She skillfully works out her metaphor of the road and the crossroads and closes with a nice vignette of her triumph.

Possible Writing Topics

1. Compose a draft that responds to an assignment asking you to write about "Beginnings" in 500 words or less (no more than two double-spaced pages). You might write about how you started as a dancer, a chess player, a baseball player, or a youth minister for your church—any occupation or preoccupation that is important in your life. Keeping in mind that it's always better to show than to tell, give details about a person who influenced you early in your development and the effect that person had on you. This writing could be a narrative to post on your personal web page, the script for a short talk in front of a group you feel comfortable with, as Naylor's was, or a feature in your church's weekly newsletter.

2. In no more than 500 words (two double-spaced pages or less), create a profile piece about a person who has had a strong influence on your life—on the personal choices you've made, the place where you live, the career you're preparing for, the college you chose, your political opinions. Remember that a person's physical appearance may not be the most significant thing about him or her— notice that Naylor never tells you how her mother looks. Look also at the essay "American Ingenuity" (page 364) to see how the author sketches the character of David Griffin by showing you how he acts and talks. Your audience could be the readers of your college newspaper or your class's web site.

NARRATION
AND
DESCRIPTION

The writer who *narrates* tells a story to make a point. The writer who *describes* evokes the senses to create a picture. Although you can use either strategy by itself, you will probably discover that they work best in combination if you want to write a detailed account of some memorable experience— your first trip alone, a last-minute political victory, a picnic in some special place. When you want to explain what happened, you will need to tell the story in some kind of chronological order, putting the most important events—I took the wrong turn, she made the right speech, we picked the perfect spot—in the most prominent position. When you want to

can't fit these 2 in any almost combination

21

give the texture of the experience, you will need to select
words and images that help your readers see, hear, and feel
what happened—the road snaked to a dead end, the crowd
thundered into applause, the sunshine softened our scowls.
When you show and tell in this way, you can help your readers see the meaning of the experience you want to convey.

I like those examples

PURPOSE

① You can use narration and description for three purposes.
Most simply, you can use them to introduce or illustrate a
complicated subject. You might begin an analysis of the energy crisis, for example, by telling a personal anecdote that
dramatizes wastefulness. Or you might conclude an argument for gun control by giving a graphic description of a
shooting incident. In each case, you are using a few sentences
or a detailed description to support some other strategy such
as causal analysis or argument.

Writers use narration and description most often not as
② isolated examples but as their primary method when they are
analyzing an issue or theme. For example, you might spend a
whole essay telling how you came to a new awareness of patriotism because of your experience in a foreign country.
Even though your personal experience would be the center
of the essay, your narrative purpose (what happened) and
your descriptive purpose (what it felt like) might be linked to
other purposes. You might want to *explain* what caused your
new awareness (why it happened) or to *argue* that everyone
needs such awareness (why everyone should reach the same
conclusion you did).

The writers who use narration and description most often
③ are those who write autobiography, history, and fiction. If
you choose to write in any of these forms, your purpose will
be not so much to introduce an example or tell about an experience as to throw light on your subject. You may explain
why events happened as they did or argue that such events
should never happen again, but you may choose to suggest
your ideas subtly through telling a story or giving a descrip-

tion rather than stating them as direct assertions. Your primary purpose is to report the actions and describe the feelings of people entangled in the complex web of circumstance.

AUDIENCE

As you think about writing an essay using narration and description, consider how much you will need to tell your readers and how much you will need to show them. If you are writing from personal experience, few readers will know the story before you tell it. They may know similar stories or have had similar experiences, but they do not know your story. Because you can tell your story in so many different ways—adding or deleting material to fit the occasion—you need to decide how much information your readers will need. Do they need to know every detail of your story, only brief summaries of certain parts, or some mixture of detail and summary?

In order to decide what details you should provide, you need to think about how much your readers know and what they are going to expect. If your subject is unusual (a trip to see an erupting volcano), your readers will need a lot of information, much of it technical, to understand the novel experience you are going to describe. They will expect an efficient, matter-of-fact description of volcanoes but also want you to give them some sense of how it feels to see one erupting. If your subject is familiar to most people (your experience with lawn sprinklers), your readers will need few technical details to understand your subject. But they will expect you to give them new images and insights that create a fresh vision of your subject—for example, portraying lawn sprinklers as the languid pulse of summer.

STRATEGIES

The writers in this section demonstrate that you need to use certain strategies to write a successful narrative and descriptive essay. For openers, you must recognize that an

Where's the point of creating images w/o too many metaphors?

experience and an essay about that experience are not the same thing. When you have any experience, no matter how long it lasts, your memory of that experience is going to be disorganized and poorly defined, but the essay you write about that experience must have a purpose and be sharply focused. When you want to transform your experience into an essay, start by locating the central **conflict.** It may be (1) between the writer and himself or herself, as when George Orwell finds himself in a quandary about whether to shoot the elephant; (2) between the writer and others, as when Jill McCorkle describes her reaction to the "mullet girls"; or (3) between the writer and the environment, as when Judith Ortiz Cofer tries to explain the difference between *individuals* and *social stereotypes.*

[Handwritten margin note: Are those ALL the combos?]

Once you have identified the conflict, arrange the action so that your readers know how the conflict started, how it developed, and how it was resolved. This coherent sequence of events is called a **plot.** Sometimes you may want to create a plot that sticks to a simple chronological pattern. In "Memories of a Dead Man Walking," Sister Helen Prejean begins her account of the original events at the beginning and describes them as they occur. At other times you may want to start your essay in the middle or even near the end of the events you are describing. In "Digging," Andre Dubus concludes his narrative by speculating about a different "middle." The authors choose a pattern according to their purpose: Sister Helen Prejean wants to describe the evolution of the events leading up to the execution; Dubus wants to describe why coming home for lunch would have changed the whole story.

[Handwritten margin note: How can a story beginning @ the middle make sense?]

When you figure out what the beginning, middle, and end of your plot should be, you can establish how each event in those sections should be paced. **Pace** is the speed at which the writer recounts events. Sometimes you can narrate events quickly by omitting details, compressing time, and summarizing experience. For example, Cofer summarizes several episodes that reveal her contact with a stereotype. At other times you may want to pace events more slowly and carefully because they are vital to your purpose. You will need to include every detail, expand on time, and present the situation as a fully realized scene rather than in summary form. Dubus creates such a scene when he describes his first morning of "digging."

the detailed account must only cover a short experience

You can make your scenes and summaries effective by your careful **selection of details.** Just adding more details doesn't satisfy this requirement. You must select those special details that satisfy the needs of your readers and further your purpose in the essay. For example, sometimes you will need to give *objective* or *technical* details to help your readers understand your subject. Cofer provides this kind of detail when she describes the cultural customs of Puerto Rico. At other times you will want to give *subjective* or *impressionistic* details to appeal to your readers' senses. Orwell provides much of this sort of detail as he tries to re-create his physical and psychological response to shooting the elephant. Finally, you may want to present your details so they form a *figurative image* or create a *dominant impression.* Dubus uses both of these strategies: the first when he describes his father's conversation, and the second when he describes his lunch hour.

How do you decide which you want?

In order to identify the conflict, organize the plot, vary the pace, and select details for your essay, you need to determine your **point of view:** the person and position of the narrator (*point*) and the attitude toward the experience being presented (*view*). You choose your *person* by deciding whether you want to tell your story as "I" saw it (as Sister Helen Prejean does in her story about her experiences with death row inmates) or as "he" saw it (as Dubus does when he describes his father's life).

You choose your *position* by deciding how close you want to be to the action in time and space. You may be involved in the action or view it from the position of an observer, or you may tell about the events as they are happening or many years after they have taken place. For example, George Orwell, the young police officer, is the chief actor in his narrative, but George Orwell, the author, still wonders, years after the event, why he shot the elephant. You create your attitude—

Which is more effective?

How do you tell.

how you view the events you intend to present and interpret—by the person and position you choose for writing your essay. The attitudes of the narrators in the following essays might be characterized as reticent (Dubus), nostalgic (McCorkle), perplexed (Cofer), tormented (Prejean), and ambivalent (Orwell).

those are great diction

USING NARRATION AND DESCRIPTION IN PARAGRAPHS

Here are two narration and description paragraphs. The first is written by a professional writer and is followed by an analysis. The second is written by a student writer and is followed by questions.

Professional →

MAXINE HONG KINGSTON
A Song for a Barbarian Reed Pipe

Not all of the children who were silent at American school found a voice at Chinese school. One new teacher said each of us had to get up and recite in front of the class, who was to listen. My sister and I had memorized the lesson perfectly. We said it to each other at home, one chanting, one listening. The teacher called on my sister to recite first. It was the first time a teacher had called on the second-born to go first. My sister was scared. She glanced at me and looked away; I looked down at my desk. I hoped that she could do it because if she couldn't, then I would have to. She opened her mouth and a voice came out that wasn't a whisper, but it wasn't a proper voice either. I hoped that she would not cry, fear breaking up her voice like twigs underfoot. She sounded as if she were trying to sing though weeping and strangling. She did not pause or stop to end the embarrassment. She kept going until she said the last word, and

Sets up conflict

Conflict slows pace; heightens suspense

Appeals to sense

then she sat down. When it was my turn, the same voice came out, a <u>crippled animal running on broken legs.</u> You could hear splinters in my voice, bones rubbing jagged against one an- other. I was loud, though. I was glad I didn't whisper.

Confirms point of view (margin note)

Creates new image (margin note)

Comment This paragraph, taken from the final section of *The Woman Warrior*, recounts an embarrassing scene involving two Chinese sisters. Kingston describes how she and her sister prepare for the expected recitation. The conflict occurs when the teacher calls on the second-born sister first—a breach of Chinese etiquette. By describing how she looks down at her desk, Kingston slows the pace and heightens the anxiety of the situation. She then selects details and images to evoke the sound of her sister's and then her own voice as they complete the lesson.

Student → (margin note)

LAUREN BRINER
Deloris

"All right, how do you say 'dollars' in Spanish?" Mrs. Tyrrel was setting the rules for Spanish II, but we wanted the old rules. Last year Mr. Kreuger, who taught Spanish I, loved to throw parties. I guess he thought fiestas would make us want to learn Spanish. What we really wanted was more fiestas. But now, according to Mrs. Tyrrel, the party was over. She peered at us over the top of her glasses looking for a snitch. We avoided her eyes by thumbing the sides of our new books. "Lauren? How about you?" I looked for help. No luck! My party friends were faking it, staring at the unintelligible sentences in *Spanish II*. I was on my own. I looked up at Mrs. Tyrrel. "Lauren?" I was desperate, caught in her gaze. I panicked. In a really hokey accent, I suggested a possible answer, "Dellores?"

Slowing pace (margin note)

I like this description (margin note)

Conflict w/ students (margin note)

Is she mocking her or does she have a sense of humor?

"Deloris? Who's Deloris? Is she a friend of yours?" Mrs. Tyrrel was laughing. The whole class began laughing, "Deloris! Deloris! Deloris!" The blood rushed to my face and tears welled in my eyes. So much for old rules and old friends.

1. How does Briner's description of the two teachers establish the conflict in this episode?
2. How do the responses of the teacher and the class to Lauren's answer reveal the writer's point of view?

NARRATION AND DESCRIPTION

Points to Remember

1. Focus your narrative on the "story" in your story— that is, focus on the conflict that defines the plot.
2. Vary the pace of your narrative so that you can summarize some events quickly and render others as fully realized scenes.
3. Supply evocative details to help your readers experience the dramatic development of your narrative.
4. Establish a consistent point of view so that your readers know how you have positioned yourself in your story.
5. Represent the events in your narrative so that your story makes its point.

The effect that she isn't even in the photo are very powerful—it erases difference

they're taunting the principle

In this excerpt from her graphic novel, Persepolis: The Story of a Childhood *(2003), Marjane Satrapi recounts the reaction of young schoolgirls to the law requiring them to wear "the veil." Some argue that the veil debases and even erases female identity. Others argue that it provides women with safety and secret power. How do the characters in Satrapi's narrative feel about this regulation? Write a narrative describing your own reactions to some obligatory dress code.*

Andre Dubus (1936–1999) was born in Lake Charles, Louisiana, and educated at McNeese State College and the University of Iowa. He taught writing at universities such as the University of Alabama and Boston University. His work includes novels such as *The Lieutenant* (1967), *Voices from the Moon* (1984), and several collections of short stories, including *Finding a Girl in America* (1980) and *Dancing After Hours* (1996). In 1986, he barely survived a devastating traffic accident that cost him his leg. He writes about confronting his disability in a series of essays, *Meditations from a Movable Chair* (1998). In "Digging," reprinted from that collection, Dubus remembers the lessons he learned from physical labor.

the accident must have impacted his perspective on life [handwritten margin note]

Digging

THAT HOT JUNE in Lafayette, Louisiana, I was sixteen, I would be seventeen in August, I weighed 105 pounds, and my ruddy, broad-chested father wanted me to have a summer job. I only wanted the dollar allowance he gave me each week, and the dollar and a quarter I earned caddying for him on weekend and Wednesday afternoons. With a quarter I could go to a movie, or buy a bottle of beer, or a pack of cigarettes to smoke secretly. I did not have a girlfriend, so I did not have to buy drinks or food or movie tickets for anyone else. I did not want to work. I wanted to drive around with my friends, or walk with them downtown, to stand in front of the department store, comb our ducktails, talk, look at girls.

My father was a civil engineer, and the district manager for 2

I like the indifferent teenage attitude set up [handwritten margin note] the Gulf States Utilities Company. He had been working for them since he left college, beginning as a surveyor, wearing boots and khakis and, in a holster on his belt, a twenty-two caliber pistol for cottonmouths. At home he was quiet; in the evenings he sat in his easy chair, and smoked, and read: *Time, The Saturday Evening Post, Collier's, The Reader's Digest,* detective novels, books about golf, and Book-of-the-Month Club novels. He loved to talk, and he did this at parties I listened to from my bedroom, and with his friends on the golf course, and drinking in the clubhouse after playing eighteen holes. I listened to more of my father's conversations about

---

It is time to thank my father for wanting me to work and telling me I had to work . . . and buying me lunch and a pith helmet instead of taking me home to my mother and sister.

I LOVE THIS ↑

politics and golf and his life and the world than I ever engaged in, during the nearly twenty-two years I lived with him. I was afraid of angering him, seeing his blue eyes, and reddening face, hearing the words he would use to rebuke me; but what I feared most was his voice, suddenly and harshly rising. He never yelled for long, only a few sentences, but they emptied me, as if his voice had pulled my soul from my body. His voice seemed to empty the house, too, and, when he stopped yelling, the house filled with silence. He did not yell often. That sound was not part of our family life. The fear of it was part of my love for him.

I was shy with him. Since my forties I have believed that he was shy with me too, and I hope it was not as painful for him as it was for me. I think my shyness had very little to do with my fear. Other boys had fathers who yelled longer and more

he set-up an amiable, strong image of his father

he's slowed the pace & filled w/ descrip.

3

often, fathers who spanked them or, when they were in their teens, slapped or punched them. My father spanked me only three times, probably because he did not know of most of my transgressions. My friends with harsher fathers were neither afraid nor shy; they quarreled with their fathers, provoked them. My father sired a sensitive boy, easily hurt or frightened, and he worried about me; I knew he did when I was a boy, and he told me this on his deathbed, when I was a Marine captain.

there's a strong father-son relationship

My imagination gave me a dual life: I lived in my body, and at the same time lived a life no one could see. All my life I have told myself stories, and have talked in my mind to friends. Imagine my father sitting at supper with my mother and two older sisters and me: I am ten and small and appear distracted. Every year at school there is a bully, sometimes a new one, sometimes the one from the year before. I draw bullies to me, not because I am small, but because they know I will neither fight nor inform on them. I will take their pushes or pinches or punches, and try not to cry, and I will pretend I am not hurt. My father does not know this. He only sees me at supper, and I am not there. I am riding a horse and shooting bad men. My father eats, glances at me. I know he is trying to see who I am, who I will be.

he seems to want to look strong to his dad

Before my teens, he took me to professional wrestling matches because I wanted to go; he told me they were fake, and I did not believe him. We listened to championship boxing matches on the radio. When I was not old enough to fire a shotgun he took me dove hunting with his friends: we crouched in a ditch facing a field, and I watched the doves fly toward us and my father rising to shoot, then I ran to fetch the warm, dead and delicious birds. In summer he took me fishing with his friends; we walked in woods to creeks and bayous and fished with bamboo poles. When I was ten he learned to play golf and stopped hunting and fishing, and on weekends I was his caddy. I did not want to be, I wanted to play with my friends, but when I became a man and left home, I was grateful that I had spent those afternoons watching him, listening to him. A minor league baseball team

the transition of admiration to wanting to be w/ friend to thankfulness is well-developed

made our town its home, and my father took me to games, usually with my mother. When I was twelve or so, he taught me to play golf, and sometimes I played nine holes with him; more often and more comfortably, I played with other boys.

If my father and I were not watching or listening to something and responding to it, or were not doing something, but were simply alone together, I could not talk, and he did not, and I felt that I should, and I was ashamed. That June of my seventeenth year, I could not tell him that I did not want a job. He talked to a friend of his, a building contractor, who hired me as a carpenter's helper; my pay was seventy-five cents an hour.

On a Monday morning my father drove me to work. I would ride the bus home and, next day, would start riding the bus to work. Probably my father drove me that morning because it was my first day; when I was twelve he had taken me to a store to buy my first pair of long pants; we boys wore shorts and, in fall and winter, knickers and long socks till we were twelve; and he had taken me to a barber for my first haircut. In the car I sat frightened, sadly resigned, and feeling absolutely incompetent. I had the lunch my mother had put in a brown paper bag, along with a mason jar with sugar and squeezed lemons in it, so I could make lemonade with water from the cooler. We drove to a street with houses and small stores and parked at a corner where, on a flat piece of land, men were busy. They were building a liquor store, and I assumed I would spend my summer handing things to a carpenter. I hoped he would be patient and kind.

As a boy in Louisiana's benevolent winters and hot summers I had played outdoors with friends: we built a clubhouse, chased each other on bicycles, shot air rifles at birds, tin cans, bottles, trees; in fall and winter, wearing shoulder pads and helmets, we played football on someone's very large side lawn; and in summer we played baseball in a field that a father mowed for us; he also built us a backstop of wood and chicken wire. None of us played well enough to be on a varsity team; but I wanted that gift, not knowing that it was a gift, and I felt ashamed that I did not have it. Now we drove

he seems almost ashamed of his lazy life

cars, smoked, drank in nightclubs. This was French Catholic country; we could always buy drinks. Sometimes we went on dates with girls, but more often looked at them and talked about them; or visited them, when several girls were gathered at the home of a girl whose parents were out for the evening. I had never done physical work except caddying, pushing a lawn mower, and raking leaves, and I was walking from the car with my father toward working men. My father wore his straw hat and seersucker suit. He introduced me to the foreman and said: "Make a man of him."

Then he left. The foreman wore a straw hat and looked old; everyone looked old; the foreman was probably thirty-five. I stood mutely, waiting for him to assign me to some good-hearted Cajun carpenter. He assigned me a pickaxe and a shovel and told me to get into the trench and go to work. In all four sides of the trench were files of black men, swinging picks, and shoveling. The trench was about three feet deep and it would be the building's foundation; I went to where the foreman pointed, and laid my tools on the ground; two black men made a space for me, and I jumped between them. They smiled and we greeted each other. I would learn days later that they earned a dollar an hour. They were men with families and I knew this was unjust, as everything else was for black people. But on that first morning I did not know what they were being paid, I did not know their names, only that one was working behind me and one in front, and they were good to me and stronger than I could ever be. All I really knew in those first hours under the hot sun was raising the pickaxe and swinging it down, raising it and swinging, again and again till the earth was loose; then putting the pick on the ground beside me and taking the shovel and plunging it into dirt that I lifted and tossed beside the trench.

he has respect for the black

I did not have the strength for this: not in my back, my legs, my arms, my shoulders. Certainly not in my soul. I only wanted it to end. The air was very humid, and sweat dripped on my face and arms, soaked my shirts and jeans. My hands gripping the pick or shovel were sore, my palms burned, the muscles in my arms ached, and my breath was quick. Some-

work is pain

9

10

times I saw tiny black spots before my eyes. Weakly I raised the pick, straightening my back, then swung it down, bending my body with it, and it felt heavier than I was, more durable, this thing of wood and steel that was melting me. I laid it on the ground and picked up the shovel and pushed it into the dirt, lifted it, grunted, and emptied it beside the trench. The sun, always my friend till now, burned me, and my mouth and throat were dry, and often I climbed out of the trench and went to the large tin water cooler with a block of ice in it and water from a hose. At the cooler were paper cups and salt tablets, and I swallowed salt and drank and drank, and poured water onto my head and face; then I went back to the trench, the shovel, the pick.

Nausea came in the third or fourth hour. I kept swinging the pick, pushing and lifting the shovel. I became my sick and hot and tired and hurting flesh. Or it became me; so, for an hour or more, I tasted a very small piece of despair. At noon in Lafayette a loud whistle blew, and in the cathedral the bell rang. I could not hear the bell where we worked, but I heard the whistle, and lowered the shovel and looked around. I was dizzy and sick. All the men had stopped working and were walking toward shade. One of the men with me said it was time to eat, and I climbed out of the trench and walked with black men to the shade of the tool shed. The white men went to another shaded place; I do not remember what work they had been doing that morning, but it was not with picks and shovels in the trench. Everyone looked hot but comfortable. The black men sat talking and began to eat and drink. My bag of lunch and jar with lemons and sugar were on the ground in the shade. Still I stood, gripped by nausea. I looked at the black men and at my lunch bag. Then my stomach tightened and everything in it rose, and I went around the corner of the shed where no one could see me and, bending over, I vomited and moaned and heaved until it ended. I went to the water cooler and rinsed my mouth and spat, and then I took another paper cup and drank. I walked back to the shade and lay on my back, tasting vomit. One of the black men said: "You got to eat."

"I threw up," I said, and closed my eyes and slept for the   12
rest of the hour that everyone—students and workers—had
for the noon meal. At home my nineteen-year-old sister and
my mother and father were eating dinner, meat and rice and
gravy, vegetables and salad and iced tea with a loaf of mint;
and an oscillating fan cooled them. My twenty-two-year-old
sister was married. At one o'clock the whistle blew, and I
woke up and stood and one of the black men said: "Are you
all right?"

I nodded. If I had spoken, I may have wept. When I was a   13
boy I could not tell a man what I felt, if I believed what I felt
was unmanly. We went back to the trench, down into it, and I
picked up the shovel I had left there at noon, and shoveled
out all the loose earth between me and the man in front of
me, then put the shovel beside the trench, lifted the pick,
raised it over my shoulder, and swung it down into the dirt. I
was dizzy and weak and hot; I worked for forty minutes or
so; then, above me, I heard my father's voice, speaking my
name. I looked up at him; he was here to take me home, to
forgive my failure, and in my great relief I could not know
that I would not be able to forgive it. I was going home. But
he said: "Let's go buy you a hat."

Every man there wore a hat, most of them straw, the oth-   14
ers baseball caps. I said nothing. I climbed out of the trench,
and went with my father. In the car, in a voice softened with
pride, he said: "The foreman called me. He said the Nigras
told him you threw up, and didn't eat, and you didn't tell
him."

"That's right," I said, and shamefully watched the road,   15
and cars with people who seemed free of all torment, and let
my father believe I was brave, because I was afraid to tell him
that I was afraid to tell the foreman. Quietly we drove to
town and he parked and took me first to a drugstore with air-
conditioning and a lunch counter, and bought me a 7-Up
for my stomach, and told me to order a sandwich. Sweet-
smelling women at the counter were smoking. The men in
the trench had smoked while they worked, but my body's
only desire had been to stop shoveling and swinging the pick,

to be with no transition at all in the shower at home, then to lie on my bed, feeling the soft breath of the fan on my damp skin. I would not have smoked at work anyway, with men. Now I wanted a cigarette. My father smoked, and I ate a bacon and lettuce and tomato sandwich.

Then we walked outside, into humidity and the heat and glare of the sun. We crossed the street to the department store where, in the work clothes section, my father chose a pith helmet. I did not want to wear a pith helmet. I would happily wear one in Africa, hunting lions and rhinoceroses. But I did not want to wear such a thing in Lafayette. I said nothing; there was no hat I wanted to wear. I carried the helmet in its bag out of the store and, in the car, laid it beside me. At that place where sweating men worked, I put it on; a thin leather strap looped around the back of my head. I went to my two comrades in the trench. One of them said: "That's a good hat."   16

I jumped in.   17

The man behind me said: "You going to be all right now."   18

I was; and I still do not know why. A sandwich and a soft drink had not given me any more strength than the breakfast I had vomited. An hour's respite in the car and the cool drugstore and buying the helmet that now was keeping my wet head cool certainly helped. But I had the same soft arms and legs, the same back and shoulders I had demanded so little of in my nearly seventeen years of stewardship. Yet all I remember of that afternoon is the absence of nausea.   19

At five o'clock the whistle blew downtown and we climbed out of the trench and washed our tools with the hose, then put them in the shed. Dirt was on my arms and hands, my face and neck and clothes. I could have wrung sweat from my shirt and jeans. I got my lunch from the shade. My two comrades said, See you tomorrow. I said I would see them. I went to the bus stop at the corner and sat on the bench. My wet clothes cooled my skin. I looked down at my dirty tennis shoes; my socks and feet were wet. I watched people in passing cars. In one were teenaged boys, and they laughed and shouted something about my helmet. I   20

[handwritten margin notes:] He seems to be gaining respect for everyday simple life

He's a dirty man working now

watched the car till it was blocks away, then took off the helmet and held it on my lap. I carried it aboard the bus; yet all summer I wore it at work, maybe because my father bought it for me and I did not want to hurt him, maybe because it was a wonderful helmet for hard work outdoors in Louisiana.

My father got home before I did and told my mother and sister the story, the only one he knew, or the only one I assumed he knew. The women proudly greeted me when I walked into the house. They were also worried. They wanted to know how I felt. They wore dresses, they smelled of perfume or cologne, they were drinking bourbon and water, and my sister and father were smoking cigarettes. Standing in the living room, holding my lunch and helmet, I said I was fine. I could not tell the truth to these women who loved me, even if my father were not there. I could not say that I was not strong enough and that I could not bear going back to work tomorrow, and all summer, anymore than I could tell them I did not believe I was as good at being a boy as other boys were: not at sports, or with girls; and now not with a man's work. I was home, where vases held flowers, and things were clean, and our manners were good.

Next morning, carrying my helmet and lunch, I rode the bus to work and joined the two black men in the trench. I felt that we were friends. Soon I felt this about all the black men at work. We were digging the foundation; we were the men and the boy with picks and shovels in the trench. One day the foundation was done. I use the passive voice, because this was a square or rectangular trench, men were working at each of its sides. I had been working with my comrades on the same side for weeks, moving not forward but down. Then it was done. Someone told us. Maybe the contractor was there, with the foreman. Who dug out that last bit of dirt? I only knew that I had worked as hard as I could, I was part of the trench, it was part of me, and it was finished; it was there in the earth to receive concrete and probably never to be seen again. Someone should have blown a bugle, we should have climbed exultant from the trench, gathered to wipe sweat from our brows, drink water, shake hands, then walk to-

21

22

He has a more "pretty" look on life

he under-stands now

gether to each of the four sides and marvel at what we had
made.

On that second morning of work I was not sick, and at
noon I ate lunch with the blacks in the shade, then we all
slept on the grass till one o'clock. We worked till five, said
goodbye to each other, and they went to the colored section
of town, and I rode the bus home. When I walked into the
living room, into cocktail hour, and my family asked me
about my day, I said it was fine. I may have learned something if I had told them the truth: the work was too hard, but
after the first morning I could bear it. And all summer it
would be hard; after we finished the foundation, I would be
transferred to another crew. We would build a mess hall at a
Boy Scout camp and, with a black man, I would dig a septic
tank in clay so hard that the foreman kept hosing water into it
as we dug; black men and I would push wheelbarrows of
mixed cement; on my shoulder I would carry eighty-pound
bags of dry cement, twenty-five pounds less than my own
weight; and at the summer's end my body would be twenty
pounds heavier. If I had told these three people who loved
me that I did not understand my weak body's stamina, they
may have taught me why something terrible had so quickly
changed to something arduous.

It is time to thank my father for wanting me to work and
telling me I had to work and getting the job for me and buying me lunch and a pith helmet instead of taking me home to
my mother and sister. He may have wanted to take me home.
But he knew he must not, and he came tenderly to me. My
mother would have been at home that afternoon; if he had
taken me to her she would have given me iced tea and, after
my shower, a hot dinner. When my sister came home from
work, she would have understood, and told me not to de-
spise myself because I could not work with a pickaxe and a
shovel. And I would have spent the summer at home, nestled
in the love of the two women, peering at my father's face, and
yearning to be someone I respected, a varsity second base-
man, a halfback, someone cheerleaders and drum major-
ettes and pretty scholars loved; yearning to be a man among

[handwritten margin notes: "23", "I think work is growing on him", "he's changed physically & mentally", "24", "weighing amounts"]

men, and that is where my father sent me with a helmet on
my head.

*I love his respect +
thankfulness*

For Study and Discussion

QUESTIONS FOR RESPONSE

1. Have you ever had a summer job that required hard physical labor? How did your body respond to the demands of this work?
2. In what ways did your parents teach you about work?

QUESTIONS ABOUT PURPOSE

1. How do Dubus's father's instructions to the foreman—"Make a
man of him"—reveal the narrator's purpose?
2. How is the narrator's admission that he lived a "dual life" revealed in his story?

QUESTIONS ABOUT AUDIENCE

1. How does Dubus's characterization of himself as sensitive and
shy help him establish a connection with his audience?
2. How does his friendship with black workmen help him teach his
audience something about justice?

QUESTIONS ABOUT STRATEGIES

1. How does Dubus pace his first day at work to reveal the intensity of his efforts?
2. How do Dubus's speculations about what would have happened if he had gone home to lunch help clarify the purpose of
the narrative?

QUESTIONS FOR DISCUSSION

1. Why is it difficult—according to Dubus—to tell the truth to
friends and family?
2. What does his father's decision to take him to lunch and buy
him a pith helmet reveal about the nature of many father-son
relationships?

JILL McCORKLE

Jill McCorkle was born in Lumberton, North Carolina, in 1958 and was educated at the University of North Carolina and Hollins College. After a career as a public school teacher and a librarian, she began teaching creative writing—first at the University of North Carolina, then at Harvard University, and currently at Bennington College. Her novels, many of them focusing on small-town life in the South, include *The Cheerleader* (1984), *July 7th* (1984), *Tending to Virginia* (1987), *Ferris Beach* (1990), and *Carolina Moon* (1996). Her short stories have been collected in *Crash Diet* (1992), *Final Vinyl Days* (1997), and *Creatures of Habit* (2001). In "The Mullet Girls," reprinted from the *Washington Post Magazine*, McCorkle remembers the summer she turned thirteen, when an encounter with two overly friendly strangers caused her to see her family in a new way.

The Mullet Girls

E VERY SUMMER MY family spent a week at the beach—for years going to the same house at Holden Beach, N.C. This house had (pre-Hurricane Hazel, 1954) been set back from the ocean a couple of rows but now in the late '60s and early '70s was oceanfront, high tide reaching and lapping beneath the wooden steps leading up to the screened-in porch. My dad's best friend, who owned the house, continued to pay a meager amount of property tax (seventy-odd cents a year) on the land that was already submerged. In spite of many efforts, sandbags and sea oats, the ocean has continued

1

that sounds gorgeous

to devour this small part of the world such that what I re-member is far removed from what now remains.

I had just turned 13 and for the first time was dividing my days between my mom and older sister, who liked to sun and read, and my dad, who spent the entire day either fishing or getting ready to fish. The house was full of people that sum-mer, various friends and relatives, our teenage boy cousins we didn't see very often. We spent a lot of time playing cards, our cousins' united goal being to get us to say "the ace of spades," which sent them into convulsive laughter about how we sounded just like we had stepped out of "The Andy

---

Temptation had come knocking on our door, and my dad, with gentle Southern kindness, had more or less said, Thank you very much but no thanks.

Griffith Show." They were, after all, from Maryland, which was the North by our standards.

Out of the blue on one of those afternoons, two women in bikini tops and short shorts appeared at the screen door. They called out my father's name in shrill girlish yoo-hoos, "Johnny! Oh, Johnny!"

We all froze. Even though the whole exchange took only a few minutes it became the event of the week and one we re-ferred to often for years after. We called them the Bathing Beauties, the Beach Walkers, the Mullet Girls.

Any other year and I would not have been the one to go to the door. I would have been with my dad fishing. I was his fishing buddy (or at least he allowed me to think that); his surrogate son. I prided myself on being the daughter who could touch anything stinky and slimy without flinching. I reached into the rich loamy earth and plucked my own fat squirmy bloodworm from the plastic carton. I speared, twisted and looped it on my hook, wiped the blood and goo on the butt of my swimsuit. I had spent hours learning how to cast, my thumb poised and ready to slow the momentum smoothly instead of giving it a jerk that would result in my dad having to sit and unwrap and untangle—something he had already done many, many times.

Once we caught a spiney sharp-toothed fish, his struggling mouth like serrated scissors. It looked prehistoric, spiked and dangerous, and I am still not sure to this day what kind of fish it was. My dad gave up trying to extract the bloody hook where it was firmly wedged and simply cut the line up close and tossed the creature back into the surf. "Poor old fella," he said, "his wife is going to be so disappointed when he gets home." Just the way he said it with such conviction and compassion left me saddened for the rest of the day as I imagined that silver briney body cutting its way against the tide, the hook already rusting. All day I saw him swimming out into the coldest, darkest depths in search of his mate.

The women at the door were as surprised to see all of us as we were to see them. I just stood and stared at them through the dark mesh of the screen. I had seen them earlier as I rocked on the porch and used the binoculars to spot dolphins and the large shrimp boats that were always hovering on the horizon. I had watched them strolling back and forth on the beach, bending to pick up shells in a way that made their shorts ride up even higher. They had stopped several times and peered into the yellow bucket beside my dad's sand chair, which we had just given him for Father's Day, curious about his catch. I knew there was probably nothing in the bucket. I knew that he often stopped baiting his hook so that he had an excuse to sit and stare at the ocean.

What I had seen from a distance as the Mullet Girls strolled back and forth were two bronzed bodies in bikinis. Up close they were not at all what I had expected.

"Is Johnny here?" the one with bobbypinned rollers hidden up under her scarf asked. I did not like the sound of his name coming out of her mouth. It made me mad. It made me feel just as I had as a 6-year-old, when, after seeing "The

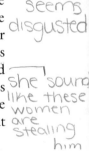

sounds like smtg happened between her parents

Sound of Music," my dad commented on how pretty he thought Julie Andrews was. I worried for the next two months that my parents would leave each other for Julie Andrews and Christopher Plummer, and there I'd be with eight siblings instead of one. My sister would do okay; she could sing. But where would I ever fit in with that crew?

"Well, is he still fishing somewhere?" This was the short   10
one, her hair bleached to a shade of yellow that would only be considered natural on an egg yolk. She closed one eye against the trail of smoke from the cigarette she held in the corner of her mouth. Her hands, I noticed, were clutching a big canvas bag.

why are the cousins obsessed w/ accents?

"He's not here," I said, hoping that my cousins were hear-   11
ing their accents, slow and flat even to my ear. The folks from Mayberry sounded like British royalty by comparison. "And I'm not sure where he is."

"Well, you tell him we were by," the short one said. "He'll   12
know who you mean. We promised him some mullet if we had us some luck, and, boy, did we have us some luck."

"We'll stop by after dark," the other one said, and I stood   13
and watched as they walked down the road to an old blue Chevrolet.

I knew exactly where my dad was. Every day, late after-   14
noon, low tide, and he walked way down the beach to what we referred to as the point, a place where a small channel connected the ocean to the inland waterway. At low tide we could walk across the channel and find live starfish and sand dollars and conchs along the way. He could sit there for

sounds like typical dad

hours, just watching the water, tending his fishing pole, puffing on his pipe, sipping a beer. He liked to think about all that he would do when his ship came in—a long, long list— only to make his way back around to say that things were pretty good the way that they were, he really wouldn't want to change a whole lot. Maybe he'd ask for two weeks vacation from his job at the post office instead of one.

He talked about depression long before it was an accept-   15
able thing to talk about, taking great solace in the knowledge that both Lincoln and Churchill had been fellow sufferers.

He had also found a way to put a positive spin on that condi- *[he's a good guy]*
tion, saying about at least one acquaintance, "I don't know
that I think that fella is smart enough to be depressed." He
told me how some of the greatest moments of his life were
when he fished with my mother's father long before he had
married into the family. How my grandfather had tied a rope
to his belt, the other end to a sack of beers which he allowed
to roll and wash under the waves where it was cool.

For years my dad had entrusted me with a special assign- *[16]*
ment. When he left for the point, he handed me an alarm
clock with strict instructions that when the alarm sounded I
should run to the refrigerator and grab the brown paper bag
and run as fast as I could down to his special fishing spot. For
a long time I thought that I was carrying bait, the bait that
would land the huge fish that had just gotten away. What I
ultimately discovered was that in those pre-Playmate cooler
days, I was making a beer run—two iced Falstaffs wrapped in
aluminum foil and swaddled in paper towels in the paper
sack. I was a two-legged Saint Bernard. I was part of a legacy
my maternal grandfather had started. My dad fancied the
idea of Smoky, our black shepherd mix who hated anyone
who was not in our immediate family, with a keg on his neck,
but by then he had his cooler. And he still had me. *[it's amazing how much time & effort men will put into getting a beer]*

"Who were they?" my mother asked. "Have you ever seen *[17]*
such skimpy outfits?" If there was a flush to her cheeks, it was
well concealed by her annual sunburn. Fair and freckled, she
was trying to get a tan even if it meant the occasional burn
and a dousing of QT lotion. "And what did they want with
Johnny?"

I told her how up close they looked nothing like they did *[18]* *[she gets it from her mother]*
from a distance. They were old looking. Coarse. Rough and
worn out. They were wrinkled like old prunes and they
smelled fishy.

"Something's fishy," she said, and though I knew it was a *[19]*
joke, I found it hard to laugh. I kept thinking how she had
said, "What did they want with Johnny?" Not your daddy,
but Johnny, leaving me to feel left out the same way I did
when I looked at photographs before I was born: a young

family of three, or before my sister; a couple of newlyweds. They had known each other their whole lives; they had dated since they were 16. They had been married for 20 years and were in their early forties, and it was the first time since "The Sound of Music" that I had ever really thought of them as people who might attract others, or worse be attracted to another, especially another who did not resemble Julie Andrews in the slightest.

It's odd but very true

"One of them had her hair rolled up," I said. "Where's she going, Surfside or Van Werry's?"—the one and only grocery store down near the drawbridge. Everybody else just laughed and went back to playing spades. There was nowhere to go in that neck of the woods other than Surfside Pavilion, a squat, pink cinderblock building with two pool tables and a few pinball machines and a miniature golf course that was always soggy and warped from years of damp salt air and rain.

She sounds jealous

20

I had seen girls hanging out of car windows hooting and hollering at boys who stood around outside the pavilion smoking cigarettes and waxing their surfboards. My mother liked to use loud girls who hung out of car windows with cigarettes in their mouths and breasts spilling from tight bathing suits as examples of what not to grow up and be.

21

"Don't you ever let me catch you looking like that," my mother said.

22

"So we should hide?" my sister asked without cracking a smile. She was 16 and had far more clout than I did.

23

We had heard all the stories about what girls NOT to be like. It was for this very reason that we had stopped going to Ocean Drive and Myrtle Beach, which had become a haven for teenagers and college kids who wanted to party, have sex, fall into violent and drunken sidewalk brawls and enter the shag contests at places like the Pad and the Spanish Galleon, where the music of the Tams and the Drifters and Maurice Williams and the Zodiacs blasted all through the night. People said that you could go to South Carolina and get married, get a drink or two, buy some fireworks, get a divorce and still be home in time for the 11 o'clock news.

24

Surfside Pavilion paled by comparison, but we had gotten

25

used to it. The quiet; the women like my mother who, if they wore a swimsuit at all, wore a one-piece with boy legs or little skirts. Suits that hid all evidence that children had ever sprung from their bodies.

That summer I wore bikinis and I was working on my tan and spraying lemon juice into my hair, as Glamour magazine suggested, more than I was fishing. I braided my long hair into pigtails and wore a beaded headband. I wore a large silver peace sign strung on a piece of rawhide (both items that I had purchased at the pier after reading all the dirty postcards that were prominently displayed on a revolving rack). My sister spent most of the late afternoons strumming her guitar and singing Joan Baez and Bob Dylan songs. She wrapped her guitar in a blanket and placed it on the empty bottom bunk below me so that the salt air wouldn't damage it. Her boyfriend had driven down to see her a couple of days earlier, then a couple of friends came by with some friends who brought some friends and so on. My mom said that she didn't like how one of those boys looked at me, with me barely 13 years old, and that even if I had wanted to tag along and walk down the beach with them when asked she would not have let me.

Somebody was looking at me that way? I asked again. After all, I would never wear that beaded headband once I got home and the fire engine nail polish would come off, too. I didn't mind hearing that I had been looked at; I just didn't want to hear it my mom. And I did want to know just what had led him to look at me. What had I said that might have lured his attention? That I really liked Cat Stevens's song "Wild World," that I had been to a Steppenwolf concert? Or was it that I was still on those hot late afternoons willing to go down to the point to crab, dragging a stinking, half-rotten fish head behind me.

And now here were the Mullet Girls—live and in Technicolor. This wasn't a picture of a couple of young wild beach babes. This was the after picture: the wild young girls who got old quick after a lot of fast and rough living. Bad men and bad marriages. The flat, tired eyes, the smear of cheap *nice descrip'*

lipstick, the way that they seemed to crane their necks to look longingly into the cottage where my mother sat in her long shorts, hair blown back from her smooth, clean face. The Mullet Girls made me stop and look at my mother in a whole new way.

They did return later that night, long after my dad had come home with an empty bucket, long after the last boiled shrimp was eaten and we were all out on the porch—no lights so we could see the stars and the flash of the beacon from the Fort Caswell lighthouse. At high tide the waves lapped up under the house, the beginning of a cycle that would—over the next 20 years—claim all of the shore where all of this took place. My own adolescent Atlantis.

I like that

The Mullet Girls arrived in fancy white slacks rolled up so that they didn't get wet, shiny spiked-heel sandals swinging from their fingers. The blonde carried the sack, this time held far away from her low-cut silky blouse. They were definitely dressed for an evening out. They came with a gift of mullets and who knows what else had they not found an entire family perched in the dark.

My dad politely opened the door and invited them in while I held tight to Smoky's collar. The blonde put one bare foot forward and then stopped short when she saw us there.

"Oh my," she laughed nervously and looked over to get her friend's reaction. "You all look like a bunch of owls up here." They both watched my dad, who flipped the switch of the yellow bulb beside the door. She handed him the bag of mullets, which he graciously accepted even though I knew that he would toss them in the freezer below for the next visitor. He wasn't going to clean them and I knew my mother wasn't. He turned and introduced us all—his wife, his kids, his dog. By then their speech was animated, their polite nods to us stiff and hurried. And then they were going—over to the Blockade Runner at Wrightsville Beach, where there was a comedy show—cover charge covered two of your drinks, they said. They wiggled off in a cloud of cologne and whiskey-voiced giggles and we never saw them again.

the father is very polite

The Mullet Girls. Temptation had come knocking on our

29

30

31

32

33

door, and my dad, with gentle Southern kindness, had more
or less said, Thank you very much but no thanks. I know they
had been hoping for a different scenario, and I often pictured
them returning from vacation to dark and cold places, imag-
ining how different their lives might be if they had ever
landed someone like my dad. How different it might be if
that stretch of the coast had not been gradually washed over
by the ocean, and if parents never got older, never got sick,
never died. There are times when I hear an alarm clock and
before I can pull myself up and through the years I am thinking "grab the bag, grab the bag" and then I am off and running down to the point, fine white sand sifting under my feet.
I am only 13; my dad is 42.

For Study and Discussion

QUESTIONS FOR RESPONSE

1. What special events do you remember from your family's summer vacation?
2. What advice did your father or mother give you about how to
   dress and behave?

QUESTIONS ABOUT PURPOSE

1. How does McCorkle's description of her fishing abilities and
   her attempt to acquire a good tan reveal the source of her confusion about the Mullet Girls?
2. Why does the use of the word *Johnny* by the Mullet Girls make
   McCorkle see her father and mother in new ways?

QUESTIONS ABOUT AUDIENCE

1. How do McCorkle's references to South Carolina help her
   readers understand her family's choice of a vacation site?
2. How does McCorkle's response to her father's reference to Julie
   Andrews in *The Sound of Music* enable her readers to understand
   her concern about the Mullet Girls?

QUESTIONS ABOUT STRATEGIES

1. How does McCorkle's description of the Mullet Girls to her mother establish the conflict in the narrative?
2. How does McCorkle's interpretation of her father's response to the Mullet Girls' gift resolve that conflict?

QUESTIONS FOR DISCUSSION

1. How does McCorkle's description of her father's "depression" explain why she is worried about his "temptation"?
2. Why does McCorkle's concern about how "those boys" looked at her explain her confusion about her mother and father?

Judith Ortiz Cofer was born in Hormigueros, Puerto Rico, in 1952. She emigrated to the United States in 1956 and was educated at Augusta College, Florida Atlantic University, and Oxford University. She has taught in the public schools of Palm Beach County, Florida, as well as at several universities such as Miami University and the University of Georgia. Her poetry is collected in *Reading for the Mainland* (1987) and *Terms of Survival* (1987), and her first novel, *The Line of the Sun* (1989), was nominated for the Pulitzer Prize. Her recent books include *The Latin Deli: Prose and Poetry* (1993) and *An Island like You: Stories of the Barrio* (1995). In "The Myth of the Latin Woman: I Just Met a Girl Named María," reprinted from *The Latin Deli*, Cofer describes several experiences that taught her about the pervasive stereotypes of Latin women.

The Myth of the Latin Woman: I Just Met a Girl Named María

O N A BUS trip to London from Oxford University where I was earning some graduate credits one summer, a young man, obviously fresh from a pub, spotted me and as if struck by inspiration went down on his knees in the aisle. With both hands over his heart he broke into an Irish tenor's rendition of "María" from *West Side Story*. My politely amused fellow passengers gave his lovely voice the round of gentle applause it deserved. Though I was not

1

that is a typical assumption

quite as amused, I managed my version of an English smile:
no show of teeth, no extreme contortions of the facial muscles—I was at this time of my life practicing reserve and cool.
Oh, that British control, how I coveted it. But María had
followed me to London, reminding me of a prime fact of my
life: you can leave the Island, master the English language,
and travel as far as you can, but if you are a Latina, especially
one like me who so obviously belongs to Rita Moreno's
gene pool, the Island travels with you.

This is sometimes a very good thing—it may win you that   2
extra minute of someone's attention. But with some people,

When a Puerto Rican girl dressed in her
idea of what is attractive meets a man
from the mainstream culture who has been
trained to react to certain types of clothing,
a clash is likely to take place.

---

the same things can make *you* an island—not so much a tropical paradise as an Alcatraz, a place nobody wants to visit. As a
Puerto Rican girl growing up in the United States and wanting like most children to "belong," I resented the stereotype
that my Hispanic appearance called forth from many people
I met.

Our family lived in a large urban center in New Jersey dur-   3
ing the sixties, where life was designed as a microcosm of my
parents' casas on the island. We spoke in Spanish, we ate
Puerto Rican food bought at the bodega, and we practiced
strict Catholicism complete with Saturday confession and
Sunday mass at a church where our parents were accommodated into a one-hour Spanish mass slot, performed by a Chinese priest trained as a missionary for Latin America.

As a girl I was kept under strict surveillance, since virtue   4
and modesty were, by cultural equation, the same as family

[handwritten margin note, left: It's funny cause even by mistake I associate matches as such]

[handwritten margin note, bottom left: they're very religious]

honor. As a teenager I was instructed on how to behave as a proper señorita. But it was a conflicting message girls got, since the Puerto Rican mothers also encouraged their daughters to look and act like women and to dress in clothes our Anglo friends and their mothers found too "mature" for our age. It was, and is, cultural, yet I often felt humiliated when I appeared at an American friend's party wearing a dress more suitable to a semiformal than to a playroom birthday celebration. At Puerto Rican festivities, neither the music nor the colors we wore could be too loud. I still experience a vague sense of letdown when I'm invited to a "party" and it turns out to be a marathon conversation in hushed tones rather than a fiesta with salsa, laughter, and dancing—the kind of celebration I remember from my childhood.

I remember Career Day in our high school, when teachers told us to come dressed as if for a job interview. It quickly became obvious that to the barrio girls, "dressing up" sometimes meant wearing ornate jewelry and clothing that would be more appropriate (by mainstream standards) for the company Christmas party than as daily office attire. That morning I had agonized in front of my closet, trying to figure out what a "career girl" would wear because, essentially, except for Marlo Thomas on TV, I had no models on which to base my decision. I knew how to dress for school: at the Catholic school I attended we all wore uniforms; I knew how to dress for Sunday mass, and I knew what dresses to wear for parties at my relatives' homes. Though I do not recall the precise details of my Career Day outfit, it must have been a composite of the above choices. But I remember a comment my friend (an Italian-American) made in later years that coalesced my impressions of that day. She said that at the business school she was attending the Puerto Rican girls always stood out for wearing "everything at once." She meant, of course, too much jewelry, too many accessories. On that day at school, we were simply made the negative models by the nuns who were themselves not credible fashion experts to any of us. But it was painfully obvious to me that to the others, in their tailored skirts and silk blouses, we must have seemed "hopeless" and "vulgar." Though I now know that most adolescents feel out of step much of the time, I also know that for the Puerto Rican girls of my generation that sense was intensified. The way our teachers and classmates looked at us that day in school was just a taste of the culture clash that awaited us in the real world, where prospective employers and men on the street would often misinterpret our tight skirts and jingling bracelets as a come-on.

Mixed cultural signals have perpetuated certain stereotypes—for example, that of the Hispanic woman as the "Hot Tamale" or sexual firebrand. It is a one-dimensional view that the media have found easy to promote. In their special vocabulary, advertisers have designated "sizzling" and "smoldering" as the adjectives of choice for describing not only the foods but also the women of Latin America. From conversations in my house I recall hearing about the harassment that Puerto Rican women endured in factories where the "boss men" talked to them as if sexual innuendo was all they understood and, worse, often gave them the choice of submitting to advances or being fired.

It is custom, however, not chromosomes, that leads us to choose scarlet over pale pink. As young girls, we were influenced in our decisions about clothes and colors by the women—older sisters and mothers who had grown up on a tropical island where the natural environment was a riot of primary colors, where showing your skin was one way to keep cool as well as to look sexy. Most important of all, on the island, women perhaps felt freer to dress and move more provocatively, since, in most cases, they were protected by the traditions, mores, and laws of a Spanish/Catholic system of morality and machismo whose main rule was: *You may look at my sister, but if you touch her I will kill you.* The extended family and church structure could provide a young woman with a circle of safety in her small pueblo on the island; if a man "wronged" a girl, everyone would close in to save her family honor.

This is what I have gleaned from my discussions as an

I really like her diction here

Nice :)

adult with older Puerto Rican women. They have told me about dressing in their best party clothes on Saturday nights and going to the town's plaza to promenade with their girlfriends in front of the boys they liked. The males were thus given an opportunity to admire the women and to express their admiration in the form of *piropos:* erotically charged street poems they composed on the spot. I have been subjected to a few piropos while visiting the Island, and they can be outrageous, although custom dictates that they must never cross into obscenity. This ritual, as I understand it, also entails a show of studied indifference on the woman's part; if she is "decent," she must not acknowledge the man's impassioned words. So I do understand how things can be lost in translation. When a Puerto Rican girl dressed in her idea of what is attractive meets a man from the mainstream culture who has been trained to react to certain types of clothing as a sexual signal, a clash is likely to take place. The line I first heard based on this aspect of the myth happened when the boy who took me to my first formal dance leaned over to plant a sloppy overeager kiss painfully on my mouth, and when I didn't respond with sufficient passion said in a resentful tone: "I thought you Latin girls were supposed to mature early"—my first instance of being thought of as a fruit or vegetable—I was supposed to *ripen,* not just grow into womanhood like other girls.

It is surprising to some of my professional friends that some people, including those who should know better, still put others "in their place." Though rarer, these incidents are still commonplace in my life. It happened to me most recently during a stay at a very classy metropolitan hotel favored by young professional couples for their weddings. Late one evening after the theater, as I walked toward my room with my new colleague (a woman with whom I was coordinating an arts program), a middle-aged man in a tuxedo, a young girl in satin and lace on his arm, stepped directly into our path. With his champagne glass extended toward me, he exclaimed, "Evita!"

Our way blocked, my companion and I listened as the man   10
half-recited, half-bellowed "Don't Cry for Me, Argentina."
When he finished, the young girl said: "How about a round
of applause for my daddy?" We complied, hoping this would
bring the silly spectacle to a close. I was becoming aware that
our little group was attracting the attention of the other
guests. "Daddy" must have perceived this too, and he once
more barred the way as we tried to walk past him. He began
to shout-sing a ditty to the tune of "La Bamba"—except the
lyrics were about a girl named María whose exploits all
rhymed with her name and gonorrhea. The girl kept saying
"Oh, Daddy" and looking at me with pleading eyes. She
wanted me to laugh along with the others. My companion
and I stood silently waiting for the man to end his offensive
song. When he finished, I looked not at him but at his
daughter. I advised her calmly never to ask her father what he
had done in the army. Then I walked between them and to
my room. My friend complimented me on my cool handling
of the situation. I confessed to her that I really had wanted to
push the jerk into the swimming pool. I knew that this same
man—probably a corporate executive, well educated, even
worldly by most standards—would not have been likely to re-
gale a white woman with a dirty song in public. He would
perhaps have checked his impulse by assuming that she could
be somebody's wife or mother, or at least *somebody* who
might take offense. But to him, I was just an Evita or a María:
merely a character in his cartoon-populated universe.

Because of my education and my proficiency with the   11
English language, I have acquired many mechanisms for
dealing with the anger I experience. This was not true for my
parents, nor is it true for the many Latin women working at
menial jobs who must put up with stereotypes about our ethnic group such as: "They make good domestics." This is another facet of the myth of the Latin woman in the United
States. Its origin is simple to deduce. Work as domestics,
waitressing, and factory jobs are all that's available to women
with little English and few skills. The myth of the Hispanic

menial has been sustained by the same media phenomenon that made "Mammy" from *Gone with the Wind* America's idea of the black woman for generations; María, the housemaid or counter girl, is now indelibly etched into the national psyche. The big and the little screens have presented us with the picture of the funny Hispanic maid, mispronouncing words and cooking up a spicy storm in a shiny California kitchen.

This media-engendered image of the Latina in the United States has been documented by feminist Hispanic scholars, who claim that such portrayals are partially responsible for the denial of opportunities for upward mobility among Latinas in the professions. I have a Chicana friend working on a Ph.D. in philosophy at a major university. She says her doctor still shakes his head in puzzled amazement at all the "big words" she uses. Since I do not wear my diplomas around my neck for all to see, I too have on occasion been sent to that "kitchen," where some think I obviously belong. 12

One such incident that has stayed with me, though I recognize it as a minor offense, happened on the day of my first public poetry reading. It took place in Miami in a boat-restaurant where we were having lunch before the event. I was nervous and excited as I walked in with my notebook in my hand. An older woman motioned me to her table. Thinking (foolish me) that she wanted me to autograph a copy of my brand new slender volume of verse, I went over. She ordered a cup of coffee from me, assuming that I was the waitress. Easy enough to mistake my poems for menus, I suppose. I know that it wasn't an intentional act of cruelty, yet of all the good things that happened that day, I remember that scene most clearly, because it reminded me of what I had to overcome before anyone would take me seriously. In retrospect I understand that my anger gave my reading fire, that I have almost always taken doubts in my abilities as a challenge—and that the result is, most times, a feeling of satisfaction at having won a convert when I see the cold, appraising eyes warm to my words, the body language change, the smile 13

I wonder what triggers such an assumption

that indicates that I have opened some avenue for communication. That day I read to that woman and her lowered eyes told me that she was embarrassed at her little faux pas, and when I willed her to look up at me, it was my victory, and she graciously allowed me to punish her with my full attention. We shook hands at the end of the reading, and I never saw her again. She has probably forgotten the whole thing but maybe not.

Yet I am one of the lucky ones. My parents made it possible for me to acquire a stronger footing in the mainstream culture by giving me the chance at an education. And books and art have saved me from the harsher forms of ethnic and racial prejudice that many of my Hispanic *compañeras* have had to endure. I travel a lot around the United States, reading from my books of poetry and my novel, and the reception I most often receive is one of positive interest by people who want to know more about my culture. There are, however, thousands of Latinas without the privilege of an education or the entrée into society that I have. For them life is a struggle against the misconceptions perpetuated by the myth of the Latina as whore, domestic or criminal. We cannot change this by legislating the way people look at us. The transformation, as I see it, has to occur at a much more individual level. My personal goal in my public life is to try to replace the old pervasive stereotypes and myths about Latinas with a much more interesting set of realities. Every time I give a reading, I hope the stories I tell, the dreams and fears I examine in my work, can achieve some universal truth which will get my audience past the particulars of my skin color, my accent, or my clothes.

I once wrote a poem in which I called us Latinas "God's brown daughters." This poem is really a prayer of sorts, offered upward, but also, through the human-to-human channel of art, outward. It is a prayer for communication, and for respect. In it, Latin women pray "in Spanish to an Anglo God / with a Jewish heritage," and they are "fervently hoping / that if not omnipotent, / at least He be bilingual."

For Study and Discussion

QUESTIONS FOR RESPONSE

1. In what ways have people misread your behavior—by focusing on your clothes, your language, or your looks?
2. What strategies do you use to control your anger and resentment when you are misread?

QUESTIONS ABOUT PURPOSE

1. Why does Cofer introduce the conflict between *custom* and *chromosomes*? How does this conflict help explain the concept of *stereotype*?
2. How does this narrative help accomplish Cofer's "personal goal in her public life"?

QUESTIONS ABOUT AUDIENCE

1. In what ways does Cofer use the references to *María* and *Evita* to identify her audience?
2. How does she use the example of the *piropos* to educate her audience?

QUESTIONS ABOUT STRATEGIES

1. How does Cofer use the details of Career Day to explain how a cultural stereotype is perpetuated?
2. How does she manipulate point of view at her "first public poetry reading" to illustrate how she intends to change that stereotype?

QUESTIONS FOR DISCUSSION

1. How does Cofer use *Gone with the Wind* to illustrate how the media create stereotypes?
2. Why does she put so much emphasis on education? What can it do *for* you? What might it do *to* you?

Helen Prejean was born in 1939 in Baton Rouge, Louisiana. At the age of eighteen, she entered the Order of the Sisters of St. Joseph of Medaille and taught English in various Catholic schools until she moved into a New Orleans housing project and co-founded a community service agency. When a friend suggested that she write to Patrick Sonnier, an inmate on death row, Prejean began a correspondence that prompted her to visit him in prison and eventually become his spiritual adviser. These experiences became the subject of her best-selling book, *Dead Man Walking: An Eyewitness Account of the Death Penalty in the United States* (1993). The book was adapted to the screen, and the film version earned Susan Sarandon an Oscar for Best Performance by an Actress in 1996. In "Memories of a Dead Man Walking," Sister Helen watches the making of the movie and is "sucked back into the original scene."

Memories of a Dead Man Walking

T HERE SHE WAS during the filming of *Dead Man Walk-* 1 *ing,* Susan Sarandon being me, going into the women's room in the death house, putting her head against the tile wall, grabbing the crucifix around her neck, praying, "Please God, don't let him fall apart." It's something to watch a film of yourself happening in front of your eyes, kind of funny to hear somebody saying that she's you, but I don't stay long with this mirror stuff. What happens is that I'm sucked back into the original scene, the white-hot fire of what actually happened.

How would my life story look? [handwritten marginal note]

There in the Louisiana death house on April 4, 1984, I was scared out of my mind. I had never watched anybody be killed. I was supposed to be the condemned man's spiritual advisor. I was in over my head. All I had agreed to in the beginning was to be a pen pal to Patrick Sonnier. Sure, I said, I could write letters. But the man was all alone. He had no one to visit him, and it was like a current in a river: I got sucked in, and the next thing I was saying was, Okay, sure, I'll come to visit you, and when I filled out the prison application form

What is it like, to watch someone die?

The torture happens when conscious human beings are condemned to death and begin to anticipate that death and die a thousand times before they die.

---

to be approved as his visitor, he suggested spiritual advisor, and I said, Sure. He was Catholic, and I'm a Catholic nun, and it seemed right, but I didn't know that at the end, on the evening of the execution, everybody has to leave the death house at 5:45 p.m. Everybody but the spiritual advisor. The spiritual advisor stays to the end. The spiritual advisor witnesses the execution.

People ask me all the time, What's a nun doing getting involved with these murderers? You know how people have these stereotypical images of nuns—nuns teach, nuns nurse the sick. I tell people: Look at who Jesus hung out with—lepers, prostitutes, thieves, the throwaways of his day. People don't get it. There's a lot of "biblical quarterbacking" in death penalty debates, with people tossing in quotes from the Bible to back up what they've already decided on, people wanting to practice vengeance and have God agree with them. The same thing happened in this country in the slavery debates and in the debates over women's suffrage. Quote that Bible. God said torture. God said get revenge. Religion is tricky business.

I like her personalized grasp of religion

Her childhood is a big influence

But here's the real reason I got involved with death row   4
inmates: I got involved with poor people. And everybody
who lives on this planet and has at least one eye open knows
that only poor people get selected for death row. On June 1,
1981, I drove a little brown truck into St. Thomas, a black,
inner-city housing project in New Orleans, and began to live
there with four other sisters (with my scared Catholic Mama
kneeling on crushed glass and saying her rosary, praying that
her daughter wouldn't be shot). ("Kneeling on crushed
glass" is just an expression. Read *fervently*.)

Growing up a Southern white girl in Baton Rouge, right   5
on the cusp of the upper class, I had only known black people
as my servants. I went to an all-white high school—this was
in the fifties—and black people had to sit in the back of
the bus and up in the balcony of the Paramount and Hart
theaters.

I got a whole other kind of education in the St. Thomas   6
Projects. I still go there every Monday to keep close to
friends I made there and to keep close to the struggle. Living
there, it didn't take long to see that there was a greased track
to prison and death row. As one Mama put it: "Our boys
leave here in a police car or a hearse."

When I began visiting Pat Sonnier in 1982, I couldn't   7
have been more naïve about prisons. The only other experience with prisoners I'd had was in the '60s when Sister Cletus
and I—decked in full head-to-toe habits—went to Orleans
Parish Prison one time to play our guitars and sing with the
prisoners. This was the era of singing nuns, the "Dominica-
nica-nica" era, and the guards brought us all into this big
room with over one hundred prisoners and I said, "Let's do
'If I Had a Hammer,'" and the song took off like a shot. The
men really got into it and started making up their own verses:
"*If I had a switchblade* . . ." laughing and singing loud, and
the guards were rolling their eyes. Sister Cletus and I weren't
invited back to sing there again. And the movie got this scene
right, at least the telling of it. Sister Helen/Susan tells this
story to the chaplain who has asked her if she's had any experience in prisons. He's not amused.

Nuns can have fun.

I wrote Patrick Sonnier about life in St. Thomas, and he [8] wrote me about life in a six-by-eight foot cell. He and forty other men were confined twenty-three out of twenty-four hours a day in cells of this size, and he'd say how glad he was when summer was over because there was no fresh air in their unventilated cells, and he'd sometimes wet the sheet from his bunk and put it on the cement floor to try to cool off, or he'd clean out his toilet bowl and stand in it and use a small plastic container to get water from his lavatory and pour it over his body. Patrick was on death row four years before they killed him.

I made a bad mistake. When I found out about Patrick [9] Sonnier's crime—he and his brother were convicted of killing two teenage kids—I didn't go to see the victims' families. I stayed away because I wasn't sure how to deal with such raw pain. The movie's got this part down pat. It really takes you over to the victims' families and helps you see their pain and my awful tension with them. In real life I was a coward. I stayed away and only met the victims' families at Patrick's pardon board hearing. They were there to demand the execution. I was there to ask the board to show mercy. It was not a good time to meet.

Here were two sets of parents whose children had been [10] ripped from them, condemned in their pain and loss to a kind of death row of their own. I felt terrible. I was powerless to assuage their grief. It would take me a long time to learn how to help victims' families, a long time before I would sit at their support group meetings and hear their unspeakable stories of loss and grief and rage and guilt. I would learn that the divorce rate for couples who lose a child is over seventy percent—a new twist to "until death do us part." I would learn that often after a murder, friends stay away because they don't know how to respond to the pain. I would learn that black families or Hispanic families or poor families who have a loved one murdered not only don't expect the district attorney's office to pursue the death penalty but are surprised when the case is prosecuted at all. In Louisiana, murder victims' families are allowed to sit on the front row in the execution chamber to watch the murderer die. Some families. Not all. But black families almost never witness the execution of someone who has killed their loved one, because in Louisiana, the hangman's noose, then the electric chair, and now the lethal injection gurney, are almost exclusively reserved for those who killed whites. Ask Virginia Smith's African-American family. She was fourteen when three white youths took her into the woods, raped, and stabbed her to death. None of them got the death penalty. They had all-white juries.

Patrick tried to protect me from watching him die. He 11 told me he'd be okay, I didn't have to come with him into the execution chamber. "Electric chair's not a pretty sight, it could scare you," he told me, trying to be brave. I said, "No, no, Pat, if they kill you, I'll be there," and I said to him, "You look at me, look at my face, and I will be the face of Christ for you, the face of love." I couldn't bear it that he would die alone. I said, "God will help me." And there in the women's room, just a few hours before the execution, my only place of privacy in that place of death, God and I met, and the strength was there, and it was like a circle of light, and it was just in the present moment. If I tried to think ahead to what would happen at midnight, I started coming unraveled, but there in the present I could hold together, and Patrick was strong and kept asking me, "Sister Helen, are you all right?"

Being in the death house was one of the most bizarre, con- 12 fusing experiences I have ever had because it wasn't like visiting somebody dying in a hospital, where you can see the person getting weaker and fading. Patrick was so fully alive, talking and responding to me and writing letters to people and eating, and I'd look around at the polished tile floors— everything so neat—all the officials following a protocol, the secretary typing up forms for the witnesses to sign, the coffee pot percolating, and I kept feeling that I was in a hospital, and the final act would be to save this man's life. It felt strange and terrifying because everyone was so polite. They kept asking Patrick if he needed anything. The chef came by to ask him if he liked his last meal—the steak (medium rare), the potato salad, the apple pie for dessert.

When the warden with the strap-down team came for 13 Patrick at midnight, I walked behind him. In a hoarse, child-like voice he asked the warden, "Can Sister Helen touch my arm?" I put my hand on his shoulder and read to him from Isaiah, Chapter 43; "I have called you by your name . . . if you walk through fire I will be with you." God heard his prayer, "Please, God, hold up my legs." It was the last piece of dignity he could muster. He wanted to walk. I saw this dignity in him, and I have seen it in the other two men I have accompanied to their deaths. I wonder how I would hold up if I were walking across a floor to a room where people were waiting to kill me. The essential torture of the death penalty is not finally the physical method: a bullet or rope or gas or electrical current or injected drugs. The torture happens when conscious human beings are condemned to death and begin to anticipate that death and die a thousand times before they die.

dignity gives a lot of meaning

I'm not saying that Patrick Sonnier or any of the con-14 demned killers I've accompanied were heroes. I do not glorify them. I do not condone their terrible crimes. But each of these men was a human being, and each had a transcendence, a dignity, which should assure them of two very basic human rights that the United Nations Universal Declaration of Human Rights calls for: the right not to be tortured, the right not to be killed. To have a firm moral bedrock for our societies we must establish that no one is permitted to kill—and that includes governments.

At the end I was amazed at how ordinary Patrick Sonnier's 15 last moments were. He walked to the dark oak chair and sat in it. As guards were strapping his legs and arms and trunk, he found my face and his voice and his last words of life were words of love to me and I took them in like a lightning rod and I have been telling his story ever since.

ordinary?

When they filmed the execution scene of *Dead Man* 16 *Walking* on a set in New York City, I was there for the whole last week, watching Sean Penn, as the death row inmate Matthew Poncelet, get executed by lethal injection. It was tense, it was slow, it was hard. They shot each scene ten or more times. It took forever. Sean dying, Susan accompanying him, me remembering. Once, during a break, Sean stayed strapped to the gurney and Susan went to visit with him for a while. He's strapped at his neck, trunk, legs, arms, ankles. The cameras are over him. There's a hushed buzz from other actors and technicians. Susan's standing close and talking softly to him. I notice she's holding his hand. It's just a movie. He's not really dying, but there she is holding his hand. Even playing at dying and killing can be real, real hard on you.

that's amazingly powerful!

For Study and Discussion

QUESTIONS FOR RESPONSE

1. How has your attitude toward capital punishment been shaped by the movies?
2. How has your attitude toward nuns been shaped by the movies?

QUESTIONS ABOUT PURPOSE

1. How does Prejean's narrative support the United Nations Universal Declaration of Human Rights?
2. What does Prejean's description of the filming of the execution scene contribute to the purpose of her narrative?

QUESTIONS ABOUT AUDIENCE

1. How does Prejean's reference to "biblical quarterbacking" anticipate the reactions of some of her readers?
2. How does her experience in poor neighborhoods help explain to her readers how she got involved with her "pen pal," Patrick Sonnier?

QUESTIONS ABOUT STRATEGIES

1. How does Prejean's explanation of the role of the "spiritual advisor" establish the conflict in her narrative?
2. How does Prejean use the shooting of the film to develop her narrative about the real events?

QUESTIONS FOR D·

1. How does Prejean provide a "new .
   part'"?
2. In what ways does Prejean's narrative .
   ward the death penalty?

GEORGE ORWELL

George Orwell, the pen name of Eric Blair (1903–1950), was born in Motihari, Bengal, where his father was employed with the Bengal civil service. He was brought to England at an early age for schooling (Eton), but rather than completing his education at the university, he served with the Indian imperial police in Burma (1922–1927). He wrote about these experiences in his first novel, *Burmese Days*. Later he returned to Europe and worked at various jobs (described in *Down and Out in Paris and London,* 1933) before fighting on the Republican side in the Spanish civil war (see *Homage to Catalonia,* 1938). Orwell's attitudes toward war and government are reflected in his most famous books: *Animal Farm* (1945), *1984* (1949), and *Shooting an Elephant and Other Essays* (1950). In the title essay from the last volume, Orwell reports a "tiny incident" that gave him deeper insight into his own fears and "the real motives for which despotic governments act."

Shooting an Elephant

I N MOULMEIN, IN lower Burma, I was hated by large num- 1
bers of people—the only time in my life that I have been important enough for this to happen to me. I was subdivisional police officer of the town, and in an aimless, petty kind of way anti-European feeling was very bitter. No one had the guts to raise a riot, but if a European woman went through the bazaars alone somebody would probably spit betel juice over her dress. As a police officer I was an obvious target and was baited whenever it seemed safe to do so.

where is Burma?

When a nimble Burman tripped me up on the football field and the referee (another Burman) looked the other way, the crowd yelled with hideous laughter. This happened more than once. In the end the sneering yellow faces of young men that met me everywhere, the insults hooted after me when I was at a safe distance, got badly on my nerves. The young Buddhist priests were the worst of all. There were several thousands of them in the town and none of them seemed to have anything to do except stand on street corners and jeer at Europeans.

All this was perplexing and upsetting. For at that time I had already made up my mind that imperialism was an evil thing and the sooner I chucked up my job and got out of it

It's odd that the white man is the weak soul

2

As soon as I saw the elephant I knew with perfect certainty that I ought not to shoot him.

---

the better. Theoretically—and secretly, of course—I was all for the Burmese and all against their oppressors, the British. As for the job I was doing, I hated it more bitterly than I can perhaps make clear. In a job like that you see the dirty work of Empire at close quarters. The wretched prisoners huddling in the stinking cages of the lock-ups, the gray, cowed faces of the long-term convicts, the scarred buttocks of the men who had been flogged with bamboos—all these oppressed me with an intolerable sense of guilt. But I could get nothing into perspective. I was young and ill educated and I had had to think out my problems in the utter silence that is imposed on every Englishman in the East. I did not even know that the British Empire is dying, still less did I know that it is a great deal better than the younger empires that are going to supplant it. All I knew was that I was stuck between my hatred of the empire I served and my rage against the

Conflict

why guilt?

evil-spirited little beasts who tried to make my job impossible. With one part of my mind I thought of the British Raj as an unbreakable tyranny, as something clamped down, in *saecula saeculorum,* upon the will of prostrate peoples; with another part I thought that the greatest joy in the world would be to drive a bayonet into a Buddhist priest's guts. Feelings like these are the normal by-products of imperialism; ask any Anglo-Indian official, if you can catch him off duty.

One day something happened which in a roundabout way   3
was enlightening. It was a tiny incident in itself; but it gave me a better glimpse than I had had before of the real nature of imperialism—the real motives for which despotic governments act. Early one morning the sub-inspector at a police station the other end of town rang me up on the 'phone and said that an elephant was ravaging the bazaar. Would I please come and do something about it? I did not know what I could do, but I wanted to see what was happening and I got on to a pony and started out. I took my rifle, an old .44 Winchester and much too small to kill an elephant, but I thought the noise might be useful *in terrorem.* Various Burmans stopped me on the way and told me about the elephant's doings. It was not, of course, a wild elephant, but a tame one which had gone "must." It had been chained up, as tame elephants always are when their attack of "must" is due, but on the previous night it had broken its chain and escaped. Its mahout, the only person who could manage it when it was in that state, had set out in pursuit, but had taken the wrong direction and was now twelve hours' journey away, and in the morning the elephant had suddenly reappeared in the town. The Burmese population had no weapons and were quite helpless against it. It had already destroyed somebody's bamboo hut, killed a cow and raided some fruit-stalls and devoured the stock; also it had met the municipal rubbish van and, when the driver jumped out and took to his heels, had turned the van over and inflicted violences upon it.

The Burmese sub-inspector and some Indian constables   4
were waiting for me in the quarter where the elephant had

been seen. It was a very poor quarter, a labyrinth of squalid bamboo huts, thatched with palm-leaf, winding all over a steep hillside. I remember that it was a cloudy, stuffy morning at the beginning of the rains. We began questioning the people as to where the elephant had gone and, as usual, failed to get any definite information. That is invariably the case in the East; a story always sounds clear enough at a distance, but the nearer you get to the scene of events the vaguer it becomes. Some of the people said that the elephant had gone in one direction, some said that he had gone in another, some professed not even to have heard of any elephant. I had almost made up my mind that the whole story was a pack of lies, when we heard yells a little distance away. There was a loud, scandalized cry of "Go away, child! Go away this instant!" and an old woman with a switch in her hand came round the corner of a hut, violently shooing away a crowd of naked children. Some more women followed, clicking their tongues and exclaiming; evidently there was something that the children ought not to have seen. I rounded the hut and saw a man's dead body sprawling in the mud. He was an Indian, a black Dravidian coolie, almost naked, and he could not have been dead many minutes. The people said that the elephant had come suddenly upon him round the corner of the hut, caught him with its trunk, put its foot on his back and ground him into the earth. This was the rainy season and the ground was soft, and his face had scored a trench a foot deep and a couple of yards long. He was lying on his belly with arms crucified and head sharply twisted to one side. His face was coated with mud, the eyes wide open, the teeth bared and grinning with an expression of unendurable agony. (Never tell me, by the way, that the dead look peaceful. Most of the corpses I have seen looked devilish.) The friction of the great beast's foot had stripped the skin from his back as neatly as one skins a rabbit. As soon as I saw the dead man I sent an orderly to a friend's house nearby to borrow an elephant rifle. I had already sent back the pony, not wanting it to go mad with fright and throw me if it smelt the elephant.

[handwritten margin note: Does this dead man have any affect on him?]

[handwritten note at bottom: I didn't know there was a conflict here]

The orderly came back in a few minutes with a rifle and five cartridges, and meanwhile some Burmans had arrived and told us that the elephant was in the paddy fields below, only a few hundred yards away. As I started forward practically the whole population of the quarter flocked out of the houses and followed me. They had seen the rifle and were all shouting excitedly that I was going to shoot the elephant. They had not shown much interest in the elephant when he was merely ravaging their homes, but it was different now that he was going to be shot. It was a bit of fun to them, and it would be to an English crowd; besides they wanted the meat. It made me vaguely uneasy. I had no intention of shooting the elephant—I had merely sent for the rifle to defend myself if necessary—and it is always unnerving to have a crowd following you. I marched down the hill, looking and feeling a fool, with the rifle over my shoulder and an ever-growing army of people jostling at my heels. At the bottom, when you got away from the huts, there was a metalled road and beyond that a miry waste of paddy fields a thousand yards across, not yet ploughed but soggy from the first rains and dotted with coarse grass. The elephant was standing eight yards from the road, his left side toward us. He took not the slightest notice of the crowd's approach. He was tearing up bunches of grass, beating them against his knees to clean them, and stuffing them into his mouth.

I had halted on the road. As soon as I saw the elephant I knew with perfect certainty that I ought not to shoot him. It is a serious matter to shoot a working elephant—it is comparable to destroying a huge and costly piece of machinery— and obviously one ought not to do it if it can possibly be avoided. And at that distance, peacefully eating, the elephant looked no more dangerous than a cow. I thought then and I think now that his attack of "must" was already passing off; in which case he would merely wander harmlessly about until the mahout came back and caught him. Moreover, I did not in the least want to shoot him. I decided that I would watch him for a little while to make sure that he did not turn savage again, and then go home.

But at that moment I glanced round at the crowd that had 7
followed me. It was an immense crowd, two thousand at the
least and growing every minute. It blocked the road for a
long distance on either side. I looked at the sea of yellow
faces above the garish clothes—faces all happy and excited
over this bit of fun, all certain that the elephant was going to
be shot. They were watching me as they would watch a con-
jurer about to perform a trick. They did not like me, but with
the magical rifle in my hands I was momentarily worth
watching. And suddenly I realized that I should have to
shoot the elephant after all. The people expected it of me and
I had got to do it; I could feel their two thousand wills pressing me forward, irresistibly. And it was at this moment, as I
stood there with the rifle in my hands, that I first grasped the
hollowness, the futility of the white man's dominion in the
East. Here was I, the white man with his gun, standing in
front of the unarmed native crowd—seemingly the leading
actor of the piece; but in reality I was only an absurd puppet
pushed to and fro by the will of those yellow faces behind. I
perceived in this moment that when the white man turns ty-
rant it is his own freedom that he destroys. He becomes a
sort of hollow, posing dummy, the conventionalized figure of
a sahib. For it is the condition of his rule that he shall spend
his life in trying to impress the "natives," and so in every crisis he has got to do what the "natives" expect of him. He
wears a mask, and his face grows to fit it. I had got to shoot
the elephant. I had committed myself to doing it when I sent
for the rifle. A sahib has got to act like a sahib; he has got to
appear resolute, to know his own mind and do definite
things. To come all that way, rifle in hand, with two thousand
people marching at my heels, and then to trail feebly away,
having done nothing—no, that was impossible. The crowd
would laugh at me. And my whole life, every white man's life
in the East, was one long struggle not to be laughed at.

But I did not want to shoot the elephant. I watched him 8
beating his bunch of grass against his knees with that preoccupied grandmotherly air that elephants have. It seemed to
me that it would be murder to shoot him. At that age I was

not squeamish about killing animals, but I had never shot an elephant and never wanted to. (Somehow it always seems worse to kill a *large* animal.) Besides, there was the beast's owner to be considered. Alive, the elephant was worth at least a hundred pounds; dead, he would only be worth the value of his tusks, five pounds, possibly. But I had got to act quickly. I turned to some experienced-looking Burmans who had been there when we arrived, and asked them how the elephant had been behaving. They all said the same thing: he took no notice of you if you left him alone, but he might charge if you went too close to him.

It was perfectly clear to me what I ought to do. I ought to walk up to within, say, twenty-five yards of the elephant and test his behavior. If he charged, I could shoot; if he took no notice of me, it would be safe to leave him until the mahout came back. But also I knew that I was going to do no such thing. I was a poor shot with a rifle and the ground was soft mud into which one would sink at every step. If the elephant charged and I missed him, I should have about as much chance as a toad under a steam-roller. But even then I was not thinking particularly of my own skin, only of the watchful yellow faces behind. For at that moment, with the crowd watching me, I was not afraid in the ordinary sense, as I would have been if I had been alone. A white man mustn't be frightened in front of "natives"; and so, in general, he isn't frightened. The sole thought in my mind was that if anything went wrong those two thousand Burmans would see me pursued, caught, trampled on, and reduced to a grinning corpse like that Indian up the hill. And if that happened it was quite probable that some of them would laugh. That would never do. There was only one alternative. I shoved the cartridges into the magazine and lay down on the road to get a better aim.

The crowd grew very still, and a deep, low, happy sigh, as of people who see the theater curtain go up at last, breathed from innumerable throats. They were going to have their bit of fun after all. The rifle was a beautiful German thing with cross-hair sights. I did not then know that in shooting an ele-

9

10

phant one would shoot to cut an imaginary bar running from ear-hole to ear-hole. I ought, therefore, as the elephant was sideways on, to have aimed straight at his ear-hole; actually I aimed several inches in front of this, thinking the brain would be further forward.

When I pulled the trigger I did not hear the bang or feel the kick—one never does when a shot goes home—but I heard the devilish roar of glee that went up from the crowd. In that instant, in too short a time, one would have thought, even for the bullet to get there, a mysterious, terrible change had come over the elephant. He neither stirred, nor fell, but every line of his body had altered. He looked suddenly stricken, shrunken, immensely old, as though the frightful impact of the bullet had paralyzed him without knocking him down. At last, after what seemed a long time—it might have been five seconds, I dare say—he sagged flabbily to his knees. His mouth slobbered. An enormous senility seemed to have settled upon him. One could have imagined him thousands of years old. I fired again into the same spot. At the second shot he did not collapse but climbed with desperate slowness to his feet and stood weakly upright, with legs sagging and head drooping. I fired a third time. That was the shot that did for him. You could see the agony of it jolt his whole body and knock the last remnant of strength from his legs. But in falling he seemed for a moment to rise, for as his hind legs collapsed beneath him he seemed to tower upward like a huge rock toppling, his trunk reaching skyward like a tree. He trumpeted, for the first and only time. And then down he came, his belly toward me, with a crash that seemed to shake the ground even where I lay.

I got up. The Burmans were already racing past me across the mud. It was obvious that the elephant would never rise again, but he was not dead. He was breathing very rhythmically with long rattling gasps, his great mound of a side painfully rising and falling. His mouth was wide open—I could see far down into caverns of pale pink throat. I waited a long time for him to die, but his breathing did not weaken. Finally I fired my two remaining shots into the spot where I thought

[handwritten margin notes: "Nooo!!!"; "I really hate this man now"; numerals 11, 12]

his heart must be. The thick blood welled out of him like red
velvet, but still he did not die. His body did not even jerk
when the shots hit him, the tortured breathing continued
without a pause. He was dying, very slowly and in great agony, but in some world remote from me where not even a
bullet could damage him further. I felt that I had got to put
an end to that dreadful noise. It seemed dreadful to see the
great beast lying there, powerless to move and yet powerless
to die, and not even to be able to finish him. I sent back for
my small rifle and poured shot after shot into his heart and
down his throat. They seemed to make no impression. The
tortured gasps continued as steadily as the ticking of a clock.

In the end I could not stand it any longer and went away.   13
I heard later that it took him half an hour to die. Burmans
were bringing dahs and baskets even before I left, and I was
told they had stripped his body almost to the bones by the
afternoon.

Afterward, of course, there were endless discussions about   14
the shooting of the elephant. The owner was furious, but he
was only an Indian and could do nothing. Besides, legally I
had done the right thing, for a mad elephant has to be killed,
like a mad dog, if its owner fails to control it. Among the Europeans opinion was divided. The older men said I was right,
the younger men said it was a damn shame to shoot an elephant for killing a coolie, because an elephant was worth
more than any damn Coringhee coolie. And afterward I was
very glad that the coolie had been killed; it put me legally in
the right and it gave me a sufficient pretext for shooting the
elephant. I often wondered whether any of the others
grasped that I had done it solely to avoid looking a fool.

For Study and Discussion

QUESTIONS FOR RESPONSE

1. How do you feel when you are laughed at? What do you do in
   order to avoid looking like a fool?

2. How did you react to Orwell's long introduction (paragraphs 1 and 2) to the incident? Were you attentive, bored, or confused? Now that you have finished the essay, reread these two paragraphs. How does your second reading compare with your first?

QUESTIONS ABOUT PURPOSE

1. What thesis about "the real nature of imperialism" does Orwell prove by narrating this "tiny incident"?
2. List the reasons Orwell considers when he tries to decide what to do. According to his conclusion, what was his main purpose in shooting the elephant?

QUESTIONS ABOUT AUDIENCE

1. How does Orwell wish to present himself to his readers in paragraphs 6 through 9? Do you follow the logic of his argument?
2. Which of the three positions stated in the final paragraph does Orwell expect his readers to agree with? Why is he "glad that the coolie had been killed"?

QUESTIONS ABOUT STRATEGIES

1. Although Orwell begins narrating the incident in paragraph 3, we do not see the elephant until the end of paragraph 5. What details do we see? How do they intensify the dramatic conflict?
2. How does Orwell pace the shooting of the elephant in paragraphs 11 and 12? How does the elephant's slow death affect Orwell's point of view toward what he has done?

QUESTIONS FOR DISCUSSION

1. Orwell was young, frightened, and tormented by strangers in a strange land. What parallels do you see between Orwell's plight and the plight of young American soldiers who have served in Afghanistan and Iraq?
2. Much of Orwell's essay assumes a knowledge of the words *imperialism* and *despotism*. What do these words mean? How do they apply to the essay? What current events can you identify in which these words might also apply?

ALICE ADAMS

Alice Adams (1926–1999) was born in Fredericks-
burg, Virginia, and educated at Radcliffe College.
After twelve years of marriage, she began working
at various office jobs, including secretary, clerk,
and bookkeeper, while she mastered the skills of a
writer. Adams published her first book of fiction,
Careless Love (1966), at the age of forty. Later she
published five widely acclaimed novels, *Families
and Survivors* (1975), *Listening to Billie* (1978)—
the title refers to the legendary blues singer Billie
Holiday—*Rich Rewards* (1980), *Superior Women*
(1984), and *Caroline's Daughter* (1991), as well
as three collections of short stories, *Beautiful Girl*
(1979), *To See You Again* (1982), and *Return
Trips* (1985). She contributed numerous short
stories to magazines such as *The New Yorker, The
Atlantic,* and *Paris Review.* Her most recent
novel, entitled *After the War* (2000), was published posthumously. The narrator of "Truth or
Consequences," reprinted from *To See You Again,*
tries to understand the "consequences" that resulted from her truthful answer in a childhood
game.

Truth or Consequences

T HIS MORNING, WHEN I read in a gossip column that a
man named Carstairs Jones had married a famous former movie star, I was startled, thunderstruck, for I knew that
he must certainly be the person whom I knew as a child, one
extraordinary spring, as "Car Jones." He was a dangerous
and disreputable boy, one of what were then called the
"truck children," with whom I had a most curious, brief and
frightening connection. Still, I noted that in a way I was

pleased at such good fortune; I was "happy for him," so to speak, perhaps as a result of sheer distance, so many years. And before I could imagine Car as he might be now, Carstairs Jones, in Hollywood clothes, I suddenly saw, with the most terrific accuracy and bright sharpness of detail, the schoolyard of all those years ago, hard and bare, neglected. And I relived the fatal day, on the middle level of that schoolyard, when we were playing truth or consequences, and I said that I would rather kiss Car Jones than be eaten alive by ants.

Our school building then was three stories high, a formi- 2 dable brick square. In front a lawn had been attempted, some years back; graveled walks led up to the broad, forbidding entranceway, and behind the school were the playing fields, the playground. This area was on three levels: on the upper level, nearest the school, were the huge polished steel frames for the creaking swings, the big green splintery wooden see-saws, the rickety slides—all for the youngest children. On the middle level older girls played hopscotch, various games, or jumped rope—or just talked and giggled. And out on the lowest level, the field, the boys practiced football, or baseball, in the spring.

To one side of the school was a parking space, usually filled 3 with the bulging yellow trucks that brought children from out in the country in to town: truck children, country children. Sometimes they would go back to the trucks at lunchtime to eat their sandwiches, whatever; almost always there were several overgrown children, spilling out from the trucks. Or Car Jones, expelled from some class, for some new acts of rebelliousness. That area was always littered with trash, wrappings from sandwiches, orange peel, Coke bottles.

Beyond the parking space was an empty lot, overgrown 4 with weeds, in the midst of which stood an abandoned trellis, perhaps once the support of wisteria; now wild honeysuckle almost covered it over.

The town was called Hilton, the seat of a distinguished 5 university, in the middle South. My widowed mother, Charlotte Ames, had moved there the previous fall (with me,

Emily, her only child). I am still not sure why she chose
Hilton; she never much liked it there, nor did she really like
the brother-in-law, a professor, into whose proximity the
move had placed us.

An interesting thing about Hilton, at that time, was that   6
there were three, and only three, distinct social classes. (Negroes could possibly make four, but they were so separate,
even from the poorest whites, as not to seem part of the social system at all; they were in effect invisible.) At the scale's
top were professors and their families. Next were the towns-
people, storekeepers, bankers, doctors and dentists, none of
whom had the prestige nor the money they were later to acquire. Country people were the bottom group, families living
out on the farms that surrounded the town, people who sent
their children in to school on the yellow trucks.

The professors' children of course had a terrific advantage,   7
academically, coming from houses full of books, from parental respect for learning; many of those kids read precociously
and had large vocabularies. It was not so hard on most of the
town children; many of their families shared qualities with
the faculty people; they too had a lot of books around. But
the truck children had a hard and very unfair time of it. Not
only were many of their parents near-illiterates, but often the
children were kept at home to help with chores, and sometimes, particularly during the coldest, wettest months of winter, weather prevented the trucks' passage over the slithery
red clay roads of that countryside, that era. A child could
miss out on a whole new skill, like long division, and fail tests,
and be kept back. Consequently many of the truck children
were overage, oversized for the grades they were in.

In the seventh grade, when I was eleven, a year ahead of   8
myself, having been tested for and skipped the sixth (attest-
ing to the superiority of Northern schools, my mother
thought, and probably she was right), dangerous Car Jones,
in the same class, was fourteen, and taller than anyone.

There was some overlapping, or crossing, among those   9
three social groups; there were hybrids, as it were. In fact, I
was such a crossbreed myself: literally my mother and I were
town people—my dead father had been a banker, but since

his brother was a professor we too were considered faculty people. Also my mother had a lot of money, making us further élite. To me, being known as rich was just embarrassing, more freakish than advantageous, and I made my mother stop ordering my clothes from Best's; I wanted dresses from the local stores, like everyone else's.

Car Jones too was a hybrid child, although his case was less visible than mine: his country family were distant cousins of the prominent and prosperous dean of the medical school, Dean Willoughby Jones. (They seem to have gone in for fancy names, in all the branches of that family.) I don't think his cousins spoke to him.

In any case, being richer and younger than the others in my class made me socially very insecure, and I always approached the playground with a sort of excited dread: would I be asked to join in a game, and if it were dodge ball (the game I most hated) would I be the first person hit with the ball, and thus eliminated? Or, if the girls were just standing around and talking, would I get all the jokes, and know which boys they were talking about?

Then, one pale-blue balmy April day, some of the older girls asked me if I wanted to play truth or consequences with them. I wasn't sure how the game went, but anything was better than dodge ball, and, as always, I was pleased at being asked.

"It's easy," said Jean, a popular leader, with curly red hair; her father was a dean of the law school. "You just answer the questions we ask you, or you take the consequences."

I wasn't at all sure what consequences were, but I didn't like to ask.

They began with simple questions. How old are you? What's your middle name?

This led to more complicated (and crueler) ones.

"How much money does your mother have?"

"I don't know." I didn't, of course, and I doubt that she did either, that poor vague lady, too young to be a widow, too old for motherhood. "I think maybe a thousand dollars," I hazarded.

At this they all frowned, that group of older, wiser girls,

whether in disbelief or disappointment, I couldn't tell. They moved a little away from me and whispered together.

It was close to the end of recess. Down on the playing field 20 below us one of the boys threw the baseball and someone batted it out in a long arc, out to the farthest grassy edges of the field, and several other boys ran to retrieve it. On the level above us, a rutted terrace up, the little children stood in line for turns on the slide, or pumped with furious small legs on the giant swings.

The girls came back to me. "Okay, Emily," said Jean. "Just 21 tell the truth. Would you rather be covered with honey and eaten alive by ants, in the hot Sahara Desert—or kiss Car Jones?"

Then, as now, I had a somewhat literal mind: I thought of 22 honey, and ants, and hot sand, and quite simply I said I'd rather kiss Car Jones.

Well. Pandemonium: Did you hear what she said? Emily 23 would kiss Car Jones! *Car Jones.* The truth—Emily would like to kiss Car Jones! Oh, Emily if your mother only knew! Emily and Car! Emily is going to kiss Car Jones! Emily said she would! Oh, Emily!

The boys, just then coming up from the baseball field, cast 24 bored and pitying looks at the sources of so much noise; they had always known girls were silly. But Harry McGinnis, a glowing, golden boy, looked over at us and laughed aloud. I had been watching Harry timidly for months; that day I thought his laugh was friendly.

Recess being over, we all went back into the schoolroom, 25 and continued with the civics lesson. I caught a few ambiguous smiles in my direction, which left me both embarrassed and confused.

That afternoon, as I walked home from school, two of the 26 girls who passed me on their bikes called back to me, "Car Jones!" and in an automatic but for me new way I squealed out, "Oh no!" They laughed, and repeated, from their distance, "Car Jones!"

The next day I continued to be teased. Somehow the boys 27 had got wind of what I had said, and they joined in with remarks about Yankee girls being fast, how you couldn't tell about quiet girls, that sort of wit. Some of the teasing sounded mean; I felt that Jean, for example, was really out to discomfit me, but most of it was high-spirited friendliness. I was suddenly discovered, as though hitherto I had been invisible. And I continued to respond with that exaggerated, phony squeal of embarrassment that seemed to go over so well. Harry McGinnis addressed me as Emily Jones, and the others took that up. (I wonder if Harry had ever seen me before.)

Curiously, in all this new excitement, the person I thought of least was the source of it all: Car Jones. Or, rather, when I saw the actual Car, hulking over the water fountain or lounging near the steps of a truck, I did not consciously connect him with what felt like social success, new popularity. (I didn't know about consequences.)

Therefore, when the first note from Car appeared on my desk, it felt like blackmail, although the message was innocent, was even kind. "You mustn't mind that they tease you. You are the prettiest one of the girls. C. Jones." I easily recognized his handwriting, those recklessly forward-slanting strokes, from the day when he had had to write on the blackboard, "I will not disturb the other children during Music." Twenty-five times. The note was real, all right.

Helplessly I turned around to stare at the back of the room, where the tallest boys sprawled in their too small desks. Truck children, all of them, bored and uncomfortable. There was Car, the tallest of all, the most bored, the least contained. Our eyes met, and even at that distance I saw that his were not black, as I had thought, but a dark slate blue; stormy eyes, even when, as he rarely did, Car smiled. I turned away quickly, and I managed to forget him for a while.

Having never witnessed a Southern spring before, I was astounded by its bursting opulence, that soft fullness of petal and bloom, everywhere the profusion of flowering shrubs and trees, the riotous flower beds. Walking home from school, I was enchanted with the yards of the stately houses (homes of professors) that I passed, the lush lawns, the rows of brilliant iris, the flowering quince and dogwood trees, crepe myrtle, wisteria vines. I would squint my eyes to see the tiniest pale-green leaves against the sky.

My mother didn't like the spring. It gave her hay fever, 32 and she spent most of her time languidly indoors, behind heavily lined, drawn draperies. "I'm simply too old for such exuberance," she said.

"Happy" is perhaps not the word to describe my own state 33 of mind, but I was tremendously excited, continuously. The season seemed to me so extraordinary in itself, the colors, the enchanting smells, and it coincided with my own altered awareness of myself: I could command attention, I was pretty (Car Jones was the first person ever to say that I was, after my mother's long-ago murmurings to a late-arriving baby).

Now everyone knew my name, and called it out as I 34 walked onto the playground. Last fall, as an envious, un- known new girl, I had heard other names, other greetings and teasing-insulting nicknames, "Hey, Red," Harry Mc- Ginnis used to shout, in the direction of popular Jean.

The new note from Car Jones said, "I'll bet you hate it 35 down here. This is a cruddy town, but don't let it bother you. Your hair is beautiful. I hope you never cut it. C. Jones."

This scared me a little: the night before I had been arguing 36 with my mother on just that point, my hair, which was long and straight. Why couldn't I cut it and curl it, like the other girls? How had Car Jones known what I wanted to do? I forced myself not to look at him; I pretended that there was no Car Jones; it was just a name that certain people had made up.

I felt—I was sure—that Car Jones was an "abnormal" per- 37 son. (I'm afraid "different" would have been the word I used, back then.) He represented forces that were dark and strange, whereas I myself had just come out into the light. I had joined the world of the normal. (My "normality" later included three marriages to increasingly "rich and promi- nent" men; my current husband is a surgeon. Three children, and as many abortions. I hate the symmetry, but there you are. I haven't counted lovers. It comes to a normal life, for a woman of my age.) For years, at the time of our coming to

Hilton, I had felt a little strange, isolated by my father's death, my older-than-most-parents mother, by money. By being younger than other children, and new in town. I could clearly afford nothing to do with Car, and at the same time my literal mind acknowledged a certain obligation.

Therefore, when a note came from Car telling me to meet him on a Saturday morning in the vacant lot next to the school, it didn't occur to me that I didn't have to go. I made excuses to my mother, and to some of the girls who were getting together for Cokes at someone's house. I'd be a little late, I told the girls. I had to do an errand for my mother.   38

It was one of the palest, softest, loveliest days of that spring. In the vacant lot weeds bloomed like the rarest of flowers; as I walked toward the abandoned trellis I felt myself to be a sort of princess, on her way to grant an audience to a courtier.   39

Car, lounging just inside the trellis, immediately brought me up short. "You're several minutes late," he said, and I noticed that his teeth were stained (from tobacco?) and his hands were dirty: couldn't he have washed his hands, to come and meet me? He asked, "Just who do you think you are, the Queen of Sheba?"   40

I am not sure what I had imagined would happen between us, but this was wrong; I was not prepared for surliness, this scolding. Weakly I said that I was sorry I was late.   41

Car did not acknowledge my apology; he just stared at me, stormily, with what looked like infinite scorn.   42

Why had he insisted that I come to meet him? And now that I was here, was I less than pretty, seen close up?   43

A difficult minute passed, and then I moved a little away. I managed to say that I had to go; I had to meet some girls, I said.   44

At that Car reached and grasped my arm. "No, first we have to do it."   45

Do it? I was scared.   46

"You know what you said, as good as I do. You said kiss Car Jones, now didn't you?"   47

I began to cry.   48

Car reached for my hair and pulled me toward him; he   49
bent down to my face and for an instant our mouths were
mashed together. (Christ, my first kiss!) Then, so suddenly
that I almost fell backward, Car let go of me. With a last look
of pure rage he was out of the trellis and striding across the
field, toward town, away from the school.

For a few minutes I stayed there in the trellis; I was no   50
longer crying (that had been for Car's benefit, I now think)
but melodramatically I wondered if Car might come back
and do something else to me—beat me up, maybe. Then a
stronger fear took over: someone might find out, might have
seen us, even. At that I got out of the trellis fast, out of the
vacant lot. (I was learning conformity fast, practicing up for
the rest of my life.)

I think, really, that my most serious problem was my utter   51
puzzlement: what did it mean, that kiss? Car was mad, no
doubt about that, but did he really hate me? In that case, why
a kiss? (Much later in life I once was raped, by someone to
whom I was married, but I still think that counts; in any case,
I didn't know what he meant either.)

Not sure what else to do, and still in the grip of a monu-   52
mental confusion, I went over to the school building, which
was open on Saturdays for something called Story Hours, for
little children. I went into the front entrance and up to the library where, to the surprise of the librarian, who may have
thought me retarded, I listened for several hours of tales of
the Dutch Twins, and Peter and Polly in Scotland. Actually it
was very soothing, that long pasteurized drone, hard even to
think about Car while listening to pap like that.

When I got home I found my mother for some reason in a   53
livelier, more talkative mood than usual. She told me that a
boy had called while I was out, three times. Even before my
heart had time to drop—to think that it might be Car, she
babbled on, "Terribly polite. Really, these *bien élevé* Southern
boys." (No, not Car.) "Harry something. He said he'd call
again. But, darling, where were you, all this time?"

I was beginning to murmur about the library, homework,   54
when the phone rang. I answered, and it was Harry

McGinnis, asking me to go to the movies with him the following Saturday afternoon. I said of course, I'd love to, and I giggled in a silly new way. But my giggle was one of relief; I was saved, I was normal, after all. I belonged in the world of light, of lightheartedness. Car Jones had not really touched me.

I spent the next day, Sunday, in alternating states of agitation and anticipation.

On Monday, on my way to school, I felt afraid of seeing Car, at the same time that I was both excited and shy at the prospect of Harry McGinnis—a combination of emotions that was almost too much for me, that dazzling, golden first of May, and that I have not dealt with too successfully in later life.

Harry paid even less attention to me than he had before; it was a while before I realized that he was conspicuously not looking in my direction, not teasing me, and that that in itself was a form of attention, as well as being soothing to my shyness.

I realized too, after a furtive scanning of the back row, that Car Jones was *not at school* that day. Relief flooded through my blood like oxygen, like spring air.

Absences among the truck children were so unremarkable, and due to so many possible causes, that any explanation at all for his was plausible. Of course it occurred to me, among other imaginings, that he had stayed home out of shame for what he did to me. Maybe he had run away to sea, had joined the Navy or the Marines? Coldheartedly, I hoped so. In any case, there was no way for me to ask.

Later that week the truth about Car Jones did come out— at first as a drifting rumor, then confirmed, and much more remarkable than joining the Navy: Car Jones had gone to the principal's office, a week or so back, and had demanded to be tested for entrance (immediate) into high school, a request so unprecedented (usually only pushy academic parents would ask for such a change) and so dumbfounding that it was acceded to. Car took the test and was put into the sophomore high-school class, on the other side of town, where he by age and size—and intellect, as things turned out; he tested high—most rightfully belonged.

I went to a lot of Saturday movies with Harry McGinnis, 61 where we clammily held hands, and for the rest of that spring, and into summer, I was teased about Harry. No one seemed to remember having teased me about Car Jones.

Considering the size of Hilton at that time, it seems sur- 62 prising that I almost never saw Car again, but I did not, except for a couple of tiny glimpses, during the summer that I was still going to the movies with Harry. On both those occasions, seen from across the street, or on the other side of a dim movie house, Car was with an older girl, a high-school girl, with curled hair, and lipstick, all that. I was sure that his hands and teeth were clean.

By the time I had entered high school, along with all those 63 others who were by now my familiar friends, Car was a freshman in the local university, and his family had moved into town. Then his name again was bruited about among us, but this time was an underground rumor: Car Jones was reputed to have "gone all the way"—to have "done it" with a pretty and most popular senior in our high school. (It must be remembered that this was more unusual among the young then than now.) The general (whispered) theory was that Car's status as a college boy had won the girl; traditionally, in Hilton, the senior high-school girls began to date the freshmen in the university, as many and as often as possible. But this was not necessarily true; maybe the girl was simply drawn to Car, his height and his shoulders, his stormy eyes. Or maybe they didn't do it after all.

The next thing I heard about Car, who was by then an au- 64 thentic town person, a graduate student in the university, was that he had written a play which was to be produced by the campus dramatic society. (Maybe that is how he finally met his movie star, as a playwright? The column didn't say.) I think I read this item in the local paper, probably in a clipping forwarded to me by my mother; her letters were always thick with clippings, thin with messages of a personal nature.

My next news of Car came from my uncle, the French pro-   65
fessor, a violent, enthusiastic partisan in university affairs, especially in their more traditional aspects. In scandalized
tones, one family Thanksgiving, he recounted to me and my
mother, that a certain young man, a graduate student in English, named Carstairs Jones, had been offered a special sort of
membership in D.K.E., his own beloved fraternity, and
"Jones had *turned it down*." My mother and I laughed later
and privately over this; we were united in thinking my uncle a
fool, and I am sure that I added, Well, good for him. But I
did not, at that time, reconsider the whole story of Car Jones,
that most unregenerate and wicked of the truck children.

But now, with this fresh news of Carstairs Jones, and his   66
wife the movie star, it occurs to me that we two, who at a certain time and place were truly misfits, although quite differently—we both have made it: what could be more American
dream-y, more normal, than marriage to a lovely movie star?
Or, in my case, marriage to the successful surgeon?

And now maybe I can reconstruct a little of that time; spe-   67
cifically, can try to see how it really was for Car, back then.
Maybe I can even understand that kiss.

Let us suppose that he lived in a somewhat better than   68
usual farmhouse; later events make this plausible—his family's move to town, his years at the university. Also, I wish
him well. I will give him a dignified white house with a broad
front porch, set back among pines and oaks, in the red clay
countryside. The stability and size of his house, then, would
have set Car apart from his neighbors, the other farm families, other truck children. Perhaps his parents too were somewhat "different," but my imagination fails at them; I can easily imagine and clearly see the house, but not its population.
Brothers? sisters? Probably, but I don't know.

Car would go to school, coming out of his house at the   69
honk of the stained and bulging, ugly yellow bus, which was
crowded with his supposed peers, toward whom he felt both
contempt and an irritation close to rage. Arrived at school, as
one of the truck children, he would be greeted with a total
lack of interest; he might as well have been invisible, or been

black, *unless* he misbehaved in an outright, conspicuous way.
And so he did: Car yawned noisily during history class, he
hummed during study hall and after recess he dawdled
around the playground and came in late. And for these and
other assaults on the school's decorum he was punished in
one way or another, and then, when all else failed to curb his
ways, he would be *held back*, forced to repeat an already in-
sufferably boring year of school.

One fall there was a minor novelty in school: a new girl   70
(me), a Yankee, who didn't look much like the other girls,
with long straight hair, instead of curled, and Yankee clothes,
wool skirts and sweaters, instead of flowery cotton dresses
worn all year round. A funny accent, a Yankee name: Emily
Ames. I imagine that Car registered those facts about me,
and possibly the additional information that I was almost as
invisible as he, but without much interest.

Until the day of truth or consequences. I don't think Car   71
was around on the playground while the game was going on;
one of the girls would have seen him, and squealed out,
"Oooh, there's Car, there *he is!*" I rather believe that some
skinny little kid, an unnoticed truck child, overheard it all,
and then ran over to where Car was lounging in one of the
school buses, maybe peeling an orange and throwing the
peel, in spirals, out the window. "Say, Car, that little Yankee
girl, she says she'd like to kiss you."

"Aw, go on."   72

He is still not very interested; the little Yankee girl is as   73
dumb as the others are.

And then he hears me being teased, everywhere, and   74
teased with his name. "Emily would kiss Car Jones—Emily
Jones!" Did he feel the slightest pleasure at such notoriety? I
think he must have; a man who would marry a movie star
must have at least a small taste for publicity. Well, at that
point he began to write me those notes: "You are the prettiest one of the girls" (which I was not). I think he was casting
us both in ill-fitting roles, me as the prettiest, defenseless girl,
and himself as my defender.

He must have soon seen that it wasn't working out that   75 way. I didn't need a defender, I didn't need him. I was having a wonderful time, at his expense, if you think about it, and I am pretty sure Car did think about it.

Interestingly, at the same time he had his perception of my triviality, Car must have got his remarkable inspiration in regard to his own life: there was a way out of those miserably boring classes, the insufferable children who surrounded him. He would demand a test, he would leave this place for the high school. 76

Our trellis meeting must have occurred after Car had taken the test, and had known that he did well. When he kissed me he was doing his last "bad" thing in that school, was kissing it off, so to speak. He was also insuring that I, at least, would remember him; he counted on its being my first kiss. And he may have thought that I was even sillier than I was, and that I would tell, so that what had happened would get around the school, waves of scandal in his wake. 77

For some reason, I would also imagine that Car is one of those persons who never look back; once kissed, I was readily dismissed from his mind, and probably for good. He could concentrate on high school, new status, new friends. Just as, now married to his movie star, he does not ever think of having been a truck child, one of the deprived, the disappointed. In his mind there are no ugly groaning trucks, no hopeless littered playground, no squat menacing school building. 78

But of course I could be quite wrong about Car Jones. He could be another sort of person altogether; he could be as haunted as I am by everything that ever happened in his life. 79

COMMENT ON "TRUTH OR CONSEQUENCES"

"Truth or Consequences" is an excellent illustration of how narration and description are used in short fiction. The catalyst for the story is the narrator's reading in a gossip column about Car Jones's marriage to a famous former movie star. His name sparks a memory, and the narrator (Emily) tries to reconstruct the events that occurred during her school years.

The story is paced at two speeds: the opening is slow as Emily describes the various social divisions on the playground; the action speeds up once Emily says she would rather kiss Car Jones than be eaten by ants. The plot reaches its climax when Car Jones calls Emily's bluff and asks her to meet him by the trellis near the school. The story concludes as Emily (older and wiser?) continues to wonder about the "truth" and "consequences" of this brief encounter.

Narration and Description as a Writing Strategy

1. Recount the details of an accident or disaster in which you were a witness or a victim. You may wish to retell the events as a reporter would for a front-page story in the local newspaper, or you may recount the events from a more personal point of view, as Sisten Helen Prejean does in her account of her experiences on death row. If you were a witness, consider the points of view of the other people involved so that you can give your readers an objective perspective on the event. If you were a victim, slow the pace of the major conflict, which probably occurred quickly, so you can show your readers its emotional impact.

2. Report an experience in which you had to commit an extremely difficult or distasteful deed. You may wish to begin, as George Orwell does, by telling your readers about the conditions you encountered before you confronted the problem of whether to commit the questionable act. Be sure to list all the options you considered before you acted, and conclude by reflecting on your attitude toward your choice. And, of course, make sure to plot your essay so that the *act* is given the central and most dramatic position.

3. In "The Mullet Girls," Jill McCorkle looks at pictures of her family before she was born. Study your family album and select a photograph that shows your parents when they were young. Then write a narrative about one of the photographs describing how one of your parents felt or behaved when he or she was your age.

4. Describe a significant event in your life when you were unfairly stereotyped. You may want to point out certain features of your dress or behavior that sent—unknown to you—mixed signals. Like Cofer, you may want to speculate on how these signals were the result of custom or caricature.

5. Describe how people who are different are treated within your community. Like Andre Dubus, you may want to document how the shy and sensitive feel shame and attract bullies. Or you may want to describe how you discovered an injustice in your community's way of acknowledging those who are different.

6. Demonstrate the effects of perception on values (how "seeing is believing"). All the writers in this section deal with this subject. Dubus recounts how his summer of physical labor changed his body and his thinking. McCorkle remembers how the visit of the "Mullet Girls" changed her perception of her mother and father. Cofer reveals how people from mainstream culture believe that they should be applauded for their ability to perpetuate stereotypes. Sister Helen Prejean relives her own experiences on death row when watching an actress (Susan Sarandon) play her in the making of a movie. Orwell shows how seeing the crowd's mocking faces convinces him to shoot the elephant. And Emily Ames, the narrator in Alice Adams's short story, tells how her concern for social acceptance made her misread the actions of someone who was different.

PROCESS
ANALYSIS

A **process** is an operation that moves through a series of steps
to bring about a desired result. You can call almost any procedure a process, whether it is getting out of bed in the morning or completing a transaction on the stock exchange. A
useful way to identify a particular kind of process is by its
principal function. A process can be *natural* (the birth of a
baby), *mechanical* (starting a car engine), *physical* (dancing),
or *mental* (reading).

    Analysis is an operation that divides something into its
parts in order to understand the whole more clearly. For example, poetry readers analyze the lines of a poem to find
meaning. Doctors analyze a patient's symptoms to prescribe

How do you make it interesting?

treatment. Politicians analyze the opinions of individual voters and groups of voters to plan campaigns.

If you want to write a process-analysis essay, you need to
go through three steps: (1) divide the process you are going
to explain into its individual steps; (2) show the movement of
the process, step by step, from beginning to end; and (3) explain how each step works, how it ties into other steps in the
sequence, and how it brings about the desired result.

Do you talk of each step?

PURPOSE

Usually you will write a process analysis to accomplish two
purposes: *to give directions* and *to provide information*. Sometimes you might find it difficult to separate the two purposes.
After all, when you give directions about how to do something (hit a baseball), you also have to provide information
on how the whole process works (rules of the game—strike
zone, walks, hits, base running, outs, scoring). But usually
you can separate the two because you're trying to accomplish
different goals. When you give directions, you want to help
your readers do something (change a tire). When you give information, you want to satisfy your readers' curiosity about
some process they'd like to know about but are unlikely to
perform (pilot a space shuttle).

You might also write a process analysis to demonstrate that
(1) a task that looks difficult is really easy or (2) a task that
looks easy is really quite complex. For instance, you might
want to show that selecting a specific tool can simplify a complex process (using a microwave oven to cook a six-course
dinner). You might also want to show why it's important to
have a prearranged plan to make a process seem simple (explaining the preparations for an informal television interview).

Does it have to be a how to how to

AUDIENCE

When you write a process-analysis essay, you must think carefully about who your audience will be. First, you need to de-

cide whether you're writing *to* an audience (giving directions) or writing *for* an audience (providing information). If you are writing *to* an audience, you can address directly readers who are already interested in your subject: "If you want to plant a successful garden, you must follow these seven steps." If you are writing *for* an audience, you can write from a more detached point of view, but you have to find a way to catch the interest of more casual readers: "Although many Americans say they are concerned about nuclear power, few understand how a nuclear power plant works."

Second, you have to determine how wide the knowledge gap is between you and your readers. Writing about a process suggests you are something of an expert in that area. If you can be sure your readers are also experts, you can make certain assumptions as you write your analysis. For instance, if you're outlining courtroom procedure to a group of fellow law students, you can assume you don't have to define the special meaning of the word *brief.*

On the other hand, if you feel sure your intended audience knows almost nothing about a process (or has only general knowledge), you can take nothing for granted. If you are explaining how to operate a VCR to readers who have never used one, you will have to define special terms and explain all procedures. If you assume your readers are experts when they are not, you will confuse or annoy them. If you assume they need to be told everything when they don't, you will bore or antagonize them. And, finally, remember that to analyze a process effectively, you must either research it carefully or have firsthand knowledge of its operation. It's risky to try to explain something you don't really understand.

STRATEGIES

The best way to write a process analysis is to organize your essay according to five parts:

> Overview
> Special terms

[handwritten in margin: kind of like our senior papers \ ugh]

Sequence of steps

Examples

Results

The first two parts help your readers understand the process, the next two show the process in action, and the last one evaluates the worth of the completed process.

Begin your analysis with an *overview* of the whole process. To make such an overview, you take these four steps:

1. Define the objective of the process
2. Identify (and number) the steps in the sequence
3. Group some small steps into larger units
4. Call attention to the most important steps or units

For example, Julia Alvarez begins her analysis of how she writes a story by breaking down this process into short steps. Nikki Giovanni makes her recommendations for black students in sequence and then goes on to illustrate some of the common problems that occur with each recommendation.

Each process has its own *special terms* to describe tools, tasks, and methods, and you will have to define those terms for your readers. You can define them at the beginning so your readers will understand the terms when you use them, but often you do better to define them as you use them. Your readers may have trouble remembering specialized language out of context, so it's often practical to define your terms throughout the course of the essay, pausing to explain their special meaning or use the first time you introduce them. Serena Nanda follows this strategy by defining what Indians mean by the bride's "dowry."

When you write a process-analysis essay, you must present the *sequence of steps* clearly and carefully. As you do so, give the reason for each step and, where appropriate, provide these reminders:

1. *Do not omit any steps.* A sequence is a sequence because all steps depend on one another. Nikki Giovanni explains the

importance of going to class to establish "a consistent presence in the classroom."

2. *Do not reverse steps.* A sequence is a sequence because each step must be performed according to a necessary and logical pattern. Barbara Ehrenreich describes a cleaning sequence that must be followed exactly.

3. *Suspend certain steps.* Occasionally, a whole series of steps must be suspended and another process completed before the sequence can resume. P. J. O'Rourke suggests that a whole sequence of steps can be avoided if you suspend the sequence and give everybody "big wads of American money."

4. *Do not overlook steps within steps.* Each sequence is likely to have a series of smaller steps buried within each step. Julia Alvarez reminds her readers that collecting curious information is not the same as researching it.

5. *Avoid certain steps.* It is often tempting to insert steps that are not recommended but that appear "logical." Serena Nanda discovers that her American logic does not work in an Indian context.

these are contra- dicting

You may want to use several kinds of examples to explain the steps in a sequence:

1. *Pictures.* You can use graphs, charts, and diagrams to illustrate the operation of the process. Although none of the writers in this section uses pictures, Barbara Ehrenreich describes the pictures she sees in the training films.

blah!

2. *Anecdotes.* Since you're claiming some level of expertise by writing a process analysis, you can clarify your explanation by using examples from your own experience. O'Rourke uses this method—for comic effect—when he describes roadblocks and animals in the right of way.

3. *Variants.* You can mention alternative steps to show that the process may not be as rigid or simplistic as it often appears. Ehrenreich suggests that her mother adheres to a style of cleaning that is concerned more with germs than cosmetics.

4. *Comparisons.* You can use comparisons to help your readers see that a complex process is similar to a process they already know. Nanda uses this strategy when she compares the complexities of arranging an Indian marriage to the "love matches" made in America.

Although you focus on the movement of the process when you write a process-analysis essay, finally you should also try to evaluate the *results* of that process. You can move to this last part by asking two questions: How do you know it's done? How do you know it's good? Sometimes the answer is simple: the car starts; the trunk opens. At other times, the answer is not so clear: the student may need further instruction; the jury may have difficulty reaching a decision.

USING PROCESS ANALYSIS IN PARAGRAPHS

Here are two process-analysis paragraphs. The first is written by a professional writer and is followed by an analysis. The second is written by a student writer and is followed by questions.

HENRY PETROSKI
The Book on the Bookshelf

Putting a book back on the shelf in such circumstances can be as difficult as putting a sardine back in a can. A bookshelf appears to abhor a vacuum, and so the void that is created when one book is removed is seldom adequate to receive the book again. Like a used air mattress or roadmap, which can never seem to be folded back into the shape in which it came, the book opened seems to have a new dimension when reclosed. Where it once fit it no longer does, and it has to be used as a wedge to pry apart its formerly tolerant neighbors in order to get a foothold on the shelf. Invariably, the book I push

Makes comparison to another process

Makes another comparison

back into its place scrapes along its neighbors and pushes them back a little. Where there is ample room above them, the disturbed books can be realigned with a little effort. However, in my office, where I cannot easily reach in to pull the books back out and align their spines, I find myself pushing the whole shelf back a bit to re-align them. I cannot just push the books all the way to the rear of the shelf, of course, because they do not all have the same width, and so the shelf of them would present a rather ragged appearance. In time, however, so many of the books end up pushed all the way back that I have to take a whole section of them out and re-position them near the front edge of the shelf.

Describes personal anecdote

Provides warning

Comment   This paragraph, excerpted from *The Book on the Bookshelf,* analyzes the difficult process of removing and then replacing a book on a bookshelf so that all the books on the shelf remain aligned. The opening sentence creates a vivid image—putting a sardine back in a can—that establishes the difficulty of the process. Petroski makes sure his readers anticipate all the things that can go wrong when trying to re-align books. And even after the books are realigned, they are so far back on the shelf that he must move whole sections out toward "the front edge of the shelf."

It's hardly that interesting

SARA TEMPLE
Making Stained Glass

Before you begin making stained glass, you will need to purchase the right tools—most of which you can find at your local hardware store. First, select a glass cutter. It looks like a steel fork with a wheel at one end. The wheel is the blade that allows you to cut out the shape of each piece of glass. Second, you will need another tool to "break" the glass along the line you have scored with your cutter. I've always called this object "the tool." Tell the hardware clerk what you want and she'll show you what you need. Third, pick out a glass grinder to polish each piece of glass to the right size. Finally, buy a soldering iron to fuse the various pieces of glass into your design. These last two tools can be "pricey," so you may want to find a partner to share the cost. In the process, you may discover that your stained glass will become more creative when you design it with a friend.

can you make these fun?

1. How does Temple list and describe the special tools needed in the process?
2. What advice does Temple provide about how to purchase and use the "pricey" tools?

PROCESS ANALYSIS

Points to Remember

1. Arrange the steps in your process in an orderly sequence.
2. Identify and explain the purpose of each of the steps in the process.
3. Describe the special tools, terms, and tasks needed to complete the process.
4. Provide warnings, where appropriate, about the consequences of omitting, reversing, or overlooking certain steps.
5. Supply illustrations and personal anecdotes to help clarify aspects of the process.

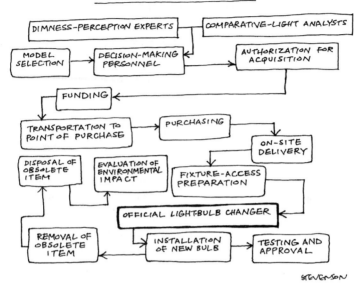

HOW MANY IT TAKES

In this comic drawing, James Stevenson offers yet another variation on the old joke, "How many [fill in the blank] does it take to change a light bulb?" Trace the various steps in this overwrought flow chart. Has Stevenson missed a step or placed steps out of sequence? Construct your own flow chart for a simple process such as making an ATM transaction or hitting a golf ball. Then write an analysis of your chart demonstrating why this simple process contains hidden steps or must be explained in a larger context.

BARBARA EHRENREICH

Barbara Ehrenreich was born in 1941 in Butte, Montana, and was educated at Reed College and Rockefeller University. She began her career working for the Health Policy Advisory Center in New York City. When she focused her attention on writing, she worked as an editor for *Seven Days* magazine and as a columnist for *Mother Jones, Time,* and the *Guardian.* The author of numerous reviews and essays, Ehrenreich has written many books, including *The Hearts of Men: American Dreams and the Flight from Commitment* (1983), *Fear of Falling: The Inner Life of the Middle Class* (1989), *The Snarling Citizen: Essays* (1995), *Nickel and Dimed: On (Not) Getting By in America* (2001), and *Global Woman: Nannies, Maids and Sex Workers in the New Economy* (2003). In "Scrubbing in Maine," excerpted from *Nickel and Dimed,* Ehrenreich explains the steps in the tedious process of working as a maid for a cleaning service.

Scrubbing in Maine

I AM RESTED and ready for anything when I arrive at The 1 Maids' office suite Monday at 7:30 A.M. I know nothing about cleaning services like this one, which, according to the brochure I am given, has over three hundred franchises nationwide, and most of what I know about domestics in general comes from nineteenth-century British novels and *Upstairs, Downstairs.* Prophetically enough, I caught a rerun of that very show on PBS over the weekend and was struck by how terribly correct the servants looked in their black-and-white uniforms and how much wiser they were than their

callow, egotistical masters. We too have uniforms, though they are more oafish than dignified—ill-fitting and in an overloud combination of kelly-green pants and a blinding sunflower-yellow polo shirt. And, as is explained in writing and over the next day and a half of training, we too have a special code of decorum. No smoking anywhere, or at least not within fifteen minutes of arrival at a house. No drinking, eating, or gum chewing in a house. No cursing in a house,

maid code (!)

---

*Liza, a good-natured women in her thirties
. . . explains that we are given only so many
minutes per house, ranging from under
sixty for a 1½-bathroom apartment to
two hundred or more for a multibathroom
"first timer."*

---

even if the owner is not present, and—perhaps to keep us in practice—no obscenities even in the office. So this is Downstairs, is my chirpy first thought. But I have no idea, of course, just how far down these stairs will take me.

Forty minutes go by before anyone acknowledges my presence with more than a harried nod. During this time the other employees arrive, about twenty of them, already glowing in their uniforms, and breakfast on the free coffee, bagels, and doughnuts The Maids kindly provides for us. All but one of the others are female, with an average age I would guess in the late twenties, though the range seems to go from prom-fresh to well into the Medicare years. There is a pleasant sort of bustle as people get their breakfasts and fill plastic buckets with rags and bottles of cleaning fluids, but surprisingly little conversation outside of a few references to what people ate (pizza) and drank (Jell-O shots are mentioned) over the weekend. Since the room in which we gather contains only two folding chairs, both of them occupied, the other new girl

2 exciting) how

and I sit cross-legged on the floor, silent and alert, while the regulars get sorted into teams of three or four and dispatched to the day's list of houses. One of the women explains to me that teams do not necessarily return to the same houses week after week, nor do you have any guarantee of being on the same team from one day to the next. This, I suppose, is one of the advantages of a corporate cleaning service to its customers: there are no sticky and possibly guilt-ridden relationships involved, because the customers communicate almost entirely with Tammy, the office manager, or with Ted, the franchise owner and our boss. The advantage to the cleaning person is harder to determine, since the pay compares so poorly to what an independent cleaner is likely to earn—up to $15 an hour, I've heard. While I wait in the inner room, where the phone is and Tammy has her desk, to be issued a uniform, I hear her tell a potential customer on the phone that The Maids charges $25 per person-hour. The company gets $25 and we get $6.65 for each hour we work? I think I must have misheard, but a few minutes later I hear her say the same thing to another inquirer. So the only advantage of working here as opposed to freelancing is that you don't need a clientele or even a car. You can arrive straight from welfare or, in my case, the bus station—fresh off the boat.

At last, after all the other employees have sped off in the company's eye-catching green-and-yellow cars, I am led into a tiny closet-sized room off the inner office to learn my trade via videotape. The manager at another maid service where I'd applied had told me she didn't like to hire people who had done cleaning before because they were resistant to learning the company's system, so I prepare to empty my mind of all prior housecleaning experience. There are four tapes—dusting, bathrooms, kitchen, and vacuuming—each starring an attractive, possibly Hispanic young woman who moves about serenely in obedience to the male voiceover: For vacuuming, begin in the master bedroom; when dusting, begin with the room directly off the kitchen. When you enter a room, mentally divide it into sections no wider than your reach. Begin in the section to your left and, within each sec-

3

[handwritten margin notes: "Welcome to business" and "this is just funny"]

tion, move from left to right and top to bottom. This way nothing is ever overlooked.

I like *Dusting* best, for its undeniable logic and a certain   4
kind of austere beauty. When you enter a house, you spray a white rag with Windex and place it in the left pocket of your green apron. Another rag, sprayed with disinfectant, goes into the middle pocket, and a yellow rag bearing wood polish in the right-hand pocket. A dry rag, for buffing surfaces, occupies the right-hand pocket of your slacks. Shiny surfaces get Windexed, wood gets wood polish, and everything else is wiped dust-free with disinfectant. Every now and then Ted pops in to watch with me, pausing the video to underscore a particularly dramatic moment: "See how she's working *this* around the vase? That's an accident waiting to happen." If *man* Ted himself were in a video, it would have to be a cartoon, because the only features sketched onto his pudgy face are *really* brown buttonlike eyes and a tiny pug nose; his belly, encased *needs* in a polo shirt, overhangs the waistline of his shorts. "You know, all this was figured out with a stopwatch," he tells me *a life* with something like pride. When the video warns against oversoaking our rags with cleaning fluids, he pauses it to tell me there's a danger in undersoaking too, especially if it's going to slow me down. "Cleaning fluids are less expensive than your time." It's good to know that *something* is cheaper than my time, or that in the hierarchy of the company's values I rank above Windex.

Vacuuming is the most disturbing video, actually a double   5
feature beginning with an introduction to the special backpack vacuum we are to use. Yes, the vacuum cleaner actually straps onto your back, a chubby fellow who introduces himself as its inventor explains. He suits up, pulling the straps tight across and under his chest and then says proudly into the camera: "See, I *am* the vacuum cleaner." It weighs only ten pounds, he claims, although, as I soon find out, with the attachments dangling from the strap around your waist, the total is probably more like fourteen. What about my petulant and much-pampered lower back? The inventor returns to the theme of human/machine merger: when properly strapped

in, we too will be vacuum cleaners, constrained only by the cord that attaches us to an electrical outlet, and vacuum cleaners don't have backaches. Somehow all this information exhausts me, and I watch the second video, which explains the actual procedures for vacuuming, with the detached interest of a cineast. Could the model maid be an actual maid and the model home someone's actual dwelling? And who are these people whose idea of decorating is matched pictures of mallard ducks in flight and whose house is perfectly characterless and pristine even before the model maid sets to work?

At first I find the videos on kitchens and bathrooms baffling, and it takes me several minutes to realize why: there is no *water*, or almost no water, involved. I was taught to clean by my mother, a compulsive housekeeper who employed water so hot you needed rubber gloves to get into it and in such Niagara-like quantities that most microbes were probably crushed by the force of it before the soap suds had a chance to rupture their cell walls. But germs are never mentioned in the videos provided by The Maids. Our antagonists exist entirely in the visible world—soap scum, dust, counter crud, dog hair, stains, and smears—and are to be attacked by damp rag or, in hardcore cases, by Dobie (the brand of plastic scouring pad we use). We scrub only to remove impurities that might be detectable to a customer by hand or by eye; otherwise our only job is to wipe. Nothing is said about the possibility of transporting bacteria, by rag or by hand, from bathroom to kitchen or even from one house to the next. It is the "cosmetic touches" that the videos emphasize and that Ted, when he wanders back into the room, continually directs my eye to. Fluff up all throw pillows and arrange them symmetrically. Brighten up stainless steel sinks with baby oil. Leave all spice jars, shampoos, etc., with their labels facing outward. Comb out the fringes of Persian carpets with a pick. Use the vacuum cleaner to create a special, fernlike pattern in the carpets. The loose ends of toilet paper and paper towel rolls have to be given a special fold (the same one you'll find in hotel bathrooms). "Messes" of loose paper, clothing, or toys are to be stacked into "neat messes." Finally, the house is to be sprayed with the cleaning service's signature floral-scented air freshener, which will signal to the owners, the moment they return home, that, yes, their house has been "cleaned."

FAKE

After a day's training I am judged fit to go out with a team, where I soon discover that life is nothing like the movies, at least not if the movie is *Dusting*. For one thing, compared with our actual pace, the training videos were all in slow motion. We do not walk to the cars with our buckets full of cleaning fluids and utensils in the morning, we run, and when we pull up to a house, we run with our buckets to the door. Liza, a good-natured woman in her thirties who is my first team leader, explains that we are given only so many minutes per house, ranging from under sixty for a 1½-bathroom apartment to two hundred or more for a multi-bathroom "first timer." I'd like to know why anybody worries about Ted's time limits if we're being paid by the hour but hesitate to display anything that might be interpreted as attitude. As we get to each house, Liza assigns our tasks, and I cross my fingers to ward off bathrooms and vacuuming. Even dusting, though, gets aerobic under pressure, and after about an hour of it—reaching to get door tops, crawling along floors to wipe baseboards, standing on my bucket to attack the higher shelves—I wouldn't mind sitting down with a tall glass of water. But as soon as you complete your assigned task, you report to the team leader to be assigned to help someone else. Once or twice, when the normal process of evaporation is deemed too slow, I am assigned to dry a scrubbed floor by putting rags under my feet and skating around on it. Usually, by the time I get out to the car and am dumping the dirty water used on floors and wringing out rags, the rest of the team is already in the car with the motor running. Liza assures me that they've never left anyone behind at a house, not even, presumably, a very new person whom nobody knows.

physical work

In my interview, I had been promised a thirty-minute lunch break, but this turns out to be a five-minute pit stop at a convenience store, if that. I bring my own sandwich—the same turkey breast and cheese every day—as do a couple of the others; the rest eat convenience store fare, a bagel or doughnut salvaged from our free breakfast, or nothing at all. The two older married women I'm teamed up with eat best—sandwiches and fruit. Among the younger women, lunch consists of a slice of pizza, a "pizza pocket" (a roll of dough surrounding some pizza sauce), or a small bag of chips. Bear in mind we are not office workers, sitting around idling at the basal metabolic rate. A poster on the wall in the office cheerily displays the number of calories burned per minute at our various tasks, ranging from about 3.5 for dusting to 7 for vacuuming. If you assume an average of 5 calories per minute in a seven-hour day (eight hours minus time for travel between houses), you need to be taking in 2,100 calories in addition to the resting minimum of, say, 900 or so. I get pushy with Rosalie, who is new like me and fresh from high school in a rural northern part of the state, about the meagerness of her lunches, which consist solely of Doritos— a half bag from the day before or a freshly purchased small-sized bag. She just didn't have anything in the house, she says (though she lives with her boyfriend and his mother), and she certainly doesn't have any money to buy lunch, as I find out when I offer to fetch her a soda from a Quik Mart and she has to admit she doesn't have eighty-nine cents. I treat her to the soda, wishing I could force her, mommylike, to take milk instead. So how does she hold up for an eight- or even nine-hour day? "Well," she concedes, "I get dizzy sometimes."

For Study and Discussion

QUESTIONS FOR RESPONSE

1. Make a list of the part-time jobs you have had since you were young. How were you trained to complete the steps in each job?

2. How do you respond to the service people—clerks, custodians, cashiers—you meet every day?

QUESTIONS ABOUT PURPOSE

1. How does Ehrenreich's criticism of the training films anticipate her criticism of her job?
2. How does her discussion of the pay scale support the overall purpose of her book as suggested by its title, *Nickel and Dimed: On (Not) Getting By in America?*

QUESTIONS ABOUT AUDIENCE

1. How does Ehrenreich's reference to her mother anticipate her readers' response to the cleaning procedure that is taught in the training films?
2. How do Ted's comments enable Ehrenreich's readers to identify with her?

QUESTIONS ABOUT STRATEGIES

1. How does Ehrenreich's characterization of the training films— "Hispanic young woman who moves about serenely in obedience to the male voiceover"—suggest the power relationship in her job?
2. How does she demonstrate that "life is nothing like the movies"?

QUESTIONS FOR DISCUSSION

1. What does the emphasis on "cosmetic touches" suggest about the quality of the work performed by the cleaning service?
2. What does the discussion of lunch food and the calories required for the job suggest about the potential health problems of service workers?

P. J. O'ROURKE

Patrick Jake O'Rourke was born in 1947 in To-
ledo, Ohio, and was educated at Miami University and Johns Hopkins University. He began his
writing career working for underground newspapers such as *Harry* in Baltimore before landing
jobs as a feature editor and freelance writer for the
New York Herald, executive editor for *National
Lampoon,* and correspondent for *Rolling Stone*
and *Atlantic Monthly.* His humorous style is
showcased in *The 1964 High School Yearbook Par-
ody* (1974), *Modern Manners: An Etiquette Book
for Rude People* (1983), *The Bachelor's Home
Companion: A Practical Guide to Keeping House
like a Pig* (1987), and *Holidays in Hell* (1988).
O'Rourke's humor always has a political edge, evident in books such as *Republican Party Reptile:
Essays and Outrages* (1987), *Give War a Chance:
Eyewitness Accounts of Mankind's Struggle Against
Tyranny, Injustice and Alcohol-Free Beer* (1992),
and *The CEO of the Sofa* (2001). In "Third World
Driving Hints and Tips," reprinted from *Holidays
in Hell,* O'Rourke analyzes the rules of the road
for driving in a different country.

Third World Driving Hints and Tips

DURING THE PAST couple of years I've had to do my 1
share of driving in the Third World—in Mexico,
Lebanon, the Philippines, Cyprus, El Salvador, Africa and
Italy. (Italy is not technically part of the Third World, but no
one has told the Italians.) I don't pretend to be an expert,

At least he's got potential to be interesting

Hey now,

I'm Italian

112

but I have been making notes. Maybe these notes will be useful to readers who are planning to do something really stupid with their Hertz #1 Club cards.

ROAD HAZARDS

What would be a road hazard anywhere else, in the Third World is probably the road. There are two techniques for coping with this. One is to drive very fast so your wheels "get on top" of the ruts and your car sails over the ditches and gullies. Predictably, this will result in disaster. The other technique is to drive very slowly. This will also result in disaster. No matter how slowly you drive into a ten-foot hole, you're

---

Never look where you're going—
you'll only scare yourself.

---

still going to get hurt. You'll find the locals themselves can't make up their minds. Either they drive at 2 m.p.h.—which they do every time there's absolutely no way to get around them. Or else they drive at 100 m.p.h.—which they do coming right at you when you finally get a chance to pass the guy going 2 m.p.h.

BASIC INFORMATION

It's important to have your facts straight before you begin piloting a car around an underdeveloped country. For instance, which side of the road do they drive on? This is easy. They drive on your side. That is, you can depend on it, any oncoming traffic will be on your side of the road. Also, how do you translate kilometres into miles? Most people don't know this, but one kilometre = ten miles, exactly. True, a kilometre is only 62 per cent of a mile, but if something is one hundred

kilometres away, read that as one thousand miles because the
roads are 620 per cent worse than anything you've ever seen.
And when you see a 50-k.p.h. speed limit, you might as well
figure that means 500 *m.p.h.* because nobody cares. The
Third World does not have Broderick Crawford and the
Highway Patrol. Outside the cities, it doesn't have many police at all. Law enforcement is in the hands of the army. And
soldiers, if they feel like it, will shoot you no matter what
speed you're going.

TRAFFIC SIGNS AND SIGNALS

Most developing nations use international traffic symbols.   4
Americans may find themselves perplexed by road signs that
look like Boy Scout merit badges and by such things as an
iguana silhouette with a red diagonal bar across it. Don't
worry, the natives don't know what they mean, either. The
natives do, however, have an elaborate set of signals used to
convey information to the traffic around them. For example,
if you're trying to pass someone and he blinks his left turn
signal, it means go ahead. Either that or it means a large truck
is coming around the bend, and you'll get killed if you try.
You'll find out in a moment.

Signalling is further complicated by festive decorations   5
found on many vehicles. It can be hard to tell a hazard flasher
from a string of Christmas-tree lights wrapped around the
bumper, and brake lights can easily be confused with the
dozen red Jesus statuettes and the ten stuffed animals with
blinking eyes on the package shelf.

DANGEROUS CURVES

Dangerous curves are marked, at least in Christian lands, by   6
white wooden crosses positioned to make the curves even
more dangerous. These crosses are memorials to people
who've died in traffic accidents, and they give a rough statistical indication of how much trouble you're likely to have at
that spot in the road. Thus, when you come through a curve

in a full-power slide and are suddenly confronted with a veritable forest of crucifixes, you know you're dead.

LEARNING TO DRIVE LIKE A NATIVE

It's important to understand that in the Third World most driving is done with the horn, or "Egyptian Brake Pedal," as it is known. There is a precise and complicated etiquette of horn use. Honk your horn only under the following circumstances:

[handwritten: 7 NICE!!!]

1. When anything blocks the road.
2. When anything doesn't.
3. When anything might.
4. At red lights.
5. At green lights.
6. At all other times.

[handwritten: Can you get a horn to continually beep.]

ROAD-BLOCKS

One thing you can count on in Third World countries is trouble. There's always some uprising, coup or Marxist insurrection going on, and this means military road-blocks. There are two kinds of military road-block, the kind where you slow down so they can look you over, and the kind where you come to a full stop so they can steal your luggage. The important thing is that you must *never* stop at the slow-down kind of road-block. If you stop, they'll think you're a terrorist about to attack them, and they'll shoot you. And you must *always* stop at the full-stop kind of road-block. If you just slow down, they'll think you're a terrorist about to attack them, and they'll shoot you. How do you tell the difference between the two kinds of road-block? Here's the fun part: you can't!

[handwritten: 8]

[handwritten: well that shakes things up]

(The terrorists, of course, have road-blocks of their own. They always make you stop. Sometimes with land mines.)

[handwritten: 9]

ANIMALS IN THE RIGHT OF WAY

As a rule of thumb, you should slow down for donkeys, speed   10
up for goats and stop for cows. Donkeys will get out of your
way eventually, and so will pedestrians. But never actually
stop for either of them or they'll take advantage, especially
the pedestrians. If you stop in the middle of a crowd of Third
World pedestrians, you'll be there buying Chiclets and bogus
antiquities for days.

Drive like hell through the goats. It's almost impossible to   11
hit a goat. On the other hand, it's almost impossible *not* to
hit a cow. Cows are immune to horn-honking, shouting,
swats with sticks and taps on the hind quarters with the
bumper. The only thing you can do to make a cow move is
swerve to avoid it, which will make the cow move in front of
you with lightning speed.

Actually, the most dangerous animals are the chickens. In   12
the United States, when you see a ball roll into the street, you
hit your brakes because you know the next thing you'll see is
a kid chasing it. In the Third World, it's not balls the kids are
chasing, but chickens. Are they practising punt returns with a
leghorn? Dribbling it? Playing stick-hen? I don't know. But
Third Worlders are remarkably fond of their chickens and,
also, their children (population problems not withstanding).
If you hit one or both, they may survive. But you will not.

chickens should be worshipped

ACCIDENTS

Never look where you're going—you'll only scare yourself.   13
Nonetheless, try to avoid collisions. There are bound to be
more people in that bus, truck or even on that moped than
there are in your car. At best you'll be screamed deaf. And if
the police do happen to be around, standard procedure is to
throw everyone in jail regardless of fault. This is done to fore-
stall blood feuds, which are a popular hobby in many of these
places. Remember the American consul is very busy fretting
about that Marxist insurrection, and it may be months before
he comes to visit.

If you do have an accident, the only thing to do is go on 14
the offensive. Throw big wads of American money at everyone, and hope for the best.

SAFETY TIPS

One nice thing about the Third World, you don't have to fas- 15
ten your safety belt. (Or stop smoking. Or cut down on saturated fats.) It takes a lot off your mind when average life ex-
pectancy is forty-five minutes.

He's done this before

For Study and Discussion

QUESTIONS FOR RESPONSE

1. How were you taught to drive? What procedures—for example,
   parallel parking—gave you the most trouble?
2. What difficulties have you encountered driving in a strange car
   or in an unfamiliar place?

QUESTIONS ABOUT PURPOSE

1. How do O'Rourke's travels establish his credentials to provide
   advice to drivers?
2. At what point in the essay do you realize that his purpose is to
   entertain rather than inform?

QUESTIONS ABOUT AUDIENCE

1. How does O'Rourke identify his readers when he refers to
   "Hertz #1 Club cards" and "big wads of American money"?
2. How might the "natives" referred to in this essay respond to
   O'Rourke's characterization of their driving habits?

QUESTIONS ABOUT STRATEGIES

1. How does O'Rourke's analysis of the "Egyptian Brake Pedal"
   and the road-blocks reveal that his hints are not really meant to
   help?

2. How does his discussion of "animals in the right of way" and children complicate his analysis?

QUESTIONS FOR DISCUSSION

1. To what extent does O'Rourke's use of the words *Third World* and *underdeveloped* suggest an attitude of smug, cultural superiority?
2. How might some of his analysis apply to the driving habits you have encountered in your hometown?

NIKKI GIOVANNI

Nikki Giovanni was born in 1943 in Knoxville, Tennessee, and was educated at Fisk University, the University of Pennsylvania, and Columbia University. She has taught creative writing at Rutgers University and Virginia Tech and worked for the Ohio Humanities Council and the Appalachian Community Fund. Her poems have appeared in the collections *My House* (1972), *The Women and the Men* (1975), and *Those Who Ride the Night Winds* (1983). Her nonfiction work appears in books such as *Gemini: An Extended Autobiographical Statement on My First Twenty-five Years Being a Black Poet* (1971), *Sacred Cows . . . and Other Edibles* (1988), and *Racism 101* (1994). In "Campus Racism 101," Giovanni tells black students how to succeed at predominantly white colleges.

Is she black?

Campus Racism 101

T HERE IS A bumper sticker that reads: TOO BAD IGNO- 1
RANCE ISN'T PAINFUL. I like that. But ignorance is. We just seldom attribute the pain to it or even recognize it when we see it. Like the postcard on my corkboard. It shows a young man in a very hip jacket smoking a cigarette. In the background is a high school with the American flag waving. The caption says: "Too cool for school. Yet too stupid for the real world." Out of the mouth of the young man is a bubble enclosing the words "Maybe I'll start a band." There could be a postcard showing a jock in a uniform saying, "I don't need school. I'm going to the NFL or NBA." Or one showing a young man or woman studying and a group of young people saying, "So you want to be white." Or something equally demeaning. We need to quit it.

agree

119

I am a professor of English at Virginia Tech. I've been here 2
for four years, though for only two years with academic rank.
I am tenured, which means I have a teaching position for life,
a rarity on a predominantly white campus. Whether from
malice or ignorance, people who think I should be at a predominantly Black institution will ask, "Why are you at Tech?"
Because it's here. And so are Black students. But even if Black
students weren't here, it's painfully obvious that this nation
and this world cannot allow white students to go through
higher education without interacting with Blacks in authori-
tative positions. It is equally clear that predominantly Black

> *Your job is not to educate white people; it is
> to obtain an education.*

colleges cannot accommodate the numbers of Black students
who want and need an education.

Is it difficult to attend a predominantly white college? 3
Compared with what? Being passed over for promotion because you lack credentials? Being turned down for jobs because you are not college-educated? Joining the armed forces
or going to jail because you cannot find an alternative to the
streets? Let's have a little perspective here. Where can you go
and what can you do that frees you from interacting with the
white American mentality? You're going to interact; the only
question is, will you be in some control of yourself and your
actions, or will you be controlled by others? I'm going to recommend self-control.

What's the difference between prison and college? They 4
both prescribe your behavior for a given period of time.
They both allow you to read books and develop your writing.
They both give you time alone to think and time with your
peers to talk about issues. But four years of prison doesn't
give you a passport to greater opportunities. Most likely that

time only gives you greater knowledge of how to get back in. Four years of college gives you an opportunity not only to lift yourself but to serve your people effectively. What's the difference when you are called nigger in college from when you are called nigger in prison? In college you can, though I admit with effort, follow procedures to have those students who called you nigger kicked out or suspended. You can bring issues to public attention without risking your life. But mostly, college is and always has been the future. We, neither less nor more than other people, need knowledge. There are discomforts attached to attending predominantly white colleges, though no more so than living in a racist world. Here are some rules to follow that may help:

Go to class. No matter how you feel. No matter how you think the professor feels about you. It's important to have a consistent presence in the classroom. If nothing else, the professor will know you care enough and are serious enough to be there.

Meet your professors. Extend your hand (give a firm handshake) and tell them your name. Ask them what you need to do to make an A. You may never make an A, but you have put them on notice that you are serious about getting good grades.

Do assignments on time. Typed or computer-generated. You have the syllabus. Follow it, and turn those papers in. If for some reason you can't complete an assignment on time, let your professor know before it is due and work out a new due date—then meet it.

Go back to see your professor. Tell him or her your name again. If an assignment received less than an A, ask why, and find out what you need to do to improve the next assignment.

Yes, your professor is busy. So are you. So are your parents who are working to pay or help with your tuition. Ask early what you need to do if you feel you are starting to get into academic trouble. Do not wait until you are failing.

Understand that there will be professors who do not like you; there may even be professors who are racist or sexist or both.

You must discriminate among your professors to see who will give you the help you need. You may not simply say, "They are all against me." They aren't. They mostly don't care. Since you are the one who wants to be educated, find the people who want to help.

Don't defeat yourself. Cultivate your friends. Know your   11
enemies. You cannot undo hundreds of years of prejudicial thinking. Think for yourself and speak up. Raise your hand in class. Say what you believe no matter how awkward you may think it sounds. You will improve in your articulation and confidence.

Participate in some campus activity. Join the newspaper   12
staff. Run for office. Join a dorm council. Do something that involves you on campus. You are going to be there for four years, so let your presence be known, if not felt.

You will inevitably run into some white classmates who are   13
troubling because they often say stupid things, ask stupid questions—and expect an answer. Here are some comebacks to some of the most common inquiries and comments:

Q: What's it like to grow up in a ghetto?   14
A: I don't know.   15

Q (from the teacher): Can you give us the Black perspective   16
on Toni Morrison, Huck Finn, slavery, Martin Luther King, Jr., and others?
A: I can give you *my* perspective. (Do not take the burden of   17
22 million people on your shoulders. Remind everyone that you are an individual, and don't speak for the race or any other individual within it.)

Q: Why do all the Black people sit together in the dining   18
hall?
A: Why do all the white students sit together?   19

Q: Why should there be an African-American studies course?   20
A: Because white Americans have not adequately studied   21
the contributions of Africans and African-Americans. Both

Black and white students need to know our total common history.

Q: Why are there so many scholarships for "minority" students?
A: Because they wouldn't give my great-grandparents their forty acres and the mule.

Q: How can whites understand Black history, culture, literature, and so forth?
A: The same way we understand white history, culture, literature, and so forth. That is why we're in school: to learn.

Q: Should whites take African-American studies courses?
A: Of course. We take white-studies courses, though the universities don't call them that.

Comment: When I see groups of Black people on campus, it's really intimidating.
Comeback: I understand what you mean. I'm frightened when I see white students congregating.

Comment: It's not fair. It's easier for you guys to get into college than for other people.
Comeback: If it's so easy, why aren't there more of us?

Comment: It's not our fault that America is the way it is.
Comeback: It's not our fault, either, but both of us have a responsibility to make changes.

It's really very simple. Educational progress is a national concern; education is a private one. Your job is not to educate white people; it is to obtain an education. If you take the racial world on your shoulders, you will not get the job done. Deal with yourself as an individual worthy of respect, and make everyone else deal with you the same way. College is a little like playing grown-up. Practice what you want to be. You have been telling your parents you are grown. Now is your chance to act like it.

For Study and Discussion

QUESTIONS FOR RESPONSE

1. How have you responded to situations in which you were convinced that your teacher did not like you?
2. How have you felt when a teacher or fellow student placed you in a group (characterized by stereotypes) and then asked you to speak *for* that group?

QUESTIONS ABOUT PURPOSE

1. How does Giovanni explain her reasons for teaching at a predominantly white school?
2. In what ways does the issue of control, particularly self-control, explain the purpose of her advice?

QUESTIONS ABOUT AUDIENCE

1. How do the examples in the first paragraph and the advice in the last paragraph identify Giovanni's primary audience?
2. How does Giovanni's status as professor at a predominantly white college establish her authority to address her audience on "Racism 101"?

QUESTIONS ABOUT STRATEGIES

1. How does Giovanni arrange her advice? Why is her first suggestion—"Go to class"—her *first* suggestion? Why is her last suggestion—"Participate in some campus activity"—her *last* suggestion?
2. How does she use sample questions and answers to illustrate the experience of learning on a white campus?

QUESTIONS FOR DISCUSSION

1. What does Giovanni's attitude toward *individual* as opposed to *group* perspective suggest about the nature of "racism"?
2. How might white students learn as much as black students from following her advice?

Julia Alvarez was born in New York City in 1950, but was raised in the Dominican Republic until her family was forced to flee the country because her father's involvement in the plot to overthrow dictator Rafael Trujillo was uncovered. She was educated at Middlebury College, Syracuse University, and Bread Loaf School of English and worked as a Poet-in-the-Schools in several states. She then began teaching writing at George Washington University, the University of Illinois, and Middlebury College. Her major works of fiction include *How the Garcia Girls Lost Their Accents* (1991), *In the Time of Butterflies* (1994), *¡YO!* (1996), and *In the Name of Salomé: A Novel* (2000). Her poems appear in *Homecoming* (1984) and *The Other Side/El Otro Lado* (1995). In "Grounds for Fiction," reprinted from *Something to Declare* (1998), Alvarez analyzes the sources and strategies of her writing process.

Grounds for Fiction

E VERY ONCE IN a while after a reading, someone in the audience will come up to me. *Have I got a story for you!* They will go on to tell me the story of an aunt or sister or next-door neighbor, some moment of mystery, some serendipitous occurrence, some truly incredible story. "You should write it down," I always tell them. They look at me as if they've just offered me their family crown jewels and I've refused them. "I'm no writer," they tell me. "You're the writer."

"Oh, you never know," I reply, so as to encourage them. What I should tell them is that writing ideas can't really be traded in an open market. If they could be, writers would be multimillionaires. Who knows what mystery (or madness) it is that drives us to our computers for two, three, four years, in pursuit of some sparkling possibility that looks like dull fact to everyone else's eyes. One way to define a writer is she who is able to make what obsesses her into everyone's obsession. I am thinking of Goethe, whose *Sorrows of Young Werther*, published in 1774, caused a spate of suicides in imitation of its young hero. Young Werther's blue frock coat and yellow waistcoat became the fad. We have all been the victims of someone's too-long slide show of their white-

Been there

I told the young man that if he didn't want to spend hours and hours finding out if the kernel of an idea, the glimmer of an inspiration, the flash of a possibility would make a good story, he should give up the idea *of wanting to be a writer.*

---

water rafting trip or their recounting of a convoluted, boring dream. But a Mark Twain can turn that slide show into the lively backdrop of a novel, or a Jorge Luis Borges can take the twist and turn of a dream and wring the meaning of the universe from it.

But aside from talent—and granted, that is a big aside, one that comes and goes and shifts and grows and diminishes, so it is also somewhat unpredictable—how can we tell when we've got it: that seed of experience, of memory, that voice of a character or fleeting image that might just be grounds for fiction? The answer is that we can never tell. And so another way to define a writer is someone who is willing to find out. As James Dickey once explained to an audience, "I work on the process of refining low-grade ore. I get maybe a couple of nuggets of gold out of fifty tons of dirt. It is tough for me. No, I am not inspired."

"Are you all here because you want to muck around in fifty tons of dirt?" I ask my workshop of young writers the first day. Not one hand goes up unless I've told them the Dickey story first. *yup*

In fact, my students want to know ahead of time if some idea they have will make a good story. "I mean, before I spend hours and hours on it," one young man explained. I told my students what Mallarmé told his friend the painter Degas, when Degas complained that he couldn't seem to write well although he was "full of ideas." Mallarmé's famous answer was, "My dear Degas, poems are not made out of ideas. Poems are made out of words." I told my student that if a young writer had come up to me and told me that he was going to write a story about a man who wakes up one morning and finds out that he has been turned into a cockroach, I would have told him to forget it. That story would never work. "And I would have stopped Kafka from writing his 'Metamorphosis,'" I concluded, smiling at my student, as if he might be a future Kafka. *hmmm*

"Well, it's just two pages," he grumbled. "And I have this other idea that might be better. About a street person who is getting Alzheimer's."

"Write both stories, and I'll read them and tell you what I think of them," I said. He looked alarmed. So I leveled with him. I told him that if he didn't want to spend hours and hours finding out if the kernel of an idea, the glimmer of an inspiration, the flash of a possibility would make a good story, he should give up the *idea* of wanting to be a writer. *only an idea*

As much as I can break down the process of writing stories, I would say that this is how it begins. I find a detail or image or character or incident or cluster of events. A certain luminosity surrounds them. I find myself attracted. I come forward. I pick it up, turn it around, begin to ask questions, and spend hours and weeks and months and years trying to answer them.

I keep a folder, a yellow folder with pockets. For a long time it had no label because I didn't know what to label it: WHATCHAMACALLITS, filed under *W,* or also under *W,* STORY-POEM-WANNABES. Finally, I called the folder CURIOSIDADES, in Spanish so I wouldn't have to commit myself to what I was going to do in English with these random little things. I tell my students this, too, that writing begins before you ever put pen to paper or your fingers down on the keyboard. It is a way of being alive in the world. Henry James's advice to the young writer was to be someone on whom nothing is lost. And so this is my folder of the little things that have not been lost on me; news clippings, headlines, inventory lists, bits of gossip that I've already sensed have an aura about them, the beginnings of a poem or a short story, the seed of a plot that might turn into a novel or a query that might needle an essay out of me.

Periodically, when I'm between writing projects and sometimes when I'm in the middle of one and needing a break, I go through my yellow folder. Sometimes I discard a clipping or note that no longer holds my attention. But most of my curiosidades have been in my folder for years, though some have migrated to new folders, the folders of stories and poems they have inspired or found a home in.

Here's one of these curiosidades that is now in a folder that holds drafts of a story that turned into a chapter of my novel *¡YO!* This chapter is in the point of view of Marie Beaudry, a landlady who, along with other narrators, gets to tell a story on Yolanda García, the writer. The little curiosity that inspired Marie's voice was a note I found in the trash of an apartment I moved into. It has nothing at all to do with what happens in my story.

Re and Mal: Here's the two keys to your father's apt.
Need I say more excepting that's such a rotten thing you

I like the verbs here [handwritten margin note]

9

10

11

pulled on him. My doing favors is over as of this morn-
ing. Good luck to you two hard-hearted hannahs. I got
more feeling in my little finger than the two of you got
in your whole body.

Jinny

I wonder what they did

I admit that when I read this note, I wanted to move out   12
of that apartment. I felt the place was haunted by the ghost
of the last tenant against whom some violation had been perpetrated by these two hard-hearted hannahs, Re and Mal.
Over the years that handwritten note stayed in my yellow
folder and eventually gave me the voice of my character
Marie Beaudry.

Here's another scrap from deep inside one of the pockets.   13
It's the title of an article in one of my husband's ophthal-
mological journals: "Treatment of Chronic Postfiltration
Hypotony by Intrableb Injection of Autologous Blood." I
think I saved that choice bit of medical babble because of the
delight I took in the jabberwocky phenomenon of that title.

> *'Twas brillig and the slithy toves*
> *Did gyre and postfiltrate the wabe;*
> *All hypotonious was the blood,*
> *And autologous the intrableb.*

I have not yet used it in a story or poem, but who knows,
maybe someday you will look over the shoulder of one of my
characters and see that he is reading this article or writing it. I
can tell you that this delight in words and how we use and
misuse them is a preoccupation of mine.

Maybe because I began my writing life as a poet, the nam-   14
ing of things has always interested me:

> *Mother, unroll the bolts and name*
> *the fabrics from which our clothing came,*
> *dress the world in vocabulary:*
> *broadcloth, corduroy, denim, terry.*

Actually, that poem, "Naming the Fabrics," besides being inspired, of course, by the names of fabrics, was also triggered by something I picked up while reading *The 1961 Better Homes and Garden Sewing Book,* page 45: "During a question and answer period at a sewing clinic, a woman in the audience asked this question: 'I can sew beautifully; my fitting is excellent; the finished dress looks as good as that of any professional—but how do I get up enough courage to cut the fabric?'" I typed out this passage and put it away. A few months later, this fear found its way from my yellow folder to my poem, "Naming the Fabrics":

> *I pay a tailor to cut his suits*
> *from seersucker, duck, tweed, cheviot,*
> *those names make my cutting hand skittish—*
> *either they sound like sex or British.*

[handwritten margin note: What?]

Since I myself have no sewing skills to speak of, I didn't know about this fear that seamstresses experience before cutting fabric. Certainly, the year 1961, when this sewing book was published, brings other fears to mind: the Berlin Wall going up; invaders going down to the Bay of Pigs; Trujillo, our dictator of thirty-one years, being assassinated in the Dominican Republic. But this housewife in Indiana had her own metaphysical fears to work out on cloth. "How do I get up enough courage to cut the fabric?" Her preoccupation astonished me and touched me for all kinds of reasons I had to work out on paper.

You might wonder what a "serious writer" was doing   15
reading *The 1961 Better Homes and Garden Sewing Book.* Wouldn't my time have been better spent perusing Milton or Emily Dickinson or even the *New York Review of Books* or *The Nation?* All I can say in my defense is that I believe in Henry James's advice: be someone on whom nothing is lost. Or what Deborah Kerr said in *Night of the Iguana,* "Nothing human disgusts me." I once heard a writer on *Fresh Air* tell Terry Gross that one of the most important things he had ever learned in his life was that you could learn a lot from

[handwritten margin note: I bet some things (would)]

people who were dumber than you. You can also learn a lot from publications that are below your literary standards: housekeeping books, cookbooks, manuals, cereal boxes, and the local newspapers of your small town. These last are the best. Even if some of this "news" is really 16 glorified gossip—so what? Most of our classics are glorified gossip. Think of the Wife of Bath's inventory of husbands or the debutante's hair-rape in "The Rape of the Lock." How about Madame Bovary's seamy affair? Is what happened to Abelard over his Héloïse or to Jason for pissing off Medea any less infamous than the John and Lorena Bobbit story of several years ago? The wonderful Canadian writer Alice Munro admits that she likes reading *People* magazine, and "not just at the checkout stand. I sometimes buy it." She goes on to say that gossip is "a central part of my life. I'm interested in small-town gossip. Gossip has that feeling in it, that one wants to know about life."

Are we supposed to know these?

I've gotten wonderful stories from the *Addison Independent,* the *Valley Voice,* even the *Burlington Free Press* that 17 would never be reported in the *Wall Street Journal* or the *New York Times:*

11-YEAR-OLD GIRLS TAKE CAR
ON TWO-STATE JOYRIDE

Two 11-year-old girls determined to see a newborn niece secretly borrowed their grandfather's car, piled clothes on the front seat so they could see over the steering wheel and drove more than 10 hours.

Neither one of them had ever driven a car before, said Michael Ray, Mercer County's juvenile case worker. The youngsters packed the Dodge Aries with soda, snacks, and an atlas for their trek from West Virginia to the central Kentucky town of Harrodsburg. "They were determined to see that baby," said caseworker Ray.

You could write a whole novel about that. In fact, in Mona 18 Simpson's latest novel, *A Regular Guy,* eleven-year-old Jane di Natali is taught by her mother to drive their pickup with wood blocks strapped to the pedals so her short legs can reach them. Little Jane takes off on her own to see her estranged father hundreds of miles away. I wonder if Mona Simpson got her idea for Jane's odyssey from reading about these two eleven-year-olds.

Here's another article I've saved in my yellow folder: 19

MISDIAGNOSED PATIENT FREED AFTER 2 YEARS

A Mexican migrant worker misdiagnosed and kept sedated in an Oregon mental hospital for two years because doctors couldn't understand his Indian dialect is going home.

Adolfo Gonzales, a frail 5-foot-4-inch grape picker who doesn't speak English or Spanish, had been trying to communicate in his native Indian dialect of Trique.

Gonzales, believed to be in his 20s, was born in a village in Oaxaca, Mexico. He was committed in June 1990 after being arrested for indecent exposure at a laundromat. Charges later were dropped.

I couldn't get this story out of my head. First, I was—and am—intensely interested in the whole Scheherazade issue of how important it is to be able to tell our stories to those who have power over us. Second, and more mundanely, I was intensely curious about those charges that were later dropped: indecent exposure at a laundromat. What was Adolfo Gonzales doing taking his clothes off in a laundromat? Why was he in town after a hard day of grape picking? I had to find answers to these questions, and so I started writing a poem. "It's a myth that writers write what they know," the writer Marcie Hershman has written. "We write what it is that we need to know."

The next payday you went to town
to buy your girl and to wash your one
set of working clothes.

In the laundromat, you took them off
to wring out the earth you wanted
to leave behind you.
              from "Two Years Too Late"

Of course, you don't even have to go to your local paper. 20
Just take a walk downtown, especially if you live in a small
town, as I do. All I have to do is have a cup of coffee at
Steve's Diner or at Jimmy's Weybridge Garage and listen to
my neighbors talking. Flannery O'Connor claimed that most
beginners' stories don't work because "they don't go very far
inside a character, don't reveal very much of the character.
And this problem is in large part due to the fact that these
characters have no distinctive speech to reveal themselves
with." Here are some examples of my fellow Vermonters
talking their very distinctive and revealing speech.

> He's so lazy he married a pregnant woman. *haha*
>
> I'm so hungry I could eat the north end out of a
> southbound skunk.
>
> The snow's butt-high to a tall cow.
>
> More nervous than a long-tailed cat in a room full of
> rocking chairs.
>
> I'm so sick that I'd have to get well to die.

Of course if, like Whitman, you do nothing but listen, you
will also hear all kinds of bogus voices these days, speaking
the new doublespeak. In our litigious, politically overcor- *nice*
rected, dizzily spin-doctored age, politicians and public
figures have to use language so that it doesn't say anything
that might upset anyone. Here's a list of nonterms and what
they really stand for:

Sufferer of fictitious disorder syndrome: Liar
Suboptimal: Failed
Temporarily displaced inventory: Stolen
Negative gain in test scores: Lower test scores
Substantive negative outcome: Death

We're back to "Treatment of Chronic Postfiltration Hypo-tony by Intrableb Injection of Autologous Blood," what Ken Macrorie in his wonderful book about expository writing, *Telling Writing,* calls "Engfish"—homogenized, doctored-up, approximate language that can't be traced to a human being.

I tend to agree with what Dickinson once said about po-   21
etry, "There are no approximate words in a poem." Auden even went so far as to say that he could pick out a potential poet by a student's answer to the question, "Why do you want to write poetry?" If the student answered, "I have im-portant things to say," then he was not a poet. If he an-swered, "I like hanging around words listening to what they say," then maybe he was going to be a poet.

I got enmeshed in one such string of words when I visited   22
the United Nations to hear my mother give a speech on vio-lation of human rights. At the door an aide handed me the list of voting member countries and the names caught my eye: Dem Kampuchea, Dem Yemen, Denmark, Djibouti, Dominica, Dominican Republic, Ecuador, Egypt. . . . When I got home, I started writing a poem, ostensibly about hearing my mother give that speech, but really because I wanted to use the names of those countries:

> *I scan the room for reactions,*
> *picking out those countries*
> *guilty of her sad facts.*
> *Kampuchea is absent,*
> *absent, too, the South African delegate.*
> *I cannot find the United States.*
> *Nervous countries predominate,*
> *Nicaragua and Haiti,*
> *Iraq, Israel, Egypt.*
> *from "Between Dominica and Ecuador"*

But of course, it's not just words that intrigue writers, but the stories, the possibilities of human character that cluster around a bit of history, trivia, gossip.

For instance, Anne Macdonald's book, *Feminine Ingenuity,* inspired a character trait of the mother in *How the García Girls Lost Their Accents.* According to Macdonald, at the beginning of the twentieth century, 5,535 American women were granted patents for inventions, including a straw-weaving device, an open-eye needle for sewing hot-air balloons, and special planking designed to discourage barnacles from attaching themselves to warships. These intriguing facts gave me a side of the mother's character I would never have thought up on my own. Inspired by the gadgetry of her new country, Laura García sets out to make her mark: soap sprayed from the nozzle head of a shower when you turn the knob a certain way; instant coffee with creamer already mixed in; time-released water capsules for your potted plants when you were away; a key chain with a timer that would go off when your parking meter was about to expire. (And the ticking would help you find your keys easily if you mislaid them.)

Sometimes the inspiration is history. History . . . that subject I hated in school because it was so dry and all about dead people. I wish now my teachers had made me read novels to make the past spring alive in my imagination. For years, I wanted to write about the Mirabal sisters, but I admit I was put off by these grand historical abstractions. It wasn't until I began to accumulate several yellow folders' worth of vivid little details about them that these godlike women became accessible to me. One of my first entries came from my father, who had just returned from a trip to the Dominican Republic: "I met the man who sold the girls pocketbooks at El Gallo before they set off over the mountain. He told me he warned them not to go. He said he took them out back to the stockroom supposedly to show them inventory and explained they were going to be killed. But they did not believe him." I still get goosebumps reading my father's letter dated June 5, 1985. It went in my yellow folder. That pocketbook-buying scene is at the end of the novel I published nine years later.

So what are you to conclude from this tour of my yellow folder? That this essay is just an excuse to take you through my folder and share my little treasures with you? Well, one thing I don't want you to conclude is that this preliminary woolgathering is a substitute for the real research that starts once you have a poem or story going. In "Naming the Fabrics," for instance, though I was inspired by the plaintive question asked at a sewing clinic, I still had to go down to the fabric store and spend an afternoon with a very kind and patient saleslady who taught me all about gingham and calico, crepe and gauze. I spent days reading fabric books, and weeks working on the poem, and years going back to it, revising it, tinkering with it. For my story, "The Tent," I had to call up the National Guard base near Champaign, Illinois, and get permission from the base commander to go observe his men setting up a tent. ("What exactly do you need this for?" he asked at least half a dozen times.) Sometimes I think the best reason for a writer to have a reputable job like being a professor at a university or a vice president of Hartford Insurance Company is so you can call up those base commanders or bother those salesladies in fabric stores as if you do have a real job. Otherwise, they might think you are crazy and lock you up like poor Adolfo Gonzales.

On the whole, I have found people to be kind and generous with their time, especially when you ask them to talk about something they know and care about. Many people have actually gone beyond kindness in helping me out. I remember calling up the local Catholic priest, bless his heart, who really deserves, I don't know, a plenary indulgence for tolerance in the face of surprise. Imagine getting an early-morning call (my writing day starts at 6:30, but I really don't do this kind of phone calling till about 7:30 since I do want my sources to be lucid). Anyhow, imagine an early-morning call at your rectory from a woman you don't know who asks you what is the name of that long rod priests have with a hole on one end to sprinkle people with holy water? I'd be lying if I tried to make drama out of the phone call and say there was a long pause. Nope. Father John spoke right up, "Ah yes, my aspergill."

One thing I should add—the bad news part of all this fun,

but something writers do have to think about in this litigious age—what is grounds for fiction can also be, alas, grounds for suing. All three of my novels have been read by my publisher's lawyer for what might be libelous. Thank goodness Algonquin's lawyer is also a reader who refuses to vacuum all the value out of a book in order to play it safe. Still, I have had to take drinks out of characters' hands and make abused ladies disabused and make so many changes in hair coloring and hairstyle that I could start a literary beauty parlor.

But even if your fictional ground is cleared of litigious material, there might still be grounds for heartache. Your family and friends might feel wounded when they can detect—even if no one else can—the shape of the real behind the form of your fiction. And who would want to hurt those very people you write for, those very people who share with you the world you are struggling to understand in your fiction for their sake as well as your own?

I don't know how to get around this and I certainly haven't figured out what the parameters of my responsibility are to the real people in my life. One of my theories, which might sound defensive and self-serving, is that there is no such thing as straight-up fiction. There are just levels of distance from our own life experience, the thing that drives us to write in the first place. In spite of our caution and precaution, bits of our lives will get into what we write. I have a friend whose mother finds herself in all his novels, even historical novels set in nineteenth-century Russia or islands in the Caribbean where his mother has never been. A novelist writing about Napoleon might convey his greedy character by describing him spooning gruel into his mouth, only to realize that her image of how a greedy man eats comes from watching her fat Tío Jorge stuff his face with sweet habichuelas.

I think that if you start censoring yourself as a novelist—*this is out of bounds, that is sacrosanct*—you will never write anything. My advice is to write it out, and then decide, by whatever process seems fair to you—three-o'clock-in-the-morning insomniac angst sessions with your soul, or a phone

[handwritten marginalia: "I like the opinion of the editor"]

[handwritten marginalia: "where's the line"]

28

29

30

call with your best friend, or a long talk with your sister—
what you are going to do about it. More often than not, an
upset reaction has more to do with people's wounded vanity
or their own unresolved issues with *you* rather than what
you've written. I'm not speaking now of meanness or revenge thinly masquerading as fiction, but of a writer's serious
attempts to render justice to the world she lives in, which includes, whether she wants it to or not, the people she loves or
has tried to love, the people who have been a part of the
memories, details, life experiences that form the whole cloth
of her reality—out of which, with fear and a trembling hand,
she must perforce cut her fiction.

But truly, this is a worry to put out of your head while you   31
are writing. You'll need your energy for the hard work ahead:
tons and tons of good *ideas* to process in order to get those
nuggets of pure prose. What Yeats once said in his poem,
"Dialogue of Self and Soul," could well be the writer's
pledge of allegiance:

> *I am content to follow to its source,*
> *every event in action or in thought.*

And remember, no one is probably going to pay you a whole
lot of money to do this. You also probably won't save anyone's life with anything you write. But so much does depend
on seeing a world in a grain of sand and a heaven in a
wildflower. Maybe we are here only to say: house, bridge,
aspergill, gingham, calico, gauze. "But to say them," as Rilke
said, "remember oh, to say them in a way that the things
themselves never dreamed of existing so intensely."

But this is too much of an orchestral close for the lowly lit-   32
tle ditty that starts with a newspaper clipping or the feel of a
bolt of gingham or a cup of coffee at the Weybridge Garage.
The best advice I can give writers is something so dull and
simple you'd never save it in your yellow folder. But go ahead
and engrave it in your writer's heart. If you want to be a
writer, anything in this world is grounds for fiction.

For Study and Discussion

QUESTIONS FOR RESPONSE

1. Have you ever read a news story or overheard some gossip that you think would make a good story? Explain the features that made it "good."
2. Have you ever tried to write about a personal experience that meant a great deal to you? Why were you satisfied or disappointed with the results?

QUESTIONS ABOUT PURPOSE

1. How does Alvarez use Henry James's advice—to be someone on whom nothing is lost—to explain the purpose of the process she is trying to analyze?
2. How does she use "the Scheherazade issue" to explain the purpose of writing?

QUESTIONS ABOUT AUDIENCE

1. In what ways do the people who attend Alvarez's poetry readings serve as the imaginary audience for her essay?
2. How does she use Auden's question to student writers (page 134) to expand her audience?

QUESTIONS ABOUT STRATEGIES

1. Identify the steps in the little paragraph Alvarez uses to "break down the process of writing fiction." What steps are hidden within this sequence?
2. How does Alvarez's "tour" of her CURIOSIDADES help her illustrate the way she *finds* stories?

QUESTIONS FOR DISCUSSION

1. How does Alvarez suggest you solve the problem of the conflict between grounds for fiction and grounds for suing?
2. How does Alvarez support her argument that there is no such thing as "straight-up fiction"?

Serena Nanda was educated at New York University and taught cultural anthropology at John Jay College of Criminal Justice at City University of New York. Her books include *Cultural Anthropology* (1998), *American Cultural Pluralism and Law* (1996), *Neither Man nor Woman: The Hijras of India* (1999), and *Gender Diversity: Cross-Cultured Variations* (2000). Nanda's current research focuses on non-European representations of Europeans in art and performance. In "Arranging a Marriage in India," reprinted from *The Naked Anthropologist: Tales from Around the World* (1992), Nanda contrasts the Indian and American processes of getting married.

Arranging a Marriage in India

Sister and doctor brother-in-law invite correspondence from North Indian professionals only, for a beautiful, talented, sophisticated, intelligent sister, 5′ 3″, slim, M.A. in textile design, father a senior civil officer. Would prefer immigrant doctors, between 26–29 years. Reply with full details and returnable photo.

A well-settled uncle invites matrimonial correspondence from slim, fair, educated South Indian girl, for his nephew, 25 years, smart, M.B.A., green card holder, 5′ 6″. Full particulars with returnable photo appreciated.
—*Matrimonial Advertisements,* India Abroad

I N INDIA, ALMOST all marriages are arranged. Even among   1
the educated middle classes in modern, urban India, marriage is as much a concern of the families as it is of the individuals. So customary is the practice of arranged marriage that there is a special name for a marriage which is not arranged: It is called a "love match."

On my first field trip to India, I met many young men and   2
women whose parents were in the process of "getting them
married." In many cases, the bride and groom would not
meet each other before the marriage. At most they might
meet for a brief conversation, and this meeting would take

---

*I found it difficult to accept the docile
manner in which this well-education young
woman awaited the outcome of a process
that would result in her spending the rest of
her life with a man she hardly knew, a
virtual stranger, picked out by her parents.*

---

*It
shouldn't
be
solely
on
the
parents*

place only after their parents had decided that the match was
suitable. Parents do not compel their children to marry a person who either marriage partner finds objectionable. But
only after one match is refused will another be sought.

As a young American woman in India for the first time, I   3
found this custom of arranged marriage oppressive. How
could any intelligent young person agree to such a marriage
without great reluctance? It was contrary to everything I believed about the importance of romantic love as the only basis of a happy marriage. It also clashed with my strongly held
notions that the choice of such an intimate and permanent
relationship could be made only by the individuals involved.
Had anyone tried to arrange my marriage, I would have been
defiant and rebellious!

I agree

At the first opportunity, I began, with more curiosity than   4
tact, to question the young people I met on how they felt
about this practice. Sita, one of my young informants, was a
college graduate with a degree in political science. She had
been waiting for over a year while her parents were arranging
a match for her. I found it difficult to accept the docile manner in which this well-educated young woman awaited the
outcome of a process that would result in her spending the

Smart

rest of her life with a man she hardly knew, a virtual stranger, picked out by her parents.

"How can you go along with this?" I asked her, in frustration and distress. "Don't you care who you marry?" 5

"Of course I care," she answered. "This is why I must let 6 my parents choose a boy for me. My marriage is too important to be arranged by such an inexperienced person as myself. In such matters, it is better to have my parents' guidance."

I had learned that young men and women in India do not 7 date and have very little social life involving members of the opposite sex. Although I could not disagree with Sita's reasoning, I continued to pursue the subject.

"But how can you marry the first man you have ever met? 8 Not only have you missed the fun of meeting a lot of different people, but you have not given yourself the chance to know who is the right man for you."

"Meeting with a lot of different people doesn't sound like 9 any fun at all," Sita answered. "One hears that in America the girls are spending all their time worrying about whether they will meet a man and get married. Here we have the chance to enjoy our life and let our parents do this work and worrying for us."

She had me there. The high anxiety of the competition to 10 "be popular" with the opposite sex certainly was the most prominent feature of life as an American teenager in the late fifties. The endless worrying about the rules that governed our behavior and about our popularity ratings sapped both our self-esteem and our enjoyment of adolescence. I reflected that absence of this competition in India most certainly may have contributed to the self-confidence and natural charm of so many of the young women I met.

And yet, the idea of marrying a perfect stranger, whom 11 one did not know and did not "love," so offended my American ideas of individualism and romanticism, that I persisted with my objections.

"I still can't imagine it," I said. "How can you agree to 12 marry a man you hardly know?"

"But of course he will be known. My parents would never 13 arrange a marriage for me without knowing all about the boy's family background. Naturally we will not rely only on what the family tells us. We will check the particulars out ourselves. No one will want their daughter to marry into a family that is not good. All these things we will know beforehand."

Duh!

Impatiently, I responded, "Sita, I don't mean know the 14 family, I mean, know the man. How can you marry someone you don't know personally and don't love? How can you think of spending your life with someone you may not even like?"

"If he is a good man, why should I not like him?" she said. 15 "With you people, you know the boy so well before you marry, where will be the fun to get married? There will be no mystery and no romance. Here we have the whole of our married life to get to know and love our husband. This way is better, is it not?"

there's something called attraction

Her response made further sense, and I began to have second thoughts on the matter. Indeed, during months of meeting many intelligent young Indian people, both male and female, who had the same ideas as Sita, I saw arranged marriages in a different light. I also saw the importance of the family in Indian life and realized that a couple who took their marriage into their own hands was taking a big risk, particularly if their families were irreconcilably opposed to the match. In a country where every important resource in life—a job, a house, a social circle—is gained through family connections, it seemed foolhardy to cut oneself off from a supportive social network and depend solely on one person for happiness and success. 16

Six years later I returned to India to again do fieldwork, 17 this time among the middle class in Bombay, a modern, sophisticated city. From the experience of my earlier visit, I decided to include a study of arranged marriages in my project. By this time I had met many Indian couples whose marriages had been arranged and who seemed very happy. Particularly in contrast to the fate of many of my married friends in the

seemed is the key word here

[handwritten margin note: I do agree that divorce is too common]

United States who were already in the process of divorce, the positive aspects of arranged marriages appeared to me to outweigh the negatives. In fact, I thought I might even participate in arranging a marriage myself. I had been fairly successful in the United States in "fixing up" many of my friends, and I was confident that my matchmaking skills could be easily applied to this new situation, once I learned the basic rules. "After all," I thought, "how complicated can it be? People want pretty much the same things in a marriage whether it is in India or America."

An opportunity presented itself almost immediately. A   18
friend from my previous Indian trip was in the process of arranging for the marriage of her eldest son. In India there is a perceived shortage of "good boys," and since my friend's family was eminently respectable and the boy himself personable, well educated, and nice looking, I was sure that by the end of my year's fieldwork, we would have found a match.

The basic rule seems to be that a family's reputation is   19
most important. It is understood that matches would be arranged only within the same caste and general social class, although some crossing of subcastes is permissible if the class positions of the bride's and groom's families are similar. Although dowry is now prohibited by law in India, extensive gift exchanges took place with every marriage. Even when the boy's family do not "make demands," every girl's family nevertheless feels the obligation to give the traditional gifts, to the girl, to the boy, and to the boy's family. Particularly when the couple would be living in the joint family—that is, with the boy's parents and his married brothers and their families, as well as with unmarried siblings—which is still very common even among the urban, upper-middle class in India, the girl's parents are anxious to establish smooth relations between their family and that of the boy. Offering the proper gifts, even when not called "dowry," is often an important factor in influencing the relationship between the bride's and groom's families and perhaps, also, the treatment of the bride in her new home.

In a society where divorce is still a scandal and where, in   20

[handwritten note: It should always be]

fact, the divorce rate is exceedingly low, an arranged marriage is the beginning of a lifetime relationship not just between the bride and groom but between their families as well. Thus, while a girl's looks are important, her character is even more so, for she is being judged as a prospective daughter-in-law as much as a prospective bride. Where she would be living in a joint family, as was the case with my friend, the girl's ability to get along harmoniously in a family is perhaps the single most important quality in assessing her suitability.

[margin note: that goes for ALL marriage]

My friend is a highly esteemed wife, mother, and daughter-in-law. She is religious, soft-spoken, modest, and deferential. She rarely gossips and never quarrels, two qualities highly desirable in a woman. A family that has the reputation for gossip and conflict among its womenfolk will not find it easy to get good wives for their sons. Parents will not want to send their daughter to a house in which there is conflict. *[21]*

My friend's family were originally from North India. They had lived in Bombay, where her husband owned a business, for forty years. The family had delayed in seeking a match for their eldest son because he had been an Air Force pilot for several years, stationed in such remote places that it had seemed fruitless to try to find a girl who would be willing to accompany him. In their social class, a military career, despite its economic security, has little prestige and is considered a drawback in finding a suitable bride. Many families would not allow their daughters to marry a man in an occupation so potentially dangerous and which requires so much moving around. *[22]*

[margin note: that's definitely opposite of here]

The son had recently left the military and joined his father's business. Since he was a college graduate, modern, and well traveled, from such a good family and, I thought, quite handsome, it seemed to me that he, or rather his family, was in a position to pick and choose. I said as much to my friend. *[23]*

While she agreed that there were many advantages on their side, she also said, "We must keep in mind that my son is both short and dark; these are drawbacks in finding the right match." While the boy's height had not escaped my notice, "dark" seemed to me inaccurate; I would have called *[24]*

[margin note: dark?]

him "wheat" colored perhaps, and in any case, I did not realize that color would be a consideration. I discovered, however, that while a boy's skin color is a less important consideration than a girl's, it is still a factor.

An important source of contacts in trying to arrange her   25
son's marriage was my friend's social club in Bombay. Many
of the women had daughters of the right age, and some had
already expressed an interest in my friend's son. I was most
enthusiastic about the possibilities of one particular family
who had five daughters, all of whom were pretty, demure,
and well educated. Their mother had told my friend, "You
can have your pick for your son, whichever one of my daughters appeals to you most."

I saw a match in sight. "Surely," I said to my friend, "we   26
will find one there. Let's go visit and make our choice." But
my friend held back; she did not seem to share my enthusiasm, for reasons I could not then fathom.

When I kept pressing for an explanation of her reluctance,   27
she admitted, "See, Serena, here is the problem. The family
has so many daughters, how will they be able to provide
nicely for any of them? We are not making any demands, but
still, with so many daughters to marry off, one wonders
whether she will even be able to make a proper wedding.
Since this is our eldest son, it's best if we marry him to a girl
who is the only daughter, then the wedding will truly be a
gala affair." I argued that surely the quality of the girls themselves made up for any deficiency in the elaborateness of the
wedding. My friend admitted this point but still seemed reluctant to proceed.

"Is there something else," I asked her, "some factor I have   28
missed?" "Well," she finally said, "there is one other thing.
They have one daughter already married and living in Bombay. The mother is always complaining to me that the girl's
in-laws don't let her visit her own family often enough. So it
makes me wonder, will she be that kind of mother who always wants her daughter at her own home? This will prevent the girl from adjusting to our house. It is not a good
thing." And so, this family of five daughters was dropped as a
possibility.

Somewhat disappointed, I nevertheless respected my friend's reasoning and geared up for the next prospect. This was also the daughter of a woman in my friend's social club. There was clear interest in this family and I could see why. The family's reputation was excellent; in fact, they came from a subcaste slightly higher than my friend's own. The girl, who was an only daughter, was pretty and well educated and had a brother studying in the United States. Yet, after expressing an interest to me in this family, all talk of them suddenly died down and the search began elsewhere.

29

"What happened to that girl as a prospect?" I asked one day. "You never mention her any more. She is so pretty and so educated, what did you find wrong?"

30

"She is too educated. We've decided against it. My husband's father saw the girl on the bus the other day and thought her forward. A girl who 'roams about' the city by herself is not the girl for our family." My disappointment this time was even greater, as I thought the son would have liked the girl very much. But then I thought, my friend is right, a girl who is going to live in a joint family cannot be too independent or she will make life miserable for everyone. I also learned that if the family of the girl has even a slightly higher social status than the family of the boy, the bride may think herself too good for them, and this too will cause problems. Later my friend admitted to me that this had been an important factor in her decision not to pursue the match.

31

I would be pushing for independence

The next candidate was the daughter of a client of my friend's husband. When the client learned that the family was looking for a match for their son, he said, "Look no further, we have a daughter." This man then invited my friends to dinner to see the girl. He had already seen their son at the office and decided that "he liked the boy." We all went together for tea, rather than dinner—it was less of a commitment—and while we were there, the girl's mother showed us around the house. The girl was studying for her exams and was briefly introduced to us.

32

bc she wanted to?

After we left, I was anxious to hear my friend's opinion. While her husband liked the family very much and was impressed with his client's business accomplishments and

33

reputation, the wife didn't like the girl's looks. "She is short, no doubt, which is an important plus point, but she is also fat and wears glasses." My friend obviously thought she could do better for her son and asked her husband to make his excuses to his client by saying that they had decided to postpone the boy's marriage indefinitely.

By this time almost six months had passed and I was becoming impatient. What I had thought would be an easy matter to arrange was turning out to be quite complicated. I began to believe that between my friend's desire for a girl who was modest enough to fit into her joint family, yet attractive and educated enough to be an acceptable partner for her son, she would not find anyone suitable. My friend laughed at my impatience: "Don't be so much in a hurry," she said. "You Americans want everything done so quickly. You get married quickly and then just as quickly get divorced. Here we take marriage more seriously. We must take all the factors into account. It is not enough for us to learn by our mistakes. This is too serious a business. If a mistake is made we have not only ruined the life of our son or daughter, but we have spoiled the reputation of our family as well. And that will make it much harder for their brothers and sisters to get married. So we must be very careful."

What she said was true and I promised myself to be more patient, though it was not easy. I had really hoped and expected that the match would be made before my year in India was up. But it was not to be. When I left India my friend seemed no further along in finding a suitable match for her son than when I had arrived.

Two years later, I returned to India and still my friend had not found a girl for her son. By this time, he was close to thirty, and I think she was a little worried. Since she knew I had friends all over India, and I was going to be there for a year, she asked me to "help her in this work" and keep an eye out for someone suitable. I was flattered that my judgment was respected, but knowing now how complicated the process was, I had lost my earlier confidence as a matchmaker. Nevertheless, I promised that I would try.

34

35

36

It was almost at the end of my year's stay in India that I   37
met a family with a marriageable daughter whom I felt might
be a good possibility for my friend's son. The girl's father was
related to a good friend of mine and by coincidence came
from the same village as my friend's husband. This new family had a successful business in a medium-sized city in central
India and were from the same subcaste as my friend. The
daughter was pretty and chic; in fact, she had studied fashion
design in college. Her parents would not allow her to go off
by herself to any of the major cities in India where she could
make a career, but they had compromised with her wish to
work by allowing her to run a small dressmaking boutique
from their home. In spite of her desire to have a career, the
daughter was both modest and home-loving and had had a
traditional, sheltered upbringing. She had only one other sister, already married, and a brother who was in his father's
business.

Sounds like an American

I mentioned the possibility of a match with my friend's   38
son. The girl's parents were most interested. Although their
daughter was not eager to marry just yet, the idea of living in
Bombay—a sophisticated, extremely fashion-conscious city
where she could continue her education in clothing design—
was a great inducement. I gave the girl's father my friend's
address and suggested that when they went to Bombay on
some business or whatever, they look up the boy's family.

Returning to Bombay on my way to New York, I told my   39
friend of this newly discovered possibility. She seemed to feel
there was potential but, in spite of my urging, would not
make any moves herself. She rather preferred to wait for the
girl's family to call upon them. I hoped something would
come of this introduction, though by now I had learned to
rein in my optimism.

— that's sad

A year later I received a letter from my friend. The family   40
had indeed come to visit Bombay, and their daughter and my
friend's daughter, who were near in age, had become very
good friends. During that year, the two girls had frequently
visited each other. I thought things looked promising.

Are they truly happy?

Last week I received an invitation to a wedding: My friend's son and the girl were getting married. Since I had found the match, my presence was particularly requested at the wedding. I was thrilled. Success at last! As I prepared to leave for India, I began thinking, "Now, my friend's younger son, who do I know who has a nice girl for him . . . ?"

FURTHER REFLECTIONS ON ARRANGED MARRIAGE

The previous essay was written from the point of view of a family seeking a daughter-in-law. Arranged marriage looks somewhat different from the point of view of the bride and her family. Arranged marriage continues to be preferred, even among the more educated, Westernized sections of the Indian population. Many young women from these families still go along, more or less willingly, with the practice, and also with the specific choices of their families. Young women do get excited about the prospects of their marriage, but there is also ambivalence and increasing uncertainty, as the bride contemplates leaving the comfort and familiarity of her own home, where as a "temporary guest" she has often been indulged, to live among strangers. Even in the best situation, she will now come under the close scrutiny of her husband's family. How she dresses, how she behaves, how she gets along with others, where she goes, how she spends her time, her domestic abilities—all of this and much more—will be observed and commented on by a whole new set of relations. Her interaction with her family of birth will be monitored and curtailed considerably. Not only will she leave their home, but with increasing geographic mobility, she may also live very far from them, perhaps even on another continent. Too much expression of her fondness for her own family, or her desire to visit them, may be interpreted as an inability to adjust to her new family, and may become a source of conflict. In an arranged marriage, the burden of adjustment is clearly heavier for a woman than for a man. And that is in the best of situations.

this is what they worry about

knowing helps

In less happy circumstances, the bride may be a target of resentment and hostility from her husband's family, particularly her mother-in-law or her husband's unmarried sisters, for whom she is now a source of competition for the affection, loyalty, and economic resources of a son or brother. If she is psychologically or even physically abused, her options are limited, as returning to her parents' home or getting a divorce is still very stigmatized. For most Indians, marriage and motherhood are still considered the only suitable roles for a woman, even for those who have careers, and few women can comfortably contemplate remaining unmarried. Most families still consider "marrying off" their daughters as a compelling religious duty and social necessity. This increases a bride's sense of obligation to make the marriage a success, at whatever cost to her own personal happiness.

[handwritten marginalia: ridiculous]

The vulnerability of a new bride may also be intensified by the issue of dowry that, although illegal, has become a more pressing issue in the consumer conscious society of contemporary urban India. In many cases, where a groom's family is not satisfied with the amount of dowry a bride brings to her marriage, the young bride will be harassed constantly to get her parents to give more. In extreme cases, the bride may even be murdered, and the murder disguised as an accident or a suicide. This also offers the husband's family an opportunity to arrange another match for him, thus bringing in another dowry. This phenomenon, called dowry death, calls attention not just to the "evils of dowry" but also to larger issues of the powerlessness of women as well.

[handwritten marginalia: why?]

[handwritten marginalia: So this is a better alternative]

For Study and Discussion

QUESTIONS FOR RESPONSE

1. Have you ever been fixed up on a blind date? How did you feel about spending an evening with someone you didn't know? How did it work out?

2. Have you ever tried to fix people up? Why were you so sure that they would make a good match? How did it work out?

QUESTIONS ABOUT PURPOSE

1. How does Nanda's conversation with Sita help illustrate her thesis that in India marriage is a family, not an individual, decision?
2. How does Sita's criticism of American marriages help Nanda clarify her purpose?

QUESTIONS ABOUT AUDIENCE

1. In what ways does Nanda address her essay to American rather than Indian readers?
2. How does Nanda serve as a substitute for her readers? For example, how does she, and thus her readers, learn about the criteria for a good marriage?

QUESTIONS ABOUT STRATEGIES

1. How does Nanda use the example of the family with five daughters to illustrate the importance of social caste and financial status in Indian marriages?
2. How does Nanda use the example of the well-educated girl to illustrate the importance of finding a good daughter-in-law—as opposed to finding a good wife?

QUESTIONS FOR DISCUSSION

1. What arguments would you use to defend "love matches" as opposed to "arranged marriages"? Compare Anne Roiphe's observation on these issues (pages 203–212).
2. How do issues such as "dowry death" enable Nanda to present the arranged marriage from the point of view of the bride and her family?

Elizabeth Winthrop was born in 1948 in Washington, D.C., and educated at Sarah Lawrence College. She worked for Harper and Row editing Harper Junior Books before she began her own career as author of books for children. She has written more than thirty such books, including *Bunk Beds* (1972), *Potbellied Possums* (1977), *In My Mother's House* (1988), *The Battle for the Castle* (1993), and *As the Crow Flies* (1998). Winthrop has twice won the PEN Syndicated Fiction Contest, once in 1985 with her story "Bad News" and again in 1990 with "The Golden Darters." In the latter story, reprinted from *American Short Fiction,* a young girl betrays her father by using their creation for the wrong purpose.

The Golden Darters

I WAS TWELVE years old when my father started tying flies. It was an odd habit for a man who had just undergone a serious operation on his upper back, but, as he remarked to my mother one night, at least it gave him a world over which he had some control.

The family grew used to seeing him hunched down close to his tying vise, hackle pliers in one hand, thread bobbin in the other. We began to bandy about strange phrases—foxy quills, bodkins, peacock hurl. Father's corner of the living room was off limits to the maid with the voracious and destructive vacuum cleaner. Who knew what precious bit of calf's tail or rabbit fur would be sucked away never to be seen again?

Because of my father's illness, we had gone up to our

summer cottage on the lake in New Hampshire a month early. None of my gang of friends ever came till the end of July, so in the beginning of that summer I hung around home watching my father as he fussed with the flies. I was the only child he allowed to stand near him while he worked. "Your brothers bounce," he muttered one day as he clamped the vise onto the curve of a model-perfect hook. "You can stay and watch if you don't bounce."

So I took great care not to bounce or lean or even breathe   4
too noisily on him while he performed his delicate maneu-
vers, holding back hackle with one hand as he pulled off the
final flourish of a whip finish with the other. I had never been
so close to my father for so long before, and while he studied
his tiny creations, I studied him. I stared at the large pores of
his skin, the sleek black hair brushed straight back from the
soft dip of his temples, the jaw muscles tightening and slack-
ening. Something in my father seemed always to be ticking.
He did not take well to sickness and enforced confinement.

When he leaned over his work, his shirt collar slipped   5
down to reveal the recent scar, a jagged trail of disrupted tissue. The tender pink skin gradually paled and then tough-
ened during those weeks when he took his prescribed afternoon nap, lying on his stomach on our little patch of front
lawn. Our house was one of the closest to the lake and it
seemed to embarrass my mother to have him stretch himself
out on the grass for all the swimmers and boaters to see.

"At least sleep on the porch," she would say. "That's why   6
we set the hammock up there."

"Why shouldn't a man sleep on his own front lawn if he so   7
chooses?" he would reply. "I have to mow the bloody thing.
I might as well put it to some use."

And my mother would shrug and give up.   8

At the table when he was absorbed, he lost all sense of any-   9
thing but the magnified insect under the light. Often when
he pushed his chair back and announced the completion of
his latest project to the family, there would be a bit of down
or a tuft of dubbing stuck to the edge of his lip. I did not tell

him about it but stared, fascinated, wondering how long it would take to blow away. Sometimes it never did, and I imagine he discovered the fluff in the bathroom mirror when he went upstairs to bed. Or maybe my mother plucked it off with one of those proprietary gestures of hers that irritated my brothers so much.

In the beginning, Father wasn't very good at the fly-tying. 10 He was a large, thick-boned man with sweeping gestures, a robust laugh, and a sudden terrifying temper. If he had not loved fishing so much, I doubt he would have persevered with the fussy business of the flies. After all, the job required tools normally associated with woman's work. Thread and bobbins, soft slippery feathers, a magnifying glass, and an instruction manual that read like a cookbook. It said things like, "Cut off a bunch of yellowtail. Hold the tip end with the left hand and stroke out the short hairs."

But Father must have had a goal in mind. You tie flies be- 11 cause one day, in the not-too-distant future, you will attach them to a tippet, wade into a stream, and lure a rainbow trout out of his quiet pool.

There was something endearing, almost childish, about his 12 stubborn nightly ritual at the corner table. His head bent under the standing lamp, his fingers trembling slightly, he would whisper encouragement to himself, talk his way through some particularly delicate operation. Once or twice I caught my mother gazing silently across my brothers' heads at him. When our eyes met, she would turn away and busy herself in the kitchen.

Finally, one night, after weeks of allowing me to watch, he 13 told me to take his seat. "Why, Father?"

"Because it's time for you to try one." 14

"That's all right. I like to watch." 15

"Nonsense, Emily. You'll do just fine." 16

He had stood up. The chair was waiting. Across the room, 17 my mother put down her knitting. Even the boys, embroiled in a noisy game of double solitaire, stopped their wrangling for a moment. They were all waiting to see what I would do. It was my fear of failing him that made me hesitate. I knew that my father put his trust in results, not in the learning process.

"Sit down, Emily."   18

I obeyed, my heart pounding. I was a cautious, secretive   19
child, and I could not bear to have people watch me doing
things. My piano lesson was the hardest hour in the week.
The teacher would sit with a resigned look on her face while
my fingers groped across the keys, muddling through a so-
nata that I had played perfectly just an hour before. The difference was that then nobody had been watching.

"—so we'll start you off with a big hook." He had been   20
talking for some time. How much had I missed already?

"Ready?" he asked.   21

I nodded.   22

"All right then, clamp this hook into the vise. You'll be   23
making the golden darter, a streamer. A big flashy fly, the
kind that imitates a small fish as it moves underwater."

Across the room, my brothers had returned to their game,   24
but their voices were subdued. I imagined they wanted to
hear what was happening to me. My mother had left the
room.

"Tilt the magnifying glass so you have a good view of the   25
hook. Right. Now tie on with the bobbin thread."

It took me three tries to line the thread up properly on the   26
hook, each silken line nesting next to its neighbor. "We're
going to do it right, Emily, no matter how long it takes."

"It's hard," I said quietly.   27

Slowly I grew used to the tiny tools, to the oddly enlarged   28
view of my fingers through the magnifying glass. They
looked as if they didn't belong to me anymore. The feeling in
their tips was too small for their large, clumsy movements.
Despite my father's repeated warnings, I nicked the floss
once against the barbed hook. Luckily it did not give way.

"It's Emily's bedtime," my mother called from the   29
kitchen.

"Hush, she's tying in the throat. Don't bother us now."   30

I could feel his breath on my neck. The mallard barbules   31
were stubborn, curling into the hook in the wrong direction.

Behind me, I sensed my father's fingers twisting in imitation
of my own.

"You've almost got it," he whispered, his lips barely mov-   32
ing. "That's right. Keep the thread slack until you're all the
way around."

I must have tightened it too quickly. I lost control of the   33
feathers in my left hand, the clumsier one. First the gold mylar came unwound and then the yellow floss.   *yup*

"Damn it all, now look what you've done," he roared, and   34
for a second I wondered whether he was talking to me. He
sounded as if he were talking to a grown-up. He sounded the
way he had just the night before when an antique teacup had
slipped through my mother's soapy fingers and shattered
against the hard surface of the sink. I sat back slowly, resting
my aching spine against the chair for the first time since we'd
begun.

"Leave it for now, Gerald," my mother said tentatively   35
from the kitchen. Out of the corner of my eye, I could see
her sponging the kitchen counter with small, defiant sweeps
of her hand. "She can try again tomorrow."

"What happened?" called a brother. They both started   36   *no name*
across the room toward us but stopped at a look from my
father.

"We'll start again," he said, his voice once more under   37
control. "Best way to learn. Get back on the horse."

With a flick of his hand, he loosened the vise, removed my   38
hook, and threw it into the wastepaper basket.

"From the beginning?" I whispered.   39

"Of course," he replied. "There's no way to rescue a mess   40
like that."

My mess had taken almost an hour to create.   41

"Gerald," my mother said again. "Don't you think—"   42

"How can we possibly work with all these interruptions?"   43   *that's an exp. mood*
he thundered. I flinched as if he had hit me. "Go on upstairs,
all of you. Emily and I will be up when we're done. Go on,
for God's sake. Stop staring at us."

At a signal from my mother, the boys backed slowly away   44
and crept up to their room. She followed them. I felt all

alone, as trapped under my father's piercing gaze as the hook
in the grip of its vise.

We started again. This time my fingers were trembling so   45
much that I ruined three badger hackle feathers, stripping off
the useless webbing at the tip. My father did not lose his temper again. His voice dropped to an even, controlled mono-
tone that scared me more than his shouting. After an hour of
painstaking labor, we reached the same point with the stubborn mallard feathers curling into the hook. Once, twice, I
repinched them under the throat, but each time they slipped
away from me. Without a word, my father stood up and
leaned over me. With his cheek pressed against my hair, he
reached both hands around and took my fingers in his. I
longed to surrender the tools to him and slide away off the
chair, but we were so close to the end. He captured the curling stem with the thread and trapped it in place with three
quick wraps.

"Take your hands away carefully," he said. "I'll do the   46
whip finish. We don't want to risk losing it now."

I did as I was told, sat motionless with his arms around   47
me, my head tilted slightly to the side so he could have the
clear view through the magnifying glass. He cemented the
head, wiped the excess glue from the eye with a waste feather,
and hung my golden darter on the tackle box handle to dry.
When at last he pulled away, I breathlessly slid my body back
against the chair. I was still conscious of the havoc my clumsy
hands or an unexpected sneeze could wreak on the table,
which was cluttered with feathers and bits of fur.

"Now, that's the fly you tied, Emily. Isn't it beautiful?"   48
I nodded. "Yes, Father."   49

"Tomorrow, we'll do another one. An olive grouse.   50
Smaller hook but much less complicated body. Look. I'll
show you in the book."

As I waited to be released from the chair, I didn't think he   51
meant it. He was just trying to apologize for having lost his
temper, I told myself, just trying to pretend that our time together had been wonderful. But the next morning when I
came down, late for breakfast, he was waiting for me with the

materials for the olive grouse already assembled. He was ready to start in again, to take charge of my clumsy fingers with his voice and talk them through the steps.

That first time was the worst, but I never felt comfortable at the fly-tying table with Father's breath tickling the hair on my neck. I completed the olive grouse, another golden darter to match the first, two muddler minnows, and some others. I don't remember all the names anymore.

Once I hid upstairs, pretending to be immersed in my summer reading books, but he came looking for me.

"Emily," he called. "Come on down. Today we'll start the lead-winged coachman. I've got everything set up for you."

I lay very still and did not answer.

"Gerald," I heard my mother say. "Leave the child alone. You're driving her crazy with those flies."

"Nonsense," he said, and started up the dark, wooden stairs, one heavy step at a time.

I put my book down and rolled slowly off the bed so that by the time he reached the door of my room, I was on my feet, ready to be led back downstairs to the table.

Although we never spoke about it, my mother became oddly insistent that I join her on trips to the library or the general store.

"Are you going out again, Emily?" my father would call after me. "I was hoping we'd get some work done on this minnow."

"I'll be back soon, Father," I'd say. "I promise."

"Be sure you do," he said.

And for a while I did.

Then at the end of July, my old crowd of friends from across the lake began to gather and I slipped away to join them early in the morning before my father got up.

The girls were a gang. When we were all younger, we'd held bicycle relay races on the ring road and played down at the lakeside together under the watchful eyes of our mothers. Every July, we threw ourselves joyfully back into each other's lives. That summer we talked about boys and smoked illicit

its a circus

cigarettes in Randy Kidd's basement and held leg-shaving parties in her bedroom behind a safely locked door. Randy was the ringleader. She was the one who suggested we pierce our ears.

"My parents would die," I said. "They told me I'm not al- 66
lowed to pierce my ears until I'm seventeen."

"Your hair's so long, they won't even notice," Randy said. 67
"My sister will do it for us. She pierces all her friends' ears at college."

In the end, only one girl pulled out. The rest of us sat in a 68
row with the obligatory ice cubes held to our ears, waiting for the painful stab of the sterilized needle.

Randy was right. At first my parents didn't notice. Even 69
when my ears became infected, I didn't tell them. All alone in my room, I went through the painful procedure of twisting the gold studs and swabbing the recent wounds with alcohol. Then on the night of the club dance, when I had changed my clothes three times and played with my hair in front of the mirror for hours, I came across the small plastic box with di-viders in my top bureau drawer. My father had given it to me so that I could keep my flies in separate compartments, un-tangled from one another. I poked my finger in and slid one of the golden darters up along its plastic wall. When I held it up, the mylar thread sparkled in the light like a jewel. I took out the other darter, hammered down the barbs of the two hooks, and slipped them into the raw holes in my earlobes.

made w/ your father

Someone's mother drove us all to the dance, and Randy 70
and I pushed through the side door into the ladies' room. I put my hair up in a ponytail so the feathered flies could twist and dangle above my shoulders. I liked the way they made me look—free and different and dangerous, even. And they made Randy notice.

"I've never seen earrings like that," Randy said. "Where 71
did you get them?"

"I made them with my father. They're flies. You know, for 72
fishing."

"They're great. Can you make me some?" 73

I hesitated. "I have some others at home I can give you," I said at last. "They're in a box in my bureau." 74

"Can you give them to me tomorrow?" she asked. 75

"Sure," I said with a smile. Randy had never noticed anything I'd worn before. I went out to the dance floor, swinging my ponytail in time to the music. 76

My mother noticed the earrings as soon as I got home. 77

"What has gotten into you, Emily? You know you were forbidden to pierce your ears until you were in college. This is appalling." 78

that's a long time

I didn't answer. My father was sitting in his chair behind the fly-tying table. His back was better by that time, but he still spent most of his waking hours in that chair. It was as if he didn't like to be too far away from his flies, as if something might blow away if he weren't keeping watch. 79

I saw him look up when my mother started in with me. His hands drifted ever so slowly down to the surface of the table as I came across the room toward him. I leaned over so that he could see my earrings better in the light. 80

like his daughter

"Everybody loved them, Father. Randy says she wants a pair, too. I'm going to give her the muddler minnows." 81

"I can't believe you did this, Emily," my mother said in a loud, nervous voice. "It makes you look so cheap." 82

earings?

"They don't make me look cheap, do they, Father?" I swung my head so he could see how they bounced, and my hip accidentally brushed the table. A bit of rabbit fur floated up from its pile and hung in the air for a moment before it settled down on top of the foxy quills. 83

"For God's sake, Gerald, speak to her," my mother said from her corner. 84

He stared at me for a long moment as if he didn't know who I was anymore, as if I were a trusted associate who had committed some treacherous and unspeakable act. "That is not the purpose for which the flies were intended," he said. 85

you're a stranger

"Oh, I know that," I said quickly. "But they look good this way, don't they?" 86

He stood up and considered me in silence for a long time   87
across the top of the table lamp.

"No, they don't," he finally said. "They're hanging upside   88
down."

Then he turned off the light and I couldn't see his face   89
anymore.

[handwritten: gotcha girly]

[handwritten: does this show the end of their relationship?]

COMMENT ON "THE GOLDEN DARTERS"

"The Golden Darters" questions the purpose of learning a particular process. Emily's father decides to tie fishing flies to help him recuperate from back surgery. Although he is clumsy at first, he masters the tools, the procedure, and the artistry of tying. He has a goal in mind—to "attach [the flies] to a tippet, wade into a stream, and lure a rainbow trout out of his quiet pool." Emily's father decides to teach her what he has learned, even though his presence makes her nervous and her mistakes complicate the work process. Emily eventually escapes his obsession and joins her girlfriends to learn other procedures—smoking, leg-shaving, ear-piercing. The last procedure enables Emily to experiment—to wear two yellow darters as earrings to the club dance. Although she dazzles her friends, she disappoints her father, who sees her experiment as a betrayal.

[handwritten: when did these become cool]

Process Analysis as a Writing Strategy

1. Write an essay for readers of a popular magazine in which you give directions on how to complete a mechanical or artistic project. Like Julia Alvarez, anticipate the resistance of those readers who are certain before they start that they can't do it.

2. Provide information for the members of your writing class on the steps you followed to complete an educational project such as writing a research paper. Like Nikki Giovanni, you may want to explain these steps to a particular group of students.

3. Barbara Ehrenreich raises significant questions about rules that govern the behavior of service workers. Construct a portrait of a conscientious worker who completes a job effectively—in his or her own way—without following the rules of some system.

4. Analyze the various steps in a political process (casting a vote), an economic process (purchasing stock), or a social process (getting married). Assume that your audience watches a lot of television. Explain how the process you are analyzing (such as finding a spouse) differs from the process they see represented on the tube.

5. Analyze a process that tests the ability to reach consensus and capture others. Like P. J. O'Rourke, you may want to describe the common courtesy required if drivers are going to avoid accidents. Or you may want to analyze the process illustrated in children's play, athletic contests, or human mating games.

6. Analyze a process that confuses or intimidates people, particularly when other people are watching. Elizabeth Winthrop's short story "The Golden Darters" is obviously a good source for this assignment. Your job is to describe the intricate steps of the physical tasks and to speculate on why the presence of the observer (a teacher, a relative, a friend) makes the task so difficult.

COMPARISON AND CONTRAST

Technically speaking, when you **compare** two or more things, you're looking for similarities; and when you **contrast** them, you're looking for differences. In practice, of course, the operations are opposite sides of the same coin, and one implies the other. When you look for what's similar, you will also notice what is different. You can compare things at all levels, from the trivial (plaid shoelaces and plain ones) to the really serious (the differences between a career in medicine and one in advertising). Often when you compare things at a serious level, you do so to make a choice. That's why it's helpful to know how to organize your thinking so that you can analyze similarities and differences in a systematic, useful way that brings out significant differences. It's particularly helpful to have such a system when you are going to write a comparison-and-contrast essay.

PURPOSE

You can take two approaches to writing comparison-and-contrast essays; each has a different purpose. You can make a *strict* comparison, exploring the relationship between things in the same class, or you can do a *fanciful* comparison, looking at the relationship among things from different classes.

When you write a *strict* comparison, you compare only things that are truly alike—actors with actors, musicians with musicians, but *not* actors with musicians. You're trying to find similar information about both your subjects. For instance, what are the characteristics of actors, whether they are movie or stage actors? How are jazz musicians and classical musicians alike, even if their music is quite different? In a strict comparison, you probably also want to show how two things in the same class are different in important ways. Often when you focus your comparison on differences, you do so in order to make a judgment and, finally, a choice. That's one of the main reasons people make comparisons, whether they're shopping or writing.

When you write a *fanciful* comparison, you try to set up an imaginative, illuminating comparison between two things that don't seem at all alike, and you do it for a definite reason: to help explain and clarify a complex idea. For instance, the human heart is often compared to a pump—a fanciful and useful comparison that enables one to envision the heart at work. You can use similar fanciful comparisons to help your readers see new dimensions to events. For instance, you can compare the astronauts landing on the moon to Columbus discovering the New World, or you can compare the increased drug use among young people to an epidemic spreading through part of our culture.

You may find it difficult to construct an entire essay

this one sounds more exciting

what about contrast

around a fanciful comparison—such attempts tax the most creative energy and can quickly break down. Probably you can use this method of comparison most effectively as a device for enlivening your writing and highlighting dramatic similarities. When you're drawing fanciful comparisons, you're not very likely to be comparing to make judgments or recommend choices. Instead, your purpose in writing a fanciful comparison is to catch your readers' attention and show new connections between unlike things.

AUDIENCE

As you plan a comparison-and-contrast essay, think ahead about what your readers already know and what they're going to expect. First, ask yourself what they know about the items or ideas you're going to compare. Do they know a good deal about both—for instance, two popular television programs? Do they know very little about either item—for instance, Buddhism and Shintoism? Or do they know quite a bit about one but little about the other—for instance, football and rugby?

If you're confident that your readers know a lot about both items (the television programs), you can spend a little time pointing out similarities and concentrate on your reasons for making the comparison. When readers know little about either (Eastern religions), you'll have to define each, using concepts they are familiar with, before you can point out important contrasts. If readers know only one item in a pair (football and rugby), then use the known to explain the unknown. Emphasize what is familiar to them about football, and explain how rugby is like it but also how it is different.

As you think about what your readers need, remember they want your essay to be fairly balanced, not 90 percent about Buddhism and 10 percent about Shintoism, or two paragraphs about football and nine or ten about rugby. When your focus seems so unevenly divided, you appear to be using one element in the comparison only as a springboard to talk about the other. Such an imbalance can disappoint your readers, who expect to learn about both.

STRATEGIES

You can use two basic strategies for organizing a comparison-and-contrast essay. The first is the *divided* or *subject-by-subject* pattern. The second is the *alternating* or *point-by-point* pattern.

When you use the *divided* pattern, you present all your information on one topic before you bring in information on the other topic. Mark Twain uses this method in "Two Views of the River." First he gives an apprentice's poetic view, emphasizing the beauty of the river; then he gives the pilot's practical view, emphasizing the technical problems the river poses.

When you use the *alternating* pattern, you work your way through the comparison point by point, giving information first on one aspect of the topic, then on the other. If Mark Twain had used an alternating pattern, he would have given the apprentice's poetic view of a particular feature of the river, then the pilot's pragmatic view of that same feature. He would have followed that pattern throughout, commenting on each feature—the wind, the surface of the river, the sunset, the color of the water—by alternating between the apprentice's and the pilot's points of view.

Although both methods are useful, you'll find that each has benefits and drawbacks. The divided pattern lets you present each part of your essay as a satisfying whole. It works especially well in short essays, such as Twain's, where you're presenting only two facets of a topic and your reader can easily keep track of the points you want to make. Its drawback is that sometimes you slip into writing what seems like two separate essays. When you're writing a long comparison essay about a complex topic, you may have trouble organizing your material clearly enough to keep your readers on track.

The alternating pattern works well when you want to show

the two subjects you're comparing side by side, emphasizing the points you're comparing. You'll find it particularly good for longer essays, such as Laura Bohannan's "Shakespeare in the Bush," when you want to show many complex points of comparison and need to help your readers see how those points match up. The drawback of the alternating pattern is that you may reduce your analysis to an exercise. If you use it for making only a few points of comparison in a short essay on a simple topic, your essay sounds choppy and disconnected, like a simple list.

Often you can make the best of both worlds by *combining strategies*. For example, you can start out using a divided pattern to give an overall, unified view of the topics you're going to compare. Then you can shift to an alternating pattern to show how many points of comparison you've found between your subjects. Paco Underhill uses a version of this strategy in "Shop like a Man." He begins by establishing the difference between the traditional ways men and women shop; then he uses the alternating pattern to demonstrate how changing gender roles may affect shopping styles.

When you want to write a good comparison-and-contrast analysis, keep three guidelines in mind: (1) *balance parts,* (2) *include reminders,* and (3) *supply reasons.* Look, for example, at how Sarah Vowell balances the American and Canadian approaches to frontier law.

Laura Bohannan uses similar strategies when she contrasts her version of *Hamlet* with the African elders' reinterpretation of the play.

USING COMPARISON AND CONTRAST IN PARAGRAPHS

Here are two comparison-and-contrast paragraphs. The first is written by a professional writer and is followed by an analysis. The second is written by a student writer and is followed by questions.

DAVID McCULLOUGH
FDR and Truman

Uses alternating pattern

Both [FDR and Truman] were men of exceptional determination, with great reserves of personal courage and cheerfulness. They were alike too in their enjoyment of people. (The human race, Truman once told a reporter, was an "excellent outfit.") Each had an active sense of humor and was inclined to be dubious of those who did not. But Roosevelt, who loved stories, loved also to laugh at his own, while Truman was more of a listener and laughed best when somebody else told "a good one." Roosevelt enjoyed flattery, Truman was made uneasy by it. Roosevelt loved the subtleties of human relations. He was a master of the circuitous solution to problems, of the pleasing if ambiguous answer to difficult questions. He was sensitive to nuances in a way Harry Truman never was and never would be. Truman, with his rural Missouri background, and partly, too, because of the limits of his education, was inclined to see things in far simpler terms, as right or wrong, wise or foolish. He dealt little in abstractions. His answers to questions, even complicated questions, were nearly always direct and assured, plainly said, and followed often by a conclusive "And that's all there is to it," an old Missouri expression, when in truth there may have been a great deal more "to it."

Establishes point of comparison

Sets up points of contrast

Expands on significant difference between two men (circuitous versus direct)

he pulls off a lot of talks about

Comment This paragraph illustrates how the alternating pattern can be used to point out many levels of comparison between two subjects. McCullough acknowledges that President Roosevelt and President Truman shared many common virtues—determination, courage, and cheerfulness. But he also contrasts (point by point) how the two men's personal

styles—love of complex subtleties (FDR) versus preference
for direct simplicity (Truman)—contributed to their unique-
ness.

NATHAN M. HARMS
Howard and Rush

Howard [Stern] and Rush [Limbaugh] seem
like the ying and yang of talk radio. Howard is
thin and shaggy and loves to bash entrenched,
stodgy Republicans. Rush is fat and dapper and
loves to bash traditional liberal Democrats.
Howard, the defender of individual freedom,
wants to sleep with every woman in America.
Rush, the defender of family values, wants every
American woman to stay home and take care of
the kids. Although they may think the world
works in different ways, Howard and Rush work
in the world in the same way. They focus their
shows on controversy, belittle those who disagree with them, package their "philosophies"
in best-selling books, and thrive on their ability
to create publicity and fame for themselves.

1. What specific points of difference does Harms see between
   Howard Stern and Rush Limbaugh?
2. What major personality trait does Harms suspect they share?

COMPARISON AND CONTRAST

Points to Remember

1. Decide whether you want the pattern of your comparison to focus on complete units (*divided*) or specific features (*alternating*).
2. Consider the possibility of combining the two patterns.
3. Determine which subject should be placed in the first position and why.
4. Arrange the points of your comparison in a logical, balanced, and dramatic sequence.
5. Make sure you introduce and clarify the reasons for making your comparison.

In this photograph, Don Hong-Oai recreates the look of a classical Chinese landscape scroll. The Chinese characters in the upper right provide the title: "At Play, Tianzi Mountains." In what ways do the line strokes in these words resemble the lines pictured in the limbs of the trees and the gibbon monkeys "at play"? Select a particularly evocative photograph and then explain why your picture is worth a thousand words, or why it takes a thousand words (to explain).

Mark Twain (the pen name of Samuel Clemens, 1835–1910) was born in Florida, Missouri, and grew up in the river town of Hannibal, Missouri, where he watched the comings and goings of the steamboats he would eventually pilot. Twain spent his young adult life working as a printer, a pilot on the Mississippi, and a frontier journalist. After the Civil War, he began a career as a humorist and storyteller, writing such classics as *The Adventures of Tom Sawyer* (1876), *Life on the Mississippi* (1883), *The Adventures of Huckleberry Finn* (1885), and *A Connecticut Yankee in King Arthur's Court* (1889). His place in American writing was best characterized by editor William Dean Howells, who called Twain the "Lincoln of our literature." In "Two Views of the River," taken from *Life on the Mississippi*, Twain compares the way he saw the river as an innocent apprentice to the way he saw it as an experienced pilot.

Two Views of the River

N OW WHEN I had mastered the language of this water, and had come to know every trifling feature that bordered the great river as familiarly as I knew the letters of the alphabet, I had made a valuable acquisition. But I had lost something, too. I had lost something which could never be restored to me while I lived. All the grace, the beauty, the poetry, had gone out of the majestic river! I still keep in mind a certain wonderful sunset which I witnessed when steamboating was new to me. A broad expanse of the river was turned to blood; in the middle distance the red hue brightened into gold, through which a solitary log came

I like these personifications

1

floating black and conspicuous; in one place a long, slanting
mark lay sparkling upon the water; in another the surface
was broken by boiling, tumbling rings that were as many-
tinted as an opal; where the ruddy flush was faintest, was a
smooth spot that was covered with graceful circles and radiating lines, ever so delicately traced; the shore on our left
was densely wooded, and the somber shadow that fell from
this forest was broken in one place by a long, ruffled trail
that shone like silver; and high above the forest wall a clean-
stemmed dead tree waved a single leafy bough that glowed
like a flame in the unobstructed splendor that was flowing

beau-
tiful

ima-
gery

> *When I mastered the language of this*
> *water . . . I had made a valuable*
> *acquisition. But I had lost something too.*

---

from the sun. There were graceful curves, reflected images,
woody heights, soft distances; and over the whole scene, far
and near, the dissolving lights drifted steadily, enriching it
every passing moment with new marvels of coloring.

I stood like one bewitched. I drank it in, in a speechless
rapture. The world was new to me, and I had never seen anything like this at home. But as I have said, a day came when I
began to cease from noting the glories and the charms which
the moon and the sun and the twilight wrought upon the
river's face; another day came when I ceased altogether to
note them. Then, if that sunset scene had been repeated, I
should have looked upon it without rapture, and should have
commented upon it, inwardly, after this fashion: "This sun
means that we are going to have wind to-morrow; that floating log means that the river is rising, small thanks to it; that
slanting mark on the water refers to a bluff reef which is going to kill somebody's steamboat one of these nights, if it
keeps on stretching out like that; those tumbling 'boils' show

2

*nice
desc*

a dissolving bar and a changing channel there; the lines and circles in the slick water over yonder are a warning that that troublesome place is shoaling up dangerously; that silver streak in the shadow of the forest is the 'break' from a new snag, and he has located himself in the very best place he could have found to fish for steamboats; that tall dead tree, with a single living branch, is not going to last long, and then how is a body ever going to get through this blind place at night without the friendly old landmark?"

No, the romance and beauty were all gone from the river. All the value any feature of it had for me now was the amount of usefulness it could furnish toward compassing the safe piloting of a steamboat. Since those days, I have pitied doctors from my heart. What does the lovely flush in a beauty's cheek mean to a doctor but a "break" that ripples above some deadly disease? Are not all her visible charms sown thick with what are to him the signs and symbols of hidden decay? Does he ever see her beauty at all, or doesn't he simply view her professionally, and comment upon her unwholesome condition all to himself? And doesn't he sometimes wonder whether he has gained most or lost most by learning his trade?

For Study and Discussion

QUESTIONS FOR RESPONSE

1. Mark Twain is one of America's most famous historical personalities. Which of his books or stories have you read? What ideas and images from this selection do you associate with his other works?

2. Do you agree with Twain when he argues that an appreciation of beauty depends on ignorance of danger? Explain your answer.

QUESTIONS ABOUT PURPOSE

1. What does Twain think he has gained and lost by learning the river?

2. What does Twain accomplish by *dividing* the two views of the river rather than *alternating* them beneath several headings?

QUESTIONS ABOUT AUDIENCE

1. Which attitude—poetic or pragmatic—does Twain anticipate his readers have toward the river? Explain your answer.
2. How does he expect his readers to answer the questions he raises in paragraph 3?

QUESTIONS ABOUT STRATEGIES

1. What sequence does Twain use to arrange the points of his comparison?
2. Where does Twain use transitional phrases and sentences to match up the parts of his comparison?

QUESTIONS FOR DISCUSSION

1. Besides the pilot and the doctor, can you identify other professionals who lose as much as they gain by learning their trade?
2. How would people whose job is to create beauty—writers, painters, musicians, architects, gardeners—respond to Twain's assertion that knowledge of their craft destroys their ability to appreciate beauty?

Sarah Vowell was born in 1969, raised in rural Oklahoma, and educated at Montana State University and School of the Art Institute in Chicago. She started contributing her witty essays to the radio program *This American Life* (Public Radio International) and the Internet magazine *Salon.com*. Her experience with radio is documented in *Radio On: A Listener's Diary* (1997). Her other essays are collected in *Take the Cannoli: Stories from the New World* (2000) and *The Partly Cloudy Patriot* (2002). In "Cowboys v. Mounties," reprinted from *The Partly Cloudy Patriot*, Vowell compares the American and Canadian frontier experience.

Cowboys v. Mounties

C ANADA HAUNTS ME. The United States's neighbor to the north first caught my fancy a few years back when I started listening to the CBC. I came for the long-form radio documentaries; I stayed for the dispatches from the Maritimes and Guelph. On the CBC, all these nice people, seemingly normal but for the hockey obsession, had a likable knack for loving their country in public without resorting to swagger or hate.

A person keen on all things French is called a Francophile. One who has a thing for England is called an Anglophile. An admirer of Germany in the 1930s and '40s is called Pat Buchanan. But no word has been coined to describe Americans obsessed with Canada, not that dictionary publishers have been swamped with requests. The comedian Jon Stewart used to do a bit in which a Canadian woman asked him to come clean with what Americans *really* think of Canada. "We don't," he said.

Keeping track of Canadians is like watching a horror 3 movie. It's *Invasion of the Body Snatchers* in slow-mo. They look like us, but there's something slightly, eerily off. Why is that? The question has nagged me for years. Asking why they are the way they are begs the follow-up query about how we ended up this way too.

There's a sad sack quality to the Canadian chronology I 4 find entirely endearing. I once asked the CBC radio host Ian Brown how on earth one could teach Canadian school-

---

Everyone knows what the individualistic American cowboy fetish gets us: shot.

---

children their history in a way that could be remotely inspiring, and he answered, "It isn't inspiring."

Achieving its independence from Britain gradually and 5 cordially, through polite meetings taking place in nice rooms, Canada took a path to sovereignty that is one of the most hilariously boring stories in the world. One Canadian history textbook I have describes it thus, "British North Americans moved through the 1850s and early sixties towards a modestly spectacular resolution of their various ambitions and problems." Modestly spectacular. Isn't that adorable?

One day, while nonchalantly perusing the annals of Cana- 6 dian history, I came across mention of the founding of the Mounties. The Royal Canadian Mounted Police, called the North-West Mounted Police at its inception, was created, I read, to establish law and order on the Canadian frontier in anticipation of settlement and the Canadian Pacific Railroad. In 1873, Canada's first prime minister, John Macdonald, saw what was happening in the American Wild West and organized a police force to make sure Canada steered clear of America's bloodbath.

That's it. Or, as they might say in Quebec, voilà! That ex-   7
plains how the Canadians are different from Americans. No
cowboys for Canada. Canada got Mounties instead—Dudley
Do-Right, not John Wayne. It's a mind-set of "Here I come
to save the day" versus "Yippee-ki-yay, motherfucker." Or
maybe it's chicken and egg: The very idea that the Canadian
head of state would come to the conclusion that establishing
law and order *before* large numbers of people migrated west,
to have rules and procedures and authorities waiting for
them, is anathema to the American way.

Not only did the Mounties aim to avoid the problems we   8
had faced on our western frontier, especially the violent,
costly Indian wars, they had to clean up after our spillover
mess. In a nineteenth-century version of that drug-war movie
Traffic, evil American whiskey traders were gouging and poi-
soning Canadian Indian populations. Based in Fort Benton,
Montana, they sneaked across the border to peddle their rot-
gut liquor, establishing illegal trading posts, including the infamous Fort Whoop-up, in what is now Alberta. You can't
throw a dart at a map of the American West without hitting
some mass grave or battleground—Sand Creek, Little Bighorn, Wounded Knee—but it's fitting that the most famous
such Canadian travesty, the Cypress Hills Massacre, happened because American whiskey and fur traders were exacting revenge on a few Indians believed to have stolen their
horses. The Americans slaughtered between one and two
hundred Assiniboine men, women, and children. Never
mind that the horse thieves had been Cree. That was 1873.
The Mounties were under formation, but they hadn't yet
marched west.

The most remarkable thing about the Mounties was their   9
mandate: one law. One law for everyone, Indian or white.
The United States makes a big to-do about all men being
created equal, but we're still working out the kinks of turning
that idea into actual policy. Reporting to the force's commissioner in 1877, one Mountie wrote of Americans in his jurisdiction, "These men always look upon the Indians as their
natural enemies, and it is their rule to shoot at them if they

approach after being warned off. I was actually asked the other day by an American who has settled here, if we had the same law here as on the other side, and if he was justified in shooting any Indian who approached his camp after being warned not to in advance."

Word of the Canadians' fairness got around. Some north-   10
western tribes referred to the border between the United States and Canada as the "medicine line." Robert Higheagle, a Lakota Sioux from Sitting Bull's band, recalled, "They told us this line was considered holy. They called that a holy trail. They believe things are different when you cross from one side to another. You are altogether different. On one side you are perfectly free to do as you please. On the other you are in danger."

[margin handwriting: ťo ly ? huh]

To Canada's dismay, the northern side of the medicine line   11
became an attractive destination for American Indians, including the most famous, most difficult one of all, Sitting Bull. On the run after Little Bighorn, Sitting Bull and entourage settled near Canada's Fort Walsh, under the command of Major James Walsh. Walsh and, as he called him, Bull became such great friends that the Canadian government had Walsh transferred to another post to separate him from Sitting Bull. Sitting Bull was an American problem and the Canadian government wanted to boot him south. Walsh even defied orders and went to Chicago to lobby on Sitting Bull's behalf, but to no avail, ensuring that Sitting Bull would die south of the medicine line.

All the Sitting Bull complications make Walsh my favorite   12
Mountie. But he's a very American choice—he bucked the system, he played favorites for a friend, he defied policy, he stuck out. (Apparently, even having a favorite Mountie is an American trait. When I asked the twentieth commissioner of Mounties, Giuliano "Zach" Zaccardelli, who was his favorite RCMP commissioner in history, he answered Canadianly, "Every one of them has contributed tremendously to the legacy of the RCMP, and I hope that during my tenure I will be able to add some value to the legacy that those nineteen who came before me left for this organization.") When Walsh

heard that Sitting Bull had been fatally shot in Minnesota, he wrote, "Bull's ambition is I am afraid too great to let him settle down and be content with an uninteresting life." This strikes me as almost treasonously individualistic, with American shades of "pursuit of happiness" and "liberty or death."

Everyone knows what the individualistic American cowboy fetish gets us: shot. It all comes down to guns. The population of the United States is ten times that of Canada, but we have about thirty times more firearms. Two-thirds of our homicides are committed with firearms, compared with one-third of theirs. (Which begs the question, just what are Canadian killers using, hair dryers tossed into bathtubs?)   13

The famous (well, in Canada) historian Pierre Berton, in his surprisingly out-of-print book *Why We Act Like Canadians*, informs an American friend that it has to do with weather. Having been to Edmonton in January, I cede his point. He wrote,   14

> *Hot weather and passion, gunfights and race riots go together. Your mythic encounters seem to have taken place at high noon, the sun beating down on a dusty Arizona street. I find it difficult to contemplate a similar gunfight in Moose Jaw, in the winter, the bitter rivals struggling vainly to shed two pairs of mitts and reach under several layers of parka for weapons so cold that the slightest touch of flesh on steel would take the skin off their thumbs.*

Most of the time, I feel Canadian. I live a quiet life. I own no firearms (though, as a gunsmith's daughter, I stand to inherit a freaking arsenal). I revere the Bill of Rights, but at the same time I believe that anyone who's using three or more of them at a time is hogging them too much. I'm a newspaper-reading, French-speaking, radio-documentary-loving square. A lot of my favorite comedians, such as Martin Short, Eugene Levy, the Kids in the Hall, are Canadian. I like that self-deprecating Charlie Brown sense of humor. As Canadian-born *Saturday Night Live* producer Lorne Michaels once put   15 it in a panel discussion devoted to the question of why Canadians are so funny at the Ninety-second Street Y, a Canadian would never have made a film called *It's a Wonderful Life* because "that would be bragging." The Canadian version, he said, would have been titled "It's an All Right Life."

So I mostly walk the Canadian walk, but the thing about a lot of Canadian talk is that it sounds bad. When I went to Ottawa, the "Washington of the North," to see the RCMP's Musical Ride, which is sort of like synchronized swimming on horseback, I was telling a constable in the Mounties about a new U.S. Army recruiting ad. The slogan was "an army of one." It aimed to reassure American kids that they wouldn't be nameless, faceless nobodies, that they could join the army and still do their own thing.

The Mountie was horrified. He said, "I think we have to try and work as a team and work together. If you start to be an individualist, then everybody's going their own way. One person might be doing something and the other person might be doing something else and everybody wants to put their word in and thinks, I'm better than him or My idea's better than his. You need conformity. You need everybody to stick together and work as a team."

It hurt my ears when he said "you need conformity." I know he's probably right, and what organization more than a military one requires lockstep uniformity so that fewer people get killed? But still. No true American would ever talk up the virtue of conformity. Intellectually, I roll my eyes at the cowboy outlaw ethic, but in my heart I know I buy into it a little, that it's a deep part of my identity. Once, when I was living in Holland, I went to the movies, and when a Marlboro Man ad came on the screen, I started bawling with homesickness. I may be the only person who cried all the way through *Don't Tell Mom the Babysitter's Dead*.

The Mounties on the Musical Ride dress in the old-fashioned red serge suits and Stetson hats, like Dudley Do-Right. Seeing them on their black horses, riding in time to music, was entirely lovable, yet lacking any sort of, for lack of a better word, edge. I tried to ask some of them about it.

I say, "In the States, the Mountie is a squeaky-clean icon. 20
Does that ever bother you that the Mountie is not 'cool'?"

He stares back blankly. I ask him, "You know what I 21
mean?"

"No, I don't." 22

"There's no dark side," I tell him. "The Mounties have no 23
dark side."

He laughs. "That might be one of the things that upset 24
the Americans, because we're just that much better." Then
he feels so bad about this little put-down that he repents,
backtracking about how "there's good and bad in everybody," that Americans and Canadians "just have different
views," and that "Canadians are no better than anyone else."

Another constable, overhearing, says, "Our country is far 25
younger than the United States, but at the same time, the
United States is a young country when you compare it to the
countries of Europe."

"Yeah," I answer, "but you're a very well-behaved young 26
country."

"Well"—he smiles—"that's just the way my mum raised 27
me."

For Study and Discussion

QUESTIONS FOR RESPONSE

1. How have the movies shaped your perception of "cowboys" and
   "mounties"?
2. How much do you know about the history and culture of Canada? For example, can you name its provinces and their capitals?

QUESTIONS ABOUT PURPOSE

1. In what ways does Vowell's characterization of Canadian history
   help her reinterpret American history?
2. How does Vowell reverse her friend's assertion that Canadian
   history "isn't inspiring"?

QUESTIONS ABOUT AUDIENCE

1. How does Vowell anticipate her readers when she quotes an American as saying he doesn't think about Canada?
2. What does Vowell mean when she says she feels Canadian? Is she trying to connect with her Canadian readers or help her American readers understand the appeal of Canadian values?

QUESTIONS ABOUT STRATEGIES

1. How does Vowell use the "medicine line" to distinguish between American and Canadian culture?
2. How does Pierre Berton use weather to explain the difference between Americans and Canadians?

QUESTIONS FOR DISCUSSION

1. What cultural values are embedded in the U.S. Army recruiting ad? Why does the Mountie object to the ad?
2. What is the difference—according to Vowell—between being "cool" and "well-behaved"?

Paco Underhill was born in 1952 and was educated at Ewha University and Vassar College. After graduation, Underhill founded Environmental
Analysis and Planning Consultants (now Enviro-
sell), a consulting firm that tracks consumers to
determine their shopping habits and preferences.
He uses this research to advise businesses on how
to increase sales. He published his findings in *Why
We Buy: The Science of Shopping* (1999). In "Shop
like a Man," reprinted from *Why We Buy*, Underhill contrasts the way men and women shop.

Shop like a Man

W HEN THEY WERE a client I used to tell Woolworth's, if 1
you would just hold Dad's Day at your stores once a
week, you'd bring in a lot more money.

They didn't listen. You may have heard. 2

Men and women differ in just about every other way, so 3
why shouldn't they shop differently, too? The conventional
wisdom on male shoppers is that they don't especially like to
do it, which is why they don't do much of it. It's a struggle
just to get them to be patient company for a woman while
she shops. As a result, the entire shopping experience—from
packaging design to advertising to merchandising to store
design and fixturing—is generally geared toward the female
shopper.

Women do have a greater affinity for what we think of as 4
shopping—walking at a relaxed pace through stores, examin-
ing merchandise, comparing products and values, interacting
with sales staff, asking questions, trying things on and ultimately making purchases. Most purchasing traditionally falls
to women, and they usually do it willingly—even when shop-

186

ping for the mundane necessities, even when the experience brings no particular pleasure, women tend to do it in dependable, agreeable fashion. Women take pride in their ability to shop prudently and well. In a study we ran of baby products, women interviewed insisted that they knew the price of products by heart, without even having to look. (Upon further inquiry, we discovered that they were mostly wrong.) As women's roles change, so does their shopping be-

---

The manufacturers, retailers and display designers who pay attention to male ways, and are willing to adapt the shopping experience to them, will have an edge in the twenty-first century.

---

havior—they're becoming a lot more like men in that regard—but they're still the primary buyer in the American marketplace.

In general, men, in comparison, seem like loose cannons. We've timed enough shoppers to know that men always move faster than women through a store's aisles. Men spend less time looking, too. In many settings it's hard to get them to look at anything they hadn't intended to buy. They usually don't like asking where things are, or any other questions, for that matter. (They shop the way they drive.) If a man can't find the section he's looking for, he'll wheel about once or twice, then give up and leave the store without ever asking for help. You can watch men just shut down.

You'll see a man impatiently move through a store to the section he wants, pick something up, and then, almost abruptly, he's ready to buy, having taken no apparent joy in the process of finding. You've practically got to get out of his way. When a man takes clothing into a dressing room, the only thing that stops him from buying it is if it doesn't fit.

Women, on the other hand, try things on as only part of the consideration process, and garments that fit just fine may still be rejected on other grounds. In one study, we found that 65 percent of male shoppers who tried something on bought it, as opposed to 25 percent of female shoppers. This is a good argument for positioning fitting rooms nearer the men's department than the women's, if they are shared accommodations. If they are not, men's dressing rooms should be very clearly marked, because if he has to search for it, he may just decide it's not worth the trouble.

Here's another statistical comparison: Eighty-six percent   7 of women look at price tags when they shop. Only 72 percent of men do. For a man, ignoring the price tag is almost a measure of his virility. As a result, men are far more easily upgraded than are women shoppers. They are also far more suggestible than women—men seem so anxious to get out of the store that they'll say yes to almost anything.

Now, a shopper such as that could be seen as more trouble   8 than he's worth. But he could also be seen as a potential source of profits, especially given his lack of discipline. Either way, men now do more purchasing than ever before. And that will continue to grow. As they stay single longer than ever, they learn to shop for things their fathers never had to buy. And because they marry women who work long and hard too, they will be forced to shoulder more of the burden of shopping. The manufacturers, retailers and display designers who pay attention to male ways, and are willing to adapt the shopping experience to them, will have an edge in the twenty-first century.

The great traditional arena for male shopping behavior has   9 always been the supermarket. It's here, with thousands of products all within easy reach, that you can witness the carefree abandon and restless lack of discipline for which the gender is known. In one supermarket study, we counted how many shoppers came armed with lists. Almost all of the women had them. Less than a quarter of the men did. Any wife who's watching the family budget knows better than to send her husband to the supermarket unchaperoned. Giving him a vehicle to commandeer, even if it is just a shopping cart, only emphasizes the potential for guyness in the experience. Throw a couple of kids in with Dad and you've got a lethal combination; he's notoriously bad at saying no when there's grocery acquisitioning to be done. Part of being Daddy is being the provider, after all. It goes to the heart of a man's self-image.

hee hee

I've spent hundreds of hours of my life watching men moving through supermarkets. One of my favorite video moments starred a dad carrying his little daughter on his shoulders. In the snacks aisle, the girl gestures toward the animal crackers display. Dad grabs a box off the shelf, opens it and hands it up—without even a thought to the fact that his head and shoulders are about to be dusted with cookie crumbs. It's hard to imagine Mom in such a wanton scenario. Another great lesson in male shopping came about watching a man and his two small sons pass through the cereal aisle. When the boys plead for their favorite brand, he pulls down a box and instead of carefully opening it along the reclosable tab, he just rips the top, knowing full well that once the boys start in, there won't be any need to reclose it.

10

Supermarkets are places of high impulse buying for both sexes—fully 60 to 70 percent of purchases there were unplanned, grocery industry studies have shown us. But men are particularly suggestible to the entreaties of children as well as eye-catching displays.

11

There's another profligate male behavior that invariably shows itself at supermarkets, something we see over and over on the video we shoot at the registers: The man almost always pays. Especially when a man and woman are shopping together, he insists on whipping out his wad and forking it over, lest the cashier mistakenly think it's the woman of the house who's bringing home the bacon. No wonder retailers commonly call men wallet carriers. Or why the conventional wisdom is, sell to the woman, close to the man. Because while the man may not love the experience of shopping, he gets a definite thrill from the experience of paying. It allows him to feel in charge even when he isn't. Stores that sell prom

12

pro liferate

we do?

totally true ✓M

gowns depend on this. Generally, when Dad's along, the girl will get a pricier frock than if just Mom was there with her.

In some categories, men shoppers put women to shame. 13 We ran a study for a store where 17 percent of the male customers we interviewed said they visited the place more than once a week! Almost one-quarter of the men there said they had left the house that day with no intention of visiting the store—they just found themselves wandering in out of curiosity. The fact that it was a computer store may have had something to do with it, of course. Computer hardware and software have taken the place of cars and stereo equipment as the focus of male love of technology and gadgetry. Clearly, most of the visits to the store were information-gathering forays. On the videotape, we watched the men reading intently the software packaging and any other literature or signage available. The store was where men bought software, but it was also where they did most of their learning about it. This underscores another male shopping trait—just as they hate to ask directions, they like to get their information firsthand, preferably from written materials, instructional videos or computer screens.

A few years back we ran a study for a wireless phone pro- 14 vider that was developing a prototype retail store. And we found that men and women used the place in very different ways. Women would invariably walk right up to the sales desk and ask staffers questions about the phones and the various deals being offered. Men, however, went directly to the phone displays and the signs that explained the agreements. They then took brochures and application forms and left the store—all without ever speaking to an employee. When these men returned to the store, it was to sign up. The women, though, on average required a third visit to the store, and more consultation, before they were ready to close.

For the most part, men are still the ones who take the lead 15 when shopping for cars (though women have a big say in most new-car purchases), and men and women perform the division of labor you'd expect when buying for the home: She buys anything that goes inside, and he buys everything

Interesting ...

that goes outside—mower and other gardening and lawn-care equipment, barbecue grill, water hose and so on. This is changing as the percentage of female-headed households rises, but it still holds.

Even when men aren't shopping, they figure prominently in the experience. We know that across the board, how much customers buy is a direct result of how much time they spend in a store. And our research has shown over and over that when a woman is in a store with a man, she'll spend less time there than when she's alone, with another woman or even with children. Here's the actual breakdown of average shopping time from a study we performed at one branch of a national housewares chain: 16

> woman shopping with a female companion:
> 8 minutes, 15 seconds
>
> woman with children: 7 minutes, 19 seconds
>
> woman alone: 5 minutes, 2 seconds
>
> woman with man: 4 minutes, 41 seconds

Nice!

In each case, what's happening seems clear: When two women shop together, they talk, advise, suggest and consult to their hearts' content, hence the long time in the store; with the kids, she's partly consumed with herding them along and keeping them entertained; alone, she makes efficient use of her time. But with him—well, he makes it plain that he's bored and antsy and likely at any moment to go off and sit in the car and listen to the radio or stand outside and watch girls. So the woman's comfort level plummets when he's by her side; she spends the entire trip feeling anxious and rushed. If he can somehow be occupied, though, she'll be a happier, more relaxed shopper. And she'll spend more time and money. There are two main strategies for coping with the presence of men in places where serious shopping is being done.   17

The first one is passive restraint, which is not to say handcuffs. Stores that sell mainly to women should all be figuring   18

what?

out some way to engage the interest of men. If I owned The Limited or Victoria's Secret, I'd have a place where a woman could check her husband—like a coat. There already exists a traditional space where men have always felt comfortable waiting around. It's called the barbershop. Instead of some ratty old chairs and back issues of *Playboy* and *Boxing Illustrated*, maybe there could be comfortable seats facing a big-screen TV tuned to ESPN or the cable channel that runs the bass-fishing program. Even something that simple would go a long way toward relieving wifely anxiety, but it's possible to imagine more: *Sports Illustrated* in-store programming, for instance—a documentary on the making of the swimsuit issue, perhaps, or highlights of last weekend's NFL action.

If I were opening a brand-new store where women could shop comfortably, I'd find a location right next to an emporium devoted to male desire—a computer store, for instance, somewhere he could happily kill half an hour. Likewise, if I were opening a computer software store, I'd put it next to a women's clothing shop and guarantee myself hordes of grateful male browsers.   19

But you could also try to sell to your captive audience. A women's clothing store could prepare a video catalog designed especially for men buying gifts—items like scarves or robes rather than shoes or trousers. Gift certificates would sell easily there; he already knows that she likes the store. Victoria's Secret could really go to town with a video catalog for men. They could even stage a little fashion show.   20

(The only precaution you'd need to take is in where to place such a section. You want customers to be able to find it easily, but you don't want it so near the entrance that the gaze of window shoppers falls on six lumpy guys in windbreakers slumped in BarcaLoungers watching TV.)   21

The second, and ultimately more satisfying, strategy would be to find a way to get the man involved in shopping. Not the easiest thing to do in certain categories, but not impossible either.   22

We were doing a study for Pfaltzgraff, the big stoneware dish manufacturer and retailer. Their typical customer will fall   23

in love with one particular pattern and collect the entire set—
many, many pieces, everything from dinner plate and coffee
cup to mustard pot, serving platter and napkin ring. It is very
time-consuming to shop the store, especially when you figure
in how long it takes to ring the items up and wrap them so
that they don't break. Just the kind of situation designed to
drive most men nuts. A typical sale at Pfaltzgraff outlet stores
can run into the hundreds of dollars—all the more reason to
find a way to get men involved.

As we watched the videotape, we noticed that for some   24
unknown reason men were tending to wander over toward
the glassware section of the store. They were steering clear of
the gravy boats and the spoon rests and drifting among the
tumblers and wineglasses. At one point we saw two guys me-
ander over to the beer glasses, where one of them picked one
up and with the other hand grabbed an imaginary beer tap,
pulled it and tilted the glass as if to fill it. And I thought, well,
of course—when company's over for dinner and the woman's
cooking in the kitchen, what does the man do? He makes
drinks. That's his socially acceptable role. And so he's interested in all the accoutrements, all the tools of the bartender
trade—every different type of glass and what it's for, and the
corkscrew and ice tongs and knives and shakers. They're being guys about it.

My first thought was that the stores should put in fake   25
beer taps, like props, for men to play with. We ended up ad-
vising them to pull together all the glassware into a barware
section—to put up on the wall some big graphic, like a photo
of a man pulling a beer, or making some martinis in a nice
chrome shaker. Something so that men would walk in and
see that there was a section meant for them, somewhere they
could shop. All the bottle openers in the different patterns,
say, would be stocked there, too. And because men prefer to
get their information from reading, the store could put up a
chart showing what type of glass is used for what—the big
balloons and the long stems and the flutes and the rocks glass
and steins.

And by doing all that you could take the man—who had   26
been seen as a drag on business and an inconvenience to the
primary shopper—and turn him into a customer himself. Or
at least an interested bystander.

We did a study for Thomasville, the furniture maker, and   27
thought that there, too, getting the man more involved
would make it easier to sell such big-ticket items. The solution was simple: Create graphic devices, like displays and
posters, showing the steps that go into making the furniture,
and use visuals, like cross sections and exploded views, to
prove that in addition to looking good, the pieces were well
made. Emphasizing construction would do a lot toward
overcoming male resistance to the cost of new furniture, but
the graphics would also give men something to study while
their wives examined upholstery and styling.

One product where men consistently outshop women is   28
beer. And that's in every type of setting—supermarket or
convenience store, men buy the beer. (They also buy the junk
food, the chips and pretzels and nuts and other entertainment food.) So we advised a supermarket client to hold a
beer-tasting every Saturday at 3 p.m., right there in the beer
aisle. They could feature some microbrew or a new beer from
one of the major brewers, it didn't matter. The tastings
would probably help sell beer, but even that wasn't the point.
It would be worth it just because it would bring more men
into the store. And it would help transform the supermarket
into a more male-oriented place.

That should be the goal of every retailer today. All aspects   29
of business are going to have to anticipate how men's social
roles change, and the future is going to belong to whoever
gets there first. A good general rule: Take any category where
women now predominate, and figure out how to make it appealing to men.

Look, for instance, at what's happened to the American   30
kitchen over the past decade or so. Once upon a time Mom
did all the grocery shopping and all the cooking. Now Mom
works. As a result, men have to know how to cook, clean and
do laundry—it's gone from being cute to being necessary.

Spenser, Robert Parker's tough detective hero, cooks. A man in the kitchen is sexy.

Is it a coincidence that as that change took place, kitchen appliances have become so butch? Once upon a time you chose from avocado and golden harvest when selecting a refrigerator or a stove. Now the trendiest stoves are industrial-strength six-burner numbers with open gas grills, and the refrigerators are huge, featureless boxes of stainless steel, aluminum and glass. If you go into a fancy kitchenware store like Williams-Sonoma you'll see that a popular gadget is the little blowtorch used for crystallizing the top of crème brûlée. Have Americans just now fallen in love with preparing elaborate, fatty French desserts? Or does cooking just seem more appealing to men when it involves firing up your own personal flamethrower?

(Similarly, as women stay single longer and sometimes become single more than once, the old-fashioned, boys-only hardware store is being killed off by Home Depot, where female homeowners can become tool-happy do-it-yourselfers in a nurturing, gender-nonspecific environment.)

Look at how microwave ovens are sold—the most prominent feature on the description sheet is the wattage. Likewise, when we interviewed men shopping for vacuum cleaners and asked which feature was most important, their (predictable) answer: "Suck." Read: *Power.* As a result, vacuum makers now boast amperage. In both cases, home appliances have gotten more macho as men have gotten less so. They seem determined to meet somewhere in the middle.

Even washday miracles and other household products are being reimagined with men in mind. I can't say for sure how Procter & Gamble or Lever Brothers came to their decisions, but why else would paper towels be called Bounty or laundry detergents be called Bold, except to make themselves respectable items for men to bring to the checkout? How many women wish they had Hefty Bags? Now: How many men? The manliest monikers used to go on cars; now they go on suds. A very successful soap introduction in the '90s wasn't anything frilly or lavender. It was Lever 2000, a name that would also sound right on a computer or a new line of power tools. I'd drive a Lever 2000 any day.

Look beyond shopping to the most elemental expressions 35 of contemporary male desire—just think of the difference between Marilyn Monroe and Elle Macpherson. Elle's biceps are probably bigger than Frank Sinatra's and Bobby Kennedy's combined. She's downright muscle-bound and hipless compared with the pinups of three decades ago.

Men have always bought their own suits and shoes, but 36 women, traditionally, shopped for everything in between. Especially they bought men's socks and underwear. Now, though, that's changing—men are more involved in their clothing, and women have enough to do without buying boxer shorts. In Kmart menswear departments, you'll still sometimes find a female-male ratio of 2 to 1 or even 3 to 1. But in expensive apparel stores, among more affluent men, males shopping for menswear now—finally—outnumber females. We caught a signal moment in the life of the modern American male on videotape. A man was browsing thoughtfully at an underwear display when he suddenly reached around, grabbed a handful of his waistband, pulled it out and craned his neck so he could learn—finally!—what size shorts he wears. Try to imagine a woman who doesn't know her underwear size. Impossible. Someday soon, we can all hope, every man will know his.

(Conversely, I am told that women frequently won't buy 37 lingerie without trying it on—over their own, I am assured. I don't know if I'll live long enough to ever see a man take a package of Fruit of the Looms into a fitting room.)

As women stop buying men's underwear, will men begin 38 buying women's? I met a jeweler who told me, "A lot of my business is with men trying to buy their way back inside the house." Many a husband or beau would choose fancy lingerie or jewelry as gift items, but the stores that sell them, and the merchandise itself, make it daunting. If he can't remember his own size, how can he remember hers, especially when she has bra and underpants to think about, not to mention robe, nightgown, etcetera? And how can he be sure he's buying the ring or necklace she wants, in a color that suits her? We frequently see men tentatively enter these lairs of femininity, cast anxious glances around, maybe study an item or two, and then flee in fear and uncertainty. Salesclerks have to be trained to lure these men in like the skittish beasts they are. Making a personal shopper available for heavy-duty handholding isn't a bad idea, especially considering the costliness of jewelry or even lingerie.

There also must be a way to simplify apparel sizes to make such cross-buying possible. Perhaps the simplest solution would be for women to register their sizes at clothing stores of their liking, then just point their men in the right direction. The first store that tries this is going to benefit from lots of latent desire among men to buy frilly underthings.

Another gender-related problem that clothing retailers have to solve is this: How do you subtly tell shoppers where the men's and women's apparel is in a store that sells both? Not so long ago it was unthinkable that men's and women's clothing would be sold side by side, from the same site. That wall was knocked down in the '60s, but some of the bugs still need to be worked out. The cueing now being used, for instance, even in dual-gender pioneers such as The Gap and J. Crew, doesn't always work, as you can tell when you suddenly realize that you spent ten minutes browsing through shoes, sweaters or jeans meant for the other sex.

Remember when the only men who saw babies being born were obstetricians? Today the presence of Dad in the delivery room is almost as required as Mom's. Men are going to have to be accommodated as they redefine their role as fathers. It's a seismic change that's being felt on the shopping floor just like everywhere else.

For example, almost no man of my father's generation had the habit of loading Junior, a bottle or two and some diapers into the stroller and going out for a Saturday morning jaunt. Today it's almost a cliché. That's why progressive men's rooms now feature baby changing stations, and it's why the McDonald's commercials invariably show Dad and the kids piling in—sans Mom, who's probably spending Saturday at the office. (Mom won't let them order Big Macs anyway.) This isn't just an American phenomenon, either—my informal Saturday observation of Milan's most fashionable districts detected that roughly half of all baby strollers were being pushed by Papa.

We tested a prototype jeans section at a department store   43
in Boston, part of an effort to improve the store's appeal to men in their twenties and thirties. We caught video of a young man walking down the aisle toward the section, accompanied by his wife and baby, whose stroller he pushed. They reached the jeans, and he clearly wanted to shop the shelves on the wall. But there were racks of clothing standing between him and the jeans, positioned so close together that he couldn't nudge the stroller past. You can see him thinking through his choice—do I leave my wife and child in the aisle just to buy jeans? He did what most people would do in that situation. He skipped the pants. You'd be amazed at how much of America's aggregate selling floor is still off-limits to anyone pushing a stroller. This is the equivalent of barring a large percentage of all shoppers in their twenties and thirties.

Two decades ago it was the rare father who ever bought   44
clothing for the little ones; today it's more common to see men shopping the toddler section. Clothing manufacturers haven't caught up with this yet, however, as evidenced by the fact that children's sizes are the most confusing in all of apparel—guaranteed to frustrate all but the most parental of shoppers. The day that size corresponds directly to the age of the child is when men will be able to pull even more of the weight for outfitting the kids. It'll be Dad who springs for the outrageous indulgences here, too—the velvet smoking jacket for his son or the miniature prom gown for his daughter.

And when Saturday morning rolls around and Pop goes to   45
pack the bottles and zwieback and diapers and baby powder and ointment and wipes and all the rest of that stuff, what does he put it in? Not the big pink nylon bag his wife lugs. In fact, he's probably disposed against any of the available op-

tions—even a plain black diaper bag says Mommy. But what if he could choose a Swiss Army diaper bag? How about a nylon Nike one that looks just like his gym bag? Even better, what if he could push a studly Harley-Davidson-brand baby stroller that came with a built-in black leather diaper bag? The whole baby category needs to be reinvented.

that'd be some sight

Other traditional female strongholds can also accommodate men, but it's got to be on masculine terms. You've got to be aware of the wimp factor. There are many stores where the floors and the walls and everything hanging on them whisper loudly to the foolhardy male trespasser, "Get the hell out of here—you don't belong!" Near my office there's a store that sells dishes and glasses and such, and it's remarkable because I can walk in and not feel like a bull in a china shop. Whereas in Bloomingdale's Royal Doulton section, I feel as though I'm back in my grandmother's dining room, and it's the grandmother who scared me.

46

There are other such places that men would gladly shop—actually want and even need to shop—if only they felt just a little bit wanted. For example, there are more health and grooming products for men than ever. But if you look at how they're sold, you see that most men will never become avid buyers.

47

In the chain drugstores and supermarket sections where these products are sold, the atmosphere is overwhelmingly feminine. Shampoo, soap and other products that can be used by either sex are invariably packaged and named with the assumption that women will be doing all the buying. It becomes a self-fulfilling prophecy. The products made especially for men, like shaving cream, hair ointment and deodorant, are stocked in a dinky little section sandwiched in among all the fragrant female goods. No-man's-land, in other words, so how's a guy to shop it?

48

fun

I can think of one item in particular where men suffer as a result of female-oriented packaging and merchandising. There is an untapped market for moisturizing creams and sunblock among men who work outdoors—police, construction workers, cable TV and telephone line installers, road

49

crews. Given all we know about skin cancer, these guys truly need access to these products. But they're not going to traipse through the blushers and concealers to find them. And they're not going to buy a product that presents itself as intended for women and children. If you went through your typical health and beauty section, you'd think that men don't have skin. But they do, and it needs help.

Clinique makes a complete line of shaving and skin prod-   50
ucts for men. But at the very sophisticated Bergdorf Goodman department store in New York City, a man has to visit the all-female cosmetics bazaar on the ground floor to find the stuff. It's not even available at the men's store across Fifth Avenue. Who would guess that the shaving cream is right next to the lipstick? I've no doubt that many women buy shaving products for their men, but that's the old-fashioned approach, not the way of the future. Gillette makes shaving creams for a variety of skin types, and there's no doubt that it's for men. But how is a man supposed to know which type of skin he has? A simple wall chart display would do the trick, but I've yet to see one. I recently visited a national chain's drugstore in Manhattan's Chelsea section, the epicenter of gay life here. Even this store shortchanges men—their section (which consisted only of deodorant, a few hair-grooming products, some Old Spice, a tube of Brylcreem) was jammed into a corner shelf between the film-processing booth and the disposable razors. This store would be a perfect place to create a prototype men's section. Instead, it was the same old dreariness.

Giving men their own products, and a place to buy them,   51
would be a good start. But that still smacks of the health, beauty and cosmetics section designed for women. Someone needs to start from scratch in designing a "men's health" department, where you'd find skin products, grooming aids, shaving equipment, shampoo and conditioner, fragrance, condoms, muscle-pain treatments, over-the-counter drugs and the vitamins, supplements and herbal remedies for ailments that afflict men as well as women. There might also be some athletic wear, like socks, T-shirts, supporters, elastic

bandages and so on. There should also be a display of books and magazines on health, fitness and appearance. The section itself would have a masculine feeling, from the fixtures to the package designs. And it would be merchandised with men in mind—the signs would be big and prominent, and everything would be easy to find. The number-one magazine success story of the past decade has been the amazing growth of a periodical called *Men's Health*, which sells over 1.5 million copies a month, more than *GQ, Esquire, Men's Journal* and all the others. If the magazine can thrive, why not the store section, too?

For Study and Discussion

QUESTIONS FOR RESPONSE

1. How would you describe your shopping style?
2. What kinds of difficulties have you encountered when you have had to shop with someone who follows a different style?

QUESTIONS ABOUT PURPOSE

1. What kind of research does Underhill use to reveal the difference between the ways men and women shop?
2. How does he use this research to demonstrate how retailers should cater to the shopping styles of men?

QUESTIONS ABOUT AUDIENCE

1. How does Underhill use videotapes to convince his readers that he is not describing mere stereotypes?
2. How does his discussion of changing gender roles expand his audience?

QUESTIONS ABOUT STRATEGIES

1. Which of the many examples Underhill cites—dressing room, price tags, wallet carriers, shopping time—makes his case most effectively about the traditional shopping styles of men and women?

2. Which of his two solutions—passive restraint or customer involvement—seems the most effective way to engage male shoppers?

QUESTIONS FOR DISCUSSION

1. To what extent does Underhill provide evidence that shopping can be studied scientifically?
2. What ads, packages, or displays can you identify that appeal most to men and/or women?

Anne Roiphe was born in New York City in 1935 and educated at Sarah Lawrence College. Perhaps best known for the novel *Up the Sandbox!* (1970), her works explore a woman's search for identity in the wake of marriage and divorce. In some of her fiction, *The Pursuit of Happiness* (1991), and nonfiction, *Generation Without Memory: A Jewish Journey in Christian America* (1981), *A Season of Healing: Reflections on the Holocaust* (1988), and *1185 Park Avenue: A Memoir* (1999), Roiphe explores the special issues confronted by Jewish women. In "A Tale of Two Divorces," reprinted from *Women on Divorce* (1995), Roiphe compares two marriages, one that should have ended in divorce and one that did.

A Tale of Two Divorces

E VERY DIVORCE IS a story, and while they can begin to sound the same—sad and cautionary—each one is as unique as a human face. My divorce is the tale of two divorces, one that never was and one that was. The first is the story of my parents' marriage.

My mother was the late fifth child, raised in a large house on Riverside Drive in New York City. Her father, who came to America as a boy from a town outside of Suvalki, Poland, had piled shirts on a pushcart and wandered the streets of the Lower East Side in the 1880s. His pushcart turned into a loft with twenty women sewing shirts for him and before he was twenty-five he owned a small company called Van Heusen Shirts. He was one of the founding members of Beth Israel Hospital and I have a photo of him, shovel in hand, black hat on his head, as the foundation stone is placed in the ground.

1

2

odd

My mother grew up, small, plump, nervous, fearful of   3
horses, dogs, cats, cars, water, balls that were hit over nets,
tunnels, and bridges. She was expected to marry brilliantly
into the world of manufacturers of coats, shoes, gowns, store

---

*In twentieth-century America we place so
much emphasis on romance that we barely
notice the other essentials of marriage that
include economics and child rearing.*

Pessimistic

owners, prosperous bankers whose sons attended the dozens
of teas and charity events where she—always afraid her hair
was wrong, her conversation dull, her dress wrinkled—tried
to obey the instructions of her older sister and sparkle. A girl
after all had to sparkle. She was under five feet. She was near-
sighted. Without her thick glasses she stumbled, recognized
no one, groped the wall for comfort. Her lipstick tended to
smear. She chain-smoked. She lost things. She daydreamed.
Her father died of a sudden heart attack when she was just
thirteen. Her older sisters married millionaires, her brothers
inherited the business. She was herself considered an heiress,
a dangerous state for a tremulous girl, whose soul was perpet-
ually fogged in uncertainty.

*I like
that
word*

*does
she like
her?*

At a Z.B.T. Columbia University fraternity party she met   4
my father. He was the Hungarian-born son of a drug salesman who bet the horses and believed that he had missed his
grander destiny. My paternal grandfather was never able to
move his family out from the railroad flat under the Third
Avenue El. His wife, my grandmother, was a statuesque
woman, taller than her husband but overwhelmed by noise,
the turmoil of her American days. She never learned English.
She stayed home in her nightgown and slippers, sleeping
long hours. My father was in law school. He was tall and
handsome with black hair slicked down like Valentino and

cold eyes set perfectly in an even face. He was an athlete who had earned his college expenses by working summers as a lifeguard in the Catskills. His shoes were perfectly polished. His white shirt gleamed. He loathed poverty. He claimed to speak no other language than English though he had arrived in America at age nine. He told my mother he loved her. Despite the warnings of her siblings, she believed him. If she was not his dream girl, she was his American dream. They went on their honeymoon to Europe and purchased fine china and linen at every stop.

My father became a lawyer for the family shirt company. He was edgy, prone to yell at others; he ground his teeth. He suffered from migraines. He could tolerate nothing out of place, nothing that wasn't spotless. He joined a club where men played squash, steamed in the sauna, and drank at the bar. He stayed long hours at his club. He told his wife she was unbeautiful. She believed him although the pictures of her at the time tell a different story. They show a young woman with soft amused eyes and a long neck, with a shy smile and a brave tilt of the head. My father explained to my mother that he could never admire a short woman, that long legs were the essence of glamour.

My father began to have other ladies. He would meet them under the clock at the Biltmore, at motels in Westchester. He had ice in his heart, but he looked good in his undershirt. He looked good in his monogrammed shirts. He lost his nonfamily clients. They didn't like his temper, his impatience. It didn't matter. He took up golf and was gone all day Saturday and Sunday in the good weather. He made investments in the stock market. He had a genius for bad bets. My mother made up the heavy losses. She had two children and she lived just as she was expected to do, with servants to take care of the details, to wake with the babies, to prepare the food, to mop the floors. She spent her days playing cards and shopping. She went to the hairdresser two, sometimes three times a week. A lady came to the house to wax her legs and do her long red nails. She had ulcers, anxiety attacks,

the random
sent.
have a
nice
affect

panic attacks. In the evening at about five o'clock she would begin to wait for my father to come home. She could do the crossword puzzle in five minutes. She was a genius at canasta, Oklahoma, bridge, backgammon. She joined a book club. She loved the theater and invested cleverly in Broadway shows. She took lessons in French and flower arranging.

At the dinner table, as the food was being served, my fa-   7
ther would comment that he didn't like the way my mother wore the barrette in her hair. She would say bitterly that he never liked anything she wore. He would say that she was stupid. She would say that she was not. Their voices would carry. In the kitchen the maid would clutch the side of the sink until her fingernails were white. My mother would weep. My father would storm out of the house, slamming doors, knocking over lamps. She would shout after him, "You don't love me." He would scream at her, "Who could love you?" She would lie in bed with ice cubes on her swollen eyes, chain-smoking Camel cigarettes. She would call her sister for comfort. Her sister would say, "Don't give him an argument." She would say, "I'll try to do better, I really will."

When I was seven years old, she lay in the bathtub soaking   8
and I was sitting on the rim keeping her company. "I could divorce him," she said. "I could do it." Her eyes were puffed. I felt a surge of electricity run through me, adrenaline flowed. "Leave him?" I asked. "Yes," she said. "Should I?" she asked me. "Should I leave him? Would you mind?" I was her friend, her confidante. I did not yet know enough of the world to answer the question. I thought of my home split apart. I thought my father would never see me again. I wondered what I would tell my friends. No one I knew had parents who were divorced. I was afraid. "Who will take care of us?" I asked. My mother let the ashes of her cigarette fall into the tub. "God!" she said. "Help me," she said. But she'd asked the wrong person.

relate

Then she did a brave thing. She went to a psychiatrist. I   9
would wait for her downstairs in the lobby. She would emerge from the elevator after her appointment with her

mascara smeared over her cheeks. "When I'm stronger," she said, "I'll leave him." But the years went on. He said she was demanding. He said, "I spend enough time with you. Go to Florida with your sister. Go to Maine with your brother. Stop asking me to talk to you. I've already said everything I want to say." She said, "I need you to admire me. I need you to say you love me." "I do," he said, but then they had a party and I found him in the coat closet with a lady and lipstick all over his face.

Ouch

He talked about politics. He read history books. He hit on the chin a man who disagreed with him. He yelled at my mother that she had no right to an opinion on anything. He said, "Women with opinions smell like skunks." She said, "He's so smart. He knows so much." She said, "If I leave him no other man will marry me." She said, "I can't leave him."

10 *strong minded*

Fear

Week after week, she would say something that irritated him. He would make her cry and then he would scream at her for crying. His screams were howls. If you listened to the sound you would think an animal was trapped and in pain. Dinner after dinner my brother and I would silently try to eat our food as the same old fight began again, built and reached its crescendo.

11

Finally I was old enough. "Leave him," I said. "I don't know," she said, "maybe." But she couldn't and she wouldn't and the dance between them had turned into a marathon. She quit first. She died at age fifty-two, still married, still thinking, if only I had been taller, different, better. He inherited her money and immediately wed a tall woman, with whom he had been having an affair for many years, whose hands shook when she spoke to him. He called her: "That stupid dame." "That dumb broad," he would say. He went off to his club. He went for long walks. He had migraines.

12 *the child sees*

This was a story of a divorce that should have been.

13

When I was twenty-seven I found myself checking into a fleabag hotel in Juárez. My three-year-old daughter was trying to pull the corncob out of the parrot cage and the parrot

14

learned from parents

was trying to bite her fingers. I was there, my room squeezed between those of the local drunks and prostitutes, to get a divorce. This was a divorce that should have been and was. I had married a man whom I thought was just the opposite of my father. He was a playwright, a philosopher. He was from an old southern family. He talked to me all the time and let me read and type his manuscripts. I worked as a receptionist to support him. Our friends were poets and painters, beatniks and their groupies. I had escaped my mother's home or so I thought. What I didn't notice was that my husband was handsome and thought me plain, that my husband was poor and thought me a meal ticket, that my husband—like my father—was dwarfed of spirit and couldn't imagine another soul beside himself. What I didn't know was that I—like my mother—had no faith, no confidence, no sense that I could fly too. I could even write.

diff. reaction

funny — isn't it

My husband had other women and I thought it was an artist's privilege. My husband said, "If Elizabeth Taylor is a woman, then you must be a hamster." I laughed. My husband went on binges and used up all our money. I thought it was poetic although I was always frightened; bill collectors called. I was always apologizing. We didn't fight so I thought I had achieved matrimonial heaven, a place where of course certain compromises were necessary.

Then after I had a child I thought of love as oxygen and I felt faint. In the middle of the night when I was nursing the baby and my husband was out at the local bar I discovered that loneliness was the name of my condition. I noticed that my husband could not hold his child because he was either too drunk, out of the house, closed into his head, or consumed with nervousness about the applause the outside world was giving or withholding from him. I discovered that I had married a man more like my father than not and that, more like my mother than not, I had become a creature to be pitied. Like moth to flame I was drawn to repeat. My divorce was related to her undivorce, so the generations unfold back to back handing on their burdens—by contamination, memory, experience, identification, one's failure becomes the

it always happens

15

16

other's. The courage it takes to really make things better, to
change, is rare and won only at great cost. Yes, we are responsible for ourselves, but nevertheless our family stories course *Unfort*
and curse through our veins: our memories are not free.

If my mother had been brave enough to go it alone I   17
might have seen myself differently. I might have been brave
enough to let myself be loved the first time around. At least I
didn't wait for my entire life to pass before leaping up and
away. So this is why I listen with tongue in cheek to all the
terrible tales of what divorce has done to the American family. I know that if my mother had left my father not only her
life but mine too might have been set on more solid ground.
I know that if I had stayed in my marriage my child would
have lived forever in the shadow of my perpetual grief and
thought of herself as I had, unworthy of the ordinary moments of affection and connection.   *everyone deserves those*

In twentieth-century America we place so much emphasis   18
on romance that we barely notice the other essentials of marriage that include economics and child rearing. My mother
was undone by the economic equation in her marriage.
Money, which we know to be a part of the bitterness of divorce, is in there from the beginning, a thread in the cloak of
love, whether we like it or not.

History clunking through our private lives certainly af-   19
fected my mother's marriage and my bad marriage. Woman's
proper role, woman's masochistic stance, immigration, push
to rise in social status, the confusion of money damned my
mother to a lifetime of tears and almost caught me there too.
But history is always present without our always being able to
name its nasty work.

The women's movement, which came too late for my   20
mother, sent some women off adventure bound, free of sub-
urb, unwilling to be sole caretakers to find, at the end of their
rainbow isolation, disappointment, bitterness. The sexual
revolution, which soon after burned like a laser through our
towns and sent wives running in circles in search of multiple
pleasures, freedom from convention, and distance from the

burdens of domesticity, was a balloon that popped long before the arrival of AIDS. We found we were not, after all, in need of the perfect orgasm. We were in need of a body to spoon with in bed, a story we could tell together as well as sexual equality.

But there is more. Divorce is also the terrible knife that   21
rends family asunder, and for the children it can be the tilting, defining moment that marks them ever after, walking wounded, angry, sad souls akimbo, always prone to being lost in a forest of despair. They can be tough, too tough. They can be helpless, too helpless. They can never trust. They can be too trusting. They can accept a stepparent for a while and then revoke their acceptance. They can protest the stepparent for a while and then change their mind, but either way their own parents' divorce hangs over them, threat, reminder, betrayal always possible. My stepdaughter, now a married woman and a mother herself, speaks of her own parents' breakup, which came when she was only seven, as the most terrible moment in her life. As she says this I have only to listen to the tightness in her voice, watch the slight tremble in her hand to know that the divorce seemed to her like an earthquake. The divorce caused a before and after and everything after is tarnished, diminished by what went before.

I wish this were not so. I wish that we could marry a new   22
mate, repair, go on to undo the worst of our mistakes without leaving ugly deep scars across our children's psyches, but we can't. And furthermore the children will never completely forgive us, never understand how our backs were against the wall: They may try to understand our broken vows but they don't. Of course there are other things our children don't forgive us for. If we die, if we withdraw, if we let ourselves drown in misery, addictions, if we fail at work or lose our courage in the face of economic or other adversity, that too will eat at their hearts and spoil their chances for the gold ring on life's carousel. There are, in other words, many ways to damage children, and divorce is only the most effective and perhaps most common of them.

For a while, in the seventies, divorce was everywhere, a   23 panacea for the heart burdened. We were too excited by the prospects of freedom to see the damage that was done. The wounds are very severe for both partners and children. It may be worth it as it would have been for my mother. It may be necessary, but divorce is never nice. I felt as if the skin had been stripped from my body the first months after my divorce, and I was only twenty-seven years old. I felt as if I had to learn anew how to walk in the streets, how to set my face, how to plot a direction, how to love. I had to admit to failure, take back my proud words, let others help me. It was a relief, but it was a disaster. I had lost confidence in my decisions. It took a long while to gain back what I had lost. I understand why my mother did not have the strength to do it, although she should have.

This would be the hardest part

I cannot imagine a world in which divorce would not sometimes occur. Men and women will always fail each other, miss each others' gestures, change in fatally different ways. There are men who cannot love, who abuse their wives or themselves or some substance. There are women who do the same. There are some disasters that wreck a marriage, a sick or damaged child, an economic calamity, a professional failure. There are marriages that are simply asphyxiated by daily life. 24

But I can imagine a world in which divorce would be rare, in which the madness, meanness, mess of everyday life were absorbed and managed without social cataclysm. It is perhaps our American obsession with the romantic that leads to so much trouble. If we were able to see marriage as largely an economic, child-rearing institution, as a social encounter involving ambition, class, money, we might be better off. Never mind our very up-to-date goals of personal fitness and fulfillment; we are still characters, all of us, in a nineteenth-century novel. 25

At the moment, now that my children are of marriageable age I have become a believer in the arranged betrothal. Such marriages could not possibly cause more mischief than those that were created by our free will rushing about in heavy traffic with its eyes closed. Perhaps we should consider love as 26 a product of marriage instead of the other way around. Of course those societies that arrange marriages have other tragic stories of bride burning, lifelong miserable submission experienced by women, sexual nightmares, poor young girls and dirty old men. We are the only animal species that cannot seem to figure out how to pair off and raise children without maiming ourselves in the process.

We can bemoan the social disorder caused by divorce until   27
the moon turns to cream cheese, but we are such fragile souls, so easily cast adrift, wounded, set upon by devils of our own making, that no matter how we twist or turn, no system will protect us from the worst. There is cruelty in divorce. There is cruelty in forced or unfortunate marriage. We will continue to cry at weddings because we know how bitter-sweet, how fragile is the troth. We will always need legal divorce just as an emergency escape hatch is crucial in every submarine. No sense, however, in denying that after every divorce someone will be running like a cat, tin cans tied to its tail: spooked and slowed down.

For Study and Discussion

QUESTIONS FOR RESPONSE

1. How have your friends or members of your family reacted to a divorce?
2. How do you characterize divorce—as a failure or liberation? Can you tell a story about a couple that might fit into each category?

QUESTIONS ABOUT PURPOSE

1. In what ways does Roiphe's sentence—"my divorce is the tale of two divorces, one that never was and one that was"—state the purpose of her essay?
2. How do her stories demonstrate her thesis that marriage requires more than romance?

QUESTIONS ABOUT AUDIENCE

1. How does Roiphe's assertion that all divorce stories sound the same, and yet each is as "unique as a human face," help her identify her audience?
2. These two contemporary tales focus on women. How does Roiphe anticipate the responses of her male readers?

QUESTIONS ABOUT STRATEGIES

1. How does Roiphe balance her two stories to demonstrate that although they seem different, her husband was like her father and she was like her mother?
2. How does Roiphe use her stepdaughter's experience to make a transition to the final part of her essay?

QUESTIONS FOR DISCUSSION

1. What effects does Roiphe think the women's movement has had on divorce?
2. How does she justify her assertion that we will always need divorce as "an emergency escape hatch"?

Laura Bohannan was born in New York City in 1922 and educated at Smith College, the University of Arizona, and Oxford University. She has taught anthropology at Northwestern University, the University of Chicago, and the University of Illinois, Chicago Circle. She has held several fellowships to conduct research in East Africa which have resulted in books such as *The Tiv of Central Nigeria* (1953) and *A Sourcebook on Tiv Religion* (1972). In "Shakespeare in the Bush," reprinted from *Natural History* magazine, Bohannan compares her version of *Hamlet* with the interpretation of the elders of an African tribe.

Shakespeare in the Bush
An American Anthropologist Set Out to Study the Tiv of West Africa and Was Taught the True Meaning of Hamlet

J UST BEFORE I left Oxford for the Tiv in West Africa, conversation turned to the season at Stratford. "You Americans," said a friend, "often have difficulty with Shakespeare. He was, after all, a very English poet, and one can easily misinterpret the universal by misunderstanding the particular."

I protested that human nature is pretty much the same the whole world over; at least the general plot and motivation of the greater tragedies would always be clear—everywhere—although some details of custom might have to be explained and difficulties of translation might produce other slight changes. To end an argument we could not conclude, my friend gave me a copy of *Hamlet* to study in the African bush: it would, he hoped, lift my mind above its primitive surroundings, and possibly I might, by prolonged meditation, achieve the grace of correct interpretation.

It was my second field trip to that African tribe, and I thought myself ready to live in one of its remote sections—an area difficult to cross even on foot. I eventually settled on the hillock of a very knowledgeable old man, the head of a home-

---

Before the end of the second month, grace descended on me. I was quite sure that Hamlet *had only one possible interpretation, and that one universally obvious.*

---

stead of some hundred and forty people, all of whom were either his close relatives or their wives and children. Like the other elders of the vicinity, the old man spent most of his time performing ceremonies seldom seen these days in the more accessible parts of the tribe. I was delighted. Soon there would be three months of enforced isolation and leisure, between the harvest that takes place just before the rising of the swamps and the clearing of new farms when the water goes down. Then, I thought, they would have even more time to perform ceremonies and explain them to me.

I was quite mistaken. Most of the ceremonies demanded the presence of elders from several homesteads. As the swamps rose, the old men found it too difficult to walk from one homestead to the next, and the ceremonies gradually ceased. As the swamps rose even higher, all activities from one came to an end. The women brewed beer from maize and millet. Men, women, and children sat on their hillocks and drank it.

People began to drink at dawn. By midmorning the whole homestead was singing, dancing, and drumming. When it rained, people had to sit inside their huts: there they drank and sang or they drank and told stories. In any case, by noon or before, I either had to join the party or retire to my own hut and my books. "One does not discuss serious matters when there is beer. Come, drink with us." Since I lacked their capacity for the thick native beer, I spent more and more time with *Hamlet*. Before the end of the second month, grace descended on me. I was quite sure that *Hamlet* had only one possible interpretation, and that one universally obvious.

Early every morning, in the hope of having some serious   6 talk before the beer party, I used to call on the old man at his reception hut—a circle of posts supporting a thatched roof above a low mud wall to keep out wind and rain. One day I crawled through the low doorway and found most of the men of the homestead sitting huddled in their ragged cloths on stools, low plank beds, and reclining chairs, warming themselves against the chill of the rain around a smoky fire. In the center were three pots of beer. The party had started.

The old man greeted me cordially. "Sit down and drink." I   7 accepted a large calabash full of beer, poured some into a small drinking gourd, and tossed it down. Then I poured some more into the same gourd for the man second in seniority to my host before I handed my calabash over to a young man for further distribution. Important people shouldn't ladle beer themselves.

"It is better like this," the old man said, looking at me approvingly and plucking at the thatch that had caught in my   8 hair. "You should sit and drink with us more often. Your servants tell me that when you are not with us, you sit inside your hut looking at a paper."

The old man was acquainted with four kinds of "papers":   9 tax receipts, bride price receipts, court fee receipts, and letters. The messenger who brought him letters from the chief used them mainly as a badge of office, for he always knew what was in them and told the old man. Personal letters for the few who had relatives in the government or mission stations were kept until someone went to a large market where there was a letter writer and reader. Since my arrival, letters were brought to me to be read. A few men also brought me bride price receipts, privately, with requests to change the figures to a higher sum. I found moral arguments were of no avail, since in-laws are fair game, and the technical hazards of forgery difficult to explain to an illiterate people. I did not wish them to think me silly enough to look at any such papers for days on end, and I hastily explained that my "paper" was one of the "things of long ago" of my country.

"Ah," said the old man. "Tell us." 10

I protested that I was not a storyteller. Storytelling is a 11
skilled art among them; their standards are high, and the audiences critical—and vocal in their criticism. I protested in vain. This morning they wanted to hear a story while they drank. They threatened to tell me no more stories until I told them one of mine. Finally, the old man promised that no one would criticize my style "for we know you are struggling with our language." "But," put in one of the elders, "you must explain what we do not understand, as we do when we tell you our stories." Realizing that here was my chance to prove *Hamlet* universally intelligible, I agreed.

The old man handed me some more beer to help me on 12
with my storytelling. Men filled their long wooden pipes and knocked coals from the fire to place in the pipe bowls; then, puffing contentedly, they sat back to listen. I began in the proper style, "Not yesterday, not yesterday, but long ago, a thing occurred. One night three men were keeping watch outside the homestead of the great chief, when suddenly they saw the former chief approach them."

"Why was he no longer their chief?" 13

"He was dead," I explained. "That is why they were trou- 14
bled and afraid when they saw him."

"Impossible," began one of the elders, handing his pipe 15
on to his neighbor, who interrupted, "Of course it wasn't the dead chief. It was an omen sent by a witch. Go on."

Slightly shaken, I continued. "One of these three was a 16
man who knew things"—the closest translation for scholar, but unfortunately it also meant witch. The second elder looked triumphantly at the first. "So we spoke to the dead chief saying, 'Tell us what we must do so you may rest in your grave,' but the dead chief did not answer. He vanished, and

they could see him no more. Then the man who knew things—his name was Horatio—said this event was the affair of the dead chief's son, Hamlet."

There was a general shaking of heads round the circle. 17
"Had the dead chief no living brothers? Or was this son the chief?"

"No," I replied. "That is, he had one living brother who 18 became the chief when the elder brother died."

The old men muttered: such omens were matters for 19 chiefs and elders, not for youngsters; no good could come of going behind a chief's back; clearly Horatio was not a man who knew things.

"Yes, he was," I insisted, shooing a chicken away from my 20 beer. "In our country the son is next to the father. The dead chief's younger brother had become the great chief. He had also married his elder brother's widow only about a month after the funeral."

"He did well," the old man beamed and announced to the 21 others, "I told you that if we knew more about Europeans, we would find they really were very like us. In our country also," he added to me, "the younger brother marries the elder brother's widow and becomes the father of his children. Now, if your uncle, who married your widowed mother, is your father's full brother, then he will be a real father to you. Did Hamlet's father and uncle have one mother?"

His question barely penetrated my mind; I was too upset 22 and thrown too far off balance by having one of the most important elements of *Hamlet* knocked straight out of the picture. Rather uncertainly I said that I thought they had the same mother, but I wasn't sure—the story didn't say. The old man told me severely that these genealogical details made all the difference and that when I got home I must ask the elders about it. He shouted out the door to one of his younger wives to bring his goatskin bag.

Determined to save what I could of the mother motif, I 23 took a deep breath and began again. "The son Hamlet was very sad because his mother had married again so quickly. There was no need for her to do so, and it is our custom for a widow not to go to her next husband until she has mourned for two years."

"Two years is too long," objected the wife, who had appeared with the old man's battered goatskin bag. "Who will hoe your farms for you while you have no husband?"

"Hamlet," I retorted without thinking, "was old enough to hoe his mother's farms himself. There was no need for her to remarry." No one looked convinced. I gave up. "His mother and the great chief told Hamlet not to be sad, for the great chief himself would be a father to Hamlet. Furthermore, Hamlet would be the next chief: therefore he must stay to learn the things of a chief. Hamlet agreed to remain, and all the rest went off to drink beer."

While I paused, perplexed at how to render Hamlet's disgusted soliloquy to an audience convinced that Claudius and Gertrude had behaved in the best possible manner, one of the younger men asked me who had married the other wives of the dead chief.

"He had no other wives," I told him.

"But a chief must have many wives! How else can he brew beer and prepare food for all his guests?"

I said firmly that in our country even chiefs had only one wife, that they had servants to do their work, and that they paid them from tax money.

It was better, they returned, for a chief to have many wives and sons who would help him hoe his farms and feed his people; then everyone loved the chief who gave much and took nothing—taxes were a bad thing.

I agreed with the last comment, but for the rest fell back on their favorite way of fobbing off my questions: "That is the way it is done, so that is how we do it."

I decided to skip the soliloquy. Even if Claudius was here thought quite right to marry his brother's widow, there remained the poison motif, and I knew they would disapprove of fratricide. More hopefully I resumed, "That night Hamlet kept watch with the three who had seen his dead father. The

how common are multiple wives?

24

25

26

27

28

29

30

31

32

dead chief again appeared, and although the others were
afraid, Hamlet followed his dead father off to one side. When
they were alone, Hamlet's dead father spoke."

"Omens can't talk!" The old man was emphatic.   33

"Hamlet's dead father wasn't an omen. Seeing him might   34
have been an omen, but he was not." My audience looked as
confused as I sounded. "It *was* Hamlet's dead father. It was a
thing we call a 'ghost.'" I had to use the English word, for
unlike many of the neighboring tribes, these people didn't
believe in the survival after death of any individuating part of
the personality.

"What is a 'ghost'? An omen?"   35

"No, a 'ghost' is someone who is dead but who walks   36
around and can talk, and people can hear him and see him
but not touch him."

They objected. "One can touch zombis."   37

"No, no! It was not a dead body the witches had animated   38
to sacrifice and eat. No one else made Hamlet's dead father
walk. He did it himself."

"Dead men can't walk," protested my audience as one   39
man.

I was quite willing to compromise. "A 'ghost' is the dead   40
man's shadow."

But again they objected. "Dead men cast no shadows."   41

"They do in my country," I snapped.   42

The old man quelled the babble of disbelief that arose im-   43
mediately and told me with that insincere, but courteous,
agreement one extends to the fancies of the young, ignorant,
and superstitious, "No doubt in your country the dead can
also walk without being zombis." From the depths of his bag
he produced a withered fragment of kola nut, bit off one end
to show it wasn't poisoned, and handed me the rest as a
peace offering.

"Anyhow," I resumed, "Hamlet's dead father said that his   44
own brother, the one who became chief, had poisoned him.
He wanted Hamlet to avenge him. Hamlet believed this in
his heart, for he did not like his father's brother." I took another swallow of beer. "In the country of the great chief,

living in the same homestead, for it was a very large one, was
an important elder who was often with the chief to advise and
help him. His name was Polonius. Hamlet was courting his
daughter, but her father and her brother . . . [I cast hastily
about for some tribal analogy] warned her not to let Hamlet
visit her when she was alone on her farm, for he would be a
great chief and so could not marry her."

"Why not?" asked the wife, who had settled down on the
edge of the old man's chair. He frowned at her for asking stupid questions and growled, "They lived in the same homestead."

"That was not the reason," I informed them. "Polonius
was a stranger who lived in the homestead because he helped
the chief, not because he was a relative."

"Then why couldn't Hamlet marry her?"

"He could have," I explained, "but Polonius didn't think
he would. After all, Hamlet was a man of great importance
who ought to marry a chief's daughter, for in his country a
man could have only one wife. Polonius was afraid that if
Hamlet made love to his daughter, then no one else would
give a high price for her."

"That might be true," remarked one of the shrewder elders, "but a chief's son would give his mistress's father
enough presents and patronage to more than make up the
difference. Polonius sounds like a fool to me."

"Many people think he was," I agreed. "Meanwhile
Polonius sent his son Laertes off to Paris to learn the things
of that country, for it was the homestead of a very great chief
indeed. Because he was afraid that Laertes might waste a lot
of money on beer and women and gambling, or get into
trouble by fighting, he sent one of his servants to Paris secretly, to spy out what Laertes was doing. One day Hamlet
came upon Polonius's daughter Ophelia. He behaved so
oddly he frightened her. Indeed"—I was fumbling for words
to express the dubious quality of Hamlet's madness—"the
chief and many others had also noticed that when Hamlet
talked one could understand the words but not what they
meant. Many people thought that he had become mad." My

audience suddenly became much more attentive. "The great chief wanted to know what was wrong with Hamlet, so he sent for two of Hamlet's age mates [school friends would have taken long explanation] to talk to Hamlet and find out what troubled his heart. Hamlet, seeing that they had been bribed by the chief to betray him, told them nothing. Polonius, however, insisted that Hamlet was mad because he had been forbidden to see Ophelia, whom he loved."

"Why," inquired a bewildered voice, "should anyone be-   51
witch Hamlet on that account?"

"Bewitch him?"   52

"Yes, only witchcraft can make anyone mad, unless, of   53
course, one sees the beings that lurk in the forest."

I stopped being a storyteller, took out my notebook and   54
demanded to be told more about these two causes of madness. Even while they spoke and I jotted notes, I tried to calculate the effect of this new factor on the plot. Hamlet had
not been exposed to the beings that lurk in the forests. Only
his relatives in the male line could bewitch him. Barring relatives not mentioned by Shakespeare, it had to be Claudius
who was attempting to harm him. And, of course, it was.

For the moment I staved off questions by saying that the   55
great chief also refused to believe that Hamlet was mad for
the love of Ophelia and nothing else. "He was sure that
something much more important was troubling Hamlet's
heart."

"Now Hamlet's age mates," I continued, "had brought   56
with them a famous storyteller. Hamlet decided to have this
man tell the chief and all his homestead a story about a man
who had poisoned his brother because he desired his
brother's wife and wished to be chief himself. Hamlet was
sure the great chief could not hear the story without making
a sign if he was indeed guilty, and then he would discover
whether his dead father had told him the truth."

The old man interrupted, with deep cunning, "Why   57
should a father lie to his son?" he asked.

I hedged: "Hamlet wasn't sure that it really was his dead   58

father." It was impossible to say anything, in that language,
about devil-inspired visions.

"You mean," he said, "it actually was an omen, and he
knew witches sometimes send false ones. Hamlet was a fool
not to go to one skilled in reading omens and divining the
truth in the first place. A man-who-sees-the-truth could have
told him how his father died, if he really had been poisoned,
and if there was witchcraft in it; then Hamlet could have
called the elders to settle the matter."

The shrewd elder ventured to disagree. "Because his father's brother was a great chief, one-who-sees-the-truth
might therefore have been afraid to tell it. I think it was for
that reason that a friend of Hamlet's father—a witch and an
elder—sent an omen so his friend's son would know. Was the
omen true?"

"Yes," I said, abandoning ghosts and the devil; a witch-
sent omen it would have to be. "It was true, for when the
storyteller was telling his tale before all the homestead, the
great chief rose in fear. Afraid that Hamlet knew his secret he
planned to have him killed."

The stage set of the next bit presented some difficulties of
translation. I began cautiously. "The great chief told Hamlet's mother to find out from her son what he knew. But because a woman's children are always first in her heart, he had
the important elder Polonius hide behind a cloth that hung
against the wall of Hamlet's mother's sleeping hut. Hamlet
started to scold his mother for what she had done."

There was a shocked murmur from everyone. A man
should never scold his mother.

"She called out in fear, and Polonius moved behind the
cloth. Shouting, 'A rat!' Hamlet took his machete and
slashed through the cloth." I paused for dramatic effect. "He
had killed Polonius!"

The old men looked at each other in supreme disgust.
"That Polonius truly was a fool and a man who knew nothing! What child would not know enough to shout, 'It's me!'"
With a pang, I remembered that these people are ardent
hunters, always armed with bow, arrow, and machete; at the

first rustle in the grass an arrow is aimed and ready, and the hunter shouts "Game!" If no human voice answers immediately, the arrow speeds on its way. Like a good hunter Hamlet had shouted, "A rat!"

I rushed in to save Polonius's reputation. "Polonius did speak. Hamlet heard him. But he thought it was the chief and wished to kill him to avenge his father. He had meant to kill him earlier that evening. . . ." I broke down, unable to describe to these pagans, who had no belief in individual afterlife, the difference between dying at one's prayers and dying "unhousell'd, disappointed, unaneled." 66

This time I had shocked my audience seriously. "For a man to raise his hand against his father's brother and the one who has become his father—that is a terrible thing. The elders ought to let such a man be bewitched." 67

I nibbled at my kola nut in some perplexity, then pointed out that after all the man had killed Hamlet's father. 68

"No," pronounced the old man, speaking less to me than to the young men sitting behind the elders. "If your father's brother has killed your father, you must appeal to your father's age mates; *they* may avenge him. No man may use violence against his senior relatives." Another thought struck him. "But if his father's brother had indeed been wicked enough to bewitch Hamlet and make him mad that would be a good story indeed, for it would be his fault that Hamlet, being mad, no longer had any sense and thus was ready to kill his father's brother." 69

There was a murmur of applause. *Hamlet* was again a good story to them, but it no longer seemed quite the same story to me. As I thought over the coming complications of plot and motive, I lost courage and decided to skim over dangerous ground quickly. 70

"The great chief," I went on, "was not sorry that Hamlet had killed Polonius. It gave him a reason to send Hamlet away, with his two treacherous age mates, with letters to a chief of a far country, saying that Hamlet should be killed. But Hamlet changed the writing on their papers, so that the 71 chief killed his age mates instead." I encountered a reproachful glare from one of the men whom I had told undetectable forgery was not merely immoral but beyond human skill. I looked the other way.

"Before Hamlet could return, Laertes came back for his father's funeral. The great chief told him Hamlet had killed Polonius. Laertes swore to kill Hamlet because of this, and because his sister Ophelia, hearing her father had been killed by the man she loved, went mad and drowned in the river."   72

"Have you already forgotten what we told you?" The old man was reproachful. "One cannot take vengeance on a madman; Hamlet killed Polonius in his madness. As for the girl, she not only went mad, she was drowned. Only witches can make people drown. Water itself can't hurt anything. It is merely something one drinks and bathes in."   73

why not?

I began to get cross. "If you don't like the story, I'll stop."   74

The old man made soothing noises and himself poured me some more beer. "You tell the story well, and we are listening. But it is clear that the elders of your country have never told you what the story really means. No, don't interrupt! We believe you when you say your marriage customs are different, or your clothes and weapons. But people are the same everywhere; therefore, there are always witches and it is we, the elders, who know how witches work. We told you it was the great chief who wished to kill Hamlet, and now your own words have proved us right. Who were Ophelia's male relatives?"   75

→ ooo... that's good

"There were only her father and her brother." Hamlet was clearly out of my hands.   76

"There must have been many more; this also you must ask of your elders when you get back to your country. From what you tell us, since Polonius was dead, it must have been Laertes who killed Ophelia, although I do not see the reason for it."   77

We had emptied one pot of beer, and the old men argued the point with slightly tipsy interest. Finally one of them demanded of me, "What did the servant of Polonius say on his return?"   78

With difficulty I recollected Reynaldo and his mission. "I   79
don't think he did return before Polonius was killed."

"Listen," said the elder, "and I will tell you how it was and   80
how your story will go, then you may tell me if I am right.
Polonius knew his son would get into trouble, and so he did.
He had many fines to pay for fighting, and debts from gambling. But he had only two ways of getting money quickly.
One was to marry off his sister at once, but it is difficult to
find a man who will marry a woman desired by the son of a
chief. For if the chief's heir commits adultery with your wife,
what can you do? Only a fool calls a case against a man who
will someday be his judge. Therefore Laertes had to take the
second way: he killed his sister by witchcraft, drowning her so
he could secretly sell her body to the witches."

I raised an objection. "They found her body and buried it.   81
Indeed Laertes jumped into the grave to see his sister once
more—so, you see, the body was truly there. Hamlet, who
had just come back, jumped in after him."

"What did I tell you?" The elder appealed to the others.   82
"Laertes was up to no good with his sister's body. Hamlet
prevented him, because the chief's heir, like a chief, does not
wish any other man to grow rich and powerful. Laertes
would be angry, because he would have killed his sister without benefit to himself. In our country he would try to kill
Hamlet for that reason. Is this not what happened?"

"More or less," I admitted. "When the great chief found   83
Hamlet was still alive, he encouraged Laertes to try to kill
Hamlet and arranged a fight with machetes between them.
In the fight both the young men were wounded to death.
Hamlet's mother drank the poisoned beer that the chief
meant for Hamlet in case he won the fight. When he saw his
mother die of poison, Hamlet, dying, managed to kill his fa-
ther's brother with his machete."

"You see, I was right!" exclaimed the elder.   84

"That was a very good story," added the old man, "and   85
you told it with very few mistakes. There was just one more

error, at the very end. The poison Hamlet's mother drank was obviously meant for the survivor of the fight, whichever it was. If Laertes had won, the great chief would have poisoned him, for no one would know that he arranged Hamlet's death. Then, too, he need not fear Laertes' witchcraft; it takes a strong heart to kill one's only sister by witchcraft.

"Sometime," concluded the old man, gathering his ragged toga about him, "you must tell us some more stories of your country. We, who are elders, will instruct you in their true meaning, so that when you return to your own land your elders will see that you have not been sitting in the bush, but among those who know things and who have taught you wisdom."

For Study and Discussion

QUESTIONS FOR RESPONSE

1. What has been your experience reading *Hamlet*? What aspects of the play confuse you?
2. Have you ever tried to tell a story to a group of people who interrupted and misunderstood you? How did you react to the situation?

QUESTIONS ABOUT PURPOSE

1. What belief convinces Bohannan that *Hamlet* is universally intelligible?
2. How does her attempt to tell Hamlet's story prove that her friend was right: "one can easily misinterpret the universal by misunderstanding the particular"?

QUESTIONS ABOUT AUDIENCE

1. How does Bohannan translate concepts—*chief* for *king*, *farm* for *castle*—to help her African audience understand her story?
2. How does she reveal her frustration and anger in trying to tell her audience what she thought was a simple story?

QUESTIONS ABOUT STRATEGIES

1. How does Bohannan's discussion of Hamlet's *madness* reveal differences in the English and African culture?
2. Ironically, what feature of her version of Hamlet's story convinces her African audience that "people are the same everywhere"?

QUESTIONS FOR DISCUSSION

1. How does Bohannan's audience interpret Hamlet's story? What convinces them that Bohannan's elders have not told her the true story?
2. How do the elders suggest that Hamlet should have resolved his conflict with Claudius? What does this solution suggest about the presumed superiority of the English culture?

WITI IHIMAERA

Witi Ihimaera was born in 1944 in Gisborne, New Zealand, and educated at the University of Auckland. After working as a newspaper reporter, he accepted a position as a diplomatic officer in New Zealand's Ministry of Foreign Affairs. He began writing to document the two landscapes of New Zealand, the Maori (the indigenous people) and the Pakeha (the Europeans). In particular, he wanted to ensure that "my Maori people were taken into account." His short stories have been collected in *Pounamu, Pounamu* (1972) and *The New Net Goes Fishing* (1976). His novels include *Tangi* (1973) and *Whanau* (1974). He has also edited a collection of Maori writing, *Into the World of Light* (1978). "His First Ball," reprinted from *Dear Miss Mansfield* (1989), recalls a similar story by a Pakeha New Zealander who spent most of her life in England, Katherine Mansfield.

His First Ball

J UST WHY IT was that he, Tuta Wharepapa, should receive the invitation was a mystery to him. Indeed, when it came, in an envelope bearing a very imposing crest, his mother mistook it for something entirely different—notice of a traffic misdemeanour, a summons perhaps, or even worse, an overdue account. She fingered it gingerly, holding it as far away from her body as possible—just in case a pair of hands came out to grab her fortnightly cheque—and said, "Here, Tuta. It must be a bill." She thrust it quickly at her son before he could get away and, wriggling her fingers to get rid of the taint, waited for him to open it.

[handwritten margin note: this says a lot about him]

1

"Hey—" Tuta said as he stared down at the card. His face 2
dropped such a long way that his mother—her name was
Coral—became alarmed. Visions of pleading in court on his
behalf flashed through her mind. "Oh, Tuta, how bad is it?"
she said as she prepared to defend her son against all-comers.
But Tuta remained speechless and Coral had to grab the card
from his hands. "What's this?" she asked. The card was edged
with gold:

The Aide-de-Camp in Waiting
Is Desired By Their Excellencies

"Oh, Tuta, what have you done?" Coral said. But Tuta was
still in a state of shock. Then, "Read on, Mum," he said.

To Invite Mr Tuta Wharepapa
To A Dance At Government House

Coral's voice drifted away into speechlessness like her son's.
Then she compressed her lips and jabbed Tuta with an elbow.
"I'm tired of your jokes," she said. "It's not my joke, Mum,"
Tuta responded. "I know you, Tuta," Coral continued.
"True, Mum, honest. One of the boys must be having me
on." Coral looked at Tuta, unconvinced. "Who'd want to
have *you* at their flash party?" she asked. "Just wait till I get
the joker who sent this," Tuta swore to himself. Then Coral
began to laugh. "You? Go to Government House? You don't
even know how to bow!" And she laughed and laughed so
much at the idea that Tuta couldn't take it. "Where are you
going, Your Highness?" Coral asked. "To find out who sent
this," Tuta replied, waving the offending invitation in her
face. "By the time I finish with him—or her—" because he
suddenly realised Coral herself might have sent it—"they'll
be laughing on the other side of their face." With that, he
strode out of the kitchen. "Oh, Tuta?" he heard Coral call, all
la-di-da, "If you ore gooing pahst Government Howse please
convay may regahrds to—" and she burst out laughing again.

Tuta leapt on to his motorbike and, over the rest of the 3
day, roared around the city calling on his mates from the factory. "It wasn't me, Tuta," Crazy-Joe said as he sank a red

ball in the billiard saloon, "but I tell you, man, you'll look great in a suit." Nor was it Blackjack over at the garage, who said, "But listen, mate, when you go grab some of those Diplo number plates for me, ay?" And neither was it Des, who moonlighted as Desirée Dawn at the strip club, or Sheree, who worked part time at the pinball parlour. "You couldn't take a partner, could you?" Desirée Dawn breathed hopefully. "Nah, you wouldn't be able to fit on my bike," Tuta said—apart from which he didn't think a six-foot transvestite with a passion for pink boas and slit satin dresses would enjoy it all that much. By the end of the day Tuta was no wiser, and when he arrived at Bigfoot's house and found his mate waiting for him in a tiara, he knew that word was getting around. Then it came to him that perhaps the invitation was real after all. Gloria Simmons would know—she was the boss's secretary and knew some lords.

"Oh," Mrs. Simmons whispered reverently as Tuta handed her the crested envelope. She led Tuta into the sitting-room. "It looks real," she said as she held it to the light. Then she opened the envelope and, incredulous, asked, "*You* received this?" Tuta nodded. "You didn't just pick it up on the street," Mrs. Simmons continued, "and put your name on it?" Offended, Tuta shook his head, saying "You don't think I want to go, do you?" Mrs. Simmons pursed her lips and said, "Perhaps there's another Tuta Wharepapa, and you got his invitation in error." And Mrs. Simmons's teeth smiled and said, "In that case, let me ring Government House and let them know." With that, Mrs. Simmons went into another room, where Tuta heard her dialling. Then *her* voice went all la-di-da too as she trilled, "Ooo, Gahverment Howse? May ay speak to the Aide-de-Camp? Ooo, har do yoo do. So sorry to trouble you but ay am ringing to advayse you—" Tuta rolled his eyes—how come everybody he told about the invitation got infected by some kind of disease! Then he became acutely aware that Mrs. Simmons had stopped talking. He heard her gasp. He heard her say in her own lingo, "You mean to tell me that this is for real? That you people actually sent an invite to a—a—boy who packs batteries in a factory?" She put down the telephone and returned to the sitting-room. She was pale but calm as she said, "Tuta dear, difficult though this may be, can you remember the woman who came to look at the factory about two months ago?" Tuta knitted his eyebrows. "Yeah, I think so. That must have been when we opened the new extension." Mrs. Simmons closed her eyes. "The woman, Tuta. The woman." Tuta thought again. "Oh yeah, there *was* a lady, come to think of it, a horsey-looking lady who—" Mrs. Simmons interrupted him. "Tuta, dear, that lady was the wife of the Governor-General."

Dazed, Tuta said, "But she didn't say who she was." And 5 he listened as Mrs. Simmons explained that Mrs. Governor-General had been very impressed by the workers at the factory and that Tuta was being invited to represent them. "Of course you will have to go," Mrs. Simmons said. "One does not say 'No' to the Crown." Then Mrs. Simmons got up and telephoned Tuta's mother. "Coral? Gloria here. Listen, about Tuta, you and I should talk about what is required. What for? Why, when he goes to the ball of course! Now—" *Me? Go to a ball?* Tuta thought. *With all those flash people, all those flash ladies with their crowns and diamonds and emeralds? Not bloody likely—Bigfoot can go, he's already got a tiara, yeah. Not me. They'll have to drag me there. I'm not going. Not me. No fear. No WAY.* But he knew, when he saw the neighbours waiting for him at home that, of course, his mother had already flapped her mouth to everybody. "Oh yes," she was telling the neighbours when Tuta walked in, "it was delivered by special messenger. This dirty big black car came and a man, must have been a flunkey, knocked on the door and—" Then Coral saw Tuta and, "Oh Tuta," she cried, opening her arms to him as if she hadn't seen him for days.

After that, of course, there was no turning back. The boss 6 from the factory called to put the hard word on Tuta. Mrs. Simmons RSVPeed by telephone and—"Just in case, Tuta dear"—by letter and, once that was done, he had to go. The rest of his mates at the factory got into the act, also, cancelling the airline booking he made to get out of town and, from thereoñ in, followed him everywhere. "Giz a break, fellas," Tuta pleaded as he tried to get out, cajole or bribe himself out of the predicament. But Crazy-Joe only said, "Lissen, if you don't get there then I'm—" and he drew a finger across his throat, and Blackjack said, "Hey, man, I know a man who knows a man who can get us a Rolls for the night—" and Bigfoot just handed him the tiara. And boy, did Coral ever turn out to be the walking compendium of What To Do And How To Do It At A Ball. "Gloria says that we have to take you to a tailor so you can hire a suit. Not just any suit and none of your purple numbers either. A black *conservative* suit. And then we have to get you a bowtie and you have to wear black shoes—so I reckon a paint job on your brown ones will do. You've got a white shirt, thank goodness, but we'll have to get some new socks—calf length so that when you sit down people won't see your hairy legs. Now, what else? Oh yes, I've already made an appointment for you to go to have your hair cut, no buts, Tuta, and the boys are taking you there, so don't think you're going to wriggle out of it. By the time that dance comes around we'll have you decked out like the Prince of Wales—" which was just what Tuta was afraid of.

why must we fit this image?

But that was only the beginning. Not only did his appearance have to be radically altered, but his manners had to be brushed up also—and Mrs. Simmons was the first to have a go. "Tuta dear," she said when he knocked on her door. "Do come in. Yes, take your boots off but on THE NIGHT, the shoes stay *on*. Please, come this way. No, Tuta, *after* me, just a few steps behind. Never barge, Tuta and don't shamble along. Be PROUD, Tuta, be HAUGHTY"—and she showed him how to put his nose in the air. Tuta followed her, his nose so high that he almost tripped, into the dining-room. "Voila!" she said. "Ay?" Tuta answered. Mrs. Simmons then realised that this was going to be very difficult. "I said, 'Ta ra!'" She had set the table with a beautiful cloth—and it appeared to be laid with thousands of knives, forks and spoons. "This is what it will be like at the ball," she explained. "Oh boy," Tuta said. "Now, because I'm a lady you must escort

7

NICE diction

me to my seat," Mrs. Simmons said. "Huh? Can't you walk there yourself?" Tuta asked. "Just *do* it," Mrs. Simmons responded dangerously, "and *don't* push me all the way under the table, Tuta, just to the edge will do—" and then, under her breath "—Patience, Gloria dear, *patienza*." Once seated, she motioned Tuta to a chair opposite her. "Gee, thanks," he said. Mrs. Simmons paused, thoughtfully, and said, "Tuta dear, when in doubt don't say *anything*. Just shut your mouth." She shivered, but really, the boy would only understand common language, "—and keep it shut." Then she smiled. "Now follow every action that I make." Exaggerating the movements for Tuta's benefit, Mrs. Simmons said, "First, take up the spoon. No, not that one, *that* one. That's for your soup, that's for the second course, that's for the third course, that's for the fourth—" Tuta looked helplessly at her. "Can't I use the same knives and things all the time?" he asked. "*Never*," Mrs. Simmons shivered. "Well, what's all these courses for?" Tuta objected. "Why don't they just stick all the kai on the table at once?" Mrs. Simmons deigned not to answer. Instead she motioned to the glasses, saying, "Now *this* is for white wine, this for red wine, this for champagne and this for cognac." Tuta sighed, saying "No beer? Thought as much." Refusing to hear him, Mrs. Simmons proceeded, "You sip your wine just like you sip the soup. Like *so*," and she showed him. "No, Tuta, not too fast. And leave the bowl *on* the table, *don't* put it to your lips. No, *don't* slurp. Oh my goodness. Very GOOD, Tuta! Now wipe your lips with the napkin." Tuta looked puzzled. "Ay?" he asked. "The paper napkin on your lap," Mrs. Simmons said. "This hanky thing?" Tuta responded. "Why, Tuta!" Mrs. Simmons's teeth said, "How clever of you to work that out. Shall we proceed to the second course? Good!" Mrs. Simmons felt quite sure that Professor Higgins didn't have it *this* bad.

Then, of course, there was the matter of learning how to 8 dance—not hot rock but slow *slow* dancing, holding a girl, "You know," Mrs. Simmons said, "*together*," adding, "and young ladies at the ball are never allowed to decline." So Tuta made a date with Desirée Dawn after hours at the club.

Desirée was just overwhelmed to be asked for advice and told her friends Alexis Dynamite and Chantelle Derrier to help her. "Lissun, honey," Desirée said as she cracked her gum. "No matter what the dance is, there's always a basic rhythm." Chantelle giggled and said, "Yeah, very basic." Ignoring her, Desirée hauled Tuta on to the floor, did a few jeté's and, once she had limbered up, said, "Now *you* lead," and "Oo, honey, I didn't know you were so masterful." Alexis fluttered her false eyelashes and, "You two don't need music at *all*," she whispered. Nevertheless, Alexis ran the tape and the music boomed across the club floor. "This isn't ball music," Tuta said as he heard the raunch scream out of the saxes. "How do *you* know?" Chantelle responded. And Tuta had the feeling that he wasn't going to learn how to dance in any way except improperly. "Lissun," Desirée said, "Alexis and I will show you. Move your butt over here, Lexie. Now, Tuta honey, just watch. Can ya hear the rhythum? Well you go *boom* and a *boom* and a *boom boom boom*." And Alexis screamed and yelled, "Desirée, he wants to dance with the girl, not *make* her in the middle of the floor." And Chantelle only made matters worse by laughing, "Yeah, you stupid slut, you want him to end up in prison like you?" At which Desirée gasped, walked over to Chantelle, peeled off both Chantelle's false eyelashes, said, "Can you see better? Good," and lammed her one in the mouth. As he exited, Tuta knew he would have better luck with Sheree at the pinball parlour—she used to be good at roller skating and could even do the splits in mid-air.

So it went on. The fitting at the tailor's was duly accomplished ("Hmmmmmnnnn," the tailor said as he measured Tuta up. "Your shoulders are too wide, your hips too large, you have shorter legs than you should have but—Hmmmmmnnnn"), his hair was trimmed to within an inch of propriety, and he painted his brown shoes black. His lessons continued with Mrs. Simmons, Tuta's mother, the workers from the factory—even the boss—all pitching in to assist Tuta in the etiquette required. For instance: "If you're talking you ask about the weather. This is called polite conversation. You say "Isn't it lovely?" to everything, even if it isn't.

You always say "Yes" if you're offered something, even if you don't want it. The man with the medals is *not* the waiter. He is His Excellency. The lady who looks like a horse is not in drag and you should *not* ask if her tiara fell off the same truck as Bigfoot's."

Then, suddenly it was time for Tuta to go to the ball. "Yes, Mum," he said to Coral as she fussed around him with a clothes brush, "I've got a hanky, I've brushed my teeth three times already, the invite is in my pocket—" And when Tuta stepped out the door the whole world was there—the boss, Mrs. Simmons, Crazy-Joe, Blackjack, Bigfoot and others from the factory, Desirée Dawn and the neighbours. "Don't let us down," the boss said. "Not too much food on the fork," Mrs. Simmons instructed. "The third boom is the one that does it," Desirée Dawn called. "Don't forget the Diplo plates," Blackjack whispered. "And don't drink too much of the beer," Coral said. Then, there was the car, a Jaguar festooned with white ribbons and two small dolls on the bonnet. "It's a ball I'm off to," Tuta said sarcastically, "not a wedding." Blackjack shrugged his shoulders. "Best I could do, mate, and this beauty was just sitting there outside the church and—" He got in and started the motor. Tuta sat in the back and, suddenly, Bigfoot and Crazy-Joe were in either side. "The boss's orders," they said. "We deliver you to the door or else—" Outside, Tuta saw the boss draw a line across their necks. The car drew away and as it did so, Mrs. Simmons gave a small scream. "Oh my goodness, I forgot to tell Tuta that if Nature calls he should not use the bushes," she said.

Looking back, Tuta never quite understood how he ever survived that journey. At one point a police car drew level on the motorway, but when they looked over at the Jaguar and saw Tuta he could just imagine their disbelief, Nah. Couldn't possibly . . . Nah. His head was whirling with all the etiquette he had learnt and all the instructions he had to remember. He trembled, squirmed, palpitated and sweated all over the seat. Then he was there, and Blackjack was showing the invitation, and the officer at the gate was looking doubtfully at the wedding decorations, and then "Proceed ahead, sir," the officer said. *What a long drive,* Tuta thought. *What a big palace. And look at all those flash people. And they're all going in.* "Well, mate," Blackjack said, "Good luck. Look for us in the car park." And Crazy-Joe said, "Hey, give the missus a whirl for me, ay?" and with that, and a squeal of tires (Blackjack was always such a show-off), they were gone.

He was alone. Him. Tuta Wharepapa. Standing there. At the entrance way. Inside he heard music and the laughter of the guests. Then someone grabbed his arm and said, "Come along!" and before he knew it he was inside and being propelled along a long hallway. And the young woman who had grabbed him was suddenly pulled away by her companion, and Tuta was alone again. *Oh boy,* he thought. *Look at this red carpet.* He felt quite sure that the paint was running off his shoes and that there were great big black footmarks all the way to where he was now standing. Then a voice BOOMED ahead, and Tuta saw that there was a line of people in front and they were handing their invitations in to the bouncer. Tuta joined them. The bouncer was very old and very dignified—he looked, though, as if he should have been retired from the job years ago. *Nah,* Tuta thought. *He couldn't be a bouncer. Must be a toff.* The toff looked Tuta up and down and thrust out his white-gloved hand. "I got an invitation," Tuta said. "True. I got one." The toff read the card and his eyebrows arched. "Your name?" he BOOMED. "Tuta." Couldn't he read? Then the toff turned away in the direction of a huge ballroom that stretched right to the end of the world. The room seemed to be hung with hundreds of chandeliers and *thousands* of people were either dancing or standing around the perimeter. There were steps leading down to the ballroom and, at the bottom, was a man wearing medals and a woman whose tiara wasn't as sparkly as Bigfoot's—*them.* And Tuta felt *sure,* when the Major-Domo—for that was who the toff was—stepped forward and opened his mouth to announce him, that *everybody* must have heard him BOOM—

"Your Excellencies, Mr. Tutae Tockypocka."

Tuta looked for a hole to disappear into. He tried to   14
backpedal down the hallway but there were people behind
him. "No, you got it wrong," he said between clenched teeth
to the Major-Domo. "Tutae's a rude word." But the Major-
Domo simply sniffed, handed back the invitation, and motioned Tuta down the stairs. Had *they* heard? In trembling
anticipation Tuta approached the Governor-General. "Mr.
Horrynotta?" the Governor-General smiled. "Splendid that
you were able to come along. Dear? Here's Mr. Tutae." And
in front of him was Mrs. Governor-General. "Mr. Forri-
moppa, how kind of you to come. May I call you Tutae?
Please let me introduce you to Lord Wells." And Lord Wells,
too. "Mr. Mopperuppa, quite a mouthful, what. Not so with
Tutae, what?" *You don't know the half of it,* Tuta thought
gloomily. And then Mrs. Governor-General just *had* to, did-
n't she, giggle and pronounce to all and sundry, "Everybody,
you must meet Mr. Tutae." And that's who Tuta became all
that evening. "Have you met Mr. Tutae yet? No? Mr. Tutae,
this is Mr.—" And Tuta would either shake hands or do a stiff
little bow and look around for that hole in the floor. He once
made an attempt to explain what "tutae" was but heard Mrs.
Simmons's voice: "If in doubt, Tuta, *don't.*" So instead he
would draw attention away from that word by asking about
the weather. "Do you think it will rain?" he would ask. "Oh,
not inside, Mr. Tutae!"—and the word got around that Mr.
Tutae was such a wit, so funny, so quaint, that he soon found
himself exactly where he didn't want to be—at the centre of
attention. In desperation, he asked every woman to dance.
"Why, certainly, Mr. Tutae!" they said, because ladies never
said no. So he danced with them all—a fat lady, a slim lady, a
lady whose bones cracked all the time—and, because he was
nervous, he went *boom* at every third step, and *that* word got
around too. And as the Governor-General waltzed past he
shouted, "Well done, Tutae, jolly good show."

No matter what he tried to do Tuta could never get away   15
from being at the centre of the crowd or at the centre of attention. Instead of being gratified, however, Tuta became
more embarrassed. Everybody seemed to laugh at his every

word, even when it wasn't funny, or to accept his way of dancing because it was so *daring*. It seemed as if he could get away with anything. At the same time, Tuta suddenly realised that he was the only Maori there and that perhaps people were mocking him. He wasn't a real person to them, but *hmm* ... rather an Entertainment. Even when buffet dinner was served, the crowd still seemed to mock him, pressing in upon him with "Have some hors d'oeuvres, Mr. Tutae. Some *escalope* of veal, perhaps? You must try the pâté de foie gras! A slice of *jambon*? What about some langouste? Oh, the raspberry gâteau is just divine!" It was as if the crowd knew very well his ignorance of such delicacies and, by referring to them, was putting him down. In desperation Tuta tried some caviar. "Oh, Mr. Tutae, we can see that you just love caviar!" Tuta gave a quiet, almost dangerous, smile. "Yes," he said. "I *II* think it's just divine."

So it went on. But then, just after the buffet, a Very Im- *16* portant Person arrived and, relieved, Tuta found himself deserted. Interested, he watched as the one who had just arrived became the centre of attention. "It always happens this way," a voice said behind Tuta. "I wouldn't worry about it." Startled, Tuta turned around and saw a huge fern. "Before you," the fern continued, "it was me." Then Tuta saw that a young woman was sitting behind the fern. "I'm not worried," he said to her, "I'm glad." The woman sniffed and said, "You certainly looked as if you were enjoying it." Tuta parted the fronds to get a good look at the woman's face—it was a pleasant face, one which could be pretty if it didn't *ouch* frown so much. "Shift over," Tuta said. "I'm coming to join you." He sidled around the plant and sat beside her. "My name is—" he began. "Yes, I know," the woman said quickly, "Mr. Tutae." Tuta shook his head vigorously, "*No*, not Tutae. Tuta." The woman looked at him curiously and, "Is there a difference?" she asked. "You better believe it," Tuta said. "Oh—" the woman sniffed. "I'm Joyce."

The music started to play again. Joyce squinted her eyes *17* and Tuta sighed, "Why don't you put on your glasses?" Joyce squealed, "How did you know?" before popping them on and parting the fronds. "I'm a sociology student," Joyce muttered. "Don't you think people's behaviour is just amaz-ing? I mean ay-*may*zing?" Tuta shrugged his shoulders and wondered if Joyce was looking at something he couldn't see. "I mean," Joyce continued, "look at them out there, just *look* at them. This could be India under the Raj. All this British Imperial graciousness and yet the carpet is being pulled from right beneath their feet." Puzzled, Tuta tried to see the ball through Joyce's eyes, but failed. "Ah well," Joyce sighed. Then she put her hand out to Tuta so that he could shake it, saying "Goodbye, Mr. Tuta." Tuta looked at her and, "Are you going?" he asked. "Oh no," Joyce said, "I'm staying here until everybody leaves. But *you* must go out and reclaim at-tention." Tuta laughed. "That new guy's welcome," he said. "But don't you want to fulfil their expectations?" Joyce asked. Tuta paused, and "If that means what I think it means, no," he said. "Good," Joyce responded, "You are perfectly capable of beating them at their own game. Good luck."

Then, curious, Tuta asked, "What did you mean when you said that before me it had been *you?*" Joyce shifted uneasily, took off her glasses and said, "Well, I'm not a Maori, but I thought it would have been obvious—" *Oh,* Tuta thought, *she's a plain Jane and people have been making fun of her.* "But that doesn't matter to me," Tuta said gallantly. "Really?" Joyce asked. "I'll prove it," Tuta said. "How about having the next dance." Joyce gasped, "Are you *sure?*" Taken aback, Tuta said, "Of course, I'm sure." And Joyce said, "But are you *sure* you're sure!" To show her, Tuta stood up and took her hand. Joyce sighed and shook her head. "Well, don't say I didn't warn you." Then she stood up . . . and up . . . and UP.

"Oh," Tuta said as he parted the fronds to look up at Joyce's face. She must have been six feet six at least. He and Joyce regarded each other miserably. Joyce bit her lip. *Well you asked for it,* Tuta thought. "Come on," he said, "let's have a good time." He reached up, grabbed her waist, put his face against her chest, and they waltzed into the middle of the floor. There, Tuta stood as high on his toes as possible.

18

19

Oh, why did I come? he thought. Then the music ended and he took Joyce back to the fern. "I'm sorry I'm such a bad dancer," she apologised. "I always took the man's part at school." Tuta smiled at her. "That's no sweat. Well—" And he was just about to leave her when he suddenly realised that after all he and Joyce were both outsiders really. And it came to him that, bloody hell, if you could not join them—as if he would really want to do *that*—then, yes, he could beat them if he wanted to. Not by giving in to them, but by being strong enough to stand up to them. Dance, perhaps, but using his own steps. Listen, also, not to the music of the band but to the music in his head. He owed it, after all, to generous but silly wonderful mixed-up Mum, Mrs. Simmons, Desirée Dawn, and the boys—Crazy-Joe, Blackjack and Bigfoot—who were out *there* but wanting to know enough to get *in*. But they needed to come in on their own terms— that's what they would have to learn—as the real people they were and not as carbon copies of the people already on the inside. Once they learnt that, *oh, world, watch out, for your walls will come down in a flash, like Jericho.*

"Look," Tuta said, "how about another dance!" Joyce   20 looked at him in disbelief. "You're a sucker for punishment, aren't you!" she muttered. "Why?" Tuta bowed, mockingly. "Well, for one thing, it would be just divine." At that, Joyce let out a peal of laughter. She stood up again. "Thank you," Joyce whispered. Then, "You know, this is my first ball." And Tuta smiled and "It's *my* first ball too," he said. "From now on, balls like these will never be the same again." He took her hand and the band began to wail a sweet but *oh-so-mean* saxophone solo as he led her on to the floor.

COMMENT ON
"HIS FIRST BALL"

"His First Ball" is a vivid and humorous comparison of cross-cultural misunderstanding. Tuta Wharepapa, a Maori factory worker, is invited to a formal ball thrown by the British government of New Zealand. With coaching from his friends,

Tuta polishes his manners and dancing, trying to transform himself into something he is not—a British gentleman. When he arrives at the ball, the British treat him as entertainment rather than as a guest. At the end of this colonial *Pygmalion,* Tuta realizes that he must be his own person—not the creation of the dominant culture.

Comparison and Contrast as a Writing Strategy

1. Select a place in your childhood neighborhood—perhaps a garden, a playground, or a movie theater. Then, in an essay addressed to your writing class, write a short comparison of the way the place used to be and the way it is now. Consider the example of Mark Twain's "Two Views of the River" as you compare your childhood and adult visions. Consider also what you have learned about the place or about yourself by making the comparison. That lesson should help control your decisions about purpose and audience.

2. Select two people who exhibit different styles. Then, like Paco Underhill, compare their strengths and weaknesses. Include information on how they might see each other. Cite biographical information that accounts for their similarities and differences.

3. Conduct some research on the conversational patterns in your home (or dormitory) and in your classroom. Keep track of who talks, what they talk about, and how they use conversation—for example, to make friends, to report information, to win approval. Keep track of who doesn't talk and in what situations they are likely to stay silent. Then write an essay in which you compare the patterns of home and school conversation.

4. In "A Tale of Two Divorces," Anne Roiphe contrasts two women's reaction to the same situation. Select a subject you know well—a family celebration—and then compare your version with the way it is represented on television.

5. Write an essay comparing the way two magazines or newspapers cover the same story. Or like Laura Bohannan, compare the way a story might be told in one culture with the way it might be told in another. For example, how would you compare the way the American media and the African media might tell the story of America's last presidential election?

6. Compare and contrast arguments on both sides of a controversial issue such as welfare reform or gun control. Such issues produce controversy because there are legitimate arguments on each side. They also produce controversy because people can simplify them in slogans (Reading is good; television is bad). Select two slogans that present the opposing sides of the controversy you are writing about. Compare and contrast the assumptions, evidence, and logic of both slogans. Like Sarah Vowell, use your research to advance a larger argument about cultural differences.

DIVISION
AND
CLASSIFICATION

Division and **classification** are mental processes that often work together. When you *divide,* you separate something (a college, a city) into sections (departments, neighborhoods). When you *classify,* you place examples of something (restaurants, jobs) into categories or classes (restaurants: moderately expensive, very expensive; jobs: unskilled, semiskilled, and skilled).

When you divide, you move downward from a concept to the subunits of that concept. When you classify, you move upward from specific examples to classes or categories that share a common characteristic. For example, you could *divide* a television news program into subunits such as news, features, editorials, sports, and weather. And you could *classify* some element of that program—such as the editorial commentator on the six o'clock news—according to his or her style, knowledge, and trustworthiness. You can use either division or classification singly, depending on your purpose, but most of the time you will probably use them together when you are writing a classification essay. First you might identify the subunits in a college sports program—football, basketball, hockey, volleyball, tennis; then you could classify them according to their budgets—most money budgeted for football, the least budgeted for volleyball.

PURPOSE

When you write a classification essay, your chief purpose is to *explain*. You might want to explain an established method for organizing information, such as the Library of Congress system, or a new plan for arranging data, such as the Internal Revenue Service's latest schedule for itemizing tax deductions. On one level, your purpose in such an essay is simply to show how the system works. At a deeper level, your purpose is to define, analyze, and justify the organizing principle that underlies the system.

You can also write a classification essay to *entertain* or to *persuade*. If you classify to entertain, you have an opportunity to be clever and witty. If you classify to persuade, you have a chance to be cogent and forceful. If you want to entertain, you might concoct an elaborate scheme for classifying fools, pointing out the distinguishing features of each category and giving particularly striking examples of each type. But if you want to persuade, you could explain how some new or controversial plan, such as the metric system or congressional redistricting, is organized, pointing out how the schemes use new principles to identify and organize information. Again, although you may give your readers a great deal of information in such an essay, your main purpose is to persuade them that the new plan is better than the old one.

AUDIENCE

As with any writing assignment, when you write a classification essay, you need to think carefully about what your readers already know and what they need to get from your writing. If you're writing on a new topic (social patterns in a primitive society) or if you're explaining a specialized system of classification (the botanist's procedure for identifying plants), your readers need precise definitions and plenty of illustrations for each subcategory. If your readers already know about your subject and the system it uses for classification (the movies' G, PG, PG–13, R, and NC–17 rating codes), then you don't need to give them an extensive demonstration. In that kind of writing situation, you might want to sketch the system briefly to refresh your readers' memories but then move on, using examples of specific movies to analyze whether the system really works.

like?

You also need to think about how your readers might use the classification system that you explain in your essay. If you're classifying rock musicians, your readers are probably going to regard the system you create as something self-enclosed—interesting and amusing, perhaps something to quibble about, but not something they're likely to use in their everyday lives. On the other hand, if you write an essay classifying stereo equipment, your readers may want to use your system when they shop. For the first audience, you can use an informal approach to classification, dividing your subject into interesting subcategories and illustrating them with vivid examples. For the other audience, you need to be careful and strict in your approach, making sure you divide your topic into all its possible classes and illustrating each class with concrete examples.

how do you decide

STRATEGIES

When you write a classification essay, your basic strategy for organization should be to *divide your subject* into major categories that exhibit a common trait, then subdivide those categories into smaller units. Next, *arrange your categories* into a sequence that shows a logical or a dramatic progression. Finally, *define each of your categories*. First, show how each category is different from the others; then discuss its most vivid examples.

To make this strategy succeed, you must be sure that your classification system is *consistent, complete, emphatic,* and *significant*. Here is a method for achieving this goal. First, when you divide your subject into categories, *apply the same principle of selection to each class*. You may find this hard to do if you're trying to explain a system that someone else has already established but that is actually inconsistent. You have undoubtedly discovered that record stores use overlapping and inconsistent categories. CDs by Shania Twain, for example, may be found in sections labeled *country, pop,* and *female vocal*. You can avoid such tangles if you create and control your own classification system.

For instance, James H. Austin classifies "four kinds of chance." By contrast, the other four writers in this section explain existing systems of classification. In "Shades of Black" Mary Mebane classifies the arbitrary and unfair assessment of students by color and class. In "Modern Friendships," Phillip Lopate classifies friendships according to age. In "Democracy for All?" James Q. Wilson classifies the conditions necessary for democracy. And in "The Dramaturgy of Death," Garry Wills classifies the fourteen motives for capital punishment.

After you have divided your subject into separate and consistent categories, *make sure your division is complete*. The simplest kind of division separates a subject into two categories: A and Not-A (for example, conformists and nonconformists). This kind of division, however, is rarely encouraged. It allows you to tell your readers about category A (conformists), but you won't tell them much about Not-A (nonconformists). For this reason, you should try to exhaust your subject by finding at least three separate categories and by acknowledging any examples that don't fit into the system. When an author writes a formal classification essay, like Phillip Lopate in this section, he or she tries to be definitive—

to include everything significant. Or if an author realizes that his or her divisions do not exhaust the subject, he or she may, like Garry Wills, admit that the categories may conflict with each other on one level and reinforce each other on another level.

Once you have completed your process of division, *arrange your categories and examples in an emphatic order.* Lopate arranges his categories of friendship from childhood to adulthood. Austin arranges his classification of chance from blind luck to personal sensibility. Mebane arranges her categories into increasingly subtle codes of class and color. Wilson arranges the conditions for democracy from the most obvious—*isolation*—to the most complex—*tradition.* The authors of these essays reveal the principal purpose underlying their classification schemes: to show variety in similarity, to challenge the arbitrariness of an established system, and to point out how concepts change.

Finally, *you need to show the significance of your system of classification.* The strength of the classification process is that you can use it to analyze a subject in any number of ways. Its weakness is that you can use it to subdivide a subject into all kinds of trivial or pointless categories. You can classify people by their educational backgrounds, their work experience, or their significant achievements. You can also classify them by their shoe size, the kind of socks they wear, or their tastes in ice cream. Notice that when Mary Mebane explains her classification system, she questions the social and psychological impact it has on self-esteem, and that Garry Wills classifies the historical reasons for capital punishment in order to demonstrate its ineffectiveness.

USING DIVISION AND CLASSIFICATION IN PARAGRAPHS

Here are two division-and-classification paragraphs. The first is written by a professional writer and is followed by an analysis. The second is written by a student writer and is followed by questions.

WENDELL BERRY
Conservation Is Good Work

Divides conservation into three categories:
1. preservation of wild or "scenic"
2. conservation of natural resources
3. limit, stop, or remedy abuses

There are, as nearly as I can make out, three kinds of conservation currently operating. The first is the preservation of places that are grandly wild or "scenic" or in some other way spectacular. The second is what is called "conservation of natural resources"—That is, of the things of nature that we intend to use: soil, water, timber, and minerals. The third is what you might call industrial troubleshooting: the attempt to limit or stop or remedy the most flagrant abuses of the industrial system. All three kinds of conservation are inadequate, both separately and together.

Concludes that all three are inadequate.

Comment In this paragraph, Wendell Berry points out the "three kinds of conservation currently operating" in our culture. As his last sentence suggests, Berry's purpose for establishing these categories is to demonstrate—in subsequent paragraphs—why they are "inadequate, both separately and together."

GARETH TUCKER
Gentlemen! Start Your Engines

On a typical weekend, most couch potatoes can channel-surf past about a dozen car races. As they watch brightly colored machines circling the track again and again, like images on some manic video game, they may conclude that a race is a race is a race. Actually automobile racing is divided into many subtle subcategories. For example, the three most popular forms can be identified by the image of the car and driver. Stock cars are perceived as souped-up versions of "stock" cars driven by "good ole boys" who talk as if they have just outrun the local police. Indy cars are perceived as masterpieces of engineering driven by "test pilots" who speak the techno-babble of rocket scientists. Formula One cars are almost as technologically advanced as Indy cars, but they still retain the image of the European "Grand Prix" car—the sports car driven by some count who talks as if he's just finished a jolly little tour through the countryside.

1. What principle does Tucker use to establish his three categories?
2. How does his characterization of the race car driver help clarify each category?

DIVISION AND CLASSIFICATION

Points to Remember

1. Determine whether you want to (a) explain an existing system of classification or (b) create your own system.
2. Divide your subject into smaller categories by applying the same principle of selection to each category.
3. Make sure that your division is complete by establishing separate and consistent types of categories.
4. Arrange your categories (and the examples you use to illustrate each category) in a logical and emphatic sequence.
5. Demonstrate the significance of your system by calling your readers' attention to its significance.

CLOUD CHART

LONERS

Single clouds that like to hang out in an otherwise cloudless sky.

SHEEP

Little clouds that always appear in bunches.

SPEEDY GONZALI

Clouds in a huge hurry to get to the next sky.

BLOCKERS

Mischievous clouds with a fondness for popping up just as one decides to go in the ocean.

GRAY BLANKET

One vast gray cloud that usually covers several states at once.

INDUSTRIOS

Beautiful clouds that are most often seen over large manufacturing plants.

SIGMUNDS

Clouds with an uncanny ability to make you feel anxious or depressed.

DUHS

No-name, generic clouds having no meteorological significance whatsoever.

R. Chst

In this quirky cartoon, Roz Chast classifies the different kinds of clouds one can see in the sky. Examine the various categories in her "Cloud Chart." Reflect on your own experience watching clouds. What categories has she omitted or mislabeled? Write an essay that explains how meteorologists classify clouds, or, alternatively, how clouds figure metaphorically in expressions (e.g., "his face clouded over"), literature (including song lyrics), or art.

JAMES H. AUSTIN

James H. Austin was born in 1925 in Cleveland,
Ohio, and educated at Brown University and
Harvard University Medical School. After an in-
ternship at Boston City Hospital and a residency
at the Neurological Institute of New York, Austin
established a private practice in neurology, first in
Portland, Oregon, and then in Denver, Colorado.
He currently serves as professor and head of the
department of neurology at the University of
Colorado Medical School. His major publication,
*Chase, Chance, and Creativity: The Lucky Art of
Novelty* (1978), addresses the issue of how
"chance and creativity interact in biomedical research." His most recent book is *Zen and the
Brain: Toward an Understanding of Meditation
and Consciousness* (1999). In this essay, published
originally in *Saturday Review,* Austin distinguishes four kinds of chance by the way humans
react to their environment.

Four Kinds of Chance

W
HAT IS CHANCE? Dictionaries define it as something   1
fortuitous that happens unpredictably without dis-
cernible human intention. Chance is unintentional and capricious, but we needn't conclude that chance is immune
from human intervention. Indeed, chance plays several distinct roles when humans react creatively with one another
and with their environment.

We can readily distinguish four varieties of chance if we   2
consider that they each involve a different kind of motor activity and a special kind of sensory receptivity. The varieties of
chance also involve distinctive personality traits and differ in
the way one particular individual influences them.

253

Chance I is the pure blind luck that comes with no effort 3
on your part. If, for example, you are sitting at a bridge table
of four, it's "in the cards" for you to receive a hand of all 13
spades, but it will come up only once in every 6.3 trillion
deals. You will ultimately draw this lucky hand—with no intervention on your part—but it does involve a longer wait
than most of us have time for.

Chance II evokes the kind of luck Charles Kettering had in 4
mind when he said: "Keep on going and the chances are you

The term serendipity *describes the facility
for encountering unexpected good luck, as
the result of accident, general exploratory
behavior, or sagacity.*

---

will stumble on something, perhaps when you are least expecting it. I have never heard of anyone stumbling on something sitting down."

In the sense referred to here, Chance II is not passive, but 5
springs from an energetic, generalized motor activity. A certain basal level of action "stirs up the pot," brings in random
ideas that will collide and stick together in fresh combinations, lets chance operate. When someone, *anyone,* does
swing into motion and keeps on going, he will increase the
number of collisions between events. When a few events are
linked together, they can then be exploited to have a fortuitous outcome, but many others, of course, cannot. Kettering
was right. Press on. Something will turn up. We may term
this the Kettering Principle.

In the two previous examples, a unique role of the individ- 6
ual person was either lacking or minimal. Accordingly, as we
move on to Chance III, we see blind luck, but in camouflage.
Chance presents the clue, the opportunity exists, but it
would be missed except by that one person uniquely

equipped to observe it, visualize it conceptually, and fully grasp its significance. Chance III involves a special receptivity and discernment unique to the recipient. Louis Pasteur characterized it for all time when he said: "Chance favors only the prepared mind."

Pasteur himself had it in full measure. But the classic example of his principle occurred in 1928, when Alexander Fleming's mind instantly fused at least five elements into a conceptually unified nexus. His mental sequences went something like this: (1) I see that a mold has fallen by accident into my culture dish; (2) the staphylococcal colonies residing near it failed to grow; (3) the mold must have secreted something that killed the bacteria; (4) I recall a similar experience once before; (5) if I could separate this new "something" from the mold, it could be used to kill staphylococci that cause human infections.

Actually, Fleming's mind was exceptionally well prepared for the penicillin mold. Six years earlier, while he was suffering from a cold, his own nasal drippings had found their way into a culture dish, for reasons not made entirely clear. He noted that nearby bacteria were killed, and astutely followed up the lead. His observations led him to discover a bactericidal enzyme present in nasal mucus and tears, called lysozyme. Lysozyme proved too weak to be of medical use, but imagine how receptive Fleming's mind was to the penicillin mold when it later happened on the scene!

One word evokes the quality of the operations involved in the first three kinds of chance. It is *serendipity*. The term describes the facility for encountering unexpected good luck, as the result of: accident (Chance I), general exploratory behavior (Chance II), or sagacity (Chance III). The word itself was coined by the Englishman-of-letters Horace Walpole, in 1754. He used it with reference to the legendary tales of the Three Princes of Serendip (Ceylon), who quite unexpectedly encountered many instances of good fortune on their travels. In today's parlance, we have usually watered down *serendipity* to mean the good luck that comes solely by accident. We think of it as a result, not an ability. We have tended to lose sight of the element of sagacity, by which term Walpole wished to emphasize that some distinctive personal receptivity is involved.

There remains a fourth element in good luck, an unintentional but subtle personal prompting of it. The English Prime Minister Benjamin Disraeli summed up the principle underlying Chance IV when he noted that "we make our fortunes and we call them fate." Disraeli, a politician of considerable practical experience, appreciated that we each shape our own destiny, at least to some degree. One might restate the principle as follows: *Chance favors the individualized action.* 10

In Chance IV the kind of luck is peculiar to one person, and like a personal hobby, it takes on a distinctive individual flavor. This form of chance is one-man-made, and it is as personal as a signature. . . . Chance IV has an elusive, almost miragelike, quality. Like a mirage, it is difficult to get a firm grip on, for it tends to recede as we pursue it and advance as we step back. But we still accept a mirage when we see it, because we vaguely understand the basis for the phenomenon. A strongly heated layer of air, less dense than usual, lies next to the earth, and it bends the light rays as they pass through. The resulting image may be magnified as if by a telescopic lens in the atmosphere, and real objects, ordinarily hidden far out of sight over the horizon, are brought forward and revealed to the eye. What happens in a mirage then, and in this form of chance, not only appears farfetched but indeed is farfetched. 11

About a century ago, a striking example of Chance IV took place in the Spanish cave of Altamira.* There, one day in 1879, Don Marcelino de Sautuola was engaged in his hobby of archaeology, searching Altamira for bones and stones. With him was his daughter, Maria, who had asked him if she could come along to the cave that day. The indulgent father had said she could. Naturally enough, he first looked where he had always found heavy objects before, on the *floor* of the cave. But Maria, unhampered by any such 12

---

*The cave had first been discovered some years before by an enterprising hunting dog in search of game. Curiously, in 1932 the French cave of Lascaux was discovered by still another dog.

preconceptions, looked not only at the floor but also all around the cave with the open-eyed wonder of a child! She looked up, exclaimed, and then he looked up, to see incredible works of art on the cave ceiling! The magnificent colored bison and other animals they saw at Altamira, painted more than 15,000 years ago, might lead one to call it "the Sistine Chapel of Prehistory." Passionately pursuing his interest in archaeology, de Sautuola, to his surprise, discovered man's first paintings. In quest of science, he happened upon Art.

Yes, a dog did "discover" the cave, and the initial receptivity was his daughter's, but the pivotal reason for the cave paintings' discovery hinged on a long sequence of prior events originating in de Sautuola himself. For when we dig into the background of this amateur excavator, we find he was an exceptional person. Few Spaniards were out probing into caves 100 years ago. The fact that he—not someone else—decided to dig that day in the cave of Altamira was the culmination of his passionate interest in his hobby. Here was a rare man whose avocation had been to educate himself from scratch, as it were, in the science of archaeology and cave exploration. This was no simple passive recognizer of blind luck when it came his way, but a man whose unique interests served as an active creative thrust—someone whose own actions and personality would focus the events that led circuitously but inexorably to the discovery of man's first paintings.

Then, too, there is a more subtle matter. How do you give full weight to the personal interests that imbue your child with your own curiosity, that inspire her to ask to join you in your own musty hobby, and that then lead you to agree to her request at the critical moment? For many reasons, at Altamira, more than the special receptivity of Chance III was required—this was a different domain, that of the personality and its actions.

A century ago no one had the remotest idea our caveman ancestors were highly creative artists. Weren't their talents rather minor and limited to crude flint chippings? But the paintings at Altamira, like a mirage, would quickly magnify this diminutive view, bring up into full focus a distant, hidden era of man's prehistory, reveal sentient minds and well-developed aesthetic sensibilities to which men of any age might aspire. And like a mirage, the events at Altamira grew out of de Sautuola's heated personal quest and out of the invisible forces of chance we know exist yet cannot touch. Accordingly, one may introduce the term *altamirage* to identify the quality underlying Chance IV. Let us define it as the facility for encountering unexpected good luck as the result of highly individualized action. *Altamirage* goes well beyond the boundaries of serendipity in its emphasis on the role of personal action in chance.

Chance IV is favored by distinctive, if not eccentric, hobbies, personal life-styles, and modes of behavior peculiar to one individual, usually invested with some passion. The farther apart these personal activities are from the area under investigation, the more novel and unexpected will be the creative product of the encounter.   16

For Study and Discussion

QUESTIONS FOR RESPONSE

1. Would you consider yourself a lucky or an unlucky person? What evidence would you use to support your case?
2. Do you agree with Austin's assessment of the dictionary's definitions of the word *chance*? How would you define the word?

QUESTIONS ABOUT PURPOSE

1. What elements of human behavior and attitude does Austin demonstrate by dividing chance into four varieties?
2. What relationship does Austin discover between the words "luck," "serendipity," "sagacity," and "altamirage"?

QUESTIONS ABOUT AUDIENCE

1. What assumptions does Austin make about his readers when he offers them *the best example* rather than several examples to illustrate each category?

2. How does Austin's attitude toward his audience change during the essay? For example, why does he speak directly to his readers when he explains Chance I but address them more formally in his discussion of other categories?

QUESTIONS ABOUT STRATEGIES

1. How does Austin arrange his four categories? Why doesn't he give equal treatment to each category?
2. How does Austin use transitions and summaries to clarify the differences between the major categories? In particular, see paragraphs 6 and 9.

QUESTIONS FOR DISCUSSION

1. What incidents in your personal experience would support Austin's classification system? How many examples can you cite in each category?
2. What do you think is the relationship between *ability* and *result*? For example, what is your opinion of Disraeli's assertion that "we make our fortunes and we call them fate"?

Mary Mebane was born in 1933 in Durham, North Carolina, and educated at North Carolina Central University and the University of North Carolina. She taught in the public schools of North Carolina before moving on to teaching writing at the University of South Carolina and the University of Wisconsin. She has written essays for the *New York Times;* a two-act play, *Take a Sad Song* (1975); and two volumes of her autobiography, *Mary: An Autobiography* (1981) and *Mary, Wayfarer* (1983). In "Shades of Black," excerpted from the first autobiographical volume, Mebane reveals how class and color have been used to classify members of the African-American community.

Shades of Black

D URING MY FIRST week of classes as a freshman, I was 1 stopped one day in the hall by the chairman's wife, who was indistinguishable in color from a white woman. She wanted to see me, she said.

This woman had no official position on the faculty, except 2 that she was an instructor in English; nevertheless, her summons had to be obeyed. In the segregated world there were (and remain) gross abuses of authority because those at the pinnacle, and even their spouses, felt that the people "under" them had no recourse except to submit—and they were right except that sometimes a black who got sick and tired of it would go to the whites and complain. This course of action was severely condemned by the blacks, but an interesting thing happened—such action always got positive results. Power was thought of in negative terms: I can deny someone something, I can strike at someone who can't strike back, I [*new outlook*] can ride someone down; that proves I am powerful. The concept of power as a force for good, for affirmative response to people or situations, was not in evidence.

When I went to her office, she greeted me with a big smile. 3 "You know," she said, "you made the highest mark on the verbal part of the examination." She was referring to the examination that the entire freshman class took upon entering the college. I looked at her but I didn't feel warmth, for in spite of her smile her eyes and tone of voice were saying, "How could this black-skinned girl score higher on the verbal than some of the students who've had more advantages than she? It must be some sort of fluke. Let me talk to her." I felt it, but I managed to smile my thanks and back off. For here at North Carolina College at Durham, as it had been since the beginning, social class and color were the primary [*ouch*] criteria used in determining status on the campus.

First came the children of doctors, lawyers, and college 4 teachers. Next came the children of public-school teachers, businessmen, and anybody else who had access to more money than the poor black working class. After that came the

---

At my college . . . social class and color were the primary criteria used in determining status on the campus.

---

bulk of the student population, the children of the working class, most of whom were the first in their families to go beyond high school. The attitude toward them was: You're here because we need the numbers, but in all other things defer to your betters. [*true*]

The faculty assumed that light-skinned students were 5 more intelligent, and they were always a bit nonplussed when a dark-skinned student did well, especially if she was a girl.

They had reason to be appalled when they discovered that I planned to do not only well but better than my light-skinned peers.

I don't know whether African men recently transported to the New World considered themselves handsome or, more important, whether they considered African women beautiful in comparison with Native American Indian women or immigrant European women. It is a question that I have never heard raised or seen research on. If African men considered African women beautiful, just when their shift in interest away from black black women occurred might prove to be an interesting topic for researchers. But one thing I know for sure: by the twentieth century, really black skin on a woman was considered ugly in this country. This was particularly true among those who were exposed to college.

Hazel, who was light brown, used to say to me, "You are *dark,* but not *too* dark." The saved commiserating with the damned. I had the feeling that if nature had painted one more brushstroke on me, I'd have had to kill myself.

Black skin was to be disguised at all costs. Since a black face is rather hard to disguise, many women took refuge in ludicrous makeup. Mrs. Burry, one of my teachers in elementary school, used white face powder. But she neglected to powder her neck and arms, and even the black on her face gleamed through the white, giving her an eerie appearance. But she did the best she could.

I observed all through elementary and high school that for various entertainments the girls were placed on the stage in order of color. And very black ones didn't get into the front row. If they were past caramel-brown, to the back row they would go. And nobody questioned the justice of these decisions—neither the students nor the teachers.

One of the teachers at Wildwood School, who was from the Deep South and was just as black as she could be, had been a strict enforcer of these standards. That was another irony—that someone who had been judged outside the realm of beauty herself because of her skin tones should have adopted them so wholeheartedly and applied them herself without question.

One girl stymied that teacher, though. Ruby, a black cherry of a girl, not only got off the back row but off the front row as well, to stand alone at stage center. She could outsing, outdance, and outdeclaim everyone else, and talent proved triumphant over pigmentation. But the May Queen and her Court (and in high school, Miss Wildwood) were always chosen from among the lighter ones.

as it should be 11

When I was a freshman in high school, it became clear that 12 a light-skinned sophomore girl named Rose was going to get the "best girl scholar" prize for the next three years, and there was nothing I could do about it, even though I knew I was the better. Rose was caramel-colored and had shoulder-length hair. She was highly favored by the science and math teacher, who figured the averages. I wasn't. There was only one prize. Therefore, Rose would get it until she graduated. I was one year behind her, and I would not get it until after she graduated.

To be held in such low esteem was painful. It was difficult 13 not to feel that I had been cheated out of the medal, which I felt that, in a fair competition, I perhaps would have won. Being unable to protest or do anything about it was a traumatic experience for me. From then on I instinctively tended to avoid the college-exposed, dark-skinned male, knowing that when he looked at me he saw himself and, most of the time, his mother and sister as well, and since he had rejected his blackness, he had rejected theirs and mine.

Oddly enough, the lighter-skinned black male did not 14 seem to feel so much prejudice toward the black black woman. It was no accident, I felt, that Mr. Harrison, the eighth-grade teacher, who was reddish-yellow himself, once protested to the science and math teacher about the fact that he always assigned sweeping duties to Doris and Ruby Lee, two black black girls. Mr. Harrison said to them one day, right in the other teacher's presence, "You must be some bad girls. Every day I come down here ya'll are sweeping." The science and math teacher got the point and didn't ask them to sweep anymore.

Uneducated black males, too, sometimes related very well   15
to the black black woman. They had been less firmly indoctrinated by the white society around them and were more securely rooted in their own culture.

Because of the stigma attached to having dark skin, a black   16
black woman had to do many things to find a place for herself. One possibility was to attach herself to a light-skinned woman, hoping that some of the magic would rub off on her. A second was to make herself sexually available, hoping to attract a mate. Third, she could resign herself to a more chaste life-style—either (for the professional woman) teaching and work in established churches or (for the uneducated woman) domestic work and zealous service in the Holy and Sanctified churches.

Even as a young girl, Lucy had chosen the first route. Lucy   17
was short, skinny, short-haired, and black black, and thus unacceptable. So she made her choice. She selected Patricia, the lightest-skinned girl in the school, as her friend, and followed her around. Patricia and her friends barely tolerated Lucy, but Lucy smiled and doggedly hung on, hoping that some who noticed Patricia might notice her, too. Though I felt shame for her behavior, even then I understood.

As is often the case of the victim agreeing with and adopt-   18
ing the attitudes of oppressor, so I have seen it with black black women. I have seen them adopt the oppressor's attitude that they are nothing but "sex machines," and their supposedly superior sexual performance becomes their sole reason for being and for esteeming themselves. Such women learn early that in order to make themselves attractive to men they have somehow to shift the emphasis from physical beauty to some other area—usually sexual performance. Their constant talk is of their desirability and their ability to gratify a man sexually.

I knew two such women well—both of them black black.   19
To hear their endless talk of sexual conquests was very sad. I

have never seen the category that these women fall into described anywhere. It is not that of promiscuity or nymphomania. It is the category of total self-rejection: "Since I am black, I am ugly, I am nobody. I will perform on the level that they have assigned to me." Such women are the pitiful results of what not only white America but also, and more important, black America has done to them.

Some, not taking the sexuality route but still accepting black society's view of their worthlessness, swing all the way across to intense religiosity. Some are staunch, fervent workers in the more traditional Southern churches—Baptist and Methodist—and others are leaders and ministers in the lower status, more evangelical Holiness sects.

Another avenue open to the black black woman is excellence in a career. Since in the South the field most accessible to such women is education, a great many of them prepared to become teachers. But here, too, the black black woman had problems. Grades weren't given to her lightly in school, nor were promotions on the job. Consequently, she had to prepare especially well. She had to pass examinations with flying colors or be left behind; she knew that she would receive no special consideration. She had to be overqualified for a job because otherwise she didn't stand a chance of getting it—and she was competing only with other blacks. She had to have something to back her up: not charm, not personality—but training.

The black black woman's training would pay off in the 1970s. With the arrival of integration the black black woman would find, paradoxically enough, that her skin color in an integrated situation was not the handicap it had been in an all-black situation. But it wasn't until the middle and late 1960s, when the post-1945 generation of black males arrived on college campuses, that I noticed any change in the situation at all. *He* wore an afro and *she* wore an afro, and sometimes the only way you could tell them apart was when his afro was taller than hers. Black had become beautiful, and the really black girl was often selected as queen of various campus activities. It was then that the dread I felt at dealing with the college-educated black male began to ease. Even now, though, when I have occasion to engage in any type of transaction with a college-educated black man, I gauge his age. If I guess he was born after 1945, I feel confident that the transaction will turn out all right. If he probably was born before 1945, my stomach tightens, I find myself taking shallow breaths, and I try to state my business and escape as soon as possible.

what happened w/ the teacher

For Study and Discussion

QUESTIONS FOR RESPONSE

1. How do you respond when you or your friends are judged by some physical feature—weight, height, hair?
2. How do you and your friends identify various social classes? What assumptions do you make about people in each class?

QUESTIONS ABOUT PURPOSE

1. Why does Mebane use the concept of power to introduce her classification?
2. How does Mebane use her essay to explain the impulse of the victim to adopt the attitudes of the oppressor?

QUESTIONS ABOUT AUDIENCE

1. Does Mebane envision her readers as primarily black or primarily white, primarily men or primarily women? Explain your answer.
2. In what way do you think Mebane's system may apply to the attitudes of today's African-American students? Explain your answer.

QUESTIONS ABOUT STRATEGIES

1. How does Mebane classify her college classmates by color and class? What assumptions do her teachers make about black black working-class women?

2. What options does Mebane suggest are available to black black women? How are these options enforced?

QUESTIONS FOR DISCUSSION

1. How did the civil rights movement of the 1950s and black consciousness movement of the 1960s change the African-American community's definition of beauty?
2. Do subtle judgments about class and color still control the power structure of the African-American community? In what way?

PHILLIP LOPATE

Phillip Lopate was born in Jamaica Heights, New York, in 1943 and educated at Columbia University. He taught creative writing with the Teachers and Writers Collaborative in the New York Public Schools before devoting his full attention to his own writing. He has contributed fiction to *Paris Review*, poetry to *Yale Literary Review*, and film criticism to the *Cinemabook*. His essays have appeared in collections such as *Against Joie de Vivre* (1989); he has also edited numerous writing collections such as *The Anchor Essay Annual* (1997) and *Writing New York: A Literary Anthology* (2000). In "Modern Friendships," reprinted from *Against Joie de Vivre*, Lopate classifies his changing attitude toward various kinds of "friends."

Modern Friendships

IS THERE ANYTHING left to say about friendship after so 1
many great essayists have picked over the bones of the subject? Probably not. Aristotle and Cicero, Seneca and Montaigne, Bacon and Samuel Johnson, Hazlitt, Emerson, and Lamb have all taken their cracks at it; since the ancients, friendship has been a sort of examination subject for the personal essayist. It is partly the very existence of such wonderful prior models that lures the newcomer to follow in the others' footsteps, and partly a self-referential aspect of the genre, since the personal essay is itself an attempt to establish a friendship on the page between writer and reader.

Friendship has been called "love without wings," implying 2
a want of lyrical afflatus. On the other hand, the Stoic definition of love ("Love is the attempt to form a friendship inspired by beauty") seems to suggest that friendship came

268

first. Certainly a case can be made that the buildup of affection and the yearning for more intimacy, without the release
of sexual activity, keeps friends in a state of sweet-sorrowful
itchiness that has as much romantic quality as a love affair. We
know that a falling-out between two old friends can leave a
deeper and more perplexing hurt than the ending of a love
affair, perhaps because we are more pessimistic about the latter's endurance from the start.

nice words

Our first attempted friendships are within the family. It is
here we practice the techniques of listening sympathetically

attempted? 3

> *Friendship is a school for character,*
> *allowing us the chance to study in great*
> *detail and over time temperaments*
> *very different from our own.*

and proving that we can be trusted, and learn the sort of
kindness we can expect in return. I have a sister, one year
younger than I, who often took care of me when I was growing up. Once, when I was about fifteen, unable to sleep and
shivering uncontrollably with the start of a fever, I decided in
the middle of the night to go into her room and wake her.
She held me, performing the basic service of a friend—presence—and the chills went away.

There is something tainted about these family friendships,
however. This same sister, in her insecure adolescent phase,
told me: "You love me because I'm related to you, but if you
were to meet me for the first time at a party, you'd think I was
a jerk and not worth being your friend." She had me in a
bind: I had no way of testing her hypothesis. I should have
argued that even if our bond was not freely chosen, our decision to work on it had been. Still, we are quick to dismiss the
partiality of our family members when they tell us we are

nice verb 4

good pt

true

strong verb talented, cute, or lovable; we must go out into the world and seduce others.

It is just a few short years from the promiscuity of the sandbox to the tormented, possessive feelings of a fifth grader who has just learned that his best and only friend is playing at another classmate's house after school. *that's harsh for that age* There may be worse betrayals in store, but probably none is more influential than the sudden fickleness of an elementary school friend who has dropped us for someone more popular after all our careful, patient wooing. Often we lose no time inflicting the same betrayal on someone else, just to ensure that we have got the victimization dynamic right.

What makes friendships in childhood and adolescence so poignant is that we need the chosen comrade to be everything in order to rescue us from the gothic inwardness of family life. Even if we are lucky enough to have several companions, there must be a Best Friend, knightly dubbed as though victor of an Arthurian tournament.

I clung to the romance of the Best Friend all through high school, college, and beyond, until my university circle began to disperse. At that point, in my mid-twenties, I also "acted out" the dark competitive side of friendship that can exist between two young men fighting for a place in life and love, by *ooo ... nice* doing the one unforgivable thing: sleeping with my best friend's girl. I was baffled at first that there was no way to repair the damage. I lost this friendship forever, and came away from that debacle much more aware of the amount of injury that friendship can and cannot sustain. Perhaps I needed to prove to myself that friendship was not an all-permissive, resilient bond, like a mother's love, but something quite fragile. Precisely because Best Friendship promotes such a merging of identities, such seeming boundarylessness, the first major *add new perspective* transgression of trust can cause the injured party to feel he is fighting for his violated soul against his darkest enemy. There is not much room to maneuver in a best friendship between unlimited intimacy and unlimited mistrust.

Still, it was not until the age of thirty that I reluctantly abandoned the Best Friend expectation and took up a more

pluralistic model. At present, I cherish a dozen friends for
their unique personalities, without asking that any one be my
soul-twin. Whether this alteration constitutes a movement
toward maturity or toward cowardly pragmatism is not for
me to say. It may be that, in refusing to depend so much on
any one friend, I am opting for self-protection over intimacy.
Or it may be that, as we advance into middle age, the life
problem becomes less that of establishing a tight dyadic bond
and more one of making our way in a broader world, "society." Indeed, since Americans have so indistinct a notion of
society, we often try to put friendship networks in its place. If
a certain intensity is lost in the pluralistic model of friendship,
there is also the gain of being able to experience all of one's
potential, half-buried selves, through witnessing the spectacle of the multiple fates of our friends. Since we cannot be
polygamists in our conjugal life, at least we can do so with
friendship. As it happens, the harem of friends, so tantalizing
a notion, often translates into feeling pulled in a dozen different directions, with the guilty sense of having disappointed
everyone a little. It is also a risky, contrived enterprise to try
to make one's friends behave in a friendly manner toward
each other: if the effort fails one feels obliged to mediate; if it
succeeds too well, one is jealous.

Whether friendship is intrinsically singular and exclusive,
or plural and democratic, is a question that has vexed many
commentators. Aristotle distinguished three types of friendship in *The Nicomachean Ethics:* "friendship based on utility,"
such as businessmen cultivating each other for benefit;
"friendship based on pleasure," like young people interested
in partying; and "perfect friendship." The first two categories
Aristotle calls "qualified and superficial friendships," because
they are founded on circumstances that could easily change;
the last, which is based on admiration for another's good
character, is more permanent, but also rarer, because good
men "are few." Cicero, who wrote perhaps the best treatise
on friendship, also insisted that what brings true friends together is "a mutual belief in each other's goodness." This insistence on virtue as a precondition for true friendship may

strike us as impossibly demanding: who, after all, feels himself good nowadays? And yet, if I am honest, I must admit that the friendships of mine which have lasted longest have been with those whose integrity, or humanity, or strength to bear their troubles I continue to admire. Conversely, when I lost respect for someone, however winning he otherwise remained, the friendship petered away almost immediately. "Remove respect from friendship," said Cicero, "and you have taken away the most splendid ornament it possesses."

I agree

Montaigne distinguished between friendship, which he   10
saw as a once-in-a-lifetime experience, and the calculating worldly alliances around him, which he thought unworthy of the name. In paying tribute to his late friend Etienne de la Boetie, Montaigne wrote: "Having so little time to last, and having begun so late, for we were both grown men, and he a few years older than I, it could not lose time and conform to the pattern of mild and regular friendships, which need so many precautions in the form of long preliminary association. Our friendship has no other model than itself, and can be compared only with itself. It is not one special consideration, nor two, nor three, nor four, nor a thousand: it is I know not what quintessence of all this mixture, which, having seized my whole will, led it to plunge and lose itself in his; which, having seized his whole will, led it to plunge and lose itself in mine, with equal hunger, equal rivalry. . . . So many coincidences are needed to build up such a friendship that it is a lot if fortune can do it once in three centuries." This seems a bit high hat: since the sixteenth century, our expectations of friendship may have grown more plebeian. Even Emerson, in his grand romantic essay on the subject, allowed as how he was not up to the Castor-and-Pollux standard: "I am not quite so strict in my terms, perhaps because I have never known so high a fellowship as others." Emerson contents himself with a circle of intelligent men and women, but warns us not to throw them together: "You shall have very useful and cheering discourse at several times with two several men, but let all three of you come together, and you shall not have one new and hearty word. Two may talk and one

may hear, but three cannot take part in a conversation of the most sincere and searching sort."

Friendship is a long conversation. I suppose I could imagine a nonverbal friendship revolving around shared physical work or sport, but for me, good talk is the point of the thing. Indeed, the ability to generate conversation by the hour is the most promising indication, during its uncertain early stages, that a possible friendship will take hold. In the first few conversations there may be an exaggeration of agreement, as both parties angle for adhesive surfaces. But later on, trust builds through the courage to assert disagreement, through the tactful acceptance that differences of opinion will have to remain.

Some view like-mindedness as both the precondition and product of friendship. Myself, I distrust it. I have one friend who keeps assuming that we see the world eye-to-eye. She is intent on enrolling us in a flattering aristocracy of taste, on the short "we" list against the ignorant "they"; sometimes I do not have the strength to fight her need for consensus with my own stubborn disbelief in the existence of any such inner circle of privileged, cultivated sensibility. Perhaps I have too much invested in a view of myself as idiosyncratic to be eager to join any coterie, even a coterie of two. What attracts me to friends' conversation is the give-and-take, not necessarily that we come out at the same point.

"Our tastes and aims and views were identical—and that is where the essence of a friendship must always lie," wrote Cicero. To some extent, perhaps, but then the convergence must be natural, not, as Emerson put it, "a mush of concession. Better be a nettle in the side of your friend than his echo." And Francis Bacon observed that "the best preservative to keep the mind in health is the faithful admonition of a friend."

Friendship is a school for character, allowing us the chance to study in great detail and over time temperaments very different from our own. These charming quirks, these contradictions, these nobilities, these blind spots of our friends we track not out of disinterested curiosity: we must have this information before knowing how far we may relax our guard, how much we may rely on them in crises. The learning curve of friendship involves, to no small extent, filling out this picture of the other's limitations and making peace with the results. (With one's own limitations there may never be peace.) Each time I hit up against a friend's inflexibility I am relieved as well as disappointed: I can begin to predict, and arm myself in advance against repeated bruises. I have one friend who is always late, so I bring a book along when I am to meet her. If I give her a manuscript to read and she promises to look at it over the weekend, I start preparing myself for a month-long wait.

Not that one ever gives up trying to educate the friend to   15
one's needs. I approach such matters experimentally: sometimes I will pride myself in tactfully circumventing the friend's predicted limitation, even if it means relinquishing all hope of getting the response I want; at other times I will confront a problem with intentional tactlessness, just to see if any change is still possible.

I have a dear old friend, Richard, who shies away from per-   16
sonal confidences. Years go by without my learning anything about his love life, and he does not encourage the baring of my soul either, much as I like that sort of thing. But we share so many other interests and values that that limitation seems easily borne, most of the time. Once, however, I found myself in a state of emotional despair; I told him I had exhausted my hopes of finding love or success, that I felt suicidal, and he changed the topic, patently embarrassed. I was annoyed both at his emotional rigidity and at my own stupidity—after all, I'd enough friends who ate up this kind of confessional talk, why foist on Richard what I might have predicted he couldn't, or wouldn't, handle? For a while I sulked, annoyed at him for having failed me, but I also began to see my despair through his eyes as melodramatic, childish petulance, and I began to let it go. As it happened, he found other ways during our visit to be so considerate that I ended up feeling better, even without our having had a heart-to-heart talk. I suppose the moral is that a friend can serve as a corrective

to our insular miseries simply by offering up his essential otherness.

Though it is often said that with a true friend there is no need to hold anything back ("A friend is a person with whom I may be sincere. Before him I may think aloud," wrote Emerson), I have never found this to be entirely the case. Certain words may be too cruel if spoken at the wrong moment—or may fall on deaf ears, for any number of reasons. I also find with each friend, as they must with me, that some initial resistance, restlessness, psychic weather must be overcome before that tender ideal attentiveness may be called forth. *17*

I have a good friend, Charlie, who is often very distracted whenever we first get together. If we are sitting in a cafe he will look around constantly for the waiter, or be distracted by a pretty woman or the restaurant's cat. It would be foolish for me to broach an important subject at such moments, so I resign myself to waiting the half hour or however long it takes until his jumpiness subsides. Or else I draw this pattern grumpily to his attention. Once he has settled down, however, I can tell Charlie virtually anything, and he me. But the candor cannot be rushed. It must be built up to with the verbal equivalent of limbering exercises. *18*

The Friendship Scene—a flow of shared confidences, recognitions, humor, advice, speculation, even wisdom—is one of the key elements of modern friendships. Compared to the rest of life, this ability to lavish one's best energies on an activity utterly divorced from the profit motive and free from the routines of domination and inequality that affect most relations (including, perhaps, the selfsame friendship at other times) seems idyllic. The Friendship Scene is by its nature not an everyday occurrence. It represents the pinnacle, the fruit of the friendship, potentially ever-present but not always arrived at. Both friends' dim yet self-conscious awareness that they are wandering conversationally toward a goal that they have previously accomplished but which may elude them this time around creates a tension, an obligation to communicate as sincerely as possible, like actors in an improvisation *19* exercise struggling to shape their baggy material into some climactic form. This very pressure to achieve "quality" communication may induce a sort of inauthentic epiphany, not unlike what happens sometimes in the last ten minutes of a psychotherapy session. But a truly achieved Friendship Scene can be among the best experiences life has to offer.

I remember one such afternoon when Michael, a close 20 writer-friend, and I met at a cafeteria on a balmy Saturday in early spring and talked for three and a half hours. There were no outside time pressures that particular afternoon, a rare occurrence for either of us. At first we caught up with our latest business, the sort of items that might have gone into a biweekly bulletin sent to any number of acquaintances. Then gradually we settled into an area of perplexing unresolved impressions. I would tell Michael about A's chance, seemingly hostile remark toward me at a gathering, and he would report that the normally ebullient B looked secretly depressed. These were the memory equivalents of food grains stuck in our teeth, which we were now trying to free with our tongues: anecdotal fragments I was not even sure had any point, until I started fashioning them aloud for Michael's interest. Together we diagnosed our mutual acquaintances, each other's character, and, from there, the way of the world. In the course of our free associations we eventually descended into what was really bothering us. I learned he was preoccupied with the fate of an old college friend who was dying of AIDS; he, that my father was in poor health and needed two operations. We had touched bottom—mortality—and it was reassuring to settle there awhile. Gradually we rose again, drawn back to the questions of ego and career, craft and romance. It was, as I've said, a pretty day, and we ended up walking through a new mall in Houston, gawking at the window displays of that bland emporium with a reawakened curiosity about the consumer treats of America, our attentions turned happily outward now that we had dwelt long enough in the shared privacies of our psyches.

Contemporary urban life, with its tight schedules and 21 crowded appointment books, has helped to shape modern friendship into something requiring a good deal of intentionality and pursuit. You phone a friend and make a date a week or more in advance; then you set aside an evening, like a tryst, during which to squeeze in all your news and advice, confession and opinion. Such intimate compression may add a romantic note to modern friendships, but it also places a strain on the meeting to yield a high quality of meaning and satisfaction, closer to art than life, thereby increasing the chance for disappointment. If I see certain busy or out-of-town friends only once every six months, we must not only catch up on our lives but convince ourselves within the allotted two hours together that we still share a special affinity, an inner track to each other's psyches, or the next meeting may be put off for years. Surely there must be another, saner rhythm to friendship in rural areas—or maybe not? I think about "the gold old days" when friends would go on walking tours through England together, when Edith Wharton would bundle poor Henry James into her motorcar and they'd drive to the South of France for a month. I'm not sure my friendships could sustain the strain of travel for weeks at a time, and the truth of the matter is that I've gotten used to this urban arrangement of serial friendship "dates," where the pleasure of the rendezvous is enhanced by the knowledge that it will only last, at most, six hours. If the two of us don't happen to mesh that day (always a possibility)—well, it's only a few hours; and if it should go beautifully, one needs an escape hatch from exaltation as well as disenchantment. I am capable of only so much intense, exciting communication before I start to fade; I come to these encounters equipped with a six-hour oxygen tank. Is this an evolutionary pattern of modern friendship, or only a personal limitation?

Perhaps because I conceive of the modern Friendship Scene as a somewhat theatrical enterprise, a one-act play, I tend to be very affected by the "set," so to speak. A restaurant, a museum, a walk in the park through the zoo, even accompanying a friend on shopping errands—I prefer public turf where the stimulation of the city can play a backdrop to our dialogue, feeding it with details when inspiration flags. True, some of the most cherished friendship scenes have occurred around a friend's kitchen table. The problem with restricting the date to one another's houses is that the entertaining friend may be unable to stop playing the host, or may sink too passively into his or her surroundings. Subtle struggles may also develop over which domicile should serve as the venue.

I have a number of *chez moi* friends, friends who always invite me to come to their homes while evading offers to visit mine. What they view as hospitality I see as a need to control the *mise-en-scène* of friendship. I am expected to fit in where they are most comfortable, while they play lord of the manor, distracted by the props of decor, the pool, the unexpected phone call, the swirl of children, animals, and neighbors. Indeed, *chez moi* friends often tend to keep a sort of open house, so that in going over to see them—for a *tête-à-tête*, I had assumed—I will suddenly find their other friends and neighbors, whom they have also invited, dropping in all afternoon. There are only so many Sundays I care to spend hanging out with a friend's entourage before becoming impatient for a private audience.

Married friends who own their own homes are much more apt to try to draw me into their domestic fold, whereas single people are often more sensitive about establishing a discreet space for the friendship to occur. Perhaps the married assume that a bachelor like myself is desperate for home cooking and a little family life. I have noticed that it is not an easy matter to pry a married friend away from mate and milieu. For married people, especially those with children, the home often becomes the wellspring of all their nurturing feelings, and the single friend is invited to partake in the general flow. Maybe there is also a certain tendency on their parts to kill two birds with one stone: they don't see enough of their spouse and kids, and figure they can visit with you all at the same time. And maybe they need one-on-one friendship less, hampered as they are by responsibilities that no amount of camaraderie or discussion can change. Often friendship in these circumstances is not even a pairing, but a mixing together of two sets of parents and children willy-nilly. What would the ancients say about this? In Rome, according to Bacon, "the whole senate dedicated an altar to Friendship, as to a goddess. . . ." From my standpoint, friendship is a jealous goddess. Whenever a friend of mine marries, I have to fight to overcome the feeling that I am being "replaced" by the spouse. I don't mind sharing a friend with his family milieu— in fact I like it, up to a point—but eventually I must get the friend alone, or else, as a bachelor at a distinct power disadvantage, I risk becoming a mere spectator of familial rituals instead of a key player in the drama of friendship.

I like that

A person living alone usually has more control over his or her schedule, hence more energy to give to friendship. If anything, the danger is of investing too much emotional energy in one's friends. When a single person is going through a romantic dry spell he or she often tries to extract the missing passion from a circle of friends. This works only up to a point: the frayed nerves of protracted celibacy can lead to hypersensitive imaginings of slights and rejections, during which times one's platonic friends seem to come particularly into the line of fire. 25

Today, with the partial decline of the nuclear family and the search for alternatives to it, we also see attempts to substitute the friendship web for intergenerational family life. Since psychoanalysis has alerted us to regard the family as a minefield of unrequited love, manipulation, and ambivalence, it is only natural that people may look to friendship as a more supportive ground for relation. But in our longing for an unequivocally positive bond, we should beware of sentimentalizing friendship, as saccharine "buddy" movies or certain feminist novels do, of neutering its problematic, destructive aspects. Besides, friendship can never substitute for the true meaning of family: if nothing else, it will never be able to duplicate the family's wild capacity for concentrating neurosis. 26

In short, friends can't be your family, they can't be your lovers, they can't be your psychiatrists. But they can be your 27 friends, which is plenty. For, as Cicero tells us, "friendship is the noblest and most delightful of all the gifts the gods have given to mankind." And Bacon adds: "It is a mere and miserable solitude to want true friends, without which the world is but a wilderness. . . ."

nice

When I think about the qualities that characterize the best friendships I've known, I can identify five: rapport, affection, need, habit, and forgiveness. Rapport and affection can only take you so far; they may leave you at the formal, outer gate of goodwill, which is still not friendship. A persistent need for the other's company, for their interest, approval, opinion, will get you inside the gates, especially when it is reciprocated. In the end, however, there are no substitutes for habit and forgiveness. A friendship may travel for years on cozy habit. But it is a melancholy fact that unless you are a saint you are bound to offend every friend deeply at least once in the course of time. The friends I have kept the longest are those who forgave me for wronging them, unintentionally, intentionally, or by the plain catastrophe of my personality, time and again. There can be no friendship without forgiveness.

ain't that the truth

For Study and Discussion

QUESTIONS FOR RESPONSE

1. In your life as a student, how many times have you had to write or read an essay on *friendship*? Which ones made the biggest impression on you?
2. How often do you enact the Friendship Scene (page 275)? What is your favorite setting for this scene?

QUESTIONS ABOUT PURPOSE

1. In what way does Lopate distinguish between the classical definition of friendship and friendships shaped by "contemporary urban life"?

2. What evidence does he supply for his argument that "friends can't be your family"?

QUESTIONS ABOUT AUDIENCE

1. Lopate acknowledges that many classical essayists have written about friendship. How does he help his readers understand what these essayists said? Does he agree or disagree with them?
2. He suggests, "The personal essay is an attempt to establish a friendship on the page between writer and reader." In what passages in the essay do you sense that Lopate is trying to establish such a friendship with his readers?

QUESTIONS ABOUT STRATEGIES

1. How does Lopate use maturity as a principle for classifying friendships? What kind of problems occur among "pluralistic" friends?
2. How does he use the scenes with Richard, Charlie, and Michael to demonstrate the difficulties of sustaining a friendship?

QUESTIONS FOR DISCUSSION

1. Only one of the friends Lopate mentions in this essay is a woman. How do you respond to the famous line in the movie *When Harry Met Sally* that "men and women can't be friends"?
2. What do you think about the five qualities Lopate identifies as characterizing the best friendships? Has he left out an important quality? Explain your answer.

James Quinn Wilson was born in 1931 in Denver, Colorado, and was educated at the University of Redlands and the University of Chicago. Wilson has taught political science at Harvard University, Massachusetts Institute of Technology, and UCLA and is currently the Ronald Reagan Professor of Public Policy at Pepperdine University. He has served as chairman of the council of academic advisors of the American Enterprise Institute and as chairman of the White House Task Force on Crime, the President's Foreign Intelligence Advisory Board, and the President's Council on Bioethics. He is a frequent contributor to magazines such as *Commonweal* and *National Review;* his many books include *Thinking About Crime* (1983), *Bureaucracy: What Government Agencies Do and Why They Do It* (1991), *The Moral Sense* (1993), *Two Nations* (1998), *American Government* (2002), and *The Marriage Problem: How Our Culture Has Weakened Families* (2002). In "Democracy for All?" reprinted from *Commentary,* Wilson classifies the conditions that, historically, have been required to produce and sustain a democracy.

Democracy for All?

we do?

T ODAY WE WONDER whether the whole world might be- 1
come democratic. Acting on the belief that it can, our government has bent its energies toward encouraging the birth or growth of democracy in places around the globe from Haiti to Russia, from Kosovo to the People's Republic of China. In doing so, it has enjoyed a kind of sanction from

the century just past, which was indeed marked by the growth of regimes resting on popular consent and a commitment to human freedom.

That has hardly been the only salient characteristic of the age; the 20th century was also an era of mass murder, in which more than 170 million people were killed by their own governments. In some ways, in fact, it is easier to explain *that* phenomenon than to explain the increase in the number of democratic regimes. Living for most of their history in tiny

really??

In the long run, democracy and human freedom are good for everyone even though they may create some mischief in the near term.

---

villages, people have customarily viewed those in other villages as at best distant strangers and at worst mortal enemies. When agriculture and industry brought people together into large cities, the stage was set for dictatorial leaders, driven by power and ideology and aided by modern technology, to seize and maintain political control by destroying not only their personal rivals but entire populations who could be depicted as the enemies of the state. In the worst cases, this destruction has amounted to genocide.

not friends?

But if hostility and mass murder can, alas, be easily explained, democracy is an oddity. How do people who evolved in small, homogeneous villages become tolerant of those whom they do not know and who may differ from them in habits and religion? How can village government, based on tradition and consensus, be transformed into national government based on votes cast by strangers?

family?

Democratic government cannot rest simply on written constitutions. Many Latin American nations have had constitutions similar to that of the United States but have practiced

2

3

4

not democracy but oligarchy. Religion may help foster tolerance, if people take the Golden Rule seriously. But we know
that some religious people are fanatics and some agnostics
tolerant. We also know that in some faiths, such as Islam,
there is no separation between religious and secular law, and
that the absence of this distinction tempts religious leaders to
impose authoritarian rule on their followers. Voltaire once
said that a nation with one church will have oppression; with
two, civil war; with a hundred, freedom. Religious freedom
strengthens political freedom, but religious freedom exists
only after political freedom has been secured.

In what follows I do not intend to dwell on the ideas that   5
have inspired, shaped, and informed democratic government. Rather, I want to suggest some conditions that to my
mind have underlain the emergence and survival of our oldest democracies. They come under four headings.

The first is *isolation*. The freest nations have been pro-   6
tected from invasion by broad oceans or high mountains.
England, Australia, New Zealand, and the United States enjoy ocean boundaries; Switzerland has a mountainous one.
The significance of isolation is that it minimizes the need for
a large standing army commanded by a single ruler, thus
minimizing the need for high taxes to sustain the army and
unfettered authority to empower the ruler. By contrast, in
nations without secure boundaries—France, Austria, Hun-
gary, Prussia—demands for popular rule and for a weak central government had to be subordinated to the need for a
powerful army.

Imagine what life in the United States would have been   7
like if Spain had remained in Florida and France had retained
the Louisiana territory. To manage the inevitable skirmishes
and wars, our national government would have grown more
powerful more quickly and would have taxed and regulated
more heavily.

The second condition is *property*. For many modern think-   8
ers, private property is the enemy of human equality and
therefore of democracy. Property is theft, wrote Proudhon.

The *Communist Manifesto* promised the abolition of private property, and generations of social planners have sought to diminish its reach. But in fact private property is the friend of democracy. Aristotle understood that it stimulates work by providing rewards to the owner, reduces arguments by supplying a basis for allocating goods, and enhances pleasure by creating a physical object for human affection. In his *Politics* he first describes the private household and how it is managed before going on to argue that government exists to perfect the character of the householders.

I don't agree

But private property furthers democracy only if ownership is widespread. If one rich man has almost all the property and many poor men have none, a struggle will ensue between the landowner and the landless. A central question, therefore, is which historical forces produce the widespread ownership of property and which do not. To this question, Alan Mac-Farlane of Cambridge University has given powerful answers in *The Origins of English Individualism* (1978).

9

In much of medieval Europe outside England, land was owned by clans or extended families, which managed their land collectively. Farms produced goods chiefly for families rather than for markets, and, as children were required to run the farm, marriages were arranged at an early age for the convenience of the clan.

10

Since clan control of property meant that land rarely changed hands, hardly any law was created to govern such transactions. Since farm produce was seldom sold, little law was developed to govern exchanges. Since marriages were arranged, there was little law to govern conjugal matters. In short, little law was developed of the sort we now recognize. And, with little law, few courts were needed to interpret or apply it. Such tribunals as existed were not independent of other sources of authority; their rulings reflected the personal decision or will of the feudal prince.

11

ugh, hard to read

In England and perhaps elsewhere in northwestern Europe, MacFarlane shows, matters were very different. From at least the 13th century on, individual ownership of land was common. Though parents exercised a great deal of authority

12

over their households, and thus over their land, they did not do so as representatives of a clan that collectively controlled it. Land could be bought, sold, bequeathed, and inherited. Many people were poor, but most were not landless.

Individual ownership was so important in England that a man had to own land before starting a family. Since it might take a long time for this to happen, marriages occurred later in life than was the case in Eastern Europe. In England, too, the prospective husband and wife usually had to agree to the union, including one arranged by their parents. Many married over parental objections.

Because land in England could change hands easily, a body of rulings grew up to manage such transactions. This collection of individual decisions, later accepted and codified by others, became the common law of England. It was produced by courts that to a large degree were independent of the king, and it contained judgments independent of his authority. The legal claims granted by this law constituted a set of rights—not broad rights aimed at political power but rights of ownership, sale, and title. Once the language of rights entered public consciousness, however, it was only a matter of time before these selfsame rights, interpreted and applied by the independent courts, became claims against the king.

Just why England and a few other nations of northwestern Europe took this path of individual property rights and helped create a property-oriented legal system is not well understood. But having taken that path, they also laid the groundwork for democratic rule that was to come several centuries later—the same groundwork that was then exported to America, English Canada, Australia, and New Zealand.

The third condition is *homogeneity*. During the cold war we could be excused for thinking that the great drivers of human life were ideology and economics. In fact, however, as Daniel P. Moynihan has observed, the deepest and most pervasive source of human conflict is ethnic rivalry. Russia has

broken apart on ethnic lines; much of Africa and the Middle
East is split along ethnic lines; Yugoslavia has sundered
on ethnic lines. World War I was a struggle over "national"
—that is, ethnic—self-determination, and World War II,
though it might have been waged by Hitler under any circumstances, was justified by him in the name of the alleged
superiority of "Aryans" and their presumed right to be politically reunited with their follow "Aryans" in other nations.

Several democratic nations are today ethnically diverse, 17
but at the time democracy was being established, that diversity was so limited that it could be safely ignored. England
was an Anglo-Saxon nation; America, during its founding period, was overwhelmingly English; so also, by and large, were
Australia, Canada, and New Zealand.

Then there is Switzerland—ethnically quite a diverse soci- 18
ety that nonetheless managed to create a democracy out of an
alliance among French, German, and Italian speakers who
were divided almost equally between Protestants and Catholics. The Swiss model—a democratic nation in which much
authority, especially that of the courts, was left in the hands of
the cantons and only modest powers were bequeathed to the
national president—is a fascinating one, but so far it has
hardly served as a guide to other nations.

I am not suggesting that ethnic homogeneity is a good 19
thing or ought to be preserved at any cost; nor am I denying
that democracies can become ethnically heterogeneous. Certainly one of the great glories of the United States is to have
become both vigorously democratic and ethnically diverse.
But it is a rare accomplishment. Historically, and with few exceptions, the growth of democracy and of respect for human
rights was made easier—often much easier—to accomplish in
nations that had a more or less common culture.

Indeed, in the formative years of a nation, ethnic diversity 20
can be as great a problem as foreign enemies. The time,
power, and money that must be devoted to maintaining one
ethnic group in power is at least equivalent to the resources
needed to protect against a foreign enemy. When one part of
a people thinks another part is unworthy of rights, it is hard

for a government to act in the name of the "rights of the people." That is why democracy in England preceded democracy in the United Kingdom: because many parts of that kingdom—the Scots, the Irish—had very different views about who should rule them and how. They still do.

Finally, *tradition*. Democratic politics is rarely produced overnight. In 1914, Europe had only three democracies. By the end of World War I, that number had grown to thirteen; but by the time of the next war, the number had fallen again as Germany, Italy, and other nations became authoritarian. Between 1950 and 1990, there were roughly as many authoritarian regimes as democratic ones, and the rate at which democratic regimes changed into authoritarian ones was about the same as the rate at which authoritarian systems changed into democratic ones. 21

The oldest democracy, England, relied heavily on a tradition of human rights to move slowly toward modern democratic rule. Its problem—one that every nation must eventually face, and usually over a much briefer period—was how to get a government to respect the rights of people who did not necessarily support it. In this connection, the great event in English history was the signing of Magna Carta in 1215. 22

At the time, Magna Carta hardly resembled the American Bill of Rights. It was not a constitution or part of a constitution; much of it concerned taxes, debts, fines, licenses, and inheritances. Except for a few passages about not delaying or denying justice and not imprisoning people save by the judgment of their peers, it had little to do with human rights, let alone modern government. 23

But as the late Erwin Griswold of the Harvard Law School once put it, "Magna Carta is not primarily significant for what it was, but rather for what it came to be." Five centuries after it was written, it had become the touchstone for English liberties. 24

How so? Because it was constantly invoked whenever the king was at odds with his barons or his people. On at least 40 occasions over several centuries, the document was con- 25 firmed by the king, usually as a way of settling some current grievance; and every time the king restated his loyalty to it, Magna Carta gained authority. When the Puritan revolutionaries came to power, they did so in part in order to restore Magna Carta, a document most of them had probably never read.

As it passed into English folklore, so also was it exported to America. American colonists spoke of having "the rights of Englishmen," by which they meant the rights specified in Magna Carta and the subsequent decisions allegedly justified by it. Andrew Hamilton defended Peter Zenger's right to publish freely by reference to Magna Carta, even though the document says nothing about free speech. The constitutions of the United States and of several individual states put into writing the assumptions of Magna Carta: government has limited and defined powers, the judiciary should be independent, private property is important, and the "law of the land"—that is, British common law—should be the basis for settling disputes.

26

In America, the Declaration of Independence acquired a power similar to that of Magna Carta, but this time for reasons that could be more easily discerned in the text, with its "self-evident" truths that all men are entitled to life, liberty, and "the pursuit of happiness," and that these entitlements can be abridged only by due process of law. The Declaration and the Bill of Rights have become icons of American politics, to which people instantly give loyalty even though they may in practice disagree with one or more of their provisions.

27

gov't lines

For an illustration, finally, of the crucial importance of democratic tradition, we need only look to Japan. It is geographically isolated, its people own property, and it is ethnically homogeneous. But until 1945 it lacked any strong tradition of personal liberty and democratic rule. And so democracy came late to Japan, and at the point of a bayonet.

28

Will, then, the whole world become democratic? Unless history offers no lessons at all, one must wonder. None of the conditions I have mentioned—isolation, private property,

29

ethnic homogeneity, and deeply felt traditions of human rights—can be found in China or Russia or in much of Africa or the Middle East. Bits and pieces exist in parts of Latin America, more so lately than earlier, but that region's welcome flirtation with democratic rule is still relatively short-lived.

There are two ways democracy can spread despite the absence of the historical forces that have produced it elsewhere. One is through military conquest. In the 19th century, English rule provided the basis for democracy in India, just as in the 20th century the victorious Allies provided it for Germany and, as I have noted, Japan. In all three cases, nations having little experience with democracy had its lessons forcibly imposed, and so successfully that it has survived and shows every sign of entrenchment. But since democracies rarely conquer other nations, this mechanism will seldom be available.

The other way is economic globalization. Not every nation with free markets is democratic, but every democratic nation has something akin to a free market. Free markets both foster and require an openness to new ideas and scientific inquiry, opportunity for innovation, and a prudent level of regulation—qualities hard to come by in undemocratic regimes. The arrival of globalization and the Internet are making it clear to everybody in every nation just where one can buy the best goods at the lowest prices. In the face of widespread knowledge about what efficiency can achieve, nondemocratic governments will have to scramble to maintain inefficiency.

Of course, scramble they will. Singapore believes that it can be both prosperous and undemocratic, and so far it has managed. China has bet that it can do the same. But will these successes endure? No one can be certain. An optimistic friend of mine has predicted that, because it wishes to be rich, China will become democratic by the year 2013. Perhaps. My question is whether it will still be democratic in the year 2033.

In the long run, democracy and human freedom are good for everyone even though they may create some mischief in the near term. But the good they bring can only be appreciated when people are calm and tolerance is accepted. The late Edward C. Banfield, perhaps the best student of American politics in modern times, said something about political systems in general that applies with particular force to democracies:

> *A political system is an accident. It is an accumulation of habits, customs, prejudices, and principles that have survived a long process of trial and error and of ceaseless response to changing circumstances. If the system works well on the whole, it is a lucky accident—the luckiest, indeed, that can befall a society, for all of the institutions of the society, and thus its entire character and that of the human types formed within it, depend ultimately on the government and the political order.*

nice new, blunt idea

To this I would add that a workable democracy is the happiest accident of all. By nourishing ours, we may perhaps hope that others will acquire something equally worthy of nurturance.

34

For Study and Discussion

QUESTIONS FOR RESPONSE

1. In your civics or political science class, what were you taught about the conditions required to create a democratic form of government?
2. How do you account for the inability of countries to make democracy work?

QUESTIONS ABOUT PURPOSE

1. How does Wilson distinguish between the *ideas* that have shaped democracies and the *conditions* that have made democracies possible?
2. If countries do not meet his conditions, how can they still become democratic?

QUESTIONS ABOUT AUDIENCE

1. What assumptions does Wilson make about his readers' historical and cultural knowledge? For example, what does he expect them to know about the history and culture of Japan?
2. How does Wilson help his readers understand the connection between globalization and democracy?

QUESTIONS ABOUT STRATEGIES

1. How does Wilson illustrate the importance of widespread ownership of private property?
2. How does Wilson explain the condition of homogeneity in countries that are ethnically and racially diverse—such as America?

QUESTIONS FOR DISCUSSION

1. What is the track record for countries that have had democracy forced on them by military conquest?
2. What is the relationship between economic prosperity and political democracy?

GARRY WILLS

Garry Wills was born in 1934 in Atlanta, Georgia, and was educated at St. Louis University, Xavier University, and Yale University. He has taught humanities at Johns Hopkins University and American culture and public policy at Northwestern University. His many books on American politics and history include *Nixon Agonistes: The Crisis of the Self-Made Man* (1970), *Inventing America: Jefferson's Declaration of Independence* (1978), *Reagan's America: The Innocents at Home* (1987), *Lincoln at Gettysburg: The Words That Remade America* (1992), and *James Madison* (2002). In "The Dramaturgy of Death," reprinted from *The New York Review of Books*, Wills classifies fourteen reasons for killing someone to demonstrate that capital punishment is an ineffective ritual.

The Dramaturgy of Death

1. CAPITAL PUNISHMENT: THE RATIONALES

A slight perusal of the laws by which the measures of vindictive and coercive justice are established will discover so many disproportions between crimes and punishments, such capricious distinctions of guilt, and such confusion of remissness and severity as can scarcely be believed to have been produced by public wisdom, sincerely and calmly studious of public happiness.
—SAMUEL JOHNSON, *Rambler* 114

N IETZSCHE DENIED THAT capital punishment ever arose from a single or consistent theory of its intent or effect. It erupted from a tangle of overlapping yet conflicting urges, which would be fitted out with later rationalizations.

The only common denominator he found in the original urges was some form of grievance (he used the French term *ressentiment*). One can expand his own list of such urges:

Killing as Exclusion. This occurs when society does not   2 want to admit any responsibility for persons considered outsiders. Abandonment of wounded or captured people one does not want to feed or support is an example, or exposure of unwanted children, or exiling the defenseless (as the blind

handwritten note in margin: like high school

The bad faith of the [death penalty] process shows in the insistence on using the deterrence argument when it has been discredited by all the most reputable studies.

---

and old Oedipus was extruded from Thebes), or "outlawing"—leaving people without protection to any predators on them. Outlawing was an English practice continued in our colonies. In fact, Thomas Jefferson, when he revised the laws of Virginia for the new republic, left certain categories of offenders "out of the protection of the laws"—freed slaves who either enter the state or refuse to leave it, a white woman bearing a black child who does not leave the state within a year. These could be killed or mistreated in any way without remedy at law. The ancient Greeks denied offenders recourse to law by the penalty of *atimia* (loss of rights). There were lesser degrees of this, but the full degree of "atimia . . . and condemnation to death are interchangeable." Nietzsche calls this "Punishment as the expulsion of a degenerate element . . . as a means of preserving the purity of a race or maintaining a social type."

Killing as Cleansing. Outlawing abandons people to possi-   3 ble or probable death but does not directly bring it about. Other forms of extrusion require society's purification by *destruction* of a polluted person. Unless society or its agents effect this purification, the pollution continues to taint them. Lesser pollutions can be robbed of their effect by simply driving away the affected person. But deeper taints are removed only by accompanying the expulsion with something like stoning the polluter to death or throwing him off a cliff. Plato said that the murderer of anyone in his own immediate family was to be killed by judicial officers and magistrate, then "thrown down naked on a designated crossroads outside the city; whereupon every official present must throw his own stone at the head of the corpse, to cleanse the whole city, and finally must take him beyond the land's outer boundaries and cast him out, all rites of burial denied" (*Laws* 873b–c).

Killing as Execration. Sometimes the community must thrust away contamination by ritual curses *(arai),* joining the punitive cry of the Furies, who are also called Arai (Aeschylus, *Eumenides* 417). When Prometheus is punished by exposure as the penalty of theft, Brute Force (Bia) tells the technician clamping him to the rock (Hephaistos) that he should curse as well as immobilize him (Aeschylus, *Prometheus* 38, 67–68). Southern lynch mobs stayed to curse with fury their hanged victim from a similar impulse.

Killing to Maintain Social Order. Superiors dramatize their dominance by showing that it is easy for those higher in the social scale to kill those lower, but harder for the lower to kill the higher. Plato's legal code devised a penalty for a slave who kills a free man—public scourging to death before the free man's tomb and family—that had no symmetrical penalty for a free man who kills a slave (*Laws* 872b–c). In Jefferson's legal code, slaves could not testify against whites, but whites could testify against slaves. In parts of this country still, a black killing a white is far more likely to receive a death sentence than a white killing a black. Nietzsche calls this "Punishment as a means of inspiring fear of those who determine and execute the punishment."

Killing to Delegitimize a Former Social Order. Revolutionary tribunals execute officials of an overthrown regime. Even without a coup, critics of Athenian democracy claimed that mass juries were too ready to condemn their leaders. When

[handwritten margin notes: "horrible", "how does power over death control that?"]

[handwritten margin numbers: 4, 6]

the Turkish general Lala Mustafa Pasha captured Cyprus from the Venetians in 1570, the podestà who had held out against him, Marcantonio Bragadin, was mutilated (nose and ears cut off), dragged around the city walls, dangled from a ship's mast, tied naked to a post, skinned alive, beheaded, and "quartered" (his four limbs cut off). Then his skin, stuffed with straw, was tied to a cow and led through the streets of the Famagusta, before being returned as a victory prize to Constantinople. Venetian rule was pulverized in its representative. Nietzsche calls this "Punishment as a festival, namely as the rape and mockery of a finally defeated enemy."

Killing as Posthumous Delegitimation. Some inquisitors   7
tried dead men and symbolically executed them. The leaders of the Gowrie Plot that tried to supplant King James VI of Scotland in 1600 were tried posthumously and their corpses were hanged, drawn (eviscerated), and quartered. In 897, Stephen VI had the corpse of his predecessor, Pope Formosus, exhumed, propped up in his papal garb, tried and condemned for usurpation, stripped of his vestments, his head (that had borne the tiara) cut off, along with the three fingers of his right hand used in benediction, and head, fingers, and body then thrown in the Tiber—all to declare Formosus's consecration of bishops and ordination of priests invalid.

Killing as Total Degradation. The previous three forms of   8
execution punished an offender as a member of a class (lower or higher); but other humiliating deaths are contrived to deprive a person of humanity as such. Public torture before death was one means for this—scourging that makes the offender scream and writhe, losing dignity along with his composure. The Greek punishment for theft was *apotympanismos,* the beating of a naked man clamped down in a crouched position before he was left to die of exposure (it is the punishment given to Prometheus in his play, though he cannot die). The death for traitors in Elizabethan England was an elaborate piece of theater. First the offender was dragged backward on a hurdle to the place of execution—signifying, said the attorney general Sir Edward Coke, that the man was "not wor-

thy any more to tread upon the face of the earth whereof he was made; also for that he hath been retrograde to nature, therefore is he drawn backward at a horse-tail." Then the man (it was a male punishment) was stripped, hanged, cut down living, castrated, disemboweled, his heart and viscera thrown in boiling water, decapitated, quartered, and his head exposed on Tower Bridge. When Jesuit priests were hanged, drawn, and quartered, their head, members, torso, and clothes were hidden away to prevent the taking of relics.

Killing and Posthumous Degradation. Refusal of burial led   9
the ancient Greeks to let bodies be exposed for ravaging by dogs and kites (Creon's treatment of Polyneices in Sophocles' *Antigone*). Romans let crucified bodies hang to be pecked at and decompose. Florentines in the Renaissance dangled the corpses of criminals from the high windows of the Bargello till they rotted, and commissioned artists like Andrea del Sarto to depict them there, prolonging the shame after they were gone. Joan of Arc was killed by a slow fire that consumed her clothes and skin, then the flames were raked away, to expose her body as a woman's and to show that no demon had spirited her away. Then intense fire was mounted to burn her down to ashes for scattering in the Seine, to prevent any collection of relics.

Killing by Ordeal. In this punishment, the innocent were   10
supposed to be protected if subjected to ordeal by combat, ordeal by fire (walking through it, as Saint Francis is supposed to have done in Egypt), or ordeal by water. The latter was especially reserved for suspected witches, who would sink only if innocent. A less lethal form of this punishment survived in the "ducking stool" for immersing witches. Jefferson's revised code says this: "All attempts to delude the people, or to abuse their understanding by exercise of the pretended [claimed] arts of witchcraft, conjuration, enchantment, or sorcery or by pretended prophecies, shall be punished by ducking and whipping at the discretion of a jury, not exceeding 15 stripes."

Threatened Killing as Inducement to Remorse. Refusal to   11
undergo trial by ordeal could be taken as a confession,

leading to a lesser penalty than death. Recanting could have the same effect. Joan of Arc, when first brought out to the stake with its kindling, renounced her voices as "idolatry" (devil worship), and was given life imprisonment. Only when she abjured her recantation was she actually put to the stake. Scaffold repentance could reduce the sentence to less than death—or, at the least, make officials perform a "merciful" (a swifter, not a lingering) execution—e.g., letting a man die in the noose before being cut down for disemboweling. Nietzsche calls this punishment for the "improvement" of the criminal.

Killing as Repayment. The *lex talionis,* as it exacts "an eye   12 for an eye," must exact a life for a life. We say, "You're going to *pay* for this." Jefferson followed the logic of his state's *lex talionis:*

> *Whosoever shall be guilty of Rape, Polygamy, or Sodomy with man or woman shall be punished, if a man, by castration, if a woman, by cutting thro' the cartilage of her nose a hole of one half inch diameter at the least . . . Whosoever on purpose and of malice forethought shall maim another, or shall disfigure him, by cutting out or disabling the tongue, slitting or cutting off a nose, lip or ear, branding, or otherwise, shall be maimed or disfigured in like sort: or if that cannot be for want of the same part, then as nearly as may be in some other part of at least equal value and estimation in the opinion of a jury, and moreover shall forfeit one half of his lands and goods to the sufferer.*

Taking a life for a life on this principle is called by Nietzsche "Punishment as recompense to the injured party for the harm done."

Killing as Repayment-Plus. In Athenian law, repayment   13 was of equal value if the crime was unintentional, but of double if it was intentional. On that principle, death has not been reserved only for taking a life, but can be considered an added penalty for crimes like major theft, rape, treasonous speech, and the like.

Killing as Victim Therapy. The Attic orator Antiphon has [14] the father of a son killed by accident plead that the unintentional killer must be punished; the death leaves the father aggrieved (*epithymion*—much like Nietzsche's *ressentiment*). The grievance, of course, would be even greater if the killing were intentional. Soothing this sense of grievance is now called "giving closure" to the ordeal of victims.

Killing as a Form of Pedagogy. We say that punishing a man [15] will "teach him a lesson." More important, it may teach others the consequence of crime, deterring anyone who contemplates a similar offense. Kant said that the person should be treated as his own end, not as a means for others' advantage. But the person executed is, by this theory, turned into a teaching instrument for the benefit of others.

2. PUBLIC EXECUTION

Experience of past times gives us little reason to hope that any reformation will be effected by a periodical havoc of our fellow beings.

—SAMUEL JOHNSON, *Rambler* 114

The fourteen types of capital punishment listed above do not [16] exhaust all the possible urges expressed in our havocking of others. And as Nietzsche said, they are not neat little separate rationales. They conflict with each other at an intellectual level, but they reinforce each other at the emotional level. They are more powerful for certain people in certain combinations. But they have one thing in common: *they all demand, in logic, maximum display and publicity.* The outlaw's status must be proclaimed for people to act on it. The other effects sought—whether cleansing, order enforcement, delegitimation, humiliation, repayment, therapy, deterrence—can only be achieved if an audience sees what is being done to satisfy, intimidate, soothe, or instruct it.

[handwritten marginalia: "Therapy is an effective word"]

that seems backwards to me

In fact, various means to dramatize the process, to make its 17
meaning clear, to show the right way to "read" it, were invented. Those going to the scaffold often had their crimes
blazoned on their backs. Joan of Arc wore a fool's cap with
her four crimes printed on it. A crucified man had his crime
posted on the cross. Lesser criminals were branded to sustain
the memory of their crime. Ingenious means of execution
were invented to express society's horror, anger, power, and
the like. Any punishment that fits the crime should be *seen* to
fit the crime. Indeed, the only urges that people now commonly admit to—the last four in the above list (repayment of
two kinds, "closure," and deterrence)—are closely linked
with publicity. The repayment is to us, to society as well as to
the victims, the therapy is for the victims' contemplation, and
an act meant to deter should vividly catch the attention of
those who might benefit from it. How can they "learn their
lesson" if it is not spelled out for them?

Our unconfessed difficulty is that we have given up what- 18
ever logic there was to the death penalty, since we have become unable to embrace most of the practices of the past. We
no longer believe in a divine miasma to be purged, or divine
guidance to be revealed in survival by ordeal. We have given
up the desecration of corpses, killing as a reinforcement of
class distinctions, torture, maiming, evisceration, and all the
the what's difference? multiple methods used to reduce the criminal to a *corpus vile*.
Even Jefferson wavered on the *lex talionis* when it came to
blinding an offender (he could go as far as a nose for a
nose, but not as far as an eye for an eye). Our Constitution
forbids cruel and unusual punishment, and we take that to
mean that there will be no gratuitous humiliation of the convict—we do not even put people in the stocks anymore,
much less invite the public to see a condemned man being
strapped onto a gurney. We want painless executions, so we
have recurred to one of the few humane-looking methods of
the Greeks—lethal injection (hemlock), though among the
many deterrents to becoming a philosopher, Socrates' quiet
(and self-chosen) death in his seventies has never ranked very
high.

So far from stigmatizing or humiliating the inmate of death row, we now provide him with a long and costly process meant to ascertain guilt, with free legal aid if he cannot afford his own, with counseling and family visits, with reading of his choice and TV, a last meal to his specifications, a last request, religious attendance, guaranteed burial, a swift and nearly painless death. We shut up his last hours from the general public, and act as if this secret rite will deter by some magic of mere occurrence. We treat the killing as a dirty little secret, as if we are ashamed of it. Well, we should be ashamed. Having given up on most of the previous justifications for the death penalty, we cling to a mere vestige of the practice, relying most urgently on one of the least defensible defenses of it.

3 . DETERRENCE

The gibbet, indeed, certainly disables those who die upon it from infesting the community; but their death seems not to contribute more to the reformation of their associates than any other method of separation.
—SAMUEL JOHNSON, *Rambler* 114

The bad faith of the process shows in the insistence on using the deterrence argument when it has been discredited by all the most reputable studies. This is an old story. In the eighteenth century, Samuel Johnson, who liked to defend any tradition he could, discovered no deterrent effect following on traditional executions, though they were far more numerous and far more public than they are now (factors, some people think, that add to deterrent effect). In the middle of the twentieth century, Arthur Koestler could refer to a strong scholarly record on the matter:

> *This belief in the irreplaceable deterrent value of the death-penalty has been proved to be a superstition by the long and patient inquiries of the Parliamentary Select Committee of 1930 and the Royal Commission on Capital Punishment of 1948; yet it pops up again and*

again. Like all superstitions, it has the nature of a Jack-in-the-box; however often you hit it over the head with facts and statistics, it will solemnly pop up again, because the hidden spring inside it is the unconscious and irrational power of traditional beliefs.

Present and former presidents of the most prestigious criminological societies, polled in 1995, overwhelmingly said they did not think the death penalty significantly reduces the homicide rate (94 percent), and they knew of no empirical evidence that would support such a claim (94.1 percent). They held (79.2 percent) that execution causes no reduction in crime—a finding confirmed by the fact that states with the death penalty have higher murder rates than those without (the region with the highest number of homicides, the South, accounts for over 80 percent of the nation's executions). Furthermore, countries in Europe that have given up the death penalty have far lower murder rates than does the United States (since those countries *do* have gun control laws). Disbelief in the deterring power of execution is also expressed, though not so overwhelmingly, by police chiefs and sheriffs—not a far-left part of the community—surveyed by Peter D. Hart Research Associates in 1995. They did not think (67 percent) that executions significantly reduce homicides. In fact, New York's former police chief Patrick V. Murphy responded that "the flimsy notion that the death penalty is an effective law enforcement tool is being exposed as mere political puffery."

Expert criminologists said (100 percent, joined in this by 21 85 percent of the police chiefs) that politicians support the death penalty for symbolic reasons, to show they are tough on crime, though that distracts them (86.6 percent of the criminologists, 56 percent of the police chiefs) from addressing better methods of reducing the homicide rate. The police listed four things that would be more effective in fighting crime, including longer sentences, more police, and gun control. It takes little observation of actual politicians to confirm that politicians support the death penalty for electoral reasons. Now-Senator Dianne Feinstein, who had opposed capital punishment as a very active member of the California parole board, embraced it in 1990 when she ran for governor. When I asked her during that campaign what had made her change her position, she said that she had become convinced that executions do deter other criminals. I said that most studies I had seen denied this, but she told me she had read new and better research, though she could not name it for me. "I'll send it to you," she promised—but she never did. The only empirical evidence that mattered to her was her knowledge of the way Rose Bird had been resoundingly defeated for reelection as the chief justice of the Supreme Court of California because she opposed capital punishment.

(research smtg useful)

When Andrew Young ran for governor of Georgia in 1990, he too abandoned his early opposition to the death penalty (though his daughter remained an activist opponent of it, because of its disproportionate rate among blacks—the NAACP Legal Defense Fund discovered that a black's chance of being executed in Georgia was eleven times that of a white). I asked Young if he too had been convinced that executions deter. He said that he had not, but that as mayor of Atlanta he had listened to police tell him that it discouraged them to catch criminals and see them escape execution—"I did it for their morale." (He did it, though, only when he was leaving the mayor's office and addressing a much whiter constituency in his race for governor.)   22

Other politicians obviously look to the polls, not to policy studies, when taking their stand on executions. Campaigning to become the senator from New York, Hillary Clinton knew how much support the state's former governor Mario Cuomo had lost because of his resolute stand against executions. William Weld, while he was still governor of Massachusetts, said that he relied not on studies but on "my gut": "My gut is that . . . capital punishment is deterrent." The deft use of the death penalty issue by Bob Graham as governor of Florida and in his 1986 race for the Senate is studied in a book that Timothy McVeigh is known to have read in prison.   23

(horrible how it works like that)

In 1984, Graham dismissed scholarly studies on the death penalty by saying, "This is an issue that is inherently beyond what empirical research can validate," making him another gut-truster like Weld. But if we cannot know the deterrent effect, we are certainly killing one man for a hypothetical effect on others that is uncertain.

Actually, the deterrent theory of capital punishment, always weak, is especially flimsy now, when a rash of cases—some involving DNA evidence—has proved that some innocent men are on death row. The evidence of incompetent defenses, faked evidence, and negligent procedures has led to announced or informal moratoria on executions. In Oklahoma alone, where Timothy McVeigh's crime was committed, the evidence in approximately three thousand cases is now tainted by the defective lab work of one technician, Joyce Gilchrist. The execution of the innocent is not a new issue, but widespread public awareness of it is. The British study by the Select Committee on Capital Punishment, cited by Arthur Koestler, found cases of mistaken executions, including "many" reported by the governor of Sing Sing in America.

Some try to separate the problem of killing the *right* person from the question of whether we should execute *any* person at all. But since the principal prop of the death penalty is deterrence theory, that prop is knocked out when uncertainty of guilt enters the national consciousness. Even if we were to grant that executions deter, they may not deter people who think it is a random matter whether the right person is caught. If they might get off while guilty, or be killed while innocent, that fact is not a very stable basis for forswearing a particular homicide. And executing the mentally defective or marginally juvenile, like the disproportionate killing of blacks, cannot much intimidate a would-be murderer who is mentally sound, of mature age, or white.

These considerations join longer-term flaws in the deterrence argument. Juries are readiest to convict people for

[marginal note: well, which one is worse?]

[marginal numbers: 24, 25, 26]

crimes of passion, sexually charged rape-murders, child-abuse murders, or serial killings. To see these offenders caught will not necessarily affect the person most likely to have the coolness and calculation that deterrence requires. And obviously they do not affect other people in the grip of obsessions, mental instability, or drug- or alcohol-induced frenzy. Plato was against executing those guilty of a crime of passion (*Laws* 867c–d), but our juries reflect more the anger of society than the didactic strategies of deterrence. In doing this, the juries fail to make the calculations that we are told future murderers will make. The whole theory is senseless.

[handwritten: And what exactly does that entail?]

4. "CLOSURE"

[People come] in thousands to the legal massacre and look with carelessness, perhaps with triumph, on the utmost exacerbations of human misery.
—Samuel Johnson, *Rambler* 114

"Closure" has become a buzzword, not only for discussing the death penalty but for addressing any kind of social discontent. When the unmarried mother of Jesse Jackson's child sued Reverend Jackson, it was not about anything so crass as money, it was to find "closure" for herself and her child. Who can deprive a grieving person of solace? This is the argument Antiphon's prosecutor made when he demanded emotional relief for the loss of his child to an accident. Attorney General John Ashcroft endorsed the argument by arranging for the families of Timothy McVeigh's victims to see him die. This conflicts with the logic of deterrence, since the families are not viewing the event to deter them from becoming mass murderers. If the real point of executions is to act *in terrorem* for other criminals, the Oklahoma families are the least appropriate audience. 27

[handwritten: great point]

Ashcroft's response to the hot pressures of the McVeigh case is just that of Dianne Feinstein or Andrew Young to less emotionally charged instances of capital punishment, where 28 no mass murder is involved. McVeigh, the cold killer revealed in *American Terrorist,* by Lou Michel and Dan Herbeck, triggers all the upsurges of emotion Nietzsche described. We feel that the very existence of a McVeigh is an affront to society, a pollutant of our life, a thing we cannot be clean of without execration. But the politician does not want to be seen ministering to atavistic reactions in their raw state. So he invokes deterrence where it does not apply, or says that humane consideration of the victims' sympathies trumps all other considerations. Seeing the murderer die, we are told, will just help the families to "close a chapter of their lives."

But is this really likely? The aim of emotional healing is to bring inflamed emotions of loss and *ressentiment* back into a manageable relationship with other parts of one's life. Does that happen when, for many years in most cases (six years so far in McVeigh's case), a victim's survivors focus on seeing that someone pays for his or her loss? This tends to reenact the outrage in a person's mind, rather than to transcend it. It prolongs the trauma, delaying and impeding the healing process. When I asked Sister Helen Prejean, the author of *Dead Man Walking,* what she has observed, she said that families are asked by prosecutors to attend the trial of a relative's murderer, but to show no emotion lest they cause a mistrial. "They learn new details of the crime, and with each new turn of the trial and its aftermath the media call them to get a reaction." This is less like healing than like tearing scabs open again and again. Some relatives who want to escape this process are accused by their own of not loving the victim, says Sister Helen: "I have seen families torn apart over the death penalty."

What's more, the sterile, anodyne, and bureaucratic procedures of a modern execution can baffle the desire for revenge encouraged before its performance. Sister Helen recalls a man who said he wished to see more suffering, and who comes with pro-death demonstrators to all later executions. This is hardly one who has found "closure." The eeriness of

29

30

the closure language was revealed when McVeigh himself, through his lawyer, Rob Nigh, expressed sympathy for the relatives' "disappointment" after his execution was delayed. He is more the manipulator of these grieving people than an offering to them.

Emotional counselors work toward reconciliation with the facts, as religious leaders recommend forgiveness. Many church bodies oppose the death penalty, drawing on rich traditions in the various faiths. Saint Augustine resisted the killing of murderers, even of two men who had murdered one of his own priests, arguing that the fate of souls is in God's hands (Letters 133, 134). It is true that Thomas Aquinas likened the killing of murderers to the amputation of a limb for the good of the whole body, but his fellow Dominican Niceto Blázquez points out how defective this argument is: Thomas was drawing an analogy with the excommunication of sinners from the Church, the body of Christ—but that is a move meant to promote reunion, to rescue a person from the death of his soul, not to impose a death on the body.

31

[handwritten marginalia: I don't think I'll ever understand why that's likeable?]

Conservative Catholics, who are aghast at fellow believers' willingness to ignore the pope on matters like contraception, blithely ignore in their turn papal pleas to renounce the death penalty (addressed most recently to the McVeigh case). And I have not seen Bible-quoting fundamentalists refer to the one place in the Gospels where Jesus deals with capital punishment. At John 8:3–11, he interrupts a legal execution (for adultery) and tells the officers of the state that their own sinfulness deprives them of jurisdiction. Jesus himself gives up any jurisdiction for this kind of killing: "Neither do I condemn you." George W. Bush said during the campaign debates of [2002] that Jesus is his favorite philosopher—though he did not hesitate to endorse the execution of 152 human beings in Texas, where half of the public defenders of accused murderers were sanctioned by the Texas bar for legal misbehavior or incompetence. Mr. Bush clearly needs some deeper consultation with the philosopher of his choice.

32

[handwritten marginalia: hmm...]

[handwritten marginalia: odd new point to add ☺ end]

For Study and Discussion

QUESTIONS FOR RESPONSE

1. In the court cases you know something about, has the punishment fit the crime?
2. In what ways do you think punishment teaches a lesson?

QUESTIONS ABOUT PURPOSE

1. How does Wills' detailed—and often gruesome—classification of the motives for killing someone support his argument against the death penalty?
2. How does Wills dispute the argument that capital punishment teaches would-be criminals not to commit a crime?

QUESTIONS ABOUT AUDIENCE

1. How does Wills use quotations from historical figures—such as Plato and Jefferson—to shock his readers?
2. How does he anticipate the reactions of those readers who believe that capital punishment provides healing and closure?

QUESTIONS ABOUT STRATEGIES

1. How does Wills explain why some of the motives he lists overlap one another?
2. How does Wills use statistical research to counteract the "gut" responses of politicians?

QUESTIONS FOR DISCUSSION

1. How do you account for our culture's preference for "secret ritual" over "public execution"?
2. How does Wills use Sister Helen Prejean's observations to explain why families have been "torn apart over the death penalty"?

Flannery O'Connor (1925–1964) was born in Savannah, Georgia, and was educated at the Women's College of Georgia and the University of Iowa. She returned to her mother's farm near Milledgeville, Georgia, when she discovered that she had contracted lupus erythematosus, the systemic disease that had killed her father and of which she herself was to die. For the last fourteen years of her life, she lived a quiet, productive life on the farm—raising peacocks, painting, and writing the extraordinary stories and novels that won her worldwide acclaim. Her novels, *Wise Blood* (1952), which was adapted for film in 1979, and *The Violent Bear It Away* (1960), deal with fanatical preachers. Her thirty-one carefully crafted stories, combining grotesque comedy and violent tragedy, appear in *A Good Man Is Hard to Find* (1955), *Everything That Rises Must Converge* (1965), and *The Complete Stories* (1971), which won the National Book Award. "Revelation" dramatizes the ironic discoveries a woman makes about how different classes of people fit into the order of things.

Revelation

THE DOCTOR'S WAITING room, which was very small, was almost full when the Turpins entered and Mrs. Turpin, who was very large, made it look even smaller by her presence. She stood looming at the head of the magazine table set in the center of it, a living demonstration that the room was inadequate and ridiculous. Her little bright black eyes took in all the patients as she sized up the seating situation. There was one vacant chair and a place on the sofa occupied by a blond child in a dirty blue romper who should have been told to move over and make room for the lady. He was five or six, but Mrs. Turpin saw at once that no one was going to tell him to move over. He was slumped down in the seat, his arms idle at his sides and his eyes idle in his head; his nose ran unchecked.

Mrs. Turpin put a firm hand on Claud's shoulder and said   2
in a voice that included anyone who wanted to listen, "Claud, you sit in that chair there," and gave him a push down into the vacant one. Claud was florid and bald and sturdy, somewhat shorter than Mrs. Turpin, but he sat down as if he were accustomed to doing what she told him to.

Mrs. Turpin remained standing. The only man in the   3
room besides Claud was a lean stringy old fellow with a rusty hand spread out on each knee, whose eyes were closed as if he were asleep or dead or pretending to be so as not to get up and offer her his seat. Her gaze settled agreeably on a well-dressed gray-haired lady whose eyes met hers and whose expression said: if that child belonged to me, he would have some manners and move over—there's plenty of room there for you and him too.

Claud looked up with a sigh and made as if to rise.   4

"Sit down," Mrs. Turpin said. "You know you're not sup-   5
posed to stand on that leg. He has an ulcer on his leg," she explained.

Claud lifted his foot onto the magazine table and rolled   6
his trouser leg up to reveal a purple swelling on a plump marble-white calf.

"My!" the pleasant lady said. "How did you do that?"   7

"A cow kicked him," Mrs. Turpin said.   8

"Goodness!" said the lady.   9

Claud rolled his trouser leg down.   10

"Maybe the little boy would move over," the lady sug-   11
gested, but the child did not stir.

"Somebody will be leaving in a minute," Mrs. Turpin said.   12
She could not understand why a doctor—with as much money as they made charging five dollars a day to just stick

their head in the hospital door and look at you—couldn't afford a decent-sized waiting room. This one was hardly bigger than a garage. The table was cluttered with limp-looking magazines and at one end of it there was a big green glass ash tray full of cigarette butts and cotton wads with little blood spots on them. If she had had anything to do with the running of the place, that would have been emptied every so often. There were no chairs against the wall at the head of the room. It had a rectangular-shaped panel in it that permitted a view of the office where the nurse came and went and the secretary listened to the radio. A plastic fern in a gold pot sat in the opening and trailed its fronds down almost to the floor. The radio was softly playing gospel music.

Just then the inner door opened and a nurse with the highest stack of yellow hair Mrs. Turpin had ever seen put her face in the crack and called for the next patient. The woman sitting beside Claud grasped the two arms of her chair and hoisted herself up; she pulled her dress free from her legs and lumbered through the door where the nurse had disappeared.

Mrs. Turpin eased into the vacant chair, which held her tight as a corset. "I wish I could reduce," she said, and rolled her eyes and gave a comic sigh.

"Oh, *you* aren't fat," the stylish lady said.

"Ooooo I am too," Mrs. Turpin said. "Claud he eats all he wants to and never weighs over one hundred and seventy-five pounds, but me I just look at something good to eat and I gain some weight," and her stomach and shoulders shook with laughter. "You can eat all you want to, can't you, Claud?" she asked, turning to him.

Claud only grinned.

"Well, as long as you have such a good disposition," the stylish lady said, "I don't think it makes a bit of difference what size you are. You just can't beat a good disposition."

Next to her was a fat girl of eighteen or nineteen, scowling into a thick blue book which Mrs. Turpin saw was entitled *Human Development*. The girl raised her head and directed her scowl at Mrs. Turpin as if she did not like her looks. She appeared annoyed that anyone should speak while she tried to read. The poor girl's face was blue with acne and Mrs. Turpin thought how pitiful it was to have a face like that at that age. She gave the girl a friendly smile but the girl only scowled the harder. Mrs. Turpin herself was fat but she had always had good skin, and, though she was forty-seven years old, there was not a wrinkle in her face except around her eyes from laughing too much.

Next to the ugly girl was the child, still in exactly the same 20
position, and next to him was a thin leathery old woman in a cotton print dress. She and Claud had three sacks of chicken feed in their pump house that was in the same print. She had seen from the first that the child belonged with the old woman. She could tell by the way they sat—kind of vacant and white-trashy, as if they would sit there until Doomsday if nobody called and told them to get up. And at right angles but next to the well-dressed pleasant lady was a lank-faced woman who was certainly the child's mother. She had on a yellow sweat shirt and wine-colored slacks, both gritty-looking, and the rims of her lips were stained with snuff. Her dirty yellow hair was tied behind with a little piece of red paper ribbon. Worse than niggers any day, Mrs. Turpin thought.

The gospel hymn playing was, "When I looked up and He 21
looked down," and Mrs. Turpin, who knew it, supplied the last line mentally, "And wona these days I know I'll weear a crown."

Without appearing to, Mrs. Turpin always noticed peo- 22
ple's feet. The well-dressed lady had on red and gray suede shoes to match her dress. Mrs. Turpin had on her good black patent leather pumps. The ugly girl had on Girl Scout shoes and heavy socks. The old woman had on tennis shoes and the white-trashy mother had on what appeared to be bedroom slippers, black straw with gold braid threaded through them—exactly what you would have expected her to have on.

Sometimes at night when she couldn't go to sleep, Mrs. 23
Turpin would occupy herself with the question of who she

would have chosen to be if she couldn't have been herself. If Jesus had said to her before he made her, "There's only two places available for you. You can either be a nigger or white-trash," what would she have said? "Please, Jesus, please," she would have said, "just let me wait until there's another place available," and he would have said, "No, you have to go right now and I have only those two places so make up your mind." She would have wiggled and squirmed and begged and pleaded but it would have been no use and finally she would have said, "All right, make me a nigger then—but that don't mean a trashy one." And he would have made her a neat clean respectable Negro woman, herself but black.

real sense of where she stands

Next to the child's mother was a red-headed youngish woman, reading one of the magazines and working a piece of chewing gum, hell for leather, as Claud would say. Mrs. Turpin could not see the woman's feet. She was not white-trash, just common. Sometimes Mrs. Turpin occupied herself at night naming the classes of people. On the bottom of the heap were most colored people, not the kind she would have been if she had been one, but most of them; then next to them—not above, just away from—were the white-trash; then above them were the home-owners, and above them the home-and-land-owners, to which she and Claud belonged. Above she and Claud were people with a lot of money and much bigger houses and much more land. But here the complexity of it would begin to bear in on her, for some of the people with a lot of money were common and ought to be below she and Claud and some of the people who had good blood had lost their money and had to rent and then there were colored people who owned their homes and land as well. There was a colored dentist in town who had two red Lincolns and a swimming pool and a farm with registered white-face cattle on it. Usually by the time she had fallen asleep all the classes of people were moiling and roiling around in her head, and she would dream they were all crammed in together in a box car, being ridden off to be put in a gas oven.

24

division

"That's a beautiful clock," she said and nodded to her   25
right. It was a big wall clock, the face encased in a brass
sunburst.

"Yes, it's very pretty," the stylish lady said agreeably. "And   26
right on the dot too," she added, glancing at her watch.

The ugly girl beside her cast an eye upward at the clock,   27
smirked, then looked directly at Mrs. Turpin and smirked
again. Then she returned her eyes to her book. She was obviously the lady's daughter because, although they didn't look
anything alike as to disposition, they both had the same shape
of face and the same blue eyes. On the lady they sparkled
pleasantly but in the girl's seared face they appeared alter-
nately to smolder and to blaze.

What if Jesus had said, "All right, you can be white-trash   28
or a nigger or ugly"!

Mrs. Turpin felt an awful pity for the girl, though she   29
thought it was one thing to be ugly and another to act ugly.

The woman with the snuff-stained lips turned around in   30
her chair and looked up at the clock. Then she turned back
and appeared to look a little to the side of Mrs. Turpin. There
was a cast in one of her eyes. "You want to know wher you
can get you one of themther clocks?" she asked in a loud
voice.

"No, I already have a nice clock," Mrs. Turpin said. Once   31
somebody like her got a leg in the conversation, she would be
all over it.

"You can get you one with green stamps," the woman   32
said. "That's most likely wher he got hisn. Save you up
enough, you can get you most anythang. I got me some
joo'ry."

Ought to have got you a wash rag and some soap, Mrs.   33
Turpin thought.

"I get contour sheets with mine," the pleasant lady said.   34

The daughter slammed her book shut. She looked straight   35
in front of her, directly through Mrs. Turpin and on through
the yellow curtain and the plate glass window which made
the wall behind her. The girl's eyes seemed lit all of a sudden
with a peculiar light, an unnatural light like night road signs

detail

nice

give. Mrs. Turpin turned her head to see if there was anything going on outside that she should see, but she could not see anything. Figures passing cast only a pale shadow through the curtain. There was no reason the girl should single her out for her ugly looks.

"Miss Finley," the nurse said, cracking the door. The gum-chewing woman got up and passed in front of her and Claud and went into the office. She had on red high-heeled shoes. 36

Directly across the table, the ugly girl's eyes were fixed on Mrs. Turpin as if she had some very special reason for disliking her. 37

"This is wonderful weather, isn't it?" the girl's mother said. 38

"It's good weather for cotton if you can get the niggers to pick it," Mrs. Turpin said, "but niggers don't want to pick cotton any more. You can't get the white folks to pick it and now you can't get the niggers—because they got to be right up there with the white folks." 39

stuck in the past

"They gonna *try* anyways," the white-trash woman said, leaning forward. 40

"Do you have one of the cotton-picking machines?" the pleasant lady asked. 41

"No," Mrs. Turpin said, "they leave half the cotton in the field. We don't have much cotton anyway. If you want to make it farming now, you have to have a little of everything. We got a couple of acres of cotton and a few hogs and chickens and just enough white-face that Claud can look after them himself." 42

"One thang I don't want," the white-trash woman said, wiping her mouth with the back of her hand. "Hogs. Nasty stinking things, a-gruntin and a-rootin all over the place." 43

ironic

Mrs. Turpin gave her the merest edge of her attention. "Our hogs are not dirty and they don't stink," she said. "They're cleaner than some children I've seen. Their feet never touch the ground. We have a pig-parlor—that's where you raise them on concrete," she explained to the pleasant lady, "and Claud scoots them down with the hose every afternoon and washes off the floor." Cleaner by far than that 44

child right there, she thought. Poor nasty little thing. He had
not moved except to put the thumb of his dirty hand into his
mouth.

The woman turned her face away from Mrs. Turpin. "I   45
know I wouldn't scoot down no hog with no hose," she said
to the wall.

You wouldn't have no hog to scoot down, Mrs. Turpin   46
said to herself.

"A-gruntin and a-rootin and a-groanin," the woman mut-   47
tered.

"We got a little of everything," Mrs. Turpin said to the   48
pleasant lady. "It's no use in having more than you can handle yourself with help like it is. We found enough niggers to
pick our cotton this year but Claud he has to go after them
and take them home again in the evening. They can't walk
that half a mile. No they can't. I tell you," she said and
laughed merrily, "I sure am tired of buttering up niggers, but
you got to love em if you want em to work for you. When
they come in the morning, I run out and I say, 'Hi yawl this
morning?' and when Claud drives them off to the field I just
wave to beat the band and they just wave back." And she
waved her hand rapidly to illustrate.

"Like you read out of the same book," the lady said, show-   49
ing she understood perfectly.

"Child, yes," Mrs. Turpin said. "And when they come in   50
from the field, I run out with a bucket of icewater. That's the
way it's going to be from now on," she said. "You may as well
face it."

"One thang I know," the white-trash woman said. "Two   51
thangs I ain't going to do: love no niggers or scoot down no
hog with no hose." And she let out a bark of contempt.

The look that Mrs. Turpin and the pleasant lady ex-   52
changed indicated they both understood that you had to
have certain things before you could *know* certain things. But
every time Mrs. Turpin exchanged a look with the lady, she
was aware that the ugly girl's peculiar eyes were still on her,
and she had trouble bringing her attention back to the conversation.

"When you got something," she said, "you got to look af-　53
ter it." And when you ain't got a thing but breath and
britches, she added to herself, you can afford to come to
town every morning and just sit on the Court House coping
and spit.

A grotesque revolving shadow passed across the curtain　54
behind her and was thrown palely on the opposite wall. Then
a bicycle clattered down against the outside of the building.
The door opened and a colored boy glided in with a tray
from the drugstore. It had two large red and white paper
cups on it with tops on them. He was a tall, very black boy in
discolored white pants and a green nylon shirt. He was chewing gum slowly, as if to music. He set the tray down in the
office opening next to the fern and stuck his head through to
look for the secretary. She was not in there. He rested his
arms on the ledge and waited, his narrow bottom stuck out,
swaying to the left and right. He raised a hand over his head
and scratched the base of his skull.

"You see that button there, boy?" Mrs. Turpin said. "You　55
can punch that and she'll come. She's probably in the back
somewhere."

"Is thas right?" the boy said agreeably, as if he had never　56
seen the button before. He leaned to the right and put his
finger on it. "She sometime out," he said and twisted around
to face his audience, his elbows behind him on the counter.
The nurse appeared and he twisted back again. She handed
him a dollar and he rooted in his pocket and made the
change and counted it out to her. She gave him fifteen cents
for a tip and he went out with the empty tray. The heavy door
swung too slowly and closed at length with the sound of suc-
tion. For a moment no one spoke.

"They ought to send all them niggers back to Africa," the　57
white-trash woman said. "That's wher they come from in the
first place."

"Oh, I couldn't do without my good colored friends," the　58
pleasant lady said.

"There's a heap of things worse than a nigger," Mrs. Tur-　59
pin agreed. "It's all kinds of them just like it's all kinds of us."

"Yes, and it takes all kinds to make the world go round," 60
the lady said in her musical voice.

As she said it, the raw-complexioned girl snapped her 61
teeth together. Her lower lip turned downwards and inside
out, revealing the pale pink inside of her mouth. After a second it rolled back up. It was the ugliest face Mrs. Turpin had
ever seen anyone make and for a moment she was certain that
the girl had made it at her. She was looking at her as if she
had known and disliked her all her life—all of Mrs. Turpin's
life, it seemed too, not just all the girl's life. Why, girl, I don't
even know you, Mrs. Turpin said silently.

She forced her attention back to the discussion. "It 62
wouldn't be practical to send them back to Africa," she said.
"They wouldn't want to go. They got it too good here."

"Wouldn't be what they wanted—if I had anythang to do 63
with it," the woman said.

"It wouldn't be a way in the world you could get all the 64
niggers back over there," Mrs. Turpin said. "They'd be hid-
ing out and lying down and turning sick on you and wailing
and hollering and raring and pitching. It wouldn't be a way
in the world to get them over there."

"They got over here," the trashy woman said. "Get back 65
like they got over."

"It wasn't so many of them then," Mrs. Turpin explained. 66

The woman looked at Mrs. Turpin as if here was an idiot 67
indeed but Mrs. Turpin was not bothered by the look, considering where it came from.

"Nooo," she said, "they're going to stay here where they 68
can go to New York and marry white folks and improve their
color. That's what they all want to do, every one of them, improve their color."

"You know what comes of that, don't you?" Claud asked. 69

"No, Claud, what?" Mrs. Turpin said. 70

Claud's eyes twinkled. "White-faced niggers," he said with 71
never a smile.

Everybody in the office laughed except the white-trash 72
and the ugly girl. The girl gripped the book in her lap with
white fingers. The trashy woman looked around her from

face to face as if she thought they were all idiots. The old woman in the feed sack dress continued to gaze expression-less across the floor at the high-top shoes of the man opposite her, the one who had been pretending to be asleep when the Turpins came in. He was laughing heartily, his hands still spread out on his knees. The child had fallen to the side and was lying now almost face down in the old woman's lap.

While they recovered from their laughter, the nasal chorus   73
on the radio kept the room from silence.

> *You go to blank blank*
> *And I'll go to mine*
> *But we'll all blank along*
> *To-geth-ther,*
> *And all along the blank*
> *We'll hep eachother out*
> *Smile-ling in any kind of*
> *Weath-ther!*

Mrs. Turpin didn't catch every word but she caught   74
enough to agree with the spirit of the song and it turned her thoughts sober. To help anybody out that needed it was her philosophy of life. She never spared herself when she found somebody in need, whether they were white or black, trash or decent. And of all she had to be thankful for, she was most thankful that this was so. If Jesus had said, "You can be high society and have all the money you want and be thin and svelte-like, but you can't be a good woman with it," she would have had to say, "Well don't make me that then. Make me a good woman and it don't matter what else, how fat or how ugly or how poor!" Her heart rose. He had not made her a nigger or white-trash or ugly! He had made her herself and given her a little of everything. Jesus, thank you! she said. Thank you thank you thank you! Whenever she counted her blessings she felt as buoyant as if she weighed one hundred and twenty-five pounds instead of one hundred and eighty.

"What's wrong with your little boy?" the pleasant lady   75
asked the white-trashy woman.

"He has a ulcer," the woman said proudly. "He ain't give   76
me a minute's peace since he was born. Him and her are just
alike," she said, nodding at the old woman, who was running
her leathery fingers through the child's pale hair. "Look like I
can't get nothing down them two but Co' Cola and candy."

That's all you try to get down em, Mrs. Turpin said to her-   77
self. Too lazy to light the fire. There was nothing you could
tell her about people like them that she didn't know already.
And it was not just that they didn't have anything. Because if
you gave them everything, in two weeks it would all be broken or filthy or they would have chopped it up for lightwood.
She knew all this from her own experience. Help them you
must, but help them you couldn't.

All at once the ugly girl turned her lips inside out again.   78
Her eyes fixed like two drills on Mrs. Turpin. This time there
was no mistaking that there was something urgent behind
them.

Girl, Mrs. Turpin exclaimed silently, I haven't done a thing   79
to you! The girl might be confusing her with somebody else.
There was no need to sit by and let herself be intimidated.
"You must be in college," she said boldly, looking directly at
the girl. "I see you reading a book there."

The girl continued to stare and pointedly did not answer.   80

Her mother blushed at this rudeness. "The lady asked you   81
a question, Mary Grace," she said under her breath.

"I have ears," Mary Grace said.   82

The poor mother blushed again. "Mary Grace goes to   83
Wellesley College," she explained. She twisted one of the
buttons on her dress. "In Massachusetts," she added with a
grimace. "And in the summer she just keeps right on studying. Just reads all the time, a real book worm. She's done real
well at Wellesley; she's taking English and Math and History
and Psychology and Social Studies," she rattled on, "and I
think it's too much. I think she ought to get out and have
fun."

The girl looked as if she would like to hurl them all   84
through the plate glass window.

"Way up north," Mrs. Turpin murmured and thought, 85
well, it hasn't done much for her manners.

"I'd almost rather to have him sick," the white-trash 86
woman said, wrenching the attention back to herself. "He's
so mean when he ain't. Look like some children just take natural to meanness. It's some gets bad when they get sick but
he was the opposite. Took sick and turned good. He don't
give me no trouble now. It's me waitin to see the doctor,"
she said.

If I was going to send anybody back to Africa, Mrs. Turpin 87
thought, it would be your kind, woman. "Yes, indeed," she
said aloud, but looking up at the ceiling, "it's a heap of things
worse than a nigger." And dirtier than a hog, she added to
herself.

"I think people with bad dispositions are more to be pitied 88
than anyone on earth," the pleasant lady said in a voice that
was decidedly thin.

"I thank the Lord he has blessed me with a good one," 89
Mrs. Turpin said. "The day has never dawned that I couldn't
find something to laugh at."

"Not since she married me anyways," Claud said with a 90
comical straight face.

Everybody laughed except the girl and the white-trash. 91

Mrs. Turpin's stomach shook. "He's such a caution," she 92
said, "that I can't help but laugh at him."

The girl made a loud ugly noise through her teeth. 93

Her mother's mouth grew thin and tight. "I think the 94
worst thing in the world," she said, "is an ungrateful person.
To have everything and not appreciate it. I know a girl," she
said, "who has parents who would give her anything, a little
brother who loves her dearly, who is getting a good education, who wears the best clothes, but who can never say a
kind word to anyone, who never smiles, who just criticizes
and complains all day long."

"Is she too old to paddle?" Claud asked. 95

The girl's face was almost purple. 96

"Yes," the lady said, "I'm afraid there's nothing to do but 97 *complete opposite of character of* (handwritten in left margin)

leave her to her folly. Some day she'll wake up and it'll be too late."

"It never hurt anyone to smile," Mrs. Turpin said. "It just makes you feel better all over."   98

"Of course," the lady said sadly, "but there are just some people you can't tell anything to. They can't take criticism."   99

"If it's one thing I am," Mrs. Turpin said with feeling, "it's grateful. When I think who all I could have been besides myself and what all I got, a little of everything, and a good disposition besides, I just feel like shouting, 'Thank you, Jesus, for making everything the way it is!' It could have been different!" For one thing, somebody else could have got Claud. At the thought of this, she was flooded with gratitude and a terrible pang of joy ran through her. "Oh thank you, Jesus, Jesus, thank you!" she cried aloud.   100

The book struck her directly over her left eye. It struck almost at the same instant that she realized the girl was about to hurl it. Before she could utter a sound, the raw face came crashing across the table toward her, howling. The girl's fingers sank like clamps into the soft flesh of her neck. She heard the mother cry out and Claud shout, "Whoa!" There was an instant when she was certain that she was about to be in an earthquake.   101

All at once her vision narrowed and she saw everything as if it were happening in a small room far away, or as if she were looking at it through the wrong end of a telescope. Claud's face crumpled and fell out of sight. The nurse ran in, then out, then in again. Then the gangling figure of the doctor rushed out of the inner door. Magazines flew this way and that as the table turned over. The girl fell with a thud and Mrs. Turpin's vision suddenly reversed itself and she saw everything large instead of small. The eyes of the white-trashy woman were staring hugely at the floor. There the girl, held down on one side by the nurse and on the other by her mother, was wrenching and turning in their grasp. The doctor was kneeling astride her, trying to hold her arm down. He managed after a second to sink a long needle into it.   102

Mrs. Turpin felt entirely hollow except for her heart which 103
swung from side to side as if it were agitated in a great empty
drum of flesh.

"Somebody that's not busy call for the ambulance," the 104
doctor said in the off-hand voice young doctors adopt for
terrible occasions.

Mrs. Turpin could not have moved a finger. The old man 105
who had been sitting next to her skipped nimbly into the
office and made the call, for the secretary still seemed to be
gone.

"Claud!" Mrs. Turpin called. 106

He was not in his chair. She knew she must jump up and 107
find him but she felt like some one trying to catch a train in a
dream, when everything moves in slow motion and the faster
you try to run the slower you go.

"Here I am," a suffocated voice, very unlike Claud's, said. 108

He was doubled up in the corner on the floor, pale as pa- 109
per, holding his leg. She wanted to get up and go to him but
she could not move. Instead, her gaze was drawn slowly
downward to the churning face on the floor, which she could
see over the doctor's shoulder.

The girl's eyes stopped rolling and focused on her. They 110
seemed a much lighter blue than before, as if a door that had
been tightly closed behind them was now open to admit light
and air.

Mrs. Turpin's head cleared and her power of motion re- 111
turned. She leaned forward until she was looking directly
into the fierce brilliant eyes. There was no doubt in her mind
that the girl did know her, knew her in some intense and personal way, beyond time and place and condition. "What you
got to say to me?" she asked hoarsely and held her breath,
waiting, as for a revelation.

The girl raised her head. Her gaze locked with Mrs. 112
Turpin's. "Go back to hell where you came from, you old
wart hog," she whispered. Her voice was low but clear. Her
eyes burned for a moment as if she saw with pleasure that her
message had struck its target.

Mrs. Turpin sank back in her chair.   113

After a moment the girl's eyes closed and she turned her   114
head wearily to the side.

The doctor rose and handed the nurse the empty syringe.   115
He leaned over and put both hands for a moment on the
mother's shoulders, which were shaking. She was sitting on
the floor, her lips pressed together, holding Mary Grace's
hand in her lap. The girl's fingers were gripped like a baby's
around her thumb. "Go on to the hospital," he said. "I'll call
and make the arrangements."

"Now let's see that neck," he said in a jovial voice to Mrs.   116
Turpin. He began to inspect her neck with his first two
fingers. Two little moon-shaped lines like pink fish bones
were indented over her windpipe. There was the beginning
of an angry red swelling above her eye. His fingers passed
over this also.

"Lea' me be," she said thickly and shook him off. "See   117
about Claud. She kicked him."

"I'll see about him in a minute," he said and felt her pulse.   118
He was a thin gray-haired man, given to pleasantries. "Go
home and have yourself a vacation the rest of the day," he
said and patted her on the shoulder.

Quit your pattin me, Mrs. Turpin growled to herself.   119

"And put an ice pack over that eye," he said. Then he went   120
and squatted down beside Claud and looked at his leg. After
a moment he pulled him up and Claud limped after him into
the office.

Until the ambulance came, the only sounds in the room   121
were the tremulous moans of the girl's mother, who continued to sit on the floor. The white-trash woman did not take
her eyes off the girl. Mrs. Turpin looked straight ahead at
nothing. Presently the ambulance drew up, a long dark
shadow, behind the curtain. The attendants came in and set
the stretcher down beside the girl and lifted her expertly onto
it and carried her out. The nurse helped the mother gather
up her things. The shadow of the ambulance moved silently
away and the nurse came back in the office.

"That ther girl is going to be a lunatic, ain't she?" the   122 white-trash woman asked the nurse, but the nurse kept on to the back and never answered her.

"Yes, she's going to be a lunatic," the white-trash woman said to the rest of them. 123

"Po' critter," the old woman murmured. The child's face was still in her lap. His eyes looked idly out over her knees. He had not moved during the disturbance except to draw one leg up under him. 124

peculiar

"I thank Gawd," the white-trash woman said fervently, "I ain't a lunatic." 125

Claud came limping out and the Turpins went home. 126

As their pick-up truck turned into their own dirt road and made the crest of the hill, Mrs. Turpin gripped the window ledge and looked out suspiciously. The land sloped gracefully down through a field dotted with lavender weeds and at the start of the rise their small yellow frame house, with its little flower beds spread out around it like a fancy apron, sat primly in its accustomed place between two giant hickory trees. She would not have been startled to see a burnt wound between two blackened chimneys. *hmmmm* 127

Neither of them felt like eating so they put on their house clothes and lowered the shade in the bedroom and lay down, Claud with his leg on a pillow and herself with a damp washcloth over her eye. The instant she was flat on her back, the image of a razor-backed hog with warts on its face and horns coming out behind its ears snorted into her head. She moaned, a low quiet moan. 128

"I am not," she said tearfully, "a wart hog. From hell." But the denial had no force. The girl's eyes and her words, even the tone of her voice, low but clear, directed only to her, brooked no repudiation. She had been singled out for the message, though there was trash in the room to whom it might justly have been applied. The full force of this fact struck her only now. There was a woman there who was neglecting her own child but she had been overlooked. The message had been given to Ruby Turpin, a respectable, hard-working, church-going woman. The tears dried. Her eyes began to burn instead with wrath. 129

She rose on her elbow and the washcloth fell into her   130
hand. Claud was lying on his back, snoring. She wanted to
tell him what the girl had said. At the same time, she did not
wish to put the image of herself as a wart hog from hell into
his mind.

"Hey, Claud," she muttered and pushed his shoulder.   131

Claud opened one pale baby blue eye.   132

She looked into it warily. He did not think about any   133
thing. He just went his way.

"Wha, whasit?" he said and closed the eye again.   134

"Nothing," she said. "Does your leg pain you?"   135

"Hurts like hell," Claud said.   136

"It'll quit terreckly," she said and lay back down. In a mo-   137
ment Claud was snoring again. For the rest of the afternoon
they lay there. Claud slept. She scowled at the ceiling. Occasionally she raised her fist and made a small stabbing motion
over her chest as if she was defending her innocence to invisible guests who were like the comforters of Job, reasonable-
seeming but wrong.

About five-thirty Claud stirred. "Got to go after those   138
niggers," he sighed, not moving.

She was looking straight up as if there were unintelligible   139
handwriting on the ceiling. The protuberance over her eye
had turned a greenish-blue. "Listen here," she said.

"What?"   140

"Kiss me."   141

Claud leaned over and kissed her loudly on the mouth. He   142
pinched her side and their hands interlocked. Her expression
of ferocious concentration did not change. Claud got up,
groaning and growling, and limped off. She continued to
study the ceiling.

She did not get up until she heard the pick-up truck com-   143
ing back with the Negroes. Then she rose and thrust her feet
in her brown oxfords, which she did not bother to lace, and
stumped out onto the back porch and got her red plastic
bucket. She emptied a tray of ice cubes into it and filled it half
full of water and went out into the back yard. Every afternoon after Claud brought the hands in, one of the boys

helped him put out hay and the rest waited in the back of the truck until he was ready to take them home. The truck was parked in the shade under one of the hickory trees.

"Hi yawl this evening?" Mrs. Turpin asked grimly, appearing with the bucket and the dipper. There were three women and a boy in the truck.   144

"Us doin nicely," the oldest woman said. "Hi you doin?" and her gaze stuck immediately on the dark lump on Mrs. Turpin's forehead. "You done fell down, ain't you?" she asked in a solicitous voice. The old woman was dark and almost toothless. She had on an old felt hat of Claud's set back on her head. The other two women were younger and lighter and they both had new bright green sunhats. One of them had hers on her head; the other had taken hers off and the boy was grinning beneath it.   145

Mrs. Turpin set the bucket down on the floor of the truck. "Yawl hep yourselves," she said. She looked around to make sure Claud had gone. "No, I didn't fall down," she said, folding her arms. "It was something worse than that."   146

"Ain't nothing bad happen to you!" the old woman said. She said it as if they all knew that Mrs. Turpin was protected in some special way by Divine Providence. "You just had you a little fall."   147

"We were in town at the doctor's office for where the cow kicked Mr. Turpin," Mrs. Turpin said in a flat tone that indicated they could leave off their foolishness. "And there was this girl there. A big fat girl with her face all broke out. I could look at that girl and tell she was peculiar but I couldn't tell how. And me and her mama was just talking and going along and all of a sudden WHAM! She throws this big book she was reading at me and . . ."   148

"Naw!" the old woman cried out.   149

"And then she jumps over the table and commences to choke me."   150

"Naw!" they all exclaimed, "naw!"   151

"Hi come she do that?" the old woman asked. "What ail her?"   152

Mrs. Turpin only glared in front of her.   153

"Somethin ail her," the old woman said.   154

"They carried her off in an ambulance," Mrs. Turpin con-   155
tinued, "but before she went she was rolling on the floor and
they were trying to hold her down to give her a shot and she
said something to me." She paused. "You know what she said
to me?"

"What she say?" they asked.   156

"She said," Mrs. Turpin began, and stopped, her face very   157
dark and heavy. The sun was getting whiter and whiter,
blanching the sky overhead so that the leaves of the hickory
tree were black in the face of it. She could not bring forth the
words. "Something real ugly," she muttered.

"She sho shouldn't said nothin ugly to you," the old   158
woman said. "You so sweet. You the sweetest lady I know."

"She pretty too," the one with the hat on said.   159

"And stout," the other one said. "I never knowed no   160
sweeter white lady."

"That's the truth befo' Jesus," the old woman said.   161
"Amen! You des as sweet and pretty as you can be."

Mrs. Turpin knew exactly how much Negro flattery was   162
worth and it added to her rage. "She said," she began again
and finished this time with a fierce rush of breath, "that I was
an old wart hog from hell."

There was an astounded silence.   163

"Where she at?" the youngest woman cried in a piercing   164
voice.

"Lemme see her. I'll kill her!"   165

"I'll kill her with you!" the other one cried.   166

"She b'long in the sylum," the old woman said emphati-   167
cally. "You the sweetest white lady I know."

"She pretty too," the other two said. "Stout as she can be   168
and sweet. Jesus satisfied with her!"

"Deed he is," the old woman declared.   169

Idiots! Mrs. Turpin growled to herself. You could never   170
say anything intelligent to a nigger. You could talk at them
but not with them. "Yawl ain't drunk your water," she said
shortly. "Leave the bucket in the truck when you're finished

with it. I got more to do than just stand around and pass the time of day," and she moved off and into the house.

She stood for a moment in the middle of the kitchen. The dark protuberance over her eye looked like a miniature tornado cloud which might any moment sweep across the horizon of her brow. Her lower lip protruded dangerously. She squared her massive shoulders. Then she marched into the front of the house and out the side door and started down the road to the pig parlor. She had the look of a woman going single-handed, weaponless, into battle.

[margin: 171 amaz- ing detail]

The sun was a deep yellow now like a harvest moon and was riding westward very fast over the far tree line as if it meant to reach the hogs before she did. The road was rutted and she kicked several good-sized stones out of her path as she strode along. The pig parlor was on a little knoll at the end of a lane that ran off from the side of the barn. It was a square of concrete as large as a small room, with a board fence about four feet high around it. The concrete floor sloped slightly so that the hog wash could drain off into a trench where it was carried to the field for fertilizer. Claud was standing on the outside, on the edge of the concrete, hanging onto the top board, hosing down the floor inside. The hose was connected to the faucet of a water trough nearby.

[margin: 172]

Mrs. Turpin climbed up beside him and glowered down at the hogs inside. There were seven long-snouted bristly shoats in it—tan with liver-colored spots—and an old sow a few weeks off from farrowing. She was lying on her side grunting. The shoats were running about shaking themselves like idiot children, their little slit pig eyes searching the floor for anything left. She had read that pigs were the most intelligent animal. She doubted it. They were supposed to be smarter than dogs. There had even been a pig astronaut. He had performed his assignment perfectly but died of a heart attack afterwards because they left him in his electric suit, sitting upright throughout his examination when naturally a hog should be on all fours.

[margin: 173 are you serious?]

A-gruntin and a-rootin and a-groanin.   174

"Gimme that hose," she said, yanking it away from Claud.   175
"Go on and carry them niggers home and then get off
that leg."

"You look like you might have swallowed a mad dog,"   176
Claud observed, but he got down and limped off. He paid no
attention to her humors.

Until he was out of earshot, Mrs. Turpin stood on the side   177
of the pen, holding the hose and pointing the stream of water
at the hind quarters of any shoat that looked as if it might try
to lie down. When he had had time to get over the hill, she
turned her head slightly and her wrathful eyes scanned the
path. He was nowhere in sight. She turned back again and
seemed to gather herself up. Her shoulders rose and she drew
in her breath.

"What do you send me a message like that for?" she said in   178
a low fierce voice, barely above a whisper but with the force
of a shout in its concentrated fury. "How am I a hog and me
both? How am I saved and from hell too?" Her free fist was
knotted and with the other she gripped the hose, blindly
pointing the stream of water in and out of the eye of the old
sow whose outraged squeal she did not hear.

The pig parlor commanded a view of the back pasture   179
where their twenty beef cows were gathered around the hay-
bales Claud and the boy had put out. The freshly cut pasture
sloped down to the highway. Across it was their cotton field
and beyond that a dark green dusty wood which they owned
as well. The sun was behind the wood, very red, looking over
the paling of trees like a farmer inspecting his own hogs.

"Why me?" she rumbled. "It's no trash around here, black   180
or white, that I haven't given to. And break my back to the
bone every day working. And do for the church."

She appeared to be the right size woman to command the   181
arena before her. "How am I a hog?" she demanded. "Exactly how am I like them?" and she jabbed the stream of water at the shoats. "There was plenty of trash there. It didn't
have to be me.

"If you like trash better, go get yourself some trash then,"   182 she railed. "You could have made me trash. Or a nigger. If trash is what you wanted why didn't you make me trash?" She shook her fist with the hose in it and a watery snake appeared momentarily in the air. "I could quit working and take it easy and be filthy," she growled. "Lounge about the sidewalks all day drinking root beer. Dip snuff and spit in every puddle and have it all over my face. I could be nasty.

"Or you could have made me a nigger. It's too late for me to be a nigger," she said with deep sarcasm, "but I could act like one. Lay down in the middle of the road and stop traffic. Roll on the ground."

In the deepening light everything was taking on a mysterious hue. The pasture was growing a peculiar glassy green and the streak of highway had turned lavender. She braced herself for a final assault and this time her voice rolled out over the pasture. "Go on," she yelled, "call me a hog! Call me a hog again. From hell. Call me a wart hog from hell. Put that bottom rail on top. There'll still be a top and bottom!"

A garbled echo returned to her.

A final surge of fury shook her and she roared, "Who do you think you are?"

The color of everything, field and crimson sky, burned for a moment with a transparent intensity. The question carried over the pasture and across the highway and the cotton field and returned to her clearly like an answer from beyond the wood.

She opened her mouth but no sound came out of it.

A tiny truck, Claud's, appeared on the highway, heading rapidly out of sight. Its gears scraped thinly. It looked like a child's toy. At any moment a bigger truck might smash into it and scatter Claud's and the niggers' brains all over the road.

Mrs. Turpin stood there, her gaze fixed on the highway, all her muscles rigid, until in five or six minutes the truck reappeared, returning. She waited until it had had time to turn into their own road. Then like a monumental statue coming to life, she bent her head slowly and gazed, as if through the very heart of mystery, down into the pig parlor at the hogs. They had settled all in one corner around the old sow who

great, effective diction

was grunting softly. A red glow suffused them. They appeared to pant with a secret life.

Until the sun slipped finally behind the tree line, Mrs. 191
Turpin remained there with her gaze bent to them as if she were absorbing some abysmal life-giving knowledge. At last she lifted her head. There was only a purple streak in the sky, cutting through a field of crimson and leading, like an extension of the highway, into the descending dusk. She raised her hands from the side of the pen in a gesture hieratic and profound. A visionary light settled in her eyes. She saw the streak as a vast swinging bridge extending upward from the earth through a field of living fire. Upon it a vast horde of souls were rumbling toward heaven. There were whole companies of white-trash, clean for the first time in their lives, and bands of black niggers in white robes, and battalions of freaks and lunatics shouting and clapping and leaping like frogs. And bringing up the end of the procession was a tribe of people whom she recognized at once as those who, like herself and Claud, had always had a little of everything and the God-given wit to use it right. She leaned forward to observe them closer. They were marching behind the others with great dignity, accountable as they had always been for good order and common sense and respectable behavior. They alone were on key. Yet she could see by their shocked and altered faces that even their virtues were being burned away. She lowered her hands and gripped the rail of the hog pen, her eyes small but fixed unblinkingly on what lay ahead. In a moment the vision faded but she remained where she was, immobile.

At length she got down and turned off the faucet and 192
made her slow way on the darkening path to the house. In the woods around her the invisible cricket choruses had struck up, but what she heard were the voices of the souls climbing upward into the starry field and shouting hallelujah.

finally all are equal

COMMENT ON "REVELATION"

Ruby Turpin, the central character in Flannery O'Conner's "Revelation," is obsessed with the classification process. At night she occupies herself "naming the classes of people": most "colored people" are on the bottom; "next to them— not above, just away from—are the white trash"; and so on. Mrs. Turpin puzzles about the exceptions to her system—the black dentist who owns property and the decent white folks who have lost their money—but for the most part she is certain about her system and her place in it. In the doctor's waiting room, she sizes up the other patients, placing them in their appropriate classes. But her internal and external dialogue reveals the ironies and inconsistencies in her rigid system. Self-satisfied, pleased that Jesus is on her side, she is not prepared for the book on *Human Development* that is thrown at her or the events that follow—the transparent flattery of the black workers, her cleaning of the pig parlor, and finally her vision of the highway to heaven that reveals her real place in God's hierarchy.

Division and Classification as a Writing Strategy

1. Write a column for your local newspaper in which you develop a system for classifying a concept such as trash. You may decide to interpret this word literally, developing a scheme to categorize the type of objects people throw away. Or you may decide to interpret the word figuratively, focusing on things that some people consider worthless—gossip columns, romance magazines, game shows. Here are a few possibilities: although people throw trash away, it won't go away; people's distaste for trash is the cause of its creation; people are so saturated by trash that they accept it as part of their culture with its own subtle subcategories.

2. In an essay addressed to a class in criminal justice, research the various punishments for murder. Then explain the different punishments for intentional and unintentional murder.

3. Mary Mebane argues that the system of class and color is used to impose power in a negative way. Consider some other system that uses power in a positive way. For example, you may want to classify people by the various ways they empower others.

4. Write an essay that classifies various kinds of bad luck. You may want to follow Austin's pattern by arranging the types of bad luck in an ascending order of complexity.

5. Focus on Phillip Lopate's pluralistic category in "Modern Friendships" and classify it into smaller subcategories. For example, you may wish to draft a feature in which you identify various kinds of "work friends" or you may wish to take on the *When Harry Met Sally* line—explaining why men and women can or cannot be friends.

6. Read Kurt Vonnegut's short story, "Harrison Bergeron," page 559. Then write an essay on the issue of equality. You may wish to classify the various kinds of inequality evident

in Vonnegut's story, or you may wish to support or contest Wilson's argument that widespread ownership of private property is necessary to create the equality necessary for democracy.

DEFINITION

As a writer, both in and out of college, you're likely to spend a good deal of time writing definitions. In an astronomy class, you may be asked to explain what the Doppler effect is or what a white dwarf star is. In a literature class, you may be asked to define a sonnet and identify its different forms. If you become an engineer, you may write to define problems your company proposes to solve or to define a new product your company has developed. If you become a business executive, you may have to write a brochure to describe a new service your company offers or draft a letter that defines the company's policy on credit applications.

Writers use definitions to establish boundaries, to show the essential nature of something, and to explain the special qualities that identify a purpose, place, object, or concept and distinguish it from others similar to it. Writers often write extended definitions—definitions that go beyond the one-sentence or one-paragraph explanations that you find in a dictionary or encyclopedia to expand on and examine the essential qualities of a policy, an event, a group, or a trend. Sometimes an extended definition becomes an entire book. Some books are written to define the good life; others are written to define the ideal university or the best kind of government. In fact, many of the books on any current nonfiction best-seller list are primarily definitions. The essays in this section of *The Riverside Reader* are all extended definitions.

PURPOSE

When you write, you can use definitions in several ways. For instance, you can define to *point out the special nature* of something. You may want to show the special flavor of San Francisco that makes it different from other major cities in the world, or you may want to describe the unique features that make the Macintosh computer different from other personal computers.

You can also define to *explain.* In an essay about cross-country skiing, you might want to show your readers what the sport is like and point out why it's less hazardous and less expensive than downhill skiing but better exercise. You might also define to *entertain*—to describe the essence of what it means to be a "good old boy," for instance. Often you define to *inform;* that is what you are doing in college papers when you write about West Virginia folk art or postmodern architecture. Often you write to *establish a standard,* perhaps for a good exercise program, a workable environmental policy, or even the ideal pair of running shoes. Notice that when you define to set a standard, you may also be defining to *persuade,* to convince your reader to accept the ideal you describe. Many definitions are essentially arguments.

Sometimes you may even write to *define yourself.* That is what you are doing when you write an autobiographical statement for a college admissions officer or a scholarship committee, or when you write a job application letter. You hope to give your readers the special information that will

distinguish you from all other candidates. When that is your
task, you'll profit by knowing the common strategies for
defining and by recognizing how other writers have used
them.

AUDIENCE

When you're going to use definition in your writing, you can
benefit by thinking ahead of time about what your readers
expect from you. Why are they reading, and what questions
will they want you to answer? You can't anticipate all their
questions, but you should plan on responding to at least two
kinds of queries.

First, your readers are likely to ask, "What distinguishes
what you're writing about? What's typical or different about
it? How do I know when I see one?" For example, if you
were writing about the Olympic games, your readers would
perhaps want to know the difference between today's Olympic games and the original games in ancient Greece. With
a little research, you could tell them about several major
differences.

Second, for more complex topics you should expect that
your readers will also ask, "What is the basic character or the
essential nature of what you're writing about? What do you
mean when you say 'alternative medicine,' 'Marxist theory,'
or 'white-collar crime'?" Answering questions such as these is
more difficult, but if you're going to use terms like these in
an essay, you have an obligation to define them, using as
many strategies as you need to clarify your terms. To define
white-collar crime, for instance, you could specify that it is
nonviolent, likely to happen within businesses, and involves
illegal manipulation of funds or privileged information. You
should also strengthen your definition by giving examples
that your readers might be familiar with.

STRATEGIES

You can choose from several strategies for defining, using
them singly or in combination. A favorite strategy we all use

who really asks that?

is *giving examples,* something we do naturally when we point to a special automobile we like or show a child a picture of a raccoon in a picture book. Writers use the same method when they describe a scene, create a visual image, or cite a specific instance of something.

Every author in this section uses an abundance of examples. Christopher Pizzi's piece "Doorways: A Visual Essay" depends on them almost entirely. He starts with the basic question "What is a doorway?" and answers it with two dictionary definitions taken from different eras. He then brings in his examples, eighteen sketches of doorways arranged according to type and expanded on with annotations explaining special features. Diane Ackerman also introduces a wealth of examples from across several societies to make her point that to some extent the way people experience pain is cultural.

You can define by *analyzing qualities* to emphasize what specific traits distinguish the person or thing you're defining. When you use this strategy for people, you focus on certain qualities or behaviors that reveal that individual's personality and character. William Langewiesche uses this strategy in "American Ingenuity" to define David Griffin as a man of initiative and courage who has the confidence and expertise to walk onto the wreckage site at the World Trade Center and take charge of demolition. In the opening paragraph of "Pain," Diane Ackerman shows what she calls T. E. Lawrence's "quintessential machismo" by describing him holding his hand in a candle flame.

A similar strategy is *attributing characteristics.* This is Stephen Harrigan's chief tactic in "The Tiger Is God." He begins by describing tigers' characteristic method of attack, points out that zookeepers know that tigers are dangerous, and then identifies tigers as predators whose mission is to kill. Christopher Pizzi attributes several characteristics to doorways, saying that they provide a transition from nature into shelter and give people signals about what to expect inside.

Another strategy is *defining negatively;* one of Berendt's chief strategies in "The Hoax" is showing what something is

they're really getting a lot of info. on the stories

not. Simple deception or trickery may be a prank, but it is not a hoax. In order to qualify as a hoax, a trick must have something witty and original about it. Alice Walker also defines negatively in "Everyday Use" when the character of the mother suggests that honoring one's heritage doesn't mean hanging on to relics from the past.

Another way to define is by *using analogies.* In "Pain" Ackerman draws an analogy between the painful rituals that young people go through in tribal initiation rites in some parts of the world and some of the procedures that women endure in beauty parlors to enhance their appearance. Stephen Harrigan uses analogy when he compares the window in the tiger's cage to "a portal through which mankind's most primeval terrors were allowed to pass unobstructed."

Still don't under- stand

You can also define by *showing function.* Often the most important feature about an object, agency, or institution is what it does. The element of function figures centrally in Pizzi's essay "Doorways." Doorways *do* things; they have a purpose; they have an important architectural function, providing entrance to a building. Harrigan also focuses on function in "The Tiger Is God," stressing that the primary function of a tiger is to kill for food; it's a predator.

COMBINING STRATEGIES

Even when you're writing an essay that is primarily an exercise in definition, you may want to do as professional writers often do and bring in other strategies, perhaps narration or argument or process analysis. For instance, in "A Chinaman's Chance" (page 493), Eric Liu gives his own definition of the American Dream and then argues that young people who feel they have no chance to achieve that dream are mistaken. In "Shop like a Man" (page 186), Paco Underhill is writing a comparison-and-contrast essay, but he attributes defining characteristics to men shoppers to make his point.

Some writers also combine definition with narration and description. In "The Mullet Girls" (page 41), Jill McCorkle defines the Mullet Girls by describing their characteristic taste in clothes and their mannerisms. Those traits are important elements in the narrative. Diane Ackerman uses several mini-narratives to illustrate that people in different cultures have different outlooks about the experience of pain. In "Stone Soup" (page 506), Barbara Kingsolver uses stories about children as a way of defining a strong family. So you can mix and mingle strategies even though one may dominate. As you read essays in this section, and especially as you reread them, try to be conscious of the strategies authors are using. You may find that you can incorporate some of them into your own writing.

USING DEFINITION IN PARAGRAPHS

Here are two definition paragraphs. The first is written by a professional writer and is followed by an analysis. The second is written by a student writer and is followed by questions.

JOYCE CAROL OATES
When Tristram Met Isolde

only possessions?

Romantic love isn't so much a love that defies conventions, for romantic love is of all love types the most conventional, as a love that arises with seeming spontaneity: unwilled, undirected by others' suggestions or admonitions, raw and unpremeditated and of the heart; not cerebral and not genital. Romantic love is forever in opposition to formal, cultural, and tribal prescriptions of behavior: arranged marriages, for instance, in which brides and their dowries are possessions to be handed over to a bridegroom and his family, or in which titled names are wed in businesslike arrangements that have little to do with the feelings of the individuals. Diana, Princess of Wales, would seem to have been a martyr to such an arrangement: her political marriage to Prince Charles ending in dissolution and di-

Romantic love is spontaneous

Opposed to rule and restrictions

Princess Di perfect example

vorce, and her "quest for personal happiness" (i.e., romantic love) ending in a grotesquely public death on a Parisian boulevard.

Comment In this paragraph taken from a short essay whose title, "When Tristram Met Isolde," invokes the tragic legend of two fatally smitten lovers, the novelist Joyce Carol Oates defines romantic love as an irrational, compulsive emotion that overwhelms all caution and good sense. Those who embrace it are rebelling against the practical economic and social concerns that families in non-Western cultures often value more than spontaneous feelings and individual desires. In both real life and in fiction, the surrender to romantic love often has disastrous consequences. To illustrate her point, Oates calls up what must be the most publicized example of a romantic disaster in the last decade: the death of Princess Diana and her lover in a high-speed automobile crash in that most romantic of cities, Paris.

JASON UTESCH
Personality

"She has a great personality." Translation: she goes to bed early to watch the shopping channel. "He has a great personality." Translation: he tells dirty jokes at funerals. The "p" word is troublesome not only because all the great personalities we've been told about have proved disappointing, but also because all the great personalities we know don't seem to measure up to other people's expectations. Even the old song suggests that personality is a complicated quality to define because to have it a person has to have a special walk, talk, smile, charm, love, and PLUS she (or he) has to have a great big heart.

1. What do you see as Utesch's purpose in listing so many contradictions in the way people define *personality?*
2. What does the writer imply by using the phrase "the 'p' word"?

DEFINITION

Points to Remember

1. Remember that you are obligated to define key terms that you use in your writing—such as *Marxism, alternative medicine, nontraditional student.*
2. Understand your purpose in defining: to explain, to entertain, to persuade, to set boundaries, or to establish a standard.
3. Understand how writers construct an argument from a definition. For example, by defining the good life or good government, they argue for that kind of life or government.
4. Know the several ways of defining: giving examples, analyzing qualities, attributing characteristics, defining negatively, using analogies, and showing function.
5. Learn to use definition in combination with other strategies, as a basis on which to build an argument, or as supporting evidence.

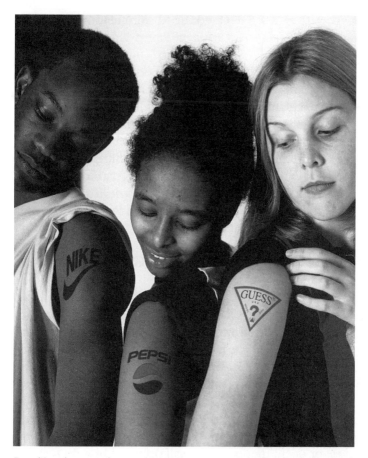

In this photograph, reprinted from an early issue of the anti-commercial, anti-consumption magazine Adbusters, *Shannon Mendes captures three high school students showing off their tattoos. In what ways do these tattoos define these students? In what ways are some of these tattoos dated? Write an essay in which you explain how your choice of some product—beverage, clothes, car—defines you.*

CHRISTOPHER M. PIZZI

Christopher M. Pizzi was born and raised in Warwick, Rhode Island, and was educated at Syracuse University. After working for several architectural firms in New York, he returned to graduate school to earn his master of architecture degree from the Yale School of Architecture. He currently works for Robert A. M. Stern Architects in New York. In "Doorways: A Visual Essay," first published in the *American Scholar,* Pizzi defines a "doorway" as an architectural and cultural object.

Doorways: A Visual Essay

WHAT IS A doorway?   1

An early edition of *Webster's Dictionary* (1864) 2 defines the *door-way-plane* as "the space between the doorway, properly so-called and the larger door-arch-way within which it is placed. It is often richly ornamented with sculptured figures." Today's *Oxford English Dictionary* defines *doorway* as "the opening or passage which a door serves to close or open; the space in a wall occupied by a door and its adjuncts; a portal."

How do we understand *doorway?* As a place? As a threshold? Or simply as a way in and out?   3

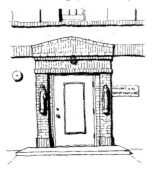 

Gallery of the Department of Art, Catholic University of America, Washington, D.C. 1917.

Dahlgren Chapel, crypt entry, Georgetown University, Washington. 1893.

Renwick Gallery (Smithsonian Institution), Washington.
James Renwick, Jr., architect, 1859-61.
Below, the portal and interior stairway.

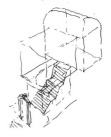

The doorway can play a mediating role between the scale of a building and the bodies entering it. It thus provides a transition between facade, door, and person.

Within, a major stairway leading to an important room is one of the great architectural motifs.

Renwick Gallery: principal facade.

National Building Museum, Washington.
Montgomery C. Meigs, engineer, 1887.

Like a room, a doorway is furnished 6
with accessories that articulate its human relationships and practical functions:

> A handle or knob to open the
> door;
> A letter slot for mail, a view,
> perhaps a hand;
> A peephole to regulate views,
> but only out;
> A lock to keep out intruders;
> A knocker or doorbell to an-
> nounce visitors.

*Townhouse at 2011 Q Street, N.W.,
Washington.*

*Townhouse at 1725 P Street, N.W.,
Washington.*

*Townhouse at 3032 Q Street, N.W.,
Washington.*

Opening a door presents us with a 7
moment of unknown physical expen-
diture: getting inside means grabbing,
leaning, and pulling. The door handle
is the site of our bodily engagement
with architecture, the moment when
we guess the weight of the door and
adjust our touch accordingly.

Smithsonian Castle, Washington (column detail below).
James Renwick, Jr., architect, 1855.

Franklin School Building, Washington, side entry,
Adolph Cluss, architect, 1869.

As a pause that separates the 8 natural from the man-made, the doorway has a privileged location in the architectural promenade. It designates the moment at which we have left nature and entered shelter. Organic motifs surrounding doorways remind us of this transition. The doorway registers our desire for interior, enclosed space, protected from the elements. Despite our ability to domesticate the landscape into outdoor rooms—an Italian Renaissance garden, a monastic courtyard, or a Roman atrium—we feel safest and most comfortable indoors.

very metaphorical

U.S. Court of Appeals for the Federal Circuit,
Washington.

Hirshhorn Museum and Sculpture Garden, Washington. Gordon Bunshaft, of Skidmore, Owings, & Merrill, architect, 1974.

Catholic University School of Law, Washington. 1994.

Today, the design of a   9
doorway is often reduced
to the selection of products
from manufacturers' cata-
logues. Economic and practical concerns, like visibility and
safety, have made every entrance—to a school, an apartment building, or a mu-
seum—visually similar to that
of almost any retail store: a
pair of aluminum and glass
doors sitting quietly in yet another rectangular opening, or
anonymously undistinguished
within a wall or large glass
windows in thin metal frames.
The revolving door was devised to regulate the flow of
people and air mechanically,
but has always been awkward
and disorienting to move
through.

but they're confusing

Franz Bader Bookstore, Washington.

Architectural products are now available globally, making any single place less distinctive. But the doorway, as a "local site," can still harbor ingenuity and creativity, as well as culturally specific ornament and decoration. The character, history, and meaning of a place can be found inscribed in its doorways.

10

It can?

Carmelite Monastery,
Mt. Carmel, Haifa.

Chapel at the Monastery of the Flagellation,
Jerusalem.

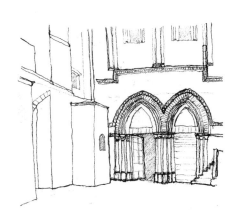

Church of the Holy Sepulchre,
Jerusalem.

Fourth Station of the Cross,
Jerusalem.

For Study and Discussion

QUESTIONS FOR RESPONSE

1. Choose a major building that you're familiar with that has a notable doorway—perhaps a library, a theater, or a state building—and describe what is notable about the doorway.
2. What two doorways in the essay do you find most impressive? Why?

QUESTIONS ABOUT PURPOSE

1. How does Pizzi hope to affect the way you look at doors and doorways?
2. What important features about all the doorways shown here does Pizzi want to draw to your attention?

QUESTIONS ABOUT AUDIENCE

1. In what ways might the size and location of the city where a reader lives affect his or her response to this essay?
2. What common experiences with doors and doorways might Pizzi assume that readers on a college campus would have?

QUESTIONS ABOUT STRATEGIES

1. Why do you think Pizzi groups the doorways on each page as he does? What features do those doorways have in common?
2. Why do you think Pizzi used line drawings instead of photographs to illustrate doorway styles?

QUESTIONS FOR DISCUSSION

1. Select an important building on your campus and analyze how its doorway introduces you to the building. What is the effect the doorway gives?
2. Contrast the residential doorways on page 348 to the museum doorways on page 347. What are the significant differences?

JOHN BERENDT

John Berendt was born in Syracuse, New York, in 1939 and was educated at Harvard University. He began his writing career as an associate editor at *Esquire*, before editing *Holiday Magazine* and writing and producing television programs such as *The David Frost Show* and *The Dick Cavett Show*. In 1979, he returned to *Esquire* as a columnist after serving as editor of *New York Magazine* from 1977 to 1979. In 1994, he published his first book, *Midnight in the Garden of Good and Evil*, a "non-fiction novel" about a controversial murder in Savannah, Georgia. The book has since been transformed into a major film by director Clint Eastwood. In "The Hoax," reprinted from *Esquire*, Berendt defines the magical ingredients of a hoax.

The Hoax

WHEN THE HUMORIST Robert Benchley was an undergraduate at Harvard eighty years ago, he and a couple of friends showed up one morning at the door of an elegant Beacon Hill mansion, dressed as furniture repairmen. They told the housekeeper they had come to pick up the sofa. Five minutes later they carried the sofa out the door, put it on a truck, and drove it three blocks away to another house, where, posing as deliverymen, they plunked it down in the parlor. That evening, as Benchley well knew, the couple living in house A were due to attend a party in house B. Whatever the outcome—and I'll get to that shortly—it was guaranteed to be a defining example of how proper Bostonians handle social crises. The wit inherent in Benchley's practical joke elevated it from the level of prank to the more respectable realm of hoax.

[handwritten: that'd be hilarious]

To qualify as a hoax, a prank must have magic in it—the   2
word is derived from *hocus-pocus,* after all. Daring and irony
are useful ingredients, too. A good example of a hoax is the
ruse perpetrated by David Hampton, the young black man
whose pretense of being Sidney Poitier's son inspired John
Guare's *Six Degrees of Separation.* Hampton managed to in-
sinuate himself into two of New York's most sophisticated
households—one headed by the president of the public-
television station WNET, the other by the dean of the
Columbia School of Journalism. Hampton's hoax touched a
number of sensitive themes: snobbery, class, race, and sex, all
of which playwright Guare deftly exploited.

Hampton is a member of an elite band of famous impos-   3
tors that includes a half-mad woman who for fifty years

To qualify as a hoax, a prank must have
magic in it. . . .

---

claimed to be Anastasia, the lost daughter of the assassinated
czar Nicholas II; and a man named Harry Gerguson, who became a Hollywood restaurateur and darling of society in the
1930s and 1940s as the ersatz Russian prince Mike
Romanoff.

Forgeries have been among the better hoaxes. Fake   4
Vermeers painted by an obscure Dutch artist, Hans van
Meegeren, were so convincing that they fooled art dealers,
collectors, and museums. The hoax came to light when Van
Meegeren was arrested as a Nazi collaborator after the war.
To prove he was not a Nazi, he admitted he had sold a fake
Vermeer to Hermann Göring for $256,000. Then he owned
up to having created other "Vermeers," and to prove he
could do it, he painted *Jesus in the Temple* in the style of
Vermeer while under guard in jail.

In a bizarre twist, a story much like Van Meegeren's be-   5 came the subject of the book *Fake!*, by Clifford Irving, who in 1972 attempted to pull off a spectacular hoax of his own: a wholly fraudulent "authorized" biography of Howard Hughes. Irving claimed to have conducted secret interviews with the reclusive Hughes, and McGraw-Hill gave him a big advance. Shortly before publication, Hughes surfaced by telephone and denied that he had ever spoken with Irving. Irving had already spent $100,000 of the advance; he was convicted of fraud and sent to jail.

As it happens, we are used to hoaxes where I come from. I grew up just a few miles down the road from Cardiff, New York—a town made famous by the Cardiff Giant. As we learned in school, a farmer named Newell complained, back in 1889, that his well was running dry, and while he and his neighbors were digging a new one, they came upon what appeared to be the fossilized remains of a man twelve feet tall. Before the day was out, Newell had erected a tent and posted a sign charging a dollar for a glimpse of the "giant"—three dollars for a longer look. Throngs descended on Cardiff. It wasn't long before scientists determined that the giant had been carved from a block of gypsum. The hoax came undone fairly quickly after that, but even so—as often happens with hoaxes—the giant became an even bigger attraction *because* it was a hoax. P. T. Barnum offered Newell a fortune for the giant, but Newell refused, and it was then that he got his comeuppance. Barnum simply made a replica and put it on display as the genuine Cardiff Giant. Newell's gig was ruined.

The consequences of hoaxes are what give them spice. Orson Welles's lifelike 1938 radio broadcast of H. G. Wells's *War of the Worlds* panicked millions of Americans, who were convinced that martians had landed in New Jersey. The forged diary of Adolf Hitler embarrassed historian Hugh Trevor-Roper, who had vouched for its authenticity, and *Newsweek* and *The Sunday Times* of London, both of which published excerpts in 1983 shortly before forensic tests proved that there were nylon fibers in the paper it was written on, which wouldn't have been possible had it originated before 1950. The five-hundred-thousand-year-old remains of

Piltdown man, found in 1912, had anthropologists confused about human evolution until 1953, when fluoride tests exposed the bones as an elaborate modern hoax. And as for Robert Benchley's game on Beacon Hill, no one said a word about the sofa all evening, although there it sat in plain sight. One week later, however, couple A sent an anonymous package to couple B. It contained the sofa's slipcovers.

why don't you speak up

For Study and Discussion

QUESTIONS FOR RESPONSE

1. What hoaxes do you know about or have you been involved in? Which of them had elements that might be described as daring or witty?
2. What's your reaction to those incidents in Berendt's account that involve criminal fraud? How do you explain that reaction?

QUESTIONS ABOUT PURPOSE

1. How do you think Berendt wants you to respond to the tricksters he describes in his essay? To what extent did you respond that way?
2. Berendt's examples of people duped by hoaxes include scientists, a historian, a college president, an eminent publisher, and curators of several museums. What does he accomplish by telling stories about such a wide range of dupes?

QUESTIONS ABOUT AUDIENCE

1. This essay originally appeared in *Esquire* magazine. What traits and attitudes do you think a writer for *Esquire* assumes characterize its readers? (If necessary, browse through an issue of *Esquire* in the library to get a feel for its audience.)
2. Berendt seems to assume that everyone enjoys stories about tricksters getting the best of their victims. In your case, is the assumption justified? Why or why not?

QUESTIONS ABOUT STRATEGIES

1. What does the writer achieve by opening and closing the essay with the anecdote about the sofa?
2. How would you characterize the tone of this essay? What attitude of the writer toward his subject do you think the tone reflects? Do you find that attitude engaging or off-putting?

QUESTIONS FOR DISCUSSION

1. Which of Berendt's anecdotes do you find the most entertaining? Why?
2. When would you say a deception ceases to be a hoax and turns into something else? What examples can you think of?

DIANE ACKERMAN

Diane Ackerman was born in 1948 in Waukegan, Illinois, and was educated at Boston University, Pennsylvania State University, and Cornell University. After jobs as a researcher and editorial assistant, Ackerman began teaching writing at schools such as Pittsburgh University; Washington University, St. Louis; and Cornell University. Her own writing includes several collections of poems (*The Planets: A Cosmic Pastoral,* 1976; and *The Senses of Animals,* 2000), a play (*Reverse Thunder: A Dramatic Poem,* 1988), two television documentaries (*Ideas,* 1990; and *The Senses,* 1995), and numerous works of nonfiction (*The Natural History of the Senses,* 1990; *A Natural History of Love,* 1994; and *A Natural History of My Garden,* 2001). In "Pain," reprinted from *A Natural History of the Senses,* Ackerman examines the difficulty of defining *pain.*

Pain

I N THE SAND-SWEPT sprawl of the panoramic film *Lawrence of Arabia* a scene of quintessential machismo stands out: T.E. Lawrence holding his hand over a candle flame until the flesh starts to sizzle. When his companion tries the same thing, he recoils in pain, crying "Doesn't that hurt you?" as he nurses his burned hand. "Yes," Lawrence replies coolly. "Then what is the trick?" the companion asks. "The trick," Lawrence answers, "is not to mind." 1

One of the great riddles of biology is why the experience of pain is so subjective. Being able to withstand pain depends to a considerable extent on culture and tradition. Many soldiers have denied pain despite appalling wounds, not even re- 2 questing morphine, although in peacetime they would have demanded it. Most people going into the hospital for an operation focus completely on their pain and suffering, whereas soldiers or saints and other martyrs can think about something nobler and more important to them, and this clouds their sense of pain. Religions have always encouraged their martyrs to experience pain in order to purify the spirit. We come into this world with only the slender word "I," and giving it up in a sacred delirium is the painful ecstasy religions

---

Being able to withstand pain depends to a considerable extent on culture and tradition.

---

demand. When a fakir runs across hot coals, his skin does begin to singe—you can smell burning flesh; he just doesn't feel it. In Bali a few years ago, my mother saw men go into trances and pick up red-hot cannonballs from an open fire, then carry them down the road. As meditation techniques and biofeedback have shown, the mind can learn to conquer pain. This is particularly true in moments of crisis or exaltation, when concentrating on something outside oneself seems to distract the mind from the body, and the body from suffering and time. Of course, there are those who welcome pain in order to surmount it. In 1989, I read about a new craze in California: well-to-do business people taking weekend classes in hot-coal-walking. Pushing the body to or beyond its limits has always appealed to human beings. There is a part of our psyche that is pure timekeeper and weather watcher. Not only do we long to know how fast we can run, how high we can jump, how long we can hold our breath under water—we also like to keep checking these limits regularly to see if they've changed. Why? What difference does it make? The human body is miraculous and beautiful, whether it can "clean and jerk" three hundred pounds, swim the English Channel, or survive a year riding the subway. In anthropological terms, we've come to be who we are by evolving sharper ways to adapt to the environment, and, from the outset, what has guided us has been an elaborate system of rewards. Small wonder we're addicted to quiz shows and lotteries, paychecks and bonuses. We've always explored our mental limits, too, and pushed them without letup. In the early eighties, I spent a year as a soccer journalist, following the dazzling legwork of Pelé, Franz Beckenbauer, and virtually every other legendary international star the New York Cosmos had signed up for equally legendary sums of American cash. Choose your favorite sport; now imagine seeing all the world's best players on one team. I was interested in the ceremonial violence of sports, the psychology of games, the charmed circle of the field, the breezy rhetoric of the legs, the anthropological spectacle of watching twenty-two barely clad men run on grass in the sunlight, hazing the quarry of a ball toward the net. The fluency and grace of soccer appealed for a number of reasons, and I wanted to absorb some of its atmosphere for a novel I was writing. I was amazed to discover that the players frequently realized only at halftime or after a match that they'd hurt themselves badly and were indeed in wicked pain. During the match, there hadn't been the rumor of pain, but once the match was over and they could afford the luxury of suffering, pain screamed like a noon factory whistle.

Often our fear of pain contributes to it. Our culture expects childbirth to be a deeply painful event, and so, for us, it is. Women from other cultures stop their work in the fields to give birth, returning to the fields immediately afterward. Initiation and adolescence rites around the world often involve penetrating pain, which initiates must endure to prove themselves worthy. In the sun dance of the Sioux, for instance, a young warrior would allow the skin of his chest to be pierced by iron rods; then he was hung from a stanchion. When I was in Istanbul in the 1970s, I saw teenage boys dressed in shiny silk fezzes and silk suits decorated with glitter. They were preparing for circumcision, a festive event in the life of a

[margin annotations: "how is $ a mental push"; "NICE"; "Howie?"]

Turk, which occurs at around the age of fifteen. No anesthetic is used; instead, a boy is given a jelly candy to chew. Sir Richard Burton's writings abound with descriptions of tribal mutilation and torture rituals, including one in which a shaman removes an apron of flesh from the front of a boy, cutting all the way from the stomach to the thighs, producing a huge white scar.

Women in some cultures go through many painful initiation rites, often including circumcision, which removes or destroys the clitoris. Being able to endure the pain of childbirth is expected of women, but there are also disguised rites of pain, pain that is endured for the sake of health or beauty. Women have their legs waxed as a matter of fashion, and have done so throughout the ages. When mine were waxed at a Manhattan beauty salon recently, the pain, which began like 10,000 bees stinging me simultaneously, was excruciating. Change the woman from a Rumanian cosmetician to a German Gestapo agent. Change the room from a cubicle in a beauty emporium to a prison cell. Keep the level of pain exactly the same, and it easily qualifies as torture. We tend to think of torture in the name of beauty as an aberration of the ancients, but there are modern scourging parlors. People have always mutilated their skins, often enduring pain to be beautiful, as if the pain chastened the beauty, gave it the special veneer of sacrifice. Many women experience extreme pain during their periods each month, but they accept the pain because they understand that it's not caused by someone else, it's not malicious, and it doesn't surprise them; and this makes all the difference.

There are also illusions of pain as vivid as optical illusions, times when the sufferer imagines he or she feels pain that cannot possibly exist. In some cultures, the father experiences a false pregnancy—*couvade* as it's called—and takes to bed with childbirth pains, going through his own arduous experience of having a baby. The internal organs don't have many pain receptors (the skin is supposed to be the guard post), so people often feel "referred pain" when one of their organs is in trouble. Heart attacks frequently produce a pain in the stomach, the left arm, or the shoulder. When this happens,

the brain can't figure out exactly where the message is coming from. In the classic phenomenon of phantom-limb pain,
the brain gets faulty signals and continues to feel pain in a
limb that has been amputated; such pain can be torturous,
perverse, and maddening, since there is nothing physically
present to hurt.

Pain has plagued us throughout the history of our species. 6
We spend our lives trying to avoid it, and, from one point of
view, what we call "happiness" may be just the absence of
pain. Yet it is difficult to define pain, which may be sharp,
dull, shooting, throbbing, imaginary, or referred. We have
many pains that surge from within as cramps and aches. And
we also talk about emotional distress as pain. Pains are often
combined, the emotional with the physical, and the physical
with the physical. When you burn yourself, the skin swells
and blisters, and when the blister breaks, the skin hurts in yet
another way. A wound may become infected. Then histamine
and serotonin are released, which dilate the blood vessels and
trigger a pain response. Not all internal injuries can be felt
(it's possible to do brain surgery under a local anesthetic),
but illnesses that constrict blood flow often are: Angina
pectoris, for example, which occurs when the coronary arter-
ies shrink too tight for blood to comfortably pass. Even intense pain often eludes accurate description, as Virginia
Woolf reminds us in her essay "On Being Ill": "English,
which can express the thoughts of Hamlet and the tragedy of
Lear, has no words for the shiver and the headache . . . let a
sufferer try to describe a pain in his head to a doctor and language at once runs dry."

For Study and Discussion

QUESTIONS FOR RESPONSE

1. If you come from our traditional Western culture, how do you
react to Ackerman's reports about the extreme pain that some
members of other cultures seem to be able to endure?

2. Ackerman says that T.E. Lawrence displays the "quintessential machismo." How do you interpret that comment?

QUESTIONS ABOUT PURPOSE

1. What assumptions about pain do you think Ackerman is challenging in this essay?
2. How might her discussion of the many ways different people deal with pain cause some people to rethink their conventional wisdom about the sensation?

QUESTIONS ABOUT AUDIENCE

1. What message about dealing with pain do you think our culture gives the average person? How is that message communicated?
2. How would you describe your most painful physical experience? What resources helped you get through it?

QUESTIONS ABOUT STRATEGIES

1. How does Ackerman's opening paragraph introduce the reader to a central concept in her essay?
2. What does Ackerman achieve by packing her essay with such a broad range of examples from diverse cultures?

QUESTIONS FOR DISCUSSION

1. What incentives can people have to endure pain? What incentive might work for you?
2. In what ways is pain management big business in this country? How might that reality affect people's attitudes about pain?

WILLIAM LANGEWIESCHE

William Langewiesche is a correspondent for the *Atlantic*. A pilot, he began his writing career submitting articles to *Flying* magazine. His books include *Cutting for Sign* (1993), an account of his experiences along the Mexican-American border; *Sahara Unveiled: A Journey Across the Desert* (1996), a description of his travels across North Africa; and *Inside the Sky: A Meditation on Flight* (1998). In "American Ingenuity," excerpted from his book about the aftermath of the September 11 disaster, *American Ground: Unbuilding the World Trade Center* (2002), Langewiesche defines the extraordinary qualities of a man who helped direct the untangling of the wreckage at Ground Zero.

American Ingenuity

WITH US AT the site of the World Trade Center was an affable, boyish-looking man named David Griffin, age thirty-four, who was the project's chief demolition consultant and its token Southerner. Demolition in this context meant the unbuilding not of all the ruins but of the standing structures, of which there were plenty—Buildings Four, Five, and Six; the stump of the Marriott hotel; and all of the intact and partially intact basement levels of the foundation hole. Griffin, as usual, was wearing immaculate golfing clothes. His site ID tag dangled from a neck strap embroidered with "I Love Jesus." He was less concerned than Rinaldi about the errant grappler, having seen much worse in his professional life, but he had gentlemanly manners, and said nothing about that now. Instead he reflected on the Trade Center work in general. He said, "It's like playing

Jenga—who's gonna pick out the last piece? Only thing is, instead of falling down on your kitchen table, the pile falls five levels down—and you're in it." I asked Griffin if he was good at playing Jenga. He grinned and said, "Yeah, I reckon I am." It was typical Griffin. He was a personable guy. He came from faraway Greensboro, North Carolina, and was the butt of a lot of NASCAR jokes. Indeed, his uncle was a NASCAR official. Griffin thought it was a pretty big deal. But he was not a complete rube. He knew all about the stereotypes, even found them funny. Once at a morning meeting

The truth is, what Griffin had grown up knowing about risk and safety, others at the site, more formally educated, were now having to learn.

at PS 89, when Griffin asked about the value of the bullion that was soon to be removed from the vault under the ruins, Mike Burton said, "It's enough to buy all of North Carolina—and they'll throw in South Carolina for free." Griffin laughed along with the rest.

But the bullion was worth only about a quarter billion dollars, and Griffin's own daddy, as he called him, was probably worth that much or more. His daddy's name was David too, though people called him "D.H." He was a tobacco farmer's boy, a ninth-grade dropout who in 1958, when he was nineteen, went to work on a cigarette production line, where he met his wife, and where he thought he'd spend his life. In his spare time he sold parts off a dozen junked cars in his front yard. In 1959, he tore down an old church to salvage the lumber and nails, and did it so well that the city inspector (who stopped by because D.H. lacked a demolition permit) asked him to handle a small apartment building next. D.H. soon realized that the value of demolition lay as much in the resale of salvaged materials as in the service rendered, and, as he liked to explain, he just kept going from there. By the time of the Trade Center collapse he had become one of the three largest demolition contractors in the United States, one of the largest scrap-metal dealers in the South, a construction magnate, and the master of more businesses and real estate in North Carolina than even he could remember.

New York was not his kind of town, and he had opposed David's impulse to get involved, but after the Griffin name became attached to the Trade Center project, D.H. arrived twice at the site to see the work, of which, of course, he was proud. He was a burly, gray-haired man of sixty-two, with a bad knee, a strong Carolina accent, and unusually quick eyes. David took him around on an all-terrain "Gator." D.H. was friendly, but didn't have much to say to the New Yorkers who passed by. He wanted to talk to David about family, and a little business. He told me about his weekend relaxation, which he called "riding around," and which amounted to an activity rather close to his work—a Sunday-drive form of looking for trades, in which the size of the deal didn't matter so much as its quality. David laughed and said that just last week his daddy, having come into 20,000 T-shirts (D.H.: "Class One T-shirts. Orange ones, white ones, blue ones") at 25 cents apiece, had taken a few boxes of them to the parking lots of local shopping centers, and for a dollar each had sold dozens out of the trunk of his car. His customers must have figured he was an old man down on his luck. Even D.H. could now chuckle about it. But later that afternoon, as we talked, I got the distinct impression that he was feeling out my interest in acquiring, say, an antique shotgun, or maybe a knife.

When the Twin Towers collapsed, D.H. Griffin, like most Americans, was so wrapped up in his affairs that he was unable to respond beyond the standard feelings of anger and surprise. David Griffin was a rich and busy man in his own right, president of the demolition company, with a wife and young children, but not quite so established as his father. He was drawn to the Trade Center site much as Ken Holden and Mike Burton were—because he had knowledge to offer, and

3

4

could not stay away. He had a business justification, too: on Thursday, September 13, he called his father and said, "Daddy, I'm going to New York. Because this is the kind of job, if it breaks—when it *does* break—they're not gonna pick up the phone book and look under 'Demolition Contractors' to see who could help them. I'm gonna leave, and if I don't have anything by Monday, all I'll feel is I wasted a weekend in New York. Nothing ventured, nothing gained."

he still says daddy?

His wife, who had been to New York only once before (for a day), insisted on accompanying him, and on bringing their children. They loaded up their Suburban, drove nine hours north, and in the middle of the night checked into the Palace Hotel, in midtown Manhattan. Griffin got a few hours' sleep, and early Friday morning, in a pouring rain, he drove downtown as far as he could, grabbed a raincoat and a hardhat out of the back of his vehicle, hung a respirator around his neck, and started walking. When he came to a police barricade at Canal Street, he did not hesitate, and he passed through unchallenged. His heart pounded. He thought, *I'm in! I'm in!* But four blocks from the site he was stopped at another barricade—this one manned by the New York National Guard. A soldier said, "Where do you think you're going?"   5

"I'm going to work."   6

"Well, lemme see your pass."   7

"I don't have a pass."   8

"If you don't have a pass, you're not going in. Who are you working for?"   9

"Well . . . Bovis." Griffin had contacts there, some names to look up.   10

why stale to help?

The soldier said, "What, you don't have a pass or anything?"   11

Griffin said, "I come from North Carolina."   12

That fixed it. The soldier said, "No pass—you can't go in."   13

Griffin stood around, unsure of what to do. The rain came down. People with passes went through. After a while a group of Red Cross volunteers showed up with drinks for the soldiers. The soldiers began talking to them. Griffin drifted   14 inside the barricade. The soldiers didn't seem to notice. He walked toward the pile, and the next thing he knew, six months had gone by.

His Bovis contacts knew him by reputation: this was   15
D.H.'s boy, a kid who'd grown up at wrecking sites from the age of two, sleeping in concrete culverts at night, with laborers standing guard. The Bovis people understood the value of the homegrown experience that Griffin could provide. They hired him for their quadrant, and introduced him around. For the first several weeks he had competition from a more flamboyant demolition man, who ultimately flamed out in the eyes of the site managers at PS 89 and was asked by Ken Holden to leave the job. People had trust in Griffin by then, as much for his lack of grandstanding as for his obvious technical competence. At Burton's request he took on the role of demolition consultant for the whole site, planning and managing the dismantling of all the standing structures. It was a crucial position, central to the entire project.

Toward the end, over a sandwich with his father and me,   16
Griffin described his early thoughts. He had considered some selective blasting at first, to drop the skeletal walls and bring down the ruined buildings. He called it "shooting" them. Holden and Burton vetoed the idea, primarily because of the jitteriness of the neighbors. As much to his father as to me, Griffin said, "These New Yorkers just flip out. You know, this ain't South Pittsburgh."

D.H. said, "Nope."   17

Griffin figured he would have the space to use a wrecking   18
ball on Buildings Four and Five, and indeed that is what he did, after pre-cutting the internal structure of the buildings, a dangerous process he called "juicing them up." It was an unusual procedure for New York, but faster and cheaper than the city's standard labor-intensive technique of incremental deconstruction.

He also figured correctly that he'd be able to topple the   19
north skeletal wall, a towering structure that had broken at the base and was leaning heavily against Building Six. This was done with five grapplers arranged side by side, pulling si-

multaneously on cables bolted to the top. Eventually he was able to rock and topple Building Six, too. But for the most part, such wholesale wrecking techniques were not going to work at the Trade Center site. Griffin said, "I knew there wasn't but one way to do it."

D.H. said, "Yep."   20

"That's to start cutting and pulling it down."   21

He meant piece by piece, and it was no big deal. He had a   22
way of making things seem simple. He brought in a few of his own people—Southern boys all, who had the hardscrabble background necessary to get the job done. They moved into some vacant apartments nearby. They were the most undaunted workers at the site. Months later Burton expressed surprise over beer one night when he discovered that Griffin had only a high school education. No one had bothered to ask before, and afterward no one thought it mattered.

The truth is, what Griffin had grown up knowing about   23
risk and safety, others at the site, more formally educated, were now having to learn. Regulation was simply not possible at the start, and even after it began to creep in, its real purpose was to exist officially on the books, playing a rearguard position while the project surged ahead and continued to allow personal responsibility and individual choice to prevail. Peter Rinaldi adapted to the freedom naturally, despite his years spent within the confines of the Port Authority, and he became Griffin's ally in the ordinarily cautious camp of the engineers. Others had a harder time accepting risk, but even they eventually came around. There was, for instance, an encounter that became well-known at PS 89, between Griffin and a DDC engineer who was nominally responsible for the aboveground structures, but whose penchant for memo-writing made him something of a misfit at the site. For weeks Griffin had been pushing the engineer to let him proceed with the demolition of the Marriott ruins, which rose three stories above the street and extended all six levels down into the foundation hole. There was no safe way to take those ruins on. Access from the sides was impossible because of the proximity of unstable structures and of the vulnerable slurry

wall. Griffin's solution—to put an excavator directly on top and wreck the Marriott from above—was obviously very risky. The DDC engineer kept blocking the action. At last Griffin came as close to losing his temper as he ever did. He said, "We're not going to *talk* it down. We gotta do *something.*"

The engineer finally gave in. He said, "Okay. I wouldn't *recommend* it, but I guess it's okay." That formulation quickly went around. It described how the site actually worked—by people turning a blind eye. 24

Given the go-ahead, a grappler operator immediately drove his machine to the top of the hotel and, at conscious risk to himself, began to tear it apart nearly underfoot. It was dangerous behavior, but typical on the pile. Griffin himself, who often stood in the thick of the action, once had a narrow escape when the counterweight of a swinging excavator hit him hard in the back, luckily knocking him down a slope rather than against the debris, which would probably have been fatal. He checked with the site doctor, and went back to work. At another time, when a large section of steel unexpectedly fell, a fire chief came rushing up to Griffin yelling, "Where's the safety zone on this job?" and Griffin calmly responded by naming the site's outer-perimeter line: "Chambers Street. Do you want to close the whole place down?" The fire chief got the message. Most people eventually did. Risk was the very nature of the Trade Center operation. 25

This was sometimes difficult to grasp for people on the outside, where there were flurries of news reports about worrisome safety violations at the site. Outsiders believed that the constant danger—along with the presence of the dead—had to be getting to people. One afternoon when Pablo Lopez stopped by the midtown engineering offices of Thornton-Tomasetti, he was offered a session with a consulting psychologist, a woman whom the company had dutifully retained to assist its Trade Center crew. The psychologist asked Lopez to make himself comfortable. She had a slow, soothing way of talking, which had the immediate effect of 26 irritating him. He told me about it the next day, exaggerating the intervals between her words.

He said, "She says, 'Close . . . your . . . eyes.'   27

"So I close my eyes. Okay, now what?   28

"She says, 'Imagine . . . a . . . safe . . . place.'   29

"I think, safe place? What's that? At least she could have   30
said 'Imagine a steak house.' I mean, where've you been, lady? I live in New York City, and there's an anthrax scare going on! I go home, and my wife is ironing the mail! And where is it I work? It's underground in the World Trade Center."

I don't know what Lopez said to the psychologist, but his   31
point to me was that he wasn't planning to move away. He lived at the center of the world because he liked the action. He worked at the Trade Center because he wanted to. He wasn't searching for safety. He didn't need to close his eyes, or to make himself comfortable. He didn't need the teddy bears that volunteers kept handing out. And he wasn't afraid of the dead.

For Study and Discussion

QUESTIONS FOR RESPONSE

1. What is your dominant impression of David Griffin? How would you describe him?
2. What is your general impression of the way the area of the World Trade Center looked a few weeks after the September 11 bombing?

QUESTIONS ABOUT PURPOSE

1. What traits of the people working at the site of the World Trade Center does Langewiesche emphasize in this selection?
2. Why does the author emphasize David Griffin's North Carolina roots and his lack of a college education?

QUESTIONS ABOUT AUDIENCE

1. What personal qualities does Langewiesche assume that his readers will value? Do you agree with that judgment?
2. Describe the kinds of readers that you think would be particularly interested in reading this article and the book it came from. Are you among those readers?

QUESTIONS ABOUT STRATEGIES

1. What does Langewiesche accomplish by focusing on one person in this part of his account of the demolition of the World Trade Center?
2. How does Langewiesche use Griffin's actions and conversations to define him?

QUESTIONS FOR DISCUSSION

1. In what ways would you say David Griffin exemplifies traits we like to think of as particularly American?
2. What kind of individuals could have obstructed and delayed the work to be done at the World Trade Center site?

STEPHEN HARRIGAN

Stephen Harrigan was born in Oklahoma City in 1948 and educated at the University of Texas. After working as a journalist, including a term as senior editor at *Texas Monthly*, Harrigan turned his attention to fiction and screenplays. His novels include *Aransas* (1980) and *Jacob's Well* (1984), and his screenplays include *The Last of His Tribe* (1992) and *The O.J. Simpson Story* (1995). Harrigan has also published two collections of essays, *A Natural State* (1988) and *Comanche Midnight* (1995). In "The Tiger Is God," reprinted from the former collection, Harrigan provides dramatic examples that help define a tiger "just being a tiger."

The Tiger Is God

WHEN TIGERS ATTACK men, they do so in a characteristic 1
way. They come from behind, from the right side, and when they lunge it is with the intent of snapping the *intense* neck of the prey in their jaws. Most tiger victims die swiftly, their necks broken, their spinal cords compressed or severed high up on the vertebral column.

Ricardo Tovar, a fifty-nine-year-old keeper at the Houston 2
Zoo, was killed by a tiger on May 12, 1988. The primary cause of death was a broken neck, although most of the ribs on the left side of his chest were fractured as well, and there were multiple lacerations on his face and right arm. No one witnessed the attack, and no one would ever know exactly how and why it took place, but the central nightmarish event was clear. Tovar had been standing at a steel door separating the zookeepers' area from the naturalistic tiger display outside. Set into the door was a small viewing window—only

slightly larger than an average television screen—made of wire-reinforced glass. Somehow the tiger had broken the glass, grabbed the keeper, and pulled him through the window to his death.

Fatal zoo accidents occur more frequently than most people realize. The year before Tovar died, a keeper in the Fort Worth Zoo was crushed by an elephant, and in 1985, an employee of the Bronx Zoo was killed by two Siberian tigers— the same subspecies as the one that attacked Tovar—when she mistakenly entered the tiger display while the animals

amazing

One point is beyond dispute: A tiger is a predator, its mission on the earth is to kill, and in doing so it often displays awesome strength and dexterity.

---

like the girl in a Jaguar in Den

were still there. But there was something especially haunting about the Houston incident, something that people could not get out of their minds. It had to do with the realization of a fear built deep into our genetic code: the fear that a beast could appear out of nowhere—through a window!—and snatch us away.

The tiger's name was Miguel. He was eleven years old— middle-aged for a tiger—and had been born at the Houston Zoo to a mother who was a wild-caught Siberian. Siberians are larger in size than any of the other subspecies, and their coats are heavier. Fewer than three hundred of them are now left in the frozen river valleys and hardwood forests of the Soviet Far East, though they were once so plentiful in that region that Cossack troops were sent in during the construction of the Trans-Baikal railway specifically to protect the workers from tiger attacks. Miguel was of mixed blood—his father was a zoo-reared Bengal—but his Siberian lineage was dominant. He was a massive 450-pound creature whose dis-

3

4

position had been snarly ever since he was a cub. Some of the other tigers at the zoo were as placid and affectionate as house cats, but Miguel filled his keepers with caution. Oscar Mendietta, a keeper who retired a few weeks before Tovar's death, remembers the way Miguel would sometimes lunge at zoo personnel as they walked by his holding cage, his claws unsheathed and protruding through the steel mesh. "He had," Mendietta says, "an intent to kill."

Tovar was well aware of Miguel's temperament. He had been working with big cats in the Houston Zoo since 1982, and his fellow keepers regarded him as a cautious and responsible man. Like many old-time zookeepers, he was a civil servant with no formal training in zoology, but he had worked around captive animals most of his life (before coming to Houston, he had been a keeper at the San Antonio Zoo) and had gained a good deal of practical knowledge about their behavior. No one regarded Miguel's aggressiveness as aberrant. Tovar and the other keepers well understood the fact that tigers were supposed to be dangerous.

In 1987 the tigers and other cats had been moved from their outdated display cages to brand-new facilities with outdoor exhibit areas built to mimic the animals' natural environments. The Siberian tiger exhibit—in a structure known as the Phase II building—comprised about a quarter of an acre. It was a wide rectangular space decorated with shrubs and trees, a few fake boulders, and a water-filled moat. The exhibit's backdrop was a depiction, in plaster and cement, of a high rock wall seamed with stress fractures.

Built into the wall, out of public view, was a long corridor lined with the cats' holding cages, where the tigers were fed and confined while the keepers went out into the display to shovel excrement and hose down the area. Miguel and the other male Siberian, Rambo, each had a holding cage, and they alternated in the use of the outdoor habitat, since two male tigers occupying the same space guaranteed monumental discord. Next to Rambo's cage was a narrow alcove through which the keepers went back and forth from the corridor into the display. The alcove was guarded by two doors.

The one with the viewing window led outside. Another door, made of steel mesh, closed off the interior corridor.

8   May 12 was a Thursday. Tovar came to work at about six-thirty in the morning, and at that hour he was alone. Rambo was secure in his holding cage and Miguel was outside—it had been his turn that night to have the run of the display.

9   Thursdays and Sundays were "fast" days. Normally the tigers were fed a daily ration of ten to fifteen pounds of ground fetal calf, but twice a week their food was withheld in order to keep them from growing obese in confinement. The animals knew which days were fast days, and on those mornings they were sometimes balky about coming inside, since no food was being offered. Nevertheless, the tigers had to be secured in their holding cages while the keepers went outside to clean the display. On this morning, Tovar had apparently gone to the viewing window to check the whereabouts of Miguel when the tiger did not come inside, even though the keepers usually made a point of not entering the alcove until they were certain that both animals were locked up in their holding cages. The viewing window was so small and the habitat itself so panoramic that the chances of spotting the tiger from the window were slim. Several of the keepers had wondered why there was a window there at all, since it was almost useless as an observation post and since one would never go through the door in the first place without being certain that the tigers were in their cages.

10   But that was where Tovar had been, standing at a steel door with a panel of reinforced glass, when the tiger attacked. John Gilbert, the senior zookeeper who supervised the cat section, stopped in at the Phase II building a little after seven-thirty, planning to discuss with Tovar the scheduled sedation of a lion. He had just entered the corridor when he saw broken glass on the floor outside the steel mesh door that led to the alcove. The door was unlocked—it had been opened by Tovar when he entered the alcove to look out the window. Looking through the mesh, Gilbert saw the shards of glass hanging from the window frame and Tovar's cap, watch, and a single rubber boot lying on the floor. Knowing

something dreadful had happened, he called Tovar's name, then pushed on the door and cautiously started to enter the alcove. He was only a few paces away from the broken window when the tiger's head suddenly appeared there, filling its jagged frame. His heart pounding, Gilbert backed off, slammed and locked the mesh door behind him and radioed for help.

Tom Dieckow, a wiry, white-bearded Marine veteran of the Korean War, was the zoo's exhibits curator. He was also in charge of its shooting team, a seldom-convened body whose task was to kill, if necessary, any escaped zoo animal that posed an immediate threat to the public. Dieckow was in his office in the service complex building when he heard Gilbert's emergency call. He grabbed a twelve-gauge shotgun, commandeered an electrician's pickup truck, and arrived at the tiger exhibit two minutes later. He went around to the front of the habitat and saw Miguel standing there, calm and unconcerned, with Tovar's motionless body lying face down fifteen feet away. Dieckow did not shoot. It was his clear impression that the keeper was dead, that the harm was already done. By that time the zoo's response team had gathered outside the exhibit. Miguel stared at the onlookers and then picked up Tovar's head in his jaws and started to drag him off.

"I think probably what crossed that cat's mind at that point," Dieckow speculated later, "is 'look at all those scavengers across there that are after my prey. I'm gonna move it.' He was just being a tiger."

Dieckow raised his shotgun again, this time with the intention of shooting Miguel, but because of all the brush and ersatz boulders in the habitat, he could not get a clear shot. He fired into the water instead, causing the startled tiger to drop the keeper, and then fired twice more as another zoo worker discharged a fire extinguisher from the top of the rock wall. The commotion worked, and Miguel retreated into his holding cage.

The Houston Zoo opened a half-hour late that day. Miguel and all the other big cats were kept inside until zoo officials could determine if it was safe—both for the cats and for the public—to exhibit them again. For a few days the zoo switchboard was jammed with calls from people wanting to express their opinion on whether the tiger should live or die. But for the people at the zoo that issue had never been in doubt.

"It's automatic with us," John Werler, the zoo director, told me when I visited his office a week after the incident. "To what end would we destroy the tiger? If we followed this argument to its logical conclusion, we'd have to destroy every dangerous animal in the zoo collection." 15

good point

Werler was a reflective, kindly looking man who was obviously weighed down by a load of unpleasant concerns. There was the overall question of zoo safety, the specter of lawsuits, and most recently the public anger of a number of zoo staffers who blamed Tovar's death on the budget cuts, staffing shortages, and bureaucratic indifference that forced keepers to work alone in potentially dangerous environments. But the dominant mood of the zoo, the day I was there, appeared to be one of simple sadness and shock. 16

so true

"What a terrible loss," read a sympathy card from the staff of the Fort Worth Zoo that was displayed on a coffee table. "May you gain strength and support to get you through this awful time." 17

The details of the attack were still hazy, and still eerie to think about. Unquestionably, the glass door panel had not been strong enough, but exactly how Miguel had broken it, how he had killed Tovar—and why—remained the subjects of numb speculation. One point was beyond dispute: A tiger is a predator, its mission on the earth is to kill, and in doing so it often displays awesome strength and dexterity. 18

absolutely

An Indian researcher, using live deer and buffalo calves as bait, found that the elapsed time between a tiger's secure grip on the animal's neck and the prey's subsequent death was anywhere from thirty-five to ninety seconds. In other circumstances the cat will not choose to be so swift. Sometimes a tiger will kill an elephant calf by snapping its trunk and waiting for it to bleed to death, and it is capable of dragging the car- 19 cass in its jaws for miles. (A full-grown tiger possesses the traction power of thirty men.) When a mother tiger is teaching her cubs to hunt, she might move in on a calf, cripple it with a powerful bite to its rear leg, and stand back and let the cubs practice on the helpless animal.

Tigers have four long canine teeth—fangs. The two in the upper jaw are tapered along the sides to a shearing edge. Fourteen of the teeth are molars, for chewing meat and grinding bone. Like other members of the cat family, tigers have keen, night-seeing eyes, and their hearing is so acute that Indonesian hunters—convinced that a tiger could hear the wind whistling through a man's nose hairs—always kept their nostrils carefully barbered. The pads on the bottom of a tiger's paws are surprisingly sensitive, easily blistered or cut on hot, prickly terrain. But the claws within, five on each front paw and four in the hind paws, are protected like knives in an upholstered box. 20

They are not idle predators; when they kill, they kill to eat. Even a well-fed tiger in a zoo keeps his vestigial repertoire of hunting behaviors intact. (Captive breeding programs, in fact, make a point of selecting in favor of aggressive predatory behavior, since the ultimate hope of these programs is to bolster the dangerously low stock of free-living tigers.) In the zoo, tigers will stalk birds that land in their habitats, and they grow more alert than most people would care to realize when children pass before their gaze. Though stories of man-eating tigers have been extravagantly embellished over the centuries, the existence of such creatures is not legendary. In the Sunderbans, the vast delta region that spans the border of India and Bangladesh, more than four hundred people have been killed by tigers in the last decade. So many fishermen and honey collectors have been carried off that a few years ago officials at the Sunderbans tiger preserve began stationing electrified dummies around the park to encourage the tigers to seek other prey. One percent of all tigers, according to a German biologist who studied them in the Sunderbans, are "dedicated" man-eaters: when they go out hunting, they're after people. Up to a third of all tigers will kill and eat a 21

human if they come across one, though they don't make a
special effort to do so.

It is not likely that Miguel attacked Ricardo Tovar out of   22
hunger. Except for the killing wounds inflicted by the tiger,
the keeper's body was undisturbed. Perhaps something about
Tovar's movements on the other side of the window intrigued the cat enough to make him spring, a powerful lunge
that sent him crashing through the glass. Most likely the tiger
was surprised, and frightened, and reacted instinctively.
There is no evidence that he came all the way through the
window. Probably he just grabbed Tovar by the chest with
one paw, crushed him against the steel door, and with unthinkable strength pulled him through the window and killed
him outside.

makes sense

John Gilbert, the senior keeper who had been the first on   23
the scene that morning, took me inside the Phase II building
to show me where the attack had taken place. Gilbert was a
sandy-haired man in his thirties, still shaken and subdued by
what he had seen. His recitation of the events was as formal
and precise as that of a witness at an inquest.

of course

"When I got to this point," Gilbert said as we passed   24
through the security doors that led to the keepers' corridor,
"I saw the broken glass on the floor. I immediately yelled Mr.
Tovar's name . . ."

The alcove in which Tovar had been standing was much   25
smaller than I had pictured it, and seeing it firsthand made
one thing readily apparent: it was a trap. Its yellow cinderblock walls were no more than four feet apart. The ceiling
was made of steel mesh and a door of the same material
guarded the exit to the corridor. The space was so confined it
was not difficult to imagine—it was impossible *not* to imagine—how the tiger had been able to catch Tovar by surprise
with a deadly swipe from his paw.

And there was the window. Covered with a steel plate now,   26
its meager dimensions were still visible. The idea of being
hauled through that tiny space by a tiger had an almost
supernatural resonance—as if the window were a portal

through which mankind's most primeval terrors were allowed to pass unobstructed.

Gilbert led me down the corridor. We passed the holding cage of Rambo, who hung his head low and let out a grumbling basso roar so deep it sounded like a tremor in the earth. Then we were standing in front of Miguel.

"Here he is," Gilbert said, looking at the animal with an expression on his face that betrayed a sad welter of emotions. "He's quite passive right now."

The tiger was reclining on the floor, looking at us without concern. I noticed his head, which seemed to me wider than the window he had broken out. His eyes were yellow, and when the great head pivoted in my direction and Miguel's eyes met mine I looked away reflexively, afraid of their hypnotic gravity. The tiger stood up and began to pace, his gigantic pads treading noiselessly on the concrete. The bramble of black stripes that decorated his head was as neatly symmetrical as a Rorschach inkblot, and his orange fur—conceived by evolution as camouflage—was a florid, provocative presence in the featureless confines of the cage.

Miguel idly pawed the steel guillotine door that covered the entrance to his cage, and then all of a sudden he reared on his hind legs. I jumped back a little, startled and dwarfed. The top of Miguel's head nestled against the ceiling mesh of his cage, his paws were spread to either side. In one silent moment, his size and scale seemed to have increased exponentially. He looked down at Gilbert and me. In Miguel's mind, I suspected, his keeper's death was merely a vignette, a mostly forgotten moment of fright and commotion that had intruded one day upon the tiger's torpid existence in the zoo. But it was hard not to look up at that immense animal and read his posture as a deliberate demonstration of the power he possessed.

I thought of Tipu Sultan, the eighteenth-century Indian mogul who was obsessed with the tiger and used its likeness as his constant emblem. Tipu Sultan's imperial banner had borne the words "The Tiger Is God." Looking up into

Miguel's yellow eyes I felt the strange appropriateness of those words. The tiger was majestic and unknowable, a beast of such seeming invulnerability that it was possible to believe that he alone had called the world into being, and that a given life could end at his whim. The truth, of course, was far more literal. Miguel was a remnant member of a species never far from the brink of extinction, and his motivation for killing Ricardo Tovar probably did not extend beyond a behavioral quirk. He had a predator's indifference to tragedy; he had killed without culpability. It was a gruesome and unhappy incident, but as far as Miguel was concerned most of the people at the zoo had reached the same conclusion: he was just being a tiger.

For Study and Discussion

QUESTIONS FOR RESPONSE

1. In your visits to zoos, how have you responded to tigers you've seen? With admiration? With awe? With fear? How do you think reading Harrigan's essay might affect your feelings on any future visit?
2. How do you respond to the zoo professionals' feeling that Miguel was "just being a tiger"? Does that reflect a callous or careless attitude?

QUESTIONS ABOUT PURPOSE

1. What attitude about the tiger do you think Harrigan wants to bring about in his readers?
2. Why does Harrigan go into minute detail about the physical arrangements of the zoo and about the schedules? Why would readers want to know these details?

QUESTIONS ABOUT AUDIENCE

1. On what basis do you think that Harrigan can assume that a general audience would want to read about tigers and about the fatal incident at the Houston Zoo?

2. What questions does Harrigan anticipate that his readers will have? How does he attempt to answer those questions?

QUESTIONS ABOUT STRATEGIES

1. What is the impact on the reader of Harrigan's first paragraph? What tone does it set for the essay?
2. What details does the author give that are most important in defining the nature of the tiger? Pick out three or four specific paragraphs that are most important.

QUESTIONS FOR DISCUSSION

1. In what ways are zoos important institutions in this country? Does their value to the public warrant their cost in money, in risk, and in the treatment of animals?
2. What do you think is the appeal of an article such as this? What special significance does it have that the animal was a tiger rather than another animal that can be just as dangerous, for instance, an elephant or rhinoceros?

Alice Walker was born in 1944 in Eatonton, Georgia, attended Spelman College in Atlanta, and graduated from Sarah Lawrence College. She then became active in the civil rights movement, helping to register voters in Georgia, teaching in the Head Start program in Mississippi, and working on the staff of the New York City welfare department. In subsequent years, she began her own writing career while teaching at Wellesley College, the University of California at Berkeley, and Brandeis University. Her writing reveals her interest in the themes of sexism and racism, themes she embodies in her widely acclaimed novels: *The Third Life of Grange Copeland* (1970), *Meridian* (1976), *The Color Purple* (1982), and *Possessing the Secret of Joy* (1992). Her stories, collected in *In Love and Trouble: Stories of Black Women* (1973) and *You Can't Keep a Good Woman Down* (1981), and essays, found in *Living by the Word* (1988) and *The Same River Twice* (1996), examine the complex experiences of black women. "Everyday Use," reprinted from *In Love and Trouble,* focuses on a reunion that reveals two contrasting attitudes toward the meaning of family heritage.

Everyday Use
For Your Grandmama

I WILL WAIT for her in the yard that Maggie and I made so   1
clean and wavy yesterday afternoon. A yard like this is more comfortable than most people know. It is not just a yard. It is like an extended living room. When the hard clay

is swept clean as a floor and the fine sand around the edges
lined with tiny, irregular grooves anyone can come and sit
and look up into the elm tree and wait for the breezes that
never come inside the house.

Maggie will be nervous until after her sister goes: she will
stand hopelessly in corners homely and ashamed of the burn
scars down her arms and legs, eyeing her sister with a mixture
of envy and awe. She thinks her sister has held life always in
the palm of one hand, that "no" is a word the world never
learned to say to her.

You've no doubt seen those TV shows where the child
who has "made it" is confronted, as a surprise, by her own
mother and father, tottering in weakly from backstage. (A
pleasant surprise, of course: What would they do if parent
and child came on the show only to curse out and insult each
other?) On TV mother and child embrace and smile into
each other's faces. Sometimes the mother and father weep,
the child wraps them in her arms and leans across the table to
tell how she would not have made it without their help. I
have seen these programs.

Sometimes I dream a dream in which Dee and I are suddenly brought together on a TV program of this sort. Out of
a dark and soft-seated limousine I am ushered into a bright
room filled with many people. There I meet a smiling, gray,
sporty man like Johnny Carson who shakes my hand and tells
me what a fine girl I have. Then we are on the stage and Dee
is embracing me with tears in her eyes. She pins on my dress a
large orchid, even though she has told me once that she
thinks orchids are tacky flowers.

In real life I am a large, big-boned woman with rough,
man-working hands. In the winter I wear flannel nightgowns
to bed and overalls during the day. I can kill and clean a hog
as mercilessly as a man. My fat keeps me hot in zero weather.
I can work all day, breaking ice to get water for washing. I can
eat pork liver cooked over the open fire minutes after it
comes steaming from the hog. One winter I knocked a bull
calf straight in the brain between the eyes with a sledge hammer and had the meat hung up to chill before nightfall. But

of course all this does not show on television. I am the way
my daughter would want me to be: a hundred pounds
lighter, my skin like an uncooked barley pancake. My hair
glistens in the hot bright lights. Johnny Carson has much to
do to keep up with my quick and witty tongue.

But that is a mistake. I know even before I wake up. Who   6
ever knew a Johnson with a quick tongue? Who can even
imagine me looking a strange white man in the eye? It seems
to me I have talked to them always with one foot raised in
flight, with my head turned in whichever way is farthest from
them. Dee, though. She would always look anyone in the
eye. Hesitation was no part of her nature.

"How do I look, Mama?" Maggie says, showing just   7
enough of her thin body enveloped in pink skirt and red
blouse for me to know she's there, almost hidden by the
door.

"Come out into the yard," I say.   8

Have you ever seen a lame animal, perhaps a dog run over   9
by some careless person rich enough to own a car, sidle up to
someone who is ignorant enough to be kind to him? That is
the way my Maggie walks. She has been like this, chin on
chest, eyes on ground, feet in shuffle, ever since the fire that
burned the other house to the ground.

Dee is lighter than Maggie, with nicer hair and a fuller fig-   10
ure. She's a woman now, though sometimes I forget. How
long ago was it that the other house burned? Ten, twelve
years? Sometimes I can still hear the flames and feel Maggie's
arm sticking to me, her hair smoking and her dress falling off
her in little black papery flakes. Her eyes seemed stretched
open, blazed open by the flames reflected in them. And Dee.
I see her standing off under the sweet gum tree she used to
dig gum out of; a look of concentration on her face as she
watched the last dingy gray board of the house fall in toward
the red-hot brick chimney. Why don't you do a dance around
the ashes? I'd wanted to ask her. She had hated the house
that much.

I used to think she hated Maggie, too. But that was before   11

we raised the money, the church and me, to send her to
Augusta to school. She used to read to us without pity; forc-
ing words, lies, other folks' habits, whole lives upon us two,
sitting trapped and ignorant underneath her voice. She
washed us in a river of make-believe, burned us with a lot of
knowledge we didn't necessarily need to know. Pressed us to
her with the serious way she read, to shove us away at just the
moment, like dimwits, we seemed about to understand.

very smart

Dee wanted nice things. A yellow organdy dress to wear to
her graduation from high school; black pumps to match a
green suit she'd made from an old suit somebody gave me.
She was determined to stare down any disaster in her efforts.
Her eyelids would not flicker for minutes at a time. Often I
fought off the temptation to shake her. At sixteen she had a
style of her own: and knew what style was.

12

mother's tone

I never had an education myself. After second grade the
school was closed down. Don't ask me why: in 1927 colored
asked fewer questions than they do now. Sometimes Maggie
reads to me. She stumbles along good-naturedly but can't
see well. She knows she is not bright. Like good looks and
money, quickness passed her by. She will marry John Thomas
(who has mossy teeth in an earnest face) and then I'll be free
to sit here and I guess just sing church songs to myself. Although I never was a good singer. Never could carry a tune. I
was always better at a man's job. I used to love to milk till I
was hoofed in the side in '49. Cows are soothing and slow
and don't bother you, unless you try to milk them the wrong
way.

13

I have deliberately turned my back on the house. It is three
rooms, just like the one that burned, except the roof is tin;
they don't make shingle roofs any more. There are no real
windows, just some holes cut in the sides, like the portholes
in a ship, but not round and not square, with rawhide holding the shutters up on the outside. This house is in a pasture,
too, like the other one. No doubt when Dee sees it she will
want to tear it down. She wrote me once that no matter
where we "choose" to live, she will manage to come see us.

14

more to the story

But she will never bring her friends. Maggie and I thought about this and Maggie asked me, "Mama, when did Dee ever *have* any friends?"

She had a few. Furtive boys in pink shirts hanging about on washday after school. Nervous girls who never laughed. Impressed with her they worshiped the well-turned phrase, the cute shape, the scalding humor that erupted like bubbles in lye. She read to them. 15

When she was courting Jimmy T she didn't have much time to pay to us, but turned all her faultfinding power on him. He *flew to marry* a cheap gal from a family of ignorant flashy people. She hardly had time to recompose herself. 16

When she comes I will meet—but there they are! 17

Maggie attempts to make a dash for the house, in her shuffling way, but I stay her with my hand. "Come back here," I say. And she stops and tries to dig a well in the sand with her toe. 18

It is hard to see them clearly through the strong sun. But even the first glimpse of leg out of the car tells me it is Dee. Her feet were always neat-looking, as if God himself had shaped them with a certain style. From the other side of the car comes a short, stocky man. Hair is all over his head a foot long and hanging from his chin like a kinky mule tail. I hear Maggie suck in her breath. "Uhnnnh," is what it sounds like. Like when you see the wriggling end of a snake just in front of your foot on the road. "Uhnnnh." 19

Dee next. A dress down to the ground, in this hot weather. A dress so loud it hurts my eyes. There are yellows and oranges enough to throw back the light of the sun. I feel my whole face warming from the heat waves it throws out. Earrings, too, gold and hanging down to her shoulders. Bracelets dangling and making noises when she moves her arm up to shake the folds of the dress out of her armpits. The dress is loose and flows, and as she walks closer, I like it. I hear Maggie go "Uhnnnh" again. It is her sister's hair. It stands straight up like the wool on a sheep. It is black as night and around the edges are two long pigtails that rope about like small lizards disappearing behind her ears. 20

"Wa-su-zo-Tean-o!" she says, coming on in that gliding 21
way the dress makes her move. The short stocky fellow with
the hair to his navel is all grinning and he follows up with
"Asalamalakim, my mother and sister!" He moves to hug
Maggie but she falls back, right up against the back of my
chair. I feel her trembling there and when I look up I see the
perspiration falling off her chin.

"Don't get up," says Dee. Since I am stout it takes some- 22
thing of a push. You can see me trying to move a second or
two before I make it. She turns, showing white heels through
her sandals, and goes back to the car. Out she peeks next with
a Polaroid. She stoops down quickly and lines up picture after
picture of me sitting there in front of the house with Maggie
cowering behind me. She never takes a shot without making
sure the house is included. When a cow comes nibbling
around the edge of the yard she snaps it and me and Maggie
and the house. Then she puts the Polaroid in the back seat of
the car, and comes up and kisses me on the forehead.

witty

Meanwhile Asalamalakim is going through the motions 23
with Maggie's hand. Maggie's hand is limp as a fish, and
probably as cold, despite the sweat, and she keeps trying to
pull it back. It looks like Asalamalakim wants to shake hands
but wants to do it fancy. Or maybe he don't know how people shake hands. Anyhow, he soon gives up on Maggie.

"Well," I say. "Dee." 24

"No, Mama," she says. "Not 'Dee,' Wangero Leewanika 25
Kemanjo!"

"What happened to 'Dee'?" I wanted to know. 26

"She's dead," Wangero said. "I couldn't bear it any longer 27
being named after the people who oppress me."

pessimistic

"You know as well as me you was named after your aunt 28
Dicie," I said. Dicie is my sister. She named Dee. We called
her "Big Dee" after Dee was born.

"But who was *she* named after?" asked Wangero. 29

"I guess after Grandma Dee," I said. 30

"And who was she named after?" asked Wangero. 31

"Her mother," I said, and saw Wangero getting tired. 32
"That's about as far back as I can trace it," I said. Though, in

fact, I probably could have carried it back beyond the Civil War through the branches.

"Well," said Asalamalakim, "there you are."   33

"Uhnnnh," I heard Maggie say.   34

"There I was not," I said, "before 'Dicie' cropped up in   35
our family, so why should I try to trace it that far back?"

He just stood there grinning, looking down on me like   36
somebody inspecting a Model A car. Every once in a while he
and Wangero sent eye signals over my head.

"How do you pronounce this name?" I asked.   37

"You don't have to call me by it if you don't want to," said   38
Wangero.

"Why shouldn't I?" I asked. "If that's what you want us to   39
call you, we'll call you."

"I know it might sound awkward at first," said Wangero.   40

"I'll get used to it," I said. "Ream it out again."   41

Well, soon we got the name out of the way. Asalamalakim   42
had a name twice as long and three times as hard. After I tripped over it two or three times he told me to just call him
Hakim-a-barber. I wanted to ask him was he a barber, but I
didn't really think he was, so I didn't ask.

"You must belong to those beef-cattle peoples down the   43
road," I said. They said "Asalamalakim" when they met you,
too, but they didn't shake hands. Always too busy: feeding
the cattle, fixing the fences, putting up salt-lick shelters,
throwing down hay. When the white folks poisoned some of
the herd the men stayed up all night with rifles in their hands,
I walked a mile and half just to see the sight.

Hakim-a-barber said, "I accept some of their doctrines,   44
but farming and raising cattle is not my style." (They didn't
tell me, and I didn't ask, whether Wangero [Dee] had really
gone and married him.)

We sat down to eat and right away he said he didn't eat   45
collards and pork was unclean. Wangero, though, went on
through the chitlins and corn bread, the greens and everything else. She talked a blue streak over the sweet potatoes.
Everything delighted her. Even the fact that we still used the

benches her daddy made for the table when we couldn't afford to buy chairs.

"Oh, Mama!" she cried. Then turned to Hakim-a-barber. 46
"I never knew how lovely these benches are. You can feel the rump prints," she said, running her hands underneath her and along the bench. Then she gave a sigh and her hand closed over Grandma Dee's butter dish. "That's it!" she said. "I knew there was something I wanted to ask you if I could have." She jumped up from the table and went over in the corner where the churn stood, the milk in its clabber by now. She looked at the churn and looked at it.

"This churn top is what I need," she said. "Didn't Uncle 47
Buddy whittle it out of a tree you all used to have?"

"Yes," I said. 48

"Uh huh," she said happily. "And I want the dasher, too." 49

"Uncle Buddy whittle that, too?" asked the barber. 50

Dee (Wangero) looked up at me. 51

"Aunt Dee's first husband whittled the dash," said Maggie 52
so low you almost couldn't hear her. "His name was Henry, but they called him Stash."

"Maggie's brain is like an elephant's," Wangero said, 53
laughing. "I can use the churn top as a centerpiece for the alcove table," she said, sliding a plate over the churn, "and I'll think of something artistic to do with the dasher."

When she finished wrapping the dasher the handle stuck 54
out. I took it for a moment in my hands. You didn't even have to look close to see where hands pushing the dasher up and down to make butter had left a kind of sink in the wood. In fact, there were a lot of small sinks; you could see where thumbs and fingers had sunk into the wood. It was beautiful light yellow wood, from a tree that grew in the yard where Big Dee and Stash had lived.

After dinner Dee (Wangero) went to the trunk at the foot 55
of my bed and started rifling through it. Maggie hung back in the kitchen over the dishpan. Out came Wangero with two quilts. They had been pieced by Grandma Dee and then Big Dee and me had hung them on the quilt frames on the front

porch and quilted them. One was in the Lone Star pattern. The other was Walk Around the Mountain. In both of them were scraps of dresses Grandma Dee had worn fifty and more years ago. Bits and pieces of Grandpa Jarrell's Paisley shirts. And one teeny faded blue piece, about the size of a penny matchbox, that was from Great Grandpa Ezra's uniform that he wore in the Civil War.

"Mama," Wangero said sweet as a bird. "Can I have these old quilts?"   56

I heard something fall in the kitchen, and a minute later the kitchen door slammed.   57

"Why don't you take one or two of the others?" I asked. "These old things was just done by me and Big Dee from some tops your grandma pieced before she died."   58

"No," said Wangero. "I don't want those. They are stitched around the borders by machine."   59

"That'll make them last better," I said.   60

"That's not the point," said Wangero. "These are all pieces of dresses Grandma used to wear. She did all this stitching by hand. Imagine!" She held the quilts securely in her arms, stroking them.   61

"Some of the pieces, like those lavender ones, come from old clothes her mother handed down to her," I said, moving up to touch the quilts. Dee (Wangero) moved back just enough so that I couldn't reach the quilts. They already belonged to her.   62

"Imagine!" she breathed again, clutching them closely to her bosom.   63

"The truth is," I said, "I promised to give them quilts to Maggie, for when she marries John Thomas."   64

She gasped like a bee had stung her.   65

"Maggie can't appreciate these quilts!" she said. "She'd probably be backward enough to put them to everyday use."   66

"I reckon she would," I said. "God knows I been saving 'em for long enough with nobody using 'em. I hope she will!" I didn't want to bring up how I had offered Dee (Wangero) a quilt when she went away to college. Then she had told me they were old-fashioned, out of style.   67

"But they're *priceless!*" she was saying now, furiously; for 68
she has a temper. "Maggie would put them on the bed and in
five years they'd be in rags. Less than that!"

"She can always make some more," I said. "Maggie knows 69
how to quilt."

Dee (Wangero) looked at me with hatred. "You just will 70
not understand. The point is these quilts, *these* quilts!"

"Well," I said, stumped. "What would *you* do with them?" 71

"Hang them," she said. As if that was the only thing you 72
could do with quilts.

Maggie by now was standing in the door. I could almost 73
hear the sound her feet made as they scraped over each other.

"She can have them, Mama," she said, like somebody used 74
to never winning anything, or having anything reserved for
her. "I can 'member Grandma Dee without the quilts."

I looked at her hard. She had filled her bottom lip with 75
checkerberry snuff and it gave her face a kind of dopey, hang-
dog look. It was Grandma Dee and Big Dee who taught her
how to quilt herself. She stood there with her scarred hands
hidden in the folds of her skirt. She looked at her sister with
something like fear but she wasn't mad at her. This was Maggie's portion. This was the way she knew God to work.

Sweet!

When I looked at her like that something hit me in the top 76
of my head and ran down to the soles of my feet. Just like
when I'm in church and the spirit of God touches me and I
get happy and shout. I did something I never had done before: hugged Maggie to me, then dragged her on into the
room, snatched the quilts out of Miss Wangero's hands and
dumped them into Maggie's lap. Maggie just sat there on my
bed with her mouth open.

"Take one or two of the others," I said to Dee. 77

But she turned without a word and went out to Hakim-a- 78
barber.

"You just don't understand," she said, as Maggie and I 79
came out to the car.

"What don't I understand?" I wanted to know. 80

"Your heritage," she said. And then she turned to Maggie, 81
kissed her and said, "You ought to try to make something of

Oh please

opposite from heritage

yourself, too, Maggie. It's really a new day for us. But from the way you and Mama still live you'd never know it."

She put on some sunglasses that hid everything above the 82 tip of her nose and her chin.

Maggie smiled; maybe at the sunglasses. But a real smile, 83 not scared. After we watched the car dust settle I asked Maggie to bring me a dip of snuff. And then the two of us sat there just enjoying, until it was time to go in the house and go to bed.

COMMENT ON "EVERYDAY USE"

Alice Walker's "Everyday Use" describes a difference between a mother's and her visiting daughter's understanding of the word "heritage." For Mama and her daughter Maggie, heritage is a matter of everyday living, of "everyday use." For Mama's other daughter, Dee (Wangero), however, heritage is a matter of style, a fashionable obsession with one's roots. These comparisons are revealed first in Walker's description of the physical appearance of the characters. Mama is fat and manly, and Maggie bears the scars from a fire. By contrast, Dee (Wangero) is beautiful and striking in her brightly colored African dress, earrings, sunglasses, and Afro hairstyle. Next, Walker compares the characters' skills. Mama can butcher a hog or break ice to get water, and Maggie is able to make beautiful quilts. Dee (Wangero), on the other hand, thinks of herself as outside this domestic world, educated by books to understand the cultural significance of her heritage. The problem posed by the debate over family possessions is whether heritage is an object to be preserved, like a priceless painting, or a process, to be learned, like the creation of a quilt.

Definition as a Writing Strategy

1. Select a category of objects in which you have a special interest and that you could illustrate with pictures or your own sketches, and put together the kind of illustrated, annotated essay that Pizzi creates in "Doorways: A Visual Essay." Several possibilities suggest themselves:

   - Bridges
   - Sports cars
   - SUVs
   - Kayaks or canoes
   - Tree houses
   - Stereo, video, and television complexes
   - Stairways

   You may think of other possibilities from your own interests or hobbies. In your comments on different examples, mention special features and the advantages or disadvantages of each one.

2. For a challenging assignment focusing on a person, pick someone you find especially interesting—an athlete such as Tiger Woods, a businessperson such as Bill Gates or Michael Dell, an entertainment personality such as Oprah Winfrey or Barbra Streisand, a public figure such as Jesse Jackson or Justice Ruth Ginsberg. Through a computer search, locate several magazine articles on that person, and read them. Be sure to use substantial articles, not just items from gossip columns. Write a definition essay in which you describe the person—his or her professional activities and personal interests—trying to bring out the unique traits that have made the person successful. Remember that anecdotes are useful in this kind of essay. Your hypothetical audience could be readers of a magazine like *Parade* or *Esquire*.

3. If you are a person with special knowledge about a particular kind of animal, reread Harrigan's essay, "The Tiger Is God," paying special attention to his strategies for

defining the nature of the tiger. Then write an essay in which you describe and define a breed or type of animal you know well. Some possibilities are the cutting horse, the dressage horse, hunting dogs or sheep dogs, a particular breed of dog such as Golden Retrievers or Weimaraners, or a particular breed of cat such as Burmese or Russian Blues. Certainly there are many other possibilities. Use concrete details and examples of particular actions that illustrate the animal's distinctive temperament and behavior.

4. Review the essay "American Ingenuity," and notice how Langewiesche illustrates the kind of man David Griffin is by showing his behavior on the job and quoting from his conversations. Then write a profile feature for your college or local newspaper of some person you know who epitomizes certain character traits. Some possibilities are someone you have watched at work, a strong personality in your family, an instructor who has been helpful to you, or a person who has contributed to the success of some enterprise by his or her diplomatic and organizational abilities. Of course, you could choose a negative example if you like—an obnoxious coach, an arrogant athlete, or an ungracious visiting celebrity. You don't necessarily have to spell out the character traits; instead, show how the person gets along with others and what he or she says. Remember that it's nearly always better to *show* your audience rather than *tell* them.

5. In "The Hoax" John Berendt defines a hoax as a special kind of practical joke that involves wit as well as a physical element, and he gives several examples. In a special feature for your college newspaper or humor magazine, explain the defining characteristics of something you have fun with. Some possibilities might be a great Halloween costume, a grade B horror movie, an April Fool's gag, or a cartoon or picture that satirizes some work of art that is so well known it's become a cliché. Have fun with this one.

6. Writers and speakers often argue from definition, trying to get their audiences to agree with or approve of something

by defining it positively (for example, a good education) or to criticize something by defining it negatively (for example, a bad grading policy). Drawing on material and information you are getting in one of your courses, write a paper suitable for that course defining a concept, policy, theory, or event either negatively or positively. For a course in early childhood development, you could define a good day-care center. For a chemistry course, you could do a process paper on how to set up a good laboratory experiment. For a government course, you could define a well-run local campaign. For a speech course, you could define an effective speaking style.

CAUSE
AND
EFFECT

If you are like most people, you're just naturally curious: you look at the world around you and wonder why things happen. But you're also curious because you want some control over your life and over your environment, and you can't have that control unless you can understand **causes.** That's why so much writing is cause-and-effect writing, writing that seeks to explain the causes for change and new developments. In almost every profession you will be asked to do writing that analyzes causes; that's why such writing has an important place in college composition courses.

You also want to understand **effects.** If A happens, will B be the effect? You want to try to predict the consequences of putting some plan into effect or look at some effect and explain what brought it about. Or you want to set a goal (the effect) and plan a strategy for reaching it. This kind of writing also prepares you for writing you're likely to do later in your career.

PURPOSE

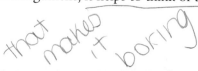

When you write cause-and-effect essays, you're likely to have one of three purposes. Sometimes you want to *explain* why something happened or what might be likely to happen under certain circumstances. Daniel Goleman is writing that kind of essay in "Peak Performance: Why Records Fall" when he explains how new knowledge about training practices and about human mental capacities have led to athletic feats that seemed impossible only a few decades ago. At other times, you might write a cause-and-effect paper to *speculate* about an interesting topic—for instance, to speculate why a new computer game has become so popular or what the effects of a new kind of body suit will be for competitive swimmers.

Writers often use a cause-and-effect essay to *argue,* or prove a point. In "Examined Life" Malcolm Gladwell argues that Stanley Kaplan proved that students could get a desired effect—a high grade on the SAT—by understanding how the test worked and preparing for it. In "Why McDonald's Fries Taste So Good," Eric Schlosser argues that the fast-food industry achieves its goal of making customers happy by hiring chemists to create tasty artificial flavors. In "Some Big Ideas Wash Up One Bulb at a Time," Andrew Revkin argues that often we are so slow to recognize bad effects—such as environmental crises—that we wait to act until it's almost too late.

AUDIENCE

When you begin to analyze your audience for a cause-and-effect argument, it helps to think of them as jurors to whom you are going to present a case. You can make up a list of questions just as a lawyer would to help him or her formulate an argument. For example:

- How should I prepare my readers for my argument? What background information do they need?
- What kind of evidence are they likely to want? Factual, statistical, anecdotal?
- How much do I have to explain? Will they have enough context to understand my points and make connections without my spelling them out?

Like a trial lawyer, you're trying to establish a chain of cause and effect. Perhaps you can't establish absolute proof, but you can show probability. The format for such arguments can be:

- State your claim early, usually in the first paragraph.
- Show the connection you want to establish.
- Present your supporting evidence.
- Repeat your claim in your conclusion.

STRATEGIES

One good strategy for cause-and-effect arguments is *drawing analogies*. Daniel Goleman draws analogies between winning performers in sports, music, chess, and feats of memory in "Peak Performances: Why Records Fall." You could use a similar strategy in drawing an analogy between a culture that glorifies male sports stars, particularly in bruising sports like professional football, and a social environment that erupts into street violence among gangs of young men. You could seek support for your thesis by doing keyword searches with entries like Violence + Sports + Gangs.

You could also use cause and effect in writing an essay about how your encounter with a person or some new activity brought about a major change in your life. That's the strategy Anna Quindlen uses in "How Reading Changed My

Life." Your version might recount how when you took piano lessons in the seventh grade, your teacher told you about a citywide choir for ten- to twelve-year-olds and encouraged you to apply. When you did and were accepted, you found you enjoyed singing so much that it became your main extra-curricular activity. That led to a role in *Guys and Dolls,* your school's senior play, and now you plan to major in voice and drama in college. You might add that although you gave up piano lessons, they did help you learn to read music, an essential skill for your career.

USING CAUSE AND EFFECT IN PARAGRAPHS

Here are two cause-and-effect paragraphs. The first is written by a professional writer and is followed by an analysis. The second is written by a student writer and is followed by questions.

JONATHAN WEINER
Elephant Evolution

For poachers, elephants with big tusks were prime targets. Elephants with small tusks were more likely to be passed over, and those with no tusks at all were not shot. In effect, though no one realized it at the time, African elephants in places where poaching was rife were under enormous selection pressure for tusklessness. And in fact, elephant watchers in the most heavily poached areas began noticing more and more tuskless elephants in the wild. Andrew Dobson, an ecologist at Princeton, has compiled graphs of this trend, tracing the evolution of tusklessness in five African wildlife preserves, Ambroseli, Mikumi, Tsavo East, Tsavo West, and Queen Elizabeth. In Ambroseli, where the elephants are relatively safe, the proportion of tuskless female elephants is small, just under a

Sets up evidence

Shows effect

Statistics that support his point

evolution

few percent. But in Mikumi, a park where the elephants are heavily poached, tusklessness is rising. The longer each generation lives the fewer tusks the elephants carry. Among females aged five through ten about 10 percent are tuskless; among females aged thirty to thirty-five, about 50 percent are tuskless.

Comment In this paragraph taken from his book *The Beak of the Finch*, which documents the evolutionary patterns two scientists have traced by measuring the beaks of finches on an isolated island in the Galápagos, the science writer Jonathan Weiner shows how poaching on elephant preserves in Africa has directly affected the physical characteristics of the elephants on those preserves. He sets up a direct "If-Then" cause-and-effect equation. When poachers killed the elephants with the largest tusks because those tusks were in the greatest demand, fewer elephants who carried the genes for that characteristic were left to breed. Therefore fewer elephants with large tusks appeared in subsequent generations. By citing the graphs that an identified academic ecologist compiled from observations in five specific wildlife preserves, Weiner shores up his cause-and-effect argument; he's not relying only on hearsay evidence or casual observation.

EMILY LINDERMAN
Barrier-Free Design

Many merchants view the Americans with Disabilities Act as expensive social engineering. They have established an attractive and affordable space for their businesses. Their customers seem satisfied. Then the federal government requires them to provide accessible ramps and elevators, wider doorways and halls, larger bathrooms, and lower drinking fountains. Seen from another perspective, however, making these changes may pay off in the long run. How many

what

good pt. but too ? . ? ✗

times have you tried to move furniture into a building or up to the third floor? How many times have you tried to find a place for your packages in a cramped bathroom stall? And how many times have you had to lift your little brother up to the fountain to get a drink? All customers, not simply disabled customers, will benefit from and reward merchants who invest in these barrier-free buildings.

1. Whom do you think Linderman is addressing with her argument for the benefits of barrier-free buildings?
2. How does the significance of the extra benefits that Linderman mentions compare with the significance of the benefits that the Disabilities Act was designed to provide?

CAUSE AND EFFECT

Points to Remember

1. Remember that in human events you can almost never prove direct, simple, cause-and-effect relationships. Qualify your claims.
2. Be careful not to oversimplify your cause-and-effect statements; be cautious about saying that a cause always produces a certain effect or that a remedy never succeeds.
3. Avoid confusing coincidence or simple sequence with cause and effect; because B follows A doesn't mean that A caused B.
4. Build your cause-and-effect argument as a trial lawyer would. Present as much evidence as you can and argue for your hypothesis.

*In this documentary photograph, Frank Hurley chronicles a
dramatic moment during Sir Ernest Shackleton's journey
across the Antarctic (1914–1916). Research the Shackleton ex-
pedition. What prompted them to go? What caused their ship,*
Endurance, *to be trapped in the ice? What happened to the ex-
pedition? Write an essay analyzing the causes and effects of this
legendary voyage.*

Andrew C. Revkin was born in Providence, Rhode Island, in 1956 and educated at Brown University and Columbia University. Revkin has worked as a journalist covering subjects ranging from murder in the Amazon to the crash of TWA Flight 800, from the plight of the working poor in America to the persistent pollution of the Hudson River. Since 1995, he has been a reporter for the *New York Times,* focusing on environmental issues affecting the metropolitan region. His books include *The Burning Season* (1990) and *Global Warming: Understanding the Forecast* (1992). His current book project, *The Last Shaman,* is the life story of a hereditary chief from a British Columbia Indian tribe. In "Some Big Ideas Wash Up One Bulb at a Time," reprinted from the *New York Times,* Revkin explains why the complex causes of environmental pollution make us feel helpless.

Some Big Ideas Wash Up One Bulb at a Time

P EOPLE REALLY GET around. From the poles to the peaks   1
to the ocean floor, humans have probed and cut and
burned and drilled and left their mark.

The human assault on the planet usually does not make   2
headlines unless there is a sudden calamity—giant fires in In-
donesia or radioactivity escaping from a nuclear plant in
Chernobyl. So we are most attuned to environmental problems of that kind—not the subtle, slow types.

But those subtle, slow-moving processes bear watching.   3
Sometimes, they creep up in surprising ways.

I got my first such surprise in 1979, when, shortly after 4
college, I ended up serving as first mate on a circumnavigating sailboat. We anchored one day in the lee of an uninhabited volcanic heap of Mars-like rock called Zuqar Island, in the south end of the Red Sea. The island was so remote that one chart labeled it "terra nullis." No one claimed it. If ever a place could be called the middle of nowhere, this was it.

No, Bailey

I felt awfully lucky to be in such an unspoiled place, with 5
black, bed-sized manta rays gliding in the shallows and no sound but the wind and waves.

ahhhh

I rowed ashore and went for a hike, clambering across a 6
sere landscape of crusty rocks, which cracked underfoot like

---

*The human assault on the planet usually
does not make headlines unless there is a
sudden calamity.*

---

nice comparison

pottery shards. I reached the windward side and walked to the beach, which was littered, heaped and piled with—light bulbs.

There were yardlong fluorescent tubes and heavy spot- 7
lights, delicate incandescent globes and flashlight bulbs as big as a pea. They lay in drifts, unbroken, above the highest tide line. Others that had shattered clinked musically with each lapping wave.

Who could have done such a thing? 8

After a moment of reflection, it dawned on me that the 9
light-bulb litter was not the fault of any individual. It must have been a consequence of the incessant parade of container and cargo ships plying the Red Sea. I envisioned a tanker crewman on his night watch unscrewing a burned-out bulb and, without a thought, tossing it over.

ship cpt

Over the years, ship after passing ship would add up to a 10
lot of bulbs bobbing around. Every once in a while, one

would be carried by a wave or the wind far enough above the island's surf line that it would remain an unseen icon of the modern age.

I was not a reporter then, but things like piles of light 11 bulbs on a faraway beach made me want to write about the effect of humans on the environment. Once I became a journalist, I began reporting on all kinds of environmental issues. One small story, in a way, summed up a lot.

It was about a construction crew in the San Fernando 12 Valley in Los Angeles that had been digging a hole for a parking-lot foundation. The crew reached a certain depth, and suddenly gasoline began welling up from the earth.

They had not struck a hidden pipeline. The gasoline, as it 13 turned out, had leaked from a buried, rusting storage tank at a service station a few hundred yards away. It had been leaking almost indiscernibly for years, quart by quart, pooling atop the aquifer in the porous soil and drifting down the block, waiting for someone to dig a hole.

no one noticed

I saw the results of a similar slow degradation a few years 14 ago when I spent time with an Indian tribe in Kitamaat Village, on the coast of British Columbia, about 500 miles north of Vancouver. The village is across a bay from a large aluminum refinery built by Alcan Aluminum.

In his office, the elected chief of the Haisla tribe, Gerald 15 Amos, showed me a glass pint jar half-filled with mercury. He said a Haisla contractor had been hired to take down a work shed on the Alcan property. While dismantling a toilet, he undid the U-shaped trap in the plumbing and found it full of the liquid metal. Someone must have been pouring something containing mercury down the toilet for years, which left a constant residue trapped in the pipes.

why?

In an ideal world, we could look ahead a few decades and 16 figure out that dumping a few dribs of mercury down a toilet, or dropping a bulb over the rail, might eventually have an undesirable effect.

But often the offending activity seems so innocuous that it 17 hardly registers on a person's consciousness, let alone his conscience. It's just one bulb, right?

And, of course, we don't live in an ideal world. We actually live in a very muddled, complicated one. As a result, even when people do think ahead, they can end up taking the wrong action.

Brazil, for example, passed laws decades ago protecting the valuable Brazil nut trees of the Amazon. When ranchers cleared rain forests, towering specimens of the tree remained—standing alone on otherwise denuded land. But without the surrounding forest, the bees that pollinated the Brazil nut flowers could not thrive, so few of the remaining trees produce nuts.

Nature's complexity can also hide early signs that we are having an impact.

Even something as big as a sharp shift in climate as a result of human pollution can be hard to see immediately. For one thing, its first manifestations—the baby steps—can be obscured by all the natural variability in the natural world.

Year by year, decade by decade, the globe has its complement of hot flashes and cold spells, thanks to El Niño and La Niña, a squiggly jet stream and the rest.

As Starley Thompson, a scientist at the National Center for Atmospheric Research in Boulder, Colo., put it, the challenge of recognizing global warming amid the ups and downs of weather is like trying to discern cornstalks rising in a weedy field.

In Dr. Thompson's scenario, at first there are lots of green sprouting things; at some point, the cornstalks finally stand out, clear for everyone to see. With climate change, it's all still a bit weedy.

What it boils down to is that you will never read a front-page headline that says "Earth's Temperature Soars Overnight—Coasts Flooded, Crops Ruined." All those things may happen, but spread over decades and scattered across the globe.

So we're a little stuck. We have the general idea that bad things may come from doubling the amount of heat-trapping gases in the air as a result of burning fossil fuels. But because there is much disagreement—and more uncertainty—about the precise dimensions of the problem, we find it hard to settle on a set of concrete actions to cut these so-called greenhouse gases.

It may be that we are condemned to mounting belated, intensive responses once the consequences of slow shifts are evident.   27

That might not be so bad. After all, humans have a good track record at crash programs: the United States did O.K. after being jogged by Sputnik, Pearl Harbor and other surprises. And there can be unanticipated benefits from doing nothing. Sometimes, problems take care of themselves.   28

Consider all those stranded light bulbs in the Red Sea. No need to go clean them up. Let global warming raise the sea level slightly, and they may simply float away.   29

For Study and Discussion

QUESTIONS FOR RESPONSE

1. What examples have you seen or do you know about where the environmental carelessness of some group caused serious damage to a place? What was your reaction to that instance?
2. What kind of regulations would be necessary to prevent such damage? What do you think public reaction would be to such regulations?

QUESTIONS ABOUT PURPOSE

1. What realizations do you think the author wants his readers to come to about how we live?
2. What specific actions, if any, do you think the author would like to have his readers take? Why?

QUESTIONS ABOUT AUDIENCE

1. This article was originally published in the *New York Times*. What assumptions do you make about the environmental awareness of regular readers of that newspaper?

2. How effective do you find the author's examples for most college students? Why?

QUESTIONS ABOUT STRATEGIES

1. How does the author set the stage for the striking scene he reveals in the last sentence of paragraph 6?
2. What is the tone of the last paragraph in the essay? Why do you think the author concludes in this way?

QUESTIONS FOR DISCUSSION

1. What practices do you see in your community or on your campus that may lead to unfortunate environmental consequences? Who can be held responsible for these practices?
2. Our American love affair with the automobile has a variety of environmental consequences. What are some of them and how could we deal with them?

DANIEL GOLEMAN

Daniel Goleman was born in 1946 in Stockton, California, and was educated at Amherst College and Harvard University. After working for several years as a professor of psychology, he began his career as an editor for *Psychology Today*. He has contributed more than fifty articles to psychology journals and has written a dozen books, including *The Meditative Mind* (1988), *The Creative Spirit* (1992), *Mind, Body Medicine: How to Use Your Mind for Better Health* (1993), *Emotional Intelligence* (1995), and *Working with Emotional Intelligence* (1998). In "Peak Performance: Why Records Fall," reprinted from a 1994 *New York Times* article, Goleman analyzes how dedication to practice contributes to peak performances.

Peak Performance: Why Records Fall

sounds familiar but can't place it

T HE OLD JOKE—How do you get to Carnegie Hall? Practice, practice, practice—is getting a scientific spin. Researchers are finding an unexpected potency from deliberate practice in world-class competitions of all kinds, including chess matches, musical recitals and sporting events. 1

Studies of chess masters, virtuoso musicians and star athletes show that the relentless training routines of those at the top allow them to break through ordinary limits in memory and physiology, and so perform at levels that had been thought impossible. 2

World records have been falling inexorably over the last century. For example, the marathon gold medalist's time in 3

nothing's impossible

412

the 1896 Olympics Games was, by 1990, only about as good as the qualifying time for the Boston Marathon.

"Over the last century Olympics have become more and more competitive, and so athletes steadily have had to put in more total lifetime hours of practice," said Dr. Michael Mahoney, a psychologist at the University of North Texas in Denton, who helps train the United States Olympic weight-lifting team. "These days you have to live your sport." 4

lifetime

That total dedication is in contrast to the relatively leisurely attitude taken at the turn of the century, when even world-class athletes would train arduously for only a few months before their competition. 5

that's the truth

"As competition got greater, training extended to a whole season," said Dr. Anders Ericsson, a psychologist at Florida 6

Through their hours of practice, elite performers of all kinds master shortcuts that give them an edge.

State University in Tallahassee who wrote an article on the role of deliberate practice for star performance recently in the journal *American Psychologist.* "Then it extended through the year, and then for several years. Now the elite performers start their training in childhood. There is a historical trend toward younger starting ages, which makes possible a greater and greater total number of hours of practice time."

To be sure, there are other factors at work: coaching methods have become more sophisticated, equipment has improved and the pool of people competing has grown. But new studies are beginning to reveal the sheer power of training itself. 7

Perhaps the most surprising data show that extensive practice can break through barriers in mental capacities, particularly short-term memory. In short-term memory, 8

I do that

information is stored for the few seconds that it is used and then fades, as in hearing a phone number which one forgets as soon as it is dialed.

The standard view, repeated in almost every psychology textbook, is that the ordinary limit on short-term memory is for seven or so bits of information—the length of a phone number. More than that typically cannot be retained in short-term memory with reliability unless the separate units are "chunked," as when the numbers in a telephone prefix are remembered as a single unit.

But, in a stunning demonstration of the power of sheer practice to break barriers in the mind's ability to handle information, Dr. Ericsson and associates at Carnegie-Mellon University have taught college students to listen to a list of as many as 102 random digits and then recite it correctly. After 50 hours of practice with differing sets of random digits, four students were able to remember up to 20 digits after a single hearing. One student, a business major not especially talented in mathematics, was able to remember 102 digits. The feat took him more than 400 hours of practice.

The ability to increase memory in a particular domain is at the heart of a wide range high-level performance, said Dr. Herbert Simon, professor of computer science and psychology at Carnegie-Mellon University and a Nobel laureate. Dr. Ericsson was part of a team studying expertise led by Dr. Simon.

"Every expert has acquired something like this memory ability" in his or her area of expertise, said Dr. Simon. "Memory is like an index; experts have approximately 50,000 chunks of familiar units of information they recognize. For a physician, many of those chunks are symptoms."

A similar memory training effect, Dr. Simon said, seems to occur with many chess masters. The key skill chess players rehearse in practicing is, of course, selecting the best move. They do so by studying games between two chess masters and guessing the next move from their own study of the board as the game progresses.

Repeated practice results in a prodigious memory for chess positions. The ability of some chess masters to play blind-

WOW

all about odds

9

10

11

12

13

14

folded, while simply told what moves their opponents make, has long been known; in the 1940s Adrian DeGroot, himself a Dutch grandmaster, showed that many chess masters are able to look at a chess board in midgame for as little as five seconds and then repeat the position of every piece on the board.

Later systematic studies by Dr. Simon's group showed that the chess masters' memory feat was limited to boards used in actual games; they had no such memory for randomly placed pieces. "They would see a board and think, that reminds me of Spassky versus Lasker," said Dr. Simon.   15

This feat of memory was duplicated by a college student who knew little about chess, but was given 50 hours of training in remembering chess positions by Dr. Ericsson in a 1990 study.   16

Through their hours of practice, elite performers of all kinds master shortcuts that give them an edge. Dr. Bruce Abernathy, a researcher at the University of Queensland in Australia, has found that the most experienced players in racquet sports like squash and tennis are able to predict where a serve will land by cues in the server's posture before the ball is hit.   17

A 1992 study of baseball greats like Hank Aaron and Rod Carew by Thomas Hanson, then a graduate student at the University of Virginia in Charlottesville, found that the all-time best hitters typically started preparing for games by studying films of the pitchers they would face, to spot cues that would tip off what pitch was about to be thrown. Using such fleeting cues demands rehearsing so well that the response to them is automatic, cognitive scientists have found.   18

The maxim that practice makes perfect has been borne out through research on the training of star athletes and artists. Dr. Anthony Kalinowski, a researcher at the University of Chicago, found that swimmers who achieved the level of national champion started their training at an average age of 10, while those who were good enough to make the United States Olympic teams started on average at 7. This is the same age difference found for national and international chess champions in a 1987 study.   19

Similarly, the best violinists of the 20th century, all with   20
international careers as soloists for more than 30 years, were
found to have begun practicing their instrument at an average age of 5, while violinists of only national prominence,
those affiliated with the top music academy in Berlin, started
at 8, Dr. Ericsson found in research reported last year in *The
Psychological Review.*

Because of limits on physical endurance and mental alert-   21
ness, world-class competitors—whether violinists or weight
lifters—typically seem to practice arduously no more than
four hours a day, Dr. Ericsson has found from studying a
wide variety of training regimens.

"When we train Olympic weight lifters, we find we often   22
have to throttle back the total time they work out," said Dr.
Mahoney. "Otherwise you find a tremendous drop in mood,
and a jump in irritability, fatigue and apathy."

Because their intense practice regimen puts them at risk   23
for burnout or strain injuries, most elite competitors also
make rest part of their training routine, sleeping a full eight
hours and often napping a half-hour a day, Dr. Ericsson
found.

Effective practice focuses not just on the key skills in-   24
volved, but also systematically stretches the person's limits.
"You have to tweak the system by pushing, allowing for more
errors at first as you increase your limits," said Dr. Ericsson.
"You don't get benefits from mechanical repetition, but by
adjusting your execution over and over to get closer to your
goal."

Violin virtuosos illustrate the importance of starting early   25
in life. In his 1993 study Dr. Ericsson found that by age 20
top-level violinists in music academies had practiced a lifetime total of about 10,000 hours, while those who were
slightly less accomplished had practiced an average of about
7,500 hours.

A study of Chinese Olympic divers, done by Dr. John Shea   26
of Florida State University, found that some 11-year-old
divers had spent as many hours in training as had 21-year-old
American divers. The Chinese divers started training at age 4.

[margin annotations: "also half of it is", "talent?", "I wish", "determination"]

"It can take 10 years of extensive practice to excel in any- 27
thing," said Dr. Simon. "Mozart was 4 when he started composing, but his world-class music started when he was about
17."

prodigy

Total hours of practice may be more important than time 28
spent in competition, according to findings not yet published
by Dr. Neil Charness, a colleague of Dr. Ericsson at Florida
State University. Dr. Charness, comparing the rankings of
107 competitors in the 1993 Berlin City Tournament, found
that the more time they spent practicing alone, the higher
their ranking as chess players. But there was no relationship
between the chess players' rankings and the time they spent
playing others.

really?

As has long been known, the extensive training of an elite 29
athlete molds the body to fit the demands of a given sport.
What has been less obvious is the extent of these changes.

"The sizes of hearts and lungs, joint flexibility and bone 30
strength all increase directly with hours of training," said Dr.
Ericsson. "The number of capillaries that supply blood to
trained muscles increases."

And the muscles themselves change, Dr. Ericsson said. 31
Until very recently, researchers believed that the percentage
of muscle fiber types was more than 90 percent determined
by heredity. Fast-twitch muscles, which allow short bursts of
intense effort, are crucial in sports like weight lifting and
sprinting, while slow-twitch muscles, richer in red blood
cells, are essential for endurance sports like marathons.
"Muscle fibers in those muscles can change from fast twitch
to slow twitch, as the sport demands," said Dr. Ericsson.

very clinical tone — boring

Longitudinal studies show that years of endurance training 32
at champion levels leads athletes' hearts to increase in size
well beyond the normal range for people their age.

Such physiological changes are magnified when training 33
occurs during childhood, puberty and adolescence. Dr.
Ericsson thinks this may be one reason virtually all top athletes today began serious practice as children or young adolescents, though some events, like weight training, may be
exceptions because muscles need to fully form before intense
lifting begins.

talk about that

The most contentious claim made by Dr. Ericsson is   34
that practice alone, not natural talent, makes for a record-
breaking performance. "Innate capacities have very little to
do with becoming a champion," said his colleague, Dr.
Charness. "What's key is motivation and temperament, not a
skill specific to performance. It's unlikely you can get just any
child to apply themselves this rigorously for so long."

But many psychologists argue that the emphasis on prac-   35
tice alone ignores the place of talent in superb performance.
"You can't assume that random people who practice a lot will
rise to the top," said Dr. Howard Gardner, a psychologist at
Harvard University. Dr. Ericsson's theories "leave out the
question of who selects themselves—or are selected—for intensive training," adding, "It also leaves out what we most
value in star performance, like innovative genius in a chess
player or emotional expressiveness in a concert musician."

Dr. Gardner said: "I taught piano for many years, and   36
there's an enormous difference between those who practice
dutifully and get a little better every week, and those students
who break away from the pack. There's plenty of room for
innate talent to make a difference over and above practice
time. Mozart was not like you and me."

For Study and Discussion

QUESTIONS FOR RESPONSE

1. Think of some top performers who started very young—for instance, violinist Midori, chess prodigy Bobby Fischer, or tennis
   player Jennifer Capriati. What do you know about their subsequent lives? To what extent can you generalize about such individuals?
2. If you hope to be a top performer in your chosen field, does this
   essay encourage you or discourage you? Explain why.

QUESTIONS ABOUT PURPOSE

1. What message do you think the experts quoted in this essay are
   giving to young people who want to excel in something? What
   do you see as the impact of that message?

2. What role do you think science plays in sports these days? What is your feeling about that role?

QUESTIONS ABOUT AUDIENCE

1. What groups of readers do you see as people who would particularly benefit from learning about the research reported here? In what way would they benefit?
2. How would the value system of a reader—that is, the complex of things that the reader thinks is important—affect the way he or she responds to this essay?

QUESTIONS ABOUT STRATEGIES

1. What is the impact of Goleman's pointing out that the marathon runner who won an Olympic gold medal a hundred years ago could barely qualify for the Boston Marathon today?
2. How does Goleman's use of diverse authorities strengthen his essay?

QUESTIONS FOR DISCUSSION

1. What impact do you think the new realities about becoming a winner will have on the families of young artists and athletes? How might it differ among families?
2. What factors in a competitor's performance that are not discussed here might affect his or her achievement? How important are those elements?

ANNA QUINDLEN

Anna Quindlen was born in 1953 in Philadelphia, Pennsylvania, and was educated at Barnard College. She began her career as a reporter for the *New York Post* and then as a reporter and columnist for the *New York Times*. Her columns are collected in *Living Out Loud* (1988) and *Thinking Out Loud: On the Personal, the Political, the Public and the Private* (1994). Quindlen continues to contribute columns to *Newsweek,* but she has devoted much of her time to writing the kinds of novels she talks about in *How Reading Changed My Life* (1998). Those best-selling novels include *Object Lessons* (1991), *One True Thing* (1995), *Black and Blue* (1998), and *Blessings* (2002). *One True Thing* was adapted to the screen and starred Renée Zellweger and Meryl Streep. In "How Reading Changed My Life," excerpted from the book of that title, Quindlen explains how her passion for reading shaped her values and work.

How Reading Changed My Life

> How many a man has dated a new era in his life from the reading of a book. The book exists for us perchance which will explain our miracles and reveal new ones.
> —HENRY DAVID THOREAU

THE STORIES ABOUT my childhood, the ones that stuck, that got told and retold at dinner tables, to dates as I sat by red-faced, to my own children by my father later on, are stories of running away. Some are stories of events I can't remember, that I see and feel only in the retelling: the tod-

dler who wandered down the street while her mother was
occupied with yet another baby and was driven home by the
police; the little girl who was seen by a neighbor ambling
down the alley a block north of her family's home; the child
who appeared on her grandparents' doorstep and wasn't
quite sure whether anyone knew she'd come so far on her
own.

Other times I remember myself. I remember taking the el- 2
evated train to downtown Philadelphia because, like Everest,
it was there, a spired urban Oz so other from the quiet flat
streets of the suburbs where we lived. I remember riding my

[handwritten margin note: so literally running away]

[handwritten margin note: typo?]

---

*I lived within the covers of books and those
books were more real to me than any other
thing in my life.*

---

bicycle for miles to the neighborhood where my aunt and
uncle lived, a narrow avenue of brick row houses with long
boxcar backyards. I remember going to the airport with my
parents when I was thirteen and reading the destinations
board, seeing all the places I could go: San Juan, Cincinnati,
Los Angeles, London. I remember loving motels; the cheap
heavy silverware on airplanes; the smell of plastic, disinfectant, and mildew on the old Greyhound buses. I remember
watching trains click by, a blur of grey and the diamond glitter of sunshine on glass, and wishing I was aboard.

The odd thing about all this is that I had a lovely child- 3
hood in a lovely place. This is the way I remember it; this is
the way it was. The neighborhood where I grew up was the
sort of place in which people dream of raising children—
pretty, privileged but not rich, a small but satisfying spread of
center-hall colonials, old roses, rhododendrons, and quiet
roads. We walked to school, wandered wild in the summer,
knew everyone and all their brothers and sisters, too. Some of

[handwritten margin note: good detail]

[handwritten margin note: ODD]

the people I went to school with, who I sat next to in sixth and seventh grade, still live there, one or two in the houses that their parents once owned.

Not long ago, when I was in town on business, I determined to test my memories against the reality and drove to my old block, my old school, the homes of my closest friends, sure that I had inflated it all in my mind. But the houses were no smaller, the flowers no less bright. It was as fine as I had remembered—maybe more so, now when so much of the rest of the world has come to seem dingy and diminished.

Yet there was always in me, even when I was very small, the sense that I ought to be somewhere else. And wander I did, although, in my everyday life, I had nowhere to go and no imaginable reason on earth why I should want to leave. The buses took to the interstate without me; the trains sped by. So I wandered the world through books. I went to Victorian England in the pages of *Middlemarch* and *A Little Princess,* and to Saint Petersburg before the fall of the tsar with *Anna Karenina.* I went to Tara, and Manderley, and Thornfield Hall, all those great houses, with their high ceilings and high drama, as I read *Gone with the Wind, Rebecca,* and *Jane Eyre.*

When I was in eighth grade I took a scholarship test for a convent school, and the essay question began with a quotation: "It is a far, far better thing that I do, than I have ever done; it is a far, far better rest that I go to, than I have ever known." Later, over a stiff and awkward lunch of tuna-fish salad, some of the other girls at my table were perplexed by the source of the quotation and what it meant, and I was certain, at that moment, weeks before my parents got the letter from the nuns, that the scholarship was mine. How many times had I gone up the steps to the guillotine with Sydney Carton as he went to that far, far better rest at the end of *A Tale of Two Cities?*

Like so many of the other books I read, it never seemed to me like a book, but like a place I had lived in, had visited and would visit again, just as all the people in them, every blessed one—Anne of Green Gables, Heidi, Jay Gatsby, Elizabeth Bennet, Scarlett O'Hara, Dill and Scout, Miss Marple, and

Hercule Poirot—were more real than the real people I knew. My home was in that pleasant place outside Philadelphia, but I really lived somewhere else. I lived within the covers of books and those books were more real to me than any other thing in my life. One poem committed to memory in grade school survives in my mind. It is by Emily Dickinson: "There is no Frigate like a Book / To take us Lands away / Nor any coursers like a Page / Of prancing Poetry."

Perhaps only a truly discontented child can become as seduced by books as I was. Perhaps restlessness is a necessary corollary of devoted literacy. There was a club chair in our house, a big one, with curled arms and a square ottoman; it sat in one corner of the living room, catty-corner to the fireplace, with a barrel table next to it. In my mind I am always sprawled in it, reading with my skinny, scabby legs slung over one of its arms. "It's a beautiful day," my mother is saying; she said that always, often, autumn, spring, even when there was a fresh snowfall. "All your friends are outside." It was true; they always were. Sometimes I went out with them, coaxed into the street, out into the fields, down by the creek, by the lure of what I knew intuitively was normal childhood, by the promise of being what I knew instinctively was a normal child, one who lived, raucous, in the world.

I have clear memories of that sort of life, of lifting the rocks in the creek that trickled through Naylor's Run to search for crayfish, of laying pennies on the tracks of the trolley and running to fetch them, flattened, when the trolley had passed. But at base it was never any good. The best part of me was always at home, within some book that had been laid flat on the table to mark my place, its imaginary people waiting for me to return and bring them to life. That was where the real people were, the trees that moved in the wind, the still, dark waters. I won a bookmark in a spelling bee during that time with these words of Montaigne upon it in gold: "When I am reading a book, whether wise or silly, it seems to me to be alive and talking to me." I found that bookmark not long ago, at the bottom of a box, when my father was moving.

In the years since those days in that club chair I have   10
learned that I was not alone in this, although at the time I
surely was, the only child I knew, or my parents knew, or my
friends knew, who preferred reading to playing kick-the-can
or ice-skating or just sitting on the curb breaking sticks and
scuffing up dirt with a sneaker in summer. In books I have
traveled, not only to other worlds, but into my own. I
learned who I was and who I wanted to be, what I might aspire to, and what I might dare to dream about my world and
myself. More powerfully and persuasively than from the
"shalt nots" of the Ten Commandments, I learned the difference between good and evil, right and wrong. One of my favorite childhood books, *A Wrinkle in Time,* described that
evil, that wrong, existing in a different dimension from our
own. But I felt that I, too, existed much of the time in a different dimension from everyone else I knew. There was waking, and there was sleeping. And then there were books, a
kind of parallel universe in which anything might happen and
frequently did, a universe in which I might be a newcomer
but was never really a stranger. My real, true world. My perfect island.

Years later I would come to discover, as Robinson Crusoe   11
did when he found Man Friday, that I was not alone in that
world or on that island. I would discover (through reading,
naturally) that while I was sprawled, legs akimbo, in that
chair with a book, Jamaica Kincaid was sitting in the glare of
the Caribbean sun in Antigua reading in that same way that I
did, as though she was starving and the book was bread.
When she was grown-up, writing books herself, winning
awards for her work, she talked in one of her memoirs of ignoring her little brother when she was supposed to be looking after him: "I liked reading a book much more than I liked
looking after him (and even now I like reading a book more
than I like looking after my own children . . .)."

While I was in that club chair with a book, Hazel   12
Rochman and her husband were in South Africa, burying an
old tin trunk heavy with hardcovers in the backyard, because
the police might raid their house and search it for banned
books. Rochman, who left Johannesburg for Chicago and

enough examples

became an editor for the American Library Association's *Booklist*, summed up the lessons learned from that night, about the power of reading, in a way I would have recognized even as a girl. "Reading makes immigrants of us all," she wrote years later. "It takes us away from home, but, most important, it finds homes for us everywhere."

While I was in that club chair with a book, Oprah Winfrey was dividing her childhood between her mother in Milwaukee and her father in Nashville, but finding her most consistent home between the covers of her books. Even decades later, when she had become the host of her eponymous talk $\Rightarrow$ show, one of the world's highest-paid entertainers, and the founder of an on-air book club that resulted in the sale of millions of copies of serious literary novels, Winfrey still felt the sting as she talked to a reporter from *Life* magazine: "I remember being in the back hallway when I was about nine—I'm going to try to say this without crying—and my mother threw the door open and grabbed a book out of my hand and said, 'You're nothing but a something-something bookworm. Get your butt outside! You think you're better than the other kids.' I was treated as thought something was wrong with me because I wanted to read all the time." 13

most parents would be happy their kid is reading

Reading has always been my home, my sustenance, my great invincible companion. "Book love," Trollope called it. "It will make your hours pleasant to you as long as you live." Yet of all the many things in which we recognize some universal comfort—God, sex, food, family, friends—reading seems to be the one in which the comfort is most undersung, at least publicly, although it was really all I thought of, or felt, when I was eating up book after book, running away from home while sitting in that chair, traveling around the world and yet never leaving the room. I did not read from a sense of superiority, or advancement, or even learning. I read because I loved it more than any other activity on earth.

oprah winfrey

By the time I became an adult, I realized that while my satisfaction in the sheer act of reading had not abated in the least, the world was often as hostile, or at least as blind, to that joy as had been my girlfriends banging on our screen 15 door, begging me to put down the book—"that stupid book," they usually called it, no matter what book it happened to be. While we pay lip service to the virtues of reading, the truth is that there is still in our culture something that suspects those who read too much, whatever reading too much means, of being lazy, aimless dreamers, people who need to grow up and come outside to where real life is, who think themselves superior in their separateness.

There is something in the American character that is even   16
secretly hostile to the act of aimless reading, a certain hale and heartiness that is suspicious of reading as anything more than a tool for advancement. This is a country that likes confidence but despises hubris, that associates the "nose in the book" with the same sense of covert superiority that Ms. Winfrey's mother did. America is also a nation that prizes sociability and community, that accepts a kind of psychological domino effect: alone leads to loner, loner to loser. Any sort of turning away from human contact is suspect, especially one that interferes with the go-out-and-get-going ethos that seems to be at the heart of our national character. The image of American presidents that stick are those that portray them as men of action: Theodore Roosevelt on safari, John Kennedy throwing a football around with his brothers. There is only Lincoln as solace to the inveterate reader, a solitary figure sitting by the fire, saying, "My best friend is a person who will give me a book I have not read."

There also arose, as I was growing up, a kind of careerism   17
in the United States that sanctioned reading only if there was some point to it. Students at the nation's best liberal arts colleges who majored in philosophy or English were constantly asked what they were "going to do with it," as though intellectual pursuits for their own sake had had their day, and lost it in the press of business. Reading for pleasure was replaced by reading for purpose, and a kind of dogged self-improvement: whereas an executive might learn far more from *Moby-Dick* or *The Man in the Grey Flannel Suit*, the book he was expected to have read might be *The Seven Habits of Highly Successful People*. Reading for pleasure, spurred on

by some interior compulsion, became as suspect as getting on
the subway to ride aimlessly from place to place, or driving
from nowhere to nowhere in a car. I like to do both those
things, too, but not half so much as reading.

For many years I worked in the newspaper business, where   18
every day the production of the product stands as a flimsy but
eloquent testimony to the thirst for words, information, experience. But, for working journalists, reading in the latter
half of the twentieth century was most often couched as a series of problems to be addressed in print: were children in
public schools reading poorly? Were all Americans reading
less? Was the printed word giving way to the spoken one?
Had television and the movies supplanted books? The jour-
nalistic answer, most often, was yes, yes, yes, yes, buttressed
by a variety of statistics that, as so often happens, were mas-
saged to prove the point: reading had fallen upon hard times.
And in circles devoted to literary criticism, among the professors of literature, the editors and authors of fiction, there was
sometimes a kind of horrible exclusivity surrounding discussions of reading. There was good reading, and there was bad
reading. There was the worthy, and the trivial. This was always couched in terms of taste, but it tasted, smelled, and felt
unmistakably like snobbery.

None of this was new, except, in its discovering, to me.   19
Reading has always been used as a way to divide a country
and a culture into the literati and everyone else, the intellectually worthy and the hoi polloi. But in the fifteenth century
Gutenberg invented the printing press, and so began the process of turning the book from a work of art for the few into a
source of information for the many. After that, it became
more difficult for one small group of people to lay an exclusive claim to books, to seize and hold reading as their own.
But it was not impossible, and it continued to be done by
critics and scholars. When I began to read their work, in college, I was disheartened to discover that many of them felt
that the quality of poetry and prose, novels and history and
biography, was plummeting into some intellectual bargain
basement. But reading saved me from despair, as it always

had, for the more I read the more I realized it had always been thus, and that apparently an essential part of studying literature, whether in 1840, 1930, or 1975, was to conclude that there had once been a golden age, and it was gone. "The movies consume so large a part of the leisure of the country that little time is left for other things," the trade magazine of the industry, *Publishers Weekly,* lamented in 1923. "The novel can't compete with cars, the movies, television, and liquor," the French writer Louis-Ferdinand Céline said in 1960.

There was certainly no talk of comfort and joy, of the lively   20
subculture of those of us who forever fell asleep with a book open on our bedside tables, whether bought or borrowed. Of those of us who comprise the real clan of the book, who read not to judge the reading of others but to take the measure of ourselves. Of those of us who read because we love it more than anything, who feel about bookstores the way some people feel about jewelers. The silence about this was odd, both because there are so many of us and because we are what the world of books is really about. We are the people who once waited for the newest installment of Dickens's latest novel and who kept battered copies of *Catcher in the Rye* in our back pockets and our backpacks. We are the ones who saw to it that *Pride and Prejudice* never went out of print.

But there was little public talk of us, except in memoirs   21
like Ms. Kincaid's. Nothing had changed since I was a solitary child being given embossed leather bookmarks by relatives for Christmas. It was still in the equivalent of the club chairs that we found one another: at the counters in bookstores with our arms full, at the front desks in libraries, at school, where teachers introduced us to one another—and, of course, in books, where book-lovers make up a lively subculture of characters. "Until I feared I would lose it, I never loved to read. One does not love breathing," says Scout in *To Kill a Mockingbird.*

Reading is like so much else in our culture, in all cultures: 22
the truth of it is found in its people and not in its pundits and its professionals. If I believed what I read about reading I would despair. But instead there are letters from readers to

never goes out of style

great book

love, love, love

attend to, like the one from a girl who had been given one of my books by her mother and began her letter, "I guess I am what some people would call a bookworm."

"So am I," I wrote back.

odd ending 23

For Study and Discussion

QUESTIONS FOR RESPONSE

1. Quindlen says, "There is still in our culture something that suspects those who read too much . . . of being lazy." What is your view of that statement?
2. For you, how does the experience of watching stories on television or in the movies compare to Quindlen's experience of reading books? Which do you prefer and why?

QUESTIONS ABOUT PURPOSE

1. Quindlen's essay is highly autobiographical, focusing on what reading means to her. What do you think she wants to convey to her readers about that experience?
2. What outcome might she hope for among young people who read this essay?

QUESTIONS ABOUT AUDIENCE

1. Many families find their recreation in games, sports, or outdoor activities rather than in reading. If you grew up in such a family, what is your reaction to Quindlen's exuberant celebration of reading?
2. If you, like Quindlen, grew up known as a child who was a "bookworm," how did your experiences match or differ from hers?

QUESTIONS ABOUT STRATEGIES

1. What image of herself as a child does Quindlen create through her anecdotes? How sympathetic are her readers likely to be with that image?
2. How does she encourage readers to trust their own taste and judgment about choosing what to read?

QUESTIONS FOR DISCUSSION

1. Many people who like to read care little about fiction. How do you think their pleasure in reading differs from Quindlen's?
2. Despite gloomy predictions about the decline of reading because of television, video games, and so on, large numbers of Americans continue to read and buy books. How might one account for this enduring interest in books?

MALCOLM GLADWELL

Malcolm Gladwell was born in 1963 in England, grew up in Canada, and graduated with a degree in history from the University of Toronto. He has worked at the *Washington Post*, first as a science writer and then as New York City bureau chief. He currently is a staff writer for the *New Yorker*, where he has written on a range of issues concerning media, education, and business. His international best-seller, *The Tipping Point: How Little Things Can Make a Big Difference* (2000), describes how ideas and trends start and spread. In "Examined Life," reprinted from the *New Yorker*, Gladwell discusses a range of problems caused by the Kaplan program that helps students improve their scores on the SAT.

Examined Life

O NCE, IN FOURTH grade, Stanley Kaplan got a B-plus on his report card and was so stunned that he wandered aimlessly around the neighborhood, ashamed to show his mother. This was in Brooklyn, on Avenue K in Flatbush, between the wars. Kaplan's father, Julius, was from Slutsk, in Belorussia, and ran a plumbing and heating business. His mother, Ericka, ninety pounds and four feet eight, was the granddaughter of the chief rabbi of the synagogue of Prague, and Stanley loved to sit next to her on the front porch, immersed in his schoolbooks while his friends were off playing stickball. Stanley Kaplan had Mrs. Holman for fifth grade, and when she quizzed the class on math equations, he would shout out the answers. If other students were having problems, Stanley would take out pencil and paper and pull them aside. He would offer them a dime

1

sometimes if they would just sit and listen. In high school, he would take over algebra class, and the other kids, passing him in the hall, would call him Teach. One classmate, Aimee Rubin, was having so much trouble with math that she was in danger of being dropped from the National Honor Society. Kaplan offered to help her, and she scored a ninety-five on her next exam. He tutored a troubled eleven-year-old

---

The SAT . . . had an ideology, and Kaplan realized that anyone who understood that ideology would have a tremendous advantage.

---

named Bob Linker, and Bob Linker ended up a successful businessman. In Kaplan's sophomore year at City College, he got a C in biology and was so certain that there had been a mistake that he marched in to see the professor and proved that his true grade, an A, had accidentally been switched with that of another, not quite so studious Stanley Kaplan. Thereafter, he became Stanley H. Kaplan, and when people asked him what the "H" stood for, he would say "Higher scores!" or, with a sly wink, "Preparation!" He graduated Phi Beta Kappa and hung a shingle outside his parent's house on Avenue K—"Stanley H. Kaplan Educational Center"—and started tutoring kids in the basement. In 1946, a high school junior named Elizabeth, from Coney Island, came to him for help on an exam he was unfamiliar with. It was called the Scholastic Aptitude Test, and from that moment forward the business of getting into college in America was never quite the same.

    The SAT, at that point, was just beginning to go into   2
widespread use. Unlike existing academic exams, it was intended to measure innate ability—not what a student had learned but what a student was capable of learning—and it

stated clearly in the instructions that "cramming or last-minute reviewing" was pointless. Kaplan was puzzled. In Flatbush you always studied for tests. He gave Elizabeth pages of math problems and reading-comprehension drills. He grilled her over and over, doing what the SAT said should not be done. And what happened? On test day, she found the SAT "a piece of cake," and promptly told all her friends, and her friends told their friends, and soon word of Stanley H. Kaplan had spread throughout Brooklyn.

A few years later, Kaplan married Rita Gwirtzman, who   3
had grown up a mile away, and in 1951 they moved to a two-story brick-and-stucco house on Bedford Avenue, a block from his alma mater, James Madison High School. He renovated his basement, dividing it into classrooms. When the basement got too crowded, he rented a podiatrist's office near King's Highway, at the Brighton Beach subway stop. In the 1970s, he went national, setting up educational programs throughout the country, creating an SAT-preparation industry that soon became crowded with tutoring companies and study manuals. Kaplan has now written a memoir, *Test Pilot*, which has as its subtitle *How I Broke Testing Barriers for Millions of Students and Caused a Sonic Boom in the Business of Education*. That actually understates his importance. Stanley Kaplan changed the rules of the game.

The SAT is now seventy-five years old, and it is in trouble.   4
Earlier this year, the University of California—the nation's largest public university system—stunned the educational world by proposing a move toward a "holistic" admissions system, which would mean abandoning its heavy reliance on standardized-test scores. The school backed up its proposal with a devastating statistical analysis, arguing that the SAT is virtually useless as a tool for making admissions decisions.

The report focused on what is called predictive validity, a   5
statistical measure of how well a high school student's performance in any given test or program predicts his or her performance as a college freshman. If you wanted to, for instance, you could calculate the predictive validity of prowess at

Scrabble, or the number of books a student reads in his senior year, or, more obviously, high school grades. What the Educational Testing Service (which creates the SAT) and the College Board (which oversees it) have always argued is that most performance measures are so subjective and unreliable that only by adding aptitude-test scores into the admissions equation can a college be sure it is picking the right students.

This is what the UC study disputed. It compared the pre-   6
dictive validity of three numbers: a student's high school GPA, his or her score on the SAT (or, as it is formally known, the SAT I), and his or her score on what is known as the SAT II, which is a so-called achievement test, aimed at gauging mastery of specific areas of the high school curriculum. Drawing on the transcripts of 78,000 University of California freshmen from 1996 through 1999, the report found that overall, the most useful statistic in predicting freshman grades was the SAT II, which explained 16 percent of the "variance" (which is another measure of predictive validity). The second most useful was high school GPA, at 15.4 percent. The SAT was the least useful, at 13.3 percent. Combining high school GPA and the SAT II explained 22.2 percent of the variance in freshman grades. Adding in SAT I scores increased that number by only 0.1 percent. Nor was the SAT better at what one would have thought was its strong suit: identifying high-potential students from bad schools. In fact, the study found that achievement tests were ten times more useful than the SAT in predicting the success of students from similar backgrounds. "Achievement tests are fairer to students because they measure accomplishment rather than promise," Richard Atkinson, the president of the University of California, told a conference on college admissions last month. "They can be used to improve performance; they are less vulnerable to charges of cultural or socioeconomic bias; and they are more appropriate for schools because they set clear curricular guidelines and clarify what is important for students to learn. Most important, they tell students that a college education is within the reach of anyone with the talent and determination to succeed."

This argument has been made before, of course. The SAT   7
has been under attack, for one reason or another, since its inception. But what is happening now is different. The University of California is one of the largest single customers of the
SAT. It was the UC system's decision, in 1968, to adopt the
SAT that affirmed the test's national prominence in the first
place. If UC defects from the SAT, it is not hard to imagine it
being followed by a stampede of other colleges. Seventy-five
years ago, the SAT was instituted because we were more interested, as a society, in what a student was capable of learning than in what he had already learned. Now, apparently, we
have changed our minds, and few people bear more responsibility for that shift than Stanley H. Kaplan.

From the moment he set up shop on Avenue K, Stanley   8
Kaplan was a pariah in the educational world. Once, in 1956,
he went to a meeting for parents and teachers at a local high
school to discuss the upcoming SAT, and one of the teachers
leading the meeting pointed his finger at Kaplan and
shouted, "I refuse to continue until *that man* leaves the
room." When Kaplan claimed that his students routinely improved their scores by a hundred points or more, he was denounced by the testing establishment as a "quack" and "the
cram king" and a "snake oil salesman." At the Educational
Testing Service, "it was a cherished assumption that the SAT
was uncoachable," Nicholas Lemann writes in his history of
the SAT, *The Big Test:*

> *The whole idea of psychometrics was that mental tests*
> *are a measurement of a psychical property of the brain,*
> *analogous to taking a blood sample. By definition, the*
> *test-taker could not affect the result. More particularly,*
> *ETS's main point of pride about the SAT was its ex-*
> *tremely high test-retest reliability, one of the best that*
> *any standardized test had ever achieved. . . . So*
> *confident of the SAT's reliability was ETS that the basic*
> *technique it developed for catching cheaters was simply*
> *to compare first and second scores, and to mount an in-*

*vestigation in the case of any very large increase. ETS
was sure that substantially increasing one's score could
be accomplished only by nefarious means.*

But Kaplan wasn't cheating. His great contribution was to   9
prove that the SAT was eminently coachable—that whatever
it was that the test was measuring was less like a blood sample
than like a heart rate, a vital sign that could be altered
through the right exercises. In those days, for instance, the
test was a secret. Students walking in to take the SAT were
often in a state of terrified ignorance about what to expect.
(It wasn't until the early eighties that the ETS was forced to
release copies of old test questions to the public.) So Kaplan
would have "Thank Goodness It's Over" pizza parties after
each SAT. As his students talked about the questions they
had faced, he and his staff would listen and take notes, trying
to get a sense of how better to structure their coaching.
"Every night I stayed up past midnight writing new questions and study materials," he writes. "I spent hours trying to
understand the design of the test, trying to think like the test
makers, anticipating the types of questions my students
would face." His notes were typed up the next day, cranked
out on a Gestetner machine, hung to dry in the office, then
snatched off the line and given to waiting students. If students knew what the SAT was like, he reasoned, they would
be more confident. They could skip the instructions and save
time. They could learn how to pace themselves. They would
guess more intelligently. (For a question with five choices, a
right answer is worth one point but a wrong answer results in
minus one-quarter of a point—which is why students were
always warned that guessing was penalized. In reality, of
course, if a student can eliminate even one obviously wrong
possibility from the list of choices, guessing becomes an intelligent strategy.) The SAT was a test devised by a particular institution, by a particular kind of person, operating from a
particular mindset. It had an ideology, and Kaplan realized
that anyone who understood that ideology would have a tremendous advantage.

Critics of the SAT have long made a kind of parlor game of 10
seeing how many questions on the reading-comprehension
section (where a passage is followed by a series of multiple-
choice questions about its meaning) can be answered without reading the passage. David Owen, in the anti-SAT account "None of the Above," gives the following example,
adapted from an actual SAT exam:

1. The main idea of the passage is that:
    A) a constricted view of [this novel] is natural and ac-
    ceptable
    B) a novel should not depict a vanished society
    C) a good novel is an intellectual rather than an emo-
    tional experience
    D) many readers have seen only the comedy [in this
    novel]
    E) [this novel] should be read with sensitivity and an
    open mind

If you've never seen an SAT before, it might be difficult to 11
guess the right answer. But if, through practice and exposure,
you have managed to assimilate the ideology of the SAT—
the kind of decent, middlebrow earnestness that permeates
the test—it's possible to develop a kind of gut feeling for the
right answer, the confidence to predict, in the pressure and
rush of examination time, what the SAT is looking for. A is
suspiciously postmodern. B is far too dogmatic. C is something that you would never say to an eager, college-bound
student. Is it D? Perhaps, but D seems too small a point. It's
probably E—and sure enough, it is.
    With that in mind, try this question: 12

2. The author of [this passage] implies that a work of art is
    properly judged on the basis of its:
    A) universality of human experience truthfully recorded
    B) popularity and critical acclaim in its own age
    C) openness to varied interpretations, including seem-
    ingly contradictory ones

D) avoidance of political and social issues of minor importance
E) continued popularity through different eras and with
different societies

Is it any surprise that the answer is A? Bob Schaeffer, the public education director of the anti-test group FairTest, says
that when he got a copy of the latest version of the SAT, the
first thing he did was try the reading comprehension section
blind. He got twelve out of thirteen questions right.

The math portion of the SAT is perhaps a better example   13
of how coachable the test can be. Here is another question,
cited by Owen, from an old SAT:

> *In how many different color combinations can 3 balls*
> *be painted if each ball is painted one color and there*
> *are 3 colors available? (Order is not considered; e.g.*
> *red, blue, red is considered the same combination as*
> *red, red, blue.)*
>   *A) 4   B) 6   C) 9   D) 10   E) 27*

This was, Owen points out, the twenty-fifth question in a   14
twenty-five-question math section. SATs—like virtually all
standardized tests—rank their math questions from easiest to
hardest. If the hardest questions came first, the theory goes,
weaker students would be so intimidated as they began the
test that they might throw up their hands in despair. So this is
a "hard" question. The second thing to understand about
the SAT is that it only really works if good students get the
hard questions right and poor students get the hard questions wrong. If anyone can guess or blunder his way into the
right answer to a hard question, then the test isn't doing its
job. So this is the second clue: the answer to this question
must not be something that an average student might blunder into answering correctly. With these two facts in mind,
Owen says, don't focus on the question. Just look at the
numbers: there are three balls and three colors. The average
student is most likely to guess by doing one of three things—

adding three and three, multiplying three times three, or, if he is feeling more adventurous, multiplying three by three by three. So six, nine, and twenty-seven are out. That leaves four and ten. Now, he says, read the problem. It can't be four, since anyone can think of more than four combinations. The correct answer must be D, ten.

Does being able to answer that question mean that a student has a greater "aptitude" for math? Of course not. It just means that he had a clever teacher. Kaplan once determined that the testmakers were fond of geometric problems involving the Pythagorean theorem. So an entire generation of Kaplan students were taught "boo, boo, boo, square root of two," to help them remember how the Pythagorean formula applies to an isosceles right triangle. "It was usually not lack of ability," Kaplan writes, "but poor study habits, inadequate instruction, or a combination of the two that jeopardized students' performance." The SAT was not an aptitude test at all.

In proving that the SAT was coachable, Stanley Kaplan did something else, which was of even greater importance. He undermined the use of aptitude tests as a means of social engineering. In the years immediately before and after World War I, for instance, the country's elite colleges faced what became known as "the Jewish problem." They were being inundated with the children of Eastern European Jewish immigrants. These students came from the lower middle class and they disrupted the genteel WASP sensibility that had been so much a part of the Ivy League tradition. They were guilty of "underliving and overworking." In the words of one writer, they "worked far into each night [and] their lessons next morning were letter perfect." They were "socially untrained," one Harvard professor wrote, "and their bodily habits are not good." But how could a college keep Jews out? Columbia University had a policy that the New York State Regents Examinations—the statewide curriculum-based high school graduation examination—could be used as the basis for admission, and the plain truth was that Jews did extraordinarily well on the Regents Exams. One solution was simply to put a quota on the number of Jews, which is what Harvard explored. The other idea, which Columbia followed, was to require applicants to take an aptitude test. According to Herbert Hawkes, the dean of Columbia College during this period, because the typical Jewish student was simply a "grind," who excelled on the Regents Exams because he worked so hard, a test of innate intelligence would put him back in his place. "We have not eliminated boys because they were Jews and do not propose to do so," Hawkes wrote in 1918.

> We have honestly attempted to eliminate the lowest grade of applicant and it turns out that a good many of the low grade men are New York City Jews. It is a fact that boys of foreign parentage who have no background in many cases attempt to educate themselves beyond their intelligence. Their accomplishment is over 100 percent of their ability on account of their tremendous energy and ambition. I do not believe however that a College would do well to admit too many men of low mentality who have ambition but not brains.

Today Hawkes's anti-Semitism seems absurd, but he was by no means the last person to look to aptitude tests as a means of separating ambition from brains. The great selling point of the SAT has always been that it promises to reveal whether the high school senior with a 3.0 GPA is someone who could have done much better if he had been properly educated or someone who is already at the limit of his abilities. We want to know that information because, like Hawkes, we prefer naturals to grinds: we think that people who achieve based on vast reserves of innate ability are somehow more promising and more worthy than those who simply work hard.

But is this distinction real? Some years ago, a group headed by the British psychologist John Sloboda conducted a study of musical talent. The group looked at 256 young musicians, between the ages of ten and sixteen, drawn from elite music academies and public school music programs alike. They interviewed all the students and their parents and recorded how each student did in England's national music-examination system, which, the researchers felt, gave them a relatively objective measure of musical ability. "What we found was that the best predictor of where you were on that scale was the number of hours practiced," Sloboda says. This is, if you think about it, a little hard to believe. We conceive musical ability to be a "talent"—people have an aptitude for music—and so it would make sense that some number of students could excel at the music exam without practicing very much. Yet Sloboda couldn't find any. The kids who scored the best on the test were, on average, practicing *800 percent more* than the kids at the bottom. "People have this idea that there are those who learn better than others, can get further on less effort," Sloboda says. "On average, our data refuted that. Whether you're a dropout or at the best school, where you end up can be predicted by how much you practice."

Sloboda found another striking similarity among the "musical" children. They all had parents who were unusually invested in their musical education. It wasn't necessarily the case that the parents were themselves musicians or musically inclined. It was simply that they wanted their children to be that way. "The parents of the high achievers did things that most parents just don't do," he said. "They didn't simply drop their child at the door of the teacher. They went into the practice room. They took notes on what the teacher said, and when they got home they would say, Remember when your teacher said do this and that. There was a huge amount of time and motivational investment by the parents."

Does this mean that there is no such thing as musical talent? Of course not. Most of those hardworking children with pushy parents aren't going to turn out to be Itzhak Perlmans; some will be second violinists in their community orchestra. The point is that when it comes to a relatively well defined and structured task—like playing an instrument or taking an exam—how hard you work and how supportive your parents are have a lot more to do with success than we

19

20

ordinarily imagine. Ability cannot be separated from effort. The testmakers never understood that, which is why they thought they could weed out the grinds. But educators increasingly do, and that is why college admissions are now in such upheaval. The Texas state university system, for example, has, since 1997, automatically admitted any student who places in the top 10 percent of his or her high school class— regardless of SAT score. Critics of the policy said that it would open the door to students from marginal schools whose SAT scores would normally have been too low for admission to the University of Texas—and that is exactly what happened. But so what? The "top 10 percenters," as they are known, may have lower SAT scores, but they get excellent grades. In fact, their college GPAs are the equal of students who scored two hundred to three hundred points higher on the SAT. In other words, the determination and hard work that propel someone to the top of his high school class—even in cases where that high school is impoverished—are more important to succeeding in college (and, for that matter, in life) than whatever abstract quality the SAT purports to measure. The importance of the Texas experience cannot be overstated. Here, at last, is an intelligent alternative to affirmative action, a way to find successful minority students without sacrificing academic performance. But we would never have got this far without Stanley Kaplan—without someone first coming along and puncturing the mystique of the SAT. "Acquiring test-taking skills is the same as learning to play the piano or ride a bicycle," Kaplan writes. "It requires practice, practice, practice. Repetition breeds familiarity. Familiarity breeds confidence." In this, as in so many things, the grind *was* the natural.

To read Kaplan's memoir is to be struck by what a representative figure he was in the postwar sociological miracle that was Jewish Brooklyn. This is the lower-middle-class, second- and third-generation immigrant world, stretching from Prospect Park to Sheepshead Bay, that ended up peopling the upper reaches of American professional life. Thou- 21 sands of students from those neighborhoods made their way through Kaplan's classroom in the fifties and sixties, many along what Kaplan calls the "heavily traveled path" from Brooklyn to Cornell, Yale, and the University of Michigan. Kaplan writes of one student who increased his score by 340 points and ended up with a Ph.D. and a position as a scientist at Xerox. "Debbie" improved her SAT by 500 points, got into the University of Chicago, and earned a Ph.D. in clinical psychology. Arthur Levine, the president of Teachers College at Columbia University, raised his SATs by 282 points, "making it possible," he writes on the book's jacket, "for me to attend a better university than I ever would have imagined." Charles Schumer, the senior senator from New York, studied while he worked the mimeograph machine in Kaplan's office, and ended up with close to a perfect 1600.

These students faced a system designed to thwart the hard worker, and what did they do? They got together with their pushy parents and outworked it. Kaplan says that he knew a "strapping athlete who became physically ill before taking the SAT because his mother was so demanding." There was the mother who called him to say, "Mr. Kaplan, I think I'm going to commit suicide. My son made only one thousand on the SAT." "One mother wanted her straight-A son to have an extra edge, so she brought him to my basement for years for private tutoring in basic subjects," Kaplan recalls. "He was extremely bright and today is one of the country's most successful ophthalmologists." Another student was "so nervous that his mother accompanied him to class armed with a supply of terry-cloth towels. She stood outside the classroom, and when he emerged from our class sessions dripping in sweat, she wiped him dry and then nudged him back into the classroom." Then, of course, there was the formidable four-foot-eight figure of Ericka Kaplan, granddaughter of the chief rabbi of the synagogue of Prague. "My mother was a perfectionist whether she was keeping the company books or setting the dinner table," Kaplan writes, still in her thrall today. "She was my best cheerleader, the reason I performed so

22

well, and I constantly strove to please her." What chance did
even the most artfully constructed SAT have against the
mothers of Brooklyn?

Stanley Kaplan graduated number two in his class at City   23
College and won the school's Award for Excellence in Natural Sciences. He wanted to be a doctor, and he applied to five
medical schools, confident that he would be accepted. To his
shock, he was rejected by every single one. Medical schools
did not take public colleges like City College seriously. More
important, in the forties there was a limit to how many Jews
they were willing to accept. "The term *meritocracy*—or success based on merit rather than heritage, wealth, or social
status—wasn't even coined yet," Kaplan writes, "and the
methods of selecting students based on talent, not privilege,
were still evolving."

That's why Stanley Kaplan was always pained by those   24
who thought that what went on in his basement was somehow subversive. He loved the SAT. He thought that the test
gave people like him the best chance of overcoming discrimination. As he saw it, he was simply giving the middle-class
students of Brooklyn the same shot at a bright future that
their counterparts in the private schools of Manhattan had.
In 1983, after years of hostility, the College Board invited
him to speak at its annual convention. It was one of the highlights of Kaplan's life. "Never, in my wildest dreams," he began, "did I ever think I'd be speaking to you here today."

The truth is, however, that Stanley Kaplan was wrong.   25
What he did in his basement *was* subversive. The SAT was designed as an abstract intellectual tool. It never occurred to its
makers that aptitude was a social matter: that what people
were capable of was affected by what they knew, and what
they knew was affected by what they were taught, and what
they were taught was affected by the industry of their teachers and parents. And if what the SAT was measuring, in no
small part, was the industry of teachers and parents, then
what did it mean? Stanley Kaplan may have loved the SAT.

But when he stood up and recited "boo, boo, boo, square root of two," he killed it.

For Study and Discussion

QUESTIONS FOR RESPONSE

1. If you took the SAT tests to be admitted to college, how does your experience mesh with Gladwell's claim that one can often choose the right answer on the test without really understanding the problem?
2. Thinking about the high achievers you know in college and other enterprises, to what extent do you believe that hard work and application had more to do with their success than a natural intelligence?

QUESTIONS ABOUT PURPOSE

1. When Gladwell explains the methods Kaplan devised for coaching students for the SAT test, what kind of commonsense wisdom emerges about test taking?
2. What weaknesses about the admissions processes of many colleges does Gladwell bring out?

QUESTIONS ABOUT AUDIENCE

1. Most high school students who plan to go to college hear about the importance of the SAT tests by the time they're in the seventh or eighth grade. How does your experience with that knowledge affect your reading of this essay?
2. If you took a Kaplan course to raise your SAT scores to increase your competitive advantage for college admission, how do you think the coaching helped (or didn't help) you?

QUESTIONS ABOUT STRATEGIES

1. How does the list of very specific examples Gladwell gives in the opening paragraph engage your interest and preview the thesis of the essay?

2. What is the intellectual and philosophical conflict that Gladwell establishes between Kaplan and the administrators of the Educational Testing Service?

QUESTIONS FOR DISCUSSION

1. Some critics say that Kaplan's coaching courses create their own kind of elite applicants: those whose parents can afford to pay for such courses. What kinds of issues does that possibility raise?
2. In the United States, tests created and administered by the Educational Testing Service—the GRE, MCAT, LSAT, and so on— act as major hurdles that any student must overcome to enter almost any professional school. Are such barriers useful or detrimental to students and to the graduate schools?

ERIC SCHLOSSER

Eric Schlosser is a correspondent for the *Atlantic* and the author of the best-selling book *Fast Food Nation: The Dark Side of the All-American Meal* (2001). Schlosser lives in New York City and is currently at work on a book about the American prison system. After he published his essay "Why McDonald's Fries Taste So Good," Schlosser became a media celebrity—being interviewed on *60 Minutes*, NPR, and CNN. His disclosure that McDonald's fries tasted so good because they were fried in "beef tallow" caused Hindus to destroy McDonald's restaurants in India and vegetarians to file class action suits against McDonald's in America.

Why McDonald's Fries Taste So Good

THE FRENCH FRY was "almost sacrosanct for me," Ray Kroc, one of the founders of McDonald's, wrote in his autobiography, "its preparation a ritual to be followed religiously." During the chain's early years french fries were made from scratch every day. Russet Burbank potatoes were peeled, cut into shoestrings, and fried in McDonald's kitchens. As the chain expanded nationwide, in the mid-1960s, it sought to cut labor costs, reduce the number of suppliers, and ensure that its fries tasted the same at every restaurant. McDonald's began switching to frozen french fries in 1966—and few customers noticed the difference. Nevertheless, the change had a profound effect on the nation's agriculture and diet. A familiar food had been transformed into a highly processed industrial commodity. McDonald's fries now come from huge manufacturing plants that can peel, slice, cook, and freeze 2 million pounds of potatoes a day. The rapid expansion of McDonald's and the popularity of its low-cost, mass-produced fries changed the way Americans eat. In 1960 Americans consumed an average of about eighty-one pounds of fresh potatoes and four pounds of frozen french fries. In 2000 they consumed an average of about fifty pounds of fresh potatoes and thirty pounds of

---

The rise and fall of corporate empires—of soft-drink companies, snack-food companies, and fast-food chains—is often determined by how their products taste.

---

frozen fries. Today McDonald's is the largest buyer of potatoes in the United States.

The taste of McDonald's french fries played a crucial role in the chain's success—fries are much more profitable than hamburgers—and was long praised by customers, competitors, and even food critics. James Beard loved McDonald's fries. Their distinctive taste does not stem from the kind of potatoes that McDonald's buys, the technology that processes them, or the restaurant equipment that fries them: other chains use Russet Burbanks, buy their french fries from the same large processing companies, and have similar fryers in their restaurant kitchens. The taste of a french fry is largely determined by the cooking oil. For decades McDonald's cooked its french fries in a mixture of about 7 percent cottonseed oil and 93 percent beef tallow. The mixture gave the fries their unique flavor—and more saturated beef fat per ounce than a McDonald's hamburger.

In 1990, amid a barrage of criticism over the amount of cholesterol in its fries, McDonald's switched to pure vegetable oil. This presented the company with a challenge: how to make fries that subtly taste like beef without cooking them in beef tallow. A look at the ingredients in McDonald's french fries suggests how the problem was solved. Toward the end of the list is a seemingly innocuous yet oddly mysterious phrase: "natural flavor." That ingredient helps to explain not only why the fries taste so good but also why most fast food—indeed, most of the food Americans eat today—tastes the way it does.

Open your refrigerator, your freezer, your kitchen cupboards, and look at the labels on your food. You'll find "natural flavor" or "artificial flavor" in just about every list of ingredients. The similarities between these two broad categories are far more significant than the differences. Both are man-made additives that give most processed food most of its taste. People usually buy a food item the first time because of its packaging or appearance. Taste usually determines whether they buy it again. About 90 percent of the money that Americans now spend on food goes to buy processed food. The canning, freezing, and dehydrating techniques used in processing destroy most of food's flavor—and so a vast industry has arisen in the United States to make processed food palatable. Without this flavor industry today's fast food would not exist. The names of the leading American fast-food chains and their best-selling menu items have become embedded in our popular culture and famous worldwide. But few people can name the companies that manufacture fast food's taste.

The flavor industry is highly secretive. Its leading companies will not divulge the precise formulas of flavor compounds or the identities of clients. The secrecy is deemed essential for protecting the reputations of beloved brands. The fast-food chains, understandably, would like the public to believe that the flavors of the food they sell somehow originate in their restaurant kitchens, not in distant factories run by other firms. A McDonald's french fry is one of countless foods whose flavor is just a component in a complex manufacturing process. The look and the taste of what we eat now are frequently deceiving—by design.

The New Jersey Turnpike runs through the heart of the 6 flavor industry, an industrial corridor dotted with refineries and chemical plants. International Flavors & Fragrances (IFF), the world's largest flavor company, has a manufacturing facility off Exit 8A in Dayton, New Jersey; Givaudan, the world's second-largest flavor company, has a plant in East Hanover. Haarmann & Reimer, the largest German flavor company, has a plant in Teterboro, as does Takasago, the largest Japanese flavor company. Flavor Dynamics has a plant in South Plainfield; Frutarom is in North Bergen; Elan Chemical is in Newark. Dozens of companies manufacture flavors in the corridor between Teaneck and South Brunswick. Altogether the area produces about two-thirds of the flavor additives sold in the United States.

The IFF plant in Dayton is a huge pale-blue building with 7 a modern office complex attached to the front. It sits in an industrial park, not far from a BASF plastics factory, a Jolly French Toast factory, and a plant that manufactures Liz Claiborne cosmetics. Dozens of tractor-trailers were parked at the IFF loading dock the afternoon I visited, and a thin cloud of steam floated from a roof vent. Before entering the plant, I signed a nondisclosure form, promising not to reveal the brand names of foods that contain IFF flavors. The place reminded me of Willy Wonka's chocolate factory. Wonderful smells drifted through the hallways, men and women in neat white lab coats cheerfully went about their work, and hundreds of little glass bottles sat on laboratory tables and shelves. The bottles contained powerful but fragile flavor chemicals, shielded from light by brown glass and round white caps shut tight. The long chemical names on the little white labels were as mystifying to me as medieval Latin. These odd-sounding things would be mixed and poured and turned into new substances, like magic potions.

I was not invited into the manufacturing areas of the IFF 8 plant, where, it was thought, I might discover trade secrets. Instead I toured various laboratories and pilot kitchens, where the flavors of well-established brands are tested or adjusted, and where whole new flavors are created. IFF's snack-and-savory lab is responsible for the flavors of potato chips, corn chips, breads, crackers, breakfast cereals, and pet food. The confectionery lab devises flavors for ice cream, cookies, candies, toothpastes, mouthwashes, and antacids. Everywhere I looked, I saw famous, widely advertised products sitting on laboratory desks and tables. The beverage lab was full of brightly colored liquids in clear bottles. It comes up with flavors for popular soft drinks, sports drinks, bottled teas, and wine coolers, for all-natural juice drinks, organic soy drinks, beers, and malt liquors. In one pilot kitchen I saw a dapper food technologist, a middle-aged man with an elegant tie beneath his crisp lab coat, carefully preparing a batch of cookies with white frosting and pink-and-white sprinkles. In another pilot kitchen I saw a pizza oven, a grill, a milk-shake machine, and a french fryer identical to those I'd seen at innumerable fast-food restaurants.

In addition to being the world's largest flavor company, 9
IFF manufactures the smells of six of the ten best-selling fine perfumes in the United States, including Estée Lauder's Beautiful, Clinique's Happy, Lancôme's Trésor, and Calvin Klein's Eternity. It also makes the smells of household products such as deodorant, dishwashing detergent, bath soap, shampoo, furniture polish, and floor wax. All these aromas are made through essentially the same process: the manipulation of volatile chemicals. The basic science behind the scent of your shaving cream is the same as that governing the flavor of your TV dinner.

Scientists now believe that human beings acquired the 10
sense of taste as a way to avoid being poisoned. Edible plants generally taste sweet, harmful ones bitter. The taste buds on our tongues can detect the presence of half a dozen or so basic tastes, including sweet, sour, bitter, salty, astringent, and umami, a taste discovered by Japanese researchers—a rich and full sense of deliciousness triggered by amino acids in foods such as meat, shellfish, mushrooms, potatoes, and seaweed. Taste buds offer a limited means of detection,

however, compared with the human olfactory system, which can perceive thousands of different chemical aromas. Indeed, "flavor" is primarily the smell of gases being released by the chemicals you've just put in your mouth. The aroma of a food can be responsible for as much as 90 percent of its taste.

The act of drinking, sucking, or chewing a substance re- 11 leases its volatile gases. They flow out of your mouth and up your nostrils, or up the passageway in the back of your mouth, to a thin layer of nerve cells called the olfactory epithelium, located at the base of your nose, right between your eyes. Your brain combines the complex smell signals from your olfactory epithelium with the simple taste signals from your tongue, assigns a flavor to what's in your mouth, and decides if it's something you want to eat.

A person's food preferences, like his or her personality, are 12 formed during the first few years of life, through a process of socialization. Babies innately prefer sweet tastes and reject bitter ones; toddlers can learn to enjoy hot and spicy food, bland health food, or fast food, depending on what the people around them eat. The human sense of smell is still not fully understood. It is greatly affected by psychological factors and expectations. The mind focuses intently on some of the aromas that surround us and filters out the overwhelming majority. People can grow accustomed to bad smells or good smells; they stop noticing what once seemed overpowering. Aroma and memory are somehow inextricably linked. A smell can suddenly evoke a long-forgotten moment. The flavors of childhood foods seem to leave an indelible mark, and adults often return to them, without always knowing why. These "comfort foods" become a source of pleasure and reassurance—a fact that fast-food chains use to their advantage. Childhood memories of Happy Meals, which come with french fries, can translate into frequent adult visits to McDonald's. On average, Americans now eat about four servings of french fries every week.

The human craving for flavor has been a largely unac- 13 knowledged and unexamined force in history. For millennia royal empires have been built, unexplored lands traversed, and great religions and philosophies forever changed by the spice trade. In 1492 Christopher Columbus set sail to find seasoning. Today the influence of flavor in the world marketplace is no less decisive. The rise and fall of corporate empires—of soft-drink companies, snack-food companies, and fast-food chains—is often determined by how their products taste.

The flavor industry emerged in the mid-nineteenth century, as processed foods began to be manufactured on a large scale. Recognizing the need for flavor additives, early food processors turned to perfume companies that had long experience working with essential oils and volatile aromas. The great perfume houses of England, France, and the Netherlands produced many of the first flavor compounds. In the early part of the twentieth century Germany took the technological lead in flavor production, owing to its powerful chemical industry. Legend has it that a German scientist discovered methyl anthranilate, one of the first artificial flavors, by accident while mixing chemicals in his laboratory. Suddenly the lab was filled with the sweet smell of grapes. Methyl anthranilate later became the chief flavor compound in grape Kool-Aid. After World War II much of the perfume industry shifted from Europe to the United States, settling in New York City near the garment district and the fashion houses. The flavor industry came with it, later moving to New Jersey for greater plant capacity. Man-made flavor additives were used mostly in baked goods, candies, and sodas until the 1950s, when sales of processed food began to soar. The invention of gas chromatographs and mass spectrometers— machines capable of detecting volatile gases at low levels —vastly increased the number of flavors that could be synthesized. By the mid-1960s flavor companies were churning out compounds to supply the taste of Pop Tarts, Bac-Os, Tab, Tang, Filet-O-Fish sandwiches, and literally thousands of other new foods.

The American flavor industry now has annual revenues of about $1.4 billion. Approximately ten thousand new processed-food products are introduced every year in the United States. Almost all of them require flavor additives. And about nine out of ten of these products fail. The latest flavor innovations and corporate realignments are heralded in publications such as *Chemical Market Reporter, Food Chemical News, Food Engineering,* and *Food Product Design.* The progress of IFF has mirrored that of the flavor industry as a whole. IFF was formed in 1958, through the merger of two small companies. Its annual revenues have grown almost fifteenfold since the early 1970s, and it currently has manufacturing facilities in twenty countries.

Today's sophisticated spectrometers, gas chromatographs,   16
and headspace-vapor analyzers provide a detailed map of a food's flavor components, detecting chemical aromas present in amounts as low as one part per billion. The human nose, however, is even more sensitive. A nose can detect aromas present in quantities of a few parts per trillion—an amount equivalent to about 0.000000000003 percent. Complex aromas, such as those of coffee and roasted meat, are composed of volatile gases from nearly a thousand different chemicals. The smell of a strawberry arises from the interaction of about 350 chemicals that are present in minute amounts. The quality that people seek most of all in a food—flavor—is usually present in a quantity too infinitesimal to be measured in traditional culinary terms such as ounces or teaspoons. The chemical that provides the dominant flavor of bell pepper can be tasted in amounts as low as 0.02 parts per billion; one drop is sufficient to add flavor to five average-size swimming pools. The flavor additive usually comes next to last in a processed food's list of ingredients and often costs less than its packaging. Soft drinks contain a larger proportion of flavor additives than most products. The flavor in a twelve-ounce can of Coke costs about half a cent.

The color additives in processed foods are usually present   17
in even smaller amounts than the flavor compounds. Many of New Jersey's flavor companies also manufacture these color additives, which are used to make processed foods look fresh

and appealing. Food coloring serves many of the same decorative purposes as lipstick, eye shadow, mascara—and is often made from the same pigments. Titanium dioxide, for example, has proved to be an especially versatile mineral. It gives many processed candies, frostings, and icings their bright white color; it is a common ingredient in women's cosmetics; and it is the pigment used in many white oil paints and house paints. At Burger King, Wendy's, and McDonald's coloring agents have been added to many of the soft drinks, salad dressings, cookies, condiments, chicken dishes, and sandwich buns.

Studies have found that the color of a food can greatly affect how its taste is perceived. Brightly colored foods frequently seem to taste better than bland-looking foods, even when the flavor compounds are identical. Foods that somehow look off-color often seem to have off tastes. For thousands of years human beings have relied on visual cues to help determine what is edible. The color of fruit suggests whether it is ripe, the color of meat whether it is rancid. Flavor researchers sometimes use colored lights to modify the influence of visual cues during taste tests. During one experiment in the early 1970s people were served an oddly tinted meal of steak and french fries that appeared normal beneath colored lights. Everyone thought the meal tasted fine until the lighting was changed. Once it became apparent that the steak was actually blue and the fries were green, some people became ill.   18

The federal Food and Drug Administration does not require companies to disclose the ingredients of their color or flavor additives so long as all the chemicals in them are considered by the agency to be GRAS ("generally recognized as safe"). This enables companies to maintain the secrecy of their formulas. It also hides the fact that flavor compounds often contain more ingredients than the foods to which they give taste. The phrase "artificial strawberry flavor" gives little hint of the chemical wizardry and manufacturing skill that can make a highly processed food taste like strawberries.   19

A typical artificial strawberry flavor, like the kind found in   20
a Burger King strawberry milk shake, contains the following
ingredients: amyl acetate, amyl butyrate, amyl valerate,
anethol, anisyl formate, benzyl acetate, benzyl isobutyrate,
butyric acid, cinnamyl isobutyrate, cinnamyl valerate, cognac
essential oil, diacetyl, dipropyl ketone, ethyl acetate, ethyl
amyl ketone, ethyl butyrate, ethyl cinnamate, ethyl hep-
tanoate, ethyl heptylate, ethyl lactate, ethyl methylphenyl-
glycidate, ethyl nitrate, ethyl propionate, ethyl valerate,
heliotropin, hydroxyphenyl-2-butanone (10 percent solution
in alcohol), α-ionone, isobutyl anthranilate, isobutyl butyrate, lemon essential oil, maltol, 4-methylacetophenone,
methyl anthranilate, methyl benzoate, methyl cinnamate,
methyl heptine carbonate, methyl naphthyl ketone, methyl
salicylate, mint essential oil, neroli essential oil, nerolin, neryl
isobutyrate, orris butter, phenethyl alcohol, rose, rum ether,
γ-undecalactone, vanillin, and solvent.

Although flavors usually arise from a mixture of many dif-   21
ferent volatile chemicals, often a single compound supplies
the dominant aroma. Smelled alone, that chemical provides
an unmistakable sense of the food. Ethyl-2-methyl butyrate,
for example, smells just like an apple. Many of today's highly
processed foods offer a blank palette: whatever chemicals are
added to them will give them specific tastes. Adding methyl-
2-pyridyl ketone makes something taste like popcorn.
Adding ethyl-3-hydroxy butanoate makes it taste like marsh-
mallow. The possibilities are now almost limitless. Without
affecting appearance or nutritional value, processed foods
could be made with aroma chemicals such as hexanal (the
smell of freshly cut grass) or 3-methyl butanoic acid (the
smell of body odor).

The 1960s were the heyday of artificial flavors in the   22
United States. The synthetic versions of flavor compounds
were not subtle, but they did not have to be, given the nature
of most processed food. For the past twenty years food processors have tried hard to use only "natural flavors" in their
products. According to the FDA, these must be derived entirely from natural sources—from herbs, spices, fruits, vegetables, beef, chicken, yeast, bark, roots, and so forth. Con-

sumers prefer to see natural flavors on a label, out of a belief that they are more healthful. Distinctions between artificial and natural flavors can be arbitrary and somewhat absurd, based more on how the flavor has been made than on what it actually contains.

"A natural flavor," says Terry Acree, a professor of food   23
science at Cornell University, "is a flavor that's been derived with an out-of-date technology." Natural flavors and artificial flavors sometimes contain exactly the same chemicals, produced through different methods. Amyl acetate, for example, provides the dominant note of banana flavor. When it is distilled from bananas with a solvent, amyl acetate is a natural flavor. When it is produced by mixing vinegar with amyl alcohol and adding sulfuric acid as a catalyst, amyl acetate is an artificial flavor. Either way it smells and tastes the same. "Natural flavor" is now listed among the ingredients of everything from Health Valley Blueberry Granola Bars to Taco Bell Hot Taco Sauce.

A natural flavor is not necessarily more healthful or purer   24
than an artificial one. When almond flavor—benzaldehyde— is derived from natural sources, such as peach and apricot pits, it contains traces of hydrogen cyanide, a deadly poison. Benzaldehyde derived by mixing oil of clove and amyl acetate does not contain any cyanide. Nevertheless, it is legally considered an artificial flavor and sells at a much lower price. Natural and artificial flavors are now manufactured at the same chemical plants, places that few people would associate with Mother Nature.

The small and elite group of scientists who create most of   25
the flavor in most of the food now consumed in the United States are called "flavorists." They draw on a number of disciplines in their work: biology, psychology, physiology, and organic chemistry. A flavorist is a chemist with a trained nose and a poetic sensibility. Flavors are created by blending scores of different chemicals in tiny amounts—a process governed by scientific principles but demanding a fair amount of art. In an age when delicate aromas and microwave ovens do not

easily coexist, the job of the flavorist is to conjure illusions about processed food and, in the words of one flavor company's literature, to ensure "consumer likeability." The flavorists with whom I spoke were discreet, in keeping with the dictates of their trade. They were also charming, cosmopolitan, and ironic. They not only enjoyed fine wine but could identify the chemicals that give each grape its unique aroma. One flavorist compared his work to composing music. A well-made flavor compound will have a "top note" that is often followed by a "dry-down" and a "leveling-off," with different chemicals responsible for each stage. The taste of a food can be radically altered by minute changes in the flavoring combination. "A little odor goes a long way," one flavorist told me.

In order to give a processed food a taste that consumers will find appealing, a flavorist must always consider the food's "mouthfeel"—the unique combination of textures and chemical interactions that affect how the flavor is perceived. Mouthfeel can be adjusted through the use of various fats, gums, starches, emulsifiers, and stabilizers. The aroma chemicals in a food can be precisely analyzed, but the elements that make up mouthfeel are much harder to measure. How does one quantify a pretzel's hardness, a french fry's crispness? Food technologists are now conducting basic research in rheology, the branch of physics that examines the flow and deformation of materials. A number of companies sell sophisticated devices that attempt to measure mouthfeel. The TA.XT2i Texture Analyzer, produced by the Texture Technologies Corporation, of Scarsdale, New York, performs calculations based on data derived from as many as 250 separate probes. It is essentially a mechanical mouth. It gauges the most important rheological properties of a food— bounce, creep, breaking point, density, crunchiness, chewiness, gumminess, lumpiness, rubberiness, springiness, slipperiness, smoothness, softness, wetness, juiciness, spreadability, springback, and tackiness.

Some of the most important advances in flavor manufacturing are now occurring in the field of biotechnology. Complex flavors are being made using enzyme reactions, fermentation, and fungal and tissue cultures. All the flavors created by these methods—including the ones being synthesized by fungi—are considered natural flavors by the FDA. The new enzyme-based processes are responsible for extremely true-to-life dairy flavors. One company now offers not just butter flavor but also fresh creamy butter, cheesy butter, milky butter, savory melted butter, and super-concentrated butter flavor, in liquid or powder form. The development of new fermentation techniques, along with new techniques for heating mixtures of sugar and amino acids, have led to the creation of much more realistic meat flavors.

The McDonald's Corporation most likely drew on these advances when it eliminated beef tallow from its french fries. The company will not reveal the exact origin of the natural flavor added to its fries. In response to inquiries from *Vegetarian Journal,* however, McDonald's did acknowledge that its fries derive some of their characteristic flavor from "an animal source." Beef is the probable source, although other meats cannot be ruled out. In France, for example, fries are sometimes cooked in duck fat or horse tallow. 28

Other popular fast foods derive their flavor from unexpected ingredients. McDonald's Chicken McNuggets contain beef extracts, as does Wendy's Grilled Chicken Sandwich. Burger King's BK Broiler Chicken Breast Patty contains "natural smoke flavor." A firm called Red Arrow Products specializes in smoke flavor, which is added to barbecue sauces, snack foods, and processed meats. Red Arrow manufactures natural smoke flavor by charring sawdust and capturing the aroma chemicals released into the air. The smoke is captured in water and then bottled, so that other companies can sell food that seems to have been cooked over a fire. 29

The Vegetarian Legal Action Network recently petitioned the FDA to issue new labeling requirements for foods that contain natural flavors. The group wants food processors to list the basic origins of their flavors on their labels. At the moment vegetarians often have no way of knowing whether a 30 flavor additive contains beef, pork, poultry, or shellfish. One of the most widely used color additives—whose presence is often hidden by the phrase "color added"—violates a number of religious dietary restrictions, may cause allergic reactions in susceptible people, and comes from an unusual source. Cochineal extract (also known as carmine or carminic acid) is made from the desiccated bodies of female *Dactylopius coccus Costa*, a small insect harvested mainly in Peru and the Canary Islands. The bug feeds on red cactus berries, and color from the berries accumulates in the females and their unhatched larvae. The insects are collected, dried, and ground into a pigment. It takes about seventy thousand of them to produce a pound of carmine, which is used to make processed foods look pink, red, or purple. Dannon strawberry yogurt gets its color from carmine, and so do many frozen fruit bars, candies, and fruit fillings, and Ocean Spray pink-grapefruit juice drink.

In a meeting room at IFF, Brian Grainger let me sample some of the company's flavors. It was an unusual taste test— there was no food to taste. Grainger is a senior flavorist at IFF, a soft-spoken chemist with graying hair, an English accent, and a fondness for understatement. He could easily be mistaken for a British diplomat or the owner of a West End brasserie with two Michelin stars. Like many in the flavor industry, he has an Old World, old-fashioned sensibility. When I suggested that IFF's policy of secrecy and discretion was out of step with our mass-marketing, brand-conscious, self-promoting age, and that the company should put its own logo on the countless products that bear its flavors, instead of allowing other companies to enjoy the consumer loyalty and affection inspired by those flavors, Granger politely disagreed, assuring me that such a thing would never be done. In the absence of public credit or acclaim, the small and secretive fraternity of flavor chemists praise one another's work. By analyzing the flavor formula of a product, Grainger can often tell which of his counterparts at a rival firm devised it. Whenever he walks down a supermarket aisle, he takes a quiet pleasure in seeing the well-known foods that contain his flavors.

Grainger had brought a dozen small glass bottles from the 32
lab. After he opened each bottle, I dipped a fragrance-testing filter into it—a long white strip of paper designed to absorb aroma chemicals without producing off notes. Before placing each strip of paper in front of my nose, I closed my eyes. Then I inhaled deeply, and one food after another was conjured from the glass bottles. I smelled fresh cherries, black olives, sautéed onions, and shrimp. Grainger's most remarkable creation took me by surprise. After closing my eyes, I suddenly smelled a grilled hamburger. The aroma was uncanny, almost miraculous—as if someone in the room were flipping burgers on a hot grill. But when I opened my eyes, I saw just a narrow strip of white paper and a flavorist with a grin.

For Study and Discussion

QUESTIONS FOR RESPONSE

1. What are some of the implications of the changes in American eating habits that Schlosser describes in his opening paragraph?
2. What is your personal reaction to learning so much about the way our food in the United States is processed and flavored?

QUESTIONS ABOUT PURPOSE

1. This essay is a chapter from Schlosser's book *Fast Food Nation*. What purpose do you think he might have had in writing a book with that title?
2. Why does he want his readers to know more about the way large food corporations flavor processed food?

QUESTIONS ABOUT AUDIENCE

1. What experience with fast food does Schlosser assume most Americans have? How justified are his assumptions?
2. This essay first appeared in the *Atlantic,* a magazine with a

relatively small circulation drawn from well-educated readers, and then appeared in book form. Why could readers like that be important for Schlosser to reach?

QUESTIONS ABOUT STRATEGIES

1. What do you think Schlosser accomplishes by using statistics (paragraphs 1 and 16) and lists (paragraphs 8, 17, and 20) to develop his explanations about how food flavors are created?
2. What does Schlosser tell you about his research and his methods in order to establish his credibility?

QUESTIONS FOR DISCUSSION

1. What do you think might be some of the consequences of ingesting the multiple chemicals that food companies use to make their products appeal to customers?
2. How could the practices Schlosser described be controlled? Should they be? Why?

Ann Beattie was born in 1947 in Washington, D.C., and was educated at American University and the University of Connecticut. She has taught writing at the University of Virginia, Harvard University, and Northwestern University. Beattie first honed her craft writing short stories for the *New Yorker*. These and other stories were gathered into collections such as *Distortions* (1976), *The Burning House* (1982), *What Was Mine* (1991), and *Park City: New and Selected Stories* (1998). Her novels include *Falling in Place* (1980), *Another You* (1995), and *The Doctor's House* (2002). In "Janus," reprinted from *Where You'll Find Me, and Other Stories* (1986), Beattie tells the story of a woman whose lucky talisman, a bowl, symbolizes her complicated emotional life.

Janus

T HE BOWL WAS PERFECT. Perhaps it was not what you'd se-   1
lect if you faced a shelf of bowls, and not the sort of thing that would inevitably attract a lot of attention at a crafts fair, yet it had real presence. It was as predictably admired as a mutt who has no reason to suspect he might be funny. Just such a dog, in fact, was often brought out (and in) along with the bowl.

Andrea was a real estate agent, and when she thought that   2
some prospective buyers might be dog lovers, she would drop off her dog at the same time she placed the bowl in the house that was up for sale. She would put a dish of water in the kitchen for Mondo, take his squeaking plastic frog out of her purse and drop it on the floor. He would pounce delightedly, just as he did every day at home, batting around his

favorite toy. The bowl usually sat on a coffee table, though recently she had displayed it on top of a pine blanket chest and on a lacquered table. It was once placed on a cherry table beneath a Bonnard still life, where it held its own.

Everyone who has purchased a house or who has wanted 3 to sell a house must be familiar with some of the tricks used to convince a buyer that the house is quite special: a fire in the fireplace in early evening; jonquils in a pitcher on the kitchen counter, where no one ordinarily has space to put flowers; perhaps the slight aroma of spring, made by a single drop of scent vaporizing from a lamp bulb.

The wonderful thing about the bowl, Andrea thought, 4 was that it was both subtle and noticeable—a paradox of a bowl. Its glaze was the color of cream and seemed to glow no matter what light it was placed in. There were a few bits of color in it—tiny geometric flashes—and some of these were tinged with flecks of silver. They were as mysterious as cells seen under a microscope; it was difficult not to study them, because they shimmered, flashing for a split second, and then resumed their shape. Something about the colors and their random placement suggested motion. People who liked country furniture always commented on the bowl, but then it turned out that people who felt comfortable with Biedermeier loved it just as much. But the bowl was not at all ostentatious, or even so noticeable that anyone would suspect that it had been put in place deliberately. They might notice the height of the ceiling on first entering a room, and only when their eye moved down from that, or away from the refraction of sunlight on a pale wall, would they see the bowl. Then they would go immediately to it and comment. Yet they always faltered when they tried to say something. Perhaps it was because they were in the house for a serious reason, not to notice some object.

Once, Andrea got a call from a woman who had not put in 5 an offer on a house she had shown her. That bowl, she said— would it be possible to find out where the owners had bought that beautiful bowl? Andrea pretended that she did not know what the woman was referring to. A bowl, somewhere in the house? Oh, on a table under the window. Yes, she would ask, of course. She let a couple of days pass, then called back to say that the bowl had been a present and the people did not know where it had been purchased.

When the bowl was not being taken from house to house, 6 it sat on Andrea's coffee table at home. She didn't keep it carefully wrapped (although she transported it that way, in a box); she kept it on the table, because she liked to see it. It was large enough so that it didn't seem fragile, or particularly vulnerable if anyone sideswiped the table or Mondo blundered into it at play. She had asked her husband to please not drop his house key in it. It was meant to be empty.

When her husband first noticed the bowl, he had peered 7 into it and smiled briefly. He always urged her to buy things she liked. In recent years, both of them had acquired many things to make up for all the lean years when they were graduate students, but now that they had been comfortable for quite a while, the pleasure of new possessions dwindled. Her husband had pronounced the bowl "pretty," and he had turned away without picking it up to examine it. He had no more interest in the bowl than she had in his new Leica.

She was sure that the bowl brought her luck. Bids were of- 8 ten put in on houses where she had displayed the bowl. Sometimes the owners, who were always asked to be away or to step outside when the house was being shown, didn't even know that the bowl had been in their house. Once—she could not imagine how—she left it behind, and then she was so afraid that something might have happened to it that she rushed back to the house and sighed with relief when the woman owner opened the door. The bowl, Andrea explained—she had purchased a bowl and set it on the chest for safekeeping while she toured the house with the prospective buyers, and she . . . She felt like rushing past the frowning woman and seizing her bowl. The owner stepped aside, and it was only when Andrea ran to the chest that the lady glanced her a little strangely. In the few seconds before Andrea picked up the bowl, she realized that the owner must have just seen that it had been perfectly placed, that the sunlight struck the bluer part of it. Her pitcher had been moved to the far side of the chest, and the bowl predominated. All the way home, Andrea wondered how she could have left the bowl behind. It was like leaving a friend at an outing—just walking off. Sometimes there were stories in the paper about families forgetting a child somewhere and driving to the next city. Andrea had only gone a mile down the road before she remembered.

In time, she dreamed of the bowl. Twice, in a waking 9 dream—early in the morning, between sleep and a last nap before rising—she had a clear vision of it. It came into sharp focus and startled her for a moment—the same bowl she looked at every day.

She had a very profitable year selling real estate. Word 10 spread, and she had more clients than she felt comfortable with. She had the foolish thought that if only the bowl were an animate object she could thank it. There were times when she wanted to talk to her husband about the bowl. He was a stockbroker, and sometimes told people that he was fortunate to be married to a woman who had such a fine aesthetic sense and yet could also function in the real world. They were a lot alike, really—they had agreed on that. They were both quiet people—reflective, slow to make value judgments, but almost intractable once they had come to a conclusion. They both liked details, but while ironies attracted her, he was more impatient and dismissive when matters became many sided or unclear. But they both knew this; it was the kind of thing they could talk about when they were alone in the car together, coming home from a party or after a weekend with friends. But she never talked to him about the bowl. When they were at dinner, exchanging their news of the day, or while they lay in bed at night listening to the stereo and murmuring sleepy disconnections, she was often tempted to come right out and say that she thought that the bowl in the living room, the cream-colored bowl, was responsible for her success. But she didn't say it. She couldn't begin to explain it.

Sometimes in the morning, she would look at him and feel guilty that she had such a constant secret.

Could it be that she had some deeper connection with the 11 bowl—a relationship of some kind? She corrected her thinking: how could she imagine such a thing, when she was a human being and it was a bowl? It was ridiculous. Just think of how people lived together and loved each other . . . But was that always so clear, always a relationship? She was confused by these thoughts, but they remained in her mind. There was something within her now, something real, that she never talked about.

The bowl was a mystery, even to her. It was frustrating, be- 12 cause her involvement with the bowl contained a steady sense of unrequited good fortune; it would have been easier to respond if some sort of demand were made in return. But that only happened in fairy tales. The bowl was just a bowl. She did not believe that for one second. What she believed was that it was something she loved.

In the past, she had sometimes talked to her husband 13 about a new property she was about to buy or sell—confiding some clever strategy she had devised to persuade owners who seemed ready to sell. Now she stopped doing that, for all her strategies involved the bowl. She became more deliberate with the bowl, and more possessive. She put it in houses only when no one was there, and removed it when she left the house. Instead of just moving a pitcher or a dish, she would remove all the other objects from a table. She had to force herself to handle them carefully, because she didn't really care about them. She just wanted them out of sight.

She wondered how the situation would end. As with a 14 lover, there was no exact scenario of how matters would come to a close. Anxiety became the operative force. It would be irrelevant if the lover rushed into someone else's arms, or wrote her a note and departed to another city. The horror was the possibility of the disappearance. That was what mattered.

She would get up at night and look at the bowl. It never   15
occurred to her that she might break it. She washed and
dried it without anxiety, and she moved it often, from coffee
table to mahogany corner table or wherever, without fearing
an accident. It was clear that she would not be the one who
would do anything to the bowl. The bowl was only handled
by her, set safely on one surface or another; it was not very
likely that anyone would break it. A bowl was a poor conduc-
tor of electricity: it would not be hit by lightning. Yet the idea
of damage persisted. She did not think beyond that—to what
her life would be without the bowl. She only continued to
fear that some accident would happen. Why not, in a world
where people set plants where they did not belong, so that
visitors touring a house would be fooled into thinking that
dark corners got sunlight—a world full of tricks?

She had first seen the bowl several years earlier, at a crafts   16
fair she had visited half in secret, with her lover. He had
urged her to buy the bowl. She didn't *need* any more things,
she told him. But she had been drawn to the bowl, and they
had lingered near it. Then she went on to the next booth,
and he came up behind her, tapping the rim against her
shoulder as she ran her fingers over a wood carving. "You're
still insisting that I buy that?" she said. "No," he said. "I
bought it for you." He had bought her other things before
this—things she liked more, at first—the child's ebony-and-
turquoise ring that fitted her little finger; the wooden box,
long and thin, beautifully dovetailed, that she used to hold
paper clips; the soft gray sweater with a pouch pocket. It was
his idea that when he could not be there to hold her hand she
could hold her own—clasp her hands inside the lone pocket
that stretched across the front. But in time she became more
attached to the bowl than to any of his other presents. She
tried to talk herself out of it. She owned other things that
were more striking or valuable. It wasn't an object whose
beauty jumped out at you; a lot of people must have passed it
by before the two of them saw it that day.

Her lover had said that she was always too slow to know   17
what she really loved. Why continue with her life the way it

was? Why be two-faced, he asked her. He had made the first
move toward her. When she would not decide in his favor,
would not change her life and come to him, he asked her
what made her think she could have it both ways. And then
he made the last move and left. It was a decision meant to
break her will, to shatter her intransigent ideas about honoring previous commitments.

Time passed. Alone in the living room at night, she often   18
looked at the bowl sitting on the table, still and safe,
unilluminated. In its way, it was perfect: the world cut in half,
deep and smoothly empty. Near the rim, even in dim light,
the eye moved toward one small flash of blue, a vanishing
point on the horizon.

COMMENT ON "JANUS"

The story focuses on a bowl that has taken on an almost magical quality for its owner, a successful real estate agent. The
bowl is never actually described; the reader learns only that
it's cream-colored with irridescent flecks. Its owner sees the
bowl as simple but perfect, a subtle but tangible presence in
her life and an important object in her home. She feels that it
brings her luck, since when she puts it on display in houses
she is showing to clients, those houses usually sell. Gradually
she becomes obsessed with the bowl, wants to protect it, see
that no harm comes to it. It's a talisman for her. She doesn't
want it used, only displayed. She feels it was meant to be
empty.

The title of the story, "Janus," a reference to the Roman
deity with two faces, one facing forward, one backward, is
puzzling until almost the end of the story. The connection
between it and the bowl emerges only in the next to the last
paragraph when the woman's lover, who gave her the bowl,
tells her she is two-faced to want to continue her affair with
him but also to stay in her comfortable and placid, but essentially sterile, marriage. Her lover refuses that arrangement
and leaves. The crux of the story seems to come in the last

paragraph: "Alone in the living room at night, she often looked at the bowl sitting on the table, still and safe, unilluminated. In its way, it was perfect: the world cut in half, deep and smoothly empty." It's a powerful image. Does it refer to her marriage? Maybe. Only the author could say for sure.

Cause and Effect as a Writing Strategy

1. Anna Quindlen has a sweeping topic in her essay "How Reading Changed My Life," but you could write something similar on a much narrower scale. For example, if you're a returning student who has come late to computers, you could write about how computers have changed your life. If LASIK surgery freed you from having to wear glasses, you could write about how that operation changed your life. If you have moved to the United States from another, very different culture, you could write about a specific way in which that move has changed your life. You could also pick out some significant way in which your life has changed in recent years and, with the help of your instructor and your fellow students, work out a closely focused topic of this kind. Your audience could be your classmates, a chat room, or the newsletter of an organization you belong to. Try to hold your project to seven hundred words or less.

2. In the last year or two, many newspaper and magazine articles and two or three books about the food industry, such as Schlosser's *Fast Food Nation,* have appeared. In them the authors have cited the rising rates of obesity in the United States, pointing out the health risks the trend poses and what the consequences are likely to be for future generations. Write an essay about the menus and ambiance of some of the restaurants you and your friends frequent near your campus or in your hometown that feature high-calorie food and drinks, many of which contain the flavor-enhancing chemicals Schlosser describes in "Why McDonald's Fries Taste So Good." Do these restaurants *cause* obesity? What do you think the effect would be if they were required to list the number of calories in each item on their menus? Would such a requirement be justified? You could write this essay for the college newspaper or post it on a web log to which you contribute. Give it some flavor-enhancing details.

3. Pick out some fairly recent innovation that you've incorporated into your life and write about the effects it has had on your day-to-day routine. Some examples might be a global positioning system either for your car or as a locating device in some outdoor activity, a DVD player (portable or at home), a wireless laptop computer, a cell phone with a visual screen, or a top-of-the-line digital camera. What have been the effects for you? Have there been drawbacks, such as difficult instructions or trouble keeping the batteries charged? What would you say is your net satisfaction from having purchased this device? Write for an audience of other owners of the device, either among your classmates or for a chat room.

4. Write an essay for your classmates telling why you have chosen the profession you currently plan to go into. What are your reasons? Why do you think it will be rewarding? What caused you to choose this profession? Whom do you know in the profession, and how have their experiences affected your choice? What kind of training and education will be necessary, and what sacrifices, both financial and personal, might be involved? What kind of conflicts, if any, do you think you might experience between your personal and professional lives? What effects do you think those conflicts might have on you?

5. Movies, on and off television, play a major role in modern culture, yet no one seems to have a clear idea of how much influence they have on young people. Write a short essay, perhaps for the movie section of your local newspaper, in which you speculate about the influence a very popular movie or kind of movie has on the under-twenty-one viewers who are a major market for Hollywood. Mention specific movies and discuss ways in which they could influence young viewers.

   As an alternative topic, consider this. American movies, particularly action movies with stars like Bruce Willis and Tom Cruise, are extremely popular in other countries. What effect do you think such movies—name some you've seen recently—may have on the image of the

United States abroad? If you're a student from another country, draw on your own experience in seeing American movies and discuss how they colored your opinions.

6. For an editorial or feature article in your local or campus newspaper, write an account of an environmental problem you have heard about in your community or your state. Such a problem might be a toxic waste dump close to a neighborhood, a leaky natural gas or oil pipeline that caused hazards, or the accumulation in the walls of a school of a substance that made students and teachers ill. Do some research in the files of your local paper or on the Web to find out the causes of the problem and how long it existed before someone noticed. Conclude by speculating what might be done to prevent such problems from developing in the future.

PERSUASION
AND
ARGUMENT

Intuitively, you already know a good deal about **argument.**
For one thing, you use it all the time as you go through the
day talking or writing and making claims and giving reasons.
But you also live surrounded by arguments. They come not
only from people you talk to and deal with in everyday personal or business situations, but also from television, radio,
newspapers, subway posters, billboards, and signs and brochures of all kinds. Any time someone is trying to persuade
you to buy something, contribute money, take action, make a
judgment, or change your mind about anything, that person
is arguing with you.

This introduction offers an overview of some important argument theory, tips about the kinds of argument that you can make, points to keep in mind as you write arguments, and some tips about pitfalls you should avoid. Remember that what we offer here barely scrapes the surface of the complex topic of argument and persuasion. If you want to learn more about argument theory and about writing good arguments, you can find several useful books in your college bookstore or through an on-line book seller.

KINDS OF ARGUMENTS

Traditionally, arguments fall into three categories: Logical, Emotional, and Ethical. *Logical arguments* appeal to the reason; they depend primarily on evidence and logic. *Emotional arguments* appeal to the feelings; they depend heavily on images and connotative language. *Ethical arguments* appeal on the basis of the writer or speaker's character. In practice, of course, most writers and speakers combine all of these appeals when they try to persuade or convince their audiences. All the writers in this section combine reason and emotion, but some appeal more strongly to the feelings, depending heavily on imagery and figurative language, while others try to make a strong rational appeal, citing historical evidence and giving examples. And all of them use various strategies to give readers the impression that they're ethical: that is, that they have integrity and character.

It's important to remember that rational arguments aren't necessarily better than emotional arguments. Some occasions call for appeals to pride, loyalty, and compassion, for using vivid metaphors and images, and for strong language that touches the passions. When someone is speaking at a political rally or at a graduation or award ceremony, the audience is probably more interested in stories and images than in logical analysis and data. The kind of writing done for such occasions is called *ceremonial discourse,* and often it's successful precisely because it is emotional. The speech by Martin Luther King, Jr., "I Have a Dream," fits into this category.

When you write arguments for your college courses or in your work, however, you should plan on appealing primarily to reason and on providing strong evidence and clear examples. Your writing situation is *not* ceremonial; you're now writing to convince a thoughtful and skeptical audience, one that expects you to make a good case for your position. Again, take your cue from courtroom lawyers: state your case and prove it.

Notice that the eight essays in this section are arranged in pairs. Each pair treats a single topic, but the two writers take a different point of view on that topic. The topic of the essays by Martin Luther King, Jr., and Eric Liu is racial discrimination. The essays by Barbara Kingsolver and Barbara Dafoe Whitehead focus on child-rearing and family values. The topic of the essays by Joan Acocella and Harold Bloom is the popular Harry Potter series of children's books. The paired essays by Francine Prose and Natalie Angier deal with human nature, people's capacity for good and evil.

PURPOSE

When you hear the term *argument,* you may automatically connect it with controversy and conflict. That's not necessarily the case, however, particularly in academic writing. There—and at other times too—you may have many purposes other than winning a dispute.

Sometimes you may argue *to support a cause.* For instance, you might write an editorial in favor of subsidized child care on your campus. You may also argue *to urge people to action* or *to promote change*—for instance, when you write a campaign brochure or a petition to reduce student fees. Sometimes you may argue *to refute a theory*—perhaps a history paper claiming that antislavery sentiment was not the chief cause of the Civil War. You can also write arguments *to arouse sympathy*—for better laws against child abuse, for example; *to stimulate interest*—for more participation in student government; *to win agreement*—to get condominium residents to agree to abolish regulations against pets; and *to provoke anger*—to arouse outrage against a proposed tax. And, of course, you might incorporate several of these purposes into one piece of writing.

AUDIENCE

When you write arguments, you must think about your readers. Who are they, what do they know, what do they believe, and what do they expect? Unless you can answer these questions at least partially, you cannot expect to write an effective argument. There simply is no such thing as a good argument in the abstract, separated from its purpose and its audience. Any argument you write is a good one only if it does what you want it to do with the particular readers who are going to read it. So by no later than the second draft of any argument you write, you need to know why you are writing and for whom you are writing.

If you are trying to choose an audience for your paper, ask yourself the following questions:

1. Who is likely to be interested in what I am writing about?
2. What groups could make the changes I'm arguing for?

When you know the answers to these questions, you can direct your writing to readers to whom you have something to say—otherwise, there's little point in writing.

Once you have settled on your audience, ask yourself these questions:

1. What do my readers already know about my topic?
   a. What experience and knowledge do they have that I can use?
   b. Can I use specialized language? Should I?
   c. How can I teach them something they want to know?
2. How do my readers feel about my topic?
   a. What shared values can I appeal to?
   b. What prejudices or preconceptions must I pay attention to?

    c. What kind of approach will work best with them—casual or formal, objective or personal, factual or anecdotal?

3. What questions will my readers want me to answer?

You may find it especially useful to write out the answers to that last question.

When you have worked your way through all of these questions, either as a brainstorming exercise or in a prewriting group discussion, you'll have a stronger sense of who your readers are and how you can appeal to them.

STRATEGIES

When you are writing arguments, you can use a wide range of strategies, but most of them will fall into one of these three categories: *emotional appeal, logical appeal,* or *ethical appeal.*

Emotional Appeal

You argue by emotional or nonlogical appeal when you appeal to the emotions, to the senses, and to personal biases or prejudices. You incorporate such appeals into your writing when you use *connotative language* that elicits feelings or reactions—words like *melancholy, crimson, slovenly,* or *villainous.* Usually you're also using nonlogical appeal when you use *figurative language*—metaphors, allusions, or colorful phrases that make the reader draw comparisons or make associations. Phrases like "environmental cancer" or "industrial Goliath" evoke images and comparisons and play on the emotions.

Creating a tone is also a nonlogical strategy and an important one. The tone you choose can exert a powerful force on your readers, catching their attention, ingratiating you into their favor, conveying an air of authority and confidence. You can establish a friendly, close-to-your-reader tone by using contractions and the pronouns *I, we,* and *you.* You can create a relaxed tone by bringing in humor or personal anecdote, or you can give your writing an air of authority and detachment by avoiding personal pronouns and writing as objectively as possible.

All writers in this group of arguments use emotional appeal, but those who rely on it most heavily are Martin Luther King, Jr., and Francine Prose. Both are writing on strongly emotional topics, King on racism and Prose on murder. Barbara Kingsolver and Natalie Angier also use emotionally appealing examples, but their language is less connotative.

Logical Appeal

You employ logical or rational strategies when you appeal mainly to your readers' intelligence, reason, and common sense. Your chief strategies are:

> Making claims and supporting them
> Giving testimony
> Citing authorities
> Arguing from precedent
> Drawing comparisons and analogies
> Arguing from cause and effect

Eric Liu argues logically when he cites the past experience of minorities in the United States to support his claim that minorities can succeed in this country. Natalie Angier's argument in "Of Altruism, Heroism, and Evolution's Gifts" starts out as an emotional appeal when she tells the stories of the firefighters who sacrificed their lives in the burning World Trade Center towers, but she moves into a more rational appeal as she gives testimony from several scientists to support her thesis about altruism and humanitarianism. Barbara Dafoe Whitehead makes a rational case that fathers are important to stable families, but there are also strong emotional undertones to her argument.

Ethical Appeal

Ethical appeal is the most subtle and often the most powerful because it comes from the character and evident expertise of the author, not directly from reason or emotion. All the writers in this section rely on their ethical appeal, but it works most effectively for Martin Luther King, Jr., because it rests on his record as a fighter for civil rights and on his having won the Nobel Peace Prize for his work. Joan Acocella's essay on the Harry Potter books has strong ethical appeal because it's evident that she understands and appreciates the generations of myths and legends that underlie the appeal of the books.

Eric Liu's ethical appeal comes from his own experience and that of his family, and Barbara Dafoe Whitehead's comes from her calm tone and obvious concern for children. Natalie Angier establishes her ethical appeal by her close knowledge of others' scientific work on the instinct for altruism and her own status as a major science writer. As a novice writer, you're not yet in a position to convince through your reputation, but if can you show your readers that you're knowledgeable, thoughtful, and have done your homework, you're likely to succeed with your arguments.

USING PERSUASION AND ARGUMENT IN PARAGRAPHS

Here are two persuasive paragraphs. The first is written by a professional writer and is followed by an analysis. The second is written by a student and is followed by questions.

NICHOLAS LEMANN
The Promised Land

During the first half of the twentieth century, it was at least possible to think of race as a Southern issue. The South, and only the South, had to contend with the contradiction between the national creed of democracy and the local reality of

Until 1950 one could think only the South had race problems

a caste system; consequently the South lacked the optimism and confidence that characterized the country as a whole. The great black migration made race a national issue in the second half of the century—an integral part of the politics, the social thought, and the organization of everyday life in the United States. Not coincidentally, by the time the migration was over, the country had acquired a good measure of the tragic sense that had previously been confined to the South. Race relations stood out nearly everywhere as the one thing most plainly wrong in America, the flawed portion of the great tableau, the chief generator of doubt about how essentially noble the whole national enterprise really was.

After 1950 black migration to North

Had to realize racism a national problem

Comment In this paragraph from the first chapter of Nicholas Lemann's book *The Promised Land*, the author lays out one of the central arguments of the book: the migration of blacks from the South to the North after World War II forced Americans to realize that racial discrimination and its consequences constituted a national problem and were not simply remnants of the South's defeat in the Civil War. They could no longer claim that America was a great democracy with liberty and justice for all. Once hundreds of thousands of blacks were living in the North, the struggle for equal rights and fair treatment began to permeate the political, economic, and social life of the whole nation. Lemann is particularly eloquent in the last sentence when he says "Race relations stood out . . . as . . . the flawed portion of the great tableau, the chief generator of doubt about how essentially noble the whole national enterprise really was."

JIM F. SALOMAN
Genetic Engineering

We need to regulate experiments in genetic engineering. Scientists can reconfigure the genetic makeup of an organism. They can literally change life. But without appropriate controls, such tampering can lead to unpredictable and violent results. What would happen if scientists were able to resurrect an extinct species that would reverse the order of natural selection? And what would happen if they produced a superior organism that destroyed the balance of our present ecosystem? And what would happen if they started "creating" people for particular tasks? They could design aggressive men to fight wars and passive women to breed children. Whole new social classes could be created, some genetically advanced, some genetically restricted. If we are to protect the rights of individuals and prevent evolutionary chaos, we must create a thoughtful public policy that protects us from our own scientific experiments.

1. How might Saloman go on to develop this paragraph into a full-length persuasive essay?
2. Saloman gives several examples of what he calls "unpredictable and violent results." How would you evaluate the persuasive value of the several generalizations that he gives as examples of such results?

PERSUASION AND ARGUMENT
Points to Remember

1. To argue well, you have to know your audience and your purpose. Do you understand your audience's interests, their backgrounds, and what questions they might have? Do you know what you want to accomplish with this particular group of readers? It's useful to write out the answers to both of these questions before you start.

2. Understand the three principal kinds of persuasive appeals.

   - Appeal to reason: Emphasizes logic, evidence, authority, cause and effect, precedent, and comparison and analogy.

   - Appeal to emotion: Emphasizes feelings, the senses, personal biases, connotative language, and images and metaphor.

   - Appeal from integrity and character: Emphasizes the writer's competence, experience, and reputation.

   The most persuasive writers usually combine elements from all three kinds of appeals.

3. Construct your arguments as a lawyer would construct a case to present to a jury: state your claim and back it up with evidence and reason, but, when appropriate, also use metaphor and connotation.

4. Always assume your audience is intelligent, if perhaps uninformed about some particulars. Be respectful; avoid a superior tone.

5. Argue responsibly.

   - Don't overstate your claim.

   - Don't oversimplify complex issues.

   - Support your claims with specific details and evidence.

In this public service advertisement created by the Leo Burnett advertising company, PALM, or Physicians Against Land Mines, presents its argument about the death, dismemberment, and disability caused by land mines. The text below Emina Uzicanin's missing leg describes how as a child playing on the outskirts of Sarajevo, she stepped on a land mine. In addition to this emotional story, the text offers other compelling evidence: "every 22 minutes another civilian is killed or maimed by a land mine"; "there are over 60 million unexploded land mines in nearly 70 countries." Select another public service advertising campaign—such as those sponsored by MADD (Mothers Against Drunk Driving) or ADL (Anti-Defamation League)—and analyze the visual and textual features that make it a persuasive argument.

A Debate About Racism

MARTIN LUTHER KING, JR.

Martin Luther King, Jr. (1929–1968), was born
in Atlanta, Georgia, and was educated at More-
house College, Crozer Theological Seminary, and
Boston University. Ordained a Baptist minister in
his father's church in 1947, King soon became involved in civil rights activities in the South. In
1957 he founded the Southern Christian Leader-
ship Conference and established himself as America's most prominent spokesman for nonviolent
racial integration. In 1963 he was named *Time*
magazine's Man of the Year; in 1964 he was given
the Nobel Peace Prize. In 1968 he was assassinated in Memphis, Tennessee. His writing includes *Letter from Birmingham Jail* (1963), *Why
We Can't Wait* (1964), and *Where Do We Go from
Here: Chaos or Community?* (1967). "I Have a
Dream" is the famous speech King delivered at
the Lincoln Memorial at the end of the March on
Washington in 1963 to commemorate the one
hundredth anniversary of the Emancipation Proclamation. King argues that realization of the
dream of freedom for all American citizens is long
overdue.

I Have a Dream

F IVE SCORE YEARS ago, a great American, in whose sym-   1
bolic shadow we stand, signed the Emancipation Proclamation. This momentous decree came as a great beacon
light of hope to millions of Negro slaves who had been

seared in the flames of withering injustice. It came as a joy-*nice* ous daybreak to end the long night of captivity. *metaphor*

But one hundred years later, we must face the tragic fact 2 that the Negro is still not free. One hundred years later, the life of the Negro is still sadly crippled by the manacles of seg- regation and the chains of discrimination. One hundred years *effective* later, the Negro lives on a lonely island of poverty in the *word* midst of a vast ocean of material prosperity. One hundred *choice* years later, the Negro is still languishing in the corners of American society and finds himself an exile in his own land. So we have come here today to dramatize an appalling con- dition.

In a sense we have come to our nation's Capitol to cash a 3 check. When the architects of our republic wrote the mag- nificent words of the Constitution and the Declaration of

> *There will be neither rest nor tranquility in America until the Negro is granted his citizenship rights.*

Independence, they were signing a promissory note to which every American was to fall heir. This note was a promise that all men would be guaranteed the unalienable rights of life, liberty, and the pursuit of happiness.

It is obvious today that America has defaulted on this 4 promissory note insofar as her citizens of color are con- *strong* cerned. Instead of honoring this sacred obligation, America *points* has given the Negro people a bad check; a check which has come back marked "insufficient funds." But we refuse to be- lieve that the bank of justice is bankrupt. We refuse to believe that there are insufficient funds in the great vaults of oppor- tunity of this nation. So we have come to cash this check—a check that will give us upon demand the riches of freedom and the security of justice. We have also come to this

I like his words

hallowed spot to remind America of the fierce urgency of *now*. This is no time to engage in the luxury of cooling off or to take the tranquilizing drug of gradualism. *Now* is the time to make real the promises of Democracy. *Now* is the time to rise from the dark and desolate valley of segregation to the sunlit path of racial justice. *Now* is the time to open the doors of opportunity to all of God's children. *Now* is the time to lift our nation from the quicksands of racial injustice to the solid rock of brotherhood.

reasons

It would be fatal for the nation to overlook the urgency of the moment and to underestimate the determination of the Negro. This sweltering summer of the Negro's legitimate discontent will not pass until there is an invigorating autumn of freedom and equality. 1963 is not an end, but a beginning. Those who hope that the Negro needed to blow off steam and will now be content will have a rude awakening if the nation returns to business as usual. There will be neither rest nor tranquility in America until the Negro is granted his citizenship rights. The whirlwinds of revolt will continue to shake the foundations of our nation until the bright day of justice emerges.

But there is something I must say to my people who stand on the warm threshold which leads into the palace of justice. In the process of gaining our rightful place we must not be guilty of wrongful deeds. Let us not seek to satisfy our thirst for freedom by drinking from the cup of bitterness and hatred. We must forever conduct our struggle on the high plane of dignity and discipline. We must not allow our creative protest to degenerate into physical violence. Again and again we must rise to the majestic heights of meeting physical force with soul force. The marvelous new militancy which has engulfed the Negro community must not lead us to a distrust of all white people, for many of our white brothers, as evidenced by their presence here today, have come to realize that their destiny is tied up with our destiny and their freedom is inextricably bound to our freedom. We cannot walk alone.

militancy =)

snap — great opinion

And as we walk, we must make the pledge that we shall   7
march ahead. We cannot turn back. There are those who are
asking the devotees of civil rights, "When will you be
satisfied?" We can never be satisfied as long as the Negro is
the victim of the unspeakable horrors of police brutality. We
can never be satisfied as long as our bodies, heavy with the fatigue of travel, cannot gain lodging in the motels of the high-
ways and the hotels of the cities. We cannot be satisfied as
long as the Negro's basic mobility is from a smaller ghetto to
a larger one. We can never be satisfied as long as a Negro in
Mississippi cannot vote and a Negro in New York believes he
has nothing for which to vote. No, no, we are not satisfied,
and we will not be satisfied until justice rolls down like waters
and righteousness like a mighty stream.

waterfall

I am not unmindful that some of you have come here out   8
of great trials and tribulations. Some of you have come fresh
from narrow jail cells. Some of you have come from areas
where your quest for freedom left you battered by the storms
of persecution and staggered by the winds of police brutality.
You have been the veterans of creative suffering. Continue to
work with the faith that unearned suffering is redemptive.

Go back to Mississippi, go back to Alabama, go back to   9
South Carolina, go back to Georgia, go back to Louisiana, go
back to the slums and ghettoes of our northern cities, knowing that somehow this situation can and will be changed. Let
us not wallow in the valley of despair.

I say to you today, my friends, that in spite of the   10
difficulties and frustrations of the moment I still have a
dream. It is a dream deeply rooted in the American dream.

I have a dream that one day this nation will rise up and live   11
out the true meaning of its creed: "We hold these truths to
be self-evident; that all men are created equal."

I have a dream that one day on the red hills of Georgia the   12
sons of former slaves and the sons of former slaveowners will
be able to sit down together at the table of brotherhood.

I have a dream that the state of Mississippi, a desert state   13
sweltering with the heat of injustice and oppression, will be
transformed into an oasis of freedom and justice.

I have a dream that my four little children will one day live   14
in a nation where they will not be judged by the color of their
skin but by the content of their character.

I have a dream today.   15

I have a dream that the state of Alabama, whose gover-   16
nor's lips are presently dripping with the words of interposi-
tion and nullification, will be transformed into a situation
where little black boys and black girls will be able to join
hands with little white boys and white girls and walk together
as sisters and brothers.

I have a dream today.   17

I have a dream that one day every valley shall be exalted,   18
every hill and mountain shall be made low, the rough places
will be made plain, and the crooked places will be made
straight, and the glory of the Lord shall be revealed, and all
flesh shall see it together.

This is our hope. This is the faith with which I return to   19
the South. With this faith we will be able to hew out of the
mountain of despair a stone of hope. With this faith we will
be able to transform the jangling discords of our nation into a
beautiful symphony of brotherhood. With this faith we will
be able to work together, to pray together, to struggle together, to go to jail together, to stand up for freedom together, knowing that we will be free one day.

This will be the day when all of God's children will be able   20
to sing with new meaning.

> My country, 'tis of thee
> Sweet land of liberty,
>   Of thee I sing:
> Land where my fathers died,
> Land of the pilgrims' pride,
> From every mountainside
>   Let freedom ring.

And if America is to be a great nation this must become   21
true. So let freedom ring from the prodigious hilltops of New
Hampshire. Let freedom ring from the mighty mountains of

New York. Let freedom ring from the heightening Alleghenies of Pennsylvania!

Let freedom ring from the snowcapped Rockies of Colorado! 22

Let freedom ring from the curvaceous peaks of California! 23

But not only that; let freedom ring from Stone Mountain of Georgia! 24

Let freedom ring from Lookout Mountain of Tennessee! 25

Let freedom ring from every hill and molehill of Mississippi. From every mountainside, let freedom ring. 26

When we let freedom ring, when we let it ring from every village and every hamlet, from every state and every city, we will be able to speed up that day when all of God's children, black men and white men, Jews and Gentiles, Protestants and Catholics, will be able to join hands and sing in the words of the old Negro spiritual, "Free at last! free at last! thank God almighty, we are free at last!" 27

For Study and Discussion

QUESTIONS FOR RESPONSE

1. What experiences of injustice have you had (or perhaps witnessed, read about, or seen in a movie) that help you to identify with King's dreams and feel the force of his speech?

2. What did you already know about the life of King and of his place in modern U.S. history that prepared you for reading "I Have a Dream"? How well did the speech live up to what you expected of it?

QUESTIONS ABOUT PURPOSE

1. King has at least two strong messages. One message is local and immediate; the other one is national and long range. How would you summarize those two messages?

2. How does King use his speech to reinforce his belief in nonviolence as the appropriate tool in the struggle for civil rights?

QUESTIONS ABOUT AUDIENCE

1. King gave this speech to a huge live audience that had come to Washington for a march for freedom and civil rights. How much larger is the national audience he is addressing, and why is that audience also important?
2. This speech is one of the most widely anthologized of modern speeches. What audiences does it continue to appeal to and why?

QUESTIONS ABOUT STRATEGIES

1. How does King draw on metaphor to engage his listeners' feelings of injustice and give them hope for a new day? What are some of the most powerful metaphors?
2. In what way do King's talents as a minister serve his purposes in the speech? What African-American leader today do you think most resembles King in style and in mission?

QUESTIONS FOR DISCUSSION

1. If King were alive today, more than forty years after this speech, how much of his dream do you think he would feel has come true? Look particularly at the visions he speaks of in paragraph 7 and paragraphs 11 through 16.
2. What elements in the speech reveal those qualities that contributed to King's power as a major civil rights leader, effective with whites as well as with blacks?

Eric Liu was born in Poughkeepsie, New York, in 1968 and was educated at Yale University. He worked as a legislative aide for Senator David Boren of Oklahoma and then as a speechwriter for Secretary of State Warren Christopher and President Bill Clinton. He is currently the publisher and editor of *The Next Progressive,* a journal of opinion, the editor of *NEXT: Young American Writers on the New Generation* (1994), and the author of *The Accidental Asian: Notes of a Native Speaker* (1998). In "A Chinaman's Chance: Reflections on the American Dream," reprinted from *NEXT,* Liu argues that the American Dream is more about seizing opportunity than about claiming prosperity.

A Chinaman's Chance: Reflections on the American Dream

A LOT OF people my age seem to think that the American Dream is dead. I think they're dead wrong. [1]

Or at least only partly right. It is true that for those of us in our twenties and early thirties, job opportunities are scarce. There looms a real threat that we will be the first American generation to have a lower standard of living than our parents. [2]

But what is it that we mean when we invoke the American Dream? [3]

In the past, the American Dream was something that held people of all races, religions, and identities together. As James Comer has written, it represented a shared aspiration among [4]

all Americans—black, white, or any other color—"to provide
well for themselves and their families as valued members of a
democratic society." Now, all too often, it seems the American Dream means merely some guarantee of affluence, a
birthright of wealth.

I wouldn't say material

At a basic level, of course, the American Dream is about   5
prosperity and the pursuit of material happiness. But to me,
its meaning extends beyond such concerns. To me, the
dream is not just about buying a bigger house than the one I
grew up in or having shinier stuff now than I had as a kid. It
also represents a sense of opportunity that binds generations

---

*I want to prove . . . that a Chinaman's
chance is as good as anyone else's.*

---

nice ¶

together in commitment, so that the young inherit not only
property but also perseverance, not only money but also a
mission to make good on the strivings of their parents and
grandparents.

The poet Robert Browning once wrote that "a man's   6
reach must exceed his grasp—else what's a heaven for?" So it
is in America. Every generation will strive, and often fail.
Every generation will reach for success, and often miss the
mark. But Americans rely as much on the next generation as
on the next life to prove that such struggles and frustrations
are not in vain. There may be temporary setbacks, cutbacks,
recessions, depressions. But this is a nation of second
chances. So long as there are young Americans who do not
take what they have—or what they can do—for granted,
progress is always possible.

good pt

My conception of the American Dream does not take   7
progress for granted. But it does demand the *opportunity* to
achieve progress—and values the opportunity as much as the
achievement. I come at this question as the son of immi-

grants. I see just as clearly as anyone else the cracks in the ide- *nice*
alist vision of fulfillment for all. But because my parents came *metaphor*
here with virtually nothing, because they did build something, I see the enormous potential inherent in the ideal.

I happen still to believe in our national creed: freedom and 8
opportunity, and our common responsibility to uphold *odd*
them. This creed is what makes America unique. More than
any demographic statistic or economic indicator, it animates
the American Dream. It infuses our mundane struggles—to
plan a career, do good work, get ahead—with purpose and
possibility. It makes America the only country that could produce heroes like Colin Powell—heroes who rise from noth- *hero?*
ing, who overcome the odds.

I think of the sacrifices made by my own parents. I appre- 9
ciate the hardship of the long road traveled by my father—
one of whose first jobs in America was painting the yellow
line down a South Dakota interstate—and by my mother—
whose first job here was filing pay stubs for a New York restaurant. From such beginnings, they were able to build a
comfortable life and provide me with a breadth of resources—through arts, travel, and an Ivy League education. *sweet*
It was an unspoken obligation for them to do so.

I think of my boss in my first job after college, on Capitol 10
Hill. George is a smart, feisty, cigar-chomping, take-no-shit
Greek-American. He is about fifteen years older than I, has *nice*
different interests, a very different personality. But like me, *details*
he is the son of immigrants, and he would joke with me that
the Greek-Chinese mafia was going to take over one day. He
was only half joking. We'd worked harder, our parents dou-
bly harder, than almost anyone else we knew. To people like
George, talk of the withering of the American Dream seems *people?*
foreign.

It's undeniable that principles like freedom and opportu- 11
nity, no matter how dearly held, are not enough. They can inspire a multiracial March on Washington, but they can not
bring black salaries in alignment with white salaries. They can
draw wave after wave of immigrants here, but they can not
provide them the means to get out of our ghettos and barrios

and Chinatowns. They are not sufficient for fulfillment of the
American Dream.

But they are necessary. They are vital. And not just to the 12
children of immigrants. These ideals form the durable thread
that weaves us all in union. Put another way, they are one of
the few things that keep America from disintegrating into a
loose confederation of zip codes and walled-in communities.

What alarms me is how many people my age look at our 13
nation's ideals with a rising sense of irony. What good is such
a creed if you are working for hourly wages in a dead-end
job? What value do such platitudes have if you live in an urban war zone? When the only apparent link between
homeboys and housepainters and bike messengers and investment bankers is pop culture—MTV, the NBA, movies,
dance music—then the social fabric is flimsy indeed.

My generation has come of age at a time when the country 14
is fighting off bouts of defeatism and self-doubt, at a time
when racism and social inequities seem not only persistent
but intractable. At a time like this, the retreat to one's own
kind is seen by more and more of my peers as an advance.
And that retreat has given rise again to the notion that there
are essential and irreconcilable differences among the races—
a notion that was supposed to have disappeared from American discourse by the time my peers and I were born in the
sixties.

Not long ago, for instance, my sister called me a "banana." 15

I was needling her about her passion for rap and hip-hop 16
music. Every time I saw her, it seemed, she was jumping and
twisting to Arrested Development or Chubb Rock or some
other funky group. She joked that despite being the daughter
of Chinese immigrants, she was indeed "black at heart." And
then she added, lightheartedly, "You, on the other hand—
well, you're basically a banana." Yellow on the outside, but
white inside.

I protested, denied her charge vehemently. But it was too 17
late. She was back to dancing. And I stood accused.

Ever since then, I have wondered what it means to be 18
black, or white, or Asian "at heart"—particularly for my gen-

eration. Growing up, when other kids would ask whether I was Chinese or Korean or Japanese, I would reply, a little petulantly, "American." Assimilation can still be a sensitive subject. I recall reading about a Korean-born Congressman who had gone out of his way to say that Asian-Americans should expect nothing special from him. He added that he was taking speech lessons "to get rid of this accent." I winced at his palpable self-hate. But then it hit me: Is this how my sister sees me?

There is no doubt that minorities like me can draw strength from our communities. But in today's environment, anything other than ostentatious tribal fealty is taken in some communities as a sign of moral weakness, a disappointing dilution of character. In times that demand ever-clearer thinking, it has become too easy for people to shut off their brains: "It's a black/Asian/Latino/white thing," says the variable T-shirt. "You wouldn't understand." Increasingly, we don't.

The civil-rights triumphs of the sixties and the cultural revolutions that followed made it possible for minorities to celebrate our diverse heritages. I can appreciate that. But I know, too, that the sixties—or at least, my generation's grainy, hazy vision of the decade—also bequeathed to young Americans a legacy of near-pathological race consciousness.

Today's culture of entitlement—and of race entitlement in particular—tells us plenty about what we get if we are black or white or female or male or old or young.

It is silent, though, on some other important issues. For instance: What do we "get" for being American? And just as importantly, What do we owe? These are questions around which young people like myself must tread carefully, since talk of common interests, civic culture, responsibility, and integration sounds a little too "white" for some people. To the new segregationists, the "American Dream" is like the old myth of the "Melting Pot": an oppressive fiction, an opiate for the unhappy colored masses.

How have we allowed our thinking about race to become so twisted? The formal obstacles and the hateful opposition to civil rights have long faded into memory. By most external

measures, life for minorities is better than it was a quarter
century ago. It would seem that the opportunities for tolerance and cooperation are commonplace. Why, then, are so
many of my peers so cynical about our ability to get along
with one another?

The reasons are frustratingly ambiguous. I got a glimpse   24
of this when I was in college. It was late in my junior year,
and as the editor of a campus magazine, I was sitting on a
panel to discuss "The White Press at Yale: What Is to Be
Done?" The assembly hall was packed, a diverse and noisy
crowd. The air was heavy, nervously electric.

Why weren't there more stories about "minority issues" in   25
the Yale *Daily News*? Why weren't there more stories on Africa in my magazine, the foreign affairs journal? How many
"editors of color" served on the boards of each of the major
publications? The questions were volleyed like artillery, one
round after another, punctuated only by the applause of an
audience spoiling for a fight. The questions were not at all
unfair. But it seemed that no one—not even those of us on
the panel who *were* people of color—could provide, in this
context, satisfactory answers.

Toward the end of the discussion, I made a brief appeal for   26
reason and moderation. And afterward, as students milled
around restlessly, I was attacked: for my narrowminded-
ness—How dare you suggest that Yale is not a fundamentally
prejudiced place!—for my simplemindedness—Have you,
too, been co-opted?

And for my betrayal—Are you just white inside?   27

My eyes were opened that uncomfortably warm early sum-   28
mer evening. Not only to the cynical posturing and the com-
bustible opportunism of campus racial politics. But more importantly, to the larger question of identity—my identity—in
America. Never mind that the aim of many of the loudest
critics was to generate headlines in the very publications they
denounced. In spite of themselves—against, it would seem,
their true intentions—they got me to think about who I am.

In our society today, and especially among people of my   29
generation, we are congealing into clots of narrow common-

ality. We stick with racial and religious comrades. This tribal consciousness-raising can be empowering for some. But while America was conceived in liberty—the liberty, for instance, to associate with whomever we like—it was never designed to be a mere collection of subcultures. We forget that there is in fact such a thing as a unique American identity that transcends our sundry tribes, sets, gangs, and cliques.

[margin annotation: true]

[margin annotation: thats what this country is]

I have grappled, wittingly or not, with these questions of identity and allegiance all my life. When I was in my early teens, I would invite my buddies overnight to watch movies, play video games, and beat one another up. Before too long, my dad would come downstairs and start hamming it up—telling stories, asking gently nosy questions, making corny jokes, all with his distinct Chinese accent. I would stand back, quietly gauging everyone's reaction. Of course, the guys loved it. But I would feel uneasy.

[margin annotation: 30]

[margin annotation: Ha – its not a racial thing]

[margin annotation: 31]

What was then cause for discomfort is now a source of strength. Looking back on such episodes, I take pride in my father's accented English; I feel awe at his courage to laugh loudly in a language not really his own.

It was around the same time that I decided that continued attendance at the community Chinese school on Sundays was uncool. There was no fanfare; I simply stopped going. As a child, I'd been too blissfully unaware to think of Chinese school as anything more than a weekly chore, with an annual festival (dumplings and spring rolls, games and prizes). But by the time I was a peer-pressured adolescent, Chinese school seemed like a badge of the woefully unassimilated. I turned my back on it.

[margin annotation: 32]

Even as I write these words now, it feels as though I am revealing a long-held secret. I am proud that my ancestors—scholars, soldiers, farmers—came from one of the world's great civilizations. I am proud that my grandfather served in the Chinese Air Force. I am proud to speak even my clumsy brand of Mandarin, and I feel blessed to be able to think idiomatically in Chinese, a language so much richer in nuance and subtle poetry than English.

[margin annotation: 33]

[margin annotation: hey now]

[handwritten margin notes: "we dad show we never appreciate what we had until its gone" and "all had a good wide"]

Belatedly, I appreciate the good fortune I've had to be the   34
son of immigrants. As a kid, I could play Thomas Jefferson in
the bicentennial school play one week and the next week play
the poet Li Bai at the Chinese school festival. I could come
home from an afternoon of teen slang at the mall and sit
down to dinner for a rollicking conversation in our family's
hybrid of Chinese and English. I understood, when I went
over to visit friends, that my life was different. At the time, I
just never fully appreciated how rich it was.

Yet I know that this pride in my heritage does not cross   35
into prejudice against others. What it reflects is pride in what
my country represents. That became clear to me when I went
through Marine Corps Officer Candidates' School. During
the summers after my sophomore and junior years of college,
I volunteered for OCS, a grueling boot camp for potential
officers in the swamps and foothills of Quantico, Virginia.

And once I arrived—standing 5'4", 135 pounds, bespecta-   36
cled, a Chinese Ivy League Democrat—I was a target straight
out of central casting. The wiry, raspy-voiced drill sergeant,
though he was perhaps only an inch or two taller than I,
called me "Little One" with as much venom as can be
squeezed into such a moniker. He heaped verbal abuse on
me, he laughed when I stumbled, he screamed when I hesitated. But he also never failed to remind me that just because
I was a little shit didn't mean I shouldn't run farther, climb
higher, think faster, hit harder than anyone else.

That was the funny thing about the Marine Corps. It is,   37
ostensibly, one of the most conservative institutions in the
United States. And yet, for those twelve weeks, it represented
the kind of color-blind equality of opportunity that the rest
of society struggles to match. I did not feel uncomfortable at
OCS to be of Chinese descent. Indeed, I drew strength from
it. My platoon was a veritable cross section of America: forty
young men of all backgrounds, all regions, all races, all levels
of intelligence and ability, displaced from our lives (if only for
a few weeks) with nowhere else to go.

Going down the list of names—Courtemanche, Dough-   38
erty, Grella, Hunt, Liu, Reeves, Schwarzman, and so on—
brought to mind a line from a World War II documentary I

once saw, which went something like this: The reason why it seemed during the war that America was as good as the rest of the world put together was that America *was* the rest of the world put together.

Ultimately, I decided that the Marines was not what I wanted to do for four years and I did not accept the second lieutenant's commission. But I will never forget the day of the graduation parade: bright sunshine, brisk winds, the band playing Sousa as my company passed in review. As my mom and dad watched and photographed the parade from the rafters, I thought to myself: this is the American Dream in all its cheesy earnestness. I felt the thrill of truly being part of something larger and greater than myself.

I do know that American life is not all Sousa marches and flag-waving. I know that those with reactionary agendas often find it convenient to cloak their motives in the language of Americanism. The "American Party" was the name of a major nativist organization in the nineteenth century. "America First" is the siren song of the isolationists who would withdraw this country from the world and expel the world from this country. I know that our national immigration laws were once designed explicitly to cut off the influx from Asia.

I also know that discrimination is real. I am reminded of a gentle old man who, after Pearl Harbor, was stripped of his possessions without warning, taken from his home, and thrown into a Japanese internment camp. He survived, and by many measures has thrived, serving as a community leader and political activist. But I am reluctant to share with him my wide-eyed patriotism.

I know the bittersweet irony that my own father—a strong and optimistic man—would sometimes feel when he was alive. When he came across a comically lost cause—if the Yankees were behind 14–0 in the ninth, or if Dukakis was down ten points in the polls with a week left—he would often joke that the doomed party had "a Chinaman's chance" of success. It was one of those insensitive idioms of a generation ago, and it must have lodged in his impressionable young

[margin notes: "39 true on some levels"; "40"; "41 not just Asia"; "42 I like how she slowly adds info on his family"]

mind when he first came to America. It spoke of a perceived stacked deck.

I know, too, that for many other immigrants, the dream simply does not work out. Fae Myenne Ng, the author of *Bone,* writes about how her father ventured here from China under a false identity and arrived at Angel Island, the detention center outside the "Gold Mountain" of San Francisco. He got out, he labored, he struggled, and he suffered "a bitter no-luck life" in America. There was no glory. For him, Ng suggests, the journey was not worth it. 43

[margin note: ironic eh?]

But it is precisely because I know these things that I want to prove that in the long run, over generations and across ethnicities, it *is* worth it. For the second-generation American, opportunity is obligation. I have seen and faced racism. I understand the dull pain of dreams deferred or unmet. But I believe still that there is so little stopping me from building the life that I want. I was given, through my parents' labors, the chance to bridge that gap between ideals and reality. Who am I to throw away that chance? 44

[margin note: wahoo]

Plainly, I am subject to the criticism that I speak too much from my own experience. Not everyone can relate to the second-generation American story. When I have spoken like this with some friends, the issue has been my perspective. *What you say is fine for you. But unless you grew up where I did, unless you've had people avoid you because of the color of your skin, don't talk to me about common dreams.* 45

[margin note: no one should]

But are we then to be paralyzed? Is respect for different experiences supposed to obviate the possibility of shared aspirations? Does the diversity of life in America doom us to a fractured understanding of one another? The question is basic: Should the failure of this nation thus far to fulfill its stated ideals incapacitate its young people, or motivate us? 46

[margin note: good question]

Our country was built on, and remains glued by, the idea that everybody deserves a fair shot and that we must work together to guarantee that opportunity—the original American Dream. It was this idea, in some inchoate form, that drew every immigrant here. It was this idea, however sullied by slavery and racism, that motivated the civil-rights movement. 47

To write this idea off—even when its execution is spotty—to let American life descend into squabbles among separatist tribes would not just be sad. It would be a total mishandling of a legacy, the squandering of a great historical inheritance.

Mine must not be the first generation of Americans to lose America. Just as so many of our parents journeyed here to find their version of the American Dream, so must young Americans today journey across boundaries of race and class to rediscover one another. We are the first American generation to be born into an integrated society, and we are accustomed to more race mixing than any generation before us. We started open-minded, and it's not too late for us to stay that way.

Time is of the essence. For in our national political culture today, the watchwords seem to be *decline* and *end*. Apocalyptic visions and dark millennial predictions abound. The end of history. The end of progress. The end of equality. Even something as ostensibly positive as the end of the Cold War has a bittersweet tinge, because for the life of us, no one in America can get a handle on the big question, "What Next?"

For my generation, this fixation on endings is particularly enervating. One's twenties are supposed to be a time of widening horizons, of bright possibilities. Instead, America seems to have entered an era of limits. Whether it is the difficulty of finding jobs from some place other than a temp agency, or the mountains of debt that darken our future, the message to my peers is often that this nation's time has come and gone; let's bow out with grace and dignity.

A friend once observed that while the Chinese seek to adapt to nature and yield to circumstance, Americans seek to conquer both. She meant that as a criticism of America. But I interpreted her remark differently. I *do* believe that America is exceptional. And I believe it is up to my generation to revive that spirit, that sense that we do in fact have control over our own destiny—as individuals and as a nation.

If we are to reclaim a common destiny, we must also reach out to other generations for help. It was Franklin Roosevelt who said that while America can't always build the future for its youth, it can—and must—build its youth for the future. That commitment across generations is as central to the American Dream as any I have enunciated. We are linked, black and white, old and young, one and inseparable.

I know how my words sound. I am old enough to perceive 53 my own naïveté but young enough still to cherish it. I realize that I am coming of age just as the American Dream is showing its age. Yet I still have faith in this country's unique destiny—to create generation after generation of hyphenates like me, to channel this new blood, this resilience and energy into an ever more vibrant future for *all* Americans.

And I want to prove—for my sake, for my father's sake, 54 and for my country's sake—that a Chinaman's chance is as good as anyone else's.

that's a good point to be at

finally

For Study and Discussion

QUESTIONS FOR RESPONSE

1. Do you endorse or discount Liu's argument? How do you think your family background and history affect your response?
2. How would you define the American Dream? To what extent do you think it has been or will be fulfilled for you?

QUESTIONS ABOUT PURPOSE

1. To what criticisms *about* his generation is Liu responding? To what criticisms *from* his generation is he responding?
2. What specific attitudes among young people does Liu challenge?

QUESTIONS ABOUT AUDIENCE

1. Liu wrote this essay for a 1994 book titled *NEXT: Young American Writers on the New Generation,* a book he conceived of and also edited. What kind of readers do you think he envisioned for the book? How do you think you fit into that group?
2. What do you think Liu's appeal might be to generations older than his? Why?

QUESTIONS ABOUT STRATEGIES

1. What is the impact of Liu's writing about his parents' experience?
2. Liu was once one of President Clinton's speechwriters. What strategies does he use that he might have learned through that experience?

QUESTIONS FOR DISCUSSION

1. What evidence, if any, do you see that students are splitting into separate groups on your campus? What is your view of such splits? Why?
2. What factors in Liu's life and experiences do you think played a significant part in his success in college and beyond? How would those factors affect his outlook on life?

A Debate About Family Values

BARBARA KINGSOLVER

Barbara Kingsolver was born in Annapolis, Maryland, in 1955 and educated at DePauw University and the University of Arizona. She began her writing career as a technical writer in the office of arid studies, then began working as a freelance journalist before publishing her first novel, *The Bean Trees* (1988). Her other novels include *Animal Dreams* (1990), *The Poisonwood Bible* (1998), and *Prodigal Summer* (2000). She has published short stories in *Homeland and Other Stories* (1989) and essays in *High Tide in Tucson: Essays from Now or Never* (1995) and *Small Wonder* (2002). In "Stone Soup," Kingsolver argues that there is not necessarily one best model for a successful family.

Stone Soup

IN THE CATALOG of family values, where do we rank an occasion like this? A curly-haired boy who wanted to run before he walked, age seven now, a soccer player scoring a winning goal. He turns to the bleachers with his fists in the air and a smile wide as a gap-toothed galaxy. His own cheering section of grown-ups and kids all leap to their feet and hug each other, delirious with love for this boy. He's Andy, my best friend's son. The cheering section includes his mother and her friends, his brother, his father and stepmother, a stepbrother and stepsister, and a grandparent. Lucky is the child with this many relatives on hand to hail a proud accomplishment. I'm there too, witnessing a family fortune. But in spite of myself, defensive words take shape in my head. I am thinking: I dare *anybody* to call this a broken home.

Families change, and remain the same. Why are our names for home so slow to catch up to the truth of where we live? →*nice!!!*   2

When I was a child, I had two parents who loved me with-   3
out cease. One of them attended every excuse for attention I ever contrived, and the other made it to the ones with higher

---

Arguing about whether nontraditional families deserve pity or tolerance is a little like the medieval debate about left-handedness as a mark of the devil.

I like her style of writing

---

production values, like piano recitals and appendicitis. So I was a lucky child too. I played with a set of paper dolls called "The Family of Dolls," four in number, who came with the factory-assigned names of Dad, Mom, Sis, and Junior. I think you know what they looked like, at least before I loved them to death and their heads fell off.

Now I've replaced the dolls with a life. I knit my days   4
around my daughter's survival and happiness, and am proud to say her head is still on. But we aren't the Family of Dolls. *satirical—* Maybe you're not, either. And if not, even though you are *very* statistically no oddity, it's probably been suggested to you in *enjoyable* a hundred ways that yours isn't exactly a real family, but an impostor family, a harbinger of cultural ruin, a slapdash sub-stitute—something like counterfeit money. Here at the tail end of our century, most of us are up to our ears in the noisy business of trying to support and love a thing called family. But there's a current in the air with ferocious moral force that finds its way even into political campaigns, claiming there is only one right way to do it, the Way It Has Always Been.

fallacy

In the face of a thriving, particolored world, this narrow 5
view is so pickled and absurd I'm astonished that it gets air-
play. And I'm astonished that it still stings.

Every parent has endured the arrogance of a child- 6
unfriendly grump sitting in judgment, explaining what those
kids of ours really need (for example, "a good licking"). If
we're polite, we move our crew to another bench in the park.
If we're forthright (as I am in my mind, only, for the rest of
the day), we fix them with a sweet imperious stare and say,
"Come back and let's talk about it after you've changed a
thousand diapers."

But it's harder somehow to shrug off the Family-of-Dolls 7
Family Values crew when they judge (from their safe distance) that divorced people, blended families, gay families,
and single parents are failures. That our children are at risk,
and the whole arrangement is messy and embarrassing. A
marriage that ends is not called "finished," it's called *failed*.
The children of this family may have been born to a happy
union, but now they are called *the children of divorce*.

I had no idea how thoroughly these assumptions overlaid 8
my culture until I went through divorce myself. I wrote to a
friend: "This might be worse than being widowed. Overnight I've suffered the same losses—companionship, financial
and practical support, my identity as a wife and partner, the
future I'd taken for granted. I am lonely, grieving, and hard-
pressed to take care of my household alone. But instead of
bringing casseroles, people are acting like I had a fit and
broke up the family china."

Once upon a time I held these beliefs about divorce: that 9
everyone who does it could have chosen not to do it. That
it's a lazy way out of marital problems. That it selfishly puts
personal happiness ahead of family integrity. Now I tremble
for my ignorance. It's easy, in fortunate times, to forget
about the ambush that could leave your head reeling: serious
mental or physical illness, death in the family, abandonment,
financial calamity, humiliation, violence, despair.

I started out like any child, intent on being the Family of 10
Dolls. I set upon young womanhood believing in most of the

doctrines of my generation: I wore my skirts four inches above the knee. I had the Barbie with her zebra-striped swimsuit and a figure unlike anything found in nature. And I understood the Prince Charming Theory of Marriage, a quest for Mr. Right that ends smack dab where you find him. I did not completely understand that another whole story *begins* there, and no fairy tale prepared me for the combination of bad luck and persistent hope that would interrupt my dream and lead me to other arrangements. Like a cancer diagnosis, a dying marriage is a thing to fight, to deny, and finally, when there's no choice left, to dig in and survive. Casseroles would help. Likewise, I imagine it must be a painful reckoning in adolescence (or later on) to realize one's own true love will never look like the soft-focus fragrance ads because Prince Charming (surprise!) is a princess. Or vice versa. Or has skin the color your parents didn't want you messing with, except in the Crayola box.

It's awfully easy to hold in contempt the straw broken home, and that mythical category of persons who toss away nuclear family for the sheer fun of it. Even the legal terms we use have a suggestion of caprice. I resent the phrase "irreconcilable differences," which suggests a stubborn refusal to accept a spouse's little quirks. This is specious. Every happily married couple I know has loads of irreconcilable differences. Negotiating where to set the thermostat is not the point. A nonfunctioning marriage is a slow asphyxiation. It is waking up despised each morning, listening to the pulse of your own loneliness before the radio begins to blare its raucous gospel that you're nothing if you aren't loved. It is sharing your airless house with the threat of suicide or other kinds of violence, while the ghost that whispers, "Leave here and destroy your children," has passed over every door and nailed it shut. Disassembling a marriage in these circumstances is as much *fun* as amputating your own gangrenous leg. You do it, if you can, to save a life—or two, or more.

I know of no one who really went looking to hoe the harder row, especially the daunting one of single parenthood. Yet it seems to be the most American of customs to blame the

[handwritten margin notes: "sounds like a real person", "Haha", "but true", "she captures every sense so well", "11", "12"]

burdened for their destiny. We'd like so desperately to believe
in freedom and justice for all, we can hardly name that rogue
bad luck, even when he's a close enough snake to bite us. In
the wake of my divorce, some friends (even a few close ones)
chose to vanish, rather than linger within striking distance of
misfortune.

But most stuck around, bless their hearts, and if I'm any   13
the wiser for my trials, it's from having learned the worth of
steadfast friendship. And also, what not to say. The least helpful question is: "Did you want the divorce, or didn't you?"
Did I want to keep that gangrenous leg, or not? How to explain, in a culture that venerates choice: two terrifying options are much worse than none at all. Give me any day the
quick hand of cruel fate that will leave me scarred but blame-
less. As it was, I kept thinking of that wicked third-grade joke
in which some boy comes up behind you and grabs your ear,
starts in with a prolonged tug, and asks, "Do you want this
ear any longer?"

Still, the friend who holds your hand and says the wrong   14
thing is made of dearer stuff than the one who stays away.
And generally, through all of it, you live. My favorite fictional
character, Kate Vaiden (in the novel by Reynolds Price), advises: "Strength just comes in one brand—you stand up at
sunrise and meet what they send you and keep your hair
combed."

Once you've weathered the straits, you get to cross the   15
tricky juncture from casualty to survivor. If you're on your
feet at the end of a year or two, and have begun putting together a happy new existence, those friends who were kind
enough to feel sorry for you when you needed it must now
accept you back to the ranks of the living. If you're truly
blessed, they will dance at your second wedding. Everybody
else, for heaven's sake, should stop throwing stones.

Arguing about whether nontraditional families deserve   16
pity or tolerance is a little like the medieval debate about left-
handedness as a mark of the devil. Divorce, remarriage, single
parenthood, gay parents, and blended families simply are.

[handwritten margin notes: "why bulk of confusing contradicting questions", "nice phrase"]

They're facts of our time. Some of the reasons listed by soci- *sadly*
ologists for these family reconstructions are: the idea of mar- *true*
riage as a romantic partnership rather than a pragmatic one; a
shift in women's expectations, from servility to self-respect
and independence; and longevity (prior to antibiotics no
marriage was expected to last many decades—in Colonial
days the average couple lived to be married less than twelve
years). Add to all this, our growing sense of entitlement to
happiness and safety from abuse. Most would agree these are
all good things. Yet their result—a culture in which serial mo-
nogamy and the consequent reshaping of families are the
norm—gets diagnosed as "failing."
such a

For many of us, once we have put ourselves Humpty- 17 *strong*
Dumpty-wise back together again, the main problem with *word*
our reorganized family is that other people think we have a
problem. My daughter tells me the only time she's uncomfortable about being the child of divorced parents is when
her friends say they feel sorry for her. It's a bizarre sympathy,
given that half the kids in her school and nation are in the *horrible*
same boat, pursuing childish happiness with the same energy
as their married-parent peers. When anyone asks how *she* feels
about it, she spontaneously lists the benefits: our house is in
the country and we have a dog, but she can go to her dad's
neighborhood for the urban thrills of a pool and sidewalks
for roller-skating. What's more, she has three sets of grandparents! *positive look*

Why is it surprising that a child would revel in a widened 18
family and the right to feel at home in more than one house?
Isn't it the opposite that should worry us—a child with no
home at all, or too few resources to feel safe? The child at risk
is the one whose parents are too immature themselves to
guide wisely; too diminished by poverty to nurture; too far
from opportunity to offer hope. The number of children in
the U.S. living in poverty at this moment is almost unfath-
omably large: twenty percent. There are families among us
that need help all right, and by no means are they new on the
landscape. The rate at which teenage girls had babies in 1957
(ninety-six per thousand) was twice what it is now. That

remarkable statistic is ignored by the religious right—probably because the teen birth rate was cut in half mainly by legalized abortion. In fact, the policy gatekeepers who coined the phrase "family values" have steadfastly ignored the desperation of too-small families, and since 1979 have steadily reduced the amount of financial support available to a single parent. But, this camp's most outspoken attacks seem aimed at the notion of families getting too complex, with add-ons and extras such as a gay parent's partner, or a remarried mother's new husband and his children.

To judge a family's value by its tidy symmetry is to purchase a book for its cover. There's no moral authority there. The famous family comprised of Dad, Mom, Sis, and Junior living as an isolated economic unit is not built on historical bedrock. In *The Way We Never Were*, Stephanie Coontz writes, "Whenever people propose that we go back to the traditional family, I always suggest that they pick a ballpark date for the family they have in mind." Colonial families were tidily disciplined, but their members (meaning everyone but infants) labored incessantly and died young. Then the Victorian family adopted a new division of labor, in which women's role was domestic and children were allowed time for study and play, but this was an upper-class construct supported by myriad slaves. Coontz writes, "For every nineteenth-century middle-class family that protected its wife and child within the family circle, there was an Irish or German girl scrubbing floors . . . a Welsh boy mining coal to keep the home-baked goodies warm, a black girl doing the family laundry, a black mother and child picking cotton to be made into clothes for the family, and a Jewish or an Italian daughter in a sweatshop making 'ladies' dresses or artificial flowers for the family to purchase."

The abolition of slavery brought slightly more democratic arrangements, in which extended families were harnessed together in cottage industries; at the turn of the century came a steep rise in child labor in mines and sweatshops. Twenty percent of American children lived in orphanages at the time;

their parents were not necessarily dead, but couldn't afford
to keep them.

During the Depression and up to the end of World War II,
many millions of U.S. households were more multi-
generational than nuclear. Women my grandmother's age
were likely to live with a fluid assortment of elderly relatives,
in-laws, siblings, and children. In many cases they spent virtually every waking hour working in the company of other
women—a companionable scenario in which it would be easier, I imagine, to tolerate an estranged or difficult spouse. I'm
reluctant to idealize a life of so much hard work and so little
spousal intimacy, but its advantage may have been resilience.
A family so large and varied would not easily be brought
down by a single blow: it could absorb a death, long illness,
an abandonment here or there, and any number of irreconcilable differences.

The Family of Dolls came along midcentury as a great
American experiment. A booming economy required a mo-
bile labor force and demanded that women surrender jobs to
returning soldiers. Families came to be defined by a single
breadwinner. They struck out for single-family homes at an
earlier age than ever before, and in unprecedented numbers
they raised children in suburban isolation. The nuclear family
was launched to sink or swim.

More than a few sank. Social historians corroborate that
the suburban family of the postwar economic boom, which
we have recently selected as our definition of "traditional,"
was no panacea. Twenty-five percent of Americans were poor
in the mid-1950s, and as yet there were no food stamps. Sixty
percent of the elderly lived on less than $1,000 a year, and
most had no medical insurance. In the sequestered suburbs,
alcoholism and sexual abuse of children were far more widespread than anyone imagined.

Expectations soared, and the economy sagged. It's hard to
depend on one other adult for everything, come what may.
In the last three decades, that amorphous, adaptable structure we call "family" has been reshaped once more by

*it
shouldn't
be*

economic tides. Compared with fifties families, mothers are far more likely now to be employed. We are statistically more likely to divorce, and to live in blended families or other extranuclear arrangements. We are also more likely to plan and space our children, and to rate our marriages as "happy." We are less likely to suffer abuse without recourse, or to stare out at our lives through a glaze of prescription tranquilizers. Our aged parents are less likely to be destitute, and we're half as likely to have a teenage daughter turn up a mother herself. All in all, I would say that if "intact" in modern family-values jargon means living quietly desperate in the bell jar, then hip-hip-hooray for "broken." A neat family model constructed to service the Baby Boom economy seems to be returning gradually to a grand, lumpy shape that human families apparently have tended toward since they first took root in the Olduvai Gorge. We're social animals, deeply fond of companionship, and children love best to run in packs. If there is a *normal* for humans, at all, I expect it looks like two or three Families of Dolls, connected variously by kinship and passion, shuffled like cards and strewn over several shoeboxes.

The sooner we can let go of the fairy tale of families func-   25
tioning perfectly in isolation, the better we might embrace the relief of community. Even the admirable parents who've stayed married through thick and thin are very likely, at present, to incorporate other adults into their families—household help and baby-sitters if they can afford them, or neighbors and grandparents if they can't. For single parents, this support is the rock-bottom definition of family. And most parents who have split apart, however painfully, still manage to maintain family continuity for their children, creating in many cases a boisterous phenomenon that Constance Ahrons in her book *The Good Divorce* calls the "binuclear family." Call it what you will—when ex-spouses beat swords into plowshares and jump up and down at a soccer game together, it makes for happy kids.

Cinderella, look, who needs her? All those evil stepsisters?   26
That story always seemed like too much cotton-picking fuss

*I love
that story*

over clothes. A childhood tale that fascinated me more was the one called "Stone Soup," and the gist of it is this: Once upon a time, a pair of beleaguered soldiers straggled home to a village empty-handed, in a land ruined by war. They were famished, but the villagers had so little they shouted evil words and slammed their doors. So the soldiers dragged out a big kettle, filled it with water, and put it on a fire to boil. They rolled a clean round stone into the pot, while the villagers peered through their curtains in amazement.

[handwritten margin note: a little violent for a child]

"What kind of soup is that?" they hooted. 27

"Stone soup," the soldiers replied. "Everybody can have 28 some when it's done."

"Well, thanks," one matron grumbled, coming out with a 29 shriveled carrot. "But it'd be better if you threw this in."

And so on, of course, a vegetable at a time, until the whole 30 suspicious village managed to feed itself grandly.

Any family is a big empty pot, save for what gets thrown 31 in. Each stew turns out different. Generosity, a resolve to turn bad luck into good, and respect for variety—these things will nourish a nation of children. Name-calling and suspicion will not. My soup contains a rock or two of hard *[handwritten: nice!]* times, and maybe yours does too. I expect it's a heck of a bouillabaise.

For Study and Discussion

QUESTIONS FOR RESPONSE

1. To what extent does the makeup of your family or the families of some of your close friends fit what Kingsolver calls the "traditional family," that is, a father, stay-at-home mother, and two or three children? How do your experiences with different kinds of families affect your response to Kingsolver's essay?

2. The phrase "family values" is an ambiguous term, used by various factions for their own political purposes. How would you define the term in what seems to you an honest and legitimate way? What do you think Kingsolver's definition of family values might be?

QUESTIONS ABOUT PURPOSE

1. In paragraphs 19 through 23, Kingsolver gives several snapshots of what so-called traditional families have actually looked like for the past several decades. What do you think she hopes to accomplish with these accounts?
2. What new insights do you think Kingsolver wants her readers to have about the divorce process?

QUESTIONS ABOUT AUDIENCE

1. What experience with divorce, single parenthood, and the stepfamilies created by second marriages do you think today's readers under forty are likely to have? How do those experiences affect the way they are likely to respond to an essay like this?
2. What details in the essay suggest that Kingsolver feels she is writing more for women than for men?

QUESTIONS ABOUT STRATEGIES

1. Kingsolver has published several successful novels, two of which—*The Bean Trees* and *Pigs in Heaven*—tell the story of a single mother who adopts and raises a child. What strategies do you see in this essay that you think might have come from her talent for writing fiction?
2. Kingsolver draws examples from two sources: from her own experience and observations and from historical examples from previous eras. What are the strengths of examples from each of these sources?

QUESTIONS FOR DISCUSSION

1. The variety of households in most communities suggests that there are several models for effective families. Drawing on your own experiences, describe one or two models that you have seen work well.
2. Kingsolver suggests that she's been severely criticized at times for being a divorced woman who is raising a child without a husband. Do you think such criticisms are common and, if so, how justified do you believe them to be?

Barbara Dafoe Whitehead was born in Rochester, Minnesota, in 1944 and educated at the University of Wisconsin and the University of Chicago. She has contributed articles to *Commonweal*, the *New York Times*, and the *Wall Street Journal*. Her most controversial article, "Dan Quayle Was Right," published in the *Atlantic*, refers to former Vice President Dan Quayle's criticism of the television show "Murphy Brown" because its title character chose to have a baby without being married. She has also written another controversial article for the *Atlantic*, "The Failure of Sex Education." These articles have led to books such as *The Divorce Culture* (1997) and *Goodbye to Girlhood: What's Troubling Girls and What We Can Do About It* (1999). In "Women and the Future of Fatherhood," excerpted from *The Divorce Culture*, Whitehead argues that even the best mothers cannot be good fathers.

Women and the Future of Fatherhood

MUCH OF OUR contemporary debate over fatherhood is governed by the assumption that men can solve the fatherhood problem on their own. The organizers of last year's Million Man March asked women to stay home, and the leaders of Promise Keepers and other grass-roots fatherhood movements whose members gather with considerably less fanfare simply do not admit women.   1

There is a cultural rationale for the exclusion of women.   2
The fatherhood movement sees the task of reinstating

masculine
women
scare
me

responsible fatherhood as an effort to alter today's norms of masculinity and correctly believes that such an effort cannot succeed unless it is voluntarily undertaken and supported by men. There is also a political rationale in defining fatherlessness as a men's issue. In the debate about marriage and parenthood, which women have dominated for at least 30 years, the fatherhood movement gives men a powerful collective voice and presence.

Yet however effective the grass-roots movement is at stirring men's consciences and raising their consciousness, the fatherhood problem will not be solved by men alone. To be sure, by signaling their commitment to accepting responsibil-

3

[This] notion of marriage as a union of two sovereign selves may be inadequate to define a relationship that carries with it the obligations, duties, and sacrifices of parenthood.

---

ity for the rearing of their children, men have taken the essential first step. But what has not yet been acknowledged is that the success of any effort to renew fatherhood as a social fact and a cultural norm also hinges on the attitudes and behavior of women. Men can't be fathers unless the mothers of their children allow it.

women are really the boss

Merely to say this is to point to how thoroughly marital disruption has weakened the bond between fathers and children. More than half of all American children are likely to spend at least part of their lives in one-parent homes. Since the vast majority of children in disrupted families live with their mothers, fathers do not share a home or a daily life with their children. It is much more difficult for men to make the kinds of small, routine, instrumental investments in their children that help forge a good relationship. It is hard to fix a flat bike tire or run a bath when you live in another neighbor-

4

hood or another town. Many a father's instrumental contribution is reduced to the postal or electronic transmission of money, or, all too commonly, to nothing at all. Without regular contact with their children, men often make reduced emotional contributions as well. Fathers must struggle to sustain close emotional ties across time and space, to "be there" emotionally without being there physically. Some may pick up the phone, send a birthday card, or buy a present, but for many fathers, physical absence also becomes emotional absence.

well they could move closer

Without marriage, men also lose access to the social and emotional intelligence of women in building relationships. Wives teach men how to care for young children, and they also encourage children to love their fathers. Mothers who do not live with the father of their children are not as likely as married mothers to represent him in positive ways to the children; nor are the relatives who are most likely to have greatest contact with the children—the mother's parents, brothers, and sisters—likely to have a high opinion of the children's father. Many men are able to overcome such obstacles, but only with difficulty. In general, men need marriage in order to be good fathers.

hmmmm . . .

If the future of fatherhood depends on marriage, however, its future is uncertain. Marriage depends on women as well as men, and women are less committed to marriage than ever before in the nation's history. In the past, women were economically dependent on marriage and assumed a disproportionately heavy responsibility for maintaining the bond, even if the underlying relationship was seriously or irretrievably damaged. In the last third of the 20th century, however, as women have gained more opportunities for paid work and the availability of child care has increased, they have become less dependent on marriage as an economic arrangement. Though it is not easy, it is possible for women to raise children on their own. This has made divorce far more attractive as a remedy for an unsatisfying marriage, and a growing number of women have availed themselves of the option.

6

very true

Today, marriage and motherhood are coming apart. 7 Remarriage and marriage rates are declining even as the rates of divorce remain stuck at historic highs and childbearing outside marriage becomes more common. Many women see single motherhood as a choice and a right to be exercised if a suitable husband does not come along in time.

The vision of the "first stage" feminism of the 1960s and 8 '70s, which held out the model of the career woman unfettered by husband or children, has been accepted by women only in part. Women want to be fettered by children, even to the point of going through grueling infertility treatments or artificial insemination to achieve motherhood. But they are increasingly ambivalent about the ties that bind them to a husband and about the necessity of marriage as a condition of parenthood. In 1994, a National Opinion Research survey asked a group of Americans. "Do you agree or disagree: one parent can bring up a child as well as two parents together." Women split 50/50 on the question; men disagreed by more than two to one.

interesting

And indeed, women enjoy certain advantages over men in 9 a society marked by high and sustained levels of family breakup. Women do not need marriage to maintain a close bond to their children, and thus to experience the larger sense of social and moral purpose that comes with raising children. As the bearers and nurturers of children and (increasingly) as the sole breadwinners for families, women continue to be engaged in personally rewarding and socially valuable pursuits. They are able to demonstrate their feminine virtues outside marriage.

brutal

ouch

Men, by contrast, have no positive identity as fathers out- 10 side marriage. Indeed, the emblematic absent father today is the infamous "deadbeat dad." In part, this is the result of efforts to stigmatize irresponsible fathers who fail to pay alimony and child support. But this image also reflects the fact that men are heavily dependent on the marriage partnership to fulfill their role as fathers. Even those who keep up their child support payments are deprived of the social importance and sense of larger purpose that comes from providing for children and raising a family. And it is the rare father who can develop the qualities needed to meet the new cultural ideal of the involved and "nurturing" father without the help of a spouse.

These differences are reflected in a growing virtue gap. 11 American popular culture today routinely recognizes and praises the achievements of single motherhood, while the widespread failure of men as fathers has resulted in a growing sense of cynicism and despair about men's capacity for virtuous conduct in family life. The enormously popular movie *Waiting to Exhale* captures the essence of this virtue gap with its portrait of steadfast mothers and deadbeat fathers, morally sleazy men and morally unassailable women. And women feel free to vent their anger and frustration with men in ways that would seem outrageous to women if the shoe were on the other foot. In *Operating Instructions* (1993), her memoir of single motherhood, Anne Lamott mordantly observes, "On bad days, I think straight white men are so poorly wired, so emotionally unenlightened and unconscious that you must approach each one as if he were some weird cross between a white supremacist and an incredibly depressing T. S. Eliot poem."

[handwritten margin note: really broad opinions]

Women's weakening attachment to marriage should not 12 be taken as a lack of interest in marriage or in a husband-wife partnership in child rearing. Rather, it is a sign of women's more exacting emotional standards for husbands and their growing insistence that men play a bigger part in caring for children and the household. Given their double responsibilities as breadwinners and mothers, many working wives find men's need for ego reinforcement and other forms of emotional and physical upkeep irksome and their failure to share housework and child care absolutely infuriating. (Surveys show that husbands perform only one-third of all household tasks even if their wives are working full-time.) Why should men be treated like babies? women complain. If men fail to meet their standards, many women are willing to do without them. Poet and polemicist Katha Pollitt captures the prevailing sentiment: "If single women can have sex, their own homes, the respect of friends and interesting work, they don't need to tell themselves that any marriage is better than none. Why not have a child on one's own? Children are a joy. Many men are not."

For all these reasons, it is important to see the fatherhood   13
problem as part of the larger cultural problem of the decline of marriage as a lasting relationship between men and women. The traditional bargain between men and women has broken down, and a new bargain has not yet been struck. It is impossible to predict what that bargain will look like—or whether there will even be one. However, it is possible to speculate about the talking points that might bring women to the bargaining table. First, a crucial proviso: there must be recognition of the changed social and economic status of women. Rightly or wrongly, many women fear that the fatherhood movement represents an effort to reinstate the status quo ante, to repeal the gains and achievements women have made over the past 30 years and return to the "separate spheres" domestic ideology that put men in the workplace and women in the home. Any effort to rethink marriage must accept the fact that women will continue to work outside the home.

Therefore, a new bargain must be struck over the division   14
of paid work and family work. This does not necessarily mean a 50/50 split in the work load every single day, but it does mean that men must make a more determined and conscientious effort to do more than one-third of the household chores. How each couple arrives at a sense of what is fair will vary, of course, but the goal is to establish some mutual understanding and commitment to an equitable division of tasks.

Another talking point may focus on the differences in the   15
expectations men and women have for marriage and intimacy. Americans have a "best friends" ideal for marriage that includes some desires that might in fact be more easily met by a best friend—someone who doesn't come with all the complicated entanglements of sharing a bed, a bank account, and a bathroom. Nonetheless, high expectations for emotional

intimacy in marriage often are confounded by the very different understandings men and women have of intimacy. Much more than men, women seek intimacy and affection through talking and emotional disclosure. Men often prefer sex to talking, and physical disrobing to emotional disclosing. They tend to be less than fully committed to (their own) sexual fidelity, while women view fidelity as a crucial sign of commitment. These are differences that the sexes need to engage with mutual recognition and tolerance.

In renegotiating the marital bargain, it may also be useful to acknowledge the biosocial differences between mothers and fathers rather than to assume an androgynous model for the parental partnership. There can be a high degree of flexibility in parental roles, but men and women are not interchangeable "parental units," particularly in their children's early years. Rather than struggle to establish identical tracks in career and family lives, it may be more realistic to consider how children's needs and well-being might require patterns of paid work and child rearing that are different for mothers and fathers but are nevertheless equitable over the course of a lifetime.

Finally, it may be important to think and talk about marriage in another kind of language than the one that suffuses our current discourse on relationships. The secular language of "intimate relationships" is the language of politics and psychotherapy, and it focuses on individual rights and individual needs. It can be heard most clearly in the personal-ad columns, a kind of masked ball where optimists go in search of partners who respect their rights and meet their emotional needs. These are not unimportant in the achievement of the contemporary ideal of marriage, which emphasizes egalitarianism and emotional fulfillment. But this notion of marriage as a union of two sovereign selves may be inadequate to define a relationship that carries with it the obligations, duties, and sacrifices of parenthood. There has always been a tension between marriage as an intimate relationship between a man and a woman and marriage as an institutional arrangement for raising children, and though the language of individual rights plays a part in defining the former, it cannot fully describe the latter. The parental partnership requires some language that acknowledges differences, mutuality, complementarity, and, more than anything else, altruism.

There is a potentially powerful incentive for women to respond to an effort to renegotiate the marriage bargain, and that has to do with their children. Women can be good mothers without being married. But especially with weakened communities that provide little support, children need levels of parental investment that cannot be supplied solely by a good mother, even if she has the best resources at her disposal. These needs are more likely to be met if the child has a father as well as a mother under the same roof. Simply put, even the best mothers cannot be good fathers.

+ dads?

18

For Study and Discussion

weak ending for where I thought she was going

QUESTIONS FOR RESPONSE

1. In paragraph 9, Whitehead says that "women enjoy certain advantages over men in a society marked by high and sustained levels of family breakup." Considering your own experience and that of people you know well, how do you respond to this claim?
2. In her first paragraph, Whitehead talks about "the fatherhood problem." How would you describe that problem in our society? Or do you think it even exists? Why do you say so?

QUESTIONS ABOUT PURPOSE

1. What changes in women's behaviors and attitudes would Whitehead like to bring about?
2. What changes in men's behaviors and attitudes would Whitehead like to bring about?

QUESTIONS ABOUT AUDIENCE

1. Whom do you see as the principal audience that Whitehead hopes to reach with this essay, men or women? On what do you base your answer?

2. What differences in responses to this article would you expect from readers over forty and those under forty?

QUESTIONS ABOUT STRATEGIES

1. Whitehead's argument is built on strong statements like this: "Today, marriage and motherhood are coming apart," and "Men have no positive identity as fathers outside marriage." In light of your own observations about today's families, how credible do you find these statements? Why?
2. Although Whitehead is writing about a topic that often generates a great deal of emotion, she is careful not to sound angry or to blame anyone. How does her argument benefit from her maintaining this moderate tone?

QUESTIONS FOR DISCUSSION

1. In paragraph 15 Whitehead says that men and women have crucial differences in their expectations about marriage and family. Judging by the people you know who have married recently or who plan to marry soon, what do you think women expect? What do men expect?
2. What important contributions (other than money) do you think a father makes to a child's upbringing that can't be adequately taken care of by a mother? Are there other individuals who can make those contributions?

A Debate About Harry Potter

JOAN ACOCELLA

Joan Acocella was born in 1945 in San Francisco and was educated at the University of California at Berkeley and Rutgers University. She began her writing career as a dance critic for *Dance Magazine,* the *New York Daily News,* and the *Wall Street Journal* before joining the staff of the *New Yorker.* Her books include *Mark Morris* (1993), *Creating Hysteria: Women and Multiple Personality Disorder* (1999), and *Willa Cather and the Politics of Criticism* (2000). In "Under the Spell," reprinted from the *New Yorker,* Acocella argues that the appeal of the Harry Potter books lies in their willingness to raise complicated moral questions.

Under the Spell

NOT SINCE Y2K have we seen a fuss like the one over "Harry Potter and the Goblet of Fire," the fourth volume in J. K. Rowling's series about a junior wizard. Biggest advance order ever (including Amazon.com's three hundred and fifty thousand), biggest first printing ever (three million eight hundred thousand copies in this country alone), biggest takeover, ever, of the *Times* best-seller list by a single writer, let alone a children's writer. As "The Goblet of Fire" was being printed, the three preceding volumes were all still in the ranking—a circumstance that resulted, last Sunday, in the creation of a separate, children's best-seller list, just what we didn't need. Prior to publication, the book was shrouded in ultra-tight, press-inflaming secrecy.

1

526

There were no copies for reviewers, or for anyone, before
publication day, July 8th. Many stores stayed open late on
July 7th—indeed, threw Harry Potter parties—and started
ringing up the sales at a minute after midnight. I myself went
to Books of Wonder, on West Eighteenth Street, and stood
in line for two hours with a lot of excited children and
bleary-eyed parents as a Harry Potter lookalike, presumably
associated with the store, cruised the sidewalk, distributing
press-on lightning-bolt tattoos and fake cheer. Around

fun,
fun
it wouldn't
be fake
cheer

---

*The subject of the Harry Potter series is
power, an important matter for children,
since they have so little of it.*

1:45 A.M., I made it to the front of the line and was allowed
to buy "The Goblet of Fire." After all that, I would love to
tell you that the book is a big nothing. In fact, it's wonderful, just like its predecessors.

odd switch of tones

Part of the secret of Rowling's success is her utter tradi-
tionalism. The Potter story is a fairy tale, plus a bildungs-
roman, plus a murder mystery, plus a cosmic war of good and
evil, and there's almost no classic in any of those genres that
doesn't reverberate between the lines of Harry's saga. The
Arthurian legend, the Superman comics, "Star Wars,"
"Cinderella," "The Lord of the Rings," the "Chronicles of
Narnia," "The Adventures of Sherlock Holmes," Genesis,
Exodus, the Divine Comedy, "Paradise Lost"—they're all
there. The Gothic paraphernalia, too: turreted castles, pur-
loined letters, surprise visitors arriving in the dark of night,
backed by forked lightning. If you take a look at Vladimir
Propp's 1928 book "Morphology of the Folk Tale," which
lists just about every convention ever used in fairy tales, you
can check off, one by one, the devices that Rowling has un-
abashedly picked up. At the beginning of the story, Propp

says, the villain harms someone in the hero's family. (The evil wizard Voldemort murdered Harry's good-wizard parents when the boy was a year old, and tried to kill him, too.) The hero is branded. (Voldemort's attack left Harry with a scar in the shape of a lightning bolt on his forehead.) The hero is banished. (Harry is forced to go live with his loathsome aunt and uncle, the Dursleys.) The hero is released. (Harry is finally informed that he is a wizard, and goes off to live at Hogwarts School of Witchcraft and Wizardry.) The hero must survive ordeals, seek things, acquire a wise helper, all of which Harry does. The villain must change form and leave bloody trails; Voldemort obliges. According to Propp, a fairy tale is supposed to end with the hero's marriage, but Rowling may break ranks here. She has said that the series will be seven novels long, one for each of Harry's years at Hogwarts. He started there at age eleven, so he will be seventeen when we say goodbye to him. In the line in front of Books of Wonder, there was heated speculation as to who is going to end up as Harry's girl. (I say Ginny Weasley.) I doubt we'll have a wedding, though. Seventeen's a little young.

So Rowling's books are chock-a-block with archetypes,   3 and she doesn't just use them; she glories in them, plays with them, postmodernly. At the Dursleys' house, Harry lives in a cupboard under the stairs, with spiders. Rowling is also a great showoff when it comes to surprise endings, and this, I think, is actually a fault of the books, or of the last two. The dénouements last for pages and pages, as red herrings are eliminated, false identities cleared up, friends unmasked as foes, and vice versa. Not only is this too complicated, the surprises are too surprising. How can Sirius Black, who has been stalking Harry throughout "The Prisoner of Azkaban," turn out to be a good guy—indeed, the boy's godfather? How can Scabbers, whom we have known and loved for three volumes as a dusty, useless little rat, snoozing in the sun, emerge at the end of that book as a deep-dyed villain in disguise? It seems to invalidate all our prior experience of the series. Not to speak of the sheer confusion. Faced with the equally counterintuitive revelations at the end of "The Goblet of

Fire," Harry thinks, "It made no sense . . . no sense at all." I
agree with him, but apparently we're in a minority.

[handwritten: really?]

Rowling has said that she has no trouble at all thinking   4
herself back to age eleven, and the novels show it. There are
toilet jokes, booger jokes. There is a ball game, Quidditch—
with four kinds of players (all flying on brooms) and three   *[handwritten: hehe]*
kinds of balls—that sounds as though it were made up by a
clever eleven-year-old. And the books are filled with children's problems. Do you have bad dreams? Did you find
your Christmas presents rather a letdown? Do you hate the
new baby in your house? Do you wish you had different parents? Is there something weird that lives under your bed and
makes noises at night? If so, Joanne Rowling is thinking
about you. Best of all is her treatment of the social nightmares of the schoolyard: cliques, bullying, ostracism, kids
who like to remind you that your family doesn't have much
money. Such problems are perhaps more pressing in the English boarding school, on which Hogwarts is modelled. (Last
year, in the *Times Book Review,* Pico Iyer claimed that
Hogwarts was a near-exact replica of Eton, where he did his
time.) But the situation clearly rings a bell with Rowling's
American readers, too.

More, even, than the Potter books' sensitivity to preteen   5
terrors, it is their wised-upness, their lack of sentimentality,
that must appeal to Rowling's audience. However much they
have to do with goodness, these are not prissy books. Harry
lies to adults again and again. He also hates certain people,
and Rowling hates them, too. Uncle Vernon Dursley is not
only cruel; he spits when he talks. Harry says the Dursleys
wish him dead, and he's right. As for the forces of good, they
are often well out of reach. In "The Sorcerer's Stone" there is
a heart-stopping scene in which Harry comes upon a mirror,
the so-called Mirror of Erised, and sees his dead parents in it.
His father waves at him; his mother weeps and smiles. Reading this, you think, Oh, good, thank God—Harry's not really
alone, not really an orphan. Yes, he's being hunted down by a
remorseless villain—in each of the books, Voldemort pursues

him—but his parents' spirits are there to protect him. Then Dumbledore, Hogwarts's wise headmaster, appears and tells Harry that the Mirror of Erised shows us not what is but what we desire. (Read "Erised" backward.) Harry is alone.

The great beauty of the Potter books is their wealth of imagination, their sheer, shining fullness. Rowling has said that the idea for the series came to her on a train trip from Manchester to London in 1990, and that, even before she started writing the first volume, she spent years just working out the details of Harry's world. We reap the harvest: the inventory of magical treats (Ice Mice, Jelly Slugs, Fizzing Whizbees—levitating sherbet balls) in the wizard candy store; the wide range of offerings (Dungbombs, Hiccup Sweets, Nose-Biting Teacups) in the wizard joke store. Hogwarts is a grand, creepy castle, a thousand years old, with more dungeons and secret passages than you can shake a stick at. There are a hundred and forty-two staircases, some of which go to different places on different days of the week. There are suits of armor that sing carols at Christmastime, and get the words wrong. There are poltergeists—Peeves, for example, who busies himself jamming gum into keyholes. We also get ghosts, notably Nearly Headless Nick, whose executioner didn't quite finish the job, so that Nick's head hangs by an "inch or so of ghostly skin and muscle"—it keeps flopping over his ruff—thus, to his grief, excluding him from participating in the Headless Hunt, which is confined to the thoroughly decapitated.

The Hogwarts staff is a display case all its own: Mad-Eye Moody, the professor of Defense Against the Dark Arts, who, apart from his ocular problems, has a chunk of his nose missing and a wooden leg ending in a clawed foot; Rubeus Hagrid, the gentle-giant gamekeeper, with his pet, Norbert, a baby dragon, whom he feeds a bucket of brandy mixed with chicken blood every half hour. Norbert isn't the only monster. There are also centaurs, basilisks, and hippogriffs, together with hinkypunks, boggarts, and, my favorites, the grindylows. Harry encounters his first grindylow in a tank in a professor's office: "A sickly green creature with sharp little horns had its face pressed against the glass, . . . flexing its long spindly fingers." (Later, the grindylow shakes its fist at him.) To deal with such encounters, and other life events, the students must learn many spells: "Expelliarmus," to get rid of something; "Waddiwasi," to extract gum from keyholes; "Peskipiksi Pesternomi," to make pixies leave you alone. Hogwarts is a whole, bursting world.

Most of Rowling's characters are types, and excellent as such, but some rise to a richness beyond the reach of British central casting. Voldemort, for example. When he failed to kill the infant Harry, Voldemort was disempowered, and it is in this weakened state that we first encounter him in "The Goblet of Fire." But he isn't just weak. He is—grotesquely, disgustingly, terrifyingly—a *baby:* "hairless and scaly-looking, a dark, raw, reddish black. Its arms and legs were thin and feeble, and its face—no child alive ever had a face like that— flat and snakelike, with gleaming red eyes." Soon—as soon as he is immersed in a potion made from Harry's blood and someone else's hacked-off hand and various other ingredients—he becomes his adult self again, which is not so handsome either, but that first sight of him, that little red thing, swaddled in blankets, is a triumph of horror fiction. *nice points*

It's horror with a difference, though. Rowling's favorite writer, she has told interviewers, is Jane Austen. She also loves Dickens. And it is in their bailiwick—English morals-and-manners realism, the world of Pip and Miss Bates, of money and position and trying to keep your head up if you have neither—that she scores her greatest victories. A nice example is the scene, in "The Sorcerer's Stone," where Harry and Ron meet for the first time, on the train that is taking them, as entering students, to Hogwarts. Each is handicapped. Harry, though he is famous throughout the wizard world (because, as an infant, he repelled Voldemort's attack), and though he has a pile of gold left to him by his parents, is without family and utterly ignorant of wizardry. Ron comes from a long line of wizards, and he has family galore, but that is his problem: five older brothers, no position. He is always dressed in hand-me-downs; his mother always forgets what *part of being in a family*

kind of sandwich he likes; he has no spending money. Together, in the train compartment, the two boys comfort and
help each other. Harry shares the wizard candies he buys
from the vender (he can afford them); Ron explains the wizard trading cards that come with the candies (he understands
them). Harry gives Ron prestige; Ron gives Harry a sense of
belonging. All this is done very Englishly, very subtly, in small
gestures, but in the end each boy, because of the other, arrives at Hogwarts slightly better armed against the harshness
of the world.

good writing here

The subject of the Harry Potter series is power, an impor-   10
tant matter for children, since they have so little of it. How
does one acquire power? How can it be used well, and ill?
Does ultimate power lie with the good? (In other words, is
there a God?) If so, why is there so much cruelty around?
These are questions that Milton, among others, addressed
before Rowling, and she is not ashamed to follow in their
wake. Voldemort is an avatar of Milton's Lucifer; Dumbledore of Milton's God, who so mysteriously permits evil in the
world.

Each of the novels approaches the problem from a differ-   11
ent angle. The first, "Harry Potter and the Sorcerer's Stone,"
is heroic. We meet our champion; he is a child; we watch him
grow into competence and faith. The second volume, "Harry
Potter and the Chamber of Secrets," is quite different: secular, topical, political. Sexism is not a major problem at
Hogwarts. The school is coed. Several of the Quidditch
champions are girls. Harry's friend Hermione, the know-it-
all girl, the hand-up-in-class girl—Rowling has said she based
the character on herself as a child—is not forced to go
through the Katharine Hepburn treatment (take off her
glasses, unpin her hair) before she becomes likable. But racism *is* a problem at Hogwarts. Yes, the student body includes
Cho Chang and Parvati Patil and Dean Thomas, who has
dreadlocks. (Rowling forgot about a few other groups,
though. I would not have minded if the evil Professor Snape

had not had a hook nose, greasy black hair, and sallow skin— *those*
standard features of the rapacious Jew—or if the chief villain *don't*
of "The Sorcerer's Stone" had not worn a purple turban, *have*
been prone to faint and weep, and had the name Quirrell, *to*
which is rather close to "queer.") But the wizard world is in *be*
the grip of an overarching race war, a campaign to rid wiz- *racist*
ardry of those with Muggle, or non-wizard, blood. This
ethnic-cleansing campaign, led by Voldemort, is the subject
of "The Chamber of Secrets." It fails, but only for the time
being. We will hear about it again.

The strangest volume is the third, "Harry Potter and the   12
Prisoner of Azkaban," the psychological installment, featur-
ing a pack of demons—operating at Voldemort's bidding—
who are the most frightening monsters in the series so far.
These are the Dementors: huge, cloaked, faceless creatures,
with rotting hands, who, if they get you, clamp their jaws on
your mouth and suck out of you every thought of happiness. *Shhh*
The Dementors represent depression. Actually, if I'm not
mistaken, they represent a specific, British theory of depression—John Bowlby's theory that loss of a parent in early
childhood is a major risk factor for that disorder. At age one,
Harry lost both his parents. (I don't know much about
Rowling's childhood, but she has told interviewers that she
suffered a period of depression as an adult, and had to get
professional help.) In any case, the Dementors are after
Harry, and he escapes them only with the help of a teacher
named Lupin. To Lupin alone can he fully confide his fears,
and Lupin's teachings are the closest thing, in the Potter series, to overt psychological counselling of child readers. At
the end of "The Prisoner of Azkaban," this nice man turns
out to be a werewolf (Rowling's antisentimentality again),
but he's a good werewolf.

The new book, "Harry Potter and the Goblet of Fire," is   13
the central pillar of the projected series of seven and is thus a
transitional volume. It introduces many new subjects, notably sex. (Harry is fourteen now, and mightily taken with Cho
Chang.) Also, the politics become more ambitious. Rowling

smart writing on her part

now asks her readers to consider the cynicism of government officials, the injustice of the law courts, the vagaries of international relations, the mendacity of the press, even the psychology of slavery. ("They're *happy*," Ron's brother says of the house-elves. Hermione does not agree.) This is a great, toppling heap of subjects, and Rowling takes seven hundred and thirty-four pages to deal with them. (Has there ever before been a children's story seven hundred and thirty-four pages long? What confidence!) Where the prior volumes moved like lightning, here the pace is slower, the energy more dispersed. At the same time, the tone becomes more grim. Voldemort has been restored to power. Things will now become harder for Harry, and for all the wizard world. Dumbledore says so.

There is much for Rowling to resolve in the remaining volumes, above all the question about power—is it reconcilable with goodness?—that she poses in the first four books. Already in "The Sorcerer's Stone," Quirrell says, "There is no good and evil, there is only power, and those too weak to seek it." As Harry has grown, he has become more powerful and ambitious and, at the same time, more virtuous. In "The Goblet of Fire," as in all the books, there is a big contest, which Harry longs to win. The contest is in three parts, and in each part, lest we miss the point, Rowling shows Harry handicapping himself, hurting his chances of victory, out of concern for others. He wins, but how will he do, thus compromised by altruism, in future contests? Remember: Voldemort is back.

Even more interesting, however, is a strange matter— something about the *kinship* of good and evil—that Rowling has been hinting at since the beginning of the series. Harry and Voldemort have a lot in common. Both have Muggle blood; both are orphans. Their wands contain feathers from the same phoenix. When they met in armed combat in "The Goblet of Fire," their wands, as they touch, produce a single stream of light, which binds them together. There is some connection between these two. (Shades of "Star Wars.") I don't know what Rowling has in mind here. Maybe it's the

Miltonic idea of evil as merely good perverted. Or maybe not.

But that is the main virtue of these books, their philosophical seriousness. Rowling is a good psychotherapist, and she teaches excellent morals. (Those parents who have objected to the Potter series on the ground that it promotes unchristian values should give it another read.) She also spins a good yarn. Undoubtedly, it is Voldemort and the Dementors and the grindylows that have gotten these books translated into forty languages and won them sales, *before* "The Goblet of Fire," of more than thirty million copies. But her great glory, and the thing that may place her in the pantheon, is that she asks her preteen readers to face the hardest questions of life, and does not shy away from the possibility that the answers may be sad: that loss may be permanent, evil ever-present, good exhaustible. In an odd, quiet moment in "The Goblet of Fire," Harry stands alone in Hogwarts's Owlery, gazing out into the twilight. He sees his friend Hagrid digging in the earth. Is Hagrid burying something? Or looking for something? Harry doesn't know, and for once he doesn't investigate. He seems tired. He just stays there, watching Hagrid, until he can see him no more, whereupon the owls in the Owlery awaken and swoosh past him, "into the night." In this volume, some darkness has fallen. With the light—the next three books—new griefs will surely come.

16

more than children books

For Study and Discussion

QUESTIONS FOR RESPONSE

1. If you've enjoyed the Harry Potter books, where do you think their appeal lies for you? If you haven't read them, what do you think accounts for your lack of interest?
2. As Acocella points out, the Harry Potter books have been cleverly marketed to build up suspense among potential buyers. To what extent do you think the marketing strategies have influenced your reaction to them?

QUESTIONS ABOUT PURPOSE

1. Although the Harry Potter books are written for children, this serious review of them was written for the *New Yorker,* a magazine for sophisticated, well-educated readers. Why do you think Acocella chose them for her audience?
2. Why does Acocella trace the traditions, from the King Arthur legends to *Star Wars,* that underlie the books, giving references that range from the Bible and literary classics to comic books?

QUESTIONS ABOUT AUDIENCE

1. Educators know that young boys are a notoriously difficult audience for writers to reach, but both boys and girls are reading Harry Potter in record numbers. How does Acocella explain this wide appeal?
2. Who besides the readers of the Potter books themselves might be interested in learning more about this publishing phenomenon?

QUESTIONS ABOUT STRATEGIES

1. Acocella goes into great detail to show the lurid and gory details of the Potter stories. How does she engage her readers with these descriptions?
2. How does Acocella present herself in this essay? How does she establish her credentials to analyze the traditions and legends that are so important to the Potter series?

QUESTIONS FOR DISCUSSION

1. Acocella says that the main virtue of the Potter books is their philosophical seriousness and the fact that Rowling, the author, is a good psychotherapist. How does she support that claim?
2. Why do you think the books have drawn so much response? How is that response different from the attention paid to movies and sports?

HAROLD BLOOM

Harold Bloom was born in 1930 in New York and was educated at Cornell University and Yale University. In his distinguished teaching career, he has taught literature at Yale, Cornell, Harvard, and New York University. A staunch defender of the Western literary tradition, his numerous critical books include *The Anxiety of Influence: A Theory of Poetry* (1973), *A Map of Misreading* (1975), *The Breaking of Vessels* (1982), *The Western Canon: The Books and School of the Ages* (1994), and most recently *Hamlet: Poem Unlimited* (2003). In "Can 35 Million Book Buyers Be Wrong? Yes," reprinted from the *Wall Street Journal,* Bloom argues that the Harry Potter books are inferior to classic children's books.

Can 35 Million Book Buyers Be Wrong? Yes.

TAKING ARMS AGAINST Harry Potter, at this moment, is to emulate Hamlet taking arms against a sea of troubles. By opposing the sea, you won't end it. The Harry Potter epiphenomenon will go on, doubtless for some time, as J.R.R. Tolkien did, and then wane.

The official newspaper of our dominant counter-culture, the *New York Times,* has been startled by the Potter books into establishing a new policy for its not very literate book review. Rather than crowd out the Grishams, Clancys, Crichtons, Kings and other vastly popular prose fictions on its fiction bestseller list, the Potter volumes will now lead a separate children's list. J. K. Rowling, the chronicler of Harry Potter, thus has an unusual distinction: She has changed the policy of the policy-maker.

IMAGINATIVE VISION

[handwritten: cynic]

I read new children's literature, when I can find some of any value, but had not tried Rowling until now. I have just concluded the 300 pages of the first book in the series, "Harry Potter and the Sorcerer's Stone," purportedly the best of the lot. Though the book is not well written, that is not in itself a crucial liability. It is much better to see the movie, "The Wizard of Oz," than to read the book upon which it was based, but even the book possessed an authentic imaginative vision.

[handwritten: wow]

> *Hogwarts enchants many of Harry's fans, perhaps because it is much livelier than the schools they attend, but it seems to me an academy more tiresome than grotesque.*

"Harry Potter and the Sorcerer's Stone" does not, so that one needs to look elsewhere for the book's (and its sequels') remarkable success. Such speculation should follow an account of how and why Harry Potter asks to be read.

The ultimate model for Harry Potter is "Tom Brown's School Days" by Thomas Hughes, published in 1857. The book depicts the Rugby School presided over by the formidable Thomas Arnold, remembered now primarily as the father of Matthew Arnold, the Victorian critic-poet. But Hughes's book, still quite readable, was realism, not fantasy. Rowling has taken "Tom Brown's School Days" and re-seen it in the magical mirror of Tolkien. The resultant blend of a schoolboy ethos with a liberation from the constraints of reality-testing may read oddly to me, but is exactly what millions of children and their parents desire and welcome at this time.

[handwritten: hell ya!]

In what follows, I may at times indicate some of the inadequacies of "Harry Potter." But I will keep in mind that a host are reading it who simply will not read superior fare, such as Kenneth Grahame's "The Wind in the Willows" or the "Alice" books of Lewis Carroll. Is it better that they read Rowling than not read at all? Will they advance from Rowling to more difficult pleasures?

maybe

Rowling presents two Englands, mundane and magical, 6 divided not by social classes, but by the distinction between the "perfectly normal" (mean and selfish) and the adherents of sorcery. The sorcerers indeed seem as middle-class as the Muggles, the name the witches and wizards give to the common sort, since those addicted to magic send their sons and daughters off to Hogwarts, a Rugby School where only witchcraft and wizardry are taught. Hogwarts is presided over by Albus Dumbledore as Headmaster, he being Rowling's version of Tolkien's Gandalf. The young future sorcerers are just like any other budding Britons, only more so, sports and food being primary preoccupations. (Sex barely enters into Rowling's cosmos, at least in the first volume.)

definite resemb-lance

Harry Potter, now the hero of so many millions of children and adults, is raised by dreadful Muggle relatives after his sorcerer parents are murdered by the wicked Voldemort, a wizard gone trollish and, finally, post-human. Precisely why poor Harry is handed over by the sorcerer elders to his piggish aunt and uncle is never clarified by Rowling, but it is a nice touch, suggesting again how conventional the alternative Britain truly is. They consign their potential hero-wizard to his nasty blood-kin, rather than let him be reared by amiable warlocks and witches, who would know him for one of their own.

danger

The child Harry thus suffers the hateful ill treatment of 8 the Dursleys, Muggles of the most Muggleworthy sort, and of their sadistic son, his cousin Dudley. For some early pages we might be in Ken Russell's film of "Tommy," the rock-opera by The Who, except that the prematurely wise Harry is much healthier than Tommy. A born survivor, Harry holds on until the sorcerers rescue him and send him off to Hogwarts, to enter upon the glory of his schooldays.

odd to put together ☺

Hogwarts enchants many of Harry's fans, perhaps because 9
it is much livelier than the schools they attend, but it seems to
me an academy more tiresome than grotesque. When the future witches and wizards of Great Britain are not studying
how to cast a spell, they preoccupy themselves with bizarre
intramural sports. It is rather a relief when Harry heroically
suffers the ordeal of a confrontation with Voldemort, which
the youth handles admirably.

[handwritten margin note: most certainly]

One can reasonably doubt that "Harry Potter and the Sor- 10
cerer's Stone" is going to prove a classic of children's literature, but Rowling, whatever the aesthetic weakness of her
work, is at least a millennial index to our popular culture. So
huge an audience gives her importance akin to rock stars,
movie idols, TV anchors, and successful politicians. Her
prose style, heavy on cliché, makes no demands upon her
readers. In an arbitrarily chosen single page—page 4—of the
first Harry Potter book, I count seven clichés, all of the
"stretch his legs" variety. *[handwritten: get a life]*

[handwritten margin note: already has]

How to read "Harry Potter and the Sorcerer's Stone"? 11
Why, very quickly, to begin with, perhaps also to make an
end. Why read it? Presumably, if you cannot be persuaded to
read anything better, Rowling will have to do. Is there any re-
deeming educational use to Rowling? Is there any to Stephen
King? Why read, if what you read will not enrich mind or
spirit or personality? For all I know, the actual wizards and
witches of Britain, or of America, may provide an alternative
culture for more people than is commonly realized.

Perhaps Rowling appeals to millions of reader non-readers 12
because they sense her wistful sincerity, and want to join her
world, imaginary or not. She feeds a vast hunger for unreal-
ity: can that be bad? At least her fans are momentarily eman-
cipated from their screens, and so may not forget wholly the
sensation of turning the pages of a book, any book.

[handwritten margin note: how smug]

INTELLIGENT CHILDREN

And yet I feel a discomfort with the Harry Potter mania, and 13
I hope that my discontent is not merely a highbrow snob-

bery, or a nostalgia for a more literate fantasy to beguile (shall we say) intelligent children of all ages. Can more than 35 million book buyers, and their offspring, be wrong? Yes, they have been, and will continue to be so for as long as they persevere with Potter. *jerkish*

A vast concourse of inadequate works, for adults and for children, crams the dustbins of the ages. At a time when public judgment is no better and no worse than what is proclaimed by the ideological cheerleaders who have so destroyed humanistic study, anything goes. The cultural critics will, soon enough, introduce Harry Potter into their college *that'd* curriculum, and the *New York Times* will go on celebrating *be* another confirmation of the dumbing-down it leads and *awesome* exemplifies. 14

For Study and Discussion

QUESTIONS FOR RESPONSE

1. What impression do you get of the author, Harold Bloom, from the reasons he gives for disliking the Harry Potter books?
2. Either from your own reading of the Potter books or from reviewing the essay "Under the Spell," what is your response to Bloom's claim that J.K. Rowling lacks imagination?

QUESTIONS ABOUT PURPOSE

1. What do you think an eminent professor of Bloom's standing hopes to accomplish by taking time to read a popular children's book and then give it—and the *New York Times*—such a scathing review?
2. What kind of reading do you think Bloom would recommend as literature that would, as he says, "enrich the mind or spirit or personality"?

QUESTIONS ABOUT AUDIENCE

1. Bloom published this essay in the *Wall Street Journal,* a national newspaper whose readers are predominantly business executives and people involved in the world of finance. To what extent

might his criticism simply be nostalgia for a "golden age of children's literature"?

2. On the other hand, why might the readers of the *Wall Street Journal* be intrigued by the Harry Potter books?

QUESTIONS ABOUT STRATEGIES

1. What persona do you think Bloom wants to present to his readers? How does his first sentence contribute to that persona?
2. Why does he liken Harry's creator, J.K. Rowling, to the "rock stars, movie idols, TV anchors, and successful politicians" of the millennium? What's his point?

QUESTIONS FOR DISCUSSION

1. In his last paragraph, when Bloom condemns "the ideological cheerleaders who have so destroyed humanistic study," he refers to faculty across the country who have, in recent years, promoted a more culturally diverse curriculum in the humanities, one that includes more women writers and more writers from minority groups. He accuses such individuals of "dumbing down" literature courses. How does his criticism of the Harry Potter books fit into this complaint?
2. To what extent do you see Bloom's criticism as valid? To what extent do you see it as nostalgia for a "golden age of children's literature"?

A Debate About Human Nature

FRANCINE PROSE

Francine Prose was born in 1947 in Brooklyn, *[rough town]* New York, and educated at Radcliffe College and Harvard University. She has taught creative writing at Harvard University, the University of Arizona, Warren Wilson College, and the Breadloaf Writers Conference. She has contributed essays and reviews to magazine such as *Harper's Bazaar, New York Times Magazine,* the *Atlantic,* and *Commentary.* Her first novel, *Judah the Pious* (1973), is a symbolic tale about religious toleration. Her subsequent novels, such as *Household Saints* (1981), *Big Foot Dreams* (1986), and *Primitive People* (1992), evoke the supernatural and hilarious cultural puzzlements. Her most recent book is *The Lives of the Muses: Nine Women and the Artists They Inspired* (2002). In "Genocide Without Apology," Prose confronts the truth that her favorite religious holiday, Passover, celebrates and justifies the killing of children.

Genocide Without Apology

A S A CHILD, I adored the ten plagues. Their ceremonial *[adored?]* 1
recitation was my favorite part of the Passover seder, which we celebrated in the basement of my great-aunt's house in Brooklyn. As each plague was named aloud, we dipped our fingers into our wine cups and transferred a single drop of the delicious, sugary wine to our plates.

It was the only time in my life when playing with food was 2
not only sanctioned but encouraged. And not just food, but

what a religion eh.?

wine, too, which I and my cousins drank until we were fairly hammered. I remember fighting the impulse to lick my finger after the dipping was finished, resisting the temptation out of some cuckoo primitive fear that by doing so, I might expose myself to one of the plagues that we had just so lovingly listed.

And what a glorious list it was! How mysterious and thrilling! Some of the plagues—frogs, locusts, boils—were irresistibly easy to visualize. I was frightened of insects, and so instantly comprehended the horror of an infestation of vermin.

great diction

3

> *Obviously, what bothers me most about [the book of] Exodus is what should make me admire it most: it tells the truth about how people behave, something I would rather not listen to.*

sense of child's curiosity

Others were more of a challenge. What was with the blood, exactly? Was it just in the rivers and the water supply . . . or did it creep over the banks and run red in the streets of Cairo? Murrain made no sense at all. What was a livestock disease to a city kid who had no idea how the food chain operated?

Such mysteries were at once illuminated and deepened by the illustrations in the Passover Haggadah—woodcuts I always thought were medieval, but that I recently learned were, more likely, seventeenth-century. All ten were crowded onto one page, each the size of a postage stamp. It was impossible to make out what was going on in the crowded images. But that, too—along with the foreign, exotic, and ancient quality of the woodcuts—only added to their creepiness. I could have stared at them forever. It was like watching certain horror films: forbidden and disturbing, therefore sexy and alluring. Like a horror film, the plagues

4

built toward a climax, a last-ditch special effect, a pulling-out
of all the stops, an orgasm of mayhem and blood—the slay-
ing of the firstborn. The technique that worked when nothing else had.

Never once, during all those years, during all those seders, 5
did I think—nor was it pointed out to me—that those
plagues had human victims, that the sufferers from boils and
blood, the ones whose houses filled with frogs and locusts,
were human beings like myself. It simply never crossed my
mind that the firstborn whom the angel slaughtered could
(except for a few particulars of place and time) just as easily
have been me. I was the oldest in our family, but I never
made the connection between myself and the dead Egyptian
children.

brutal epiphany

There are many reasons, I suppose, to enjoy and admire 6
and be inspired by the Book of Exodus. Its themes could
hardly be more stirring, or more beautiful. Oppression and
liberation, courage, self-determination: nothing less than the
human spirit yearning to break free, and breaking free; nothing less than people screwing up, suffering, wandering, and
painfully, slowly, starting to learn how to live as a new, hope-
ful nation. It's the Founding Fathers, the Emancipation
Proclamation, with highly cinematic hoodoo: the way that
Moses and his brother Aaron make people listen up is by
magically changing walking sticks into snakes.

Exodus is also—as many (including, most notably, Cecil B. 7
DeMille) have realized—action packed. There's little in the
Bible to equal, chapter for chapter, its roller-coaster narrative
of incident, suspense, structural parallelisms, magic, special
effects (the burning bush! the splitting of the Red Sea!), hesi-
tations, missteps, punishments and sufferings, renewals and
redemptions.

great literature

And brutality. From the start, the Book of Exodus involves 8
a series of bloodbaths—outbreaks of state-sponsored and di-
vinely ordained carnage directed principally at children.
Whole populations are oppressed, enslaved, tormented,

effective opening

innocent
connotation

nearly wiped out in a battle for sovereignty whose victims— with the exception of the soldiers drowned in the Red Sea— are almost entirely civilians.

After a nod to the brothers who, together with their 9
households, followed Joseph into Egypt, the Exodus narrative begins by striking an ominous note of political anxiety that will echo until the last chapters.

The Jews are prospering and multiplying; their presence is 10
a liability that makes the new Pharaoh nervous. So he enslaves them, makes them work in the building trades and the fields, but still they continue to multiply.

It has long been noted that there's always trouble when 11
one population begins to worry excessively about the birthrate of another. Once this happens, in fact, it's usually too late, and violence is inevitable.

every-
where

And so the book's first slaughter of children begins. Pha- 12
raoh directs the midwives to kill every Jewish male baby. But here, as in the rest of Exodus, women distinguish themselves by performing significant, often quiet, acts of courage and resistance. Not only do the midwives spare the male babies, but when the Pharaoh demands an explanation, they play with his head a little, claiming that the Hebrew women go into labor so rapidly that the midwives always arrive too late to assist at the births and murder the babies.

In the rabbinical commentary on the Book of Exodus, it's 13
suggested that the Pharaoh had leprosy and imagined he might be cured by bathing in the blood of Jewish male babies. Like monitoring the birthrate of another race, blood accusations are an indicator of present and future trouble.

All this is background for the story of how a hero is chosen 14
and trained. Baby Moses is found in the bulrushes and, in another act of female resistance, is adopted by Pharaoh's daughter, who knows exactly what she's doing and hands him off to his mother to nurse and raise.

sarcasm?

The rest—the burning bush, the staff turning into the ser- 15
pent—is pure heroic fairy tale, the sorts of signs and wonders that would separate a Greek hero from the crown, or reveal a

new Dalai Lama, or inspire a prophet. The voice that speaks to Moses from the burning bush is powerful and succinct. It's the voice of God introducing himself. *I am that I am.*

[margin: I love that intro]

The other magic trick that God teaches Moses to perform in order to help prove his credentials involves putting his hand into his robe and taking it out white with leprosy, then putting it back again and taking it out once more—healed. Anyone would listen to a guy who could do that. Moses speaks, Pharaoh listens. God hardens the Egyptian ruler's heart.

[margin: great sentence]

Now comes the long painful back-and-forth of *let my people go,* a battle that God warns Moses He himself will make Moses lose. And it happens just as God says. Pharaoh makes the Jews slave harder.

Warnings and threats. Promises, and failures to keep them. Warnings, promises, threats, and lies. In other words, end-stage diplomacy.

[margin: odd grammar]

And before you know it, blood.

The pools and rivers turn to blood. The fish die. There is nothing to drink. Recall, if you will, your horror at drawing a bath and finding the water dark. And that is only rust. Ecologists have probably charted the inevitable progress from the blood drought to the rain of frogs and the onslaught of locusts and the lice and the flies and the sick cattle.

The counting off of the ten plagues is surgical in its restraint, compared with the pleasure that the writer of Exodus takes in the gruesome details. The frogs in the beds and ovens, the swarms of flies, the devouring locusts stripping the trees and blackening the earth, the unprecedented and murderous hail and fire. Darkness.

[margin: interesting way to classify author]

And all this is merely a prelude to the grand finale, to the plague that succeeds where the others have not, the one that does the trick, that will cause Pharaoh, after all his stubbornness, not merely to let the Hebrews go but to expel them from Egypt. And that of course is the killing of the firstborn.

Unlike the massacre of the Hebrew male babies, which Pharaoh arranges rather casually, almost capriciously, and

[margin: ugh]

[margin: Diction]

leaves—with such unfortunate consequences for himself—to the unreliable midwives, the massacre orchestrated by God is carefully prepared for. Through Moses, God announces precisely what is about to occur.

> *And all the first-born in the land of Egypt shall die, from the first-born of Pharaoh that sitteth upon his throne, even unto the first-born of the maid-servant that is behind the mill; and all the first-born of beasts. And there shall be a great cry throughout the land of Egypt, such as there was none like it, nor shall be like it any more.*

It is genocide without apology. And at the end of this dire prophecy comes the most important sentence of all, the real beginning of what the rest of the Book of Exodus will so ferociously and zealously continue: the demarcation of difference, the establishment of a separation between Israel and the other nations and tribes, the forging of an identity, an exclusive and exclusionary proto-nationalism: "But against any of the children of Israel shall not a dog move his tongue, against man or beast; that ye may know how the Lord doth put a difference between the Egyptians and Israel." It is a difference that will prove as important, as essential, as life and death.

The killing of the firstborn is preceded by the first of the numerous series of almost obsessively meticulous instructions that appear throughout Exodus—detailed protocols that, again, will form the identity, the tradition, and the history that will forever distinguish the Hebrews from their neighbors. The time and the manner of the animal sacrifice is ordained. It must be not just any beast, but a lamb "without blemish," a year-old male. Present and future feasts—the celebration we now know as Passover—will be observed by eating unleavened bread, though, it should be noted, uncircumcised foreigners should not be permitted to partake of the ritual meal. And the blood of the lambs is to be used to mark the doors of the homes that the angel of death will spare in the otherwise merciless search for the children who

[handwritten margin note: dark & demented]

[margin numbers: 24, 25]

are to die in order that God's chosen people can win their freedom.

And it came to pass exactly as the Lord predicted, or warned: 26

> *At midnight the Lord smote all the first-born in the Land of Egypt, from the first-born of Pharaoh that sat on his throne unto the first-born of the captive that was in the dungeon: and all the first-born of cattle. And Pharaoh rose up in the night, he and all his servants, and all the Egyptians; and there was a great cry in Egypt; for there was not a house where there was not one dead.*

For there was not a house where there was not one dead. This   27
was what I was celebrating as I dipped my finger in my cup *were* and watched the little puddle of wine growing in my saucer. How ironic that I, a child, should have rejoiced in this evidence that the lives and deaths of children meant nothing, that they were merely pawns to be used or eliminated because of political exigencies. First, the Hebrew children, then the Egyptian children. And thousands of years later, an American child dipped her finger in her wine and learned— without being told—that the suffering of the innocent, the murder of children, was not merely pardonable but a holy thing when the freedom of the other group was at stake.

It all puts a peculiar slant on the Ten Commandments,   28
which Moses receives a little later in the book, together with an amazingly detailed set of architectural and decorating plans for the Ark of the Covenant and a legal system that no one would call liberal. Including, for example, the law *Thou shalt not suffer a witch to live.*

Obviously, what bothers me most about Exodus is what   29
should make me admire it most: that is, that it tells us a truth about how people behave, something I would rather not listen to. Humans clump together in arbitrary, tightly knit groups that want to kill other groups and occupy their territory. Children are merely bodies, especially other people's children, Hebrew, Egyptian, Palestinian, Afghan, Hutu,

brutal truth

Kurd. It hardly matters who they are, as long as they are not our own.

Needless to say, this way of seeing the world and its inhabitants is by no means limited to the ancient Hebrews in the Bible, or to contemporary Israelis and Palestinians. Every group is capable of behaving this way, and has behaved this way—Americans included. Though I would rather not believe it, I feel obliged to suggest that what happens in Exodus tells us something about the dark side of human nature.

ya!

One would have to be totally unconscious not to realize that all this is as true now as it was when Moses was in Egypt. Though I am willing to admit it, I don't have to celebrate it; I don't have to dip my finger in my wine glass and extract sweet drops for the time when my group, my nation, triumphed at a terrible cost, when it was our turn to show another group who was boss. Nor do I have to thank God for making this point by killing the Egyptian children, just as God first, presumably, had inspired the Egyptians to attempt to kill the Jews.

The most disturbing and depressing thing about the Book of Exodus is the proof it offers that genocide without apology is older than the Bible.

great ending

For Study and Discussion

QUESTIONS FOR RESPONSE

1. What is your first reaction to Prose's pointing out that a major book of the Old Testament not only sanctions killing the children of Israel's enemies, but encourages it?
2. What connections do you see between Prose's account of the racial hatred and slaughter in the book of Exodus and the events of September 11, 2001?

QUESTIONS ABOUT PURPOSE

1. What fresh insights about a dramatic narrative from the Old Testament do you think Prose wants her readers to get by reading this essay?

2. What change in her readers' consciousness do you think she wants to achieve through her last four paragraphs?

QUESTIONS ABOUT AUDIENCE

1. What knowledge about religious hatred and bloodshed can Prose assume that her American readers have in 2004?
2. What elements in American popular culture seem to emphasize violence as the natural solution to conflict?

QUESTIONS ABOUT STRATEGIES

1. How do Prose's opening paragraphs help her readers identify with and understand her childhood fascination with ancient plagues and bloodshed?
2. How does she dramatize the story of Exodus to set the context for the celebration of Passover?

QUESTIONS FOR DISCUSSION

1. How do you react to Prose's statement "Every group is capable of behaving this way, and has behaved this way—Americans included"?
2. What recent conflicts in the world seem to bear out Prose's conclusions about human behavior?

Natalie Angier was born in New York City in 1958 and educated at the University of Michigan and Barnard College. She worked as a staff writer for *Discover* and *Time* and as an editor for *Savvy* before becoming the science correspondent for the *New York Times,* where she won the Pulitzer Prize for best reporting. Her books include *Natural Obsessions* (1988), *The Beauty of the Beastly* (1995), and *Woman: An Intimate Geography* (1999). In "Of Altruism, Heroism, and Evolution's Gifts," reprinted from the *New York Times,* Angier argues that the best qualities of human nature often emerge in crises.

Of Altruism, Heroism, and Evolution's Gifts

[handwritten: that's a great way to open]

F OR THE WORDLESS, formless, expectant citizens of tomor- 1
row, here are some postcards of all that matters today:

- Minutes after terrorists slam jet planes into the towers of the World Trade Center, streams of harrowed humanity crowd the emergency stairwells, heading in two directions. While terrified employees scramble down, toward exit doors and survival, hundreds of New York firefighters, each laden with 70 to 100 pounds of lifesaving gear, charge upward, never to be seen again.
- As the last of four hijacked planes advances toward an unknown but surely populated destination, passengers huddle together and plot resistance against their captors, an act that may explain why the plane fails to reach its target, crashing instead into an empty field outside Pittsburgh.

- Hearing of the tragedy whose dimensions cannot be charted or absorbed, tens of thousands of people across the nation storm their local hospitals and blood banks, begging for the chance to give blood, something of themselves to the hearts of the wounded—and the heart of us all—beating against the void.

great metaphor

Altruism and heroism. If not for these twin radiant badges of our humanity, there would be no us, and we know it. And so, when their vile opposite threatened to choke us into submission last Tuesday, we rallied them in quantities so great we surprised even ourselves. 2

Nothing and nobody can fully explain the source of the emotional genius that has been everywhere on display. Politi- 3

Altruism and heroism. If not for these twin radiant badges of our humanity, there would be no us, and we know it.

---

cians have cast it as evidence of the indomitable spirit of a rock-solid America; pastors have given credit to a more celestial source. And while biologists in no way claim to have discovered the key to human nobility, they do have their own spin on the subject. The altruistic impulse, they say, is a nondenominational gift, the birthright and defining characteristic of the human species.

she has a great style of writing

As they see it, the roots of altruistic behavior far predate Homo sapiens, and that is why it seems to flow forth so readily once tapped. Recent studies that model group dynamics suggest that a spirit of cooperation will arise in nature under a wide variety of circumstances. 4

"There's a general trend in evolutionary biology toward recognizing that very often the best way to compete is to cooperate," said Dr. Barbara Smuts, a professor of anthropol- 5

I really like that

ogy at the University of Michigan, who has published papers on the evolution of altruism. "And that, to me, is a source of some solace and comfort."

Moreover, most biologists concur that the human capacity 6 for language and memory allows altruistic behavior—the desire to give, and to sacrifice for the sake of others—to flourish in measure far beyond the cooperative spirit seen in other species.

With language, they say, people can learn of individuals 7 they have never met and feel compassion for their suffering, and honor and even emulate their heroic deeds. They can also warn one another of any selfish cheaters or malign tricksters lurking in their midst.

"In a large crowd, we know who the good guys are, and 8 we can talk about, and ostracize, the bad ones," said Dr. Craig Packer, a professor of ecology and evolution at the University of Minnesota. "People are very concerned about their reputation, and that, too, can inspire us to be good."

Oh, better than good. 9

"There's a grandness in the human species that is so strik- 10 ing, and so profoundly different from what we see in other animals," he added. "We are an amalgamation of families working together. This is what civilization is derived from."

At the same time, said biologists, the very conditions that 11 encourage heroics and selflessness can be the source of profound barbarism as well. "Moral behavior is often a within-group phenomenon," said Dr. David Sloan Wilson, a professor of biology at the State University of New York at Binghamton. "Altruism is practiced within your group, and often turned off toward members of other groups."

The desire to understand the nature of altruism has occu- 12 pied evolutionary thinkers since Charles Darwin, who was fascinated by the apparent existence of altruism among social insects. In ant and bee colonies, sterile female workers labor ceaselessly for their queen, and will even die for her when the nest is threatened. How could such seeming selflessness evolve, when it is exactly those individuals that are behaving altruistically that fail to breed and thereby pass their selfless genes along?

By a similar token, human soldiers who go to war often are   13
at the beginning of their reproductive potential, and many
are killed before getting the chance to have children. Why
don't the stay-at-homes simply outbreed the do-gooders and
thus bury the altruistic impulse along with the casualties of
combat?

confusing

The question of altruism was at least partly solved when   14
the British evolutionary theorist William Hamilton formu-
lated the idea of inclusive fitness: the notion that individuals
can enhance their reproductive success not merely by having
young of their own, but by caring for their genetic relatives as
well. Among social bees and ants, it turns out, the sister
workers are more closely related to one another than parents
normally are to their offspring; thus it behooves the workers
to care more about current and potential sisters than to fret
over their sterile selves.

the comparison to ants really weird

The concept of inclusive fitness explains many brave acts   15
observed in nature. Dr. Richard Wrangham, a primatologist
at Harvard, cites the example of the red colobus monkey.
When they are being hunted by chimpanzees, the male monkeys are "amazingly brave," Dr. Wrangham said. "As the biggest and strongest members of their group, they undoubtedly could escape quicker than the others." Instead, the
males jump to the front, confronting the chimpanzee hunters
while the mothers and offspring jump to safety. Often, the
much bigger chimpanzees pull the colobus soldiers off by
their tails and slam them to their deaths.

Their courageousness can be explained by the fact that   16
colobus monkeys live in multimale, multifemale groups in
which the males are almost always related. So in protecting
the young monkeys, the adult males are defending their kin.

Yet, as biologists are learning, there is more to cooperation   17
and generosity than an investment in one's nepotistic patch
of DNA. Lately, they have accrued evidence that something
like group selection encourages the evolution of traits
beneficial to a group, even when members of the group are
not related.

In computer simulation studies, Dr. Smuts and her   18
colleagues modeled two types of group-living agents that

would behave like herbivores: one that would selfishly consume all the food in a given patch before moving on, and another that would consume resources modestly rather than greedily, thus allowing local plant food to regenerate.

Researchers had assumed that cooperators could collaborate with genetically unrelated cooperators only if they had the cognitive capacity to know goodness when they saw it. [19]

But the data suggested otherwise. "These models showed that under a wide range of simulated environmental conditions you could get selection for prudent, cooperative behavior," Dr. Smuts said, even in the absence of cognition or kinship. "If you happened by chance to get good guys together, they remained together because they created a mutually beneficial environment." [20]

This sort of win-win principle, she said, could explain all sorts of symbiotic arrangements, even among different species—like the tendency of baboons and impalas to associate together because they use each other's warning calls. [21]

Add to this basic mechanistic selection for cooperation the human capacity to recognize and reward behaviors that strengthen the group—the tribe, the state, the church, the platoon—and selflessness thrives and multiplies. So, too, does the need for group identity. Classic so-called minimal group experiments have shown that when people are gathered together and assigned membership in arbitrary groups, called, say, the Greens and the Reds, before long the members begin expressing amity for their fellow Greens or Reds and animosity toward those of the wrong "color." [22]

"Ancestral life frequently consisted of intergroup conflict," Dr. Wilson of SUNY said. "It's part of our mental heritage." [23]

Yet he does not see conflict as inevitable. "It's been shown pretty well that where people place the boundary between us and them is extremely flexible and strategic," he said. "It's possible to widen the moral circle, and I'm optimistic enough to believe it can be done on a worldwide scale." [24]

Ultimately, though, scientists acknowledge that the evolutionary framework for self-sacrificing acts is overlaid by individual choice. And it is there, when individual firefighters or [25]

[margin annotation:] can we get back to humans?

office workers or airplane passengers choose the altruistic path that science gives way to wonder.

Dr. James J. Moore, a professor of anthropology at the University of California at San Diego, said he had studied many species, including many different primates. "We're the nicest species I know," he said. "To see those guys risking their lives, climbing over rubble on the chance of finding one person alive, well, you wouldn't find baboons doing that." The horrors of last week notwithstanding, he said, "the overall picture to come out about human nature is wonderful." — 26

"For every 50 people making bomb threats now to mosques," he said, "there are 500,000 people around the world behaving just the way we hoped they would, with empathy and expressions of grief. We are amazingly civilized." — 27

True, death-defying acts of heroism may be the province of the few. For the rest of us, simple humanity will do. — 28

it rhymes

For Study and Discussion

QUESTIONS FOR RESPONSE

1. What specific altruistic and heroic acts at the World Trade Center site do you remember reading about after the attack on September 11, 2001?
2. What is your reaction to the quotation from a biologist whom Angier cites toward the end of the essay: "We're the nicest species I know"?

QUESTIONS ABOUT PURPOSE

1. What beliefs or attitudes about human nature do you think Angier wants to counteract in this essay?
2. What scenario can you imagine would take place in a major crisis such as an earthquake or flood if every person acted only from immediate self-interest?

QUESTIONS ABOUT AUDIENCE

1. Angier published this article in the *New York Times* one week after the World Trade Center bombing, and it was then posted on

the Internet. What emotions and reactions of her readers at that time do you think she seeks to address?

2. To what extent do you think altruism is an important strand in the American character (assuming there is such a character)? Can you give an example?

QUESTIONS ABOUT STRATEGIES

1. What strategies that Angier would use in her work as a science writer does she employ in this essay?

2. What range of examples does Angier use to persuade her readers that altruism and heroism are survival strategies?

QUESTIONS FOR DISCUSSION

1. What role does language seem to play among humans in fostering altruism?

2. In what ways does Angier suggest that acts of altruism may also be acts of self-interest in the long run?

KURT VONNEGUT, JR.

Kurt Vonnegut, Jr., was born in 1922 in Indianapolis, Indiana, and attended Cornell University before being drafted into the infantry in World War II. Vonnegut was captured by the Germans at the Battle of the Bulge and sent to Dresden, where he worked in the underground meat locker of a slaughterhouse. He survived the Allied firebombing of Dresden and, following the war, returned to the United States, where he studied anthropology, then worked for a news bureau, and later wrote publicity for the General Electric Research Laboratory in Schenectady, New York. In 1950 he began to devote all his time to his own writing. His first three novels, *Player Piano* (1952), *The Sirens of Titan* (1959), and *Cat's Cradle* (1963), established Vonnegut's reputation as a writer who could blend humor with serious insights into the human experience. His most successful novel, *Slaughterhouse-Five, or the Children's Crusade* (1969), is based on his wartime experiences in Dresden. Among his numerous other works are *God Bless You, Mr. Rosewater* (1966), *Galápagos* (1985), *Hocus Pocus* (1990), and *Timequake* (1997). His best-known short stories are collected in *Canary in the Cat House* (1961) and *Welcome to the Monkey House* (1968). "Harrison Bergeron," reprinted from the latter collection, is the story of the apparatus that a future society must create to make everyone equal.

Harrison Bergeron

THE YEAR WAS 2081, and everybody was finally equal. 1
They weren't only equal before God and the law.

They were equal every which way. Nobody was smarter than anybody else. Nobody was better looking than anybody else. Nobody was stronger or quicker than anybody else. All this equality was due to the 211th, 212th, and 213th Amendments to the Constitution, and to the unceasing vigilance of agents of the United States Handicapper General.

Some things about living still weren't quite right, though. April, for instance, still drove people crazy by not being springtime. And it was in that clammy month that the H-G men took George and Hazel Bergeron's fourteen-year-old son, Harrison, away. 2

It was tragic, all right, but George and Hazel couldn't think about it very hard. Hazel had a perfectly average intelligence, which meant she couldn't think about anything except in short bursts. And George, while his intelligence was way above normal, had a little mental handicap radio in his ear. He was required by law to wear it at all times. It was tuned to a government transmitter. Every twenty seconds or so, the transmitter would send out some sharp noise to keep people like George from taking unfair advantage of their brains. 3

George and Hazel were watching television. There were tears on Hazel's cheeks, but she'd forgotten for the moment what they were about. 4

On the television screen were ballerinas. 5

A buzzer sounded in George's head. His thoughts fled in panic, like bandits from a burglar alarm. 6

"That was a real pretty dance, that dance they just did," said Hazel. 7

"Huh?" said George. 8

"That dance—it was nice," said Hazel. 9

"Yup," said George. He tried to think a little about the ballerinas. They weren't really very good—no better than anybody else would have been, anyway. They were burdened with sashweights and bags of birdshot, and their faces were masked, so that no one, seeing a free and graceful gesture or a pretty face, would feel like something the cat drug in. George was toying with the vague notion that maybe danc- 10 ers shouldn't be handicapped. But he didn't get very far with it before another noise in his ear radio scattered his thoughts.

George winced. So did two of the eight ballerinas. 11

Hazel saw him wince. Having no mental handicap herself, 12
she had to ask George what the latest sound had been.

"Sounded like somebody hitting a milk bottle with a ball 13
peen hammer," said George.

"I'd think it would be real interesting, hearing all the dif- 14
ferent sounds," said Hazel, a little envious. "All the things they think up."

"Um," said George. 15

"Only, if I was Handicapper General, you know what I 16
would do?" said Hazel. Hazel, as a matter of fact, bore a strong resemblance to the Handicapper General, a woman named Diana Moon Glampers. "If I was Diana Moon Glampers," said Hazel, "I'd have chimes on Sunday—just chimes. Kind of in honor of religion."

"I could think, if it was just chimes," said George. 17

"Well—maybe make 'em real loud," said Hazel. "I think 18
I'd make a good Handicapper General."

"Good as anybody else," said George. 19

"Who knows better'n I do what normal is?" said Hazel. 20

"Right," said George. He began to think glimmeringly 21
about his abnormal son who was now in jail, about Harrison, but a twenty-one-gun salute in his head stopped that.

"Boy!" said Hazel, "that was a doozy, wasn't it?" 22

It was such a doozy that George was white and trembling, 23
and tears stood on the rims of his red eyes. Two of the eight ballerinas had collapsed on the studio floor, were holding their temples.

"All of a sudden you look so tired," said Hazel. "Why 24
don't you stretch out on the sofa, so's you can rest your handicap bag on the pillows, honeybunch." She was referring to the forty-seven pounds of birdshot in a canvas bag, which was padlocked around George's neck. "Go on and rest the bag for a little while," she said. "I don't care if you're not equal to me for a while."

George weighed the bag with his hands. "I don't mind it," 25
he said. "I don't notice it any more. It's just a part of me."

"You been so tired lately—kind of wore out," said Hazel. 26
"If there was just some way we could make a little hole in the
bottom of the bag, and just take out a few of them lead balls.
Just a few."

"Two years in prison and two thousand dollars fine for 27
every ball I took out," said George. "I don't call that a bargain."

"If you could just take a few out when you came home 28
from work," said Hazel. "I mean—you don't compete with
anybody around here. You just set around."

"If I tried to get away with it," said George, "then other 29
people'd get away with it—and pretty soon we'd be right
back to the dark ages again, with everybody competing
against everybody else. You wouldn't like that, would you?"

"I'd hate it," said Hazel. 30

"There you are," said George. "The minute people start 31
cheating on laws, what do you think happens to society?"

If Hazel hadn't been able to come up with an answer to 32
this question, George couldn't have supplied one. A siren
was going off in his head.

"Reckon it'd fall all apart," said Hazel. 33

"What would?" said George blankly. 34

"Society," said Hazel uncertainly. "Wasn't that what you 35
just said?"

"Who knows?" said George. 36

The television program was suddenly interrupted for a 37
news bulletin. It wasn't clear at first as to what the bulletin
was about, since the announcer, like all announcers, had a serious speech impediment. For about half a minute, and in a
state of high excitement, the announcer tried to say, "Ladies
and gentlemen—"

He finally gave up, handed the bulletin to a ballerina to 38
read.

"That's all right—" Hazel said to the announcer, "he 39
tried. That's the big thing. He tried to do the best he could
with what God gave him. He should get a nice raise for trying so hard."

"Ladies and gentlemen—" said the ballerina, reading the 40
bulletin. She must have been extraordinarily beautiful, because the mask she wore was hideous. And it was easy to see
that she was the strongest and most graceful of all the dancers, for her handicap bags were as big as those worn by two-
hundred-pound men.

And she had to apologize at once for her voice, which was 41
a very unfair voice for a woman to use. Her voice was a warm,
luminous, timeless melody. "Excuse me—" she said, and she
began again, making her voice absolutely uncompetitive.

"Harrison Bergeron, age fourteen," she said in a grackle 42
squawk, "has just escaped from jail, where he was held on
suspicion of plotting to overthrow the government. He is a
genius and an athlete, is under-handicapped, and should be
regarded as extremely dangerous."

A police photograph of Harrison Bergeron was flashed on 43
the screen upside down, then sideways, upside down again,
then right side up. The picture showed the full length of
Harrison against a background calibrated in feet and inches.
He was exactly seven feet tall.

The rest of Harrison's appearance was Halloween and 44
hardware. Nobody had ever borne heavier handicaps. He had
outgrown hindrances faster than the H-G men could think
them up. Instead of a little ear radio for a mental handicap, he
wore a tremendous pair of earphones, and spectacles with
thick wavy lenses. The spectacles were intended to make him
not only half blind, but to give him whanging headaches besides.

Scrap metal was hung all over him. Ordinarily, there was a 45
certain symmetry, a military neatness to the handicaps issued
to strong people, but Harrison looked like a walking junk-
yard. In the race of life, Harrison carried three hundred
pounds.

And to offset his good looks, the H-G men required that 46
he wear at all times a red rubber ball for a nose, keep his eyebrows shaved off, and cover his even white teeth with black
caps at snaggle-tooth random.

"If you see this boy," said the ballerina, "do not—I repeat, 47
do not—try to reason with him."

There was the shriek of a door being torn from its hinges.   48

Screams and barking cries of consternation came from the   49
television set. The photograph of Harrison Bergeron on
the screen jumped again and again, as though dancing to the
tune of an earthquake.

George Bergeron correctly identified the earthquake, and   50
well he might have—for many was the time his own home
had danced to the same crashing tune. "My God—" said
George, "that must be Harrison!"

The realization was blasted from his mind instantly by the   51
sound of an automobile collision in his head.

When George could open his eyes again, the photograph   52
of Harrison was gone. A living, breathing Harrison filled the
screen.

Clanking, clownish, and huge, Harrison stood in the cen-   53
ter of the studio. The knob of the uprooted studio door was
still in his hand. Ballerinas, technicians, musicians, and announcers cowered on their knees before him, expecting to
die.

"I am the Emperor!" cried Harrison. "Do you hear? I am   54
the Emperor! Everybody must do what I say at once!" He
stamped his foot and the studio shook.

"Even as I stand here—" he bellowed, "crippled, hobbled,   55
sickened—I am a greater ruler than any man who ever lived!
Now watch me become what I *can* become!"

Harrison tore the straps of his handicap harness like wet   56
tissue paper, tore straps guaranteed to support five thousand
pounds.

Harrison's scrap-iron handicaps crashed to the floor.   57

Harrison thrust his thumbs under the bars of the padlock   58
that secured his head harness. The bar snapped like celery.
Harrison smashed his headphones and spectacles against the
wall.

He flung away his rubber-ball nose, revealed a man that   59
would have awed Thor, the god of thunder.

"I shall now select my Empress!" he said, looking down   60
on the cowering people. "Let the first woman who dares rise
to her feet claim her mate and her throne!"

A moment passed, and then a ballerina arose, swaying like   61
a willow.

Harrison plucked the mental handicap from her ear,   62
snapped off her physical handicaps with marvelous delicacy.
Last of all, he removed her mask.

She was blindingly beautiful.   63

"Now—" said Harrison, taking her hand, "shall we show   64
the people the meaning of the word dance? Music!" he commanded.

The musicians scrambled back into their chairs, and Harri-   65
son stripped them of their handicaps, too. "Play your best,"
he told them, "and I'll make you barons and dukes and
earls."

The music began. It was normal at first—cheap, silly, false.   66
But Harrison snatched two musicians from their chairs,
waved them like batons as he sang the music as he wanted it
played. He slammed them back into their chairs.

The music began again and was much improved.   67

Harrison and his Empress merely listened to the music   68
for a while—listened gravely, as though synchronizing their
heartbeats with it.

They shifted their weights to their toes.   69

Harrison placed his big hands on the girl's tiny waist, let-   70
ting her sense the weightlessness that would soon be hers.

And then, in an explosion of joy and grace, into the air   71
they sprang!

Not only were the laws of the land abandoned, but the law   72
of gravity and the laws of motion as well.

They reeled, whirled, swiveled, flounced, capered, gam-   73
boled, and spun.

They leaped like deer on the moon.   74

The studio ceiling was thirty feet high, but each leap   75
brought the dancers nearer to it.

It became their obvious intention to kiss the ceiling.   76

They kissed it.   77

And then, neutralizing gravity with love and pure will,   78
they remained suspended in air inches below the ceiling, and
they kissed each other for a long, long time.

It was then that Diana Moon Glampers, the Handicapper   79
General, came into the studio with a double-barreled ten-
gauge shotgun. She fired twice, and the Emperor and the
Empress were dead before they hit the floor.

Diana Moon Glampers loaded the gun again. She aimed it   80
at the musicians and told them they had ten seconds to get
their handicaps back on.

It was then that the Bergerons' television tube burned   81
out.

Hazel turned to comment about the blackout to George.   82
But George had gone out into the kitchen for a can of beer.

George came back in with the beer, paused while a handi-   83
cap signal shook him up. And then he sat down again. "You
been crying?" he said to Hazel.

"Yup," she said.   84

"What about?" he said.   85

"I forgot," she said. "Something real sad on television."   86

"What was it?" he said.   87

"It's all kind of mixed up in my mind," said Hazel.   88

"Forget sad things," said George.   89

"I always do," said Hazel.   90

"That's my girl," said George. He winced. There was the   91
sound of a rivetting gun in his head.

"Gee—I could tell that one was a doozy," said Hazel.   92

"You can say that again," said George.   93

"Gee—" said Hazel, "I could tell that one was a doozy."   94

COMMENT ON "HARRISON BERGERON"

Known for his offbeat and sometimes bizarre vision of reality,
Kurt Vonnegut, Jr., has created in "Harrison Bergeron" a science fiction story full of black humor and grotesque details.
The society he creates in the story is reminiscent of the society pictured in Orwell's *1984*, totally controlled by a government that invades and interferes in every facet of its citizens'
lives. In a travesty of the famous declaration that "All men are
created equal," the government has set out to legislate equal-

ity. Vonnegut portrays the results of such legislation in macabre images of people forced to carry weighted bags to reduce their strength, wear grotesque masks to conceal their beauty, and wear headphones that emitted disruptive sounds to prevent them from thinking clearly. When a fourteen-year-old boy, Harrison Bergeron, shows signs of excellence, he is first arrested, then ruthlessly destroyed when he throws off his restraints and literally rises to the top.

Underneath the farce, Vonnegut has created a tragic picture of a culture so obsessed with equality that people must be leveled by decree. Mediocrity reigns; any sign of excellence or superiority threatens law and order and must be suppressed immediately. Ultimately, of course, such a society will perish because it will kill its talent and stagnate.

Vonnegut wrote this story in 1961, after the repressive Stalinist regime that wiped out thousands of leaders and intellectuals in Russia; it precedes by a few years the disastrous era of Mao's Red Guards in China, when hundreds of thousands of intellectuals and artists were killed or imprisoned in the name of equality. Is Vonnegut commenting on the leveling tendencies of these totalitarian societies? Or does he see such excesses reflected in our own society? No one knows, but it's the genius of artists to prod us to think about such concerns.

Persuasion and Argument as a Writing Strategy

1. In their essays, both Martin Luther King, Jr., and Eric Liu show how strong they still find the concept of the American Dream, the idea that in the United States a person can break away from the constraints of race and poverty and work to fulfill his or her ambition. For a short essay to post on your class web site, argue either for or against this concept. If you're skeptical about it, show what limitations you think a person faces because of race, class, or economic circumstances. If you agree that many disadvantaged people in the United States still have a good chance to achieve the American Dream, give examples to support your view. For a comparison, you might look at Gloria Naylor's brief essay in the Introduction to this reader.

2. If you're a Harry Potter fan, reread Harold Bloom's essay "Can 35 Million Book Buyers Be Wrong? Yes." and critique his argument. What are his main arguments against the books? What problems do you find with those arguments? To what extent do you think his position as an eminent professor of literature and a famous Shakespeare scholar might influence his opinions about the Potter books? You could post your essay on the web site that your hometown library maintains and to which it invites readers to contribute.

3. Reread Kingsolver's essay "Stone Soup" and Whitehead's essay "Women and the Future of Fatherhood" and compare the kinds of arguments the two authors are making. How would you describe the dominant appeal of each essay? How do the two authors use evidence to support their claims, and what kinds of evidence do they choose? Then decide which essay you find more effective and argue for your preference. Conclude your essay by briefly sketching what your experiences with family life have been, either your own or that of people close to you; then consider how those experiences have probably affected

your response to these essays. You could write for the audience of a chat room that's run for children of divorce, write for a discussion group in your writing class, or post your argument on the class web site.

4. Many liberal arts colleges require that their students do considerable volunteer work in their communities as one of the requirements for completing their degree. Such work might include tutoring in a structured program run by the local schools, being a counselor for four weeks in a summer camp for disadvantaged children, doing physical work one day a month on a Habitat for Humanity project, or serving meals at the Salvation Army charity kitchen twice a month. A student is not permitted to substitute service at his or her own church. In an editorial for your college newspaper, argue for or against this requirement. If you argue for it, give well-supported reasons about the benefits students gain; if you argue against it, do not simply claim that a college has no authority to make such a requirement—point out what you believe are real disadvantages to the students.

5. Carefully reread Francine Prose's essay "Genocide Without Apology," her analysis and interpretation of the Old Testament book of Exodus. Then critique and respond to it in an essay to be posted on the class web site for other students to read. On what evidence does she base her statement that Exodus "tells us a truth about how people behave, something I would rather not listen to"? Do you agree with her interpretation of that evidence? Argue for or against her view, drawing on statements she makes in the essay.

6. Carefully reread Natalie Angier's post–September 11 essay, "Of Altruism, Heroism, and Evolution's Gifts." Respond to it in a short essay that might be published on the op-ed page of the newspaper that published it, the *New York Times*. (Yes, even you might get on that page!) Angier is a science writer for the *Times,* and in addition to citing the altruistic behavior of many hundreds of New Yorkers to support the optimistic thesis suggested by her

title, she cites evidence from several scientists: two anthropologists, a biologist, a primatologist, and an evolutionary
theorist. They argue that altruism and cooperation are basic human traits; one says that "the overall picture to come
out about human nature [after September 11] is wonderful." In your response to Angier's essay, evaluate the quality of her evidence and explain why you agree or disagree
with her conclusions.

RESOURCES FOR WRITING: DISCOVERIES— A CASEBOOK

As you worked your way through this book, you discovered that you already possess many resources for reading and writing. You read essays on a wide variety of themes. You encountered new and complicated information shaped by unusual and unsettling assertions. But you discovered experiences and feelings that you recognize—the challenge of learning, the ordeal of disappointment, and the cost of achievement. As you examined these essays, you realized that you had something to say about your reading, something to contribute to the themes explored by the writers.

Your work with this book has also enabled you to identify and practice strategies that at each stage of the writing process helped you transform your ideas about a theme into writing. In the beginning, these strategies give rise to questions that you might ask to explore any topic.

Suppose you want to write an essay on the theme of women and science. You might begin by asking why so few women are ranked among the world's great scientists. You might continue asking questions: What historical forces have discouraged women from becoming scientists (cause and effect)? How do women scientists define problems, analyze evidence, and formulate conclusions (process analysis), and do they go about these processes differently than men (comparison and contrast)? If women scientists look at the world differently than men do, does this difference have an effect on the established notions of inquiry (persuasion and argument)? Such questions work like the different lenses you attach to a camera: each lens gives you a different perspective on a subject, a variation on a theme.

If your initial questions enable you to envision your theme from different perspectives, then answering one of these questions encourages you to develop your theme according to a purpose associated with one of the common patterns of organization. For instance, if you decide to write about the underwater discoveries you made on your first scuba dive, your choice of purpose seems obvious: to answer the question "What happened?" You would then write a narrative essay. In drafting this essay, however, you may discover questions you had not anticipated: What caused explorers to develop scuba diving equipment? What kinds of discoveries have been made using scuba diving equipment? What are the limitations of scuba diving equipment for underwater exploration? How is scuba diving similar to or different from swimming?

Responding to these new questions forces you to decide whether your new information develops or distorts your draft. The history of underwater discovery—from diving bells to diving suits to small submarines—may help your readers see a context for your narrative. On the other hand, such information may confuse them, distracting them from your original purpose—to tell about the discoveries you made scuba diving.

As you struggle with your new themes, you may decide that your original purpose no longer drives your writing. You may decide to change your purpose and write a cause-and-effect essay. Instead of telling what happened to you on your first scuba dive, you might decide to use your personal experience, together with some reading, to write a more scientific essay analyzing the effects of underwater exploration on your senses of sight and hearing.

This book has helped you make such decisions by showing you how the common patterns of organization evoke different purposes, audiences, and strategies. In this thematic unit, you will have the opportunity to make decisions about a little anthology of writing on the theme of *discoveries*.

Before you begin reading these selections, take an initial inventory:

- What kind of direct experience have you had making discoveries?
  What personal discoveries have you made?
  What technical or scientific discoveries have you made?
  What geographical discoveries have you made on camping trips or family vacations?

- What kind of indirect experience have you had making discoveries?

  What discoveries have your friends or members of your family made?

  What discoveries have you read about in your academic classes?

  What discoveries have you seen documented on film or television?

- What do you know about the significance of discoveries in cultural history?

  Who are the great explorers, and what did they discover?

  Who are the great inventors, and what did they create?

  Why do we see discovery as an adventure and those who make discoveries as heroes?

  How have the revolutions in technology enabled us to make new kinds of discoveries?

  How have the great discoveries changed what we know and what we believe?

Thinking about such questions will remind you of the extensive resources you bring to the theme of *discoveries*. It is a subject that touches all our lives in some way. And it affects our behavior in countless other ways—what we do with our time, with whom we associate, how we spend our money, what we think of ourselves and our culture.

After you have made a preliminary inventory of your knowledge and attitudes toward discoveries, read the writing in this unit. You will notice that each selection asks you to think about discoveries from a different perspective:

1. *What happened? (Narration and Description):* Andrew Sullivan recounts several stories that led to his personal discovery that he was gay.

2. *How do you do it? How is it done? (Process Analysis):* Colin Evans analyzes the process of discovering evidence that leads to an arrest.

3. *How is it similar to or different from something else?* *(Comparison and Contrast):* Dava Sobel compares the imaginary lines of latitude and longitude, which enable explorers to navigate the world.

4. *What kinds of subdivisions does it contain?* *(Division and Classification):* Lewis Thomas classifies three types of medical technology that are used to treat illness.

5. *How would you characterize it?* *(Definition):* Witold Rybczynski defines the technological discovery—the machine-made screw—that "brought the world together."

6. *How did it happen?* *(Cause and Effect):* John Fleischman analyzes how various archeological discoveries caused scholars to reassess Homer's literary epics.

7. *How do you prove it?* *(Persuasion and Argument):* Richard Doerflinger and Peggy Prichard Ross present opposing arguments about the value of pursuing stem cell research.

This collection ends with Arthur C. Clarke's story, "The Star," a science fiction tale about the discoveries of space exploration. The story raises all sorts of questions about science, religion, and the ultimate purpose of creation.

As you examine these selections, keep track of how your reading expands the theme of *discoveries*—provoking memories, adding information, and suggesting questions you had not considered when you made your initial inventory about discoveries. Because this information will give you new ways to think about your original questions, you will want to explore your thinking in writing.

The assignments that follow each selection suggest several ways that you can explore this theme in writing:

1. You can *respond* to the essay by shaping a similar experience according to its methods of organization.

2. You can *analyze* the essay to discover how the writer uses specific strategies to communicate a purpose to an audience.

3. You can use the essay as a springboard for an essay that *argues* a similar thesis in a different context.

Drawing on your experience, reading, and familiarity with writing strategies, you are ready to *discover* a writing assignment on any theme.

Andrew Sullivan was born in 1963 in Godstone, Surrey, England, and was educated at Magdalen College, Oxford, and Harvard University, where he received a Ph.D. in political science. He has worked as a staff writer and editor of the *New Republic* magazine and has contributed articles and editorials to *Commonweal,* the *New Yorker,* and the *New York Times.* His best-known book, *Virtually Normal: An Argument About Homosexuality* (1995), focuses on the issues of whether openly gay people should serve in the military and the legalization of same-sex marriages. His other books focus on the political—*The New Republic Guide to the Candidates, 1996* (1996)—and the personal—*Love Undetectable: Notes on Friendship, Sex and Survival* (1998). In "Virtually Normal," an excerpt from the book of the same title, Sullivan recollects his emotional childhood in England, where he first discovered he was homosexual.

Virtually Normal

I REMEMBER THE first time it dawned on me that I might be a homosexual. I was around the age of ten and had succeeded in avoiding the weekly soccer practice in my elementary school. I don't remember exactly how—maybe I had feigned a cold, or an injury, and claimed that because it was raining (it always seemed to be raining), I should be given the afternoon inside. I loathed soccer, partly because I wasn't very good at it and partly because I felt I didn't quite belong in the communal milieu in which it unfolded. The way it's played in English junior schools puts all the

get yourself apart ←

great diction

emphasis on team playing, and even back then this didn't appeal much to my nascent sense of *amour-propre*. But that lucky afternoon, I found myself sequestered with the girls, who habitually spent that time period doing sewing, knitting, and other appropriately feminine things. None of this, I remember, interested me much either; and I was happily engaged reading. Then a girl sitting next to me looked at me with a mixture of curiosity and disgust. "Why aren't you out with the boys playing football?" she asked. "Because I hate it," I replied. "Are you sure you're not really a girl under

---

No homosexual child, surrounded overwhelmingly by heterosexuals, will feel at home in his sexual and emotional world, even in the most tolerant of cultures.

---

there?" she asked, with the suspicion of a sneer. "Yeah, of course," I replied, stung, and somewhat shaken.

It was the first time the fundamental homosexual dilemma had been put to me so starkly. It resonated so much with my own internal fears that I remember it vividly two decades later. Before then, most of what I now see as homosexual emotions had not been forced into one or the other gender category. I didn't feel as a boy or a girl; I felt as me. I remember vividly—perhaps I was five or six—being seated in the back of a car with my second cousin, a tousle-headed, wide-grinned kid a few years older, and being suddenly, unwittingly entranced by him. It was a feeling I had never felt before, the first inkling of a yearning that was only to grow stronger as the years went by. I remember too that around the age of eight, I joined a gang of four boys—modeled perhaps on the ubiquitous, vaguely homoerotic male pop groups common at the time—and developed a crush on one of them. He was handsome and effortlessly athletic, and in

ya

great writing

2

THE SENSES OF PLACE

A VISUAL ESSAY

PHOTO 1   © *The Image Bank/Getty Images.*

"Places, as well as the landscapes that allow us to grasp them, are narratives. They would not exist as places were it not for the stories told about and through them. Stories—particularly those tales we tell ourselves about ourselves—provide the weathered bedrock that binds us to the lands we inhabit."

—Patricia L. Price, *Dry Places: Landscapes of Belonging and Exclusion*

PHOTO 2   *Lucy Rawlinson,* Jose's Dream, *1990. The Bridgeman Art Library/Getty Images.*

PHOTO 3   © *Karen Huntt Mason/CORBIS.*

Lucy Rawlinson's *Jose's Dream* (1990) and Karen Huntt-Mason's *The Porch* (1990) reveal private places where people dream, read, and reflect. Describe your favorite private place and explain why it is so meaningful for you.

P H O T O 4   *Grandma Moses,* Hoosick Falls in Winter, *1944. Copyright © 1946 (renewed 1974). Grandma Moses Properties Co., New York. The Phillips Collection, Washington, D.C.*

P H O T O 5   *Edward Hopper,* Nighhawks, *1942. Oil on canvas, 84.1 x 152.4 cm, Friends of American Art Collection. Reproduction, The Art Institute of Chicago.*

Grandma Moses' *Hoosick Falls in Winter* (1944) and Edward Hopper's *Nighthawks* (1942) depict American rural and urban places around the middle of the twentieth century. How do you think these places look today? Write about a place that has changed greatly over time and explain how you feel about that change.

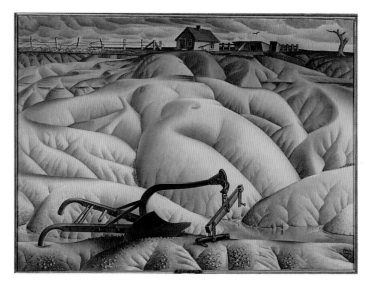

PHOTO 6 *Alexandre Hogue,* Erosion #2 Mother Earth
Laid Bare, *1936. Museum purchase, The
Philbrook Museum of Art, Tulsa, Oklahoma.*

Alexandre Hogue's *Erosion #2 Mother Earth Laid Bare,* as its title
suggests, presents an interpretative history of the American landscape. Analyze the patterns and details in the painting that support
this interpretation.

P H O T O   7   *© 2001 Ruth Fremson, The New York Times Company.*

Ruth Fremson's *Ground Zero* (2001) shows the devastation that created a tragic place on the American landscape. After the attacks of September 11, 2001, Americans debated divergent ideas about how best to honor and restore the site. After researching some of the plans that emerged, discuss and defend your own ideas about the future of the Ground Zero site.

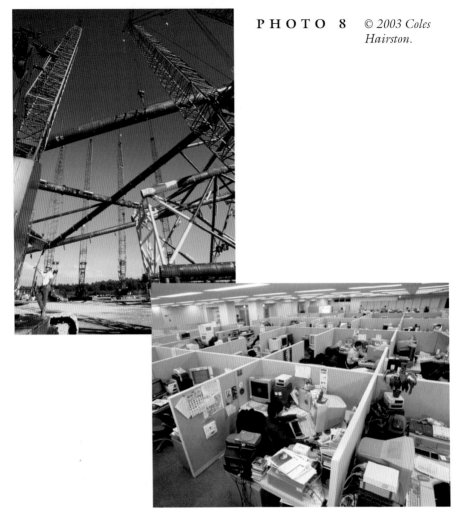

PHOTO 8 *© 2003 Coles Hairston.*

PHOTO 9 *© Tom Wagner/CORBIS SABA.*

Coles Hairston's *Building an Offshore Rig* (2003) and Tom Wagner's *Office* (2003) portray complicated workplaces that produce commodities essential to our economy—energy and information. Analyze the layout, tools, and procedures in a workplace you know well and assess the value of the product it produces.

The map of J.R.R. Tolkien's "Middle-Earth" by John Howe (2003) and Thomas Taylor's drawing (2003) of Platform Nine and Three-Quarters in J.K. Rowling's *Harry Potter and the Sorcerer's Stone* illustrate imaginary places. If you are familiar with either or both books (or films), explain how these drawings do or do not reflect the way you imagine these places. Or describe your favorite imaginary place, in a book or film—and explain why you are attracted to its landscape.

P H O T O   1 2 *© Lowell Georgia/CORBIS.*

Lowell Georgia's *Central City Cemetery, Colorado* (1976) documents the sacred resting place of a nameless child. Speculate on the events that brought "Baby Sonne" to this place. Or demonstrate how naming and story bind "us to the lands we inhabit." For example, what stories are suggested by the names on the first page of this visual essay?

my difficult attempt to cement both a companionship and a premature love affair, I felt the first strains of the homosexual hurt that is the accompaniment of most homosexual lives. It was not so much the rejection; it was the combination of acceptance and rejection. It was feeling that that part of the male-male bond that worked—the part that works with most heterosexual male-male friendships—was also the part that destroyed the possibility of another, as yet opaque but far more complete longing that for me, but not for him, was inextricable from the relationship. It was a sense that longing was based on a structural lack of reciprocity; that love was about being accepted on the condition that you suppressed what you really felt.

Looking back, this inchoate ache was all that I knew of the homosexual experience. But I knew also, because of the absence of any mention of the subject, because of the lack of any tangible visible reflections of it in the world around me, that there was something wrong with it. So when that afternoon, I was abruptly asked whether I was actually a girl, I blanched and stammered. Had my friend seen something I thought was hidden? She had, of course, merely accused me of being a sissy—something all young geeks, whatever their fledgling sexual orientation, were well used to. But I wondered whether she hadn't detected something else, something deeper. How had she known? And what, anyway, was it? By the age of ten, the only answer I had been given was that I was simply the wrong gender, something that any brief perusal of my body would discount.

Maybe I should be clearer here. The longing was not sexual. I was too young to feel any explicit sexual desire. I had no idea what an expression of sexual love might be. So far as I can remember it, it was a desire to unite with another: not to possess, but to join in some way; not to lose myself, but to be given dimension. At the time, I also had fantasies of being part of some boys' gang, or a rock group—some institution that could legitimately incorporate the half-understood, half-felt emotions that were filtering through my system. Nowhere else in the world did I see relationships that

incorporated this desire. There were many that intimated it—
the soccer team, my father and his friends, the male atmosphere of the local pub or the rugby club—but all these, I divined even then, were somehow premised on a denial of the
acknowledged intimacy I had begun to crave. They were a
simulacrum of acceptance. Because of their proximity to the
very things I felt I wanted, they had developed a visceral hostility to the very thing that I was. So I had to be careful, in
case they found out.

The secret, then, began when I was young. I hardly dared   5
mention it to anyone; and the complete absence of any note
of the subject in my family or in school, in television, newspapers, or even such books as I could get ahold of, made the secret that much more mystifying. I wondered whether there
was any physical manifestation of this unmentionable fact. I
was circumcised, unlike many other English boys: had that
done it? I remember looking up physical descriptions of men
and women in the local library to see if my own body corre-
sponded to the shape of the male (I was, I determined, not
broad-shouldered enough). When I was a little late going
through puberty, I wondered whether that might be related,
and half imagined that my voice might not break, and reveal
my difference. Eventually, I succumbed to panic and mentioned it before God. I was in the communion line at my local parish church, Our Lady and Saint Peter's, the church
that was linked to my elementary school. Please, I remember
asking of the Almighty almost offhandedly as I walked up the
aisle to receive communion from the mild-mannered Father
Simmons for the umpteenth time, please, help me with *that*.

When people ask me whether homosexuality is a choice or   6
not, I can only refer them to these experiences. They're the
only thing I know for sure. Dozens of surveys have been
written, countless questionnaires filled out, endless theories
elaborated upon; but in most of these purportedly objective
studies, opaque and troubling emotions are being reduced to
statistics in front of strangers. I distrust them. But I don't
fully distrust my own experience, or the experience of so
many homosexuals I have met over the years. This experience

is filtered, as all experience is, through the prism of reflection and self-reflection: it is not some raw datum in the empirical, verifiable world which I am presenting for review. But it is as honest a sketch as I can provide of the experience of finding oneself a homosexual.

Not that this was yet a truly sexual condition. In some sense, physical contact had, in a somewhat comic way, implanted itself in my mind. But it was still intensely abstract. I remember when I was around seven or eight seeing a bare-chested man on television one night and feeling such an intense longing for him that I determined to become a doctor. That way, I figured, I could render the man unconscious and lie on top of him when no one else was in the room. But then, I quickly realized, I would be found out and get into trouble. I spent most of the night awake, working out this scenario, and ending up as confused and as overcome by desire as when I began. But already I had divined that the expression of any kind of longing would have to take devious and subterranean forms. I would have to be an outlaw in order to be complete. I also remember making a joke in a debate competition at the age of twelve, at the time of a homosexual scandal involving the leader of the British Liberal Party. I joked that life was better under the Conservatives— or behind the Liberals, for that matter. It achieved a raucous response, but I had no idea what the analogy meant. Perhaps my schoolboy audience hadn't either. We had learned the social levers of hostility to homosexuality before we had even the foggiest clue what they referred to.

My attraction to the same sex was not a desire as natural as sneezing, or eating, or sleeping, as some people claim. It was a secondary part of my psychological and emotional makeup; it operated in that confused and confusing part of my mind that was a fusion of involuntary desire and conscious aspiration. My first explicit sexual fondlings were with girls; but they were play, and carried no threat of emotional intimacy. Looking back, I realize I had no deep emotional ties to girls at all; they were friends, sometimes companions, sometimes soul mates. At elementary school, where I was academically ahead of my class, my closest colleagues were precocious girls. Their intellect I respected. But I had no longing to unite with them, and, looking back, didn't even want to talk with them much. I preferred hanging out with boys, traipsing through the neighboring woods with them, forming secret clubs, cycling around nearby lanes, playing childhood chase games (and in much of this, I guess I was indistinguishable from any other boy). But looking back, I also remember a nascent sense of a deeper, more intuitive, more emotional longing. I have always enjoyed the company of women, sustained many deep, strong friendships, had countless, endless conversations; but I have never longed for a woman in the way that I have longed for a man, never yearned for her physical embrace or her emotional solidarity.

I was, in other words, virtually normal. Like many homosexuals, I have spent some time looking back and trying to decipher what might have caused my apparent aberration. One explanation does make some sort of sense. I had a very close relationship with my mother and a somewhat distant one with my father. My father provided very basic physical and practical support—when I had asthmatic attacks as a child, it was my father who picked me up in the middle of the night and calmed me down to help me breathe. He made my birthday cakes, picked me up from school, and provided a solid, if undemonstrative, base of emotional support. But it was my mother who filled my head with the possibilities of the world, who conversed with me as an adult, who helped me believe in my ability to do things in the wider world. It was her values that shaped and encouraged me; and my father who sought to ground me in reality, and to keep my inflated ego in some sort of check. In my adolescence I warred with my father and sided with my mother in the family fights that took place. And in all of this, I suppose, I follow a typical pattern of homosexual development.

But then so do many heterosexuals. Both my brother and sister grew up in the same atmosphere, and neither of them turned out to be homosexual. Many heterosexual boys have intense bonds with their mothers, and seek to recreate them

9

10

in the women they eventually love. Many heterosexual boys fight with their fathers and loathe organized sports. And some homosexual boys may sense in their fathers—especially those who cast an extremely heterosexual image—a rejection that they then intensify and internalize. Because the son feels he cannot be what his father wants, he seeks refuge in the understanding of a perhaps more sympathetic mother, who can temporarily shield her gay son from the disappointment and latent suspicions of his father. In other words, homosexuality may actually cause a young boy to be distant from his father and close to his mother, rather than be caused by it.

[margin: more normal]

But whatever its origins, by puberty, my nascent homosexual emotional makeup interacted with my burgeoning hormones to create the beginnings of a sexual implosion. Something like this, of course, happens to gay and straight kids alike; but gay children have a particularly weird time of it. It was then that the scope of my entire situation began to click into place in my head. My longings became so intense that I found myself drawing sketches of the men I desired; I cut out male models from glossy magazines and made catalogues of them; I moved from crushes to sexual obsessions. I could no longer hide from this explicit desire: there it was on paper, in my brain, before my eyes—an undeniable and powerful attraction to other boys and men. And of course, with all of this came an exquisite and inextricable sense of exhilaration as well as disgust. It was like getting on a plane for the first time, being exhilarated by its ascent, gazing with wonder out of the window, seeing the clouds bob beneath you, but then suddenly realizing that you are on the wrong flight, going to a destination which terrifies you, surrounded by people who inwardly appall you. And you cannot get off. You are filled with a lurching panic. You are one of them. 11

[margin: great analogy]

It is probably true that many teenagers experience something of this panic. Although there is an understandable desire to divide the world starkly into heterosexual desire and its opposite, most of us, I'd guess, have confronted the possibility at some time in our lives of the possibility of our own homosexuality. There is something of both attractions in all 12 of us, to begin with. For the majority, it is resolved quite early; our society forces such a resolution. Except for a few who seem to retain throughout their lives a capacity for attraction to both sexes, for most of us the issue is largely resolved before the teenage years set in. On this, both experience and empirical study agree. It is not always—perhaps never—easy, for either the homosexual or the heterosexual. Sometimes, the strength of the other attraction requires such a forceful suppression that it resonates much later in life. How else to explain the sometimes violent fear and hostility to homosexuals that a few heterosexual males feel? And how else to account for the sense of distance and betrayal that haunts some homosexuals? In this early, panicked resolution—one way or another—are the roots of many subsequent pathologies, pathologies that are not always pervious to reason.

But before the teenage years, panic is intermixed with pre-adult ambiguity. Many pubescent children play at sex with members of the same gender, before graduating on to the real thing. Many homosexuals do the exact opposite. For my part, my feelings were too strong and too terrifying to do anything but submerge them completely. There were, of course, moments when they took you unawares. Gay adolescents are offered what every heterosexual teenager longs for: to be invisible in the girls' locker room. But you are invisible in the boys' locker room, your desire as unavoidable as its object. In that moment, you learn the first homosexual lesson: that your survival depends upon self-concealment. I remember specifically coming back to high school after a long summer when I was fifteen and getting changed in the locker room for the first time again with a guy I had long had a crush on. But since the vacation, he had developed enormously: suddenly he had hair on his chest, his body had grown and strengthened, he was—clearly—no longer a boy. In front of me, he took off his shirt, and unknowingly, slowly, erotically stripped. I became literally breathless, overcome by the proximity of my desire. The gay teenager learns in that kind of event a form of control and sublimation, of deception and self-contempt, that never leaves his consciousness. He

13

learns that that which would most give him meaning is most
likely to destroy him in the eyes of others; that the condition
of his friendships is the subjugation of himself.

fallacy

In the development of any human being, these are power- 14
ful emotions. They form a person. The homosexual learns to
make distinctions between his sexual desire and his emotional
longings—not because he is particularly prone to objecti-
fication of the flesh, but because he needs to survive as a social and sexual being. The society separates these two entities,
and for a long time the homosexual has no option but to
keep them separate. He learns certain rules; and, as with a
child learning grammar, they are hard, later on in life, to un-
learn.

It's possible, I think, that whatever society teaches or 15
doesn't teach about homosexuality, this fact will always be
the case. No homosexual child, surrounded overwhelmingly
by heterosexuals, will feel at home in his sexual and emotional world, even in the most tolerant of cultures. And every
homosexual child will learn the rituals of deceit, imperson-
ation, and appearance. Anyone who believes political, social,
or even cultural revolution will change this fundamentally is
denying reality. This isolation will always hold. It is defini-
tional of homosexual development. And children are particularly cruel. At the age of eleven, no one wants to be the odd
one out; and in the arena of dating and hormones, the exclusion is inevitably a traumatic one.

*how did
us
that*

It's also likely to be forlorn. Most people are liable to meet 16
emotional rejection by sheer force of circumstance; but for a
homosexual, the odds are simply far, far higher. My own experience suggests that somewhere between two and five percent of the population have involuntarily strong emotional
and sexual attractions to the same sex. Which means that the
pool of possible partners *starts* at one in twenty to one in fifty.
It's no wonder, perhaps, that male homosexual culture has
developed an ethic more of anonymous or promiscuous sex
than of committed relationships. It's as if the hard lessons of
adolescence lower permanently—by the sheer dint of the
odds—the aspiration for anything more.

loot

Did I know what I was? Somewhere, maybe. But it was   17
much easier to know what I wasn't. I wasn't going to be able
to enter into the world of dating girls; I wasn't going to be
able to feel fully comfortable among the heterosexual climate
of the male teenager. So I decided, consciously or subcon-
sciously, to construct a trajectory of my life that would remove me from their company; give me an excuse, provide a
dignified way out. In Anglo-Saxon culture, the wonk has
such an option: he's too nerdy or intellectual to be absorbed
by girls. And there is something masculine and respected in
the discipline of the arts and especially the sciences. You can
gain respect and still be different.

that's how it should be

So I threw myself into my schoolwork, into (more dubi-   18
ously) plays, into creative writing, into science fiction. Other
homosexuals I have subsequently met pursued other strategies: some paradoxically threw themselves into sports, out-
jocking the jocks, gaining ever greater proximity, seeking respect, while knowing all the time that they were doomed to
rejection. Others withdrew into isolation and despair. Others
still, sensing their difference, flaunted it. At my high school,
an older boy insisted on wearing full makeup to class; and he
was accepted in a patronizing kind of way, his brazen otherness putting others at ease. They knew where they were with
him; and he felt at least comfortable with their stable contempt. The rest of us who lived in a netherworld of sexual in-
security were not so lucky.

why didn't you make a move

Most by then had a far more acute sense of appearances   19
than those who did not need to hide anything; and our sense
of irony, and of aesthetics, assumed a precociously arch form,
and drew us subtly together. Looking back, I realize that
many of my best friends in my teen years were probably
homosexual; and that somewhere in our coded, embarrassed
dialogue we admitted it. Many of us also embraced those ide-
ologies that seemed most alien to what we feared we might
be: of the sports jock, of the altar boy, of the young conservative. They were the ultimate disguises. And our recognition
of ourselves in the other only confirmed our desire to keep it
quiet.

I should add that many young lesbians and homosexuals seem to have had a much easier time of it. For many, the question of sexual identity was not a critical factor in their life choices or vocation, or even a factor at all. Perhaps because of a less repressive upbringing or because of some natural ease in the world, they affected a simple comfort with their fate, and a desire to embrace it. These people alarmed me: their very ease was the sternest rebuke to my own anxiety, because it rendered it irrelevant. But later in life, I came to marvel at the naturalness of their self-confidence, in the face of such concerted communal pressure, and to envy it. I had the more common self-dramatizing urge of the tortured homosexual, trapped between feeling wicked and feeling ridiculous. It's shameful to admit it, but I was more traumatized by the latter than by the former: my pride was more formidable a force than my guilt.

When people ask the simple question What is a homosexual? I can only answer with stories like these. I could go on, but too many stories have already been told. Ask any lesbian or homosexual, and they will often provide a similar account. I was once asked at a conservative think tank what evidence I had that homosexuality was far more of an orientation than a choice, and I was forced to reply quite simply: my life. It's true that I have met a handful of lesbians and gay men over the years who have honestly told me that they genuinely had a choice in the matter (and a few heterosexuals who claim they too chose their orientation). I believe them; but they are the exception and not the rule. As homosexual lives go, my own was somewhat banal and typical.

This is not, of course, the end of the matter. Human experience begins with such facts, it doesn't end with them. There's a lamentable tendency to try to find some definitive solution to permanent human predicaments—in a string of DNA, in a conclusive psychological survey, in an analysis of hypothalami, in a verse of the Bible—in order to cut the argument short. Or to insist on the emotional veracity of a certain experience and expect it to trump any other argument on the table. But none of these things can replace the political and moral argument about how a society should deal with the presence of homosexuals in its midst. I relate my experience here not to impress or to shock or to gain sympathy, but merely to convey what the homosexual experience is actually like. You cannot discuss something until you know roughly what it is.

It is also true, I think, that the lesbian experience is somewhat different than the homosexual male experience. Many lesbians argue that homosexuality is more often a choice for women than for men; that it involves a communal longing as much as an individual one; that it is far more rooted in moral and political choice than in ineradicable emotional or sexual orientation. Nevertheless, many lesbians also relate similar experiences to the one I have just related. Because girls and women can be less defensive about emotions and sexuality than boys and men, the sense of beleaguerment may be less profound than it is for boys, and the sense of self-contradiction less intense. But the coming to terms with something one already is, the slow unfolding of a self-realization around a basic emotional reality, is the same. In many, and probably most, cases, they cannot help it either.   23

The homosexual experience may be deemed an illness, a disorder, a privilege, or a curse; it may be deemed worthy of a "cure," rectified, embraced, or endured. *But it exists.* And it exists in something like the form I have just described. It occurs independently of the forms of its expression; it is bound up in that mysterious and unstable area where sexual desire and emotional longing meet; it reaches into the core of what makes a human being who he or she is. The origins of homosexuality are remarkably mysterious, and probably are due to a mixture of some genetic factors and very early childhood development (before the ages of five or six). But these arguments are largely irrelevant for the discussion that follows. The truth is that, for the overwhelming majority of adults, the condition of homosexuality is as involuntary as heterosexuality is for heterosexuals. Such an orientation is evident from the very beginning of the formation of a person's emotional identity. These are the only unavoidable premises of the arguments that follow.   24

Given a choice, many homosexuals along the way would   25
have preferred this were not so, which is about as good a
piece of evidence that it is. Men married happily for years
eventually crack and reveal the truth about themselves; people dedicated to extirpating homosexuality from the face of
the earth have succumbed to the realization that they too are
homosexual; individuals intent on ridding it from their systems have ended in defeat and sometimes despair; countless
thousands have killed themselves in order not to face up to it,
or often because they *have* finally faced up to it. They were
not fleeing a chimera or chasing a deception; they were expe-
riencing something real, whatever it was.

. . . By "homosexual," I mean simply someone who can   26
tell a similar story to my own; someone who has found in his
or her life that he or she is drawn emotionally and sexually to
the same gender, someone who, practically speaking, has had
no fundamental choice in the matter. Every society in human
history has devised some way to account for this phenomenon, and to accommodate it. As I write, Western society is in
the middle of a tense and often fevered attempt to find its
own way on the matter. Amid a cacophony of passion and
reason, propaganda and statistics, self-disclosures and bouts
of hysteria, the subject is being ineluctably discussed. This . . .
is an attempt to think through the arguments on all sides as
carefully and honestly as possible; to take the unalterable experience of all of us, heterosexual and homosexual, and try to
make some social and political sense of it.

Topics for Writing Narration and Description

1. *Respond.* Study the way Sullivan describes his personal discovery and his reaction to it. Consider your own personal experience. What secrets have you discovered about yourself? How have you responded to your discoveries? Write a narrative about the methods you used to explore or conceal your secret.

2. *Analyze.* Examine Sullivan's attempt to explain why homosexuality is an orientation rather than a choice. For example, what comparisons does he make between homosexuals and heterosexuals, and between homosexuals and lesbians? Consider how he responds to the question about orientation and choice asked him by those in the "conservative think tank." Write your own answer to their question.

3. *Argue.* Given Sullivan's experience, what do you think his attitude is toward same-sex marriage? You may want to read his comments on this issue in subsequent chapters of his book, *Virtually Normal.* What is your attitude toward this issue? Write an op-ed column on the subject for your local newspaper.

Colin Evans was born in 1948, in Bristol, England, and has worked as both a professional musician and a crime researcher. His many books include *Killer Doctors* (1993), *Superlawyers* (1997), *Great Feuds in History* (2001), *A Question of Evidence* (2002), and *The Encyclopedia of Forensic Detection* (2004). In "The Kelly Gang," reprinted from *The Casebook of Forensic Detection: How Science Solved 100 of the World's Most Baffling Crimes* (1996), Evans analyzes how the vivid memory of a kidnap victim enables the police to track down his captors.

The Kelly Gang

Date: 1933
Location: Oklahoma City, Oklahoma
Significance: In this extraordinary case, the victim's own fingerprints, not those of his captors, led to multiple convictions for kidnapping.

O N THE EVENING of July 22, 1933, a bridge game between Oklahoma City oil millionaire Charles Urschel, his wife, and their friends the Jarretts on the patio of Urschel's home was abruptly interrupted by the sudden appearance of two gunmen. "Which of you is Urschel?" snarled one of the bandits. When neither man at the card table responded, both were forced into a waiting car and driven off. Although ordered not to do so, Mrs. Urschel quickly called the police and the FBI. Within ninety minutes, Walter Jarrett was back at the Urschel house, shaken but otherwise unharmed. Once the kidnappers had clarified his identity, they had taken his wallet, pushed him from the car, and then driven off with Urschel.

1

Four days later, a ransom note arrived in the mail. Besides 2
a demand for two hundred thousand dollars, the kidnappers
enclosed a note in Charles Urschel's handwriting. To signify
their acceptance of the terms, the family was told to place an
advertisement in the classified column of the *Daily Oklaho-
man* reading: "FOR SALE—160 acres land, good five room
house, deep well. Also cows, tools, tractors, corn and hay.
$3,750 for quick sale. TERMS. Box H-807."

Soon afterward, another family friend, E. E. Kirkpatrick, 3
received fresh instructions to check into a Kansas City hotel.

---

*The account [the victim] gave the
FBI agents of his ordeal is unparalleled in
the annals of kidnapping: every detail,
every incident, no matter how mundane,
had been consciously logged for possible
future use as evidence.*

Later, carrying a bag stuffed with two hundred thousand dollars in marked bills, he left the hotel as arranged and was approached by a tall stranger "in a natty summer suit with a
turned down Panama hat." The man took the grip, assured
Kirkpatrick that Urschel would be returned safely, then disappeared. Twenty-four hours later, exhausted, Urschel arrived home.

EXTRAORDINARY DETAIL

Charles Urschel was clearly a remarkable man. The account 4
he gave FBI agents of his ordeal is unparalleled in the annals
of kidnapping: every detail, every incident, no matter how
mundane, had been consciously logged for possible future
use as evidence. After releasing Jarrett, the kidnappers had
blindfolded Urschel and driven through the night. At dawn,

they switched cars in a garage or barn. Urschel was told to lie down on the rear floor of a large car he guessed to be either a Buick or a Cadillac. Three hours later, they pulled into a gas station. As a woman filled the tank, one of the kidnappers idly asked about local farming conditions. The woman replied that crops in that area were "all burned up."

At the next stop, another garage or barn, Urschel over- 5 heard one gang member mention the time—2:30 P.M. After dark, he was taken on foot to a house where he spent the night. The next morning, the final leg of his journey ended at a farmhouse surrounded by cows and chickens.

Despite being blindfolded and handcuffed to a chair, 6 Urschel missed nothing. When water was being drawn from the farmhouse well, he noticed that the windlass creaked. And the water, drunk from a tin cup without a handle, had had a distinctive mineral taste. By loosening his blindfold a fraction, he was able to glimpse his watch. He noted that each morning at 9:45 and each evening at 5:45 a plane passed over the house. But on Sunday, July 30, there was a downpour of rain, and he didn't hear the morning plane.

Neither did Urschel limit his detective talents to mere ob- 7 servation. While writing the letter to his family, unnoticed by his kidnappers, he deliberately left fingerprints on every surface he could reach. On July 31, his ordeal came to an end when he was driven to Norman, on the outskirts of Oklahoma City, and released.

WIDE SEARCH

FBI efforts to locate the kidnappers' lair centered on the rain- 8 storm and the plane's failure on that Sunday to follow its usual flight pattern. All airlines that flew within a six-hundred-mile radius of Oklahoma City were contacted for details of their schedules. Meanwhile, the comment by the gas station attendant prompted calls to meteorological offices to ask if any drought-ridden regions had recently received a heavy drenching.

American Airlines reported that on Sunday, July 30, a   9
plane on the Forth Worth–Amarillo run had been forced to
swing north from its usual course to avoid a heavy storm over
an area previously afflicted by scorching drought. Calculations showed that the morning plane and the return afternoon flight would pass over Paradise, Texas, at the approximate times recalled by Urschel.

Posing as bankers seeking to extend loans to farmers, FBI   10
agents began visiting every farm in the area. Eventually they
came to the five-hundred-acre ranch of Mr. and Mrs. R. G.
Shannon. Here they arrested Harvey Bailey, a notorious
hoodlum, with seven hundred dollars of the marked ransom
bills on him. Then investigators remembered that the
Shannons' daughter Kathryn was married to George "Machine Gun" Kelly, an infamous if somewhat reluctant gang-
ster (his notoriety was almost entirely due to his wife's
mythomania). Warrants were issued for the arrest of anyone
connected with the Kellys.

When shown the Shannon home, Urschel immediately   11
identified it as his place of capture. There was the well, the
old tin cup, and the chair to which he had been handcuffed.
And he could never forget the taste of that water. Most conclusive of all, however, were Urschel's fingerprints; according
to one expert, they covered almost every square inch of
reachable surface.

Eventually the entire Kelly gang was rounded up and   12
given long jail terms.

CONCLUSION

It seemed almost inevitable that "Machine Gun" Kelly, a   13
hapless bungler who never once fired a gun in anger, should
have chosen Charles Urschel, possibly the most astute hos-
tage ever, for his one excursion into kidnapping. In such a
lopsided contest, Kelly never stood a chance. He spent the
rest of his life behind bars and died in Leavenworth in 1954.

Topics for Writing Process Analysis

1. *Respond.* How have your attitudes toward kidnapping been shaped by the movies? For example, in the movies, how do family members and police deal with the issue of ransom? Write an analysis of how you would deal with the issue of ransom if one of your family members were kidnapped.

2. *Analyze.* Analyze how the detectives used the clues to find the kidnappers. How realistic is Urschel's ability to store and plant clues? Write an essay analyzing the plots of the *CSI* television programs to demonstrate how the media have shaped our belief in the existence of physical evidence.

3. *Argue.* Argue that most criminal cases remain unsolved because there is little physical evidence. Conduct some research on unsolved crimes—those in your hometown or those you have seen discussed in the media. Then cite these cases to prove that through either accident or design most criminals leave no clues.

DAVA SOBEL

Dava Sobel was born in 1947 in New York City and was educated at the State University of New York at Binghamton. She has worked as a science reporter for the *New York Times* and the Discovery Channel Online. She has contributed articles to magazines such as *Audubon, Discover,* the *New Yorker,* and *Vogue.* Her books include *Is Anyone Out There?: The Scientific Search for Extraterrestrial Intelligence* (1992), *Longitude: The Truth Story of a Lone Genius Who Solved the Greatest Scientific Problem of His Time* (1995), and *Galileo's Daughter: A Historical Memoir of Science* (1999). In "Imaginary Lines," reprinted from *Longitude,* Sobel compares and contrasts the imaginary lines that travelers have used to navigate the world.

Imaginary Lines

When I'm playful I use the meridians of longitude and parallels of latitude for a seine, and drag the Atlantic Ocean for whales.
—MARK TWAIN, *Life on the Mississippi*

O NCE ON A Wednesday excursion when I was a little 1 girl, my father bought me a beaded wire ball that I loved. At a touch, I could collapse the toy into a flat coil between my palms, or pop it open to make a hollow sphere. Rounded out, it resembled a tiny Earth, because its hinged wires traced the same pattern of intersecting circles that I had seen on the globe in my schoolroom—the thin black lines of latitude and longitude. The few colored beads slid along the wire paths haphazardly, like ships on the high seas.

My father strode up Fifth Avenue to Rockefeller Center 2 with me on his shoulders, and we stopped to stare at the statue of Atlas, carrying Heaven and Earth on his.

The bronze orb that Atlas held aloft, like the wire toy in   3
my hands, was a see-through world, defined by imaginary
lines. The Equator. The Ecliptic. The Tropic of Cancer. The
Tropic of Capricorn. The Arctic Circle. The prime meridian.
Even then I could recognize, in the graph-paper grid imposed on the globe, a powerful symbol of all the real lands
and waters on the planet.

Today, the latitude and longitude lines govern with more   4
authority than I could have imagined forty-odd years ago, for
they stay fixed as the world changes its configuration under-

---

*The zero-degree parallel of latitude is fixed
by the laws of nature, while the zero-degree
meridian of longitude shifts like
the sands of time.*

---

neath them—with continents adrift across a widening sea,
and national boundaries repeatedly redrawn by war or peace.

As a child, I learned the trick for remembering the differ-   5
ence between latitude and longitude. The latitude lines, the
parallels, really do stay parallel to each other as they girdle the
globe from the Equator to the poles in a series of shrinking
concentric rings. The meridians of longitude go the other
way. They loop from the North Pole to the South and back
again in great circles of the same size, so they all converge at
the ends of the Earth.

Lines of latitude and longitude began crisscrossing our   6
worldview in ancient times, at least three centuries before the
birth of Christ. By A.D. 150, the cartographer and astronomer
Ptolemy had plotted them on the twenty-seven maps of his
first world atlas. Also for this landmark volume, Ptolemy
listed all the place names in an index, in alphabetical order,
with the latitude and longitude of each—as well as he could
gauge them from travelers' reports. Ptolemy himself had only

an armchair appreciation of the wider world. A common misconception of his day held that anyone living below the Equator would melt into deformity from the horrible heat. The Equator marked the zero-degree parallel of latitude 7 for Ptolemy. He did not choose it arbitrarily but took it on higher authority from his predecessors, who had derived it from nature while observing the motions of the heavenly bodies. The sun, moon, and planets pass almost directly overhead at the Equator. Likewise the Tropic of Cancer and the Tropic of Capricorn, two other famous parallels, assume their positions at the sun's command. They mark the northern and southern boundaries of the sun's apparent motion over the course of the year.

Ptolemy was free, however, to lay his prime meridian, the 8 zero-degree longitude line, wherever he liked. He chose to run it through the Fortunate Islands (now called the Canary & Madeira Islands) off the northwest coast of Africa. Later mapmakers moved the prime meridian to the Azores and to the Cape Verde Islands, as well as to Rome, Copenhagen, Jerusalem, St. Petersburg, Pisa, Paris, and Philadelphia, among other places, before it settled down at last in London. As the world turns, any line drawn from pole to pole may serve as well as any other for a starting line of reference. The placement of the prime meridian is a purely political decision.

Here lies the real, hard-core difference between latitude 9 and longitude—beyond the superficial difference in line direction that any child can see: The zero-degree parallel of latitude is fixed by the laws of nature, while the zero-degree meridian of longitude shifts like the sands of time. This difference makes finding latitude child's play, and turns the determination of longitude, especially at sea, into an adult dilemma—one that stumped the wisest minds of the world for the better part of human history.

Any sailor worth his salt can gauge his latitude well 10 enough by the length of the day, or by the height of the sun or known guide stars above the horizon. Christopher Columbus followed a straight path across the Atlantic when he "sailed the parallel" on his 1492 journey, and the technique would doubtless have carried him to the Indies had not the Americas intervened.

The measurement of longitude meridians, in comparison, is tempered by time. To learn one's longitude at sea, one needs to know what time it is aboard ship and also the time at the home port or another place of known longitude—at that very same moment. The two clock times enable the navigator to convert the hour difference into a geographical separation. Since the Earth takes twenty-four hours to complete one full revolution of three hundred sixty degrees, one hour marks one twenty-fourth of a spin, or fifteen degrees. And so each hour's time difference between the ship and the starting point marks a progress of fifteen degrees of longitude to the east or west. Every day at sea, when the navigator resets his ship's clock to local noon when the sun reaches its highest point in the sky, and then consults the home-port clock, every hour's discrepancy between them translates into another fifteen degrees of longitude. 11

Those same fifteen degrees of longitude also correspond to a distance traveled. At the Equator, where the girth of the Earth is greatest, fifteen degrees stretch fully one thousand miles. North or south of that line, however, the mileage value of each degree decreases. One degree of longitude equals four minutes of time the world over, but in terms of distance, one degree shrinks from sixty-eight miles at the Equator to virtually nothing at the poles. 12

Precise knowledge of the hour in two different places at once—a longitude prerequisite so easily accessible today from any pair of cheap wristwatches—was utterly unattainable up to and including the era of pendulum clocks. On the deck of a rolling ship, such clocks would slow down, or speed up, or stop running altogether. Normal changes in temperature encountered en route from a cold country of origin to a tropical trade zone thinned or thickened a clock's lubricating oil and made its metal parts expand or contract with equally disastrous results. A rise or fall in barometric pressure, or the subtle variations in the Earth's gravity from one latitude to another, could also cause a clock to gain or lose time. 13

For lack of a practical method of determining longitude,   14
every great captain in the Age of Exploration became lost at
sea despite the best available charts and compasses. From
Vasco da Gama to Vasco Núñez de Balboa, from Ferdinand
Magellan to Sir Francis Drake—they all got where they were
going willy-nilly, by forces attributed to good luck or the
grace of God.

As more and more sailing vessels set out to conquer or ex-   15
plore new territories, to wage war, or to ferry gold and commodities between foreign lands, the wealth of nations floated
upon the oceans. And still no ship owned a reliable means for
establishing her whereabouts. In consequence, untold numbers of sailors died when their destinations suddenly loomed
out of the sea and took them by surprise. In a single such accident, on October 22, 1707, at the Scilly Isles near the
southwestern tip of England, four home-bound British warships ran aground and nearly two thousand men lost their
lives.

The active quest for a solution to the problem of longitude   16
persisted over four centuries and across the whole continent
of Europe. Most crowned heads of state eventually played a
part in the longitude story, notably King George III of England and King Louis XIV of France. Seafaring men such as
Captain William Bligh of the *Bounty* and the great circum-
navigator Captain James Cook, who made three long voy-
ages of exploration and experimentation before his violent
death in Hawaii, took the more promising methods to sea to
test their accuracy and practicability.

Renowned astronomers approached the longitude chal-   17
lenge by appealing to the clockwork universe: Galileo Galilei,
Jean Dominique Cassini, Christiaan Huygens, Sir Isaac Newton, and Edmond Halley, of comet fame, all entreated the
moon and stars for help. Palatial observatories were founded
at Paris, London, and Berlin for the express purpose of determining longitude by the heavens. Meanwhile, lesser minds
devised schemes that depended on the yelps of wounded
dogs, or the cannon blasts of signal ships strategically anchored—somehow—on the open ocean.

In the course of their struggle to find longitude, scientists   18
struck upon other discoveries that changed their view of the
universe. These include the first accurate determinations of
the weight of the Earth, the distance to the stars, and the
speed of light.

As time passed and no method proved successful, the   19
search for a solution to the longitude problem assumed legendary proportions, on a par with discovering the Fountain
of Youth, the secret of perpetual motion, or the formula for
transforming lead into gold. The governments of the great
maritime nations—including Spain, the Netherlands, and
certain city-states of Italy—periodically roiled the fervor by
offering jackpot purses for a workable method. The British
Parliament, in its famed Longitude Act of 1714, set the highest bounty of all, naming a prize equal to a king's ransom
(several million dollars in today's currency) for a "Practicable
and Useful" means of determining longitude.

English clockmaker John Harrison, a mechanical genius   20
who pioneered the science of portable precision timekeeping,
devoted his life to this quest. He accomplished what Newton
had feared was impossible: He invented a clock that would
carry the true time from the home port, like an eternal flame,
to any remote corner of the world.

Harrison, a man of simple birth and high intelligence,   21
crossed swords with the leading lights of his day. He made a
special enemy of the Reverend Nevil Maskelyne, the fifth astronomer royal, who contested his claim to the coveted prize
money, and whose tactics at certain junctures can only be described as foul play.

With no formal education or apprenticeship to any watch-   22
maker, Harrison nevertheless constructed a series of virtually
friction-free clocks that required no lubrication and no cleaning, that were made from materials impervious to rust, and
that kept their moving parts perfectly balanced in relation to
one another, regardless of how the world pitched or tossed
about them. He did away with the pendulum, and he combined different metals inside his works in such a way that
when one component expanded or contracted with changes

in temperature, the other counteracted the change and kept the clock's rate constant.

His every success, however, was parried by members of the   23
scientific elite, who distrusted Harrison's magic box. The commissioners charged with awarding the longitude prize—Nevil Maskelyne among them—changed the contest rules whenever they saw fit, so as to favor the chances of astronomers over the likes of Harrison and his fellow "mechanics." But the utility and accuracy of Harrison's approach triumphed in the end. His followers shepherded Harrison's intricate, exquisite invention through the design modifications that enabled it to be mass produced and enjoy wide use.

An aged, exhausted Harrison, taken under the wing of   24
King George III, ultimately claimed his rightful monetary reward in 1773—after forty struggling years of political intrigue, international warfare, academic backbiting, scientific revolution, and economic upheaval.

All these threads, and more, entwine in the lines of longi-   25
tude. To unravel them now—to retrace their story in an age when a network of orbiting satellites can nail down a ship's position within a few feet in just a moment or two—is to see the globe anew.

Topics for Writing Comparison and Contrast

1. *Respond.* How were you taught the difference between latitude and longitude? How did you learn to identify the latitude and longitude of a specific place? Write an essay in which you explain the process of navigating between the latitude and longitude of your hometown and the latitude and longitude of your university.

2. *Analyze.* Analyze the historical problem of longitude. Why was it considered a political as well as a scientific problem? Conduct some historical research and then speculate on the political forces that led to the establishment of London as the prime meridian.

3. *Argue.* Read up on some of the manned space exploration journeys in the last ten to fifteen years and find out what discoveries resulted from them. Then argue for or against such space journeys, citing your reasons. Perhaps you think they cost too much money that could be spent on other projects, or you may cite the loss of life and weigh that against the value of the discoveries. Or you could compare these modern journeys of exploration with those of other eras, such as Stapleton's journey to the South Pole or Magellan's circumnavigation of the globe, and argue which have been more valuable.

LEWIS THOMAS

Lewis Thomas (1913–1993) was born in Flushing, New York, and was educated at Princeton University and Harvard University Medical School. He held appointments at numerous research hospitals and medical schools before assuming the position of president of the Sloan-Kettering Cancer Center in New York City. In 1974 his collection of essays, *The Lives of a Cell: Notes of a Biology Watcher,* won the National Book Award for Arts and Letters. His other books include *The Medusa and the Snail: More Notes of a Biology Watcher* (1979), *The Youngest Science* (1983), *Late Night Thoughts on Listening to Mahler's Ninth Symphony* (1983), and *The Fragile Species* (1992). In "The Technology of Medicine," from *The Lives of a Cell,* Thomas classifies "three quite different levels of technology in medicine."

The Technology of Medicine

T ECHNOLOGY ASSESSMENT HAS become a routine exercise   1
for the scientific enterprises on which the country is obliged to spend vast sums for its needs. Brainy committees are continually evaluating the effectiveness and cost of doing various things in space, defense, energy, transportation, and the like, to give advice about prudent investments for the future.

Somehow medicine, for all the $80-odd billion that it is   2
said to cost the nation, has not yet come in for much of this analytical treatment. It seems taken for granted that the technology of medicine simply exists, take it or leave it, and the only major technologic problem which policy-makers are in-

terested in is how to deliver today's kind of health care, with equity, to all the people.

When, as is bound to happen sooner or later, the analysts get around to the technology of medicine itself, they will have to face the problem of measuring the relative cost and effectiveness of all the things that are done in the management of disease. They make their living at this kind of thing, and I wish them well, but I imagine they will have a bewilder- 3

There are three quite different levels of technology in medicine, so unlike each other as to seem altogether different undertakings.

---

ing time. For one thing, our methods of managing disease are constantly changing—partly under the influence of new bits of information brought in from all corners of biologic science. At the same time, a great many things are done that are not so closely related to science, some not related at all.

In fact, there are three quite different levels of technology in medicine, so unlike each other as to seem altogether different undertakings. Practitioners of medicine and the analysts will be in trouble if they are not kept separate. 4

1. First of all, there is a large body of what might be termed "nontechnology," impossible to measure in terms of its capacity to alter either the natural course of disease or its eventual outcome. A great deal of money is spent on this. It is valued highly by the professionals as well as the patients. It consists of what is sometimes called "supportive therapy." It tides patients over through diseases that are not, by and large, understood. It is what is meant by the phrases "caring for" and "standing by." It is indispensable. It is not, however, a technology in any real sense, since it does not involve measures directed at the underlying mechanism of disease. 5

It includes the large part of any good doctor's time that is   6
taken up with simply providing reassurance, explaining to patients who fear that they have contracted one or another lethal disease that they are, in fact, quite healthy.

It is what physicians used to be engaged in at the bedside   7
of patients with diphtheria, meningitis, poliomyelitis, lobar pneumonia, and all the rest of the infectious diseases that have since come under control.

It is what physicians must now do for patients with intrac-   8
table cancer, severe rheumatoid arthritis, multiple sclerosis, stroke, and advanced cirrhosis. One can think of at least twenty major diseases that require this kind of supportive medical care because of the absence of an effective technology. I would include a large amount of what is called mental disease, and most varieties of cancer, in this category.

The cost of this nontechnology is very high, and getting   9
higher all the time. It requires not only a great deal of time but also very hard effort and skill on the part of physicians; only the very best of doctors are good at coping with this kind of defeat. It also involves long periods of hospitalization, lots of nursing, lots of involvement of nonmedical professionals in and out of the hospital. It represents, in short, a substantial segment of today's expenditures for health.

2. At the next level up is a kind of technology best termed   10
"halfway technology." This represents the kinds of things that must be done after the fact, in efforts to compensate for the incapacitating effects of certain diseases whose course one is unable to do very much about. It is a technology designed to make up for disease, or to postpone death.

The outstanding examples in recent years are the trans-   11
plantations of hearts, kidneys, livers, and other organs, and the equally spectacular inventions of artificial organs. In the public mind, this kind of technology has come to seem like the equivalent of the high technologies of the physical sciences. The media tend to present each new procedure as though it represented a breakthrough and therapeutic triumph, instead of the makeshift that it really is.

In fact, this level of technology is, by its nature, at the   12 same time highly sophisticated and profoundly primitive. It is the kind of thing that one must continue to do until there is a genuine understanding of the mechanisms involved in disease. In chronic glomerulonephritis, for example, a much clearer insight will be needed into the events leading to the destruction of glomeruli by the immunologic reactants that now appear to govern this disease, before one will know how to intervene intelligently to prevent the process, or turn it around. But when this level of understanding has been reached, the technology of kidney replacement will not be much needed and should no longer pose the huge problems of logistics, cost, and ethics that it poses today.

An extremely complex and costly technology for the management of coronary heart disease has evolved—involving specialized ambulances and hospital units, all kinds of electronic gadgetry, and whole platoons of new professional personnel—to deal with the end results of coronary thrombosis. Almost everything offered today for the treatment of heart disease is at this level of technology, with the transplanted and artificial hearts as ultimate examples. When enough has been learned to know what really goes wrong in heart disease, one ought to be in a position to figure out ways to prevent or reverse the process, and when this happens the current elaborate technology will probably be set to one side. 13

Much of what is done in the treatment of cancer, by surgery, irradiation, and chemotherapy, represents halfway technology, in the sense that these measures are directed at the existence of already established cancer cells, but not at the mechanisms by which cells become neoplastic. 14

It is a characteristic of this kind of technology that it costs an enormous amount of money and requires a continuing expansion of hospital facilities. There is no end to the need for new, highly trained people to run the enterprise. And there is really no way out of this, at the present state of knowledge. If the installation of specialized coronary-care units can result in the extension of life for only a few patients with coronary disease (and there is no question that this technology is effective in a few cases), it seems to me an inevitable fact of life 15 that as many of these as can be will be put together, and as much money as can be found will be spent. I do not see that anyone has much choice in this. The only thing that can move medicine away from this level of technology is new information, and the only imaginable source of this information is research.

3. The third type of technology is the kind that is so effective that it seems to attract the least public notice; it has come to be taken for granted. This is the genuinely decisive technology of modern medicine, exemplified best by modern methods for immunization against diphtheria, pertussis, and the childhood virus diseases, and the contemporary use of antibiotics and chemotherapy for bacterial infections. The capacity to deal effectively with syphilis and tuberculosis represents a milestone in human endeavor, even though full use of this potential has not yet been made. And there are, of course, other examples: the treatment of endocrinologic disorders with appropriate hormones, the prevention of hemolytic disease of the newborn, the treatment and prevention of various nutritional disorders, and perhaps just around the corner the management of Parkinsonism and sickle-cell anemia. There are other examples, and everyone will have his favorite candidates for the list, but the truth is that there are nothing like as many as the public has been led to believe.   16

The point to be made about this kind of technology—the real high technology of medicine—is that it comes as the result of a genuine understanding of disease mechanisms, and when it becomes available, it is relatively inexpensive, and relatively easy to deliver.   17

Offhand, I cannot think of any important human disease for which medicine possesses the outright capacity to prevent or cure where the cost of the technology is itself a major problem. The price is never as high as the cost of managing the same diseases during the earlier stages of no-technology or halfway technology. If a case of typhoid fever had to be managed today by the best methods of 1935, it would run to a staggering expense. At, say, around fifty days of hospitalization, requiring the most demanding kind of nursing care,   18

with the obsessive concern for details of diet that characterized the therapy of that time, with daily laboratory monitoring, and, on occasion, surgical intervention for abdominal catastrophe, I should think $10,000 would be a conservative
estimate for the illness, as contrasted with today's cost of a
bottle of chloramphenicol and a day or two of fever. The halfway technology that was evolving for poliomyelitis in the
early 1950s, just before the emergence of the basic research
that made the vaccine possible, provides another illustration
of the point. Do you remember Sister Kenny, and the cost of
those institutes for rehabilitation, with all those ceremonially
applied hot fomentations, and the debates about whether the
affected limbs should be totally immobilized or kept in passive motion as frequently as possible, and the masses of statistically tormented data mobilized to support one view or the
other? It is the cost of that kind of technology, and its relative
effectiveness, that must be compared with the cost and effectiveness of the vaccine.

Pulmonary tuberculosis had similar episodes in its history. 19
There was a sudden enthusiasm for the surgical removal of
infected lung tissue in the early 1950s, and elaborate plans
were being made for new and expensive installations for major pulmonary surgery in tuberculosis hospitals, and then
INH and streptomycin came along and the hospitals themselves were closed up.

It is when physicians are bogged down by their incomplete 20
technologies, by the innumerable things they are obliged to
do in medicine when they lack a clear understanding of disease mechanisms, that the deficiencies of the health-care system are most conspicuous. If I were a policy-maker, interested in saving money for health care over the long haul, I
would regard it as an act of high prudence to give high prior-
ity to a lot more basic research in biologic science. This is the
only way to get the full mileage that biology owes to the science of medicine, even though it seems, as used to be said in
the days when the phrase still had some meaning, like asking
for the moon.

Topics for Writing Division and Classification

1. *Respond.* What kind of medical tests have you experienced or seen conducted on friends and family? What kind of emotional reaction have you felt toward the imposing machines used for such tests? Write an essay classifying the types of medical tests that produce the least and the most emotional stress. In the process, suggest ways to avoid such stress.

2. *Analyze.* Assess Thomas's classification system. Then select a disease he does not mention—such as AIDS or SARS. Explain where such a disease would fit in his classification system.

3. *Argue.* Thomas believes strongly in "basic research in biologic science" as a way to cure disease. After conducting some preliminary research of your own, argue that the best solution to the problem of illness is wellness—that is, eating carefully, exercising regularly, and avoiding dangerous addictions such as smoking.

the human body, for they have evolved over centuries—millenniums—of trial and error. Power tools are more convenient, of course, but they lack precisely this sense of refinement. Using a clumsy nailing gun is work, but swinging a claw hammer is satisfying work.

Had a medieval carpenter come along—untutored neo-phytes, we could have used his help—he would have found most of my tools familiar. Indeed, even an ancient Roman carpenter would have found few surprises in my toolbox. He would recognize my plane, a version of his *plana;* he might

---

Without screws, entire fields of science would have languished, navigation would have remained primitive and naval warfare as well as routine maritime commerce in the 18th and 19th centuries would not have been possible.

---

admire my retractable tape measure, an improvement on his bronze folding *regula*. He would be puzzled by my brace and bit, a medieval invention, but being familiar with the Egyptian bow drill, he would readily infer its purpose. No doubt he would be impressed by my hard steel nails, so much superior to his hand-forged spikes.

Saws, hammers (and nails), chisels, drills, and squares all date from the Bronze and early Iron Ages. Many types of modern tools originated even earlier, in the Neolithic period, about 8,000 years ago. In fact, there is only one tool in my toolbox that would puzzle a Roman and a medieval carpenter: my screwdriver. They would understand the principle of screws; after all, Archimedes invented the screw in the third century B.C. Ancient screws were large wood contraptions, used for raising water. One of the earliest devices that used a

WITOLD RYBCZYNSKI

Witold Rybczynski was born in Edinburgh, Scot
land, and educated at the School of Architecture
McGill University, in Montreal, Canada. H
worked as an architect and as planner of housin
and new towns in northern Canada. In 1975 h
joined the faculty of McGill University and als
began working as a consultant to the World Banl
the United Nations, and the International Re
search Center. His books include *Taming the T
ger: The Struggle to Control Technology* (1983
Home: A Short History of an Idea (1986), an
City Life: Urban Expectations in a New Wor
(1995). In "One Good Turn," excerpted fro
*One Good Turn: A Natural History of the Scre
driver and the Screw* (2000), Rybczynski defin
the functions of the tapered and threaded screw

One Good Turn:
How Machine-Made Screws
Brought the World Together

S OME YEARS AGO my wife and I built a house. I mea
built it—ourselves, from the ground up. Electri
ing unavailable, we used hand tools. I did not have
toolbox. It contained different-size saws, a mallet ar
els, a plane, several hammers (for friends conscript
our work force) and, for correcting major mistakes,
sledge. In addition I had a number of tools for meas
tape, a square, a spirit level and a plumb line. That wa
needed.

One of the rewards of building something yourse
pleasure of using tools. Hand tools are really exten

screw to apply pressure was a Roman clothes press; presses were also used to make olive oil and wine. The Middle Ages applied the same principle to the printing press and to that fiendish torturing device, the thumbscrew. Yet the ordinary screw as a small fixing device was unknown.

Wood screws originated sometime in the 16th century. 5 The first screwdrivers were called turnscrews, flat-bladed bits that could be attached to a carpenter's brace. The inventor of the handheld screwdriver remains unknown, but the familiar tool does not appear in carpenters' toolboxes until after 1800. There was not a great call for screwdrivers, because screws were expensive. They had to be painstakingly made by hand and were used in luxury articles like clocks. It was only after 1850 that wood screws were available in large quantities.

Inexpensive screws are quintessentially modern. Their 6 mass production requires a high degree of precision and standardization. The wood screw also represents an entirely new method of attachment, more durable than nails—which can pop out if the wood dries out or expands. (This makes screws particularly useful in shipbuilding.) The tapered, gimlet-pointed wood screw—like its cousin the bolt—squeezes the two joined pieces together. The more you tighten the screw—or the nut—the greater the squeeze. In modern steel buildings, for example, high-tension bolts are tightened so hard that it is the friction between the two pieces of steel— not the bolt itself—that gives strength to the joint. On a more mundane level, screws enable a vast array of convenient attachments in the home: door hinges, drawer pulls, shelf hangers, towel bars. Perhaps that is why if you rummage around most people's kitchen drawers you will most likely find at least one screwdriver.

Wood screws are stronger and more durable than nails, 7 pegs, or staples. But the aristocrat of screws is the precision screw. This was first made roughly—by hand—and later on screw-cutting lathes, which is a chicken-and-egg story, since it was the screw that made machine lathes possible. The machined screw represented a technological breakthrough of epic proportions. Screws enabled the minute adjustment of a variety of precision instruments like clocks, microscopes, telescopes, sextants, theodolites and marine chronometers.

It is not an exaggeration to say that accurately threaded   8 screws changed the world. Without screws, entire fields of science would have languished, navigation would have remained primitive and naval warfare as well as routine maritime commerce in the 18th and 19th centuries would not have been possible. Without screws there would have been no machine tools, hence no industrial products and no Industrial Revolution. Think of that the next time you pick up a screwdriver to pry open a can of paint.

Topics for Writing Definition

1. *Respond.* What kinds of experience have you had with tools or making something, such as a bookcase or a stew? Write a humorous essay in which you define how the strange tools or difficult procedures you discovered were essential to completing your project successfully.
2. *Analyze.* Study Rybczynski's historical analysis of the screw. Then research some of the claims he makes for its importance to the Industrial Revolution. Flesh out his analysis with some other extended examples of how "machine-made screws brought the world together."
3. *Argue.* Select another technological device—such as the elevator, the rivet, the microchip—and demonstrate how this discovery changed the course of human history.

JOHN FLEISCHMAN

John Fleischman was born in 1948 in New York City and was educated at Antioch College and Nottingham University, England. He works as a science writer for the American Society for Cell Biology, has contributed articles to magazines such as the *Atlantic,* the *Smithsonian,* and *Audubon,* and has written award-winning books for children, such as *Phineas Gage: A Gruesome but True Story About Brain Science* (2002). He has also worked as a science broadcaster for Boston's WGBH and as a senior editor for *Yankee* and *Ohio* magazines. In "Homer's Bones," reprinted from *Discover* magazine, Fleischman explains how archeological excavations have caused scholars to reassess Homer's *Iliad* and *Odyssey.*

Homer's Bones

FIVE YEARS AGO, on the western edge of the Greek 1 Peloponnesus, Sharon Stocker stood before a darkened basement door and wondered if going inside was such a good idea. As a doctoral student in classics at the University of Cincinnati, Stocker was trying to track down a particular group of Bronze Age pottery sherds for her thesis work. Her search had led her to a small archaeological museum in the village of Hora and an underground storeroom that had been opened only rarely in 30 years. "The museum guards opened the door very slowly, and then they stepped back," Stocker recalls. "There were just tons of stuff in there. I immediately thought about asking the guards to close up again. Talk about looking for a needle in a haystack."

Stocker forced herself from sunlight into the dark. Then, 2 as her eyes adjusted, she made out some order among the

rough wooden boxes and sagging cardboard barrels that
were closely packed right to the ceiling. Some still carried
greetings from the American people—relics of the U.S. food
relief program during the Greek civil war in the 1940s.
Stocker began to peek under lids and poke among bundles
wrapped in yellowing newsprint, their labels fading toward
blank. She stopped to read a wooden identification tag and to
admire a Greek newspaper from the 1960s with a picture of a
young Jackie Kennedy wearing a pill-box hat. The filthier

In Mycenae, home of the legendary ruins
of King Agamemnon's palace,
[Heinrich Schliemann] found a treasure
of gold masks, bronze weapons, and stylized
vessels that marked a new civilization that
[he] named Mycenaean.

Stocker's hands got, the happier she became. There were
tons of pottery fragments and other ancient detritus stored
there. And there were animal bones, lots of them.

More than 3,000 years earlier, these animals fed the inhab-   3
itants of a great hilltop palace in the southwest corner of
Greece. Their remains had been excavated on April 4, 1939,
in what may have been the luckiest first day in archaeological
history. That day, Carl Blegen, Stocker's predecessor at the
University of Cincinnati, was digging an exploratory trench
through an olive grove when one of his workmen lifted a clay
tablet from the soil. Lightly brushing away the dirt, Blegen
saw at once that the tablet was incised in Linear B, an
undeciphered script known from Bronze Age Crete and
never before seen on the Greek mainland. That spring, before war closed in on Greece, Blegen raced to unearth hundreds more tablets, providing the critical mass for decipher-
ing the script. The tablets revealed that the people of this

hilltop palace wrote in an early form of Greek. Although they never named their king, Blegen became convinced that his name was Nestor.

Nestor. To students of classical literature, the name is a   4
piece of fiction. In Homer's *Iliad*, a sage old king named Nestor joins Agamemnon in the war on Troy and fires up the troops with tales of his youthful exploits. In Book 3 of the *Odyssey*, Telemachus begins his quest for his long-lost father, Odysseus, at "sandy Pylos," Nestor's kingdom. When Telemachus runs his ship's keel ashore at dawn, he finds the wise but long-winded king on the beach, his people assembled around him:

> *Sacrificing sleek black bulls to Poseidon,*
> *god of the sea-blue mane who shakes the earth.*
> *They sat in nine divisions, each five hundred strong,*
> *each division offering up nine bulls, and while the*
>   *people*
> *tasted the innards, burned the thighbones for the*
>   *god.*

Nestor's Pylos was one of the glories of Mycenaean civili-   5
zation. His palace straddled a strategic ridge, commanding a view south across the sandy Bay of Navarino and northward over the shoulder of Mount Aigaleon into the kingdom's rich inland province. When a great fire destroyed the palace around 1200 B.C., it heralded the collapse of Mycenaean culture across Greece. For many archaeologists since Blegen, the details of that collapse and the often-mundane lives of the people who lived through it are of far more interest than their romantic echoes in the *Iliad* and the *Odyssey*. Homer was a poet, they say, not a historian.

To Carl Blegen, the barrels and boxes, bones and pot-   6
sherds, that he packed off to the storeroom in Hora were just table scraps from an archaeological feast—carefully excavated, dutifully noted, and then forgotten. But to Stocker and a new generation of forensic archaeologists, these leftovers had their own fascinating story to tell. Stocker's first

thought was that the place desperately needed reorganization. Her next thought was that a good housecleaning might yield fresh evidence. What she didn't guess is that hidden within that archaeological mishmash, in an unremarkable wooden box, were some remains with the power to reawaken the Greek bard's ancient voice—and with it, the debate over what he was talking about.

The modern origins of the Homer question can be precisely dated—April 1870—and placed: a hill called Hissarlik in western Turkey overlooking the Dardanelles, the narrow strait between Europe and Asia. Here Heinrich Schliemann, a self-made German merchant prince turned self-made Homeric scholar, arrived with a revolutionary scientific instrument—a shovel. He was looking for Homer's Troy. The best classical scholars of his day had agreed that Troy was a myth. Schliemann had other ideas. After making a few test trenches, he returned the following year with a gang of local workmen and drove a massive trench straight through Hissarlik, slicing into a wedding cake of lost cities. He counted nine. They ranged from Troy IX, the Roman city rebuilt by the Emperor Augustus to celebrate his family's fanciful connections to the Trojan hero Aeneas, and so on down, city below city, to Troy I, a small but powerful early Bronze Age fortress. Schliemann's only problem was deciding which one was Homer's Troy.

He chose Troy II chiefly because in that layer, he had recovered a treasure of ancient gold, crystal, and bronze. If this was Homer's Troy, then Schliemann could proclaim his hoard the "Treasure of Priam," after the Trojan king, and its golden bead headdress as nothing less than the jewels of Helen of Troy.

Schliemann was the kind of founding father to make any descendant nervous, capable of sharp practice, outright fabrication, and promotional bombast. Troy II was eventually found to date from roughly 2400 B.C.—far older than Schliemann had imagined and too old to qualify as Homer's Troy. But Schliemann had found *something,* a clue to a lost

Bronze Age civilization on the Greek mainland. In 1876, assuming that he'd uncovered Homer's Trojans in Turkey, Schliemann went looking for Homer's Greeks in Greece. There in Mycenae, home of the legendary ruins of King Agamemnon's palace, he found a treasure of gold masks, bronze weapons, and stylized vessels that marked a new civilization that Schliemann named Mycenaean. The Mycenaeans, influenced heavily by the Minoan civilization on Crete, were aggressive seafarers. They lived in state-controlled economies, tightly organized from the top down by a king and his scribes. Then, late in the 13th century B.C., their power centers collapsed, one after another, leaving behind their language, their names, and little more than a memory of their grandeur.

Some 500 years later, many scholars believe, along came Homer. Tradition says he was a blind wandering bard from Ionia, the western coast and islands off what is now Turkey. Whoever Homer was, he seems to have known the geography of northern Ionia—the islands of Imbros and Tenedos, the Dardanelles, and the low coastal hills and wetlands around Troy. But even Schliemann conceded that Homer retold a very old story, "as it was handed down to him by preceding bards, clothing the traditional facts of the war and destruction of Troy in the garb of his own day."

Just as Schliemann sliced through Hissarlik, classics scholars have sliced through Homer's text in search of layers of meaning. His verse, though, is more like a fruitcake than a layer cake. The *Iliad* and *Odyssey*, scholars have concluded, contain a core of very old stories, recited and reshaped by bards over centuries. Those stories were drastically revised, most likely around the eighth century B.C., when Homer is thought to have lived. At the time, the illiterate Greeks had just begun adopting a Phoenician writing system that began "alpha, beta."

In that text are many Bronze Age details that no one in Homer's Iron Age would have known: chariots ferrying bronze-armored warriors to combat, helmets covered in boars' tusks, and semicylindrical "tower" shields so large that

10

11

12

enemy warriors must have felt as if they were dueling men behind trees. Homer rattles off roughly 30 Mycenaean kingdoms that sent ships to join Agamemnon's assault on Troy.
Except for Athens and a handful of others, these kingdoms
had vanished or sunk to insignificance by the eighth century
B.C. If archaeologists have since tracked a quarter of them
down, it's only because Homer kept them vivid in memory.

Pylos is a prime example. Between a living Homer and a   13
burning Pylos yawns an illiterate dark age, bridged at best by
oral traditions and well-worn tales. Another 400 years or so
stretches between Homer and the Athenian invention of history as a record of facts. By then the location of Pylos was
hopelessly confused. The Roman writer Strabo reported that
eager locals in the first century A.D. were promoting three
different sites as "authentic." He turned away, muttering:
"There is a Pylos before Pylos, and yet another." When the
Greeks won their modern independence from the Ottoman
Empire in 1832 and started re-Hellenizing place names, they
changed the Turkish city of Navarino to Pylos. It was a rough
guess.

On that lucky morning in 1939, Carl Blegen may have dis-   14
covered the real Pylos, but he hardly put the question of
Homer's veracity to rest. For all his attention to Bronze Age
costuming, Homer often slips into contemporary Iron Age
garb. His warriors cremate their dead, for instance, instead of
burying them as the Mycenaeans did. Achilles offers the winner of the funeral games at Troy enough iron to keep vassal
shepherds and plowmen back home well supplied with tools.
Yet iron was the rarest of metals in the Bronze Age. The animal sacrifices in the *Iliad* and *Odyssey* are just another Homeric "mistake," many scholars say. The Greeks didn't practice such sacrifices until the eighth century B.C., when the
practice was imported from the Near East. No evidence has
been found among Mycenaean remains for the kind of
animal sacrifices described in Homer. The sleek bulls that
Nestor butchers on the beach at Pylos, in other words, are
just a figment of Homer's ahistorical imagination. Or are
they?

A year after Sharon Stocker's storeroom discovery, her 15
husband, Jack Davis, decided to take a closer look at what she
had found. Davis is *the* Blegen Professor of Greek Archaeology at the University of Cincinnati, but he's a very different
sort of investigator from the man who discovered Pylos. Davis draws more on physical anthropology and hard sciences
than the classics or even the testimony of the shovel. He's a
leading proponent of survey archaeology: Rather than exca-
vate trenches in search of artifacts, he tends to focus on the
surface of a site, laying grids over large swaths of territory,
plotting any artifacts that have weathered to the surface, and
subjecting the results to statistical analysis. His sites often resemble a crime scene, with biologists and chemists brought
in to go over the evidence for organic clues.

To sort out the bones from Hora, Davis and Stocker called 16
in Paul Halstead, an animal-bone expert and a professor of
archaeology at the University of Sheffield in England.
Halstead jokes that his first summer at Pylos was "an excavation of an excavation." Barrel by barrel he and Davis carried
the contents of the basement out into the sunlight and onto
wooden tables set out under the trees behind the museum.
While Davis struggled to decipher the fading information
penciled onto the excavation labels by Blegen's trench super-
visors, Halstead happily sorted the bones by type and by appearance.

Most appeared to be standard food refuse—broken bits of 17
goat and sheep bones, mostly unburned—but one collection
"stood out like a sore thumb," Halstead says. "They were almost exclusively cow, almost exclusively femurs, humeruses,
and mandibles, and all burnt."

The following summer Halstead returned to Pylos with 18
Valasia Isaakidou, a doctoral student at University College
London with bone experience. They pored over the burnt
bones with hand lenses, noting butchering marks, species in-
dicators, age, sex, and the absence of tissue residues. The
bones had been badly fractured either by an intense roasting
fire or by Blegen's excavators, but Halstead and Isaakidou

were able to reassemble whole specimens. There were at least 10 animals, primarily bulls, plus one red deer. The parts were carefully filleted of their meat but their marrow was left intact—something no one cooking for mere mortals would have done. The burn marks weren't uneven in the way of meaty bones burned on a cooking fire or buried underneath a burning palace. They were uniform, as if the entire bone surface had been exposed to the flames at once. To Halstead the bones looked exactly like the remains of a burnt sacrifice.

These were startling words in certain ears. Last year, when 19 Halstead shared his preliminary findings at a Bronze Age roundtable discussion in Sheffield, his colleagues were nonplussed. "I hadn't been fully aware of the extent to which the absence of evidence for burnt sacrifice was quite so contentious," Halstead says. Although no one mentioned Homer at the roundtable, his name hovered in the shadows. These burnt bones could have come smoking from the beach at Pylos on the morning that Telemachus stepped ashore.

Truth be told, Homer is something of an embarrassment 20 to 21st-century archaeology. He catches the public imagination, archaeologists say, but complicates the science. "I understand the public love of Homer, but it can be dangerous," says James Wright of Bryn Mawr College in Pennsylvania. "Some archaeologists will say, 'Well, if you were really excited by the *Iliad*, let me take you to the very place.' It's right on the edge of pandering, of bending the scholarship to make it more palatable to more people." To prove that Halstead's bones were once truly burnt offerings, Wright says, archaeologists would have to point to similar remains and rituals from before and after Mycenaean times. "Until that moment," he says, "I think we need to respect the silence of the intermediate 400 years."

Yet there are those who welcome Halstead's awkward 21 bones. Cynthia Shelmerdine, a prehistorian at the University of Texas who has worked with Jack Davis at Pylos, says younger scholars and archaeologists are willing to take a new look at Homer and the problem of cultural continuity through the dark age. In some ways this is a response to the anti-Homer backlash that began in the mid-1960s. The targets of that backlash were archaeologists like Blegen who dug, if not with the *Iliad* in hand, then with a memory of it fresh in mind.

"By the mid-1970s we had people talking about Homer as   22
a liar, a pseudo-historian, and a false source of information," Shelmerdine says. "The thinking was that if you want to know about the Bronze Age, you don't read Homer. You come and look at the Bronze Age evidence. Then you can look back at the Homeric texts and say, OK, here's a yardstick for what's reliable in Homer, but you can't use Homer for the Bronze Age."

Only now are people daring to take the reverse perspective   23
again. "The world that Homer evoked through poetry and the world we evoke through archaeology have great similarities, great points of contacts," Shelmerdine says. "Animal sacrifice is what they do in both the *Iliad* and the *Odyssey*. Whenever they have a battle or an escape, they slaughter a couple of animals and have a great feast, and it's meat, meat, and more meat. Meat is what's special. You're not going to have a celebratory feast and eat lentils. The Linear B textual evidence for this has just been emerging in the past five years." Homer may not be an "officially reliable source" for the Bronze Age, Shelmerdine admits. "But there are echoes that we can't deny."

The bones at Pylos, in the end, offer archaeology a   24
magnificent opportunity to have it both ways. Whatever they say about Homer, they also suggest a great deal about the Mycenaeans at the height of their power. "Just by analyzing bone material, studying the location of pottery, and collecting evidence from frescoes," James Wright says, "archaeology can put together a story on its own, a very rich and detailed story." Stocker and Davis, for instance, were able to trace the burnt leg- and jawbones of 10 cattle to a single room near the entrance to the palace. Allowing for the burnt offerings to the gods, Stocker and Davis calculate, still leaves 4,000 pounds of beef for human consumption. If all 10 ani-

mals were sacrificed at a single event, they could have fed 6,000 people—far more than lived in and around the citadel at its height. Add in the evidence of floor plans, potsherds, and Linear B tablets, and you begin to get a picture of Pylos not just as a fortress but also as a catering complex. Just outside the central court, or *megaron,* where the king sat on his throne and received his great guests, were outdoor banqueting courtyards well served by pantries and stocked with cooking gear. Blegen found wine storage jars, mixing bowls, ladles, and thousands of examples of a delicate, two-handled drinking cup, known as a *kylix,* which stood on a narrow stem above a round foot.

In the right hands those cups alone could tell the story of Pylos in a new way. Lisa Bendall, a research fellow at the University of Cambridge, used Blegen's published excavation records to plot how many kylix stems were found in each room. A single stem was a dot; a room filled with hundreds of kylix stems became a red blob. The resulting map showed concentrations of cups in the serving pantries and in the small room just off the entrance court—a wine bar for travelers entering the palace, Blegen suggested. Red dots also outlined a large courtyard west of the megaron and a large open area in front of the palace gates where erosion had jumbled sediment layers but left a churn of kylix fragments. To a Cambridge-trained archaeologist like Bendall, these patterns suggest the "negotiations of social hierarchies." To the rest of us, it's the seating plan for a catered function.

Bendall believes the lowest-ranked guests probably drank, and presumably ate beef, on a plaza outside the palace gates. The merely second-class probably had their drinks in the gated western courtyard, where they could take pride in having been invited into the palace, if not into the megaron itself. The A-list likely joined the king in the megaron, drinking from fancier metal vessels. Bendall found signs of yet another class of "to go" diners in the palace's Linear B tablets: The king used these to order wine and other luxury foodstuffs for his subjects in the provinces.

All this feasting suggests how the palace drew smaller,   27
regional power centers into its orbit and cemented new alliances. Counting kylix stems clashes with the Homeric reading of Nestor as a piratical, warrior king: The king of Pylos
may have assembled his domain—or at least assuaged his
newly conquered constituents—with a wine cup more than
with a sword.

Archaeologists in Carl Blegen's time could make little   28
sense of such ceramic sherds and bone fragments. But
Blegen, to his enduring credit, had the foresight to preserve
the remains for his successors. "Everyone else was pitching
this stuff," Stocker says. "In that respect he was way ahead of
his time." In 1960 the Greek Archaeological Service erected
a huge metal shed over the central ruins of Pylos to protect
them from the elements. Go to Pylos today and you can trace
the passages, rooms, and courtyards where the king ruled
3,200 years ago.

Room 7 is right by the front gate of the palace, the realm   29
of clerks and their chattering tablets. On feast days the third-
class banqueters would have gathered just outside, waiting
perhaps for the king to appear at the main gate with the remains of the sacrifice. Perhaps those remains were deposited
with the clerks in Room 7 as proof that the king had kept
faith with the gods—and that he was rich enough to feed the
leg- and jawbones of 10 bulls to a roaring fire.

The Linear B tablets tell us some of the names the king   30
worshipped: Poseidon, Zeus, Hera, Dionysius, and Ares. But
in the end those gods couldn't save the palace. Circa 1200
B.C., the storehouses—stuffed with perfumed oils, fine-spun
wool, vintage wine, chariot wheels, and bronze weapons—all
went up in flames. The king's scribes abandoned their clay
ledgers to the fire. Ash rained down on the great outdoor
banqueting courts, the shelves in the pantries collapsed, and
drinking cups smashed to the floor by the thousands. From
every corner of the king's domain, the fire by night and the
smoke by day would have been clearly visible.

In time the palace rubble was overrun by *maquis,* the   31
razor-leafed Mediterranean chaparral, and Pylos was lost. If

we can see its remains today, it's only because a legendary bard had the force of imagination, some 500 years after the palace burned, to rebuild it in memory. And if that memory grows more vivid with each passing year, it's thanks to the painstaking work of Blegen and his successors—and their stubborn insistence on taking Homer, at least in part, at his word.

Topics for Writing Cause and Effect

1. *Respond.* Write an essay in which you suggest the kind of artifacts that should be saved to help future archaeologists understand the behavior and beliefs of our culture.
2. *Analyze.* What caused scholars to distrust Homer? What events caused scholars to rethink Homer? Explain how the discovery of animal bones in the small museum in Hora caused scholars to reconsider "the Homer question."
3. *Argue.* What sort of assumptions about the nature of evidence and truth are embedded in the phrase "Homer complicates science"? Select a historical novel you have read (for example, Mary Renault's *The Bull from the Sea* or Steven Pressfield's *Gates of Fire*) and argue that the writer has—or has not—given a plausible version of the events.

RICHARD DOERFLINGER

Richard Doerflinger is deputy director of the Secretariat for Pro-Life Activities at the United States Conference of Catholic Bishops in Washington, D.C. A Maryland resident, Doerflinger also serves as an adjunct fellow in bioethics and public policy at the National Catholic Bioethics Center in Boston. In "First Principles and the 'Frist Principles,'" Doerflinger presents arguments for why scientists should not conduct stem cell research.

[handwritten: religious view?]

First Principles and the "Frist Principles"

A COUPLE OF interesting things happened at a recent Senate hearing on stem cell research. News media covered one of those things, and not very well. The full picture has horrifying implications for our future. *[handwritten: common]*

The media reported that Senator Bill Frist of Tennessee, known as a pro-life Republican and the Senate's only physician member, testified in favor of funding stem cell research that requires destroying human embryos. Senator Frist claimed that while such research is "untried and untested" it also has "huge potential," and so should be funded even as we show "the highest moral regard" for the embryos we kill in the process.

So far this is the tale of another Senator who threw away his pro-life convictions citing a hope of medical benefits. Sadly, Frist's reference to "moral regard" sounded like the hypocrisy of President Clinton's National Bioethics Advisory Commission, which concluded that embryos deserve "respect" as human lives but should be killed for their stem cells. What is the "respectful" way to suck out a living being's innards and throw away the shell? *[handwritten: violent diction]*

[handwritten: ouch!]

Receiving less media attention was Frist's announcement   4
that federal funding of this research "should be contingent
on the implementation of strict new safeguards," to prevent
abuse of his newfound loophole in respect for life. Without a
trace of irony he presented these as "Frist Principles on Human Stem Cell Research."

Some of these "principles" are just silly. For example, one   5
calls for "independent scientific and ethical review" of the research by the Institute of Medicine and the Secretary of

---

*There's no negotiating with the ideologues
who want a Brave New World.*

Health and Human Services. This is like calling for independent review of the henhouse by the foxes, since IOM and Secretary Thompson both favor destructive embryo research.
Another principle would make standards for fetal tissue research "consistent" with the rules for embryo research. This
seems to mean that researchers could perform abortions *solely
to obtain fetal tissue for government research,* just as they may
kill live embryos solely to obtain stem cells.

There were also "principles" that pro-life Americans can   6
and do support: Ban human cloning; continue the ban on
directly funding destruction of human embryos; ban the
creation of embryos solely for research. These should be pursued in their own right, not as "trade-offs" for government-
sanctioned experimentation on some humans.

In this context, nonetheless, Frist proposed that it could   7
be "pro-life" for the government, for the first time in U.S.
history, to fund research on stem cells obtained by killing human embryos. Only embryos "that would otherwise be discarded" will be used—which is like saying that the government will fund abortions only for unborn children not
wanted by their parents.

Not covered at all by most media is what happened to the   8

"Frist Principles" when they were presented to Senators Arlen Specter (R-PA) and Tom Harkin (D-IA), the Senate's chief promoters of embryo research and the conveners of this hearing. The principles got massacred. *syntax*

Frist's effort to limit the number of embryos killed was denounced by Senator Specter and several like-minded scientists, who said hundreds of cell lines may be needed for valid scientific results. One researcher said that ten thousand may be needed, to obtain a close genetic "match" to most patients needing tissue. (Keep in mind that each cell line requires destroying many embryos. Recently a fertility clinic in Virginia created and destroyed over a hundred embryos to get three cell lines.) Human cloning—creating and killing embryonic "copies" of each patient to obtain genetically tailored stem cells—was called the best way to provide tissue that will not be rejected by patients' bodies, and Harkin and Specter raised no objection. 9

Senator Specter also asked a representative of the National Institutes of Health whether the NIH needs to be able to destroy its own stock of human embryos to do high-quality research. When the official hesitated at taking this step, Specter angrily threatened to make massive cuts in total NIH spending unless she expressed support for federal embryo farms. 10

In other words, proponents of this grotesque research have no need for Senator Frist's compromises. They think they have support for their real agenda: Government embryo farming, creating human life in the lab solely to destroy it, cloning to make multiple human guinea pigs. The whole frightening Brave New World is before our eyes—which should help us concentrate on what the real issue is. 11 *strong*

Senator Frist said his support for funding embryonic stem cell research is "contingent" on these principles, and the principles were ridiculed and rejected by his newfound pro-abortion friends. He now may realize they are no friends. And President Bush might learn from the fate of the hapless Bill Frist: There's no negotiating with the ideologues who want a Brave New World. The only reasonable approach to embryonic stem cell research is not to do it at all. 12

Peggy Prichard Ross grew up in Pittsburgh, Pennsylvania, and was educated at the University of Florida, where she earned a master's degree in communications. She has worked as the director of communications for AvMed Health Plan in Gainesville, Florida. In "Stem Cell Research: It's About Life and Death, Not Politics," reprinted from the *Tallahassee Democrat,* Ross provides powerful reasons why scientists should be allowed to pursue stem cell research.

Stem Cell Research: It's About Life and Death, Not Politics

I N SIX MONTHS there is a good chance I'll be dead. This doesn't bother me nearly as much as having a president who wants to jail scientists and doctors who are trying to find cures for people with my disease and other illnesses such as diabetes, Alzheimer's, Parkinson's, and so many others.

In October 2001, I was diagnosed with a grade-three astrocytoma, which is a brain cancer with no known cause and no known cure. I tried to learn all I could about the disease and medical research in the field. I learned that brain cancer is technically not really cancer. It is, in fact, a disease of stem cells.

And just like that, the political debate on stem cell research became more than a political argument to me. It became a debate of hope versus despair.

I watched President Bush's 2003 State of the Union address from my hospital bed in Shands Hospital in Gainesville. During the speech he urged Congress to ban "all human cloning." Unfortunately, "all human cloning" includes therapeutic cloning, which is one and the same with stem cell research.

The president likes to call it cloning because he knows it creates images of mutant or butchered babies, when stem cell research (also known as somatic cell nuclear transfer, or SCNT) has nothing to do with babies or fetuses. In fact, the

good point

5

The arguments against stem cell research are scientifically unfounded and at best, are based on personal religious beliefs.

---

egg cells used in therapeutic cloning have no chance of being fertilized or transplanted into a woman's womb.

The arguments against stem cell research are scientifically unfounded and at best, are based on personal religious beliefs. I take exception to the president using his religion to dictate public health policy. Policy should be based on science, not sectarian beliefs.

6

The president describes himself as a compassionate conservative. But what is compassionate about outlawing vital research? What is conservative about using the federal government to dictate religion?

7

cliché

I fully realize that my time is limited, and any cures discovered from stem cell research will be several years away. My concern is with the future generations. Almost 20,000 Americans per year will get the same type of brain cancer I did. They will be children and adults, men and women, black and white, Christian and Muslim.

8

The disease is not hereditary, yet has no known environmental cause either. There is no rhyme or reason to who gets it and why. What we don't understand about the disease far outweighs what we do understand about it. How can any of this change if studying the very root cause of the disease is made illegal?

9

There are bipartisan bills in Congress that recognize the　10
importance of stem cell research and I hope that our representatives, senators, and president will give the millions of
Americans who fight for their lives every day against life
threatening illnesses the hope they need and deserve.

hard to argue with

Topics for Writing Persuasion and Argument

1. *Respond.* How has science fiction—in novels and films— portrayed the Brave New World where cloning and robotics have become commonplace? Select one such example for analysis. Then write an essay in which you explain how much of this portrayal could be *science* and how much of it is probably *fiction*.
2. *Analyze.* Analyze the way Doerflinger and Ross slant or distort evidence to arrive at the major assertions in their argument. For example, notice how Doerflinger suggests that conducting stem cell research is similar to funding abortions, and how Ross suggests that the president is using the federal government to dictate religion.
3. *Argue.* Make your own argument for or against stem cell research. Consider the way Doerflinger's position as a pro-life advocate for the National Catholic Bioethics Center and Ross's position as a patient with a terminal disease influence the ethical appeal of their arguments. As you construct your argument, consider the claims of each side as you try to arrive at some kind of reasonable position in this controversy.

ARTHUR C. CLARKE

Arthur C. Clarke was born in 1917 in Somerset, England. He was interested in science at an early age, but his family could not afford to give him a formal university education. During World War II, he was a radar specialist with the Royal Air Force. Following the war he entered King's College, University of London, graduating with honorary degrees in math and physics. His nonfiction publications include *Interplanetary Flight* (1950), *The Exploration of Space* (1951), and *The Making of a Moon* (1957), but his science fiction about space travel brought him fame. His many short stories are collected in such volumes as *The Other Side of the Story* (1958) and *The Wind from the Sun* (1972). His novels include *The Sounds of Mars* (1951), *A Fall of Moondust* (1961), and *Rendezvous with Rama* (1974), and his screenplay for Stanley Kubrik's *2001: A Space Odyssey* is considered a classic. In "The Star," reprinted from *The Nine Billion Names of God* (1955), a Jesuit astronomer tells of a space journey that challenges his faith in God.

The Star

I T IS THREE thousand light-years to the Vatican. Once, I believed that space could have no power over faith, just as I believed that the heavens declared the glory of God's handiwork. Now I have seen that handiwork, and my faith is sorely troubled. I stare at the crucifix that hangs on the cabin wall above the Mark VI Computer, and for the first time in my life I wonder if it is no more than an empty symbol.

I have told no one yet, but the truth cannot be concealed.   2
The facts are there for all to read, recorded on the countless
miles of magnetic tape and the thousands of photographs we
are carrying back to Earth. Other scientists can interpret
them as easily as I can, and I am not one who would condone
that tampering with the truth which often gave my order a
bad name in the olden days.

The crew were already sufficiently depressed: I wonder   3
how they will take this ultimate irony. Few of them have any
religious faith, yet they will not relish using this final weapon
in their campaign against me—that private, good-natured,
but fundamentally serious war which lasted all the way from
Earth. It amused them to have a Jesuit as chief astrophysicist:
Dr. Chandler, for instance, could never get over it. (Why are
medical men such notorious atheists?) Sometimes he would
meet me on the observation deck, where the lights are always
low so that the stars shine with undiminished glory. He
would come up to me in the gloom and stand staring out of
the great oval port, while the heavens crawled slowly around
us as the ship turned end over end with the residual spin we
had never bothered to correct.

"Well, Father," he would say at last, "it goes on forever   4
and forever, and perhaps *Something* made it. But how you
can believe that Something has a special interest in us and our
miserable little world—that just beats me." Then the argument would start, while the stars and nebulae would swing
around us in silent, endless arcs beyond the flawlessly clear
plastic of the observation port.

It was, I think, the apparent incongruity of my position   5
that caused most amusement to the crew. In vain I would
point to my three papers in the *Astrophysical Journal,* my five
in the *Monthly Notices of the Royal Astronomical Society.* I
would remind them that my order has long been famous for
its scientific works. We may be few now, but ever since the
eighteenth century we have made contributions to astronomy and geophysics out of all proportion to our numbers.

Will my report on the Phoenix Nebula end our thousand
years of history? It will end, I fear, much more than that.

I do not know who gave the nebula its name, which seems   6
to me a very bad one. If it contains a prophecy, it is one that
cannot be verified for several billion years. Even the word
"nebula" is misleading: this is a far smaller object than those
stupendous clouds of mist—the stuff of unborn stars—that
are scattered throughout the length of the Milky Way. On the
cosmic scale, indeed, the Phoenix Nebula is a tiny thing—a
tenuous shell of gas surrounding a single star.

Or what is left of a star . . .   7

The Rubens engraving of Loyola seems to mock me as it   8
hangs there above the spectrophotometer tracings. What
would *you*, Father, have made of this knowledge that has
come into my keeping, so far from the little world that was all
the Universe you knew? Would your faith have risen to the
challenge, as mine has failed to do?

You gaze into the distance, Father, but I have traveled a   9
distance beyond any that you could have imagined when you
founded our order a thousand years ago. No other survey
ship has been so far from Earth: we are at the very frontiers of
the explored Universe. We set out to reach the Phoenix Nebula, we succeeded, and we are homeward bound with our
burden of knowledge. I wish I could lift that burden from my
shoulders, but I call to you in vain across the centuries and
the light-years that lie between us.

On the book you are holding the words are plain to read.   10
AD MAIOREM DEI GLORIAM, the message runs, but it is
a message I can no longer believe. Would you still believe it, if
you could see what we have found?

We knew, of course, what the Phoenix Nebula was. Every   11
year, in our Galaxy alone, more than a hundred stars explode,
blazing for a few hours or days with thousands of times their
normal brilliance before they sink back into death and obscu-
rity. Such are the ordinary novae—the commonplace disasters of the Universe. I have recorded the spectrograms and
light curves of dozens since I started working at the Lunar
Observatory.

But three or four times in every thousand years occurs   12
something beside which even a nova pales into total insignificance.

When a star becomes a *supernova*, it may for a little while   13
outshine all the massed suns of the Galaxy. The Chinese astronomers watched this happen in A.D. 1054, not knowing
what it was they saw. Five centuries later, in 1572, a supernova blazed in Cassiopeia so brilliantly that it was visible in
the daylight sky. There have been three more in the thousand
years that have passed since then.

Our mission was to visit the remnants of such a catastro-   14
phe, to reconstruct the events that led up to it, and, if possible, to learn its cause. We came slowly in through the concentric shells of gas that had been blasted out six thousand
years before, yet were expanding still. They were immensely
hot, radiating even now with a fierce violet light, but were far
too tenuous to do us any damage. When the star had exploded, its outer layers had been driven upward with such
speed that they had escaped completely from its gravitational
field. Now they formed a hollow shell large enough to engulf
a thousand solar systems, and at its center burned the tiny,
fantastic object which the star had now become—a White
Dwarf, smaller than the Earth, yet weighing a million times
as much.

The glowing gas shells were all around us, banishing the   15
normal night of interstellar space. We were flying into the
center of the cosmic bomb that had detonated millennia ago
and whose incandescent fragments were still hurtling apart.
The immense scale of the explosion, and the fact that the debris already covered a volume of space many billions of miles
across, robbed the scene of any visible movement. It would
take decades before the unaided eye could detect any motion
in these tortured wisps and eddies of gas, yet the sense of tur-
bulent expansion was overwhelming.

We had checked our primary drive hours before, and were   16
drifting slowly toward the fierce little star ahead. Once it had
been a sun like our own, but it had squandered in a few hours
the energy that should have kept it shining for a million years.

Now it was a shrunken miser, hoarding its resources as if trying to make amends for its prodigal youth.

No one seriously expected to find planets. If there had 17 been any before the explosion, they would have been boiled into puffs of vapor, and their substance lost in the greater wreckage of the star itself. But we made the automatic search, as we always do when approaching an unknown sun, and presently we found a single small world circling the star at an immense distance. It must have been the Pluto of this vanished Solar System, orbiting on the frontiers of the night. Too far from the central sun ever to have known life, its remoteness had saved it from the fate of all its lost companions.

The passing fires had seared its rocks and burned away the 18 mantle of frozen gas that must have covered it in the days before the disaster. We landed, and we found the Vault.

Its builders had made sure that we should. The monolithic 19 marker that stood above the entrance was now a fused stump, but even the first long-range photographs told us that here was the work of intelligence. A little later we detected the continent-wide pattern of radioactivity that had been buried in the rock. Even if the pylon above the vault had been destroyed, this would have remained, an immovable and all but eternal beacon calling to the stars. Our ship fell toward this gigantic bull's-eye like an arrow into its target.

The pylon must have been a mile high when it was built, 20 but now it looked like a candle that had melted down into a puddle of wax. It took us a week to drill through the fused rock, since we did not have the proper tools for a task like this. We were astronomers, not archaeologists, but we could improvise. Our original purpose was forgotten: this lonely monument, reared with such labor at the greatest possible distance from the doomed sun, could have only one meaning. A civilization that knew it was about to die had made its last bid for immortality.

It will take us generations to examine all the treasures that 21 were placed in the Vault. They had plenty of time to prepare, for their sun must have given its first warnings many years before the final detonation. Everything that they wished to preserve, all the fruit of their genius, they brought here to this distant world in the days before the end, hoping that some other race would find it and that they would not be utterly forgotten. Would we have done as well, or would we have been too lost in our own misery to give thought to a future we could never see or share?

If only they had had a little more time! They could travel 22 freely enough between the planets of their own sun, but they had not yet learned to cross the interstellar gulfs, and the nearest Solar System was a hundred light-years away. Yet even had they possessed the secret of the Transfinite Drive, no more than a few millions could have been saved. Perhaps it was better thus.

Even if they had not been so disturbingly human as their 23 sculpture shows, we could not have helped admiring them and grieving for their fate. They left thousands of visual records and the machines for projecting them, together with elaborate pictorial instructions from which it will not be difficult to learn their written language. We have examined many of these records, and brought to life for the first time in six thousand years the warmth and beauty of a civilization that in many ways must have been superior to our own. Perhaps they only showed us the best, and one can hardly blame them. But their worlds were very lovely, and their cities were built with a grace that matches anything of man's. We have watched them at work and play, and listened to their musical speech sounding across the centuries. One scene is still before my eyes—a group of children on a beach of strange blue sand, playing in the waves as children play on Earth. Curious whiplike trees line the shore, and some very large animal is wading in the shallows yet attracting no attention at all.

And sinking into the sea, still warm and friendly and life- 24 giving, is the sun that will soon turn traitor and obliterate all this innocent happiness.

Perhaps if we had not been so far from home and so vul- 25 nerable to loneliness, we should not have been so deeply moved. Many of us had seen the ruins of ancient civilizations on other worlds, but they had never affected us so profoundly. This tragedy was unique. It is one thing for a race to fail and die, as nations and cultures have done on Earth.

But to be destroyed so completely in the full flower of its achievement, leaving no survivors—how could that be reconciled with the mercy of God?

My colleagues have asked me that, and I have given what answers I can. Perhaps you could have done better, Father Loyola, but I have found nothing in the *Exercitia Spiritualia* that helps me here. They were not an evil people: I do not know what gods they worshiped, if indeed they worshiped any. But I have looked back at them across the centuries, and have watched while the loveliness they used their last strength to preserve was brought forth again into the light of their shrunken sun. They could have taught us much: why were they destroyed?

I know the answers that my colleagues will give when they get back to Earth. They will say that the Universe has no purpose and no plan, that since a hundred suns explode every year in our Galaxy, at this very moment some race is dying in the depths of space. Whether that race has done good or evil during its lifetime will make no difference in the end: there is no divine justice, for there is no God.

Yet, of course, what we have seen proves nothing of the sort. Anyone who argues thus is being swayed by emotion, not logic. God has no need to justify His actions to man. He who built the Universe can destroy it when He chooses. It is arrogance—it is perilously near blasphemy—for us to say what He may or may not do.

This I could have accepted, hard though it is to look upon whole worlds and peoples thrown into the furnace. But there comes a point when even the deepest faith must falter, and now, as I look at the calculations lying before me, I know I have reached that point at last.

We could not tell, before we reached the nebula, how long ago the explosion took place. Now, from the astronomical evidence and the record in the rocks of that one surviving planet, I have been able to date it very exactly. I know in what year the light of this colossal conflagration reached our Earth. I know how brilliantly the supernova whose corpse now dwindles behind our speeding ship once shone in terres-

26

27

28

29

30

trial skies. I know how it must have blazed low in the east before sunrise, like a beacon in that oriental dawn.

There can be no reasonable doubt: the ancient mystery is solved at last. Yet, oh God, there were so many stars you could have used. What was the need to give these people to the fire, that the symbol of their passing might shine above Bethlehem? 31

COMMENT ON "THE STAR"

The distressed narrator of this story is a Jesuit scientist who, on the basis of evidence that he cannot refute professionally or ethically, finds himself forced to acknowledge a scientific discovery that he fears may destroy his religious faith, the rock of his very existence. Two arguments are going on in the story. The first is a vocal one between the Jesuit and the crew, particularly a medical doctor who represents the traditional scientific view that although there may be order in the universe, there is no God who takes a special interest in the affairs of humans. The Jesuit represents the argument for faith in God and His concern for humankind. The second argument is the silent one that the Jesuit astrophysicist has seen building as his spaceship penetrated the outer reaches of space to investigate the origins of the Phoenix Nebula. He collects evidence from three sources: from the interstellar space debris that testifies to the explosion of a supernova; from irrefutable evidence left purposefully by a superior, cultured civilization that flourished on a lost planet several thousand years before; and, finally, from the evidence that allows him to calculate the date of the explosion that destroyed that planet. When he puts all the pieces together, the Jesuit sees the conclusion of the second argument. Ironically, it destroys the first argument but almost destroys the Jesuit also. God does indeed take special interest in the affairs of humans; the proof is that the date of the supernova that destroyed the beautiful lost civilization coincides precisely with the Star of Bethlehem announcing the birth of Jesus.

USING
AND
DOCUMENTING
SOURCES

The essays in *The Riverside Reader* are sources. Many of the writing assignments at the end of each chapter ask you to *analyze* these sources or to use them to support your own ideas. Most academic writing asks you to use sources—from books, journals, magazines, newspapers, and the Internet—to augment and advance the ideas in your writing. Every time you cite a source, or use it in some way, you must *document* it.

For example, in the student research paper at the end of this chapter, Blythe Rogers uses the Modern Language Association Style to cite print and electronic sources. This chapter explains the style recommended by the Modern Language Association (MLA) for documenting sources in academic papers. It also analyzes some of the implications of MLA style for your research and composing. More detailed information is given in the *MLA Handbook* and the *MLA Style Manual.*

MLA style has three major features. First, all sources cited in a paper are listed in a section entitled **Works Cited,** which is located at the end of the paper. Second, material borrowed from another source is documented within the text by a brief parenthetical reference that directs readers to the full citation in the list of works cited. Third, numbered footnotes or endnotes are used to present two types of supplementary information: (1) commentary or explanation that the text cannot accommodate and (2) bibliographical notes that contain several source citations.

PREPARING THE LIST OF WORKS CITED

In an academic paper that follows MLA style, the list of works cited is the *only* place where readers will find complete information about the sources you have cited. For that reason, your list must be thorough and accurate.

The list of works cited appears at the end of your paper and, as its title suggests, *lists only the works you have cited in your paper.* Occasionally, your instructor may ask you to prepare a list of works consulted. That list would include not only the sources you cite but also the sources you consulted as you conducted your research. In either case, MLA prefers Works Cited or Works Consulted to the more limited heading Bibliography (literally, "description of books") because those headings are more likely to accommodate the variety of sources—articles, films, Internet sources—that writers may cite in a research paper.

To prepare the list of works cited, follow these general guidelines:

1. Paginate the Works Cited section as a continuation of your text. If the conclusion of your paper appears on page 8, then begin your list on page 9 (unless there is an intervening page of endnotes).
2. Double-space between successive lines of an entry and between entries.
3. Begin the first line of an entry flush left, and indent successive lines five spaces or one-half inch.
4. List entries in alphabetical order according to the last name of the author.
5. If you are listing more than one work by the same author, alphabetize the works according to title (excluding the articles *a, an,* and *the*). Instead of repeating the author's name, type *three* hyphens and a period, and then give the title.
6. Underline the titles of works published independently: books, plays, long poems, pamphlets, periodicals, films.
7. Although you do not *need* to underline the spaces between words, a continuous line is easier to type and guarantees that all features of the title are underlined. Type a continuous line under titles unless you are instructed to do otherwise.
8. If you are citing a book whose title includes the title of another book, underline the main title, but do not underline the other title (for example, A Casebook on Ralph Ellison's Invisible Man).
9. Use quotation marks to indicate titles of short works that appear in larger works (for example, "Minutes of Glory." African Short Stories). Also use quotation marks for song titles and for titles of unpublished works, including dissertations, lectures, and speeches.
10. Use arabic numerals except with names of monarchs (Elizabeth II) and except for the preliminary pages of a work (ii–xix), which are traditionally numbered with roman numerals.
11. Use lowercase abbreviations to identify the parts of a

work (for example, *vol.* for *volume*), a named translator (*trans.*), and a named editor (*ed.*). However, when these designations follow a period, they should be capitalized (for example, Woolf, Virginia. A Writer's Diary. Ed. Leonard Woolf).

12. Whenever possible, use appropriate shortened forms for the publisher's name (*Random* instead of *Random House*).

13. Separate author, title, and publication information with a period followed by *one space*.

14. Use a colon and one space to separate the volume number and year of a periodical from the page numbers (for example, Trimmer, Joseph. "Memoryscape: Jean Shepherd's Midwest." Old Northwest 2 (1976): 357–69).

In addition to these guidelines, MLA recommends procedures for documenting an extensive variety of sources, including electronic sources and nonprint materials such as films and television programs. The following models illustrate sources most commonly cited.

Sample Entries: Books

When citing books, provide the following general categories of information:

Author's last name, first name. Book title. Additional information. City of publication: Publishing company, publication date.

Entries illustrating variations on this basic format appear below.

A Book by One Author

Light, Richard J. Making the Most of College: Students Speak Their Minds. Cambridge: Harvard UP, 2001.

Two or More Books by the Same Author

Garreau, Joel. Edge City: Life on the New Frontier. New York: Doubleday, 1991.

– – –. The Nine Nations of North America. Boston: Houghton, 1981.

A Book by Two or Three Authors

Vare, Ethlie Ann, and Greg Ptacek. Mothers of Invention: From the Bra to the Bomb: Forgotten Women and Their Unforgettable Ideas. New York: Morrow, 1988.

Atwan, Robert, Donald McQuade, and John W. Wright. Edsels, Luckies, and Frigidaires: Advertising the American Way. New York: Dell, 1979.

A Book by Four or More Authors

Belenky, Mary Field, et al. Women's Ways of Knowing: The Development of Self, Voice, and Mind. New York: Basic, 1986.

A Book by a Corporate Author

National Geographic Society. Cradle and Crucible: History and Faith in the Middle East. Washington: National Geographic, 2002.

A Book by an Anonymous Author

Literary Market Place: The Dictionary of American Book Publishing. 1998 ed. New York: Bowker, 1997.

A Book with an Editor

Hall, Donald, ed. The Oxford Book of American Literary
   Anecdotes. New York: Oxford UP, 1981.

A Book with an Author and an Editor

Toomer, Jean. Cane. Ed. Darwin T. Turner. New York: Norton,
   1988.

A Book with a Publisher's Imprint

Kozol, Jonathan. Illiterate America. New York: Anchor-
   Doubleday, 1985.

An Anthology or Compilation

Eggers, Dave, ed. The Best American Nonrequired Reading,
   2002. Boston: Houghton, 2002.

A Work in an Anthology

Silko, Leslie Marmon. "The Man to Send Rain Clouds." Imag-
   ining America: Stories from the Promised Land. Ed.
   Wesley Brown and Amy Ling. New York: Persea, 1991.
   191–95.

An Introduction, Preface, Foreword, or Afterword

Black, Roger. Foreword. Don't Make Me Think: A Common
   Sense Approach to Web Usability. By Steve Krug. Indianapolis, IN: New Riders, 2000.

A Multivolume Work

Blotner, Joseph. Faulkner: A Biography. 2 vols. New York:
   Random, 1974.

An Edition Other Than the First

Chaucer, Geoffrey. The Riverside Chaucer. Ed. Larry D.

Benson. 3rd ed. Boston: Houghton, 1987.

A Book in a Series

McClave, Heather, ed. Women Writers of the Short Story.

Twentieth Century Views. Englewood Cliffs: Spectrum-

Prentice, 1980.

A Republished Book

Malamud, Bernard. The Natural. 1952. New York: Avon,

1980.

A Signed Article in a Reference Book

Tobias, Richard. "Thurber, James." Encyclopedia Americana.

1991 ed.

An Unsigned Article in a Reference Book

"Tharp, Twyla." Who's Who of American Women. 17th ed.

1991–92.

A Government Document

United States. Cong. House. Committee on the Judiciary. Im-

migration and Nationality Act with Amendments and

Notes on Related Laws. 7th ed. Washington: GPO, 1980.

Published Proceedings of a Conference

Griggs, John, ed. AIDS: Public Policy Dimensions. Proc. of a

conference. 16–17 Jan. 1986. New York: United Hospital

Fund of New York, 1987.

A Translation

Giroud, Françoise. Marie Curie: A Life. Trans. Lydia Davis.

New York: Holmes, 1986.

A Book with a Title in Its Title

Habich, Robert D. Transcendentalism and the Western Mes-

senger: A History of the Magazine and Its Contributors,

1835–1841. Rutherford: Fairleigh Dickinson UP, 1985.

A Book Published Before 1900

Field, Kate. The History of Bell's Telephone. London, 1878.

An Unpublished Dissertation

Geissinger, Shirley Burry. "Openness versus Secrecy in Adop-

tive Parenthood." Diss. U of North Carolina at Greens-

boro, 1984.

A Published Dissertation

Ames, Barbara Edwards. Dreams and Painting: A Case Study

of the Relationship between an Artist's Dreams and

Painting. Diss. U of Virginia, 1978. Ann Arbor: UMI,

1979. 7928021.

Sample Entries: Articles in Periodicals

When citing articles in periodicals, provide the following
general categories of information:

Author's last name, first name. "Article title." Periodical title

Date: inclusive pages.

Entries illustrating variations on this basic format appear below.

A Signed Article from a Daily Newspaper

Barringer, Felicity. "Where Many Elderly Live, Signs of the
    Future." New York Times 7 Mar. 1993, nat. ed., sec. 1:
    12.

An Unsigned Article from a Daily Newspaper

"Infant Mortality Down; Race Disparity Widens." Washington
    Post 12 Mar. 1993: A12.

An Article from a Monthly or Bimonthly Magazine

Wills, Garry. "The Words That Remade America: Lincoln at
    Gettysburg." Atlantic June 1992: 57–79.

An Article from a Weekly or Biweekly Magazine

Sedaris, David. "Who's the Chef?" New Yorker 10 March
    2003: 40–41.

An Article in a Journal with Continuous Pagination

Hesse, Douglas. "The Place of Creative Nonfiction." College
    English 65 (2003): 237–41.

An Article in a Journal That Numbers Pages in Each Issue Separately

Seely, Bruce. "The Saga of American Infrastructure: A Re-
    public Bound Together." Wilson Quarterly 17.1 (1993):
    19–39.

An Editorial

"A Question of Medical Sight." Editorial. Plain Dealer [Cleveland, OH] 11 Mar. 1993: 6B.

A Review

Morson, Gary Soul. "Coping with Utopia." Rev. of Soviet Civilization: A Cultural History, by Andrei Sinyavsky. American Scholar 61 (1992): 132–38.

An Article Whose Title Contains a Quotation or a Title Within Quotation Marks

DeCuir, Andre L. "Italy, England and the Female Artist in George Eliot's 'Mr. Gilfil's Love-Story.'" Studies in Short Fiction 29 (1992): 67–75.

An Abstract from *Dissertation Abstracts* or *Dissertation Abstracts International*

Creek, Mardena Bridges. "Myth, Wound, Accommodation: American Literary Responses to the War in Vietnam." DAI 43 (1982): 3539A. Ball State U.

Sample Entries: CD-ROMs

When citing information from CD-ROMs, provide the following general categories of information:

Author's last name, first name. "Article title of printed source or printed analogue." Periodical title of printed source or printed analogue Date: inclusive pages. Title of database. CD-ROM. Name of vendor or computer service. Electronic publication date or date of access.

Entries illustrating variations on this basic format appear below.

CD-ROM: Periodical Publication with Printed Source or Printed Analogue

West, Cornel. "The Dilemma of the Black Intellectual." Criti-

cal Quarterly 29 (1987): 39–52. MLA International Bib-

liography. CD-ROM. Silver Platter. Feb. 1995.

CD-ROM: Nonperiodical Publication

Cinemania 97. CD-ROM. Redmond: Microsoft, 1996.

CD-ROM: A Work in More Than One Electronic Medium

Mozart. CD-ROM. Laser disk. Union City, CA: Ebook, 1992.

Sample Entries: Internet and Web Sources

When citing information from Internet and World Wide Web sources, provide the following general categories of information:

Author's last name, first name. "Article title" or Book title.

Publication information for any printed version. Or sub-

ject line of forum or discussion group. Indication of on-

line posting or home page. Title of electronic journal.

Date of electronic publication. Page numbers or the num-

bers of paragraphs or sections. Name of institution or

organization sponsoring web site. Date of access to the

source <URL>.

Enclose the URL in angle brackets. For lengthy or complex URLs, give enough information about the path so a reader can locate the exact page you are referring to from the search page of the site or the database. If you need to break a URL at the end of a line, do so only after a slash and do not add any hyphens or punctuation that is not in the original URL.

The speed of change in the electronic world means that particular features for citing Internet and web sources are constantly evolving. The best way to confirm the accuracy of your citations is to check the MLA web site (<http://www.mla.org>).

Entries illustrating variations on the basic format appear below.

A Professional Site

MLA Style. 4 April 2002. Modern Language Association of

      America. 26 Mar. 2003 <http://www.mla.org>.

A Personal Site

Hawisher, Gail. Home page. University of Illinois Urbana-

      Champaign. 26 Mar. 2003 <http://www.english.uiuc.edu/

      facpages/Hawisher.htm>.

A Book

Conrad, Joseph. Lord Jim. London: Blackwoods, 1900. Oxford

      Text Archive. 12 July 1993. Oxford University Com-

      puting Services. 20 Feb. 1998 <ftp://ota.ox.ac.uk/pub/

      ota/public/english/conrad/lordjim.1824>.

A Poem

Roethke, Theodore. "My Papa's Waltz," Favorite Poem Proj-

      ect. <http://www.favoritepoem.oralpoems/roethke/

      waltz.html>.

An Article in a Reference Database

"Women in American History." Britannica Online Vers.

    98.1.1. Nov. 1997. Encyclopedia Britannica. 10 Mar.

    1998 <http://www.britannica.com>.

An Article in a Journal

Bieder, Robert A. "The Representation of Indian Bodies in

    Nineteenth-Century American Anthropology." The

    American Indian Quarterly 20.2 (1996). 28 Mar. 1998

    <http://www.uoknor.edu/aiq/aiq202.html#bieder>.

An Article in a Magazine

Levine, Judith. "I Surf, Therefore I Am." Salon 29 July

    1997. 9 Dec. 1997 <http://www.salonmagazine.com/

    July97/mothers/surfing.970729.html>.

A Review

Roth, Martha. "A Tantalizing Remoteness." Rev. of Jane

    Austen: A Biography by Claire Tomalin. Hungry Mind

    Review Winter 1997. 10 Mar. 1998 <http://

    www.bookwire.com/HMR/nonfiction/read.review$5376>.

A Posting to a Discussion Group

Inman, James. "Re: Technologist." Online Posting. 24 Sept.

    1997. Alliance for Computers in Writing. 27 Mar. 1998

    <acw-l@unicorn.acs.ttu.edu>.

A Personal E-mail Message

Penning, Sarah. "Mentor Advice." E-mail to Rai Peterson.

    6 May 1995.

Sample Entries: Other Sources

Films; Radio and Television Programs

Chicago. Dir. Rob Marshall. With Renée Zellweger, Catherine
  Zeta-Jones, Richard Gere. Miramax, 2002.

"If God Ever Listened: A Portrait of Alice Walker." Horizons.
  Prod. Jane Rosenthal. NPR. WBST, Muncie. 3 Mar. 1984.

"The Hero's Adventure," Moyers: Joseph Campbell and the
  Power of Myth. Prod. Catherine Tatge. PBS. WNET, New
  York. 23 May 1988.

Performances

The Producers. By Mel Brooks. Dir. Susan Stroman. With
  Nathan Lane and Matthew Broderick. St. James Theater.
  8 October 2002.

Ozawa, Seiji, cond. Boston Symphony Orch. Concert. Symphony Hall, Boston. 30 Sept. 1988.

Recordings

Mozart, Wolfgang A. Cosi Fan Tutte. Record. With Kiri Te
  Kanawa, Frederica von Stade, David Rendall, and
  Philippe Huttenlocher. Cond. Alain Lombard. Strasbourg
  Philharmonic Orch. RCA, SRL3-2629, 1978.

Jones, Norah. Come Away with Me. Blue Note, 2002.

Works of Art

Botticelli, Sandro. Giuliano de' Medici. Samuel H. Kress Collection. National Gallery of Art, Washington.

Rodin, Auguste. The Gates of Hell. Rodin Museum, Paris.

Maps and Charts

Sonoma and Napa Counties. Map. San Francisco: California

  State Automobile Assn., 1984.

Cartoons and Advertisements

Addams, Charles. Cartoon. New Yorker 22 Feb. 1988: 33.

Air France. "The Fine Art of Flying." Advertisement. Travel

  and Leisure May 1988: 9.

Published and Unpublished Letters

Fitzgerald, F. Scott. "To Ernest Hemingway." 1 June 1934.

  The Letters of F. Scott Fitzgerald. Ed. Andrew Turnbull.

  New York: Scribner's, 1963. 308–10.

Stowe, Harriet Beecher. Letter to George Eliot. 25 May 1869.

  Berg Collection, New York: New York Public Library.

Interviews

Ellison, Ralph. "Indivisible Man." Interview. By James Alan

  McPherson. Atlantic Dec. 1970: 45–60.

Diamond, Carol. Telephone interview. 27 Dec. 1988.

Lectures, Speeches, and Addresses

Russo, Michael. "A Painter Speaks His Mind." Museum of

  Fine Arts. Boston, 5 Aug. 1984.

Baker, Houston A., Jr. "The Presidential Address." MLA Con-

  vention. New York, 28 Dec. 1992.

IMPLICATIONS FOR YOUR RESEARCH AND COMPOSING

MLA style emphasizes the importance of following the procedures for planning and writing the research paper outlined in any standard writing textbook. In particular, MLA style requires you to devote considerable attention to certain steps in your research and composing.

Compiling Source Information

Once you have located sources that you suspect will prove useful, create a computer file for each item. List the source in the appropriate format (use the formats shown in the guidelines for preparing the list of works cited, pages 646–659). To guarantee that each file is complete and accurate, take your information directly from the source rather than from the card or on-line catalog or a bibliographical index. Your collection of files will help you keep track of your sources throughout your research. Alphabetizing the files will enable you to prepare a provisional list of works cited.

The provisional list must be in place *before* you begin writing your paper. You may expand or refine the list as you write, but to document each source in your text, you first need to know its correct citation. Thus, although Works Cited will be the last section of your paper, you must prepare it first.

Taking Notes

Note-taking demands that you read, select, interpret, and evaluate the information that will form the substance of your paper. After you return books and articles to the library, your notes will be the only record of your research. If you have taken notes carelessly, you will be in trouble when you try to use them in the body of your paper. Many students inadvertently plagiarize because they have incorrectly copied and pasted sources into their files. (See "Avoiding Plagiarism," page 664.) As you select information from a source, use one of three methods to record it: quoting, summarizing, or paraphrasing.

Quoting Sources

Although quoting an author's text word for word is the easiest way to record information, use this method selectively and quote only the passages that deal directly with your subject in memorable language. When you copy a quotation into a file, place quotation marks at the beginning and the end of the passage. If you decide to omit part of the passage, use ellipsis points to indicate that you have omitted words from the original source. To indicate an omission from the middle of a sentence, use three periods (. . .), and leave a space before and after each period. For an omission at the end of a sentence, type three spaced periods following the sentence period.

To move a quotation from your notes to your paper, making it fit smoothly into the flow of your text, use one of the following methods.

1. Work the quoted passage into the syntax of your sentence.

Morrison points out that social context prevented the authors of slave narratives "from dwelling too long or too carefully on the more sordid details of their experience" (109).

2. Introduce the quoted passage with a sentence and a colon.

Commentators have tried to account for the decorum of most slave narratives by discussing social context: "popular taste discouraged the writers from dwelling too long or too carefully on the more sordid details of their experience" (Morrison 109).

3. Set off the quoted passage with an introductory sentence followed by a colon.

This method is reserved for long quotations (four or more lines of prose; three or more lines of poetry). Double-space the quotation, and indent it one inch (ten spaces) from the left margin. Because this special placement identifies the passage as a quotation, do not enclose it within quotation marks. Notice that the final period goes *before* rather than *after* the parenthetical reference. Leave one space after the final period. If the long quotation extends to two or more paragraphs, then indent the first line of these additional paragraphs one-quarter inch (three spaces).

Toni Morrison, in "The Site of Memory," explains how social context shaped slave narratives:

> No slave society in the history of the world wrote more
> —or more thoughtfully—about its own enslavement. The
> milieu, however, dictated the purpose and the style. The
> narratives are instructive, moral and obviously repre-
> sentative. Some of them are patterned after the senti-
> mental novel that was in vogue at the time. But what-
> ever the level of eloquence or the form, popular taste
> discouraged the writers from dwelling too long or too
> carefully on the more sordid details of their experience.
> (109)

Summarizing and Paraphrasing Sources

Summarizing and paraphrasing an author's text are the most efficient ways to record information. The terms *summary* and *paraphrase* are often used interchangeably to describe a brief restatement of the author's ideas in your own words, but they may be used more precisely to designate different procedures. A *summary* condenses the content of a lengthy passage. When you write a summary, you reformulate the main idea and outline the main points that support it. A *paraphrase* restates the content of a short passage. When you paraphrase, you reconstruct the passage phrase by phrase, recasting the author's words in your own.

A summary or a paraphrase is intended as a complete and objective presentation of an author's ideas, so be careful not to distort the original passage by omitting major points or by adding your own opinion. Because the words of a summary or a paraphrase are yours, they are not enclosed by quotation marks. But because the ideas you are restating came from someone else, you need to cite the source in your notes and in your text. (See "Avoiding Plagiarism," page 664.)

The following examples illustrate two common methods of introducing a summary or a paraphrase into your paper.

1. Summary of a long quotation

Often, the best way to proceed is to name the author of a source in the body of your sentence and place the page numbers in parentheses. This procedure informs your reader that you are about to quote or paraphrase. It also gives you an opportunity to state the credentials of the authority you are citing.

Award-winning novelist Toni Morrison argues that although slaves wrote many powerful narratives, the context of their enslavement prevented them from telling the whole truth about their lives (109).

2. Paraphrase of a short quotation

You may decide to vary the pattern of documentation by presenting the information from a source and placing the author's name and page numbers in parentheses at the end of the sentence. This method is particularly useful if you have already established the identity of your source in a previous sentence and now want to develop the author's ideas in some detail without having to clutter your sentences with constant references to his or her name.

> Slave narratives sometimes imitated the popular fiction of their era (Morrison 109).

Works Cited

Morrison, Toni. "The Site of Memory." Inventing the Truth:

The Art and Craft of Memoir. Ed. William Zinsser. Boston:

Houghton, 1987. 101–24.

Avoiding Plagiarism

Plagiarism is theft. It is using someone else's words or ideas without giving proper credit—or without giving any credit at all—to the writer of the original. Whether plagiarism is intentional or unintentional, it is a serious offense that your professor and school will deal with severely. You can avoid plagiarism by taking notes carefully, by formulating and developing your own ideas, and by using quotes responsibly to support, rather than to replace, your own work. Adhere to the advice for research and composing outlined above and demonstrated below.

The following excerpt is from Robert Hughes's *The Fatal Shore,* an account of the founding of Australia. The examples of how students tried to use this excerpt illustrate the problem of plagiarism.

Original Version

> Transportation did not stop crime in England or even slow it down. The "criminal class" was not eliminated by transportation, and could not be, because transportation did not deal with the causes of crime.

Version A

Transportation did not stop crime in England or even slow it down. Criminals were not eliminated by transportation because transportation did not deal with the causes of crime.

Version A is plagiarism. Because the writer of Version A does not indicate in the text or in a parenthetical reference that the words and ideas belong to Hughes, her readers will believe the words are hers. She has stolen the words and ideas and has attempted to cover the theft by changing or omitting an occasional word.

Version B

Robert Hughes points out that transportation did not stop crime in England or even slow it down. The criminal class was not eliminated by transportation, and could not be, because transportation did not deal with the causes of crime (168).

Version B is also plagiarism, even though the writer acknowledges his source and documents the passage with a parenthetical reference. He has worked from careless notes and has misunderstood the difference between quoting and paraphrasing. He has copied the original word for word yet has supplied no quotation marks to indicate the extent of the borrowing. As written and documented, the passage masquerades as a paraphrase when in fact it is a direct quotation.

Version C

Hughes argues that transporting criminals from England to Australia "did not stop crime. . . . The 'criminal class' was not eliminated by transportation, and could not be, be-

cause transportation did not deal with the causes of crime"
(168).

Version C is one satisfactory way of handling this source material. The writer has identified her source at the beginning of the sentence, letting readers know who is being quoted. She then explains the concept of transportation in her own words, placing within quotation marks the parts of the original she wants to quote and using ellipsis points to delete the parts she wants to omit. She provides a parenthetical reference to the page number in the source listed in Works Cited.

Works Cited

Hughes, Robert. The Fatal Shore. New York: Knopf, 1987.

SAMPLE OUTLINE AND RESEARCH PAPER

The author of the following research paper used many features of MLA style to document her paper. At her instructor's request, she first submitted a final version of her thesis and outline. Adhering to MLA style, she did not include a title page with her outline or her paper. Instead, she typed her name, her instructor's name, the course title, and the date on separate lines (double-spacing between lines) at the upper left margin. Then, after double-spacing again, she typed the title of her paper, double-spaced, and started the first line of her text. On page 1 and successive pages, she typed her last name and the page number in the upper right-hand corner, as recommended by MLA.

Rogers 1

Blythe Rogers

Mr. Johnson

English 104

17 December 1999

Assessing Coffee's Health Problems

Thesis: Coffee lovers may be able to drink their coffee and keep their health.

I. Coffee is addictive.

    A. Much addiction is psychological.

    B. Physical addiction can create negative symptoms.

    C. Coffee addiction is not a bad thing.

II. Coffee consumption is associated with heart disease.

    A. Coffee may raise cholesterol.

    B. Coffee may raise blood pressure.

    C. Experts disagree about consumption rate.

    D. Experts agree about preparation process.

III. Coffee has been connected with cancer.

    A. Older research suggests possible linkage.

    B. Recent research has not found link.

    C. Coffee may actually prevent some cancers.

IV. Coffee does have a negative effect on unborn babies.

    A. Coffee increases danger of miscarriage.

    B. Coffee may cause low-birth-weight babies.

V. Coffee's popularity prompts more research.

    A. Recent popularity of coffee raises old questions about health.

    B. Recent research suggests that moderate consumption is not harmful.

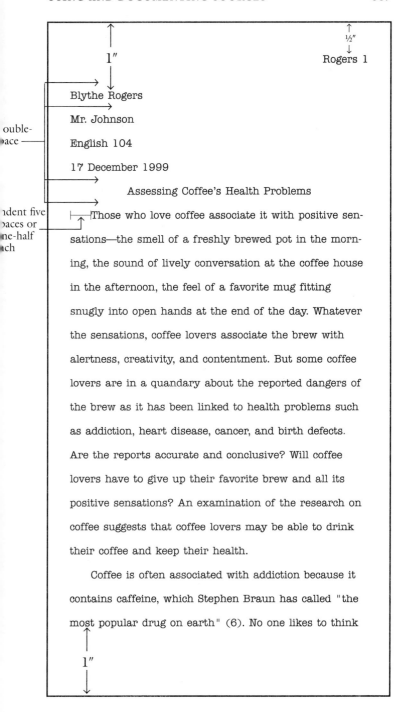

½″

Rogers 1

1″

Blythe Rogers

Mr. Johnson

English 104

17 December 1999

Assessing Coffee's Health Problems

Those who love coffee associate it with positive sensations—the smell of a freshly brewed pot in the morning, the sound of lively conversation at the coffee house in the afternoon, the feel of a favorite mug fitting snugly into open hands at the end of the day. Whatever the sensations, coffee lovers associate the brew with alertness, creativity, and contentment. But some coffee lovers are in a quandary about the reported dangers of the brew as it has been linked to health problems such as addiction, heart disease, cancer, and birth defects. Are the reports accurate and conclusive? Will coffee lovers have to give up their favorite brew and all its positive sensations? An examination of the research on coffee suggests that coffee lovers may be able to drink their coffee and keep their health.

Coffee is often associated with addiction because it contains caffeine, which Stephen Braun has called "the most popular drug on earth" (6). No one likes to think

double-space

indent five spaces or one-half inch

1″

Rogers 2

that he or she is addicted to any substance, but when people try to cut back or skip their morning coffee they realize they are hooked. Indeed, Barbara Brehm believes that Americans cannot live without coffee.

Indent ten spaces or one inch

> Caffeine's speed-you-up effects complement American lifestyle demands. Combined with easy accessibility, caffeine addiction is a common result. Addiction is marked by strong psychological and physical cravings for a substance. . . . Caffeine withdrawal symptoms include fatigue, headache, nausea and various psychological symptoms.

Long quotation: A quotation of more than four lines is set off from text and is *not* placed in quotation marks.

Use elip points t show where y have omitted words from th original

Much addiction is psychological. People believe coffee stimulates their senses and accelerates their thinking. Braun argues that coffee is associated with work, "particularly work involving thinking, reading, writing or talking" (139). Such associations explain why our culture has "institutionalized" the "coffee break" to help workers regain energy and alertness (Pendergrast 241–42). But health columnist Jane Brody explains that such positive psychological associations do not compensate for the negative physical symptoms of withdrawal: "When I recently tried to give up caffeine, my body rebelled. I developed a headache so intense that if I had

Rogers 3

not known better I would have sworn I had a brain tu-

mor or had suffered a stroke. "

Despite such horror stories, addiction does not have

to become a deadly affair like other major health con-

cerns. As Mark Pendergrast points out, "as addictions

go, [coffee] is a relatively harmless one" (417). He cites

Peter Dews, a Harvard professor, as saying "most peo-

ple are addicted to caffeine-containing beverages, just as

most are addicted to showers and regular meals. That is

not a bad thing. It is a habit that can be indulged for a

lifetime without adverse effects to health" (Pendergrast

417).

Coffee is also associated with heart disease because

it has been linked with major risk factors such as high

cholesterol, hypertension, and stress. According to Ste-

phen Cherniske, caffeine raises blood cholesterol levels

and blood pressure, "increases homocysteine (a bio-

chemical that damages artery walls), promotes arrhyth-

mia, and constricts blood vessels leading to the heart"

(5). Although not direct causes, these problems, either

alone or in combination, have a close relationship to

heart disease, and people who suffer from these

difficulties are warned to significantly reduce or elimi-

nate their consumption of coffee.

Short quotation: Author is identified at the beginning of the sentence as brackets are used to work quotation into the sentence.

Short quotation: Author is identified at the beginning of the sentence and quotation is worked into sentence.

Rogers 4

Two considerations, however, must be factored into
the connection between coffee and heart disease: the
amount of coffee consumed by the subjects in the medical study and the process by which that coffee was prepared. Marilyn Elias argues that "a few cups of coffee
should be avoided by adults with even borderline hypertension or a family history of heart attacks." In this
same report, however, Elias defines "a few" as more
than five, and goes on to explain that "people who consume fewer than four or five cups a day seem to incur
no cardiac risk, even if they already have clogged arter-
ies or irregular heart rhythms." Jane E. Brody adds to
the number confusion by arguing that "a significant rise
in blood pressure can occur after just two or three cups
of coffee."

What most of these reports fail to mention is how
coffee is prepared. For example, if the coffee is
unfiltered, then the correlation between coffee consumption and cholesterol increases. A 1996 report from the
Consumers Union of the United States explains that
"boiling ground coffee beans releases oils that contain
two compounds—cafestol and kahweol—that tend to
raise levels of low density lipoprotein (LDL) cholesterol,
the artery-clogging kind." If the coffee is instant or drip

*Short quota-
tion: Author
is identified
as an organi-
zation.*

Rogers 5

filtered, however, the cafestol and kahweol are removed.
This report suggests that such information sheds new
light on the old research studies, as "nearly all the
studies linking coffee with increased cholesterol have involved unfiltered coffee."

Thus, it would seem that if people consume "a few"
cups of coffee and are selective about how they prepare
it, they need not be alarmed about the risk of heart disease. Or to put the matter differently, if a person is
truly concerned about heart disease, coffee is not the
thing to worry about. They should be concerned with the
more dramatic risk factors—some of which can be controlled by medicine (hypertension) and some of which
can be controlled by a healthier lifestyle (obesity). For
those people who already lead a healthy lifestyle, moderate consumption of coffee will not cause heart disease
(James 163).

Another health concern associated with coffee is
cancer. Since caffeine does alter the metabolism of the
body, medical researchers have speculated that coffee
might cause cancer. Like heart disease, however, cancer
has multiple and indirect causes. If a person eats un-
healthy food and does not consume any antioxidants,
cancer <u>might</u> loom on the horizon. But no medical

Paraphrase:
Source is para-
phrased and
the author and
page are placed
within paren-
theses.

Rogers 6

Paraphrase:
Author is
identified at
beginning of
sentence;
source is para-
phrased; sin-
gle-page source
does not re-
quire a page
number.

research has demonstrated a direct link between coffee
and cancer. Brody reports that coffee has been associated with pancreatic cancer, breast cancer, and bladder
cancer, but these were "anecdotal findings," not conclusive proof. Pendergrast reports that a 1979 "epidemio-
logical study appeared to link coffee to pancreatic cancer, triggering widespread media attention and sick jokes
about coffee being 'good to the last drop'" (340). Although the study was done twenty years ago, the negative press left its mark. People believe rumors and initial warnings and distrust the later reports that correct
the findings and reassure them that it is OK to drink
coffee.

Short quota-
tion: Author
and date are
stated at begin-
ning of the
sentence, and
ellipses are
used to work
source into the
sentence.

In 1994, Barbara Brehm concluded that "most recent studies have not found a caffeine-cancer link. . . .
And researchers no longer believe that caffeine contributes to benign breast lumps." In fact, some research
shows that caffeine lowers the risk for certain cancers.
Medical Data International reports that "the risk of
colorectal cancer drops as the amount of coffee con-

Short quota-
tion: Author
and title of pe-
riodical estab-
lish credibility
of source. A
page number is
not required in
single sources.

sumed rises." In an article in Men's Health, Matt Marion
explains that "coffee increases the frequency of bowel
movements, which may limit the colon's exposure to
carcinogens." The plot thickens. Consumers who are told

Rogers 7

in one case to limit their coffee intake to a few cups daily are told in another case that a few cups more will help them avoid problems. No wonder coffee lovers are in a quandary.

Medical researchers do seem to agree that caffeine has a negative effect on unborn babies. Brehm advises pregnant women "to avoid caffeine [because] it may increase rates of miscarriage and low birth weight." Unborn babies "lack the liver enzyme to break down caffeine" (Pendergrast 415). In a study in Physician and Sportsmedicine, Nancy Clark summarizes these side effects:

> A woman who wants to start a family should be
> aware that consuming over 300 milligrams of
> caffeine a day might increase the time it takes
> to get pregnant, as well as the risk of miscar-
> riage or a low-birth-weight baby. The U.S. Food
> and Drug Administration recommends that preg-
> nant women avoid caffeine-containing foods and
> drugs or consume them only sparingly, because
> caffeine crosses the placenta and is a stimulant
> to the unborn baby. It is also transfered into
> breast milk, so women who breastfeed should
> avoid caffeine. (110)

Documentation: The parenthetical reference to a block quotation follows the final mark of punctuation.

Documentation: The parenthetical reference to a run-in quotation precedes the final mark of punctuation.

Rogers 8

No one has disproved caffeine's negative effects on the unborn. Even Pendergrast, whose positive attitude toward caffeine is often revealed in the tone of his book, agrees that pregnant women should be careful—although he does remark, lightheartedly, that coffee "turns breast milk into a kind of natural latte" (415).

In recent years, coffee has enjoyed a resurgence of popularity. Coffee lovers have become specialists in selecting designer blends and processing machinery. Coffee bars and coffee houses have become prominent features of the landscape of reality and television. This resurgence prompted medical researchers to revisit the issue of whether coffee caused health problems. But as the analysis of that research demonstrates, coffee's negative impact on health is not that severe. So coffee lovers, it would appear, need not give up their coffee or the positive sensations they associate with its consumption. If they consume coffee in moderation, coffee lovers can have their health and drink one or two cups.

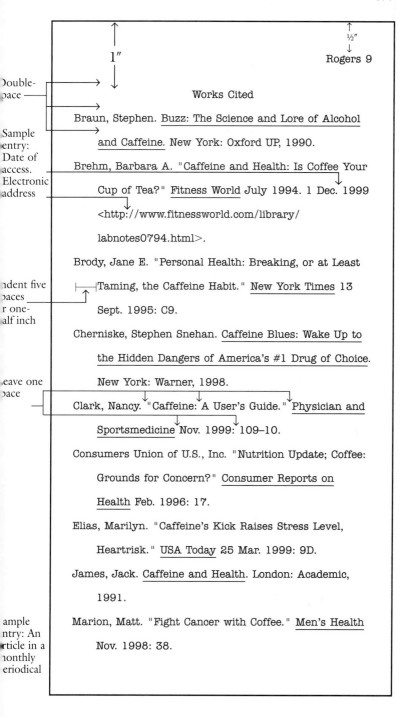

Rogers 9

Double-
space

Sample
entry:
Date of
access.
Electronic
address

indent five
spaces
or one-
half inch

Leave one
space

Sample
entry: An
article in a
monthly
periodical

Works Cited

Braun, Stephen. Buzz: The Science and Lore of Alcohol
and Caffeine. New York: Oxford UP, 1990.

Brehm, Barbara A. "Caffeine and Health: Is Coffee Your
Cup of Tea?" Fitness World July 1994. 1 Dec. 1999
<http://www.fitnessworld.com/library/
labnotes0794.html>.

Brody, Jane E. "Personal Health: Breaking, or at Least
Taming, the Caffeine Habit." New York Times 13
Sept. 1995: C9.

Cherniske, Stephen Snehan. Caffeine Blues: Wake Up to
the Hidden Dangers of America's #1 Drug of Choice.
New York: Warner, 1998.

Clark, Nancy. "Caffeine: A User's Guide." Physician and
Sportsmedicine Nov. 1999: 109–10.

Consumers Union of U.S., Inc. "Nutrition Update; Coffee:
Grounds for Concern?" Consumer Reports on
Health Feb. 1996: 17.

Elias, Marilyn. "Caffeine's Kick Raises Stress Level,
Heartrisk." USA Today 25 Mar. 1999: 9D.

James, Jack. Caffeine and Health. London: Academic,
1991.

Marion, Matt. "Fight Cancer with Coffee." Men's Health
Nov. 1998: 38.

Rogers 10

Medical Data International. "Experts Put to Sleep Cof-

    fee's Link with Heart Disease." Medical Industry

    Today July 1999: 3.

Pendergrast, Mark. Uncommon Grounds: The History of

    Coffee and How It Transformed Our World. New

    York: Basic, 1999.

RHETORICAL GLOSSARY

Abstract

Abstract qualities or characteristics are those we conceive of mentally but cannot see, touch, or hear. For example, *bravery, laziness,* and *perseverance* are abstract terms, and writers often illustrate such terms with examples in order to help readers grasp their significance. For instance, in her essay "Stone Soup" (page 506), Barbara Kingsolver sketches several scenes of children and adults together to show a variety of ways in which the abstract term *family values* can be understood. The opposite of abstract is **concrete,** meaning a term that we understand because it appeals to the senses, such as *rocky, sizzling,* or *bright yellow.*

Active Reading
A manner of reading in which one reads intently and consciously, simultaneously reading for meaning and being aware of one's responses to the content and style. An active reader often reads with a pencil and ruler in hand, underlining important phrases or sentences and writing notes in the margin. See the annotated essay "Beginnings" in the Introduction, page 9.

Allusion
A reference to a person, event, or story that is familiar to the reader, a reference that will help enrich the writer's meaning because it draws on shared knowledge with the reader. For instance, on the first page of her essay "Grounds for Fiction" (page 125), Julia Alvarez makes an allusion to *crown jewels*, assuming that all her readers will understand this reference to an object of great value. Allusions work only if the reader recognizes them; for example, when Alvarez refers to Degas later in her essay, she is careful to identify him as a painter, aware that not all her readers would be familiar with the name.

Analogy
A comparison between two things or concepts that share certain characteristics although they are not similar in most ways. Analogies are often used to help clarify an explanation. Witold Rybczynski is using an analogy in "One Good Turn" (page 611) when he says, "Hand tools are really extensions of the human body, for they have evolved over centuries of trial and error."

Annotate
To make notes or comments about a piece of writing. See the annotated essay on pages 9–10 of the Introduction.

Argument
A piece of writing or an oral presentation in which an author or speaker seeks to persuade an audience to accept a proposition or an opinion by giving reasons and evidence. An argument doesn't necessarily involve controversy or anger; often it is simply a statement that presents a claim or a particular

point of view. For example, in "Why McDonald's Fries Taste So Good" (page 447) Eric Schlosser lays out this proposition: "The canning, freezing, and dehydrating techniques used in processing destroy most of food's flavors—and so a vast industry has arisen in the United States to make processed food palatable." That's his argument in the essay, and he develops it with substantial detail.

Although most arguments combine different kinds of appeal, *emotional arguments* appeal primarily to the feelings, relying heavily on figurative language and provocative imagery to persuade. In his famous "I Have a Dream" speech (page 486), Martin Luther King, Jr., shows his great skill with metaphor and stirring language with sentences like "We will not be satisfied until justice rolls down like waters and righteousness like a mighty stream" and phrases like "battered by the storms of persecution and staggered by the winds of police brutality." *Rational arguments* rely more on appeals to reason and logic, arguing from example and working to establish cause and effect. Daniel Goleman makes a primarily rational argument in "Peak Performance: Why Records Fall" (page 412).

Writers who want to establish *ethical appeal* seek to establish their credentials as persons with authority, expertise, and integrity. Joan Acocella does this in "Under the Spell" (page 526), showing her strong background in myth, legend, and literary tradition and demonstrating that she knows the Harry Potter books. Garry Wills's essay "The Dramaturgy of Death" (page 293) also resonates with ethical appeal, not only because of his knowledgeable discussion of the death penalty over the centuries but because of his reputation as a writer on religious and historical issues.

Assumption
Something taken for granted, presumed to be true without need for further explanation or proof. Writers usually make the assumption that their readers have certain knowledge and experiences that they can count on as they present their arguments. In "Shakespeare in the Bush" (page 214), Laura Bohannan shows how her assumptions and those of the tribal

elders to whom she was trying to explain *Hamlet* were so wildly different that any understanding was impossible.

Audience

The readers for whom a piece of writing is intended. That audience may be close or distant, a small group or a large number, popular or specialized. Professional writers nearly always tailor their writing toward a particular audience about whom they know a good deal—for example, the readers of the *New York Times* or of *Parade*—and they adapt their vocabulary and style to suit that audience. In the headnote about the author before each essay in *The Riverside Reader* we usually tell you in what other publications the author's work has appeared and where that particular essay originally appeared so you can get a feeling for the kind of reader the author was writing for and how that audience might react. It's important that you, as a college student, are aware that you were not the original audience for these essays and to reflect on how your responses to them might be different from those of the original audience.

Audience Analysis

As you work to develop your writing abilities, few skills are more important to you as a writer than learning how to analyze your audience. Ask yourself: (1) Who am I writing for? (2) What do they expect of me? (3) What knowledge do they already have? (4) What kind of evidence and strategies are they most likely to respond to? And it's important that you learn to project an audience other than your instructor, such as a nonprofessional audience whose interest you must catch and hold. Often it is good practice to imagine your fellow students as the audience for whom you're writing and to gear your language and appeal to them.

Brainstorming

A way of generating ideas and material for writing by thinking about a topic intently and jotting down random thoughts as they occur to you without regard to whether they seem immediately useful and relevant.

Cause and Effect

A mode of writing that explains or persuades by setting up cause-and-effect relationships. In his essay "Some Big Ideas Wash Up One Bulb at a Time" (page 406), Andrew C. Revkin shows how apparently harmless actions—throwing used light bulbs overboard from ships—can cause a serious environmental problem—an accumulation of clinking light bulbs covering an entire tropical beach.

Central Pattern

The dominant mode of exposition in an essay. Most writers use more than one expository pattern when they construct an essay. For example, Serena Nanda combines narration and comparison and contrast in her process essay, "Arranging a Marriage in India" (page 140). In *The Riverside Reader*, however, we have chosen essays that show a central pattern in order to demonstrate how a writer may use a specific pattern as a writing strategy. For example, the central pattern of Jill McCorkle's "The Mullet Girls" (page 41) is narration; the central pattern of Paco Underhill's "Shop like a Man" (page 186) is comparison and contrast.

Classification and Division

A method of organizing an explanation or argument by dividing a topic into distinct parts or classes and discussing the characteristics of those classes. In "Four Kinds of Chance" (page 253), James H. Austin analyzes four different kinds of luck, showing how luck can range from the blind chance of gambling games to the fortuitous discovery that often comes to an energetic, knowledgeable, and prepared person who is open to new information.

Comparison and Contrast

A popular and convenient way of organizing an essay or article to highlight important ways in which two things or processes can be similar yet different. Mark Twain's classic piece, "Two Views of the River" (page 174), illustrates the method beautifully by contrasting the romantic view of someone who travels down the Mississippi for the first time with the pragmatic view of an experienced river pilot who sees the river as a dangerous waterway that he must analyze in order to navigate safely.

Concept
A broad intellectual notion that captures the essential nature of an idea, system, or process: for example, the concept of affirmative action or the concept of intellectual property. In "Modern Friendships" (page 268), for example, Phillip Lopate explains the new concept of friendship he has developed as he has matured and made friends with a broad range of people with diverse traits and abilities.

Conclusion
The final paragraph or section of an essay that brings the argument or explanation to appropriate closure and leaves the reader feeling that the author has dealt with all the issues or questions he or she has raised. Good conclusions are challenging to write, and writers sometimes go through several drafts before they are satisfied.

Concrete
Something specific and tangible that can be perceived through the senses; see **Abstract** earlier in *The Riverside Reader* glossary.

Connotation
The added psychological and emotional associations that certain words and phrases carry in addition to their simple meaning. For instance, words like *liberty* and *individualism* carry heavily positive connotations in our culture; they may carry negative connotations in a culture that puts great value on tradition and discipline. All the authors in *The Riverside Reader* use connotation, but two who employ it with particular skill are Martin Luther King, Jr., in "I Have a Dream" (page 486) and Anne Roiphe in "A Tale of Two Divorces" (page 203).

Critical Reading
The critical reader is one who asks questions and analyzes content as he or she reads in order to judge the truth, merit, and general quality of an essay or article. A critical reader might ask, "What is the source of the author's information?,"

"What evidence does he cite in support of his claim?," and "What organization or special interest might she be affiliated with?" The questions and comments in the margins of "Beginnings" (page 9) show the critical reader at work.

Definition
A type of essay that identifies and gives the qualities of a person, object, institution, pattern of behavior, or political theory in a way that highlights its special characteristics. Authors often use definition in combination with description or comparison to make their point. Paco Underhill defines male shoppers in "Shop like a Man" (page 186) by comparing their shopping patterns to those of women. In "Pain" (page 358) Diane Ackerman defines people's attitudes toward pain by showing how members of different cultures handle pain.

Description
A kind of factual writing that aims to help the reader visualize and grasp the essential nature of an object, an action, a scene, or a person by giving details that reveal the special characteristics of that person or scene. Most skilled professional writers, like those represented in *The Riverside Reader*, are good at choosing particular details that give color and interest. For example, in "American Ingenuity" (page 364) William Langewiesche shows David Griffin's confidence and ingenuity by narrating details about him, quoting snatches of his conversation, and describing how he directs the demolition of a building from a hazardous perch on top of it.

Division and Classification
See **Classification and Division.**

Documentation
A system used for giving readers information about where the writer found the sources he or she used in an academic paper, a research paper, or a technical report. Writers document their sources by inserting footnotes, endnotes, or in-text citations so that a reader who wants to know more about the topic can easily find the article or book that the author is citing or track down other related articles by the same author.

The most common system writers use for documentation in academic papers in writing classes is MLA.

While most authors writing in magazines or books for the general public seldom use formal documentation, many use an informal documentation that lets the reader know where they found the information on which they base their conclusions. Notice that Daniel Goleman does this in "Peak Performance: Why Records Fall" (page 412) by giving the names and the university associations of several researchers whose work he cites. Such informal documentation lends credibility to an article and enhances the writer's authority.

Draft

A preliminary version of a piece of writing that enables an author to get started and develop an idea as he or she writes. Authors often write and revise several drafts before they are satisfied with a piece of writing. In her essay "Grounds for Fiction" (page 125), Julia Alvarez relates how she gathers fragments of miscellaneous information and, through writing drafts, turns them into stories or poems.

Dramaturgy

The craft or technique of dramatic composition; the art of creating a drama to make a point or dramatize an idea. In "The Dramaturgy of Death" (page 293), Garry Wills describes how over the centuries the authorities in many countries created a kind of public theater by executing condemned men and women in order to give a message or warning to the onlookers. Writers often practice dramaturgy by creating little dramatic scenes or episodes to make a point. Barbara Kingsolver does this in "Stone Soup" (page 506) to illustrate different kinds of family values, and Jill McCorkle's mini-dramas reveal the story in "The Mullet Girls" (page 41).

Edit

To make small-scale changes in a piece of writing that is close to being complete. Editing may involve changing some word choices, checking for correct spelling and punctuation, eliminating repetition, rearranging sentences or paragraphs, and generally polishing a manuscript into final form before submitting it to an instructor or editor.

Essay

An article or short nonfiction composition that focuses on a specific topic or theme. *The Random House Webster's Unabridged Dictionary* says that an essay is generally "analytical, speculative, or interpretive." Thus a news story would not be an essay, but an opinion piece could be. Nearly all the selections in *The Riverside Reader* qualify as essays. Harold Bloom's piece, "Can 35 Million Book Buyers Be Wrong? Yes." (page 537), an opinion piece that was first published in the *Wall Street Journal,* is certainly an essay, and Phillip Lopate's "Modern Friendships" (page 268) is a particularly good example.

Evidence

The term suggests largely factual supporting examples such as scientific observations, the testimony of authorities, and reliable historical or eyewitness reports. Personal anecdotes or opinions aren't generally considered evidence, although they often serve as reinforcing stories. Andrew Revkin's "Some Big Ideas Wash Up One Bulb at a Time" (page 406) and Witold Rybczynski's "One Good Turn" (page 611) are good examples of solid evidence used convincingly.

Example

A specific incident, object, or anecdote used to illustrate and support a claim or expand on an assertion or generalization. Skillful writers know that readers expect and need examples to clarify a statement, develop a thesis sentence, or support an opening assertion. Every writer in *The Riverside Reader* uses examples, but John Berendt's essay "The Hoax" (page 353) consists almost entirely of specific examples that illustrate the distinction he makes between a hoax and a prank.

Figurative Language

Language that uses vivid and sometimes fanciful comparisons to enliven and enrich prose. Such language often takes the form of metaphors that explain an unfamiliar thing or process by comparing it to a familiar thing. Julia Alvarez does this early in her essay "Grounds for Fiction" (page 125) when she quotes the author James Dickey as saying that his writing process was like digging through fifty tons of low-grade ore to come up with two gold nuggets. Martin Luther King, Jr., of course, is the grand master of metaphor and figurative language. Dipping into his "I Have a Dream" (page 486) almost anywhere reveals his magnificent command of the telling image, but it's especially evident in paragraph 4 in the masterfully crafted metaphor that begins, "It is obvious today that America has defaulted on this promissory note insofar as her citizens of color are concerned."

In writing college essays, you should use figurative language carefully because often the assignment is one that calls for rational argument and a serious tone. In such situations, too much figurative language can distract the reader, although an apt metaphor can work well to explain an unfamiliar concept.

Focus
As a verb, to concentrate or emphasize; as a noun, the point of concentration or emphasis. Skillful writers know how to focus their writing on a single central idea or point; they have learned to "write more about less," to narrow their topic down to one that they can explore fully and enrich with details. Witold Rybczynski demonstrates such skill in his essay "One Good Turn" (page 611) by taking a very narrow topic, the wood screw, and writing a rich and informative essay full of fascinating details.

Free-writing
A way to generate ideas for an essay or article by writing down whatever comes into your mind about a topic you have chosen or been assigned, not concerning yourself with organization or style. In free-writing, work quickly to capture ideas. Don't stop to consider whether a phrase or sentence is pertinent or useful—just get it down. After you accumulate a substantial amount of material, you can comb through it to find a starting point for your first draft.

Generalization

A broad statement that makes a general claim or an assertion without giving specific details or supporting evidence. Writers often begin an essay with a generalization, and when readers encounter such a generalization they expect the next sentences and paragraphs to give details and information that expand on and support it. Eric Liu does this in the first sentence of "A Chinaman's Chance" (page 493) when he says, "A lot of people my age seem to think that the American Dream is dead." In "Modern Friendships" (page 268) Phillip Lopate opens with a general question: "Is there anything left to say about friendship after so many great essayists have picked over the bones of the subject?" Both writers quickly shift from the general to the specific and begin to fill out their statements with details.

Headnote

The short introductory passage that comes before each essay in *The Riverside Reader* is a headnote about its author. Its purpose is to give you enough information about the author's age, cultural heritage, and education to help put him or her in some cultural context and to give you a few other pertinent facts, such as what else he has written or where she has published other articles. We provide this information because we believe readers are likely to understand an author's point of view better when they can place his or her work in the larger context of that author's background.

Image

In writing, an impression or visual effect created by an author through the skillful use of language that appeals to the senses of sight and sound. In "Pain" (page 358) Diane Ackerman opens with a startling image of pain when she describes T. E. Lawrence holding his hand over a candle flame until the flesh starts to sizzle. In Garry Wills's "The Dramaturgy of Death" (page 293), the author opens with a series of shocking images of public executions. Andrew C. Revkin creates images of a ravaged environment by piling up detailed descriptions in "Some Big Ideas Wash Up One Bulb at a Time" (page 406).

Logic

An intellectual system or process that uses reason and evidence to arrive at conclusions. Often writers construct a logical framework for their arguments, setting up cause-and-effect relationships or establishing a chain of reasoning, but embellish the logic with some figurative and emotional language. In "Women and the Future of Fatherhood" (page 517) Barbara Dafoe Whitehead makes a logical argument that the future of fatherhood is uncertain because today's women are less economically dependent on marriage than women of previous eras, and she claims that "a new bargain must be struck over the division of paid work and family work." In "Examined Life" (page 431) Malcolm Gladwell uses logic to demonstrate that Stanley Kaplan demolished the College Board's claim that students couldn't prepare for the SAT exams.

Metaphor
See **Figurative Language.**

Mode

A style or pattern of writing or discourse that has certain features that characterize it and make it distinctive. The essays in *The Riverside Reader* are classified according to their mode: narration, process, division and classification, definition, argument, and so on. Often a writer combines two or three modes in an essay or article but emphasizes one dominant mode. For example, Andrew C. Revkin uses narration to tell his experiences in "Some Big Ideas Wash Up One Bulb at a Time" (page 406), but his main emphasis is on cause and effect.

Narration

A mode of nonfiction writing that develops an idea or makes a point by telling a story or anecdote. In "Digging" (page 30) Andre Dubus tells the story of how his initiation into hard manual labor at the age of seventeen marked his passage into the world of adults. Writers often combine narration with other patterns of writing to make a point or add human interest to an essay. Judith Ortiz Cofer uses several personal anecdotes to illustrate sexist attitudes toward Latina women in her essay "The Myth of the Latin Woman" (page 51).

Pace

The rate at which an essay or article moves. Writers can create different paces through word choice, sentence length, and the selection of certain kinds of verbs. One can see a dramatic example of changing pace by contrasting the first two paragraphs from Mark Twain's "Two Views of the River" (page 174). In the first paragraph the author creates a dreamy, leisurely pace with long sentences filled with rich description and inactive verbs. A few sentences into the second paragraph, the pace changes as he switches from contemplation to analysis. Now the tempo quickens with shorter words and phrases and verbs that depict action.

Paraphrase

A passage that briefly restates the content of another passage in such a way that it retains the original meaning.

Persona

The role or personality a writer assumes in an essay or article. Writers take on a wide range of personas. Some possibilities are the involved narrator, the committed advocate, the scolding critic, and the objective reporter. In "Stone Soup" (page 506) Barbara Kingsolver assumes the role of involved narrator, as does Anna Quindlen in "How Reading Changed My Life" (page 420). Harold Bloom plays the scolding critic in "Can 35 Million Book Buyers Be Wrong? Yes." (page 537), and William Langewiesche assumes the persona of objective reporter in "American Ingenuity" (page 364), although his admiration for the workers at the site of the September 11 disaster certainly comes through. Writers can and often do assume many different personas as they write for different audiences and different purposes.

Persuasion
The process of using language to get readers to accept opinions, beliefs, or points of view. The essays in the Persuasion and Argument section are the most strongly persuasive, but in an important sense, most essays tend to be persuasive, as we point out in the introduction to that section. For example, Anne Roiphe's essay "A Tale of Two Divorces" (page 203) seeks to persuade the reader that a romantic view of marriage can have damaging effects. In "How Reading Changed My Life" (page 420), Anna Quindlen seeks to persuade her readers that the habit of reading can enrich one's life enormously.

Plagiarism
Plagiarism is using someone else's words or ideas without giving proper credit to the person who wrote the original. See page 664 for more explanation and helpful examples about how you can credit your sources properly. Having another person write something that you turn in for credit—for instance, a term paper taken from the Internet or a commercial source—also constitutes plagiarism and can bring serious consequences.

You should always do your own work for two other important reasons. First, if you get someone else to do your work in a writing class, you're missing a golden opportunity to learn a craft that will be essential to you throughout your life, professionally and personally. People who can write well are much more likely to get what they want—in and out of their profession. No one else can learn to write for you any more than someone can exercise for you. So don't blow your opportunity to acquire an important skill by being lazy at this early stage in your adult life.

Second, your integrity is at stake here. College is the time in your life when you're making those decisions that decide, as Martin Luther King, Jr. said, "the content of your character." If you choose to be an honorable and trustworthy person, now is the time to start. You'll like yourself better and so will other people.

Plot

The chain of events that develops a story; through it a writer puts characters into a set of circumstances, describes their behavior, and shows the consequences that ensue.

Point of View

The angle or perspective from which a story or account is told. An account in which the narrator uses "I" and gives an account of an event as it appeared to him or her is called *first-person* point of view. George Orwell's "Shooting an Elephant" (page 68) illustrates this strategy. When the narrator recounts an incident as a detached but fully informed observer, he or she is using the *third-person omniscient* point of view. Flannery O'Connor employs this strategy in "Revelation" (page 309).

Purpose

Authors write with a purpose or a goal. They may wish to inform, to persuade, to explain, to support an assertion, or to entertain. Sometimes they may combine two or more of these purposes, but usually they have a primary goal, one that should be evident to the reader. For instance, in "Arranging a Marriage in India" (page 140) Serena Nanda's primary purpose is to explain why so many young people from India willingly accept the practice of arranged marriages, a custom that seems inexplicable to young Americans. In "Why McDonald's Fries Taste So Good" (page 447) Eric Schlosser's purpose is to show that much of the processed food we eat in the United States is flavored by artificial substances created through chemistry.

When you are writing a paper for a college course, you'll do well to think beyond the immediate goal of fulfilling an assignment in order to earn a grade and consider what effect you want to have on your readers. Are you writing to explain, to persuade, to argue for or against a proposal? When you know your purpose, you're better able to choose successful strategies for achieving it.

Quotation

A passage that gives the actual words a speaker or writer has used in an article, book, speech, or conversation. Authors often use quotations to support their arguments. Barbara Dafoe Whitehead employs this strategy several times in "Women and the Future of Fatherhood" (page 517). Natalie Angier uses it extensively in "Of Heroism, Altruism, and Evolution's Gifts" (page 552) to cite anthropologists and other scientists who support her claims about people's capacity for altruism.

Such passages must always appear in quotation marks in academic papers or, indeed, in any writing done by a responsible author. Writers who fail to give proper credit for a quotation risk losing the respect of their readers or, in college, of getting disciplined for plagiarism. You'll find the proper format for citing quotations in the Documentation section of *The Riverside Reader* (page 645).

Refute

To counteract an argument or seek to disprove a claim or proposition. Several of the authors in *The Riverside Reader* are writing to refute what they see as misconceptions. Judith Ortiz Cofer in "The Myth of the Latin Woman" (page 51) wants to disprove the all-too-common assumption that Latin women are sexy and hot-blooded and show that such attitudes are based on false stereotypes. Barbara Kingsolver in "Stone Soup" (page 506) wants to disprove the simplistic view that good family values can flourish only in a traditional two-parent family. Harold Bloom wrote "Can 35 Million Book Buyers Be Wrong? Yes." (page 537) to refute the popular opinion that the Harry Potter books are good children's literature.

Response

A reader's reaction to what he or she reads is a *response*. Readers can respond in different ways—analytically, critically, emotionally, or approvingly—but in nearly every case that response will come from their own experiences and background: what they know, where they grew up, what kind of culture they lived in, and so on. You might say that they look at an essay through the lens shaped by their own lives, and that lens affects what they see. Such a response is natural and legitimate. Joan Acocella's "Under the Spell" (page 526) is her response to the great popularity of the Harry Potter books; she draws on her knowledge about the appeal of fairy tales and legends from earlier centuries to explain why both children and adults enjoy the books. Laura Bohannan's essay "Shakespeare in the Bush" (page 214) also delightfully illustrates the ways in which two audiences look through such different lenses that they simply don't see the same thing.

Revise

To make substantial changes in a written draft, changes that may involve narrowing the topic, adding or deleting material, rearranging sections, or rewriting the introduction or conclusion. Don't look at revising as a process of correcting a draft; rather, you develop your essay by the process of revising and often can clarify and strengthen your ideas by the process. Many writers revise an essay through three or four drafts.

Strategy

The means or tactic a writer uses to achieve his or her purpose. In the essays in *The Riverside Reader*, authors use various strategies: narration and description, comparison and contrast, process analysis, cause and effect, and so on.

Summary

A passage that condenses the ideas and content of a long passage in a few sentences or paragraphs; a summary should be objective and accurate.

Testimony
Evidence offered in support of a claim or assertion. The term suggests factual statements given by experts or taken from sources such as historical or government records or from statistical data. Eyewitness accounts are frequently used as testimony. In "Pain" (page 358) Diane Ackerman takes many of her examples of how differently people react to pain from eyewitness accounts—men picking up red-hot cannonballs and walking with them, T. E. Lawrence holding his hand in a candle flame, men getting hurt in a bruising hockey game. Eric Schlosser depends heavily on testimony to make his argument in "Why McDonald's Fries Taste So Good" (page 447), giving an analysis of the fat in which those french fries are cooked and reporting his firsthand observations to International Flavors and Fragrance, the world's largest flavor plant.

Thesis Sentence
A comprehensive sentence, usually coming in the first paragraph or so of an essay, that summarizes and previews the main idea the author is going to develop in the essay. Daniel Goleman, in the first sentence of the second paragraph of "Peak Performance: Why Records Fall" (page 412), writes an almost classic thesis sentence that encapsulates the central idea of the essay. Here is the sentence: "Studies of chess masters, virtuoso musicians, and star athletes show that the relentless training routines of those at the top allow them to break through the ordinary limits in memory and physiology, and so perform at levels that had been thought impossible." He goes on to develop each segment of the sentence with examples and testimony.

Tone
The emotional attitude toward their topic that authors convey in their writing. They create tone through the choices they make of words—particularly verbs—of sentence and paragraph length, of styles—formal or informal—and with the kinds of images and figurative language they use. Readers sometimes have trouble finding the exact word for tone; it's an impression you get from writing rather than a quality you

discover analytically, and usually we fall back on emotional terms to describe it: angry, engaging, whimsical, passionate, blunt, sarcastic, patronizing, and so on. But tone is an important element in writing, one of which any author should be aware. If your tone antagonizes your readers, they'll quit reading.

In her essay "The Myth of the Latin Woman" (page 51) Judith Ortiz Cofer's tone shifts subtly as her account progresses. At first she seems fairly tolerant of non-Latins who misinterpret cultural dress preferences, but when she begins to tell of the humiliating incidents that she and other Latina women have endured, her tone becomes unmistakably angry. Sisten Helen Prejean's "Memories of a Dead Man Walking" (page 60) has a somber, serious tone as she tells of her close involvement with a condemned man as he goes to his execution. In "The Hoax" (page 353) John Berendt projects an amused tone of admiration for people who can think up and carry out a witty hoax.

Works Cited
The list of references and sources that appears at the end of an academic paper or report that uses MLA style and gives the readers enough information about those sources to enable them to evaluate them or use them for further research. On page 646 of the section Using and Documenting Sources you will find a full explanation of this feature.

Writing Process
While there is no single writing process that works for every writer or every writing task, writing specialists have found certain patterns when they analyze how most writers seem to work. They agree that productive writers tend to work through a series of steps in the process of creating an essay or article.

Stage 1. Invention: The process of discovering one's topic and generating material. Typical activities are reading and researching, brainstorming, free-writing, talking with fellow writers, and making rough preliminary outlines.

Stage 2. Drafting: Writing a first version of the paper that puts down ideas in some organized form. Many writers continue to generate ideas as they write and often write two or three drafts before they complete one they think is fairly satisfactory.

Stage 3. Revising and rewriting: Reviewing the completed first draft and making substantial changes, perhaps by narrowing the focus, reorganizing, adding and deleting material, or writing a new introduction or conclusion.

Stage 4. Editing, polishing, and proofreading: Making minor word changes, polishing style, and checking for spelling and typographical errors.

Writing Situation

Every piece of writing, from business memos to inaugural speeches, is created within some context; that context is the writing situation. Its components are (1) the writer, (2) the topic, (3) the audience, and (4) the purpose. To figure out what your writing situation is for any particular assignment, ask yourself,

- What is my persona or role in this situation?
- What do I want to say?
- To whom am I writing?
- What is my purpose?

By working out an answer to each of these questions before you begin to write, you'll have a good start on turning out a focused and effective product.

ACKNOWLEDGMENTS

WITI IHIMAERA From *Dear Miss Mansfield* by Witi Ihimaera, published by Penguin Books New Zealand. Reprinted by permission.

MARTIN LUTHER KING, JR. "I Have A Dream," reprinted by arrangement with The Heirs to the Estate of Martin Luther King, Jr., c/o Writers House, Inc. as agent for the proprietor. Copyright 1963 Martin Luther King Jr., copyright renewed 1991 Coretta Scott King.

BARBARA KINGSOLVER "Stone Soup" by Barbara Kingsolver. From *High Tide in Tucson: Essays from Now or Never.* © 1995 by Barbara Kingsolver. Reprinted by permission of HarperCollins Publishers.

WILLIAM LANGEWIESCHE "American Ingenuity" from *American Ground* by William Langewiesche. Copyright © 2002 by William Langewiesche. Reprinted by permission of North Point Press, a division of Farrar, Straus and Giroux, LLC.

ERIC LIU "A Chinaman's Chance: Reflections on the American Dream" by Eric Liu. Copyright © 1994 by Eric Liu, from *Next: Young American Writers on the New Generation,* edited by Eric Liu. Used by permission of the author and W.W. Norton & Company, Inc.

PHILIP LOPATE "Modern Friendships," reprinted by permission of The Wendy Weil Agency, Inc. First appeared in *Texas Monthly.* Copyright © 1989.

JILL MCCORKLE "The Mullet Girls," reprinted by permission of the author. Originally appeared in *The Washington Post Magazine,* July 30, 2000.

DAVID MCCULLOUGH Text excerpt, "FDR and Truman," from *Truman* by David McCullough.

MARY MEBANE "Shades of Black," from *Mary* by Mary Mebane, copyright © 1981 by Mary Elizabeth Mebane. Used by permission of Viking Penguin, a division of Penguin Group (USA) Inc.

SHANNON MENDES "Adbusters," courtesy Adbusters Media Foundation. Photograph Shannon Mendes.

SERENA NANDA "Arranging a Marriage in India," by Serena Nanda in *Stumbling Toward Truth: Anthropologists At Work,* Philip R. DeVita, ed. (Prospect Heights, IL: Waveland), pp. 196–204. Reprinted by permission of the author.

GLORIA NAYLOR Permission to reprint Gloria Naylor's "Beginnings" from *Three Minutes or Less: Life Lessons from America's Greatest Writers* courtesy of Bloomsbury USA, Copyright © 2000 by The PEN/Faulkner Foundation.

JOYCE CAROL OATES Text excerpt from "When Tristram Met Isolde" by Joyce Carol Oates. From *The New York Times,* April 18, 1999. Copyright © 1999 by *The New York Times.* Reprinted by permission.

FLANNERY O'CONNOR "Revelation" from *The Complete Stories* by Flannery O'Connor. Copyright © 1971 by the Estate of Mary Flannery O'Connor. Reprinted by permission of Farrar, Straus and Giroux, LLC.

P. J. O'ROURKE "Third World Driving Hints and Tips," by P. J. O'Rourke, from *Holidays in Hell* by P. J. O'Rourke. Copyright© 1988 by P. J. O'Rourke. Used by permission of Grove/Atlantic, Inc.

GEORGE ORWELL   "Shooting an Elephant" from *Shooting an Elephant and Other Essays,* by George Orwell, copyright 1950 by Harcourt, Inc. and renewed 1979 by Sonia Brownell Orwell, reprinted by permission of Harcourt, Inc.

PHYSICIANS AGAINST LAND MINES   By permission of the Center for International Rehabilitation.

CHRISTOPHER PIZZI   "Doorways: A Visual Essay," from *The American Scholar,* Summer 2003, pp. 77–83. Reprinted with permission of the author.

SISTER HELEN PREJEAN   "Memories of a Dead Man Walking," from *Oxford American* Magazine, Spring 1996. Reprinted by permission of Helen Prejean and the Watkins/Loomis Agency.

FRANCINE PROSE   "Genocide without Apology," copyright 2003 by Francine Prose. First published in *The American Scholar.* Reproduced by permission of Denise Shannon Literary Agency.

ANNA QUINDLEN   From *How Reading Changed My Life* by Anna Quindlen, copyright © 1998 by Anna Quindlen. Used by permission of Ballantine Books, a division of Random House, Inc.

ANDREW C. REVKIN   "Some Big Ideas Wash Up One Bulb at a Time," by Andrew C. Revkin. From *The New York Times,* December 8, 1998. Reprinted by permission of the author. Andrew C. Revkin writes about the environment for *The New York Times.* He is the author of *The Burning Season: The Murder of Chico Mendes and the Fight for the Amazon Rain Forest* (Houghton Mifflin, 1990) and *Global Warming: Understanding the Forecast* (Abbeville Press, 1992).

BLYTHE ROGERS   Blythe Rogers, "Assessing Coffee's Health Problems."

ANNE ROIPHE   "A Tale of Two Divorces" from *Women on Divorce: A Bedside Companion* by Penny Kaganoff and Susan Spano, copyright © 1995 by Anne Roiphe, reprinted by permission of Harcourt, Inc.

PEGGY PRICHARD ROSS   "Stem Cell Research: It's about Life and Death, Not Politics," as it appeared in the *Tallahassee Democrat* and was reprinted in The Stem Cell Research Foundation, www.stemcellresearchfoundation.org. Copyright © 2003 by Knight-Ridder Newspapers.

WITOLD RYBCZYNSKI   "One Good Turn: How Machine-Made Screws Brought the World Together" by Witold Rybczynski. From *New York Times Magazine,* April 18, 1999. Reprinted with permission from the author.

MARJANE SATRAPI   "The Veil," From *Persepolis: The Story of a Childhood* by Marjane Satrapi, translated by Mattias Ripa & Blake Ferris. Translation copyright © 2003 by L'Asociation, Paris, France. Used by permission of Pantheon Books, a Division of Random House, Inc.

ERIC SCHLOSSER   "Why McDonald's Fries Taste So Good," from *Fast Food Nation: The Dark Side of the All-American Meal* by Eric Schlosser. Excerpted and reprinted by permission of Houghton Mifflin Company. All rights reserved. First published in the *Atlantic Monthly,* January 2001.

DAVA SOBEL   "Imaginary Lines," from *Longitude,* pp. 1–10 (Walker, 1995). Published by arrangement with Walker & Co.

ANDREW SULLIVAN   From *Virtually Normal* by Andrew Sullivan, copyright © 1995 by Andrew Sullivan. Used by permission of Alfred A. Knopf, a division of Random House, Inc.

LEWIS THOMAS   "The Technology of Medicine," copyright © 1971 by The Massachusetts Medical Society, from *The Lives of a Cell* by Lewis Thomas. Used by permission of Viking Penguin, a division of Penguin Group (USA) Inc.

PACO UNDERHILL   Reprinted with the permission of Simon & Schuster Adult Publishing Group from *Why We Buy: The Science of Shopping* by Paco Underhill. Copyright © 1999 by Obat, Inc.

KURT VONNEGUT   "Harrison Bergeron," from *Welcome to the Monkey House* by Kurt Vonnegut, Jr., copyright © 1961 by Kurt Vonnegut, Jr. Used by permission of Dell Publishing, a division of Random House, Inc.

SARAH VOWELL   "Cowboys vs. Mounties," reprinted with the permission of Simon & Schuster Adult Publishing Group from *The Partly Cloudy Patriot* by Sarah Vowell. Copyright © 2002 by Sarah Vowell.

ALICE WALKER   "Everyday Use" from *In Love & Trouble: Stories of Black Women*, copyright © 1973 by Alice Walker, reprinted by permission of Harcourt, Inc.

BARBARA DAFOE WHITEHEAD   "Women and the Future of Fatherhood," from *The Divorce Culture* by Barbara Dafoe Whitehead, copyright © 1996 by Barbara Dafoe Whitehead. Used by permission of Alfred A. Knopf, a division of Random House, Inc.

ELIZABETH WINTHROP   "The Golden Darters" by Elizabeth Winthrop. First published in *American Short Fiction*. Copyright © 1991 by Elizabeth Winthrop. Reprinted by permission of the author.

GARRY WILLS   "The Dramaturgy of Death," from *New York Review of Books,* June 21, 2001. Reprinted with permission from *The New York Review of Books*. Copyright © 2001 NYREV, Inc.

JAMES Q. WILSON   "Democracy for All?" from *Commentary,* March 2000, pp. 25–28. Reprinted from *Commentary,* March 2000 by permission; all rights reserved.

INDEX

Abstract, 679
Ackerman, Diane, 358
  "Pain," 340, 341, 342, 358–363,
    685, 689, 696
Acocella, Joan, 526
  "Under the Spell," 477, 481,
    526–536, 681, 695
Action, persuasion and argument
  urging, 477
Active reading, 680
Adams, Alice, 78
  "Truth or Consequences," 78–
    92
"Adbusters" (Mendes), 345
Addresses, in Works Cited, 659
Advertisements, in Works Cited,
  659
Allusion, 680
Alternating strategy, for comparison
  and contrast, 168–169, 172
Alvarez, Julia, 125
  "Grounds for Fiction," 98, 99,
    125–139, 680, 686, 688
"American Ingenuity"
  (Langewiesche), 4, 340, 364–
    372, 685, 691–692
Analogies, 680
  in cause and effect, 401
  in definition, 341, 344
Analysis, 95–96. *See also* Process
  analysis.

Anecdotes
  in narration and description,
    22
  in process analysis, 99, 102
Angier, Natalie, 481, 552
  "Of Altruism, Heroism, and Evo-
    lution's Gifts," 477, 480, 481,
    552–558, 694
Annotating, 2, 9–10, 680
  in cause and effect, 402–403
  in comparison and contrast, 169–
    171
  in definition, 342–343
  in division and classification, 249–
    251
  in narration and description, 26–
    28
  in persuasion and argument, 481–
    483
  in process analysis, 100–102
Argument, 475–476, 680–681. *See*
  also Persuasion and argument.
"Arranging a Marriage in India"
  (Nanda), 140–152, 683, 693
Articles in periodicals, in Works
  Cited, 652–654, 677
Assumption, 681–682
"At Play, Tianzi Mountains"
  (Hong-Oai), 173
Attitude, in narration and descrip-
  tion, 25–26